Exotix Developing M

Exotix Capital

Exotix Developing Markets Guide

Debt and Risk across the Frontier

Sixth Edition

Exotix Capital
Watson House
London, UK

ISBN 978-3-030-05866-1 ISBN 978-3-030-05867-8 (eBook)
https://doi.org/10.1007/978-3-030-05867-8

Library of Congress Control Number: 2019930048

This Palgrave Macmillan imprint is published by the registered company Springer Nature Switzerland AG.
The registered company address is: Gewerbestrasse 11, 6330 Cham, Switzerland

Acknowledgements

The Exotix Developing Markets Guide is based on our vast, accumulated knowledge of illiquid and frontier emerging markets, stretching back many years. Exotix itself has been in this business for some 20 years. Much of the book is based on professional and institutional experience, as well as previous editions of the book and our other published material.

We have also drawn from a wealth of other sources. Many are noted in the text along the way, but we would highlight the following useful ones; bond prospectuses (generally available on Bloomberg or listing exchanges) and loan documentation; the IMF, especially for its invaluable country reports, World Economic Outlook and other statistical databases, Regional Economic Outlooks and annual report on exchange arrangements; the World Bank, especially its Global Development Finance, debt tables and World Development Indicators; a host of national government sources, including central banks, ministries of finance, debt management offices, statistical agencies and government websites; the Paris Club, UK Foreign Office, US State Department, UN, European Commission, IEA, US Energy Information Administration (EIA), CIA World Factbook, EBRD, Asian Development Bank and African Development Bank; Haver Analytics; national electoral commissions and the IFES Election Guide; the Economist and EIU, the BBC, Reuters, the Financial Times, Bloomberg and various local media.

We have endeavoured to ensure that the information in this book is as up-to-date and accurate as possible. In general, the cut-off for information was end-September 2018, although we tried to include new issues in October or other significant events until the publication date. But this is a moving target. We hope you will understand that, with a project of this magnitude, it is difficult to pick up everything, so please forgive any errors and omissions.

Finally, we'd like to express our sincere appreciation to the other contributors to the book and the production team, including: Tolu Alamutu, Rafael Elias and Kiti Pantskhava for their contributions on corporate bond markets, the editorial team and various other Exotix staff who have made important contributions throughout the project. This book would not have been possible without their help. We'd also like to thank Charles Blitzer (Blitzer Consulting) and Sebastian Espinosa (White Oak) for their helpful comments on the introduction and other country chapters.

In particular, we'd like to give a special thank you to Luke Richardson for his research assistance and tireless dedication and commitment throughout the project. We'd also like to thank Peder Beck-Friis and Leon Ernst for research assistance provided during their time at Exotix.

Chief Economist and Global Head of Fixed Income Research — Stuart Culverhouse

Senior Economist — Christopher Dielmann

CONTENTS

Acronyms and Abbreviations

ADB	Asian Development Bank
AfDB	African Development Bank
Afrexim	African Export-Import Bank
BADEA	Arab Bank for Economic Development in Africa
BCEAO	Central Bank of West African States
BEAC	Bank of Central African States
BOAD	West African Development Bank
BRI	Belt and Road Initiative
CABEI	Central American Bank for Economic Integration
CAF	Corporacion Andina de Fomento – Latin American Development Bank
CARICOM	Caribbean Community – promotes economic integration and free trade
CBD	Caribbean Development Bank
CEMAC	Economic and Monetary Union of Central Africa
COMESA	Common Market for Eastern and Southern Africa
CP	Completion point
CPI	Consumer price index
CRF	Common Reduction Factor
DFID	Department for International Development
DP	Decision point
EBRD	European Bank for Reconstruction and Development
EC	European Commission
ECCAS	Economic Community of Central African States
ECCB	Eastern Caribbean Central Bank
ECCU	Eastern Caribbean Currency Union

ECF	Extended credit facility – IMF programme for medium-term support to low income countries, formerly PRGF
ECOWAS	Economic Community of West African States
EFF	Extended fund facility – IMF programme for countries with medium-term financing needs, longer than under an SBA
EFSD	Eurasian Fund for Stabilisation and Development
EFSF	European financial stability facility
EIA	Energy Information Agency
EIB	European Investment Bank
EMU	European Monetary Union of the European Union
ESAF	Enhanced structural adjustment facility – IMF programme providing concessional financial assistance, replaced by PRGF
ESAP	Economic and structural adjustment program
ESF	Exogenous shock facility – IMF programme
ESM	European stability mechanism
EU	European Union
ExIm	Export-Import Bank of the United States
FCL	Flexible Credit Line
FY	Fiscal year
GDP	Gross domestic product
GFC	Global financial crisis (2007–2009)
GIZ	Deutsche Gesellschaft für Internationale Zusammenarbeit – German development agency
GNI	Gross national income
GNP	Gross national product
HIPC	Heavily indebted poor country
IADB	InterAmerican Development Bank
IBRD	International Bank for Reconstruction and Development – part of the World Bank Group
IDA	International Development Agency – part of the World Bank Group
IDFC	International Development Finance Corporation
IEA	International Energy Agency
IFAD	International Fund for Agricultural Development
IFI	International financial institution
IMF	International Monetary Fund
IsDB	Islamic Development Bank
KFW	Kreditanstalt für Wiederaufbau – German Reconstruction Credit Institute
LIC	Low income country
MAC	Market access country
MDB	Multilateral development bank
MDGs	Millennium development goals

MDRI	Multilateral debt relief initiative
MIGA	Multilateral Investment Guarantee Agency – part of the World Bank Group
MLT	Medium and long term
MOU	Memorandum of understanding
NPV	Net present value
NR	Not rated
OECD	Organisation for Economic Co-operation and Development
OFID	OPEC Fund for International Development
OPEC	Organization of Petroleum Exporting Countries
OPIC	Overseas Private Investment Corporation
OSI	Official sector involvement
PC	Paris Club; performance criteria
PDI	Past due interest
PED	Public external debt
PNG	Private non-guaranteed
PPG	Public and publicly guaranteed
PPP	Public-private partnership
PRGF	Poverty reduction and growth facility – IMF programme, replaced by ECF
PRGT	Poverty reduction and growth trust
PRSP	Poverty reduction strategy paper
PSE	Public sector enterprise
PSI	Policy support instrument; private sector involvement
PV	Present value
SADC	Southern African Development Community
SAFC	Structural adjustment facility commitment – IMF programme providing concessional balance of payments support
SAFE	State Administration of Foreign Exchange (China)
SBA	Stand-by arrangement – IMF programme for countries with balance of payments imbalances
SCF	Standby credit facility – IMF programme for countries with a short-term balance of payments financing need
SDR	Special drawing rights
SMP	Staff-monitored programme – Informal agreement for IMF staff to monitor authorities' economic policy implementation
SOE	State-owned enterprise
ST	Short term
TMU	Technical memorandum of understanding
UN	United Nations
USD	US dollar
WAEMU	West African Economic and Monetary Union
WB(G)	World Bank (Group)

Introduction

The Evolution of Frontier Fixed Income

Welcome to the latest edition of the Exotix Capital Developing Markets Guide. This is the sixth edition, the previous one having been published in February 2011, when the concept of investing in frontier[1] economies was beginning to gain traction again after being derailed by the GFC. A lot has happened since then.

Developments in Frontier Sovereign Debt: Past, Present and Future

The evolution of the frontier/EM fixed income landscape over the past decade or so has been characterised by two features. First, significantly more hard currency (eurobond) issuance, albeit mainly from sovereigns (developing market corporate issuance has generally lagged). Second, continuing sovereign defaults. Looking at the recent history of these sovereign defaults, we highlight what we think are three interesting characteristics of the recent sovereign debt restructuring experience. These are:

[1] We don't define "frontiers" in a strict sense, but such markets tend to share characteristics of illiquidity in securities trading, lack of market depth, under-developed capital markets, and weaker policy making frameworks and institutional governance than more mainstream EMs.

Exotix Capital, *Exotix Developing Markets Guide*,
https://doi.org/10.1007/978-3-030-05867-8_1

1. Proactive creditor committees;
2. Bondholders have generally done well in recent restructurings; and
3. A decline in exit yields.

Going forward, we think other issues will come to the fore to test or change the existing international financial architecture. We highlight here two issues. First, the role of China as a significant lender and investor in emerging and frontier economies and how its presence will challenge the established world order in terms of crisis prevention and resolution. Second, if the focus of international policy on emerging market sovereign debt over the past 20 years has been on trying to make debt restructurings more orderly, an agenda that has in no small part been influenced by the official sector's fears over demonstration effects of the holdout litigation in Argentina, then the future policy agenda may be shaped by current initiatives to promote sustainable lending and greater transparency in lending, which—although at an early stage—could have similarly wide-ranging implications.

The Growth in Frontier Bond Issuance[2]

Frontier sovereign hard currency bond issuance has boomed over recent years (Table 1). On our count, there were 33 debut sovereign issuers (excluding those issuing bonds through restructurings) over the period 2007–2018, of which there have been 21 since 2012. Before 2007, the frontier universe was smaller (depending on interpretation), consisting of c20 or so countries, including a number of less liquid or smaller EM issuers that could have been considered frontiers (and still are), and a few other smaller bond issues or those that came out of previous restructurings. For instance, the Dominican Republic, Ecuador, El Salvador, Jamaica, Pakistan, Ukraine and Vietnam all had bonds by then, and smaller issuers included Barbados, Fiji, Macedonia, the Seychelles and Trinidad & Tobago (for us, Argentina and Venezuela have also drifted in and out of this category over this period). Adding them together would take the universe to something like 57 countries today. In other words, with the issuance over the past decade, the number of frontiers has just about tripled.

[2] Our focus here is sovereign hard currency debt. We exclude corporate bond issuance and domestic debt (local currency) markets, where similar drivers apply and similar trends can be observed (albeit not to the same magnitude as with hard currency sovereign debt).

Table 1 Frontier hard currency debut issues

Year	*Total number*	*Debut issuers*					
2007	3	Sri Lanka-12	Ghana-17	Gabon-17			
2008	1	Georgia-13					
2009	1	Senegal-14					
2010	4	Belarus-15	Montenegro-15 EUR	Albania-15 EUR	Jordan-15		
2011	3	Nigeria-21	Serbia-21	Namibia-21			
2012	4	Angola NL-19	Zambia-22	Bolivia-22	Mongolia-22		
2013	6	Paraguay-23	Tanzania-20	Honduras-24	Rwanda-23	Armenia-20	EMATUM-20
2014	5	Azerbaijan-24	Kenya-19 and 24	Ivory Coast-24	Kazakhstan-24	Ethiopia-24	
2015	1	Cameroon 25					
2016	1	Suriname-26					
2017	3	Iraq-23	Tajikistan-27	Maldives-22			
2018	1	PNG-28					

Source: Exotix, Bloomberg

And many frontiers have also become repeat issuers since their debuts, having two or more bonds outstanding. Moreover, they are also issuing longer tenors, with 15- and 30-year maturities now more commonplace. In Sub-Saharan Africa excluding South Africa (SSA), for example, Nigeria issued the region's first 30-year bond in November 2017, and has been followed in 2018 by Kenya, Senegal, Cote d'Ivoire, Angola and Ghana (although Ghana's recently reported plans for a jumbo century bond, following in the steps of Argentina in 2017, might be stretching things a bit far).

Perhaps indicating another sign of market maturity, Ghana (2017), Gabon (2017) and Nigeria (2018) have all repaid bullet maturities on due date, with their ability to do so aided by being able to retain market access in order to refinance these debts.

A number of new issuers are included in this Guide. There have been 24 new frontier sovereign issuers since our last edition (excluding those with bonds arising out of previously restructured debt and Brady bonds). These include Azerbaijan, Kazakhstan, Mongolia, Suriname, Tajikistan and much of SSA, including Angola, Cameroon, Ethiopia, Kenya, Mozambique, Nigeria, Rwanda and Zambia. At the time of writing, Papua New Guinea had come to the market too.

Today, SSA, in particular, has US$44bn of sovereign bonds outstanding, across 16 issuers, of which 90% has been issued since 2013 (and just under half since 2017). Indeed, 2018 has seen the highest issuance ever out of the region (Fig. 1).

But frontiers are not just about Africa. As we like to say, most of the world is a frontier.

Outstanding hard currency sovereign bonds in this Guide, across 38 issuers, amount to cUS$234bn (excluding Greece). And, on a broader sweep, including another 19 frontier issuers not included in this book, with a total amount outstanding of US$99bn, that takes a rough estimate of the size of the frontier sovereign hard currency bond market to cUS$332bn in 57 countries (by comparison, we note the JPM NEXGEM index, the only frontier bond index, only covers part of this universe, comprising 35 countries at end-2017, with a nominal amount outstanding of US$116bn). Nearly one-third of these (17 countries) had not even issued a bond until four years ago (2013).

The boom in frontier bond issuance reflects a combination of push and pull factors, which have tended to increase capital flows to frontier markets and lowered their borrowing costs. Push (external) drivers comprise buoyant global liquidity conditions since the global financial crisis whereby,

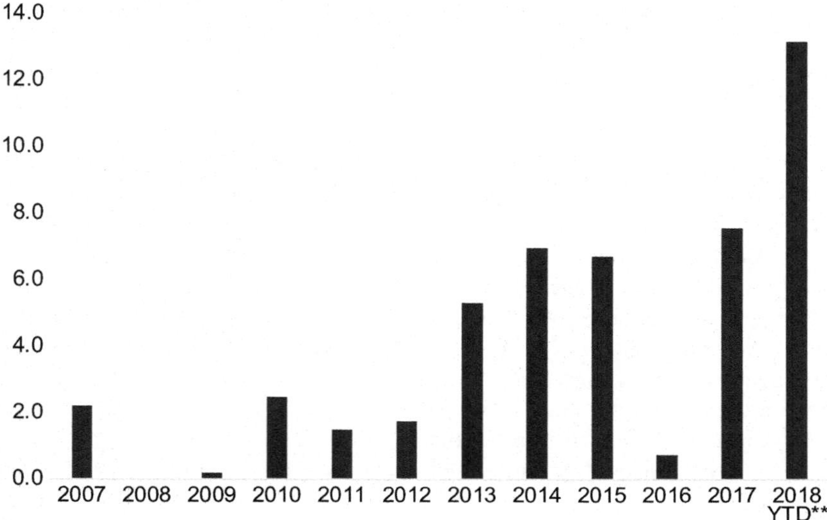

Fig. 1 Sovereign eurobond issuance in SSA (US$bn)*. Source: Exotix, Bloomberg. *Gross issuance including restructurings. **Year through end-September

until recently, markets have enjoyed low global interest rates on the back of ultra-loose monetary policy in the G3. Lower global interest rates have encouraged the search for yield into frontiers, and lower sovereign borrowing costs too. The question of what happens to frontier borrowers, who either want to issue to finance budget deficits, or to refinance upcoming maturities, when liquidity conditions are less benign will be a major theme over the next few years.

Positive external factors also include generally supportive commodity prices (notwithstanding the 2014–2016 oil and commodity price crash) and, for many, the cleaning up of sovereign balance sheets post-HIPC debt relief (leading to concerns over the financial health of some countries that have used the borrowing space that was provided by debt forgiveness to re-leverage). Pull (domestic) factors that have made these countries more attractive to foreign investors include improved domestic macroeconomic policy frameworks, stronger growth prospects and rising per capita incomes, natural resource endowments, strengthening institutions and governance, and broadening democracies. These drivers have helped to lower frontier sovereign borrowing costs through lower country risk spreads.

The stronger GDP growth prospects for frontiers (although partly a function of income convergence), and their potential for portfolio diversification and lower correlations with other asset classes (although this might in part be a function of illiquidity and the time horizon), has been among the arguments leading to more mainstream acceptance of frontier investing.

All nine of the fastest-growing countries in the world in 2018, those growing at 7% or more according to IMF WEO projections, are emerging markets, of which eight are frontier (India being the exception), with four in SSA and three in Southeast Asia. Of the eight frontiers, four have eurobonds (Ethiopia, Cote d'Ivoire, Rwanda and Senegal). Taking an average over the past decade, which includes the period of the GFC, frontiers again dominate the list of the 11 fastest-growing countries (7% or more), with eight markets, of which Rwanda, Mongolia, Ghana and Ethiopia are investable (the three non-frontiers are China, India and Qatar). But growth does not always equal returns.

Moreover, the evidence for whether such large-scale borrowing through the eurobond market has indeed been used for productive purposes to boost potential growth rates seems somewhat mixed, or at least it is too early to be certain. Although bond proceeds are often earmarked for infrastructure spending, project selection and appraisal can be weak, and there may be concerns that borrowing has merely fuelled higher current spending.

The compression of yields on hard currency frontier sovereign bonds has also led to more interest in frontier market local currency opportunities, to take advantage of higher local interest rates (carry trade) and/or prospects for currency appreciation, as well as the possibilities it offers for greater diversification and lower market correlations. The local currency market has grown, although perhaps not at the rate observers were expecting a decade ago. There may be a couple of reasons for this. First, investor interest has been punctured by episodes of global market distress, such as the GFC, the eurozone crisis of 2010–2012 and commodity price crash of 2014–2016. And it seems to take longer for investor interest to return to local markets than it does hard currency bonds. Second, local currency performance is also influenced by the performance of the US dollar. The period of US dollar strength, and hence EM currency weakness, over 2014–2016 and again throughout 2018 has dented local currency appetite, and again, it can take time to recover.

Moreover, liquidity remains an important factor for many investors and the still relatively small size of domestic government bond markets in most frontier countries can be a deterrent, with small primary issues and generally little secondary market activity. Although some frontiers have been able to tap into this source of foreign capital, with non-resident holdings of domestic government securities becoming significant in, say, Nigeria, Zambia, Egypt and Ghana, this has not been able to displace the volume that treasury managers can obtain on the international market; and of course, it can also be a source of financial instability if the capital is repatriated quickly (eg as may have been in part the case for Argentina in early 2018).

Recent Sovereign Default Experience

Since our last Guide was published, 10 countries have defaulted (classified by missed payments, announcements of a moratorium or an involuntary exchange) on their sovereign international bonds (or guaranteed issues) and there have been 14 instances of default (Belize and Mozambique have defaulted twice and the Republic of Congo three times; Table 2). And there have been 17 instances of default stretching further back over the last decade. Background to these default events is given in this Guide (except one, St. Kitts and Nevis). These defaults have tended to be in frontiers, covering small bond stocks, rather than in the more mainstream markets (Argentina, Venezuela, Ukraine and Greece being notable exceptions). We also observe that whereas some saw hard defaults (missed payments), some were cases of pre-arrears restructuring, namely Greece (2012), Ukraine (2015), Mozambique's EMATUM exchange (2016) and Belize (2017), while others saw missed payments but no action was taken by creditors as they were prepared to wait in the belief that the authorities would cure the situation later—eg in the case of Argentina (2014), the Republic of Congo (three times) and, going further back, Cote d'Ivoire (2010).

As at end-September 2018, there were three ongoing defaults on sovereign eurobonds—Barbados (US$0.5bn), Mozambique (US$0.7bn) and Venezuela (US$31.1bn)—covering cUS$32bn (nominal) in bonds (although most of this, c96%, related to Venezuela). Including defaulted PDVSA bonds in Venezuela (another US$25bn), the total sovereign and related bonds in default amounted to US$57.7bn. This, however, excludes other commercial loans in default in the case of Mozambique (two commercial loans, MAM and Proindicus, amounting to about US$1.1bn combined) and Barbados, and in Barbados's case domestic debt in default as well (cUS$6bn equivalent in BBD$ claims), which would bring defaulted commercial claims (domestic and external) to some US$65bn.

Of the three sovereign bond defaults, by end-September 2018, Mozambique's bond default was 20 months old, Venezuela's was

Table 2 Summary of recent sovereign bond defaults and restructurings[a]

		Default date[b]	*Exchange date*[c]	*US$ or foreign law bonds covered (principal, US$bn)*	*Nominal haircut (%)*	*NPV loss (%)*
2008	Seychelles	Oct-08	Jan-10	0.2[d]	50	56.2
2009	Ecuador	Nov-08	May-09[e]	3.2	65	67.7
2010	Cote d'Ivoire	Dec-10	Resolved[f]	2.3	0	n/a
2011	St Kitts[g]	Jun-11	Mar-12	0.2[d]	50	62.9
2012	Greece	Feb-12[h]	Mar-12	26.3[i]	53.5	64.6
	Belize	Aug-12[j]	Mar-13	0.5	10	29
2013	Grenada	Mar-13	Nov-15	0.2[d]	50[k]	49
2014	Argentina	Jun-14	Resolved[l]	25.3	0	n/a
2015	Ukraine	Mar-15[m]	Nov-15	18.0	20	20[n]
	Rep of Congo	Dec-15	Resolved[o]	0.4	0	0
2016	Mozambique[p]	Mar-16	Apr-16	0.85	0	n/a
	Rep of Congo	Jun-16	Resolved[q]	0.4	0	0
2017	Mozambique	Jan-17[r]	Ongoing	0.7[d]	n/a	n/a
	Belize	Nov-16[s]	Mar-17	0.5	0	20
	Rep of Congo	Jun-17	Resolved[t]	0.4	0	0
	Venezuela	Nov-17[u]	Ongoing	56.5[v]	n/a	n/a
2018	Barbados	Jun-18	Ongoing	0.5[d]	n/a	n/a

Source: Exotix, Bloomberg, IMF, Cruces and Trebesch

[a]Including government guaranteed bonds but excluding non-bond defaults (eg loans) and defaults of SOEs (except Venezuela's PDVSA)

[b]Payment due date rather than end of grace period, or date of restructuring announcement/moratorium

[c]In the cases where default was not resolved through an exchange offer, they were usually cured through payments being made at a later date. We label these "resolved" but leave undated as it is not always possible to discern when the default was actually cured (see also respective footnote for additional detail)

[d]Excludes other debt in default

[e]Cash buyback at 35 cents on the dollar

[f]No exchange took place, rather a repayment plan for missed coupons was agreed in November 2012

[g]Not covered in this book

[h]Technically Greece did not default (miss payments) on its international law bonds. Completion of a debt exchange became a prior action for the IMF's EFF programme that was approved in March 2012, and terms of a PSI offer were announced in February 2012

[i]Excludes other debt in default. We show EUR19.9bn in foreign law sovereign and government guaranteed bonds, equivalent to US$26.3bn at average US$/EUR exchange rate in March 2012, out of a total eligible debt of EUR205.6 billion (US$271.4bn) consisting of domestic and foreign law, sovereign and state-enterprise debt, including guaranteed bonds

[j]In announcing an intention to restructure, the government paid half the August coupon as a show of good faith

[k]50% nominal reduction in two tranches, second tranche being conditional on satisfactory performance under the IMF programme

[l]No exchange took place—missed payments were eventually paid when legal restrictions were lifted

[m]Debt restructuring (PSI) was part of the IMF programme approved in March 2015. The government set out the restructuring parameters in April 2015—a bond default occurred in September and October 2015

[n]Excluding GDP warrants

(continued)

Table 2 (continued)

[o]No exchange took place, payment was made within grace period
[p]Exchange of the government guaranteed EMATUM bond which may be viewed as a default as an involuntary exchange, in which the bond's CAC was activated, even though financial terms were broadly NPV neutral to positive and no payments were missed. S&P classified it as selective default. Fitch did not
[q]No exchange took place, payment was made after grace period
[r]Announcement of intention to seek a restructuring came in October 2016—the government later missed the January 2017 coupon payment on the MOZAM bond
[s]Announcement of intention to seek a restructuring came in November 2016—the government later missed the February 2017 coupon payment on the bond
[t]No exchange took place—payment was blocked by legal action, which was later overturned, and payment was made after grace period
[u]Announcement of moratorium and intention to seek a restructuring—the government later defaulted, selectively, on most of its sovereign and PDVSA bonds
[v]Comprising US$31.1bn in defaulted sovereign bonds (excluding 36s, which is subject to OFAC sanctions, where payment details are not generally available) and US$25.4bn in defaulted PDVSA bonds (all its bonds except the collateralised 20s, which are current)

10 months old and Barbados's three months old. Other than these, some other countries that have outstanding eurobonds are in some sense distressed, including the Republic of Congo (in default on some loans, and official debt, and looking to restructure large parts of its public external debt, although its own US$ bond has been excluded). And, of course, the long-running commercial debt (loan) defaults continue in Cuba, North Korea (both markets being subject to US OFAC sanctions) and Sudan, while Zimbabwe also seeks to normalise its own debt situation with arrears mainly to multilateral creditors.

What does this tell us?

Although each of the dozen or so sovereign bond restructurings over the past decade has had its own circumstances particular to it, we make three observations from these experiences:

1. **Proactive creditor committees.** We think bondholders have become more proactive in organising themselves, forming robust and well-coordinated committees. This should be a positive in terms of helping to facilitate a rapid resolution. Examples of well-organised groups include Ukraine (2015), Belize (2012, 2016), Greece (2012), Grenada (2013), Mozambique (2016–), and Barbados (2018–). The Republic of Congo's London Club restructuring (2007) is a good example of creditors organising themselves pre-emptively and agreeing restructuring terms even before an official sector treatment. This observation is counter to the prevailing view

during the 1990s/early 2000s that held that the shift in international finance away from syndicated bank lending towards more fragmented and diverse bondholders would complicate sovereign debt restructuring. In fact, it might be said that the resolution of bond defaults has been faster than with loans. The use of collective action clauses (CACs) in bonds, whereby acceptance of a super-majority of holders is binding on everyone else, might also have played a role too, in terms of speeding up the process.

2. **Bondholders have generally done well in recent restructurings.** We think bondholders have generally been able to extract good terms in recent sovereign debt restructurings, based on, for example, comparing the final outcomes to the initial restructuring request, or looking at the behaviour of bond prices over the default period. This might be attributed to two reasons. First, is creditor power, as bondholders form strong and well-coordinated committees, and therefore hold stronger bargaining power. This might be seen from Ukraine (2014–2015), Belize (2012 and 2016) and even Greece (2012). And bondholders may have been able to do just as well in bigger and more complex restructurings, such as Ukraine (with multiple bonds), as they have in the case of restructurings on a single bond (Belize). Yet it remains to be seen whether such positive outcomes apply in situations involving multiple and more diverse bonds (the inclusion of aggregation clauses is a more recent innovation), and more complex capital structures (eg in the case of Venezuela, with sovereign and PDVSA debt). Second, is better debtor government behaviour, with improved debtor-creditor dialogue (guided by the IIF principles on sovereign debt restructuring) and a stronger commitment by debtor governments to pursuing economic reforms (often in the context of IMF programmes), which is more likely to be rewarded by investors over the longer term. As such, the take it or leave it unilateral offers of Argentina (2005) or Ecuador (2009) may increasingly be seen as the exception rather than the rule. In fact, it might be that it was the very presence of the IMF (during the crisis period and workout) that meant bondholders did well in those cases compared with those instances when there was no IMF engagement.
3. **Decline in exit yields.** The exit yield (discount rate for the new restructured bonds) is an input to the calculation of recovery values (and the size of PV losses) and its downward trajectory over recent

years may be another factor explaining why bondholders have seemingly enjoyed better recoveries in recent restructuring cases compared with the past (it means discounting future cash flows at lower rates, so enhancing PV gains, and/or making it easier for bondholders to accept cash flow relief); although lower exit yields per se do not explain why creditors may have been able to get better terms. Over the past 20 years, we observe a downward trend in exit yields (Fig. 2). This trend in part mirrors the downward path in global interest rates over this period. The decline in US bond yields is part of the explanation, with the average 10-year UST yield over 2015–2017 at c2.4%, compared with c5.5% over 1998–2000 (during the restructurings of Pakistan, Ecuador and Cote d'Ivoire). Hence, on some occasions, the lower exit yields we have seen recently might be explained entirely by lower US bond yields. The spread between the exit yield and the risk free in the recent cases of Ukraine, Grenada and Belize is little different to that seen in those earlier episodes. But nominal EM yields have also fallen because of the narrowing in EM country risk premia (credit spreads) too, with

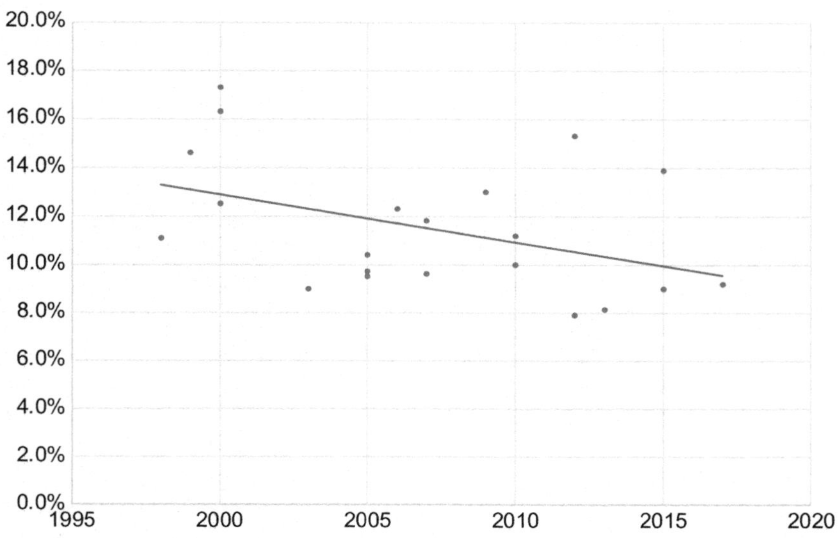

Fig. 2 Exit yields in recent sovereign debt restructurings (%). Source: Exotix, Bloomberg, IMF, Cruces and Trebesch database

the general improvement in EM fundamentals. One measure of country risk, the JPM EMBIGD spread, has fallen from 600–1000bps over 1999–2000 (admittedly, a time of systemic EM crises), to a narrow range of c225–450bps over most of the past eight years (2010–2018). So, in other cases (such as those over 2010–2013, and some of the restructurings in the mid-2000s), lower exit yields have been driven mainly by lower risk premia. Either way, this downward trend may force the need to reappraise traditional benchmark discount rates when analysing restructuring proposals, although a case-by-case approach is certainly needed (we have tended to use a benchmark rate of 12%, but see why 10% might be more relevant nowadays). That said, the tightening of post-GFC easy liquidity conditions might be a harbinger of higher yields in the future and cause exit yield assumptions to become more conservative again.

Future Issues in Frontier Debt Markets

China

Perhaps the biggest issue confronting Western policymakers (and investors) today that could test the prevailing world order is the emergence of China, and other non-traditional creditors, as a dominant lender to emerging and frontier markets, with seemingly less conditionality and transparency, as well as the emergence of other quasi-official lending institutions.

Of itself, new lending is not a bad thing, if the money has been used productively (Africa's infrastructure needs, for instance, are still in the tens of billions per annum) and a more diverse creditor base is a positive. But the rise in public debt burdens across EMs, and especially in frontiers and across SSA, only a decade after many benefitted from significant debt forgiveness from the HIPC initiative, is a concern, and the pace of new borrowing may have outpaced the borrowing countries' capacity to manage the proceeds and debt stock appropriately. For many frontiers, bond issuance is still a relatively recent phenomenon and they have yet to fully establish track records of prudent borrowing and debt management over a full economic cycle.

But the often-opaque nature of new lending from non-traditional bilateral creditors is a growing cause of concern. This is particularly an issue for Chinese lending, because of its sheer scale (Fig. 3), but the wider point is relevant to new lending provided by other lenders, including Russia, India and the Middle East. There is often very little public information on such

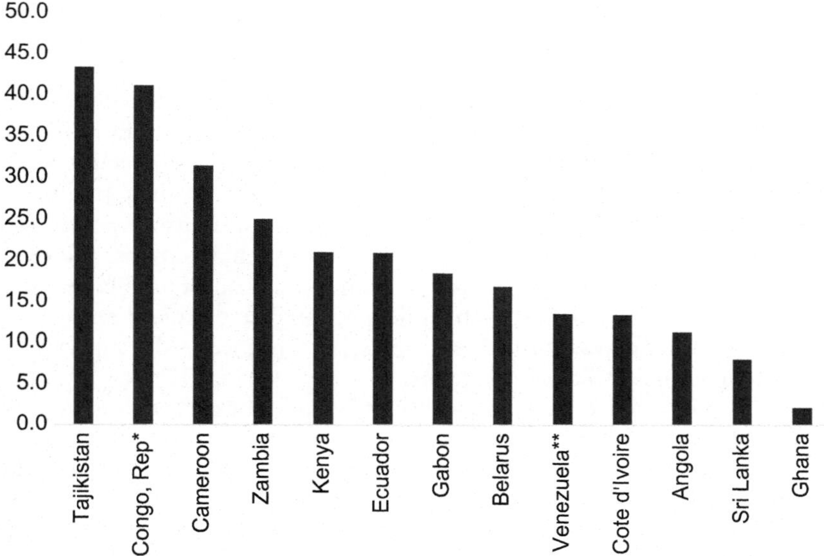

Fig. 3 Chinese debt as a share of public external debt in selected countries (%). Source: Exotix. Based on official figures. *Based on media reports. **Exotix estimate

lending, from the creditor and debtor, on both the amount and its terms, which are often at commercial rather than concessional rates. And such lending and investment is only going to increase under China's transformational Belt and Road Initiative (BRI).

The existence of such large non-traditional bilateral lending in general, and Chinese lending in particular, could provide a major test of the international financial architecture in regards to the official sector response to emerging and frontier market debt crises. Of course, non-traditional bilateral debt has been present in previous sovereign debt workouts, although it was then often much smaller than traditional bilateral lending (usually from Western governments and their export credit agencies) and easier for the Paris Club to push its principle of comparability of treatment onto smaller lenders. It is the scale of such new non-traditional bilateral lending, and the lenders' growing geopolitical clout, that makes it different and could test the traditional sovereign debt workout mechanisms (eg the Paris Club).

In managing future debt crises, there seem to be three potential scenarios:

1. Could such bilateral lenders be brought into the traditional Paris Club forum (ad hoc or permanent)? This, though, might require a degree of transparency that such lenders are not comfortable with, especially in regards to providing enough detail on their lending in order for the IMF to carry out proper debt sustainability tests and ensure suitable programme design (as in such situations, the existence of an IMF programme is often a pre-requisite for Paris Club relief). It will also test such lenders' willingness to adopt some general and well-established principles; for instance, IMF supervision and comparability of treatment.
2. Or might there be more ad hoc bilateral debt agreements outside the Paris Club, treatments that themselves are non-transparent, and that could complicate the IMF's own role in programme lending? An ad hoc treatment with China was seen in the recent case of Ethiopia Airlines' reprofiling of its Chinese debt. Ecuador and Zambia also, in 2018, and Venezuela before then, all turned to China to restructure their bilateral debt (although, to date, neither Ecuador nor Zambia have been able to restructure their Chinese debt). And the Republic of Congo, which needs an IMF programme and is seeking to restructure its debt, in which China is a significant creditor, could be a first test of whether such situations will follow the traditional route or a more ad hoc approach.
3. Or could there be a breakaway or formation of a new non-traditional bilateral lending club as direct competition to the Paris Club—the Beijing Club, say? This would require a greater degree of inter-agency cooperation and coordination amongst such lenders across countries than seen hitherto.

Moreover, such non-traditional bilateral lending sources may have implications for the role of the IMF and other official sector lending in crisis prevention. The possible fall-back of seemingly generous Chinese financing without policy conditionality could delay calls to Washington for help, or lead to one being played off against the other (or create a risk that China effectively free rides on the Fund, effectively ensuring the IMF finances the country's ability to repay its debt to China, something we think the Fund will want to avoid), while the existence of sizeable bilateral debt and its lack of transparency could complicate the IMF programme discussions themselves, given the need for the IMF to assess debt sustainability and financing gaps (the Fund cannot credibly assess these if it only knows half the picture).

Test cases of China's willingness to abide by traditional rules of the game might be provided in the Republic of Congo, Pakistan, Zambia and Venezuela. We think the Republic of Congo is likely to be the first example, albeit on a small scale, of a situation in which a country requires an IMF programme and needs to restructure its debt, and where China is a significant creditor. China needs to be part of the solution. But this immediately throws up two key issues. First, debt reconciliation and coordination across the various Chinese lending arms. Second, obtaining the necessary financing assurances from major creditors, including China, for a Fund programme to go ahead. Both of these will require greater transparency from China than seen hitherto. On a bigger scale, another test case will come from Pakistan, which has recently requested Fund support, and where China is also a significant creditor (although there is no suggestion of a restructuring of its commercial debt). Meanwhile, Zambia is seeking comfort on its Chinese debt, seemingly either before it re-engages with the IMF or decides that it does not need the IMF. Venezuela, which is already in default on most of its bonded debt, will also be an important test case of debt resolution where China is a major bilateral creditor (if and when the time comes).

Yet, it is also worth noting in some cases that even Chinese lending has its limits. It often comes at a big cost (financially and politically) when borrowers get into trouble, and they have little choice but to transfer assets in return, as we have seen in the cases of Sri Lanka and Djibouti handing over ports to China. This could prompt public unrest in the home countries. Examples where countries have shown more resistance to Chinese lending, or demanded greater scrutiny and more prudent borrowing, include Malaysia (cancelling three BRI projects), Bangladesh, Indonesia, Thailand and Sierra Leone.

Transparency in Lending

If the focus of international policy on EM sovereign debt over the past 20 years has been on trying to make debt restructuring more orderly, then the future policy agenda may be shaped by global initiatives to promote sustainable lending and greater transparency in lending, such as the IIF/G20 Debt Transparency Initiative, as a direct reaction to recent events. This should have benefits both in terms of crisis prevention and, if it comes to it, crisis resolution.

The international agenda for much of the past 20 years has in no small part been influenced by the official sector's fear of 'holdout creditors' (aka vultures), following Argentina's post-default 2001 default experience. Arguably, it was also because the debtor behaved so badly, through its 'take it or leave it' offer, but the threat of holdouts destabilising future restructurings forced the notion of mechanisms to ensure orderly restructurings up the agenda. The IIF/G20 best practice, codified in the *Principles for Stable Capital Flows and Fair Debt Restructuring* (November 2004), was an important step on this road. Specifically, bond contracts have pursued legal remedies; first, through the mainstream introduction of CACs for EM sovereign bonds (commencing with Mexico in 2003); and, second, more recently, with the introduction of aggregation clauses to better bind the majority over a series of bonds.

What next? As recent experience of some developing markets shows, perhaps there needs to be more attention paid to controlling sovereign borrowing, and shadow borrowing, in the first place. The experience of Mozambique's hidden debt saga might be another example where one incident can set a global agenda and have repercussions for some time to come. It has shone a light within the IMF and wider official sector community over borrowing and lending practices, governance and data reporting. But this is not easy for the IMF and IFIs to police, especially outside a Fund programme (when a lot of lending that could eventually cause distress occurs), when they have less influence and leverage, especially when there is always a willing lender given the size of the global capital market (private and official).

As a result, the notion of debt transparency is moving up the international policy agenda. One idea is to encourage lenders to disclose more information about the nature of their lending through a voluntary code of conduct (eg the amount of a new loan, interest rate and repayment profile) and make comprehensive debt data more accessible. One idea is even to create a central registry of lending, but this not without its difficulties. We make three observations here. First, the focus it seems is very much on private sector discipline, although, given the preceding discussion, the same emphasis should also be applied to non-traditional bilateral creditors too. Second, regarding private sector lending, while there may be little impact on the public side (bond issuance), which by nature tends to be fairly transparent, it would have wider repercussions for private placements, bank lending and the loan market, which by definition tends to be less transparent. Third, although there is no intention to promote this transparency initiative through force (the focus is on voluntary framework), private sector lenders in particular might worry that slow or limited uptake could lead to a more coercive approach. Yet, in sum, if it means less, and more expensive, but higher-quality lending, that may be applauded. It will demand greater responsibility from both sides, creditors and debtors, especially in the strengthening of debt management operations of frontier issuers with limited track records in the market and weaker institutional capacity.

Ultimately, whether the official sector takes a stick rather than carrot approach or relies on self-regulation will be determined in ongoing discussions within the various official fora on this topic, such as the new G20/IIF work on voluntary debt transparency principles launched in April 2018. However this initiative unfolds, and we think there is sufficient momentum from both the official sector and private sector, including lenders and financial firms, as well as civil society, to ensure it does not just fade away, it is likely to lead to some changes.

And Finally

This Guide is written for the serious frontier market investor, policymaker or academic analyst who is looking to maximise returns, improve policymaking or advance research through superior knowledge. We provide analysis and outlooks for 42 frontier economies (with additional countries available on our website), along with detailed descriptions of their debt histories and restructuring experiences, and with the main investable instruments in the hard currency sovereign and corporate space in each. We aim to give our clients a convenient reference point to check details on loans and illiquid bonds and include as many frontier markets, illiquid instruments, nonperforming or restructured bonds and loans as possible.

We hope you enjoy reading and using the latest edition of the Exotix Capital Guide.

Stuart Culverhouse
Chief Economist & Global Head of FI Research

Christopher Dielmann
Senior Economist

5 November 2018

Summary Statistics

Economic data

	Income per capita 2018f (USD)	*Nominal GDP 2018f (USD bn)*	*10 year average real GDP growth (%)*	*Inflation 2018f*	*Current account 2018f (% of GDP)*	*Latest reserves (USD mn)*
Angola	3924	114.5	5.7	20.5	−2.1	13,300
Argentina	10,667	475.4	2.8	31.8	−3.7	61,881
Azerbaijan	4587	45.6	8.3	3.5	6.6	5471
Barbados	18,366	5.2	0.3	4.2	−3.1	205
Belarus	6020	56.9	3.7	5.5	−2.5	6831
Belize	4830	1.9	2.4	1.3	−6.0	305
Bosnia and Herzegovina	5704	20.0	2.5	1.4	−6.0	6530
Cameroon	1545	38.4	4.3	1.0	−3.2	3235
Republic of Congo	2572	11.5	4.0	1.2	9.1	417
Cote d'Ivoire	1791	45.9	4.7	1.7	−4.6	17,600
Cuba	8129	93.2	2.2	6.9	2.2	11,553
Dominican Republic	7891	81.1	5.6	4.3	−1.6	6598
Ecuador	6301	107.3	3.5	−0.2	−0.5	3128
El Salvador	4041	25.9	2.2	1.2	−3.9	3273
Ethiopia	891	83.8	10.3	12.7	−6.2	3197
Gabon	8385	17.2	3.5	2.8	−1.6	982
Georgia	4506	16.7	4.9	2.8	−10.5	3005

(*continued*)

Exotix Capital, *Exotix Developing Markets Guide*,
https://doi.org/10.1007/978-3-030-05867-8_2

(continued)

	Income per capita 2018f (USD)	*Nominal GDP 2018f (USD bn)*	*10 year average real GDP growth (%)*	*Inflation 2018f*	*Current account 2018f (% of GDP)*	*Latest reserves (USD mn)*
Ghana	1787	51.8	6.8	9.5	−4.1	3871
Greece	20,311	218.1	−1.9	0.7	−0.8	6317
Grenada	11,032	1.2	1.4	2.6	−7.5	202
Iraq	5793	220.9	6.5	2.0	6.9	55
Jamaica	5393	15424.0	0.2	3.4	−4.9	3135
Kazakhstan	9977	184.2	5.1	6.4	−0.2	30,563
Kenya	1865	89.6	5.3	5.0	−5.6	9291
Mongolia	4098	12.7	7.5	7.6	−8.3	3256
Mozambique	481	14.6	7.0	6.0	−18.2	3188
Nigeria	2050	397.5	5.7	12.4	2.0	47,789
Pakistan	1527	306.9	3.9	3.9	−5.9	13,697
Rwanda	800	9709.0	7.8	3.3	−8.9	987
Senegal	1485	24.2	4.2	0.4	−7.7	17,600
Seychelles	16,377	1.6	4.7	4.4	−18.4	569
Sri Lanka	4265	92.5	6.1	4.8	−2.9	9248
Sudan	792	33.2	0.8	61.8	−14.2	830
Suriname	6506	3.8	2.5	7.8	−3.3	762
Tajikistan	807	7.4	6.8	5.8	−4.7	758
Tanzania	1090	55.6	6.5	3.8	−4.3	5906
Trinidad	16,931	23.3	1.4	2.3	10.7	7965
Ukraine	2964	126.4	−0.5	10.9	−3.1	17,979
Venezuela	3300	96.3	−0.3	–	6.1	8717
Vietnam	2553	241.4	6.1	3.8	2.2	42,200
Zambia	1450	25.8	6.6	8.5	−4.0	1785
Zimbabwe	1269	19.4	3.6	3.9	−5.8	201

Source: IMF WEO where available. See country chapters for definitions, details and footnotes

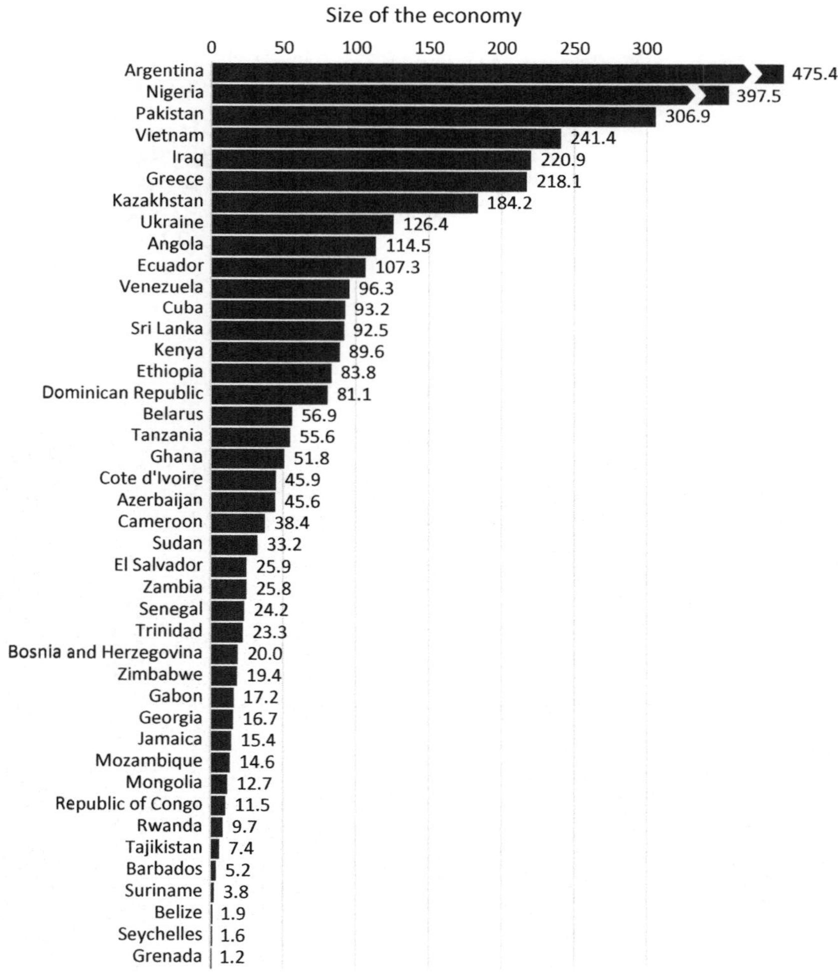
Size of the economy
0
50
100
150
200
250
300
Argentina 475.4
Nigeria 397.5
Pakistan 306.9
Vietnam 241.4
Iraq 220.9
Greece 218.1
Kazakhstan 184.2
Ukraine 126.4
Angola 114.5
Ecuador 107.3
Venezuela 96.3
Cuba 93.2
Sri Lanka 92.5
Kenya 89.6
Ethiopia 83.8
Dominican Republic 81.1
Belarus 56.9
Tanzania 55.6
Ghana 51.8
Cote d'Ivoire 45.9
Azerbaijan 45.6
Cameroon 38.4
Sudan 33.2
El Salvador 25.9
Zambia 25.8
Senegal 24.2
Trinidad 23.3
Bosnia and Herzegovina 20.0
Zimbabwe 19.4
Gabon 17.2
Georgia 16.7
Jamaica 15.4
Mozambique 14.6
Mongolia 12.7
Republic of Congo 11.5
Rwanda 9.7
Tajikistan 7.4
Barbados 5.2
Suriname 3.8
Belize 1.9
Seychelles 1.6
Grenada 1.2

Nominal GDP (USD billion, 2018 or latest available)

Debt ratios

2017 (or latest available)	*Total external debt/GDP*	*Total external debt/exports*	*External debt service ratio*	*Total external debt (USD mn)*	*Public debt/GDP*
Angola	35.2	124.2	15.1	45,700	64.2
Argentina	37.0	324.7	49.1	235,955	57.1
Azerbaijan	37.3	76.1	4.4	14,085	50.7
Barbados	41.4	83.3	8.4	2141	152.3
Belarus	73.3	109.5	4.7	40,221	46.5
Belize	75.1	138.6	8.5	1393	97.1
Bosnia and Herzegovina	61.8	157.5	19.9	11,163	41.2
Cameroon	24.8	116.1	5.6	8429	27.9
Republic of Congo	77.4	151.5	3.5	3837	114.6
Cote d'Ivoire	38.7	124.2	10.8	17,733	45.6
Cuba	33.2	222.4	–	30,466	43.5
Dominican Republic	35.0	138.7	20.9	29,067	39.4
Ecuador	38.6	159.3	35.9	41,906	45.5
El Salvador	57.1	130.6	6.8	16,420	65.5
Ethiopia	31.5	409.5	19.6	25,502	43.2
Gabon	37.4	103.4	12.5	4933	64.2
Georgia	96.8	193.9	20.2	14,244	44.5
Ghana	51.0	117.4	17.0	25,347	79.1
Greece	227.9	720.6	–	403	184.9
Grenada	129.2	229.8	10.6	1441	81.1
Iraq	33.0	85.5	4.0	64,600	58.7
Jamaica	100.5	193.5	17.1	14,437	111.6
Kazakhstan	104.1	300.5	66.4	167,485	26.7
Kenya	44.9	226.3	13.1	43,487	55.7
Mongolia	246.2	396.3	9.3	27,412	99.6
Mozambique	138.7	364.6	18.2	17,586	107.7
Nigeria	12.6	87.4	0.9	47,438	22.1
Pakistan	28.1	289.9	20.2	85,393	67.9
Rwanda	40.6	179.3	6.4	3709	48.3
Senegal	73.2	171.7	7.2	14,090	66.5
Seychelles	100.4	95.3	3.6	1487	64.9
Sri Lanka	59.2	268.8	10.9	54,323	79.7
Sudan	90.9	1035.0	33.0	29,067	96.4
Suriname	78.2	128.5	6.3	2619	63.9
Tajikistan	74.4	313.2	9.8	5385	50.1
Tanzania	37.1	190.2	8.9	20,157	41.1
Trinidad	16.2	32.9	2.0	3501	82.7
Ukraine	104.6	216.8	4.8	116,800	72.2
Venezuela	78.9	604.6	4.7	165,665	70.3
Vietnam	43.2	45.9	1.8	86,953	57.1
Zambia	70.0	169.8	6.8	17,844	53.4
Zimbabwe	74.3	243.6	5.0	12,717	80.6

Notes: See main text for definitions, details and footnotes

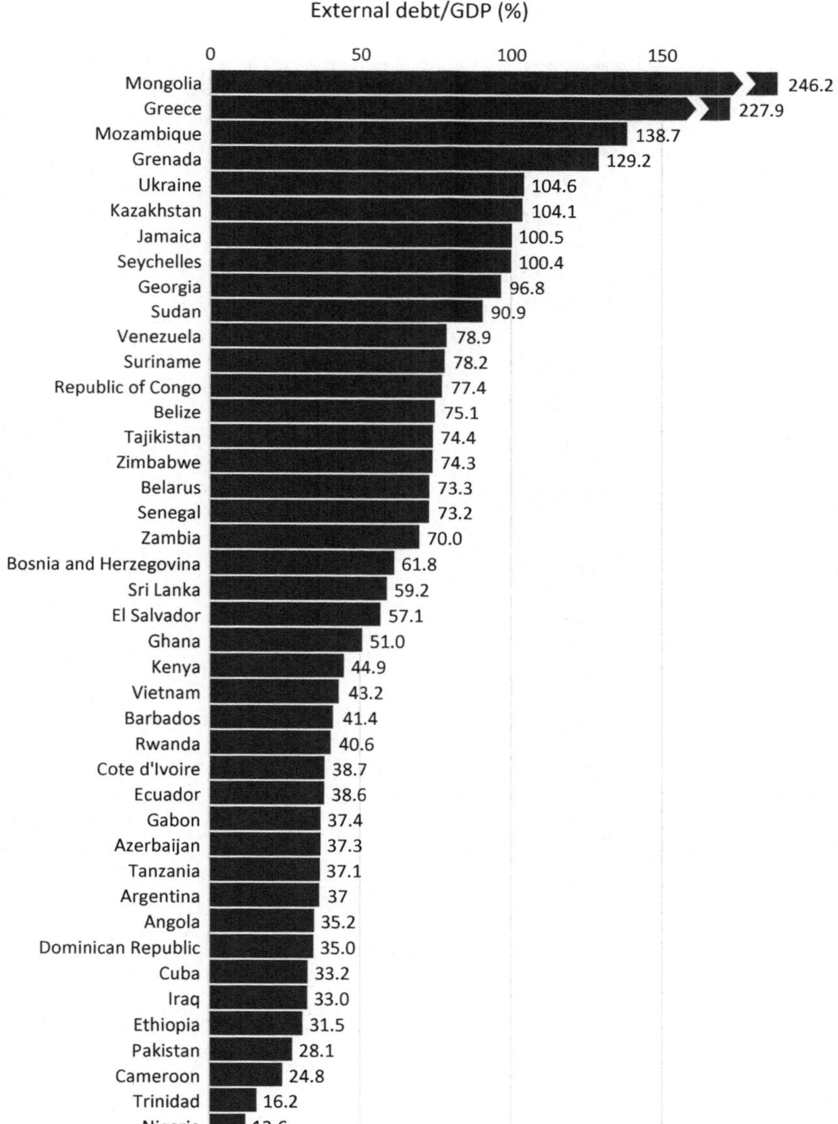

External Debt/GDP ratio for 2017 or latest available, see main text for details

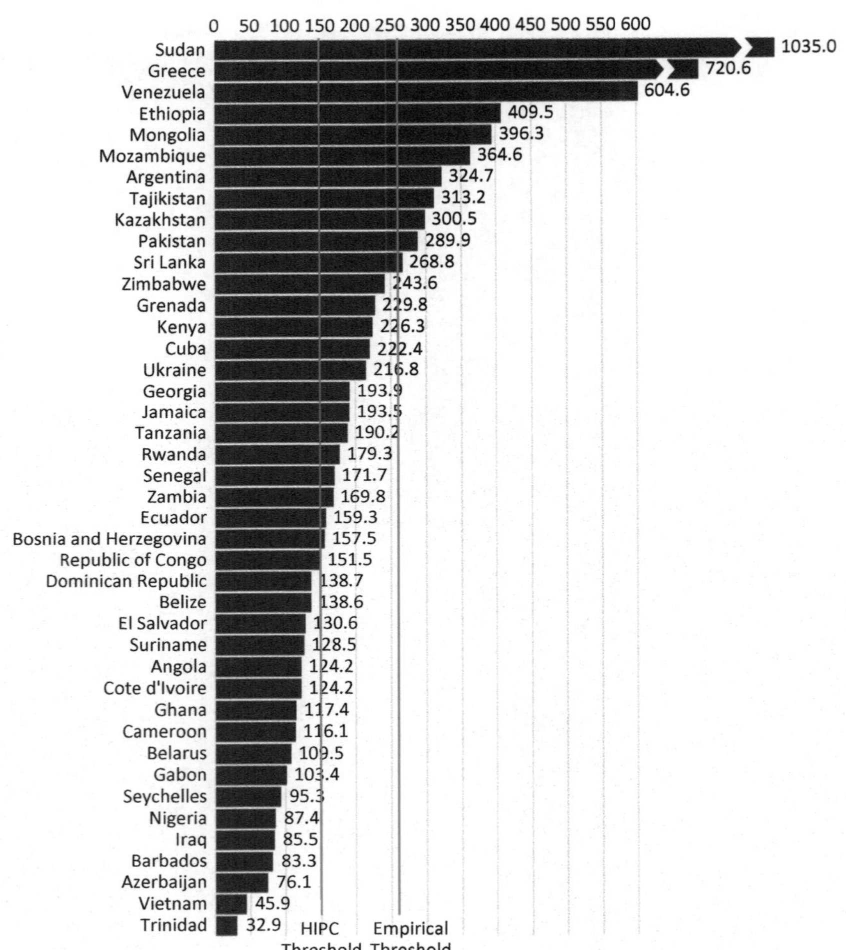

External debt/Exports ratio for 2017 or latest available, see main text for details. Indicative thresholds for debt sustainability shown

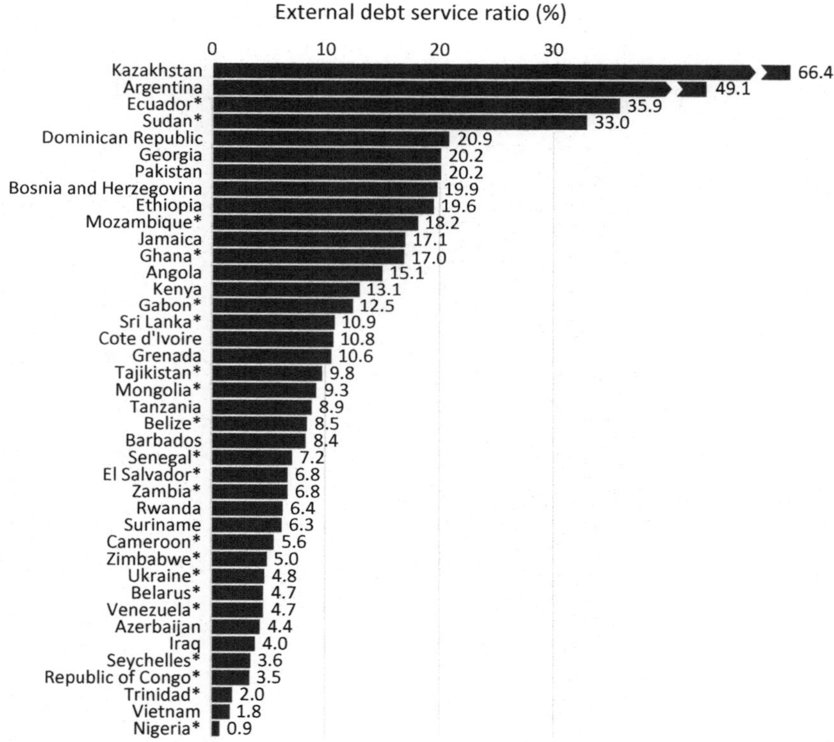

External Debt Service Ratio (%)
*PPG only

Public debt/GDP
0 20 40 60 80 100 120
Greece 184.9
Barbados 152.3
Republic of Congo 114.6
Jamaica 111.6
Mozambique 107.7
Mongolia 99.6
Belize 97.1
Sudan 96.4
Trinidad 82.7
Grenada 81.1
Zimbabwe 80.6
Sri Lanka 79.7
Ghana 79.1
Ukraine 72.2
Venezuela 70.3
Pakistan 67.9
Senegal 66.5
El Salvador 65.5
Seychelles 64.9
Angola 64.2
Gabon 64.2
Suriname 63.9
Iraq 58.7
Argentina 57.1
Vietnam 57.1
Kenya 55.7
Zambia 53.4
Azerbaijan 50.7
Tajikistan 50.1
Rwanda 48.3
Belarus 46.5
Cote d'Ivoire 45.6
Ecuador 45.5
Georgia 44.5
Cuba 43.5
Ethiopia 43.2
Bosnia and Herzegovina 41.2
Tanzania 41.1
Dominican Republic 39.4
Papua New Guinea 32.2
Cameroon 27.9
Kazakhstan 26.7
Nigeria 22.1

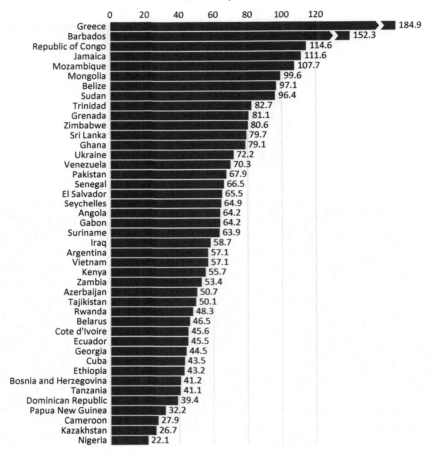

Institutional characteristics

	UN HDI 2018	*TI CPI 2017*	*FP Fragile State Index 2018*	*WB Doing Business 2018*	*HF IEF 2018*
Angola	147	167	33	175	164
Argentina	47	85	141	117	144
Azerbaijan	80	122	78	57	67
Barbados	58	25	139	132	117
Belarus	53	68	97	38	108
Belize	106	–	115	121	116
Bosnia and Herzegovina	77	92	95	86	91
Cameroon	151	153	23	163	149
Republic of Congo	137	162	29	179	177
Cote d'Ivoire	170	104	25	139	85
Cuba	73	62	119	–	178
Dominican Republic	94	135	104	99	89
Ecuador	86	117	82	118	165
El Salvador	121	114	96	73	75
Ethiopia	173	108	15	161	142
Gabon	110	119	88	167	109
Georgia	70	46	83	9	16
Ghana	140	81	108	120	122
Greece	31	59	128	67	115
Grenada	75	52	123	142	–
Iraq	120	169	11	168	–
Jamaica	97	69	118	70	40
Kazakhstan	58	124	117	36	41
Kenya	142	145	17	80	129
Mongolia	92	105	130	62	125
Mozambique	180	154	36	138	170
Nigeria	157	150	14	145	104
Pakistan	150	120	20	147	131
Rwanda	158	49	34	41	39
Senegal	164	67	62	140	126
Seychelles	62	37	125	95	88
Sri Lanka	76	94	50	111	111
Sudan	167	175	7	170	161
Suriname	100	79	114	165	166
Tajikistan	127	164	63	123	106
Tanzania	154	106	64	137	97
Trinidad	69	80	131	102	112
Ukraine	88	134	86	76	150
Venezuela	78	170	46	188	179
Vietnam	116	110	107	68	141
Zambia	144	102	41	85	132
Zimbabwe	156	160	10	159	174
Out of	189 countries	180 countries	178 countries	190 countries	180 countries
Best rank	Lower	Lower	Higher	Lower	Lower

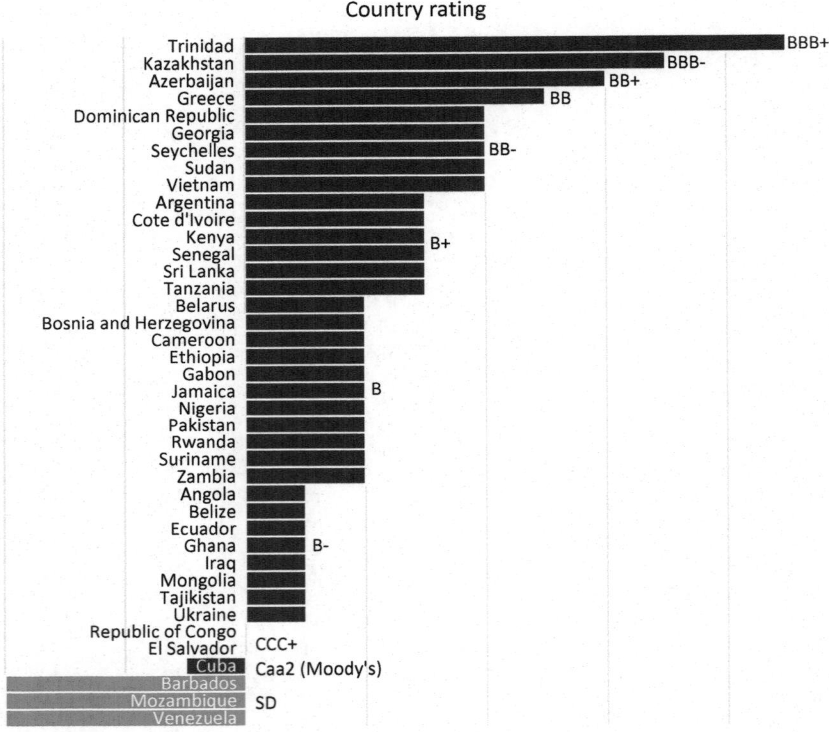

Long term foreign currency rating
Note: S&P rating, or Moody's equivalent/Fitch rating where available or Exotix assignment

Angola

Nominal GDP (US$mn, 2018)[a]		114,504
Population (thousand, 2018)[a]		29,178
GDP per capita (USD, 2018)[a]		3924
Credit ratings (long-term foreign currency)[b]	Fitch	B
	Moody's	B3
	S&P	B–

[a]IMF WEO October 2018
[b]As at end-September 2018

Country Summary

- Long-time President José Eduardo dos Santos was succeeded by João Lourenço following the legislative elections in August 2017, ending his 38 years in power. The new president has actively worked to tackle corruption and strengthen institutions, dismantling the nepotism and cronyism of the dos Santos era. He also wants to encourage private sector activity and increase investment.
- Angola is a major African oil exporter (producing about 2mn barrels per day) and is now the biggest supplier of crude oil to China, replacing Russia. There have been attempts over recent years to diversify away from oil, with potential seen in agriculture, construction, financial services, mining and others, although success will depend on infrastructural improvements, which needs external financing, and improving

Exotix Capital, *Exotix Developing Markets Guide*,
https://doi.org/10.1007/978-3-030-05867-8_3

the business environment. Angola scores badly on business environment, ranking 175 out of 190 in the 2018 World Bank's Doing Business survey.

- Angola was hit hard by the lower oil prices over 2014–2017, which led to wider fiscal and external deficits, a sharp fall in official reserves, and a rise in the public debt/GDP ratio (which doubled over 2014–2016 to 80% of GDP on IMF WEO figures), as Angola borrowed a lot from foreign creditors (official and commercial). China now accounts for over half its central government external debt. But the policy response, initially under Dos Santos and then under Lourenço, was also orthodox, including a devaluation of the exchange rate and fiscal tightening. Lourenço has also sought to buttress policy credibility through requesting IMF support.

Economic data	*Avg*[a]	*2014*	*2015*	*2016*	*2017 (e)*	*2018 (f)*	*2019 (f)*
Real GDP growth	5.7	4.8	0.9	−2.6	−2.5	−0.1	3.1
Inflation (annual average)	13.3	7.3	9.2	30.7	29.8	20.5	15.8
Current account (% of GDP)	5.0	−2.6	−8.8	−4.8	−1.0	−2.1	−1.9
Reserves (US$bn, end-period)[b]	–	27.1	24.3	20.8	13.4	13.3[c]	–
Reserves/imports (months)[d]	–	5.2	6.6	8.0	4.5	–	–
Overall fiscal balance (% of GDP)[e]	0.3	−5.7	−2.9	−4.5	−6.1	−0.8	−0.2
Currency (ticker)	Angolan kwanza (AOA)						
FX regime	The de jure exchange rate arrangement is floating, while the IMF has classed the de facto exchange rate arrangement as "other managed" since June 2015. AOA is pegged to USD and has seen a number of devaluations, most recently in January 2018, when the government announced it would let the currency trade in a wider unpublished band (the kwanza was devalued in two moves by nearly 20% against the US dollar). Prior to this, the kwanza was devalued in 2014 and three times in 2015, and before that in 2009, after the global financial crisis.						
Key exports	Oil (96%), diamonds (3.6%) in 2016. These had been 98% and 1.7%, respectively, in 2013, before the decline in oil prices.						

Source: IMF WEO Database, Haver, IMF Country Reports, OEC

[a]10-year average to 2016, unless otherwise stated

[b]Net international reserves

[c]Latest figure, June 2018

[d]In months of the current year's imports of goods, services and primary income debit, Exotix calculation

[e]Overall government net lending

Key figures		*Party*	*Since*
President	João Lourenço	MPLA	Sep. 2017
Vice president[a]	Bornito de Sousa	MPLA	Sep. 2017
Minister of state for economic and social development in the office of the president[b]	Manuel Nunes Júnior	MPLA	Sep. 2017
Minister of finance	Augusto Archer de Sousa Mangueira	MPLA	Sep. 2016
Minister of economy and planning	Pedro Luis da Fonseca	MPLA	Sep. 2017
Key opposition figure	Isaias Samakuva	UNITA	Jun. 2003
Central bank governor[c]	José de Lima Massano	–	Oct. 2017

[a]The position of vice president was created after a cabinet reshuffle in February 2010

[b]A cabinet reshuffle in October 2010 saw the president's office assume more control over certain areas of economic policymaking, including coordination of economic policies, relations with the IMF and financing, at the expense of the economy ministry. The planning ministry also emerged more powerful after the reshuffle also taking on some of the economy ministry's duties

[c]Originally governor from October 2010, President dos Santos replaced José de Lima Massano with José Pedro de Morais in January 2015, and President Lourenço re-appointed him governor in October 2017

Politics

Executive Power

Power rests with the president, who is chief of state and head of government. The president's position was further empowered after changes to the constitution approved in January 2010 that removed direct elections for the presidency, abolished the post of prime minister, created the role of vice president and allowed the president to appoint judges to the constitutional court, supreme court and court audit. The president appoints a cabinet-come-government: the Council of Ministers. The latter comprises 31 appointees and 55 deputies, and acts as the executive, with senior members, including the president, able to pass law by decree in areas of expertise. Fernando dos Santos (the former president's cousin) is president of the National Assembly. A consultative body—the Council of the Republic—is also formed by presidential appointment.

Presidential term: The leader of the winning party in the legislative election automatically becomes president, for up to two five-year terms.

Parliamentary term: Five years

Legislature

Angola has a unicameral legislature; the National Assembly, with a total of 220 seats: 130 are elected by popular vote and 90 according to equal representation of the 18 provinces (five seats each).

Elections

Next due *Legislative: August 2022*

Last legislative election (August 2017)	*Seats*	*% of vote*
Popular Movement for the Liberation of Angola (MPLA)	150	61.1
National Union for the Total Independence of Angola (UNITA)	51	26.7
Broad Convergence for the Salvation of Angola (Coalition, CASA-CE)	16	9.4
Social Renewal Party (PRS)	2	1.4
National Front for the Liberation of Angola (FNLA)	1	0.9
National Patriotic Alliance	0	0.5
Total (directly elected)	**220**	**100.0**

People

Angola's history of conflict is now seemingly behind it. Civil war raged through the country from 1975 to 2002 as different nationalist groups fought for power after independence from Portugal in 1975. The UN estimated that 4mn people were internally displaced in 2002. During the 1950s–1960s, three independence movements emerged: MPLA (communist, backed by USSR and Cuba), UNITA (sponsored by US until the early 1990s and apartheid South Africa until 1989) and FNLA (backed by Zaire). In January 1975, a coup d'etat in Portugal led to the Alvor Accord, with elections set for independence day on 11 November 1975. However, the Alvor Accord broke down. Elections were not held. MPLA seized control of the capital, Luanda, on independence day and imposed a one-party state modelled on Marxist-Leninism. An internationalised civil war erupted, and despite a UN supervised election in 1992 and the 1994 Lusaka Protocol peace agreement, lasted until 2002 after UNITA leader Jonas Savimbi was killed by government forces in February. The Luena Accord in April between MPLA and UNITA ended the war.

Legislative elections were held for the first time in 16 years in September 2008 which saw a landslide victory for the ruling MPLA as expected. In the 2012 and 2017 elections, MPLA's majority declined. These elections were considered free and fair, although received complaints from the opposition. After having made similar statements in previous years, President José Eduardo dos Santos—one of Africa's longest serving leaders after 38 years in power—announced in March 2016 that he planned to retire in 2018, although he stepped down before the 2017 legislative elections. He nominated João Lourenço, previously the defence minister, as his successor. In July 2017, parliament passed laws limiting the president's power in removing heads of the army, police and intelligence services, protecting them in their posts for eight years.

Angola has three main tribes of Bantu origin. The Ovimbundu constitute 37% and traditionally support UNITA. Other major groups include Kimbundu (25%) and Bakongo (13%). The population is very youthful, with 2017 estimates of 48% below the age of 15. Portuguese is the official language and there are other local African languages spoken. The country is predominantly Christian (with the two-fifths of those being Roman Catholic). A continuing separatist conflict simmers in the oil-rich Cabinda province, with deadly clashes between FLEC and government troops in August 2016.

Debt

	2012	*2017*
External debt ratios (%)		
Total external debt/GDP	19.8	35.2
Public external debt/GDP	19.8	35.2
Private external debt/GDP	n/a	n/a
Total external debt/exports of goods and services	31.3	124.2
External debt service ratio	2.9	15.1
Public debt ratios (%)		
Public domestic debt/GDP	10.7	29.0
Public debt/GDP	30.5	64.2

Source: Angola central bank, 2028/2048 Eurobond prospectus, IMF, Haver, Exotix

Angola's total external debt was 35.2% of GDP in 2017, up from 19.8% in 2012, according to Exotix estimates using central bank debt data and IMF GDP figures from the WEO. This is the same as the public external debt/GDP ratio. Figures for private external debt are not available. The private sector is reported to still have no external debt and Bloomberg shows that Angolan corporates have not issued any eurobonds. Total external debt was therefore 124% of exports of goods and services, up from just 31% in 2012, due to the increase in total debt and the decrease in exports over this period. Exports (mainly oil) more than halved over this period, falling to just US$34.6bn in 2017. According to the Angola's eurobond prospectus for the 2028/2048 bonds issued in May 2018, external debt service increased from US$2.1bn in 2012 to US$5.3bn in 2017, leading the external debt service ratio (external debt service as a percentage of exports of goods, services and primary income) to increase from 2.9% to 15.1% over this period.

Angola's public external debt (including arrears and Sonangol, the state-owned oil company), according to central bank figures, was US$43.7bn at the end of 2017 (35.2% of GDP as per the IMF WEO), nearly double the stock in 2012 of US$22.6bn (19.8% of GDP). Some 88% of this in 2017 (US$38.6bn) was central government debt while the remaining 12% (US$5.1bn) was owed by Sonangol. Most of Angola's public external debt has historically been owed to commercial creditors, specifically banks, as even after recent eurobond issuance, bonds remain a small part of the total. Within central government external debt (i.e. excluding debt owed by Sonangol), bank debt rose four fold between 2013 and 2017, from US$5.2bn to US$22.9bn, mostly due to increased borrowing from China, and this was the main driver in the overall increase in central government external debt (up from US$15.0bn in 2013 to US$38.6bn in 2017); as a result, the share of bank debt in central government external debt rose from 35% in 2013 to 60% in 2017. According to a detailed creditor breakdown in the 2028/48 eurobond prospectus, which is not available from central bank figures, Angola's statistics classifies what might be considered bilateral Chinese debt lent via CDB (and some official sector lenders such as JBIC and DBSA) among its commercial bank creditors. Most of the increase in bank debt occurred in one year (2016) as lending from China Development Bank (CDB) increased by US$11bn. Debt owed to CDB rose from US$1.1bn in 2015 to US$12.3bn in 2016 (rising further to US$15.5bn in 2017), as Angola sought external funding to compensate for the loss of oil export revenues. Therefore, by 2017, debt owed to CDB was about 40% of central government external debt, compared to just 2% in 2013, and was nearly 70% of all central government commercial bank debt. Meanwhile eurobonds were just 4% of central government external debt. After commercial creditors, bilaterals were the next largest creditor group, accounting for 20% of central government external debt. Bilateral debt, which has remained broadly unchanged in US$ terms over 2012–2017, was mainly owed to non Paris Club creditors following a Paris Club repayment agreement in 2007, which now leaves debt owed to Paris Club creditors at just US$0.1bn. The main bilateral creditor was China Exim Bank (owed US$5.2bn, about 67% of bilateral debt and 13.5% of central government debt), followed by Brazil (Government and National Bank for Social and Economic Development) and Portugal (Government and COSEC). Hence, overall, China (including official bilateral debt and its banks) has emerged as Angola's biggest bilateral lender by far, accounting for 54% (US$20.7bn) of Angola's central government external debt, compared to 29% (US$4.4bn) in 2013 and a low of 21% (US$5bn) in 2015. Multilaterals accounted for just 5%. There were just two multilateral creditors, the World Bank IDA and the African Development Bank's African Development Fund, owed about US$1bn each. Suppliers were 10.6%.

Included in the aggregate central bank figures is also a small amount of arrears. Arrears totalled around US$105mn and now mostly relate to suppliers and construction contracts, as lower oil export revenues constrain the government's payment ability. US$99mn of the total arrears was to commercial creditors.

Sonangol's external debt meanwhile has more than halved, according to the eurobond prospectus, falling to just US$5.1bn in 2017, down from US$13.3bn in 2013 (all of it being MLT debt). The marked fall is due to the company's own corporate restructuring and debt renegotiations, under the helm of Isobel Dos Santos, daughter of the former president, as the company's chair over 2016–2017, after the company built up sizeable arrears and expanded its business into non-core areas. Sonangol's direct debt to Chinese banks and lending consortia was US$3.8bn at end-2016, although industry executives have suggested that this has since increased. In addition, the government took out a US$6.9bn loan in 2016 from the CDB that it then lent to Sonangol. The IMF reported that US$3.8bn of this was used to refinance debt. An unnamed source was quoted in media in November 2017 saying that of Sonangol's US$3bn commercial debt, nearly US$1bn was owed to trading firms Trafigura and Vitol under oil-guaranteed loans.

Central bank data showed that the public external debt had fallen by US$1.6bn to US$42.1bn in March 2018, due mainly to a decrease in commercial bank debt. However, Angola also issued US$3bn of eurobonds in May 2018 in two maturities (2028 and 2048). Angola also tapped the 2048 bond for an additional US$500mn on 16 July 2018. These issues have therefore increased the level of debt and resulted in a further shift in its composition, other things equal. Exotix has therefore added this gross issuance (US$3.5bn) to the end March 2018 debt stock, and adjusted accordingly other items, to give a more up-to-date creditor breakdown in the table below. This shows as of July 2018 central government external debt was an estimated US$40.6bn and public external debt US$45.7bn (about 38.3% of projected 2018 GDP in the IMF WEO).

Exotix estimates that Angola's total public sector debt (including Sonangol) was 64.2% of GDP in 2017, more than double its 2012 level of 30.5% of GDP (GDP as per the IMF WEO)—according to the IMF WEO, public debt peaked at 80% of GDP in 2016, but declined in 2017 due to a rebound in US$ nominal GDP. In US$ terms, total public debt was US$79.7bn in 2017, of which public domestic debt was just under half at US$36.0bn (29.0% of GDP), according to the eurobond prospectus. This compared to total public debt of US$34.8bn in 2012, of which public domestic debt was just over a third at US$12.2bn (10.7% of GDP). Public domestic debt has therefore tripled as a share of GDP since 2012. Just over three quarters of the stock of domestic debt in 2017 was long term. The rise in total debt reflects budget deficits (due to the impact on fiscal revenues from lower oil prices) and a weakening currency. The IMF WEO projected total public debt to increase to 73% of GDP in 2018, up from 65% in 2017, due in part to the impact of the currency devaluation at the beginning of the year. The overall budget deficit is expected to narrow by some 4ppts in 2018 from 6% of GDP to 2% under the government's economic adjustment plan.

Composition of external debt

External debt by creditor (Jul. 2018e)	*Nominal amount outstanding (US$bn)*	*Share of total (%)*
Public sector external debt	**45.7**	**100.0**
o/w Central government	40.6	88.8
Official multilateral[a]	2.1	4.6
World Bank IDA[b]	1.1	2.4
AfDB/AfDF[b]	1.0	2.2
Official bilateral[a]	7.5	16.4
China[b]	5.2	11.4
Brazil[b]	1.2	2.6
Portugal[b]	0.6	1.3
Commercial creditors	26.9	58.9
Commercial banks[c]	21.9	47.9
Eurobonds[d]	5.0	10.9
Suppliers[a]	4.1	9.0
Sonangol[b]	5.1	11.2
Private non-guaranteed external debt	**n/a**	**n/a**
Total external debt	**45.7**	**100.0**

Source: National Bank of Angola, 2028/2048 Eurobond prospectus, Exotix

[a]Figure as at end-March 2018 from central bank
[b]Figure as at end-2017 from eurobond prospectus
[c]Exotix estimate based on end-March 2018 figures from central bank
[d]Includes eurobond issuance in May and July 2018

Rescheduling History

Angola has a history of debt service problems and arrears, although it only has two instances of restructuring its official debt and has not previously restructured its commercial debt, making its rescheduling history a fairly modest one. This might be because much of its debt has traditionally been owed to commercial banks, through the government or Sonangol, and hence there may have been a reluctance to reschedule this for fear of being cut off from external finance which would hurt the oil industry. It has also not tended to have IMF-supported programmes, in part due to weak policy performance, which multilateral and bilateral creditors require to complete debt rescheduling agreements.

Angola's debt problems date back a long way. Much of its external debt was contracted during the civil war, spurred by loans from Russia to finance arms purchases, and arrears began to accumulate during the 1990s after the collapse of the oil market in the mid-1980s saw government revenues slide. After the civil war, a reluctance to engage in structural and/or technical programmes with multilateral institutions prevented attempts to renegotiate its obligations. In particular, this strained relations with Paris Club members, with whom Angola had been in arrears for almost two decades, entering 2006. Angola selectively defaulted on external obligations, only remaining current where loans were securitised against oil. Angola had access to new bilateral financing from Portugal and China, for example, while state-owned oil company Sonangol took on a number of oil-backed loans. Rescheduling agreements tended to be made on a bilateral and fairly opaque basis; at least until a Paris Club agreement in December 2007 (see below).

By end-1995, public external debt (medium and long term), including arrears, stood at US$12.1bn, some 256% of GDP and 358% of exports. Over half the debt (51%) was owed to Eastern bloc creditors with most of the remainder (46%) owed to western creditors. Less than 2% was owed to multilaterals. A rescheduling agreement was reached in 1996 with Russia resulting in the elimination of ruble-denominated debt; this contributed to a fall in public external debt to US$9.7bn in 1996, equivalent to 153% of GDP and 194% of exports. However, external arrears continued to accumulate. The continued accumulation of external arrears closed Angola's access to multilateral and bilateral financing and forced the government to turn to (expensive) commercial, oil-guaranteed loans. By end-1999, oil guaranteed debt accounted for one-third of total debt and debt servicing was limited to oil guaranteed loans and some multilateral debt. Arrears had reached US$4.4bn (80% of GDP). Domestic arrears also accumulated in 1999. By September 2000, public external debt was US$8.3bn (95% of GDP), of which US$4bn was in arrears, while total public debt in 2000 was 105% of GDP (IMF WEO). Arrears to multilateral creditors were however cleared by January 2001 and, to temper a renewed build up in debt, the authorities agreed to limit the contracting of new non-concessional debt. By 2002, external debt had fallen to 80% of GDP, and total public debt fell to 71% of GDP, in part due to rapid GDP growth and limited new sources of finance rather than debt resolution. Arrears remained at about half the debt.

The oil boom during the noughties subsequently put public debt on a sharp downward path, with public debt falling to 16% of GDP in 2007, before rising again to 44% in 2010 (IMF WEO). Clearance of arrears under an IMF programme and rising oil prices in the preceding years helped it to contain the debt burden, which fell to 30% in 2012, but an increase in public spending, even before the onset of the 2014 oil price crash, saw public debt rise again to 41% in 2014. Rising fiscal deficits, increased borrowing and exchange rate depreciation saw public debt rise further in 2015 to 65% and again in 2016 to 80%. Lower tax revenues after oil price declines contributed to the accumulation of arrears and highlighted the need for economic diversification. The Debt Management Unit (DMU), created by the government in 2010, said in February 2017, that the programme to pay arrears owed to companies between 2014 and 2016 had a budget of US$3.59bn, and that about 20% of the amount had already been repaid.

Relations with Multilateral Creditors

Angola obtained its first, and until recently, only, IMF programme in November 2009. Prior to this, it had no history of financial arrangements with the Fund after it became a member in 1989, despite a history of arrears and debt service problems. Angola's relationship with the IMF was largely based on a number of failed Staff Monitored Programmes (SMP). More broadly, economic policy aimed to stabilise the economy, following the build-up of arrears in the 1990s and episodes of hyperinflation. It was hoped that a dialogue would pave the way for debt relief as the government implemented a reform programme in 1999. The Angolan authorities saw SMPs as a way to establish a policy track record and facilitate a rescheduling with Paris Club and other creditors. However, buoyant oil revenues subsequently enabled Angola to build foreign exchange reserves and work towards clearing its arrears with most creditors, such that balance of payments needs (and hence the need for an IMF programme) became redundant; until the global financial crisis exposed Angola's oil dependency and limited capacity to respond flexibly to the shock.

In fact, Angola was classified as a "severely indebted low-income country" over the late 1990s and considered for HIPC. However, poor relations with the IMF and other international financial institutions—and lack of any IMF programme—eventually made it ineligible for debt relief. Policy performance proved weak. In October 1996, a three-year programme was signed with the IMF including a pledge of US$75mn dependent on securing a peace that was not found until 2002. Angola secured a SMP over the period April–December 2000, although execution was hindered by inadequate data and controls. A new SMP was agreed for the period January–June 2001 although many of the targets were not met. There were various attempts since when the authorities stated their willingness to enter a new facility, with the intention of securing debt relief, although these never came to fruition owing to a lack of enthusiasm on the part of the authorities. During the 2003 Article IV consultation with the IMF, discussions on a new SMP were mooted, following the ceasefire in April 2002. Similar noises were made in 2004 about a possible SMP and discussions were reported to be continuing at the time of the 2004 Article IV in February 2005. In the event, a SMP was not forthcoming and subsequent developments on the debt obviated the near-term need for such an arrangement. In March 2007, then finance minister Jose Pedro de Morais terminated the development of a joint government/IMF facility citing self-sustaining economic growth and reform as negating the need for a Fund programme; although this was not a complete cessation of relations.

The IMF approved a 27-month Stand-by Arrangement (SBA) in November 2009. It came after the global financial crisis hit the country, and marked a reversal after the government had said in 2007 that it was not interested in a formally structured IMF programme but would continue to participate in Article IV consultations and other technical assistance on an ad hoc basis. However, the new programme was designed to support official reserves after Angola's balance of payments and fiscal accounts came under pressure during the global financial crisis. The collapse in oil prices in 2008–2009 meant that Angola's export earnings declined by 40% and government revenues fell by a similar amount (crude oil accounts for 95% of goods exports and typically 80% of government revenues). Official reserves fell from over US$20bn at their peak in 2008 to US$12bn and the Kwanza was eventually devalued. The IMF noted that Angola made significant improvements in normalising the economy, although overall programme implementation was mixed and large government domestic payment arrears hindered the rest of the economy. On completion of the SBA, IMF staff concluded that Angola had achieved the objectives of the programme, with a stabilisation of the exchange rate, declining inflation, strengthened reserves and settlement of arrears. Growth was recovering, after increasing each year under the programme, and a positive outlook for 2012 was given. Economic diversification was highlighted as a focus point going forward.

Angola has not had an IMF programme since 2012 and has no outstanding credit to the Fund. However, immediately after the expiry of the SBA, the IMF conducted post-programme monitoring of Angola, the first such review taking place in May 2012 and the second in March 2014. More significantly, the government did formally request further Fund support in April 2016, in response to the lower oil price environment, although this request was withdrawn in June. In June, the IMF announced in one of its regular press briefings that Angola had cancelled programme talks, and no other programme has been agreed since. However, the retraction was poorly communicated and initially sparked some market panic about the government's motivation, which the ministry of finance subsequently responded to by issuing a press release on 11 July setting out the details of its decision. The reasons given were the reversal in oil prices since the programme request was made and that the government had been able to secure new borrowing from other sources, which obviated the need for IMF financing. In particular, the finance ministry noted that it had secured US$10bn in new borrowing, from official (mainly China) and commercial sources. Meanwhile, the government remained engaged with the IMF through regular Article IV consultations. The 2016 Article IV was concluded in January 2017 and the 2018 Article IV was concluded in May 2018. The delay on the annual cycle was due to the government transition following the elections in August 2017. A staff visit had taken place in November 2017 to prepare the groundwork for the Article IV consultation mission expected in early 2018, and to hold preliminary discussions on the new government's economic policy.

The Angolan authorities formally requested IMF support through its new Policy Coordination Instrument (PCI) on 18 April 2018. Angola became only the second country to seek the new PCI (PCIs have since been approved for Seychelles and Serbia), a programme that requires the same level of policy oversight as a standby agreement but without access to Fund financing. In a statement, the IMF noted that it stood ready to help Angola address its economic challenges by supporting a comprehensive policy package to improve governance, accelerate the diversification of the economy, and promote inclusive growth, while restoring macroeconomic stability and safeguarding financial stability. Preparations for programme discussions were expected to start after the Board review of the 2018 Article IV (which was concluded on 18 May 2018).

The IMF announced on 21 August 2018 that it had received a request from the Angolan authorities to initiate discussions on an economic programme that could be supported by an EFF.

IMF programmes

Date	*Arrangements*	*Comments*
2009–2012	SBA	27-month programme approved in November 2009 for an amount of SDR858.9mn (cUS$1.4bn, 300% of quota). The programme aimed to restore macroeconomic balances and rebuild international reserves. It also sought an orderly exchange rate adjustment and to normalise conditions in the foreign exchange market. The first review was completed in May 2010 and the second and third reviews (combined) were completed in September 2010. Waivers were granted in the September review for the non-observance of targets for the accumulation of new domestic payment arrears and new external payment arrears. Each subsequent review came with waivers and the programme eventually expired fully drawn. In February 2012, when the programme was originally scheduled to expire, the IMF board agreed to a one-month extension (to end-March) to allow for the conclusion of the sixth and final review. The final review was also approved with waivers. IMF staff reported that the stabilisation programme and SBA achieved their objectives and the authorities were continuing to work on policy reform.

Source: IMF. Angola joined the IMF in 1989

The World Bank and African Development Bank are Angola's only official multilateral creditors, at least according to the classification of its own official statistics. World Bank's strategy in Angola works to promote economic diversification and the involvement of the people in achieving national development; improving human capital will be important for facilitating sustained growth and economic diversification. The African Development Bank has ten active projects in Angola, with a broad range of objectives working towards sector development and living standards improvements.

Paris Club and Bilateral Creditors

Until 2007, Angola had consistently run arrears to the Paris Club for some twenty years, despite having only one Paris Club agreement over this period (in 1989). The 1989 agreement involved rescheduling of maturities on Classic terms and has been fully repaid. A comparability clause applied under which multilaterals (the World Bank) consolidated some of its debt on similar terms although it is uncertain whether commercial creditors complied.

By 2002, discussions on clearing arrears with bilateral creditors were underway, including with Portugal and Spain (Portugal was reported to be willing to consider a bilateral deal, including debt relief, outside the Paris Club). Angola continued to service its debts to the World Bank, Brazil and international banks, providing access to some new financing. The bank loans were collateralised against future oil revenues, with the typical three-year credit facility at LIBOR plus 350bp (IMF report) and were generally criticised by the multilateral agencies as being too expensive. Despite the intention to limit new borrowing, disbursements increased to 12% of GDP in 2003–2004, with some US$3.4bn in oil-backed loans from commercial banks (including a new US$2.35bn facility) and an additional US$0.5bn from facilities with Brazil, China and Israel. By end-2004, external debt (including arrears and late interest) was US$10.9bn (55% of GDP). Further bilateral deals were negotiated with bilateral creditors, outside the Paris Club, including with Germany and Poland in 2003, Portugal in 2003–2004 and with reports of discussions with Hungary and Bulgaria. The former deals involved a 27% upfront payment on US$1bn of short-term debt, in return for the residual laid out across thirty years. Many of these credit facilities had been used by the government to support the military during conflict; hence involved considerable write-offs within various restructuring agreements. In particular, a settlement with Russia (as the former USSR) was reported to have been concluded in 1997. Russia forgave cUS$4bn in 1996 and was thought to have completed a rescheduling arrangement by 1997. In 2005, some of the commercial oil-backed loans (US$600mn) were repaid. Sonangol, the state oil company, however raised US$3bn in a new oil-backed loan. By end-2005, external public debt, including the Sonangol borrowings, was projected to have fallen to below 40% of GDP, with a quarter of the debt in arrears (mostly to the Paris Club), and to 20% of GDP by end-2006. By the end of 2006, the IMF estimated that only cUS$100mn of arrears were outstanding to non-Paris Club creditors compared with US$1bn in 2003.

Angola formally committed to fully normalise its relations with the Paris Club in December 2007, paying all arrears in full, despite most other bilateral agreements being achieved prior to 2006. This came after a long period in which relations were generally strained, although buoyant oil revenues presented the government with an opportunity to reconcile an onerous US$3.75bn of past due interest and principal owed to the Paris Club. Talks began in April 2006. By end-2007, Angola had already paid to Paris Club creditors all its arrears except late interest and resumed the normal payment of maturities, paying Paris Club creditors US$2.3bn in late 2006-early 2007 to settle principal and interest arrears, and at the end of 2017 reached agreement on US$1.5bn mostly related to penalty interest on late payments. Angola committed to pay late interest for which it was seeking favourable treatment; the terms of the deal included repayment of late interest calculated by the Paris Club in three instalments between January 2008 and January 2010. It was expected that this agreement would lead to new credits with export credit agencies.

Paris Club agreements

Date	*Terms*	*Status*	*Details*
1989	Classic	Fully repaid	
2007	Repayment	–	A formal agreement in December 2007 was reached for Angola to clear all its remaining arrears to the Paris Club, after clearance of principle and part interest arrears (excluding late interest) had already taken place. The government agreed to pay late interest in three instalments from January 2008 to January 2010.

Source: Paris Club

Bilateral debt has historically been a sizeable element of Angola's debt stock, although the particular creditors have changed, from its traditional lenders, Brazil, Spain, Portugal and France, to non-traditional lenders such as China and its commercial banks. Moreover, the share of officially classified bilateral debt in central government external debt (i.e. excluding Sonangol) has declined (from 53% in 2013 to 20% in 2017), as bilateral debt has remained relatively unchanged over the past five years (at cUS$8bn) while CG external debt increased (from US$15bn in 2013 to US$38bn in 2017). In 2017, outstanding bilateral and commercial external debt due to China and its commercial banks amounted to US$21.5bn, debt due to Brazil amounted to US$1.2bn and debt due to Russian commercial banks amounted to US$1.8bn.

China has become Angola's most significant creditor by far, a situation which occurred mainly during 2016, as Angola sought new external finance to compensate for the loss of oil revenues in order to fund wider budget deficits and to meet amortisation needs (the budget deficit was expected to rise to 6% of GDP in 2016, exceeding the budget target, while US$4.4bn of external debt fell due in the 12 months to June 2017). China's lending mainly occurred through China Development Bank (CDB) (classified as a commercial bank creditor on Angola's official debt statistics). At the time, the Angolan government stated in a ministry of finance communique on 11 July 2016 that it had negotiated cUS$11.5bn in new borrowing since November 2015, including US$5bn from the CDB, US$1.98bn from Chinese export credit facilities, and US$3.3bn in other credit facilities. The full extent of Chinese lending is now revealed in the 2028/2048 eurobond prospectus. The stock of debt owed to the CDB increased from cUS$1bn over 2013–2015 to US$12.3bn in 2016, rising further to US$15.5bn in 2017. Until then, China's exposure was mainly through official bilateral debt provided by China Exim bank, whose stock of debt had been roughly unchanged over 2013–2016 at US$4bn, rising to US$5.2bn in 2017. In June 2017, it was reported that China had agreed to write-off some of Angola's debt, in the form of a waiver for repayments of an interest-free loan, already in the repayment period. China pardoned US$14.300mn from two loans granted under economic cooperation agreements, in a deal agreed in June 2017. Previously, in 2016, the CDB suspended new funds to Sonangol due to their lack of contractual compliance, limiting Sonangol's finance options, as its debt ratios were outside of those required by international banks.

Like other major oil-exporting countries, Angola used oil as collateral for external loans, including from China. These loans had been used to develop infrastructure, but oil-backed loans increased to US$25bn in 2016 (including to China).

Sovereign Commercial Debt

Angola completed a buyback of its London Club claims in 2003. The exact value of these claims was unknown at the time the authorities mounted the operation in June. The terms of the agreement were at par, albeit with no consideration for past due interest. Exotix believes most affected creditors took part in the operation, leaving few unreconciled claims.

Angola had a number of tradeable commercial debts in the market even before its eurobond issues. Commercial pieces of Angolan debt that traded on the secondary market were typically related to loans issued by Sonangol, secured by escrow accounts which receive oil payments direct from purchasers. There were also a number of loan agreements and trade claims in existence, although these traded less frequently. Most of these claims were retired in private bilateral deals. But the situation over 2007–2008, given buoyant oil revenues and low funding needs, suggested that bond issue was not necessary, although the then minister of finance Jose Pedro de Morais commented in November 2007 that Angola would seek to extend its presence on the international capital markets in the near future, without specific details emerging.

Plans to issue a eurobond first surfaced in November 2009, when the government announced its intention to sell US$4bn of bonds on international markets between December 2009 and June 2010, in two tranches, as part of its debt management and financing strategy, as the fall in oil prices following the global financial crisis opened up a funding gap. Angola's then IMF programme originally permitted US$2bn in commercial borrowing in 2010 (the ceiling was increased to US$6bn in the Fund's first review in May 2010). However, market appetite and cost considerations pointed to a smaller debut issue. Despite market scepticism, the authorities did not at the time consider the absence of a sovereign rating would preclude an initial bond sale, but after some market discussion, the Head of the National Investment Agency confirmed in February 2010 that the country was in the process of obtaining a rating. After a further delay, the three main ratings agencies assigned B+ or equivalent ratings in May 2010. It was anticipated that a eurobond issue would duly follow before the end of the year. It did not.

Angola's debut international issue came in August 2012 with a loan participation note (LPN) issued under the Northern Lights SPV. The five-year issue, maturing in 2019, was for US$1bn and has a 7% coupon. The LPN amortises in 15 equal quarterly payments from November 2015 to August 2019 at 6.25% of principal per payment. Despite its securitised structure, the bond was eligible for the key EMBIG bond index. After the 17 May 2018 payment date, the outstanding principal was US$312.5mn.

Angola's debut eurobond came in November 2015, with a US$1.5bn ten-year bullet bond. The timing meant that the government ended up paying a relatively high 9.5% coupon (the bond was issued at par), in the aftermath of the oil price crash and subsequent market disruption. But the bond was still more than four times oversubscribed, indicating there was strong demand. The bond was rated B+ from Fitch, with Ba2 and B+ from Moody's and S&P respectively. Proceeds were for the support of long-term economic development, through a number of infrastructure projects, as organised by the Ministry of Energy and Water. These projects include electrical power network expansion (the government's 2025 target for the electrification of 60% of the population coincides with the bond's maturity), water supplies and road upgrades. The government later, in January 2018, stated its intention to issue more bonds, reported at US$2bn.

The government returned to the market in May 2018 raising US$3bn altogether in a dual tranche offering of US$1.75bn in a new 10-year (2028 bond) and US$1.25bn in a new 30 year (2048 bond). Both bonds were issued at a price just under par, at 99.987 and 99.976 respectively, although yields at issue were the same as their respective coupons. The government tapped the 2048 issue on 16 July 2018 to meet demand for HY long-dated bonds, issuing a further US$500mn, bringing the total outstanding stock of eurobonds to US$5bn.

Angola's outstanding bond issues

Description	*Amount outstanding*	*Maturity type*	*Issue date*
US$ 7.000% Due 2019[a]	US$312.5mn	Sinkable	Aug. 2012
US$ 9.500% Due 2025	US$1500mn	Bullet	Nov. 2015
US$ 8.250% Due 2028	US$1750mn	Bullet	May 2018
US$ 9.375% Due 2048	US$1750mn[b]	Bullet	May 2018

Source: Bloomberg

[a]Issued via Northern Lights SPV
[b]Following US$500mn tap in July 2018

Angola also has a number of other commercial bank facilities, over and above its eurobond borrowings. According to the 2028/2048 eurobond prospectus, commercial bank lending facilities include VTB, Gemcorp, Luminar, Soc Gen, Santander, GE, and the Development Bank of Southern Africa (DBSA). In particular, Angola undertook a significant amount of new commercial (bank) borrowing over 2015–2016, as it sought new external financing in response to the loss of oil export earnings. Exotix estimates this amounted to over US$3bn in various commercial facilities (excluding the eurobonds, China and World Bank loans). A description of a DBSA facility, which is the only commercial loan facility that Exotix is aware of that trades in the secondary market, is shown below.

Angola bond
Republic of Angola 8.25% 2028
Bloomberg ticker: ANGOL

Borrower	Republic of Angola
Issue date	9 May 2018
Form	Eurobond
ISIN	XS1819680288
Issue size	US$1750mn
Issue outstanding	US$1750mn
Currency	US dollar
Denomination	US$200,000 and US$1000 thereafter
Amortisation	Bullet
Final maturity date	9 May 2028
Coupon/interest	8.25% per annum, paid semi-annually June and December
Day count	30/360
Method of transfer	Clearstream Lux
Settlement period	T + 2
Joint lead managers	Deutsche Bank, Goldman Sachs, ICBC London
Exchange	London, Munich
Governing law	English

Source: Bloomberg

Angola bond
Republic of Angola 9.375% 2048
Bloomberg ticker: ANGOL

Borrower	Republic of Angola
Issue date	9 May 2018
Form	Eurobond
ISIN	XS1819680528
Issue size	US$1250mn
Issue outstanding	US$1750mn (tapped by US$500mn on 16 July 2018)
Currency	US dollar
Denomination	US$200,000 and US$1000 thereafter
Amortisation	Bullet
Final maturity date	8 May 2048
Coupon/interest	9.375% per annum, paid semi-annually June and December
Day count	30/360
Method of transfer	Euroclear/Clearstream
Settlement period	T + 2
Joint lead managers	Deutsche Bank, Goldman Sachs, ICBC London
Exchange	London, Munich
Governing law	English

Source: Bloomberg

DBSA Angola Loan

Borrower	Republic of Angola
Issue date	16 December 2013
Form	Term Facility
FIGI	BBG005SCDGT0
Issue size	US$700mn
Outstanding amount	US$481.25mn (as at June 2018)
Currency	US dollar
Amortisation	16 equal semi-annual instalments from June 2016, following 24-month capitalisation period and six-month grace period
Final maturity date	16 December 2023
Interest	FRN: 6M US LIBOR + 625bps
Original lender/agent	Development Bank of Southern Africa (agent role since transferred to BBVA)
Use of proceeds	For public investment projects in Angola

Source: Bloomberg

Argentina

Nominal GDP (US$mn, 2018)[a]		475,429
Population (thousand, 2018)[a]		44,570
GDP per capita (USD, 2018)[a]		10,667
Credit ratings (long-term foreign currency)[b]	Fitch	B
	Moody's	B2
	S&P	B+

[a]IMF WEO October 2018
[b]As at end-September 2018

Country Summary

- Argentina emerged from the shadow of a long default 15 years later, with President Mauricio Macri largely normalising the debt situation in 2016. A settlement with most bond holdouts was reached in February 2016 following the ground-breaking pari passu ruling in the US courts in 2012, and, freed from the shackles of litigation, Argentina returned to the international market in size, issuing some US$44bn in sovereign bonds over 2016–2018. Re-leveraging increased public debt to 57% of GDP in 2017 from just 39% in 2012.
- But Argentina has not proven immune to economic crisis; in part, a legacy of a decade of Kirchnerism and the weak state of the economy Macri inherited. The country underwent a structural break in 2015 with the election of Macri but, despite pursuing a tough reform agenda

Exotix Capital, *Exotix Developing Markets Guide*,
https://doi.org/10.1007/978-3-030-05867-8_4

and normalising its international relations, in the very short term, macroeconomic outcomes might appear to be little different as inflation accelerated during 2018 and the economy is expected to fall into recession. This came after a combination of external and domestic factors caused a currency crisis, which began in April 2018, leading eventually to a call to the IMF for help. The Fund approved a US$50bn (1110% of quota) three-year stand-by arrangement (SBA) in June 2018, which—following further macroeconomic weakness—was augmented at the time of the first review in October 2018, with access increased by US$6bn and faster front-loaded disbursements.

- Argentina faces a presidential election in 2019, which could pose a significant test for Macri. After a strong start, and a good showing in mid-term elections in 2017, the economic crisis—and policy tightening—could damage his re-election chances, although it is not clear whether the mainstream Peronists, or Kirchnerites, will be able to capitalise on this.

Economic data	*Avg*[a]	*2014*	*2015*	*2016*	*2017 (e)*	*2018 (f)*	*2019 (f)*
Real GDP growth	2.8	−2.5	2.7	−1.8	2.9	−2.6	−1.6
Inflation (annual average)	9.4	–	–	–	25.7	31.8	31.7
Current account (% of GDP)	−0.2	−1.6	−2.7	−2.7	−4.9	−3.7	−3.2
Reserves (US$mn, end-period)[b]	41.0	31.4	25.6	39.3	55.1	49.0[c]	–
Reserves/imports (months)[d]	5.9	4.0	3.4	5.3	6.1	–	–
Overall fiscal balance (% of GDP)[e]	−2.6	−4.3	−6.0	−6.6	−6.7	−5.4	−2.6
Currency (ticker)	Argentina peso (ARS)						
FX regime	De facto managed float floating since December 2015. The IMF reclassified the de facto regime from a crawl-like arrangement to floating in December 2015. Other exchange controls were also removed.						
Key exports	Foodstuffs, meat and vegetable products (64%), vehicles and transport (9.4%), chemicals (8.2%), gold (3.6%), petroleum (2.4%).						

Source: IMF WEO Database, Haver, OEC, Central Bank, Exotix

[a]10-year average to 2016 unless otherwise stated
[b]Central bank international reserves
[c]Latest figure, September 2018
[d]In months of imports of goods, services and primary income debits, Exotix calculation
[e]Overall government net lending

Key figures		*Party*	*Since*
President	Mauricio Macri	PRO	Dec. 2015
Vice president	Gabriela Michetti	PRO	Dec. 2015
Minister of the Treasury	Nicolas Dujovne	UCR	Jun. 2018[a]
Main opposition leader	Sergio Massa	UNA	–
Other opposition figure	Cristina Fernandez	UC	Dec. 2015
Other opposition figure	Juan Manuel Urtubey (Governor of Salta)	FpV/PJ	Dec. 2015
Central bank governor	Guido Sandleris	PRO	Sep. 2018

[a]The Ministry of Finance and Treasury was reunified in June 2018 after it had been divided in two in December 2016. Dujovne, who had been Treasury minister since December 2016, took over the unified ministry with Minister of Finance Luis Caputo becoming president of the central bank (until his resignation in September 2018)

Politics

Executive power

Resides with the president, who is both chief of state and head of government, and cabinet. In practice, power is concentrated around the president and parliament. The constitution provides for a balance of power across Argentina's 23 provincial governorships plus the federal district of Buenos Aires and the legislature, with each province having its own devolved constitution. The constitution separates the powers of the executive, the legislature and the judiciary (the Supreme Court). The president is directly elected by popular vote.

Presidential term: Four years (two-term limit; consecutive allowed)

Parliamentary term: Four years (Chamber of Deputies); six years (Senate)

Legislature

Bicameral legislature; the National Congress consists of the Senate (Upper House) and the Chamber of Deputies (Lower House). Popular elections are held every two years for representatives of both houses, meaning regular rotation is attempted, although each minister serves a full term and can be re-elected. Voting is compulsory.

Senate: 72 seats

Three Senators are drawn from each province. One-third of Senators exit/enter every two years.

Chamber of Deputies: 257 seats

The number of deputies per province depends on population. As such, Buenos Aires has the most. Half the Deputies exit/enter every two years.

Elections	
Next due	*Presidential and legislative: 2019*

Last legislative elections (Oct. 2017)

Senate[a]	*Seats after election (change)*	*Chamber of Deputies*[a]	*Seats after election (change)*
PJ	29 (−11)	Cambiemos	109 (+19)
Cambiemos	26 (+8)	PJ	73 (−25)
Unidad Ciudadana	7 (+4)	Unidad Ciudadana	30 (+25)
1Pais	5 (−1)	1Pais	19 (−17)
Others	5 (0)	Others	26 (−2)

Last presidential (2015)	*% of vote*
First round (October)	
Daniel Scioli (FPV)	36.9
Mauricio Macri (Cambiemos)	34.3
Sergio Massa (UNA)	21.3
Others	7.5
Second round (November)	
Mauricio Macri (Cambiemos)	51.3
Daniel Scioli (FPV)	48.7

[a]24 Senate seats were up for election and half of the Chamber of Deputies

People

Predominantly white, at 97% of the population, most Argentineans are Hispanic and of European descent, especially Spanish and Italian, although French, Polish, German and Russian origin is also found. Mestizos (mixed race indigenous) account for most of the remainder and live in the north and west of the country. Over 90% of the populace are Catholic. There is also a sizeable Jewish community. Around 15.5mn live in the metropolitan area of Buenos Aires, over one-third of the population.

Argentina has a volatile political history. The period 1946–1976 saw military/civilian governments, dominated by General Juan Peron and after his death in 1974, by his third wife (Isabel), until she was removed by a military coup in 1976. From 1976–1983, the country experienced political chaos and internal terrorism, in a period that became known as Argentina's Dirty War. A succession of military chiefs ruled with an iron hand restoring public order at the cost of public repression against suspected dissidents and subversives. Casualties range from 10,000–30,000 people. Former military rulers General Jorge Videla and Reynaldo Bigone were later sentenced to life in prison for crimes against humanity. Defeat in the Falklands war in 1982, under General Galtieri, proved the last straw with the public, and moves were made to set about the return of democracy.

The military government fell a year later and the election of Raul Alfonsin as president (1983–1989) marked a return to civilian government. Yet hyperinflation and economic collapse forced Alfonsin to resign, leading to the President Menem era (1989–1999).

(*continued*)

(continued)

People

Menem introduced convertibility (pegging the peso one to one with the US dollar) in 1992 to help control inflation and pursued privatisation and liberalisation. Great strides were made in restoring civil order and public confidence. With some successes, Menem was re-elected in 1995 after a change to the constitution the previous year allowed the president to serve two consecutive terms. Fernando De La Rua (1999–2001) presided over an economic crisis that culminated in Argentina's sovereign default in December 2001–January 2002 and forced his resignation. After a period of flux, Eduardo Duhalde (2002–2003) became interim president in January 2002 when he was selected by Congress to finish De La Rua's term. He became the country's fifth president in three weeks. The elections in 2003 saw the arrival of the Kirchners, first President Nestor Kirchner (2003–2007) and then his wife President Cristina Fernandez de Kirchner (CFK; 2007–2015). The Kirchner years saw a strong post-default economic recovery (although this was partly massaged by statistical manipulation of official statistics) but governance was marked by an increasingly confrontational style, while policies were interventionist and unorthodox; exemplified for example by the disastrous attempt in March 2008 to raise taxes on farm exports, prompting farmers' strikes, mass protests and a collapse in CFK's popularity and the nationalisation of the private pension schemes (AFJPs) in October 2008. Nestor Kirchner, who remained highly influential under his wife's administration (the key political strategist, deal-maker and main decision taker), died in October 2010 after suffering a heart attack. However, while CFK maintained some core support, the economy began to suffer as the post-default recovery waned in the wake of the global financial crisis and inflation remained high (despite the government's tampering with official figures). But it was the ongoing saga with litigating bondholders who did not participate in the country's 2005 and 2010 debt exchanges following the default ("the holdouts") that finally did it for CFK, as this ended in a second "technical" default in 2014 after the US Supreme Court rejected Argentina's appeal of a NY District Court ruling in favour of the holdout creditors. This ultimately starved the country of fresh capital and CFK's economic model proved unsustainable, especially by then as commodity prices were then beginning to fall. Failing to change the constitution to allow CFK to run for a third term in 2015, voters rejected Kirchnerism (and her chosen successor, Daniel Scioli) in favour of the pro-market and business-friendly opposition candidate, and mayor of Buenos Aries, Mauricio Macri. President Macri brought about major economic reform immediately, including increasing utility tariffs, allowing the peso to fall, easing capital controls, re-engaging with the IMF and other IFIs, and crucially, reaching a rapid agreement with the holdout creditors to settle the outstanding defaulted debt, thereby paving the way to renewed access to the international bond markets. Macri's Cambiemos coalition (formed in June 2015 from the Civic Coalition, PRO and UCR) won in mid-term parliamentary elections in October 2017, seen as an endorsement of his reformist policies. However, he also adopted a "gradualist" macroeconomic adjustment, involving a slow pace of fiscal consolidation and disinflation so as not to risk growth, a strategy that appeared to backfire during 2018 as policy missteps at the end of 2017/early 2018 and a widening current account deficit left the country exposed to fragile investor sentiment after the rise in US bond yields and a stronger US dollar in April 2018. The resulting peso crisis led the government to call in the IMF again, a decision that could have political consequences for Macri as the country approaches the 2019 presidential election with local memories still scarred by the experience of the 2000–2001 default. The IMF approved a massive US$50bn SBA in June 2018 (augmented to US$57.1bn in September 2018).

Debt

	2012	*2017*
External debt ratios (%)		
Total external debt/GDP	29.0	37.0
Public external debt/GDP	17.8	25.7
Private external debt/GDP	11.1	11.2
Total external debt/exports of goods and services	170.7	324.7
External debt service ratio[a]	15.6	49.1
Public debt ratios (%)		
Public domestic debt/GDP	25.6	34.9
Public debt/GDP	38.9	57.1

Source: IMF, Ministry of Finance, central bank, INDEC, World Bank, IIF, Exotix

Note: Figures for public external debt and public domestic debt do not add to total public debt because of different methodologies. Public domestic debt on residency basis from IMF figures

[a]IIF, ratio to G&S&I

Argentina's total external debt in 2017 was US$235.7bn, based on IMF data (staff report for SBA published in July 2018), with most of it (70%) owed by the public sector. It comprised public external debt of US$164.1bn and private external debt of US$71.6bn. These data are consistent with official data provided by INDEC under BPM6 methodology (although they are only given for 2017, and are not available on the same basis for prior years). Total external debt has increased by 40% since 2012, when it stood at just US$168.0bn, with a rise in public sector debt the main driver of the overall increase. Public external debt was US$103.3bn in 2012, still roughly the same proportion of total external debt (c62%), with private external debt of US$64.6bn. In particular, most of the increase in total external debt occurred, unsurprisingly, in 2016–2017, with the arrival of President Macri and the normalisation of the sovereign debt situation following the 2001 default. Public external debt rose by US$51bn in 2015–2017 (up by US$17bn in 2016 and US$34bn in 2017), with nearly all the increase coming from bond issues (up from a stock of US$70.2bn at end-15, a level around which it had been since at least 2011, to US$116.8bn at end-2017). Bonds accounted for 71% of public external debt at end-17 (little changed from its 67% share in 2012), while loans accounted for 29%, of which multilaterals were c45% of overall loans (and 13% of public external debt). Meanwhile, private external debt, which had generally been stable at cUS$60bn–65bn over 2011–2016, rose by cUS$12bn in 2017 as the improvement in sovereign risk opened the international market to private sector borrowers.

Total external debt was therefore 37% of GDP in 2017, up from 29% of GDP in 2012. Of this, public external debt was 26% of GDP (up from 18% in 2012) and private external debt was 11% (unchanged from 2012). As a share of exports of goods and service (based on INDEC data), total external debt rose from 171% to 325%, fuelled also by a 27% decline in goods' exports over this period. Exports of goods and services were US$73bn in 2017 (goods US$58bn, services US$14bn), compared with US$98bn in 2012 (goods US$80bn, services US$18bn). Moreover, given the public sector's additional foreign borrowing in 2018 to date (including US$9bn more bonds issued in January 2018 and an IMF disbursement of US$15bn in June 2018), as well as the fall in US$ GDP because of the weaker peso, the total external debt/GDP ratio would be expected to increase further in 2018. Exotix calculates this rising to 51.3% of GDP (from 37% in 2017), some 360% of exports. The IMF projected public external debt to rise by US$44bn in 2018 to US$208bn.

External debt service has also risen sharply in the past two years due to more public and private sector foreign borrowing, although detailed figures from public sources are not readily available. The IMF noted in the staff report for the SBA, published in July 2018, that total external debt service is high, estimated at 11% of GDP in 2017 and c100% of exports of goods and services, due to the large share of short-term debt. A detailed breakdown of external debt service between public and private sectors is also not available, although the IMF noted that c70% represented obligations of the private sector. The external debt service ratio, based on IIF data (under which, the stock of total external debt is consistent with the IMF and authorities' data mentioned above), has risen from 16% in 2012 to 49% in 2017 (equating to c6% of GDP), in part also due to the fall in the denominator (exports of goods, services and income). In USD terms, external debt service increased from US$15bn in 2012 (a level around which it remained until 2015) to US$37bn in 2017, on IIF data. It was only US$20bn in 2016. Interest has doubled, from US$5.1bn to US$10.7bn, while principal repayments nearly tripled from US$9.8bn to US$26.6bn.

Total public debt was 57.1% of GDP in 2017, according to Exotix calculations based on Ministry of Finance figures (which put it at ARS6025bn, US$320.9bn) and IMF WEO GDP; the ratio is consistent with the IMF figure in its staff report for the SBA. However, a precise breakdown between public domestic and public external debt is complicated by methodological differences between BPM6 and public finance statistics, and differences due to whether external debt is assessed on a residency or currency basis. A precise domestic/external split is clouded because Argentina issues local debt in USD and non-resident participation in the local market has also been significant. According to the IMF, for 2017, domestic debt was ARS1904bn and external debt was ARS4121bn on a currency basis (32% and 68% of the total, respectively), while domestic debt was ARS2339bn and external debt was ARS3686bn on a residency basis (39% and 61% of the total, respectively). Exotix shows public domestic debt by residency (34.9% of GDP in 2017), rather than by currency (39.0% of GDP in 2017). Implied public external debt figures, however, differ from external debt/ BPM6 methodology, so that the sum of public external debt and PDD do not add up to total public debt. Note that Exotix excludes GDP warrants from public debt (another US$13.8bn nominal on Ministry of Finance figures). Argentina's public debt figures also exclude provincial debt. According to the IMF, the total debt of all provinces at end-2017 was estimated at ARS542bn (5.3% of GDP), of which around one-third was held by the federal government. The IMF's public sector debt DSA projected the public debt ratio to increase from 57.1% of GDP in 2017 to 64.5% in 2018, under its baseline scenario. Allowing for provincial debt, at the more depreciated USD GDP, it is plausible to foresee Argentina's overall public debt/GDP ratio rise to over 70% in 2018.

Exotix shows the composition of overall public sector debt (as opposed to external debt) as at end-2017 in the table below based on Ministry of Finance figures (given the difficulty in drawing the precise distinction between public external and public domestic from official figures). Public debt amounted to US$320.9bn (excluding GDP warrants and provincial debt). Most of the debt is medium/long-term (MLT), c84% of the total, with short-term debt and central bank debt making up most of the remainder. Around 70% of the total, and 83% of all MLT debt, was owed in the form of bonds, both domestic and external. According to the Ministry of Finance figures, international bonds amounted to US$61bn (about 19% of total public debt). Ministry of Finance figures do state that MLT external debt was US$94.4bn at end-2017, just 30% of overall public debt of US$320.9bn, of which about two-thirds was bonds and 23% was owed to multilaterals. The main multilateral creditors were the IADB (accounting for over half of all multilateral debt; 55%), followed by the World Bank (30%) and CAF (14%). At end-17, Argentina had no outstanding debt to the IMF, a position that changed in June 2018 with the US$15bn disbursement under a new SBA. However, it is not clear how much of the short term and central bank debt is external versus domestic. The Ministry of Finance figures also include a small amount of arrears (US$107mn) and

US$2.9bn in claim value (principal and interest) for eligible debt (domestic and external) pending restructuring, which Exotix understands relates to the remaining holdout debt.

Composition of public debt

Public debt by creditor (end-17)	*Nominal amount outstanding (US$bn)*	*Share of total (%)*
Direct debt (1)	**317.951**	**99.1**
o/w MLT debt (excl. central bank)	268.232	83.6
o/w Bonds	221.926	69.1
o/w Domestic	56.592	17.6
External	165.334	51.5
o/w International bonds	61.627	19.2
Treasury notes	11.089	3.5
Multilaterals	21.327	6.6
o/w World Bank	6.328	2.0
IADB	11.778	3.7
CAF	3.039	0.9
Bilateral	8.280	2.6
o/w Paris Club	5.471	1.7
Commercial banks	2.434	0.8
Other creditors	2.036	0.6
Guarantees	1.139	0.4
Short-term debt (excl. central bank)	24.566	7.7
o/w Treasury notes	23.500	7.3
Central bank	25.153	7.8
Arrears (2)	**0.107**	**0.0**
Eligible debt pending restructuring (3)	**2.877**	**0.9**
o/w Principal	1.258	0.4
o/w Domestic	0.075	0.0
External	1.184	0.4
Total public debt (= (1) + (2) + (3))[a]	**320.935**	**100.0**

Source: Ministry of Finance, Paris Club, Exotix

[a]Figure excludes GDP warrants and provincial debt

Rescheduling History

Argentina has been something of a serial rescheduler stretching back many decades, on both its official debt, mainly Paris Club, and its commercial debt. Argentina defaulted in the early 1980s during the Latin America debt crisis, which saw a series of reschedulings on commercial bank debt and led, ultimately, to a Brady deal in 1993 (the third-biggest deal in size in terms of the amount of debt it covered, behind Mexico and Brazil). However, financial pressures re-emerged towards the end of the 1990s after a series of adverse shocks and an inadequate policy response, culminating in the 2001–2002 sovereign default on both bilateral Paris Club debt and domestic and international bonds.

Argentina's sovereign default in 2001–2002 was the biggest sovereign default in history at the time, since surpassed only by Greece in 2012, covering US$100bn in debt. The drivers were a mix of external and domestic factors. Brazil's currency devaluation in 1999 undermined Argentina's own competitiveness, as its currency board arrangement, adopted in 1992, pegged the peso to the US dollar (at parity). Terms-of-trade shocks (low commodity prices) also undermined the current account while the government borrowed aggressively on the domestic and international markets. Crowding out increased domestic interest rates, choking investment, while refinancing risks rose in the international market. Argentina lapsed into a period of weak growth and, ultimately, a four-year long recession from 1998–2001, from which it struggled to recover under the constraint of convertibility. Concerns over fiscal sustainability and Argentina's ability to refinance its huge external debts raised fears among investors. A US$40bn IMF-led package was approved in December 2000 and the IMF approved a further US$8bn in September 2001. Despite international assistance, the situation became untenable and, what was initially seen as a liquidity problem, turned into one of solvency. The tipping point came in autumn 2001, amid mass protests on the streets and a run on banks in late November, which prompted a freeze on bank deposits ("Corralito") and pressure on reserves, prompting the resignation of President De La Rua on 21 December 2001. A replacement, and interim president, Adolfo Rodriguez Saa, announced the intention to default on government debt on 23 December and later that a bond payment due on 3 January 2002 would be missed. Subsequently, President Eduardo Duhalde, the fifth president in three weeks, declared on 3 January 2002 a moratorium on nearly US$100bn of debt. Three days later, convertibility—the foundation of economic policy for the previous decade—was abandoned. The peso was devalued and went into freefall. The effect was to produce a sharp rise in the external debt/GDP ratio, from c50% in 2000 to 160% in 2002, while debt/exports were over 400%. The banking system was hit further by "pesification" which followed on 3 February 2002. This saw the asymmetric conversion of bank loans and deposits into pesos (banks' dollar assets and liabilities were converted at ARS1:US$1 for private sector loans and ARS1.4:US$1 for public sector loans and USD deposits).

It was, however, some time before there was any attempt to resolve the default and it took even longer to cure it completely; in fact, it took until 2016, some 15 years later (and three more presidents), and a US judge's draconian order, before most of the default had been settled. Following the election of President Nestor Kirchner in May 2003, the government presented a harsh restructuring proposal in October of that year (the Dubai terms) with a 70% haircut in face value. A take it or leave it bond exchange was finally completed in March 2005, with an exchange ratio of 33.7%, achieving an acceptance rate of 76%. But holders of cUS$20bn of bonds did not participate (ie untendered bonds). The exchange was reopened under President CFK, closing in June 2010, along similar terms to the 2005 offer to try to mop up the remaining bonds, achieving an acceptance rate of 66%. But, even after two exchanges, leading to a combined acceptance rate of 92%, cUS$6.2bn (principal) in defaulted bonds (excluding Brady's) remained, some of which was subject to litigation (the famous *pari passu* litigation of the holdout creditors), and the threat of attachment of any new bond issue or seizure of Argentina's overseas assets hamstrung the government of CFK throughout her tenure. She refused to resolve the situation, however (on ideological grounds), relying instead on non-traditional partners for finance (Venezuela) and a commodity price windfall, but did oversee an agreement in 2014 to repay its US$9bn in arrears to the Paris Club (although the likely hoped for new lending from bilaterals and export credit agencies did not materialise). Finally, a US court ruling in 2012 in favour of holdouts set in train the path to an eventual settlement, albeit under Macri in February 2016, soon after he took office.

Relations with Multilateral Creditors

Argentina has had a mixed relationship with the IMF but, after a decade of isolation (and anti-IMF sentiment) under Kirchnerism, Macri sought to reengage with the IMF and other multilaterals. Argentina has had 22 IMF arrangements, with its first dating back to 1958, and 17 of them had taken place by 2000. But, domestically, IMF-imposed austerity was (wrongly) blamed for the 2000–2001 economic crisis, and subsequent default. This view was further inflamed with the election of nationalist-leaning President Nestor Kirchner in 2003. President Kirchner cut official ties completely after the early repayment on 2 January 2006 of US$10bn of IMF borrowing, financed from central bank reserves. His successor, and wife, CFK, built on anti-IMF sentiment, and later Argentina was found to be in breach of its IMF membership obligations, leading to a declaration of censure in 2013 which could have led to its expulsion. With the last Article IV in July 2006, it took the arrival of Macri (who took office in December 2015) to repair relations with the IMF (and other multilaterals), with the first Article IV in over a decade taking place in November 2016. The next Article IV, the 2017 Article IV, was concluded in December 2017.

The IMF approved a new programme for Argentina in June 2018, the first programme in over 12 years, a three-year SBA for US$50bn (SDR35.379bn, 1110% of quota)—which is now set to be augmented (see below). The SBA aimed to restore market confidence via a consistent macroeconomic programme that reduced financing needs (via fiscal tightening), put Argentina's public debt on a firm downward trajectory, and strengthened the disinflation process by setting more realistic inflation targets and reinforcing the independence of the central bank. Approval led to the immediate disbursement of US$15bn (SDR10,614bn, 333% of quota), with half (US$7.5bn) used for budget support. The authorities indicated they would treat the remainder of the arrangement as precautionary. In fact, the IMF programme was part of an overall nearly US$60bn official sector financing package. In addition to the IMF money, other multilaterals provided US$5.65bn, comprising US$1.75bn from the World Bank, US$2.5bn from the IADB and US$1.4bn from CAF.

The IMF programme was at the upper end of market expectations. In absolute size, it was the largest IMF programme in recent times, if not history (bigger than Greece's in 2010 and 2012). In quota terms, though, it is not the biggest. It is just a bit smaller than Iceland's in 2008 (1190%), but slightly larger than Hungary's in 2008 (1015%), although well below Greece's 2010 SBA (3212%).

Programme conditionality seemed pretty light, especially in 2018. It set new fiscal and inflation targets, as expected, aiming to reach primary balance by 2020, a year sooner than the authorities had originally planned, with inflation falling to 17% in 2019, and to 9% in 2021. The inflation target for 2018 was abandoned, although there was a consultation clause for inflation in 2018–2019, whereby deviations from an inner band triggered discussion with staff on remedial measures, while deviations from an outer band required consultation with the Executive Board.

The surprise IMF programme came after Argentina saw a sharp deterioration in investor confidence, and a peso crisis, that began in late April 2018. Official reserves fell by US$5bn (8%) to US$56.6bn in the last week of April as the central bank intervened to try to support the peso, raising interest rates in three surprise steps by a cumulative amount of 12.75% by early May. The peso, which had been relatively flat in the year until then, fell by 18% against the US dollar in May, and another 13% in June. The crisis in confidence followed a combination of external events (rising risk aversion due to higher US bond yields and a stronger US dollar during April) and domestic events (policy missteps, amid dovish changes to the central bank inflation targets in December 2017 and an interest rate cut in January 2018, and a widening current account deficit), which left Argentina particularly exposed to sharp change in sentiment. In addition, perceived difficultly for Macri in pursing structural reforms and changes to LEBAC tax rates, which prompted non-resident outflows in April 2018, also hit confidence and the peso. The government, albeit amid a sense of panic with the central bank interest rate hikes, tried to oversee an orthodox crisis response with tighter monetary and fiscal policy. But it was not enough. Argentina initially sought a flexible credit line (FCL), according to media reports on 8 May 2018, perhaps because it would not appear like a bailout compared with the traditional SBA, but, maybe after realising it would not qualify (an FCL requires a country to have very strong economic fundamentals and institutional policy frameworks), the IMF Board was formally notified of the authorities' intention to request an exceptional access SBA on 18 May 2018, after reserves had fallen to US$52.4bn. The IMF reported that a staff-level agreement (SLA) on an SBA had been reached on 7 June and formal Board approval came on 20 June, a process that was completed in double-quick time.

The IMF's SBA programme was, however, augmented in October 2018, shortly after being approved. The adverse external environment over July–August 2018 caused the programme to go off track almost as soon as it started. President Macri called for IMF disbursements to be accelerated via a YouTube video on 29 August, which further eroded market sentiment. Since the approval of the programme on 20 June, the peso had fallen by an additional 13% against the US dollar, and had fallen by 50% YTD, to end-August, putting more pressure on reserves and undoing the macro assumptions. The IMF announced an SLA on 26 September on the first review of the SBA, which involved higher access, front-loading of a revised disbursement schedule and a strengthened set of policies; subject to Board approval. The IMF Board approved the first review, and an augmented programme, soon after on 26 October. Access under the programme was increased to US$56.3bn (1277% of quota), compared with the US$7bn increase stated at the time of the SLA. The increase in size was well below market expectations that had coalesced at cUS$15bn–20bn after Macri's announcement, but which had eased down to cUS$5bn just a few days prior to the IMF SLA announcement. More important than the headline increase was a bigger front-loading of the disbursement schedule, with US$19bn more available through to end-19. Furthermore, disbursements for the remainder of 2018 will more than double the original Fund-supported programme—US$13.4bn (in addition to the US$15bn already disbursed). The programme was also no longer to be treated as precautionary and the authorities intended to draw on it and use IMF financing for budget support. The revised programme was based on a strengthened set of policies, including the government's revised fiscal targets (aiming for a primary balance one year early, in 2019, and a 1% primary surplus in 2020), a shift in monetary policy from an inflation target to a money supply target (base money), and a floating exchange rate without intervention. Updated IMF projections in the first review saw the public debt/GDP ratio increase to 81.2% in 2018, from the 64.5% expected at the time of programme approval, and just 57.6% in 2017.

IMF programmes

Date	*Arrangements*	*Comments*
1980s	SBA	1983–1984, 1984–1986, 1987–1988, 1989–1991
1990s	Various	1991–1992 (SBA), 1992–1996 (EFF), 1996–1998 (SBA), 1998–2000 (EFF). The 1998–2000 EFF was for SDR2.08bn and went undrawn. It was replaced by a new SBA in March 2000.
2000–2003 2001–2002	SBA; Of which SRF	Three-year SBA agreed in March 2000 expired January 2003. SBA augmented with one-year SRF, agreed in January 2001. SBA was for SDR16.937bn of which only SDR9.756bn was drawn. The SRF was for SDR6.087bn, with SDR5.875bn drawn.
2003	SBA	Eight-month programme from January to August for SDR2.175bn which was fully drawn.
2003–2006	SBA	Three-year SBA agreed in September 2003, expired January 2006, for SDR8.981bn. Only SDR4.171bn was drawn.

(*continued*)

(continued)

Date	*Arrangements*	*Comments*
2018–2021	SBA	The Board approved a new three-year SBA for US$50bn (SDR35.379bn, 1110% of quota) in June 2018, with US$15bn (SDR10.614bn) disbursed immediately, half of which was for budget support. The remaining US$35bn was available during the programme, subject to quarterly reviews, with the first review scheduled for mid-September. The authorities' intention was to treat the arrangement as precautionary after the first tranche. The programme was in support of the authorities' economic plan, aiming to restore market confidence following a sharp decline in the peso, and allow public debt to decline. Another aim was to reduce inflation, through realistic targets and reinforcing central bank independence. However, renewed market pressure on the peso forced the authorities to seek to renegotiate access under the programme in August 2018. The IMF Board approved an augmented programme on 26 October, at the time of the first review, after having announced SLA on 26 September. The programme was increased by US$6.3bn to US$56.3bn (1277% of quota) along with a revised front-loaded disbursement schedule increasing available resources by US$19bn through end-19. The resources available under the programme would no longer be treated as precautionary and the authorities intended to use IMF financing for budget support.

Source: IMF. Argentina joined the IMF in 1956

Argentina, under President CFK, was found to be in breach of its IMF membership obligations under the articles of agreement (specifically Article VIII, Section 5—data provision) in July 2011. This was due to its inaccurate provision of CPI and GDP data. Despite requesting IMF technical assistance as early as 2010, Argentina's repeated failure to remedy the situation led the Fund's Executive Board to issue a statement of concern on 17 September 2012 and a declaration of censure on 1 February 2013. In December 2013, the IMF Board adopted a decision calling on Argentina to implement specified actions according to a specified timetable, under which Argentina demonstrated a fairly lethargic effort to address the situation, and was still judged not to be fully compliant by June 2015. However, while repeated Board meetings lamented the lack of progress, the Fund did not take further action. The declaration of censure was, however, lifted in November 2016 after the arrival of Macri made important progress in strengthening the accuracy of Argentina's statistics and the recommencing of Article IV discussions. An IMF technical mission visited Argentina in July 2016, followed by an Article IV mission in September 2016, and the Article IV Board review in November 2016—just 11 months after Macri took office. By this time, Argentina's Article IV had been delayed by 108 months (nine years).

The IMF, with the support of the international community, via the G7, provided significant financial assistance to Argentina in the run-up to its 2001 default. Although economic growth was expected to pick up in 2000, the failure of it to do so raised investor concerns, which were magnified by the failure of the government to implement structural and fiscal reforms. An uncovered domestic Treasury bill auction in September 2000 signalled the beginning of the end. In January 2001, a much-larger-than-expected IMF-led package was announced, amounting to US$40bn available over three years. This was split roughly evenly between the official sector and the private sector. With regards to official creditors, the IMF provided US$13.7bn, augmenting its SBA that was agreed in March 2000 and providing a further US$2.7bn through an SRF. The programme amounted to some 500% of quota, well beyond the usual country limit of 300% of quota. The IMF programme catalysed US$5bn in additional financing from multilaterals, with the World Bank and IADB providing US$2.5bn each, while Spain contributed a further US$1bn in a bilateral loan. Central to the package were efforts to bail-in the private sector, under the IMF's policy of private sector involvement (PSI). This involved US$20bn of financing from the private sector as the government gained voluntary commitments from banks and pension funds to purchase government securities and proposed a bond exchange to extend maturities. A "mega-bond swap" was seen as successful in May 2001, but vulnerabilities remained. Tangible progress on a new SBA failed to materialise over the year; crucially, as the government lacked the broad political support to implement fiscal and structural reforms, despite the efforts of new economy minister Cavallo. The G7 was reluctant to pull the plug, however, giving Argentina the benefit of the doubt. By summer 2001 concerns had returned, particularly the possibility of a bank run as local deposits fell. The IMF approved a further US$8bn in September 2001, although this was seen as merely marking time—it was reluctant to withdraw, for fear of being criticised for forcing the crisis it was trying to avoid, but it also did not want to lend into an insolvency situation. By December 2001, speculation was rife about default and protests were seen at banks across the country. The government announced a debt moratorium at end-December 2001 and missed an interest payment on 3 January 2002.

It also called an end to convertibility, allowing the peso to float, whereby it depreciated by 74% against the US dollar within six months. In response, the government-imposed price and capital controls and a freeze on bank deposits, which were only lifted in 2003.

Paris Club and Bilateral Creditors

Argentina remained in default on its Paris Club debt following the 2001 sovereign default until 2014. Arrears totalled US$9.69bn (US$4.96bn in principal, US$1.1bn in interest and US$3.63bn in penalty interest). Prior to the 2001 default, Argentina had a number of Paris Club rescheduling agreements, dating back to 1956 when the Paris Club group of creditors was established. There were several attempts at talks between the government and the Paris Club after the 2005 bond exchange took place, with reports usually emanating from the Argentineans and subsequently denied by the Paris Club. Eventually, by summer 2008, it seemed a break-through was close at hand, with Argentina announcing it would repay Paris Club creditors in full in cash (from central bank reserves), obviating the need for any IMF programme. The announcement was welcomed by the Paris Club in a statement on 17 September. Yet subsequent global events overtook these plans and Argentina remained in default to Paris Club creditors. Talks were said to have recommenced in 2009, but again were denied by the Paris Club. In November 2010, Argentina announced the beginning of negotiations with the Paris Club "without IMF involvement". Then Economy Minister Boudou met Paris Club officials in Paris in December. The main disagreement at that stage appeared to be the repayment period, as press reports indicated that the Paris Club was reluctant to accept anything longer than two years while the government was looking for a five- or six-year repayment period. Finally, in May 2014, an agreement was reached on ad hoc terms: the total stock of arrears was treated with a flexible repayment structure. All arrears should be cleared over five years, longer than Paris Club creditors had previously wanted, with a minimum payment of US$1.15bn by May 2015.

The IMF staff report for the SBA in June 2018 (published July 2018) noted that Argentina still has a limited amount of outstanding arrears to official bilateral creditors. The arrears are cUS$30mn claimed by the French export credit agency, relating to the building of a gas pipeline in the Tierra del Fuego region by a French company in the late 1970s. The parties are currently in arbitration in the International Chamber of Commerce International Court of Arbitration.

Paris Club agreements

Date	*Terms*	*Status*	*Details*
1956	Classic	Fully repaid	
1962	Classic	Fully repaid	
1965	Classic	Fully repaid	
1985	Classic	Fully repaid	US$1726mn treated, maturities falling due during 1985.
1987	Classic	Fully repaid	US$2156mn treated, maturities falling due between 1987 and 1988.
1989	Classic	Fully repaid	US$2400mn treated, maturities falling due between 1991 and 1992.
1991	Classic	Fully repaid	US$1476mn treated, maturities falling due between 1991 and 1992.
1992	Classic	Active	US$2700mn treated, maturities falling due between 1992 and 1995.
1997	Buyback		Argentina proposed a part prepayment at par to all PC creditors in April 1997. Each country creditor could decide whether or not to participate.
2014 May	Ad Hoc	Active	US$9690mn (US$4955mn in principal, US$1102mn in interest and US$3633mn in penalty interest) of arrears treated, to be repaid over five years, with a minimum payment of US$1150mn by May 2015.

Source: Paris Club

Sovereign Commercial Debt

Argentina has seen a number of commercial debt restructurings, including a Brady deal in 1993, but none bigger or more profound (economically and politically) than its 2001–2002 default. The government announced the intention to default on 23 December 2001. A bond payment due on 3 January 2002 was missed and a debt moratorium was declared the same day. The government formally defaulted on US$95bn of external debt and US$2.2bn of local currency bonds.

It took a long time to deal with the foreign debt after its 2001–2002 default and the government's restructuring offer, when it finally came in 2005, was seen as particularly aggressive (indeed, it took some 15 years to deal with the legacy entirely). During the September 2003 IMF annual meetings in Dubai, the Argentineans, advised by Clearly Gottlieb, unilaterally proposed a far-reaching restructuring of its commercial debt with a 70% face value haircut and partial forgiveness of unpaid interest. Such radical restructuring terms were unprecedented and shocked the creditor community. The exchange finally opened on 14 January 2005 as the government launched an offer for defaulted sovereign global bonds and Brady bonds, involving a nominal haircut of 66.3%. Eligible bonds amounted to US$81.1bn, comprising US$79.7bn in principal and US$2.1bn in accrued unpaid interest as of 31 December 2001. Accrued and unpaid interest since 31 December 2001 was not paid. The government insisted on writing off past due interest (PDI) for the 2002 and 2003 periods, but assumed other accrued interest (although at less than the contractual rate) for 2004 and early 2005. The offer closed on 25 February with a settlement date of 2 June 2005, after last-minute litigation by two creditors attempted to stall the restructuring. By contrast, an agreement on the local debt was much quicker. The local bonds represented provincial debt that was restructured by the issue of Bonos Garantizados (Bogars), peso-denominated and CER-adjusted. The exchange was open during the first part of 2002 and the effective date was set as of 4 February 2002.

In its restructuring of the foreign debt, the Republic of Argentina issued the equivalent of US$35.3bn in new bonds under the terms of the exchange prospectus issued to commercial bondholders on 27 December 2004. The government's offer comprised new par bonds, discount bonds and quasi-par bonds; the latter aimed at long-term Argentinean investors, such as pension funds. An issuance limit of US$15bn (dollar equivalent) was placed on the par bonds and the largest single tranche of bonds was the US$6.6bn pars (with US$5.3bn governed by New York law and US$1.3bn by Argentine law). The limit was reached on the par bonds. There was no limit on the discounts. The interest accrual date for the new bonds was 31 December 2003, with first interest payment date of 31 December 2005 for the discounts and 31 March 2006 for the pars. However, interest accrued on the discounts until December 2004 was paid in cash on settlement date. Interest accrued on pars until March 2005 was paid in cash on settlement date too. The government narrowed the list of currencies to include US dollars, euros and Japanese yen as well as Argentine pesos. Warrants linked to future GDP performance were also included and these became automatically detached six months after issue. The deal had an acceptance rate of 76%, according to official calculations, with reports suggesting that 97% of Argentine creditors accepted the offer and 75% of foreign creditors also did so.

The mechanics of the 2005 exchange offer were as follows:

Holders of eligible bonds were able to exchange into the following bonds:

Par bonds due December 2038	Exchange ratio 1.000 Issuance limit: If participation <=70% If participation >70%	 US$10bn US$15bn
Discount bonds due December 2033	Exchange ratio 0.337 No issuance limit	
Quasi-par bonds due December 2045	Exchange ratio 0.699 Issuance limit: ARS24.3bn	

Principal amounts of peso-denominated Pars, discount bonds and quasi-par bonds were adjusted for inflation, based on CER.

The exchange also created GDP-linked securities that expire in December 2035; initially attached to the pars, discounts and quasi-pars. GDP-linked securities were received in notional amounts equal to the accepted amount of eligible securities tendered. The first coupon payment on GDP-linked securities was paid on 15 December 2006.

The quasi-par bonds were not allowed to trade until some years after the exchange.

Some US$23bn of new exchange bonds were created, in Discounts and Pars, under foreign law, and the principal amount grew because of capitalised interest. After the second exchange, in 2010, principal (excluding capitalised interest) rose to US$29bn. By end-2017, the outstanding capitalised amount was US$34bn.

Despite the particularly egregious nature of the offer, estimates of the haircut vary. The exchange translated into an effective write off of 66.3% of total claim (face value plus factor). The NPV haircut was estimated at 76.8%, according to the Cruces and Trebesch database, based on a 10.4% discount rate (excluding the value of the GDP warrants). However, including the GDP warrants would reduce the haircut (the market price of the GDP warrants at the time of issue was US$4–5).

Commercial debt agreements

Date	*Details*
1983	Bank debt restructurings, comprising bridging loan in January of US$1.3bn and new money loan of US$0.5bn in August.
1985	Rescheduling of US$9.8bn of bank debt maturities over January 1982–January 1986, with new long-term money of US$3.6bn and maintenance of short-term credit lines of US$3.1bn.

(*continued*)

(continued)

Date	*Details*
1987	Revised rescheduling agreement covering amounts due under the 1983 and 1985 agreements and subsequent loans falling due, totalling US$24.3bn. New long-term money of US$1.3bn and maintenance of short-term credit lines of US$3.5bn.
1993 Apr.	Brady deal, covering US$29bn of debt. Argentina exchanged US$19.3bn of bonds for (1) discount bonds. 30-year bonds at a 35% discount with interest of LIBOR + 13/16%; (2) front-loaded interest reduction bonds (FLIRBs). 30-year par bonds with step-up coupons (4% in first year, rising to 6% in year seven until maturity). Discount bonds and FLIRBs were collateralised for principal and had 12-month rolling interest guarantees. PDI of US$9.3bn was also included. US$0.7bn was paid in cash on closing, US$400mn written off and the remainder exchanged for amortising bond with 17-year maturity at LIBOR + 13/16%.
2001 May	"Mega Bond" swap. A "voluntary" debt exchange that swapped US$29.5bn in debt. It reduced debt service obligations falling due over 2001–2005 but at an implied interest rate of 17%.
2005 Feb.	Exchange of US$81bn in eligible sovereign (foreign and Argentina law) debt (principal and accrued interest) into US$35bn of new bonds, at an exchange ratio of 33.7% (ie 66% reduction in nominal value of the claim). The offer opened in January and closed in February. Three new bonds created, with detachable GDP warrants. Amounts issued of the new bonds were US$15bn (pars), US$11.9bn (discounts) and ARP24.3bn (quasi-pars, cUS$8.3bn equivalent). Acceptance of the foreign debt exchange was 76%, leaving US$20bn untendered. Estimates of the NPV haircut vary.
2010 Jun.	Exchange of US$18bn in debt (certain bonds were not eligible) that remained untendered from the previous exchange. The offer opened in May and closed in June. Participation rate of 66% led to a combined participation rate (including the 2005 exchange) of 92%. Some US$6.2bn remained untendered.
2016 Feb.	After a lengthy legal process, Argentina published its global offer to holdouts on 5 February 2016. The proposal comprised two offers: (1) Basic offer. Offer of 150% for all holdouts not in the *pari passu* group in NY. (2) Pari passu offer. Offer for the *pari passu* group of a 30% reduction in: (a) the original amount recognised in money judgements granted to creditors prior to 1 February; or (b) the accrued claim, if holders did not yet have a money judgement by 1 February, subject to some conditions. There was an early acceptance premium in the form of a reduced haircut of only 27.5% if pari passu holders under either camp agreed to accept the proposal by 19 February.

Source: Exotix, World Bank GDF, IMF

Dealing with the Untendered Bonds

Around US$20bn in bonds were not tendered in the 2005 exchange. They were referred to as the "hold outs" or "untendered", with some creditors taking legal action in the US courts. There was an active market for the untendered bonds after the 2005 exchange and again after the 2010 re-opening, after which some US$6.2bn in untendered bonds (excluding Brady bonds) remained. For a time, the untendered bonds traded on a similar basis in terms of price, irrespective of the actual terms of the bond, although later, as the *pari passu* litigation gained traction from 2012, pricing and investor focus was ISIN specific, depending on coupon, maturity date and legal jurisdiction.

2010 Reopening

After the 2005 exchange, market attention shifted on-and-off to the government's strategy to deal with the holdouts, while holdouts themselves pursued legal options. During 2005, the "Lock law" bill was passed by Congress, stating that the exchange offer could not be re-opened (before 2010) whereas the 2005 exchange prospectus stated that any future offer could not be on more favourable terms. The government of Nestor Kirchner made no effort to re-open the exchange offer. But dealing with the US$20bn in untendered debt was seen as essential for Argentina to restore its international image and access to the international capital market (legal judgements precluded Argentina from being able to borrow from abroad). Hopes arose when his wife, CFK, took office in December 2007. An announcement in September 2008 that the government was studying a proposal presented by three international banks led to some optimism that a revised settlement was in the offing. It came on the heels of the announcement some weeks prior that Argentina would pay down defaulted Paris Club debt (US$6.7bn) with reserves. Both initiatives were shelved after Lehman's collapse.

Discussion on a re-opening of the exchange took some time to revive; one year later, in October 2009, Economy Minister Boudou announced the country had signed a mandate with three investment banks, which were said to represent US$10bn or half the untendered debt stock, to work on an exchange offer. As part of the process, in November a bill to temporarily suspend the Lock law was passed by Congress. Approvals by international regulators took longer than initially expected. That, coupled with tensions in the local scene and a volatile global context, led to speculation that the exchange could have been shelved one more time. Speculation proved wrong, and the final terms were announced in April 2010. The exchange opened in early May and closed, after an extension, in late June. Out of US$18.3bn in eligible debt (Brady bonds were not deemed eligible due to legal issues) US$12.1bn were tendered, with a participation rate of 66%. Combined participation between the 2005 and 2010 exchanges thus stood at 92%. But this still left cUS$6.2bn in untendered bonds.

The terms of the 2010 reopening were similar but slightly worse than in 2005 (worse because all past payments on the GDP warrants were not recognised). Large holders received discount bonds, GDP warrants (both with similar economic terms to those issued in 2005) and Global 2017 8.75% bonds to compensate for PDI on discount bonds during 2004–2009. Small holders (tendering up to US$1.0mn) could choose a par option for up to US$ 50,000, which included a par bond, GDP warrants (same economic terms as those issued in 2005) and a cash payment for PDI on par bonds in the 2004–2009 period. Par bonds' issuance was capped at US$2.0bn. In the exchange, there were issued US$3.7bn equivalent in discount bonds, US$2.0bn equivalent in par bonds, US$12.9bn equivalent in GDP warrants and US$950.5mn in Global 2017 bonds. The exchange resulted in a write off (face value) of c53%.

By end-2010, Argentina was continuing the process of regularising its debts. In December, an exchange for untendered Brady bonds was launched and the government announced that it had engaged in negotiations with the Paris Club. Aside from these, there was still over US$6bn in defaulted bonds, mostly held in the hands of experienced litigant funds. The Republic did not give any indications of what its strategy to deal with this issue would be (other than saying it will "continue to isolate litigants").

Pari Passu Litigation

A US court ruling in 2012 in favour of holdout investors marked the beginning of the end of the holdout saga. The US Court of Appeals for the Second Circuit in the case of *NML Capital v Argentina* on 26 October 2012 affirmed in part and remanded in part an order by the US District Court for the Southern District of New York designed to remedy Argentina's perceived breach of the *pari passu* (equal ranking) clause contained in the bonds that were subject to the 2005 (and 2010) debt exchanges. The District Court order was dated 23 February 2012, but it was stayed pending the appeal court's decision. Judge Griesa, who presided over the case in the District Court, had ordered that—because of the pari passu breach—whenever Argentina paid any amount due on the exchange bonds, it should concurrently or in advance make a "Ratable Payment" (as defined by the Court) to the plaintiffs (conversely, if Argentina did not want to pay the plaintiffs, it could not pay the exchange bonds either). But, although a ruling in favour of holdouts and collecting on a money judgement are not the same thing, Griesa's order was given added enforcement strength by specifying that no one in the payment chain could facilitate the payment either, so third parties could be charged with aiding and abetting Argentina. Argentina was also prevented from taking action to evade the court's order (such as changing the payment mechanism). The amount due to the plaintiffs was, at the time, cUS$1.33bn, comprising principal and PDI.

The court rulings raised the imminent prospect of another Argentina default (technical or otherwise). The next set of payments on the exchange bonds was due in December 2012 (consisting of US$42mn on 2 December on the Global 2017s, US$3bn on 15 December on the GDP warrants and US$100mn on 31 December on the discounts). After a further period, as Judge Griesa considered the issues on remand, the District Court issued another order on 21 November 2012 to the effect that, if Argentina wanted to pay the exchange bonds, it would have to make a payment to the plaintiffs into an escrow account on or before 15 December if it wanted to pay GDP warrants' holders in full. As the ruling came just days before the 2 December coupon payment on the 2017s, that payment was permitted. In the event, the payment was allowed as the appeal process continued.

The pari passu ruling was controversial. The ratable payment argument was based on the plaintiffs' interpretation of the old bonds' boilerplate pari passu clauses, a strategy that had worked earlier in the case of *Elliott v Peru* in 2000. In Argentina's case, under the 1994 fiscal agency agreement (FAA) that governed most of the defaulted bonds, this said (to paraphrase) that the securities should at all times rank pari passu among themselves and all future indebtedness. Griesa controversially upheld the plaintiffs' view. Moreover, at stake was not just the plaintiffs' US$1.3bn claim, but, if successful, it would lead to all other holdout investors (the "me-toos") seeking the same treatment. The total amount of untendered bonds (excluding Brady's), following the two exchanges in 2005 and 2010, amounted to cUS$6.2bn in principal, with a claim that was generally understood to be upwards of US$20bn (depending on the calculation of PDI).

Argentina, however, appealed the order every step of the way, all the way up to the Supreme Court, thereby buying it a bit more time. After a final ruling by the US Court of Appeals on 23 August 2013, CFK announced in a domestic TV interview a half-baked two-fold strategy to deal with the Court's order, including passing legislation to allow a reopening of the debt exchange for a third time and (surprisingly), an offer to swap exchange bonds under foreign law for local law bonds paid in Argentina. In the event, another exchange did not happen and moreover, the local law swap could have been seen as an attempt to evade the court order. Later, the government changed the trustee to a subsidiary of Banco de la Nacion (a state-owned bank) but payments remained blocked, and few holders wanted to be seen as collecting payment and thereby aiding and abetting Argentina. Eventually, the government submitted a writ of certiorari (cert) on 18 February 2014 to the Supreme Court, its last hope. Argentina's cause was supported by amicus briefs from a number of different parties, particularly noteworthy were briefs from the governments of France, Mexico and Brazil, concerned about the ruling's global impact, that it would undermine sovereign debt restructuring and New York's role as an international financial centre (arguments that were all somewhat overplayed). Notably, although the US submitted an amicus brief at an earlier stage (to the US Court of Appeals in April 2012), it did not do so in favour of Argentina's request for cert. The Supreme Court announced on 16 June 2014 that it would not hear the case.

With the Supreme Court declining to hear Argentina's case, CFK announced on 20 June 2014 that the government would negotiate with the holdouts. It marked a dramatic U-turn and came after a week of confusing and contradictory policy statements as the government was seemingly caught off guard by the US Supreme Court's decision. It also came as another payment deadline loomed, with the next scheduled payment on its exchange bonds, the discounts (both USD- and EUR-denominated), on 30 June. On 18 June 2014, the US Court of Appeals lifted the stay on payments that had protected Argentina from default, meaning that Argentina was now obliged to pay the plaintiffs the whole amount of their (now) US$1.5bn claim when it paid the discounts (although the bonds had a 30-day grace period). Argentina said on 18 June it would not make the payment. But, in her speech on 20 June, CFK appeared finally to have conceded defeat and offered to negotiate with the holdouts; as the threat of default and risk to her legacy trumped any political fallout from another policy U-turn. In the event, although Argentina deposited the funds into a trustee account on 26 June, demonstrating the government's willingness to pay, these were not disbursed by the trustee because of the third-party restrictions. By 29 July 2014, with just one day to go to reach an agreement with holdout creditors to comply with the US court ruling, the government still refused to negotiate, despite its pledge on 20 June to do so. Judge Griesa even appointed a mediator, the Special Master, Daniel Pollack, to help facilitate negotiations. Instead, under the cover of the rights upon future offers (RUFO) clause, which was due to expire on 31 December 2014, the government appeared to be preparing the country for default. The payment was still not made after the end of the 30-day grace period, so Argentina fell into default on its foreign law discount bonds. It later defaulted on its other exchange bonds too.

Argentina remained in default on its exchange bonds for the next two years, making little effort to resolve the legal situation. After its grace period default in July 2014, local reports of a private deal soon circulated, either involving local banks or foreign banks buying the plaintiffs' bonds, in order to get around the RUFO clause, before it expired at end-14, but details were sketchy and it fizzled out likely because the government was unwilling to warrant the participating banks that they would be compensated in 2015 after RUFO expired, and perhaps because of the legal risk that even such a side arrangement could also be seen as a breach of RUFO, and the potential risk of other me-too claims. Separately, a group of euro-denominated exchange bondholders subsequently brought a case against the bonds' trustee (BONY Mellon) in the English courts, arguing that the US ruling should not extend to English law bonds. But the Court's decision on 13 February 2015 was inconclusive. Optimism over a speedy resolution in early 2015, after the expiry of the RUFO clause, also faded during the year and investors soon focused on the chances of a settlement in 2016 under a new (and "better") government.

Macri's Settlement with the Holdouts

President Macri's new government moved quickly to resolve the holdout situation. Then Finance Minister Caputo held meetings with holdouts in New York on 13 January 2016 in the office of the court-appointed special master, the first meeting between the two sides since Macri took office. A proposal to creditors was reportedly going to follow soon after. Government statements from Davos also revealed its attitude towards the holdouts. Macri said they were ready to solve the debt problem "now" and that settlement needed to be approved by Congress, while the then Finance Minister Alfonso Prat-Gay (APG) reiterated that the government was committed to resolving the holdout issue, but needed to discuss whether the holdouts' claim was "fair" (ie they thought interest on some bonds was too high). Yet, although the initial signs were positive, the new government's refusal to sign a non-disclosure agreement and its confusing Davos offer were not. The *FT* reported APG saying Argentina would honour the face value of the debt while seeking to negotiate the interest, with an offer of 120 cents on each dollar, although the figure led to more confusion.

Shortly after, it was reported on 5 February 2016 that the government had reached a preliminary agreement to pay Italian holdouts US$1.35bn for a face value of US$900mn, and a claim that amounted to US$2.5bn (the Italian accord). The settlement was in cash (and made easier after the government secured US$5bn from a number of banks the previous week). The settlement implied a payment of 150% of principal and a 46% reduction in the claim. Argentina was thus able to pick off c15% of the US$6.2bn untendered principal through a strategy of divide and conquer. It also dealt with a small but vocal group of bondholders, and so proved a good piece of public relations.

The new government published its global offer to holdouts on 5 February 2016. The proposal, subject to Congress's approval, comprised two offers: (1) Basic offer. Offer of 150% for all holdouts not in the pari passu group in NY. The assumption was that this extended to EUR holders. The 150% offer was the same as the Italian retail offer. (2) Pari passu offer. Offer for the pari passu group of a 30% reduction in: (a) the original amount recognised in money judgements granted to creditors prior to 1 February; or (b) the accrued claim, if holders did not yet have a money judgement by 1 February, subject to some conditions which were not completely clear. There was an early acceptance premium in the form of a reduced haircut of only 27.5% if pari passu holders under either camp agreed to accept the proposal by 19 February. Pari passu (injunction) holders could elect to take the basic offer instead (later, the government appeared to refine the terms of the basic offer, whereby it said injunction holders could take the 150% offer as long as this did not exceed the value of any money judgement, presumably to avoid any potential criticism that some settling plaintiffs might get more than their judgement). The government was to make payments to holdouts in cash, financed by the issuance of bonds. The offer was open for 120 days from 8 February.

The offer, however, was not without controversy. First, it implied significant forgiveness of claims on some bonds, which varied widely bond by bond and by type of claim, raising questions about inter-creditor equity and equal treatment. The average haircut was large. Outside the pari passu group, for which the average haircut was 30% (falling to 27.5% for early acceptance), average haircuts for everyone else ranged broadly from 55–65% in the basic offer, depending on currency. And while pari passu holders received better treatment, that still meant accepting something like 240%, after a 30% discount, rather than 360%. Second, there was an additional uncertainty over what claim the government was going to recognise and in particular whether the claim had passed its prescribed period (ie whether the statute of limitations had lapsed or not). The statute of limitations varied by jurisdiction, and in some cases, was different for interest and principal. In New York, the statute of limitations is six years. The government's participation instructions published later, on 17 February 2016, seemed to imply that bonds for which the statute of limitations had expired were not eligible, although the government refused to publish a list of the ISINs that were time-barred. In practice, it was up to bondholders to submit their own claim and hope, and, anecdotally, it appeared that some holders were paid and some not.

But there was also a strong incentive for some holders to participate, especially for EUR holders (who had no guarantee they could get the same pari passu treatment in New York) and other USD holders outside the main litigants. That said, some investors thought the government might have to sweeten the offer to increase participation, which could have been done at little additional cost (when set against the benefits of settling), but the early acceptance by two big holdouts (Dart and Montreaux; NML settled later), together holding c14% of the claims in the New York court (their combined claim was cUS$1.3bn out of US$9bn in New York claims), and only c5–6% of the potential total claim, essentially set the tone for most of the other holdouts to follow suit.

The government submitted a motion to Judge Griesa on 11 February 2016 seeking to vacate the pari passu injunction, subject to two conditions, that it repealed legislation preventing a settlement (the Lock law) and that payment was made with the plaintiffs on or before 29 February 2016, which was duly done.

To date, most of the holdouts have been resolved, although Exotix understands some litigation is still ongoing, mainly related to claims over the statute of limitations. The Ministry of Finance has continued settling claims with untendered debt holders throughout this period, with the terms offered the same as those offered to the creditors who accepted in 2016. As at end-17, IMF figures contained in the staff report for the SBA in June 2018 (published in July) showed that settlement agreements covered US$5.5bn in principal (out of a total of US$6.7bn), with an agreement to settle at US$11.3bn out of a total claim of US$17.4bn; that is, a haircut of 35%. However, Argentina continues to have arrears to private creditors with a residual amount of untendered debt that is still unresolved and not yet subject to a settlement agreement, and where litigation continues in several jurisdictions. Another US$1.2bn in principal and US$3.3bn in claim (ie including accrued interest) is still pending.

Argentina's Return to the Market

Argentina, under the new Macri government, returned to the international debt market in April 2016 with a mega bond sale, marking the end of some 15 years in default and isolation. The government issued US$16.5bn in new bonds, one of the largest bond sales in EM history, with US$10bn to pay the holdouts (after the final lifting of the US injunction prior to the issuance) and the remainder for general budget needs for the year. The issuance was increased from an initial size of US$10bn–15bn, in the face of strong demand, with an order book reportedly amounting to nearly US$70bn, according to the *FT*. Settlement was on 22 April, which was when payments to holdouts were to be made. Four new bonds were issued, with US$2.75bn in a three-year (2019), US$4.5bn in a five-year (2021), US$6.5bn in a 10-year (2026) and US$2.75bn in a 30-year (2046). Yields ranged from 6.3% for the new three-year to 8% for the new 30-year.

The government returned to the market numerous times after the April 2016 operation, and has issued some US$43.7bn in total since then according to Exotix calculations, in 18 different bonds. It issued another US$2.75bn in July 2016, with US$1bn in a new 2028 bond and

US$1.75bn in a 20-year (2036 maturity). Euro-denominated issues followed in December, with EUR2.5bn split evenly between 2022 and 2027 issues. In January 2017, Argentina issued US$7bn, comprising US$3.25bn in a new 2022 bond and US$3.75bn in a new 2027 bond. In April 2017, Argentina issued a three-year CHF400mn bond. In June 2017, taking advantage of strong investor interest in the country's turn-around story, Argentina issued a century bond, becoming only the third EM issuer to do so (after the Mexico sovereign in 2010 and Brazil's Petrobras in 2015; and excluding a small and illiquid China 100-year bond issued in 1996), with US$2.75bn in a 2117-dated bond at a coupon of 7.125%. The bond was priced at 90 to yield 7.917%. In November 2017, Argentina issued EUR2.75bn in three bonds: EUR1bn 2023, EUR1bn 2028 and EUR0.75bn 2047. In January 2018, Argentina issued US$9bn in three bonds: US$1.75bn 2023, US$4.25bn 2028 and US$3bn 2048. As a result, Argentina issued cUS$21.8bn in 2016 (although only cUS$11bn "net" after the proceeds used to settle with the holdouts), US$12.9bn in 2017 and US$9bn in 2018.

Despite the issuance of a number of other bonds, Argentina's exchange bonds (discounts and pars; the Global 17s have matured) continue to trade. They are still liquid, with a stock of over US$30bn, and tend to be looked at against the curve. The dollar and euro exchange bonds trade regularly. Trading in the GDP warrants has, however, been negatively impacted by ongoing issues and uncertainty over what past GDP rebasings and methodological changes, under both Presidents CFK and Macri, mean for the relevant reference years and baseline triggers and, hence, the payment calculation. There has been no official clarification as to the impact or what measures the government will take to resolve the situation. There have been no payments on the warrants now for the past six years.

Argentina's new issues are summarised below and details for its century bond and GDP warrants are also given.

Argentina's selected sovereign eurobond issues

Ticker	*Coupon (%)*	*Currency*	*Issue date*	*Maturity date*	*Amount outstanding (mn)*
ARGENT	6.25	USD	22/04/2016	22/04/2019	2750
ARGENT	3.375	CHF	12/04/2017	12/10/2020	400
ARGENT	6.875	USD	22/04/2016	22/04/2021	4500
ARGENT	3.875	EUR	12/10/2016	15/01/2022	1250

(*continued*)

(continued)

Ticker	*Coupon (%)*	*Currency*	*Issue date*	*Maturity date*	*Amount outstanding (mn)*
ARGENT	5.625	USD	26/01/2017	26/01/2022	3250
ARGENT	4.625	USD	11/01/2018	11/01/2023	1750
ARGENT	3.375	EUR	09/11/2017	15/01/2023	1000
ARGENT	7.5	USD	22/04/2016	22/04/2026	6500
ARGENT	5	EUR	12/10/2016	15/01/2027	1250
ARGENT	6.875	USD	26/01/2017	26/01/2027	3750
ARGENT	5.875	USD	11/01/2018	11/01/2028	4250
ARGENT	5.25	EUR	09/11/2017	15/01/2028	1000
ARGENT	6.625	USD	06/07/2016	06/07/2028	1000
ARGENT	8.28	USD	29/11/2005	31/12/2033	3966
ARGENT	7.82	EUR	29/11/2005	31/12/2033	2270
ARGENT	7.125	USD	06/07/2016	06/07/2036	1750
ARGENT	2.5	USD	29/11/2005	31/12/2038	5297
ARGENT	2.26	EUR	29/11/2005	31/12/2038	5034
ARGENT	7.625	USD	22/04/2016	22/04/2046	2750
ARGENT	6.25	EUR	09/11/2017	09/11/2047	750
ARGENT	6.875	USD	11/01/2018	11/01/2048	3000
ARGENT	7.125	USD	28/06/2017	28/06/2117	2750

Source: Bloomberg

Argentina century bond
Republic of Argentina 7.125% 2117
Bloomberg ticker: ARGENT

Borrower	Republic of Argentina
Issue date	28 June 2017
Form	Eurobond
ISIN	USP04808AN44 (later exchanged into US040114HN39 in May 2018)
Issue size	US$2750mn
Currency	US dollar
Denomination	Minimum US$1000; increments of US$1000 thereafter
Amortisation	Bullet
Final maturity date	28 June 2117
Coupon/interest	7.125%, payable semi-annually
Day count	30/360
Method of transfer	Euroclear/Clearstream
Settlement period	T + 2 business days
Managers	Citi, HSBC
Governing law	Argentina, New York
Listing	Berlin, Buenos Aires, Dusseldorf, EuroTLX, Frankfurt, MAE, Munich, Stuttgart

Source: Bloomberg

Argentina GDP warrants
Republic of Argentina Float 12/2035
Bloomberg ticker: ARGENT

Reference amount	GDP-linked units issued with respect to the amount of eligible securities tendered.
Calculation currency	Pesos
Payment currency	Currency of the new bond to which the GDP-linked security was initially attached.
Expiration	15 December 2035
Calculation date	Annually from 1 November 2006
Payment date	Annually from 15 December 2006 and subject to specified payment conditions.
Reference year	Calendar year, which commences in 2005 and ends in 2034.
Payment amount	5% of excess GDP of any year multiplied by aggregate notional amount of GDP warrants held. This is then divided by the total aggregate amount of all eligible securities. Payments are made in December in the year following the reference year.
Excess GDP	Excess GDP for any reference year is the amount (if any) that actual real GDP exceeds the BASE case GDP (converted to nominal pesos).
Payment trigger	For the reference year: 1. Actual real GDP exceeds the BASE case GDP. 2. Annual expansion of actual real GDP exceeds the growth rate indicated for any such year in the Base case GDP. 3. Total payments made on a GDP-linked security do not exceed the payment cap.
Actual real GDP	Argentine real GDP published and calculated by INDEC using 1993 prices.
BASE case GDP	GDP table published in the prospectus for each reference year using 1993 prices.
Conversion to nominal pesos	Multiplication by GDP deflators calculated by INDEC.
Conversion to currency of payment	Multiplication by the average free exchange rate prevailing 15 days before the end of the reference year.
Payment cap	Total accumulated payments cannot exceed 0.48 per GDP unit.

Payments

Reference year	USD	EUR	ARS (in USD)
2005	0.6245	0.6618	0.6491
2006	1.3182	1.2621	1.3834
2007	2.2798	1.9852	2.4545
2008	3.1688	2.8397	3.7198
2009	0	0	0
2010	4.3828	4.1908	5.9751

(*continued*)

(continued)

Argentina GDP warrants *Republic of Argentina Float 12/2035* *Bloomberg ticker: ARGENT*				
	2011	6.2657	6.0553	9.2242
	2012	0	0	0
	2013	0	0	0
	2014	0	0	0
	2015	0	0	0
	2016	0	0	0
	2017	0	0	0
Change in the base prices	BASE case GDP will be adjusted accordingly.			

Source: Bloomberg

Provincial Debt: Eurobonds

Argentina provinces have been issuing international bonds, mainly in USD, for some 20 years. Before 2016, some provinces had been able to issue bonds since 2001, despite the sovereign default. Indeed, in H1 15, after the sovereign defaulted on its exchange bonds in 2014 following the *pari passu* ruling, both the City and Province of Buenos Aries (PBA) issued bonds, albeit at high coupons, as the City of Buenos Aires issued a US$500mn six-year bond at par with a coupon of 8.95% in February and the PBA issued a US$900mn six-year bond in June with a coupon of 9.95% and priced to yield 10.25%. Prior to this, issuance was generally clustered around the two sovereign debt exchanges (with a rash of issues in 2006 following the 2005 exchange, mainly from PBA in its own restructuring, and in 2010–2011 following the reopening of the sovereign debt exchange in 2010). The City of Buenos Aires had issued a US$250mn 10-year note in 1997 under an EMTN programme, which was amended, in 2003, along with two other instruments (in EUR and ARS), with a maturity extension to 2011 and a lower coupon. This was followed by a US$475mn five-year bond in 2010. PBA issued a US$100mn three year note in 1994 and again in 1995 under an EMTN programme, followed by a US$200mn combined in two zero coupon notes in 1999, along with two DEM issues (in 1995 and 1996), and more issues of similar size in different currencies over 1999–2001, until the disruption caused by the sovereign default. PBA issued four bonds in its restructuring in 2006 (two maturities, 2020 and 2035, both in USD and EUR), before returning to the market in 2007 with a US$400mn 2028 issue, and again in 2011 with a US$750mn 2021 issue. More PBA issues followed over 2015–2017. Yet Salta had even issued a small US$79mn bond backed by hydrocarbon royalties in February 2001, Mendoza issued a small 10-year bond in 1997 for US$250mn (which was exchanged in 2004, following default in 2002, into a new 2018 bond which has now matured), and Neuquen followed with a small debut bond in 2006 amounting to US$250mn and maturing in 2014, backed by oil royalties. After marked inactivity during 2008 and 2009, stemming from the global financial crisis, the Province of Cordoba issued a small debut bond in November 2009 for US$128mn with a coupon of 12%. Over the period 2010 to January 2011 there were five new issues (City of Buenos Aires 2015, PBA 2015 and 2021, Province of Cordoba 2017 and Province of Chubut oil and gas royalties-backed trust) for a combined total of US$2.7bn.

However, it was the normalisation of the debt situation in 2016, with the settlement of the holdout litigation, that opened the door for a rush of new issues as cash-starved provinces piggy-backed on the country's stronger rating outlook and investor demand, with some provinces making their issuance debuts. The World Bank noted that, in addition to the US$16.5bn debt restructuring operation, public sector borrowers issued bonds to the value of US$21.4bn in 2016. Other than the US$5bn or so of additional sovereign issues that year, Exotix calculates provincial issuance in 2016 of US$8.2bn, consisting of US$3.75bn in three bonds from PBA, US$890mn from the City of Buenos Aires, and other issues from Cordoba, Mendoza, Neuquen, Salta, and debuts from Santa Fe, Chubut and Chaco. Exotix calculates further provincial issuance in 2017 of US$3.9bn, with US$1.25bn in two more bonds from PBA, and other smaller issues from Cordoba, Neuquen, Santa Fe, and debuts from Jujuy, La Rioja, Rio Negro, Tierra del Fuego, and Entre Rios. Hence, provincial issuance amounted to cUS$12.1bn over 2016–2017.

Exotix calculates the outstanding stock of provincial bonds at cUS$16.0bn. This is across some 31 bonds from 15 issuers. Of this, around three-quarters (by number of issues) have been issued after 2015. The largest issuer, PBA, accounts for just over half the total outstanding (52%). See the table below for a summary of the main provincial bonds outstanding.

Selected Argentina provincial bonds

Province	*Ticker*	*Coupon (%)*	*Currency*	*Maturity date*	*Issue date*	*Amount outstanding (mn)*
City of Buenos Aires	BUEAIR	8.95	USD	19 February 2021	19 February 2015	500
City of Buenos Aires	BUEAIR	7.5	USD	1 June 2027	1 June 2016	890
Provincia de Buenos Aires	BUENOS	5.75	USD	15 June 2019	15 June 2016	750
Provincia de Buenos Aires	BUENOS	4.0	EUR	1 May 2020	12 January 2006	381
Provincia de Buenos Aires	BUENOS	10.875	USD	26 January 2021	26 January 2011	750
Provincia de Buenos Aires	BUENOS	9.95	USD	9 June 2021	9 June 2015	899.5
Provincia de Buenos Aires	BUENOS	5.375	EUR	20 January 2023	20 July 2017	500
Provincia de Buenos Aires	BUENOS	6.5	USD	15 February 2023	15 February 2017	750
Provincia de Buenos Aires	BUENOS	9.125	USD	26 March 2024	16 March 2016	1250
Provincia de Buenos Aires	BUENOS	7.875	USD	15 June 2027	15 June 2016	1750
Provincia de Buenos Aires	BUENOS	9.625	USD	18 April 2028	18 April 2007	400
Provincia de Buenos Aires	BUENOS	4.0	EUR	15 May 2035	12 January 2006	468
Provincia de Buenos Aires	BUENOS	4.0	USD	15 May 2035	12 January 2006	446
Provincia de Cordoba	PDCAR	7.125	USD	10 June 2021	10 June 2016	725
Provincia de Cordoba	PDCAR	7.45	USD	1 September 2024	1 March 2017	510
Provincia de Cordoba	PDCAR	7.125	USD	27 October 2026	27 October 2016	300
City of Cordoba	CORDOB	7.875	USD	29 September 2024	29 September 2016	150
Provincia del Chaco	CHACO	9.375	USD	18 August 2024	18 August 2016	250

(*continued*)

(continued)

Province	*Ticker*	*Coupon (%)*	*Currency*	*Maturity date*	*Issue date*	*Amount outstanding (mn)*
Provincia del Chubut	CHUBUT	7.75	USD	26 July 2026	26 July 2016	650
Provincia de Entre Rios	ENTRIO	8.75	USD	2 August 2025	2 August 2017	500
Provincia de Jujuy	JUJUYA	8.625	USD	20 September 2022	20 September 2017	210
Provincia de Mendoza	MENDOZ	8.375	USD	19 May 2024	19 May 2016	500
Provincia de Neuquen	NEUQUE	7.5	USD	27 April 2025	27 April 2017	366
Provincia de Neuquen	NEUQUE	8.625	USD	12 May 2028	12 May 2016	349
Provincia de la Rioja	PRIO	9.75	USD	24 February 2025	24 February 2017	300
Provincia de Rio Negro	PRN	7.75	USD	7 December 2025	7 December 2017	300
Provincia de Santa Fe	PROVSF	7.0	USD	23 March 2023	23 March 2017	250
Provincia de Santa Fe	PROVSF	6.9	USD	1 November 2027	1 November 2016	250
Provincia de Salta	SALTA	9.5	USD	16 March 2022	16 March 2012	76
Provincia de Salta	SALTA	9.125	USD	7 July 2024	7 July 2016	350
Pr. de Tierra Del Fuego	FUEGO	8.95	USD	17 April 2027	17 April 2017	200

Source: Bloomberg

Corporate Bond Markets

A summary of the main outstanding corporate eurobonds in Argentina is shown below. These amount to a total outstanding of US$14.7bn, across 17 issuers. The main issuer is YPF, with some US$6.9bn outstanding (including a December 2018 maturity), c47% of the total. As with the provinces, much of the issuance has taken place since 2015 after Argentina normalised its debt situation. In general, corporate issuance was fairly muted until then due to the sovereign default. The second sovereign debt exchange in 2010 resulted in a modest recovery in corporate new issues. Combining pure new issues (Arcor, Aeropuertos Argentina 2000, Clisa, IRSA, Panamerican Energy and Tarjeta Naranja), bonds issued upon restructurings (Masher and Ausol) and refinancings (Edenor, WPE-IMPSA), 2010 corporate eurobond issuance totaled US$2.3bn, compared with issuance of cUS$3.5bn in 2016 and US$4.5bn in 2017.

Selected Argentina corporate eurobonds

Corporate	*Description*	*Amount outstanding*	*Maturity type*	*Issue date*
Adecoagro (AGRO)	USD 6% Due 2027	US$350mn	Callable	Jan. 2017
Aeropuertos Argentina (AEROAR)	USD 6.875% Due 2027	US$400mn	Call/Sink	Feb. 2017
Agua y Saneamientos (AGUSAN)	USD 6.625% Due 2023	US$500mn	Callable	Feb. 2018
Arcor (ARCOR)	USD 6% Due 2023	US$500mn	Callable	Jul. 2016
Banco de Galicia y Buenos Aires (GALIAR)	USD 8.25% Due 2026	US$250mn	Callable	Jul. 2016
Banco Macro (BMAAR)	USD 6.75% Due 2026	US$400mn	Callable	Nov. 2016
Cablevision (TASFT)	USD 6.5% Due 2021	US$500mn	Callable	Jun. 2016
Empresa Distribuidora del Norte Edenor (EDNAR)	USD 9.75% Due 2022	US$176mn	Callable	Oct. 2010
Generacion Mediterranea (ALBAAR)	USD 9.625% Due 2023	US$336mn	Callable	Jul. 2016
Genneia (GNNEIA)	USD 8.75% Due 2022	US$350mn	Callable	Jan. 2017
Pampa Energia (PAMPAR)	USD 7.375% Due 2023	US$500mn	Callable	Jul. 2016
Pampa Energia (PAMPAR)	USD 7.5% Due 2027	US$750mn	Callable	Jan. 2017
Pan American Energy (PANAME)	USD 7.875% Due 2021	US$500mn	Sinkable	May 2010
Rio Energy/UGEN/UENSA (MSUNRG)	USD 6.875% Due 2025	US$600mn	Callable	Feb. 2018
Stoneway Capital (STNEWY)	USD 10% Due 2027	US$665mn	Call/Sink	Feb. 2017
Tecpetrol (TECPET)	USD 4.875% Due 2022	US$500mn	Callable	Dec. 2017

(*continued*)

(continued)

Corporate	*Description*	*Amount outstanding*	*Maturity type*	*Issue date*
Transportadora de Gas del Sur (TRAGAS)	USD 6.75% Due 2025	US$500mn	Callable	Apr. 2018
YPF (YPFDAR)	USD 8.875% Due 2018	US$861.6mn	Bullet	Dec. 2013
YPF (YPFDAR)	USD FRN Due 2020	US$750mn	Bullet	Jul. 2012
YPF (YPFDAR)	USD 8.5% Due 2021	US$1000mn	Bullet	Mar. 2016
YPF (YPFDAR)	USD 8.75% Due 2024	US$1325mn	Sinkable	Apr. 2014
YPF (YPFDAR)	USD 8.5% Due 2025	US$1500mn	Bullet	Apr. 2015
YPF (YPFDAR)	USD 6.95% Due 2027	US$750mn	Bullet	Jul. 2017
YPF (YPFDAR)	USD 7% Due 2047	US$750mn	Bullet	Dec. 2017

Source: Bloomberg

Azerbaijan

Nominal GDP (US$mn, 2018)[a]		45,592
Population (thousand, 2018)[a]		9940
GDP per capita (USD, 2018)[a]		4587
Credit ratings (long-term foreign currency)[b]	Fitch	BB+
	Moody's	Ba2
	S&P	BB+

[a]IMF WEO October 2018
[b]As at end-September 2018

Country Summary

- Acknowledged as an authoritarian regime which has seen the ruling NAP in power since the early 1990s, now under President Ilham Aliyev (since 2003), and his father for ten years before him. The country's early transition after independence in 1991 was turbulent and a ceasefire in the destructive war with Armenia was achieved only in 1994. Many development projects still focus on improving the transport infrastructure, which suffered extensive damage during the war and underinvestment since.
- The economy is dominated by oil and gas, and still hasn't fully recovered from the oil price collapse from 2014 which hit the country hard. While oil helped transform the economy, seeing income per capita rise ten-fold over 2003–2013, its over-dependence is also a key

Exotix Capital, *Exotix Developing Markets Guide*,
https://doi.org/10.1007/978-3-030-05867-8_5

vulnerability. Oil accounts for over 90% of exports, but the value of oil exports halved over 2013–2016, and the exchange rate peg became unsustainable. The currency was devalued by over 50% as official reserves fell by 60% in 2015. Government attempts to support the non-oil sectors and stimulate the economy have led to budget deficits and rising public debt (now over 50% of GDP), but considerable savings in its SWF mitigate to some extent the rise in gross public debt.

- Azerbaijan has no modern history of sovereign restructuring, having generally maintained a low public debt burden, at least until the 2014 oil price crash. The government issued its first eurobond in 2014, which is still outstanding. However, Azerbaijan suffered from a confidence crisis following the fall in commodity prices in H2 14, after which it lost its investment grade rating, and the resulting currency devaluation ultimately led one bank (IBA) to restructure its corporate eurobonds.

Economic data	*Avg*[a]	*2014*	*2015*	*2016*	*2017 (e)*	*2018 (f)*	*2019 (f)*
Real GDP growth	8.3	2.7	0.6	−3.1	0.1	1.3	3.6
Inflation (annual average)	7.5	1.5	4.1	12.6	13.0	3.5	3.3
Current account (% of GDP)	18.5	13.9	−0.4	−3.6	4.1	6.6	8.1
Reserves (US$mn, end-period)[b]	8831	13,758	5017	3974	5335	5471[c]	–
Reserves/imports (months)[d]	–	6.9	2.8	2.4	3.2	–	–
Overall fiscal balance (% of GDP)[e]	4.8	2.7	−4.8	−1.2	−1.7	4.8	6.5
Currency (ticker)	Azerbaijani manat (AZN)						
FX regime	Managed float, although the IMF reclassified it as de facto "other managed" from a stabilised arrangement in December 2015. Effective 16 February 2015, the exchange rate was devalued and repegged to a currency basket comprising the US dollar and euro, and was devalued again in December. Prior to this, since 2011, the peg was against USD.						
Key exports	Oil (94% of goods exports in 2013) is the dominant export. Oil exports halved over 2013–2016, from US$30bn to US$12bn.						

Source: IMF WEO Database, IMF Country Reports, Haver, Central Bank, Exotix

[a]10-year average to 2016 unless otherwise stated

[b]Official foreign reserves from central bank statistical bulletin, average over eight years only

[c]Latest figure, May 2018

[d]In months of the current year's imports of goods, services and primary income debits calculated by Exotix

[e]Overall government net lending

Key figures		*Party*	*Since*
President	Ilham Aliyev	New Azerbaijan Party (NAP)	2003
Prime minister	Artur Rasizade	Communist Party	2003
Minister of finance	Samir Sharifov Rauf oglu	Independent	2006
Key opposition figure	Jamil Hasanli[a]	DQMS	2013
Central bank governor	Elman Rustamov	–	2010

[a]Boycotted the 2018 presidential election after it was unexpectedly brought forward

Politics

Executive power

The President is head of state, now elected for a seven-year term, and responsible for the appointment of the Prime Minister, who is the head of government, (confirmed by the National Assembly) and all cabinet positions. The constitution denotes that power is separated between the legislative, executive and judicial branch, though governance and power is consolidated by the president. The president is elected by an absolute majority in a two-round system. A controversial constitutional amendment in 2016 gave the president the power to call early elections, as well as extending the president's term, which he did in 2018. After the previous election in October 2013, an election was called in April 2018, before the end of the full five-year term.

Presidential term: Seven years, term extended from five years in 2016 (starting next term; ie in 2018) and two-term limit abolished in 2009

Parliamentary term: Five years

Legislature

The unicameral Milli Majlis (National Assembly) has 125 members, elected for five years; single seat constituencies. The final branch of government is the Judicial body, headed by the constitutional court; it remains autonomous and independent from the other branches of government.

Elections

Next due	*Legislative: May 2020*	*Presidential: 2025*	
Last legislative election[a] (November 2015)	*Seats*	*Last presidential (April 2018)*	*% of vote*
NAP	71	Ilham Aliyev (NAP)	86.0
Civil Solidarity Party	2	Zahid Oruj (Independent)	3.1
Independents	43	Sardar Mammadov (ADP)	3.0
Other	8	Qudrat Hasanguliyev (PFPWA)	3.0
Invalidated[b]	1	Other	4.9
Total	**125**	**Total**	**100.0**

[a]The main opposition parties boycotted the National Assembly election

[b]In the Aghdash constituency, two candidates complained of irregularities and the result was annulled

People

The dominant ethnic group is Azeri (91.6%); 2% of the population are Lezghin, 1.3% Russian and 1.3% Armenian. The most widely spoken language is Azerbaijani (also spoken by 25% of Iran) with 13 other languages native to the country. 97% of the population are (mostly Shia) Muslim but the practicing proportion of this is very small, Christians amount to 3% of population. The constitution denotes the State is secular by law. Azerbaijan was one of the constituent republics of the Soviet Union in 1922 and achieved independence in August 1991, shortly before the dissolution of the USSR. However, the transition was turbulent and from 1988 to 1992 war with Armenia resulted in 30,000 deaths and the loss of 14% in the country's territory. Over a million refugees immigrated into the country, causing social unrest and poverty to rise dramatically. A ceasefire was achieved in 1994 but there had been considerable damage to infrastructure including transport links, thus disrupting regional trade. Limited economic development followed independence as the country faced a contraction in economic activity, an increase in poverty and deterioration in social services and infrastructure. Since 1995 the government has aimed to stabilise the economy and introduce structural reforms as well as attract investment from abroad. The vast reserves of mineral resources, especially oil and gas, has led to an influx of capital into the country and supported its development during the noughties, with income per capita rising six-fold between 2003 and 2008. Azerbaijan is now an upper-middle income country. However, the oil sector employs less than 1% of the labour force. 37% of the population is still employed in agriculture with crops including grapes, cotton and tobacco and c5% of the population lives below the poverty line. 55% of the population in 2017 lived in urban areas, especially in and around Baku. Yet the economic expansion of Azerbaijan has been a successful example of post-Soviet economic development, although the dependence on the hydrocarbon sector and largely unsuccessful government attempts to expand other sectors shows the ongoing need for diversification and private sector activity. The major opposition parties, including Musavat (Equality) Party, boycotted the 2015 parliamentary election, on the grounds that the government had committed huge violations, including jailing its opponents. The dominant New Azerbaijan Party (NAP) was formed in the early 1990s by Heydar Aliyev, former KGB head and father of the current president. Heydar Aliyev was the country's third president (serving from 1993–2003); the first and second presidents only served for nine months and one year respectively. The party is centrist and nationalist. Freedom House describe Azerbaijan as being ruled by an authoritarian regime characterised by intolerance for dissent and disregard for civil liberties and political rights. The disputed territory of Nagorno Karabakh is an enclave in Azerbaijan, controlled by the Republic of Artsakh (a de facto independent state) but internationally recognised as part of Azerbaijan. It suffers from violence despite a ceasefire agreement from the end of the Nagorno Karabakh War in 1994. Peace talks have continued since then over the region's disputed status, while border clashes have flared up again since 2016, and military conflict continues through 2018.

Debt

	2012	*2016*
External debt ratios (%)		
Total external debt/GDP[a]	15.0	37.3
o/w Public external debt/GDP (MLT)	8.3	27.8
Private external debt/GDP (MLT)	4.0	5.0
Total external debt/exports	27.3	76.1
External debt service ratio	0.9	4.4
Public debt ratios (%)		
Public domestic debt/GDP[b]	5.5	22.9
Public debt/GDP[c]	13.8	50.7

Source: World Bank IDS, IMF, Exotix

[a]Including short-term and IMF credit
[b]Implied (difference between overall public debt and PPG MLT external debt)
[c]IMF WEO

Timely and detailed data on Azerbaijan's public debt position is somewhat limited. The ministry of finance has published the total of public external debt since 2015 on an almost quarterly basis, but with little additional information on the composition or creditor breakdown. There are no ministry of finance (MOF) figures for public domestic debt. External public debt as of 1 January 2018 (ie end-2017) was reported at US$9398mn (AZN15,978mn), by the MOF, which amounted to 22.8% of GDP on official figures. This compared to US$6913mn (AZN12,241mn), 20.4% of GDP, at end-2016 and US$6894mn (AZN10,751mn), 19.8% of GDP, at end-2015. The figures include direct obligations of the state as well as contingent liabilities arising from sovereign guarantees. For the creditor composition, the World Bank's IDS is the most readily available, although its figures are currently only up to 2016, and the total is somewhat higher. There are no up to date IMF figures either (other than in the WEO).

With oil wealth accumulating steadily until 2014, public debt was historically very low and there was limited need to use public borrowing as a means of financing the country's development, although the government first planned a eurobond issue back in 2007. Public debt fell as low as 7% of GDP in 2008, from 24% in 2001, and stood at only 14% of GDP in 2012 (IMF WEO figures). However, the public sector debt burden rose quickly over 2014–2015, firstly with the debut eurobond issue in March 2014 and then after global oil prices fell from mid-2014. In addition to declining oil revenues, the government provided fiscal stimulus: in nominal terms, general government expenditure in 2017 was forecast at over double its 2009 level. Meanwhile real GDP growth contracted in 2016, stagnating in 2017, and the currency was devalued by c50% against the US dollar over 2015 (weakening a bit further in 2016), causing US$ GDP to half over 2014–2016. Public sector debt therefore jumped to 35% of GDP in 2015, up from 14% in 2014, and to 51% of GDP in 2016, and was projected to rise further to 55% in 2017, stabilising at this level in 2018 (IMF WEO figures).

Public and publicly guaranteed (PPG) medium- and long-term (MLT) external debt was cUS$10.5bn in 2016, according to World Bank IDS data (c27.8% of GDP, based on WEO GDP). Multilaterals held 42% of this and 31% of the total external debt stock. Only 21% of multilateral debt was at concessional rates, a source of finance no longer available as a result of the country's upper middle-income status. Bilateral creditors were owed c11% of PPG MLT external debt, all of which was on concessional terms. Commercial creditors however have become the biggest creditor group, amounting to US$5bn, nearly half the total PPG MLT external debt and c36% of total external debt. This included US$3.25bn in bonds, which Exotix believes included the one sovereign eurobond (2024) and the three State Oil Company of Azerbaijan (SOCAR) bonds that were outstanding at end-2016. By end-2017, outstanding bonds would have increased by a net amount of US$1.5bn, after the issuance of a further US$2.1bn in sovereign bonds as part of the IBA restructuring, and the repayment in February of the US$500mn SOCAR 5.45% 2017. With overall public debt at 50.7% of GDP (from the WEO), this implies public domestic debt was 22.9% of GDP (although this assumes there was no short-term public external debt).

Total external debt was US$14.1bn, as per IDS data, increasing from 15.0% of GDP in 2012 to 37.3% of GDP (using WEO GDP). PPG MLT external debt was c75% of the total (28% of GDP). Private sector (non-guaranteed) MLT external debt was c13.5% of the total (c5.0% of GDP). In nominal terms, private non-guaranteed MLT external debt decreased from US$2.75bn in 2012 to US$1.9bn in 2016. Short-term external debt, based on World Bank figures, was 10.4% of the total (cUS$1.5bn, 4.0% of GDP). The use of IMF credit, on IDS figures was 1.5% of the total (cUS$206.5mn, 0.5% of GDP). Total external debt increased to 76% of exports, due to the fall in oil revenues. The value of exports in 2016 was less than half of its 2012 level. With the declining proportion of external debt that was on concessional terms, down from 24.1% in 2012 to 14.5% in 2016, the external debt service ratio has increased from 0.9% to 4.4%.

Despite the rise in the (gross) public debt burden, net public debt is much lower (negative). The government has accumulated considerable savings in its Sovereign Wealth Fund (the State Oil Fund, SOFAZ) since 2005 (in addition to its central bank reserves). SOFAZ assets stood at US$38.4bn at end Q2 18, up from US$35.8bn at end-2017, and have remained in the US$30–40bn range since 2012 (according to Haver). The limited accumulation over the past few years is probably due to lower oil revenues and some drawdowns. The savings really began to accumulate from 2007, rising from US$2.5bn at end-2007 to US$23bn at end-2010. Standing at over 80% of GDP today, these savings ensure that Azerbaijan is a net external creditor, which therefore helps to mitigate to some extent risks from the rise in the gross debt and associated external vulnerabilities.

Composition of external debt

External debt by creditor (end-2016)	*Nominal amount outstanding (US$mn)*	*Share of total (%)*
Public sector external debt (MLT PPG)	**10,517.8**	**74.7**
o/w Official multilateral	4399.0	31.2
o/w World Bank	2544.8	18.1
Memo: official multilateral concessional	912.6	6.5
Official bilateral	1125.7	8.0
Memo: official bilateral concessional	1125.7	8.0
Commercial creditors	4993.1	35.5
Bonds	3250.0	23.1
Commercial banks and other	1743.1	12.4
Private non-guaranteed external debt (MLT)	**1899.3**	**13.5**
Short term external debt	**1461.7**	**10.3**
Use of IMF credit	**206.5**	**1.5**
Total external debt	**14,085.3**	**100.0**

Source: World Bank IDS

Rescheduling History

Azerbaijan has no history of rescheduling any of its sovereign commitments in recent times. This is probably largely because public debt had been fairly low since the ceasefire in the war with Armenia in 1994, until 2014. The International Bank of Azerbaijan (IBA), a majority state-owned bank, restructured its debt in mid-2017, including its eurobonds (see below).

Azerbaijan suffered from a liquidity-style confidence crisis following the fall in commodity prices in H2 14. With lower oil prices and falling reserves (which fell by 55% between September in 2014 and September 2015), the authorities undertook in 2015 two currency devaluations against the US dollar, to which it had been fixed for the previous five years (devaluing by 26% in February and 33% in December) and switched to a managed float on 21 December 2015. That said, after some initial flexibility following the December 2015 float, the currency has (to date) de facto been fixed against the US dollar since April 2017. In all, the currency saw a 55% cumulative devaluation against the US dollar from the time of its February 2014 devaluation to end June 2018. Azerbaijan came under ratings pressure and ultimately lost its investment grade status. S&P downgraded it from BBB– (where it had been since 2011) to BB+ in January 2016. Fitch downgraded its BBB– rating (where it had been since 2010) to BB+ in February 2016. Moody's downgraded its Baa3 rating (which it had assigned in 2014) to Ba1 in February 2016 and again to Ba2 in August 2017.

Relations with Multilateral Creditors

Azerbaijan has only had four IMF credit arrangements since becoming a member of the IMF in 1992, although two of these (a combined ECF and EFF in 1995–1996) ran concurrently, while in the mid-1990s, it drew twice on the Fund's Systemic Transformation Facility (STF), the second time being in tandem with a standby credit. In fact, Azerbaijan had almost continuous program engagement with the Fund over ten years from 1995–2005, but very little since. The IMF last entered into an agreement with Azerbaijan in July 2001 when it approved a three-year ECF of cUS$100mn, subsequently extended by one year, aimed at budget stabilisation and structural reform. International lenders led by the IMF, World Bank, Asian Development Bank, and EBRD, also approved in April 2002 a regional initiative to help the seven low-income countries of the Commonwealth of Independent States, including Azerbaijan, accelerate poverty reduction and economic growth. The country did not seek IMF assistance during the global financial crisis. Indeed, between 2001 and 2008, poverty rates fell from 49% to 16%, and Azerbaijan was named 'Top Reformer' in the World Bank's 'Doing Business Report 2009'. But its vulnerability as a result of commodity dependence was revealed during the oil price crash in 2014. After the sharp fall in reserves, successive devaluations, and the loss of its investment grade rating, there were media reports in January 2016 that Azerbaijan was in talks with the IMF and World Bank over a possible US$4bn financing arrangement (its IMF quota is only SDR392mn, about US$560mn). However this did not materialise. The authorities did impose some restrictions on the movement of capital at the time, including a 20% tax on foreign currency sent for investment abroad, and sought to strengthen the banking system. Otherwise, IMF engagement has predominately been in the form of Article IV consultations, which are meant to take place on a 12-month cycle, although staff reports are not always published. The most recent Article IV consultation (the 2017 Article IV) was concluded on 21 March 2018, on a lapse of time basis, but at the time, the authorities stated they needed more time to consider the publication of the staff report and to date not even a press release has been issued.

IMF programmes

Date	*Arrangements*	*Comments*
1995 Apr.	Systemic Transformation Facility (STF)	The IMF approved a drawing of SDR29mn (US$46mn) under the STF in April 1995 to support the government's stabilisation and systemic reform programme. It was the country's first use of IMF financing.
1995–1996	Standby credit and STF	The IMF approved credits totalling SDR88mn (US$132mn) in November 1995 to support the government's 1995–1996 reform programme. SDR58.5mn (US$88mn) was made available under a one-year stand-by credit (SBA), and SDR29.3mn (US$44mn) was disbursed as Azerbaijan's second drawing under the STF.
1996–2000	ECF[a] + EFF	Combined three-year ECF (formerly ESAF) + EFF amounting to SDR94mn and SDR59mn respectively, totalling the equivalent of SDR152.1mn (cUS$219mn), approved in December 1996 to support the government's economic programme for 1996–1999. Both programmes expired in March 2000. Neither facility was fully drawn.
2001–2005	ECF[a]	Three-year arrangement for SDR67.6mn (US$100mn, 50% of quota) was approved in July 2001. In the fourth review, the arrangement was extended until July 2005.

Source: IMF. Azerbaijan joined the IMF in 1992

[a]Formerly PRGF

The World Bank currently has 16 active projects in Azerbaijan, with the largest by commitment amount focusing on infrastructural development, especially transport systems. The combined commitment amount of all projects currently totals US$1.95bn. World Bank programmes have supported financial services, the business environment, essential infrastructure and the rural economy. The Asian Development Bank currently has 19 active projects with transport, power and water supply as key recipients.

In October 2017, the European Bank for Reconstruction and Development (EBRD) approved US$500mn in financing for an oil pipeline to Europe. For political reasons regarding dependence on Russian gas exports, the decision came despite concerns over corruption in Azerbaijan. It is part of a wider project in the Southern Gas Corridor link. The EBRD has invested in a total of 162 projects in Azerbaijan with a cumulative value of US$2.4bn. As of November 2017, the portfolio amounted to US$786mn, of which 49% were formed of private sector investments.

Paris Club and Bilateral Creditors

Azerbaijan has not undergone any Paris Club restructuring agreements.

Sovereign Commercial Debt

The government has not restructured any of its commercial debt, although it was forced to issue sovereign bonds as part of the restructuring of the state-owned International Bank of Azerbaijan (IBA) in 2017 (see below).

The government issued its first eurobond in 2014, although plans for an issue had surfaced earlier in 2007 and 2010. It was a ten-year US$1.25bn bullet bond maturing in 2024. The order book was oversubscribed at almost US$4bn. At the time of the issue, Azerbaijan had an investment grade rating, with Moody's, S&P and Fitch holding Baa3, BBB– and BBB– ratings respectively. It remains the only international sovereign bond outstanding that is not part of the IBA restructuring; seven sovereign bonds in total were issued in September 2017 as part of the IBA restructuring agreement. The restructuring created a series of five small sovereign bonds, maturing in December 2017 (now matured), and then annually over September 2018–September 2021, and two longer maturities in September 2029 and September 2032. The 2032 maturity, at US$1.077bn in size, is by far the biggest of the new sovereign issues that were created and is detailed below. With the maturity of the December 2017 issue, this means there are now (at the time of writing) seven Azerbaijan bonds outstanding.

Until 2013, in the absence of a sovereign eurobond, the main internationally traded Azeri bonds were issued by Rubrika Finance Company Ltd for financing loans of the International Bank of Azerbaijan (IBA). A US$130mn loan was issued in October 2010 and matured in October 2013. In 2016, Azerbaijan considered a second issue of US$1bn to fund the construction of a natural gas link to Europe but the issue did not materialise.

Azerbaijan bond
Azerbaijan 4.75% 2024
Bloomberg ticker: AZERBJ

Borrower	Republic of Azerbaijan
Issue date	18 March 2014
Form	Eurobond
ISIN	XS1044540547
Issued amount	US$1250mn
Currency	US dollar
Denomination	US$200,000 and US$1000 thereafter
Amortisation	Bullet
Final maturity date	18 March 2024
Coupon/interest	4.75% per annum, paid semi-annually March and September
Day count	30/360
Method of transfer	Euroclear/Clearstream
Settlement period	T + 2
Governing law	English
Listing	Berlin, Dublin, Frankfurt, Stuttgart
Joint lead managers	Barclays Bank, Deutsche Bank, Citigroup

Source: Bloomberg

Azerbaijan bond
Azerbaijan 3.5% 2032
Bloomberg ticker: AZERBJ

Borrower	Republic of Azerbaijan
Issue date	1 September 2017
Form	Eurobond
ISIN	XS1678623734
Issued amount	US$1076.578mn
Currency	US dollar
Denomination	US$150,000 and US$1000 thereafter
Amortisation	Amortises in three equal instalments in September of 2030, 2031 and 2032
Final maturity date	1 September 2032
Coupon/interest	3.5% per annum, paid semi-annually March and September
Day count	30/360
Method of transfer	Clearstream
Settlement period	T + 2
Governing law	English
Listing	Not listed

Source: Bloomberg

International Bank of Azerbaijan (IBA) Restructuring

The currency devaluations in 2015 that followed the fall in oil prices over 2014–2015 took its toll on the Azeri banking system. The central bank sought to strengthen the system through consolidation (mergers) and closed six banks in January 2016 for failing to comply with minimum capital requirements. It closed another four in May 2016. In all, numerous smaller banks were closed, accounting for 6% of the total size of the banking system, according to the IMF.

In May 2017, the state-owned IBA (Ticker: IBAZAZ), Azerbaijan's largest bank, launched a debt restructuring after missing some debt payments. Lower oil prices, manat weakness and the currency mismatch created by transactions with Agrarkredit together had a significant, negative impact on the bank's performance. With the looming maturity of one of its bonds, the bank had to take action. And as it transpired, the bank had had difficulties since February 2017 rolling over trade finance facilities. The bank had three eurobonds at the time, a 6.17% 2017 subordinated bond, due to mature on 10 May 2017, amounting to US$100mn, and two senior bonds, a 5.625% 2019 (US$500mn) and a 8.25% 2024 (US$250mn). The 2024s were solely held by the Kazakh SWF Samruk-Kazyna (SK). None of the bonds had any explicit state guarantees. In July, the Bank announced that it had enough support (94% of debtholders, two thirds was required) to implement a restructuring to treat US$3.34bn of debt, including all its eurobonds. Some foreign investors however challenged the vote in a US court, protesting that the Azeri State Oil Fund (SOFAZ) had participated, which—together with the presence of the SK—meant that it was much easier for the authorities to achieve the required majority, although the initial challenge was unsuccessful.

Creditors were offered new bank or sovereign bonds. Trade finance creditors were entitled to new sovereign bonds, a 3 month bond (maturing on 1 December 2017) and a four year interest paying principal strip, repaying in equal amounts over 2018–2021, in the proportion 21% for the three-month paper and 79% into the four-year paper. Junior bondholders, holding the US$100mn 2017 subs, were subject to a 50% nominal haircut and swapped in a new sovereign 12-year (2029) bond. Senior creditors had three options: the new sovereign 12-year (2029) bond, with a 20% haircut and 5.125% coupon, or a new sovereign 15-year (2032) bond, with no haircut and 3.5% coupon. Both were sinkers with principal payments commencing three years to final maturity. The third option was a new seven-year bullet bank bond at par for par (IBAZAZ 3.5% 2024), although the longer dated bond at a lower coupon also implied NPV reduction. Over 92% of senior creditors opted for the new 15-year sovereign bond. In late-July 2017, Moody's upgraded the Bank's local and foreign credit ratings following the agreement.

In early 2018, reports emerged that a London Court had backed two creditors of IBA in their position against the bank. The ruling came many months after the issuance of new instruments in the restructuring. At the time of writing, it was not clear what implications the court ruling would have on the bank or on instruments issued as part of the restructuring. It was also not clear if creditors that previously agreed to the restructuring (and signed a deed of release) would be impacted by the court ruling. At the time of writing, IBA was appealing the court ruling. The successful restructuring has helped the government with its plan to privatise the bank by the end of 2018.

The seven new government bonds and one new corporate bond, all in US$, were issued in September 2017 and are detailed in the tables below.

IBA restructuring: new bonds created

Issuer	*Size (US$mn)*	*Coupon*	*Issue date*	*Maturity date*	*Maturity type*
Republic of Azerbaijan	184.508	0.85%	1 Sep. 2017	1 Dec. 2017	Bullet (now matured)
Republic of Azerbaijan	173.524	2.82%	1 Sep. 2017	1 Sep. 2018	Bullet (now matured)
Republic of Azerbaijan	173.524	2.82%	1 Sep. 2017	1 Sep. 2019	Bullet
Republic of Azerbaijan	173.524	2.82%	1 Sep. 2017	1 Sep. 2020	Bullet
Republic of Azerbaijan	173.524	2.82%	1 Sep. 2017	1 Sep. 2021	Bullet
Republic of Azerbaijan	310.718	5.125%	1 Sep. 2017	1 Sep. 2029	Sinkable
Republic of Azerbaijan	1076.580	3.5%	1 Sep. 2017	1 Sep. 2032	Sinkable
International Bank of Azerbaijan	1000.000	3.5%	1 Sep. 2017	1 Sep. 2024	Bullet

Source: Bloomberg

International Bank of Azerbaijan 3.5% 2024
Bloomberg ticker: IBAZAZ

Borrower	International Bank of Azerbaijan
Issue date	1 September 2017
Form	Eurobond
Ranking	Senior unsecured
ISIN	XS1678463784
Issue size	US$1000mn
Currency	US dollar
Denomination	US$150,000 and US$1000 thereafter
Amortisation	Bullet
Final maturity date	1 September 2024
Coupon/interest	3.5% paid semi-annually, March and September
Day count	30/360
Method of transfer	Euroclear/Clearstream
Settlement period	T + 2
Governing law	English

Source: Bloomberg

Corporate Bond Markets

Azerbaijani corporates currently have four outstanding US$-denominated bonds with issues over US$500mn, including the IBA bond detailed above, two of which are issued by the state oil company (SOCAR). These are listed in the table below. SOCAR's US$500mn 5.45% 2017 bullet bond was repaid in full on its due date on 9 February 2017.

Azerbaijan corporate eurobonds

Issuer	*Ticker*	*Size (US$mn)*	*Coupon*	*Maturity date*	*Series*
State Oil Co of the Azerbaijan Republic	SOIAZ	1000	4.75%	Mar. 2023	EMTN
International Bank of Azerbaijan OJSC	IBAZAZ	1000	3.5%	Sep. 2024	RegS/144A
Southern Gas Corridor CJSC	SGCAZE	2000	6.875%	Mar. 2026	RegS/144A
State Oil Co of the Azerbaijan Republic	SOIAZ	750	6.95%	Mar. 2030	n/a

Source: Bloomberg

State Oil Co of Azerbaijan 4.75% 2023
Bloomberg ticker: SOIAZ

Borrower	State Oil Co of the Azerbaijan Republic (SOCAR)
Issue date	13 March 2013
Form	Eurobond
ISIN	XS0903465127
Issue size	US$1bn
Currency	US dollar
Denomination	US$200,000 and US$1000 thereafter
Amortisation	Bullet
Final maturity date	13 March 2023
Coupon	4.75%, paid semi annually
Day count	30/360
Settlement period	T + 2

Source: Bloomberg

State Oil Co of Azerbaijan 6.95% 2030
Bloomberg ticker: SOIAZ

Borrower	State Oil Co of the Azerbaijan Republic (SOCAR)
Issue date	18 March 2015
Form	Eurobond
ISIN	XS1196496688
Issue size	US$750mn
Currency	US dollar
Denomination	US$200,000 and US$1000 thereafter
Amortisation	Bullet
Final maturity date	18 March 2030
Coupon	6.95%, paid semi annually
Day count	30/360
Settlement period	T + 2

Source: Bloomberg

Southern Gas Corridor CJSC 6.875% 2026 *Bloomberg ticker: SGCAZE*	
Borrower	Southern Gas Corridor CJSC
Issue date	24 March 2016
Form	Eurobond
ISIN	XS1319820897
Issue size	US$2bn
Currency	US dollar
Denomination	US$200,000 and US$1000 thereafter
Amortisation	Bullet
Final maturity date	24 March 2026
Coupon	6.875%, paid semi annually
Day count	30/360
Settlement period	T + 2

Source: Bloomberg

Barbados

Nominal GDP (US$mn, 2018)[a]		5172
Population (thousand, 2018)[a]		282
GDP per capita (USD, 2018)[a]		18,366
Credit ratings (long-term foreign currency)[b]	Fitch	NR
	Moody's	Caa3
	S&P	SD

[a]IMF WEO October 2018
[b]As at end-September 2018

Country Summary

- Barbados has generally seen political stability since gaining independence from Britain in 1966 with power alternating between its two main parties, the Barbados Labour Party and the Democratic Labour Party. Legislative elections in May 2018 saw a change in government as the BLP won all 30 House of Assembly seats. The previous DLP government had faced criticism of its economic management.
- The economy is focussed on tourism and financial services, making it very sensitive to international conditions. Real GDP growth became negative following the global financial crisis and has pretty much stagnated since. Despite a small rebound in economic activity in 2016, growth has slowed again. Barbados has suffered for years from a persistently high public debt burden (175% of GDP according to the

Exotix Capital, *Exotix Developing Markets Guide*,
https://doi.org/10.1007/978-3-030-05867-8_6

new government), reflecting weak growth, a high interest burden and wide budget deficits, as well as very low reserve cover. But it had avoided debt restructuring, until now.

- New Prime Minister Mia Mottley announced on 1 June 2018 the intention to seek a comprehensive restructuring of (most of its) public debt (domestic and external), while also seeking an IMF programme, just a few weeks after taking office. The government subsequently defaulted on interest payments on its three sovereign bonds, which amount to a total nominal outstanding of US$540mn (39% of central government external debt but just 6.5% of total public debt).

Economic data	*Avg*[a]	*2014*	*2015*	*2016*	*2017 (e)*	*2018 (f)*	*2019 (f)*
Real GDP growth	0.3	−0.2	2.2	2.3	−0.2	−0.5	−0.1
Inflation (annual average)	4.3	1.8	−1.1	1.5	4.4	4.2	0.8
Current account (% of GDP)	−7.8	−9.2	−6.1	−4.3	−3.8	−3.1	−3.4
Reserves (US$mn, end-period)[b]	626	527	465	342	205	–	–
Reserves/imports (months)[c]	3.9	3.4	3.2	2.4	1.5	–	–
Overall fiscal balance (% of GDP)[d]	−6.7	−7.5	−9.1	−5.3	−4.3	−1.3	2.6
Currency (ticker)	Barbados dollar (BBD)						
FX regime	Pegged to the US dollar at USD1:BBD2						
Key exports	Rum (8.6%), chemicals (7.2%), food (5.9%), construction materials (4.2%) and sugar (0.5%). Services exports (US$1.6bn) include tourism/travel (67%), and financial services. 2017 remittances around US$150mn.						

Source: IMF WEO Database, Central Bank of Barbados, OEC

[a]10-year average to 2016 unless otherwise stated
[b]Foreign exchange reserves
[c]Converted from CBB weeks' import cover
[d]IMF general government net lending

Key figures		*Party*	*Since*
Prime minister and minister of finance	Mia Mottley	BLP	May. 2018
Key opposition figure	Freundel Stuart	DLP	May. 2018
Central bank governor	Cleviston Haynes	–	Feb. 2017[a]

Note: Barbados is a member of the Commonwealth. It gained independence from Britain in 1966. Queen Elizabeth II (UK) remains monarch, represented by the governor general, Dame Sandra Mason (since January 2018)

[a]Haynes was appointed acting governor in February 2017 after Delisle Worrell was removed from the job, and was appointed governor on 1 January 2018

Politics

Executive power

Under the constitution, power is concentrated around the prime minister and cabinet, with the Senate, which replaced the Legislative Council in 1964, acting primarily as a review body. Queen Elizabeth II remains chief of state, while the prime minister is head of government. Although the governor general provides assent for legislation, for and on behalf of the monarch, who is executive, this is essentially a formality. The governor general appoints the prime minister, usually from the ruling party.

Presidential term: Five years

Legislature

Bicameral, comprising the Senate (upper house) and the House of Assembly (lower house). Senate members are directly appointed by the governor general, as detailed below, while the House of Assembly is decided by popular vote on a first-past-the-post system

Senate: 21 seats
Twelve seats under the advisement of the prime minister usually on his/her party's consensus.
Two seats on the advice of the main opposition leader usually on his/her party's consensus.
Seven seats at the governor general's discretion to represent all groups of the Barbados people.

House of Assembly: 30 seats
Directly elected.

Next due: 2023

Last legislative election[a] *(May 2018)*	*Seats*	*% of vote*
Barbados Labour Party (BLP)	30	74.6
Democratic Labour Party (DLP)	0	22.6
Others	0	2.8
Total	**30**	**100.0**

[a]Results shown for the House of Assembly

People

Barbados's population is 92% black, 2.7% white and 3.1% mixed, with the remainder comprising East Indians and others. Christianity is the dominant religion of Barbados, at over 75% of the population. The remaining 25% is mostly non-religious and members of some smaller religious groups.

The island was a seventeenth century English colony established by Captain Henry Powell and became a sugar plantation dependent on slave labour. After its first parliament in 1639, Barbados became an English Crown possession in 1663. In 1834 slavery was abolished in all British territories. During the twentieth century, politics was reshaped in Barbados and the two dominant parties of the past 70 years, the Barbados Labour Party (BLP) and Democratic Labour Party (DLP), born of leftist labour movements, emerged. Grantley Adams founded what became the BLP after the 1937 riots over economic conditions (caused by low international sugar prices), while the DLP split from the BLP in 1955 to pursue more left-leaning policies, although the two parties have since maintained similar ideologies.

Power has alternated between them since full internal self-governance was granted in 1961, with DLP leader Errol Barrow as premier, who then became the country's first prime minister after its independence from Britain in 1966 (DLP: 1961–1976, BLP: 1976–1986, DLP: 1986–1994, BLP: 1994–2008, DLP: 2008–2018, BLP: 2018–present). The BLP governed from 1994–2008, under Owen Arthur, and won 23 out of the 30 seats in the 2003 general election, but lost power to the DLP in the 2008 general election, winning just 10 seats to the DLP's 20. The DLP, led by Prime Minister Freundel Stuart, who succeeded David Thompson as party leader following his death in 2010, won a second term in the 2013 general election, albeit on a narrow majority after losing four seats, and an advantage that equated to just 4500 votes. A desire for change after the DLP's policies during the global financial crisis was one reason for its smaller majority. Economic management was a key factor in the 2018 election and, after 10 years in power, the incumbent DLP accepted defeat as opposition BLP won all 30 seats and leader Mia Mottley became Barbados's first female prime minister.

Debt

	2012	*2017*
External debt ratios (%)		
Total external debt/GDP	44.7	41.4
Public external debt/GDP	34.4	30.8
Private external debt/GDP	10.3	10.6
Total external debt/exports of goods and services	86.9	83.3
External debt service ratio	6.4	8.4
Public debt ratios (%)		
Public domestic debt[a]/GDP	94.5	121.6

(*continued*)

(continued)

	2012	*2017*
Public debt[a]/GDP	128.9	152.3
Memo: Public debt excluding NIS holdings[b]/GDP	98.9	115.9
Memo: Gross central government debt/GDP	113.6	141.4

Source: Central Bank of Barbados, IMF, Exotix

[a]Public sector debt including domestic holdings of central bank and the National Insurance Scheme (NIS)
[b]Public sector debt excluding domestic debt held by the NIS

Barbados suffers from a persistent high public debt burden, although most of this is driven by high domestic debt, as public external debt is low (c30% of GDP) and the underlying debt burden can be overstated by significant intra-government holdings of public debt (which the previous government therefore netted out). Most public sector debt is owed by central government. At the narrowest level of government, gross central government debt (domestic and external) rose from 113.6% of GDP in 2012 to 141.4% of GDP in 2017, according to central bank data, shown in the table above as a memo item (note, IMF WEO figures for GDP are used in the denominator). The increase reflected a sharp rise in 2014 and again in 2016 in domestic debt held by the central bank. With other public sector debt (domestic and external) amounting to a further 15.4% of GDP in 2012, and 10.9% in 2017, gross public debt—the widest level of government—rose from an already high 129% in 2012 to 152% of GDP in 2017. The central bank's preferred definition of gross public sector debt produced a lower figure, however, as it nets out (1) central bank holdings of domestic debt (treasury bills, ways and means, and debentures)—which amounted to 23% of GDP in 2017, up from 6% in 2012—and (2) domestic debt held by the National Insurance Scheme (NIS)—which amounted to 36% of GDP in 2017, up from 30% in 2012. On that basis, gross public debt was a relatively stable 93% of GDP over 2012–2017 (using IMF WEO figures for GDP), although it rose from 86.7% in 2012 to 95.8% in 2017 on the central bank's own figures (which uses its own GDP figures). New IMF/World Bank guidelines on public sector debt statistics do allow the netting out of the public sector's intra-agency debt in the definition of general government debt. For Barbados, the implication is that the NIS is now included in general government and so its holdings of government debt can be excluded from the wider definition of government debt. Exotix therefore shows public debt excluding NIS holdings, but including central bank holdings of domestic debt, as a memo item, and this definition amounted to debt of 116% of GDP in 2017, up from 99% in 2012 (using WEO GDP).

Latest IMF figures, contained in the press release for the 2017 Article IV board review concluded in January 2018, show that central government gross debt (excluding NIS holdings) was 97% of GDP in 2017 (with central government external debt of 26.8% of GDP and central government domestic debt of 70.4%), but it was 132.8% including NIS holdings. Note also that nominal GDP in the latest IMF statement is now BDD$10,045mn, 4% higher than the WEO and 7% higher than the central bank figure.

The rise in public debt stems from a number of factors. A deliberate implementation of counter-cyclical fiscal policy in 2009 following the global financial crisis saw increased public spending, especially on welfare and social protection programmes. But some of the rise in the debt burden also reflects additional liabilities following the transfer onto the public sector balance sheet of loss-making entities previously operated under PPPs. However, generally weak fiscal discipline has also been a factor. Wide budget deficits have persisted, averaging 7.5% of GDP a year over FY2011/12–FY2016/17, as the primary balance turned into a deficit over FY2012/13–FY2015/16. Moreover, debt dynamics are also poor. Real GDP growth has generally stagnated since the global financial crisis, averaging just 0.4% over 2010–2015, and, despite picking up to 1.8% in 2016, it eased to 1% in 2017, while the interest burden has grown, from 5.6% of GDP to 8.1%. Interest accounts for 27% of government revenues.

Barbados's public external debt was 31% of GDP in 2017, down slightly from 34% in 2012, according to Exotix calculations based on central bank data. Most public external debt is owed by the central government. A creditor breakdown from the central bank, as of December 2017, showed that public external debt amounted to US$1.48bn, of which US$1.4bn was central government debt. Of central government external debt, most (49%) was in the form of bonds. The central bank data showed bonds of US$691mn. Multilaterals were the next biggest creditor group (owed 39% of central government external debt). Bilateral creditors were only 3% of the total. With total external debt of 41.4% of GDP in 2017 (about US$2bn), down from 44.7% in 2012, according to the IMF 2017 Article IV, this implied private external debt of 10.6% of GDP in 2012 (US$0.5bn). Total external debt was c83% of current account receipts in 2017, largely unchanged from 2012. Tourism is the main source of FX earnings, and has grown as a share of total earnings over the past several years (amounting to 44% of total earnings in 2017), but overall current account receipts have generally been flat over this period as the rise in tourism earnings has been offset by the fall in earnings from other services. The external debt service ratio edged up over this period from 6.4% to 8.4%.

The new government of Mia Mottley, after announcing on 1 June 2018 its intention to pursue a restructuring of its public debt, published a detailed breakdown of gross public debt by creditor as at March 2018. This showed total public debt (including arrears) was 175.5% of GDP. The breakdown is shown in the table below.

Composition of public debt

Public debt by creditor (Mar. 2018)	*Nominal amount outstanding (US$mn)*	*Share of external (%)*	*Share of total debt (%)*	*Share of GDP (%)*
External debt (central govt)	**1373**	**100.0**	**16.6**	**29.1**
Multilateral	473	34.5	5.7	10.0
IADB	258	18.8	3.1	5.5
CDB	102	7.4	1.2	2.2
CAF	84	6.1	1.0	1.8
World Bank	29	2.1	0.4	0.6
Bilateral	108	7.9	1.3	2.3
EDC	64	4.7	0.8	1.4
China Exim	42	3.1	0.5	0.9
ING Bank	2	0.1	0.0	0.0
Commercial	792	57.7	9.6	16.8
Eurobonds	540	39.3	6.5	11.4
Other	252	18.4	3.0	5.3
Domestic debt (central govt)	**5508**	–	**66.5**	**116.8**
Total central govt debt	**6881**	–	**83.1**	**145.9**
Other public sector	577	–	7.0	12.2
Total public sector (excl. arrears)	7458	–	90.1	158.1
Arrears	820	–	9.9	17.4
Total public sector (incl. arrears)	**8278**	–	**100.0**	**175.5**

Source: Barbados Ministry of Finance, Exotix

Rescheduling History

On 1 June 2018, after just one week in office, Mottley's new government announced its intention to pursue a debt restructuring covering most of its public debt, including both domestic and external creditors, while excluding official multilateral debt and certain domestic debt and savings instruments. Barbados subsequently defaulted on two out of its three outstanding sovereign bonds as payments fell due in June and on its third bond in August. To Exotix's knowledge, this was Barbados's first ever default. Until 2018, Barbados had no modern history of rescheduling its official or commercial debt.

The new government inherited a weak economic situation and a debt problem. Indeed, the BLP's election manifesto had set out its intention to deal with the debt, recognising that the government spent over BDD$500mn a year on interest payments. However, it spoke, perhaps ambiguously, of reprofiling rather than restructuring. In its restructuring announcement, the government reported that public debt was 175% of GDP, including arrears of 17% of GDP, while reserves were just US$220mn (seven weeks of imports). Scheduled debt service in June 2018 alone was estimated to consume 25% of reserves, according to the new government. However, some market participants had also taken comfort from the debt structure, arguing that the situation looked more like a domestic debt problem than an external debt problem. Most of Barbados's outstanding public debt was owed to domestic creditors. On the basis of central bank figures, while central government debt was 150% of GDP in March, central government external debt was only 20% of total public debt and just 29% of GDP, and the bonds were just 48% of central government external debt. A Jamaica-style domestic debt exchange rather than a restructuring of the USD bonds seemed more appropriate. Barbados only had three small bonds, with annual debt service of just US$41mn (until a 2021 principal payment), and an implied interest rate of just 6.9%, suggesting that restructuring the USD bonds would not save very much. However, the new government's disclosure of other, more expensive, commercial debt, was also a factor in its decision.

The restructuring is part of the new government's Emergency Plan for the economy. In its mini-budget on 11 June 2018, the government stated its aim to reduce public debt to below 115% of GDP after five years and to below 85% over 10 years. It aims to increase the primary surplus from 4% of GDP to 6%, based on revenue and expenditure measures, and to close the overall fiscal deficit completely in FY2018/19, before moving into surplus the following year and to have surpluses in excess of 3% from year 3. The government has, however, reaffirmed its commitment to the exchange rate peg with the US dollar.

Previous governments in contrast had always refrained from taking such action on the debt. Former finance minister Christopher Sinckler had said in March 2016 that there was no justification for Barbados to undertake debt restructuring with its creditors and that Barbados had "never defaulted" on any of its external or local loans and "so it will remain". However, in April 2017, the fiscal deficit committee of the social partnership made recommendations to the prime minister on the way towards a more sustainable future, including reducing coupon rates and extending maturities on some debt. In 2011, Barbados had the third highest debt/GDP ratio in the Caribbean, behind only Jamaica and St Kitts and Nevis, both of which have since undergone debt restructurings.

Default fears have however surfaced on occasion in recent years. Barbados has had a challenging debt situation for some time, as public debt as a share of GDP doubled from 65% in 2007 to 137% in 2016 (based on IMF WEO data), firstly in response to counter cyclical policies adopted after the global financial crisis, but latterly because of high and persistent budget deficits. Despite the debt ratio easing to a projected 133% in 2017, and forecast to fall to 128% in 2018, it remained high. Debt dynamics are also unfavourable given its generally weak growth (real GDP growth has averaged 1.1% over the last 20 years). The fixed exchange rate puts more pressure on the need for a politically costly internal devaluation. Investor concerns over default surfaced in 2013, after the budget deficit reached over 10% of GDP, and again in early 2017, when Moody's downgraded its rating to Caa3 in early March, and as the central bank governor was removed in late March because of his resistance to central bank financing of the government. Yet the IMF noted in 2014 that fiscal problems go further back than that, observing that the structural budget balance started to deteriorate in the mid-2000s as spending and investment was ramped up for various capital projects, including preparations for the Cricket World Cup in 2007, just prior to the onset of the global financial crisis.

Fiscal consolidation has however proved slow. The previous DLP government's medium-term fiscal strategy (MTFS) in 2010 went off track in its first year, due to weaker global conditions and low revenue. The aim had originally been to balance the budget over the medium term and reduce public debt to 90% of GDP by 2015. A revised strategy was announced in autumn 2011. More consolidation measures were announced in August 2013, and again in December 2013, in response to renewed financing pressures. The December announcement included a reduction in the size of the civil service in 2014/15 by c3500, or 15% of the total, further downsizing of c500 positions per year until 2018/19, wage cuts for elected and appointed officials and a two-year nominal wage freeze. After a period of respite, financing pressures returned in early 2017 after the Moody's downgrade, prompting the government to announce supplementary budget measures in May 2017.

This included a solidarity tax, the national social responsibility levy (NSRL). Again, this might have brought some temporary respite, as the government undertook its second fiscal consolidation in five years, reducing the overall fiscal deficit (cash basis) from 9.4% of GDP in FY2015/16 to 4.2% of GDP in FY2017/18, and a primary balance shifting from a deficit of 2% to a surplus of 4% over the same period (ie a 6ppt improvement), according to central bank figures. This was a fairy big adjustment in two years. However, it is now clear that the headline figures (on a cash basis) were flattered because of the build-up of sizeable arrears and, thus, the underlying fiscal position inherited by the new BLP government was somewhat weaker.

Relations with Multilateral Creditors

Barbados—until now—has only ever had two IMF programmes, both of which were a long time ago (the most recent ended in 1993). Even recent financial wobbles, such as those seen in 2013 and 2017, did not lead the authorities to approach the Fund, perhaps amid concern that this would be seen as a sign of weakness. The IMF continues to provide Article IV assessments, which are on the standard annual cycle, but even these have not been regular and the staff papers are not always published. The most recent, the 2017 Article IV, was approved by the IMF Board in January 2018. However, the staff report was not published until 30 May 2018, after the election of the new government of Mia Mottley. Crucially, the staff report said that the debt was unsustainable.

In the press statement following the 2017 Article IV review in January 2018, the IMF welcomed the authorities' progress on fiscal consolidation over the previous two years, but noted that additional effort was needed. The debt and deficit remained high, while growth had slowed (reflecting in part fiscal consolidation) and reserves were low (which could put the currency peg at risk). The fiscal deficit was estimated to have declined to 5.5% of GDP in FY2016/17 reflecting stronger revenue performance, including the introduction of the NSRL and one-off factors, and was projected at 4.1% of GDP in FY2017/18. The larger-than-expected fiscal deficit had increased funding challenges, although central bank funding of the government had been reduced. Expenditure control needed to focus on the reform of state-owned enterprises, containing the wage bill (which remains the largest expenditure), pension reform and widening the tax base.

Mottley announced on 1 June 2018 the intention to seek an IMF programme to support her government's comprehensive economic reform programme and debt restructuring. A staff team subsequently concluded a visit to the country on 7 June 2018 to discuss economic policies and possible IMF financial support. In a statement, staff said that Barbados was in a precarious economic situation, with low international reserves (just US$220mn) and an unsustainable central government debt. It noted that substantial fiscal consolidation was needed to put debt on a clear downward trajectory in conjunction with the proposed debt restructuring. Another staff visit took place in the first half of July, with the accompanying press release on 13 July 2018 stating that significant progress had been made on an economic plan that could underpin financial support from the IMF. There was no date for when discussions would conclude or when a programme would go to the Executive Board.

At the time of writing, the IMF announced on 7 September 2018 that a staff-level agreement had been reached on a two-year extended fund facility (EFF) amounting to SDR208mn (US$290mn, 220% of quota). SDR35mn (US$49mn) would be available immediately, if approved. The announcement came at the end of another staff visit in late August/early September. The IMF Executive Board was set to consider the proposed arrangement in early October.

IMF programmes

Date	*Arrangements*	*Comments*
1982–1984	SBA	Agreed in October 1982 at 125% of quota.
1992–1993	SBA	Agreed in February 1992 at 70% of quota.

Source: IMF. Barbados joined the IMF in 1970

Mottley met IADB President Luis Alberto Moreno in June 2018, shortly after the announcement of a debt restructuring, suggesting a positive engagement between the two. The IADB is Barbados's single largest multilateral creditor, accounting for over half (55%) of multilateral debt and 19% of public external debt. It is followed by the CDB (22% of multilateral debt and 7% of public external debt), CAF (18% and 6%) and World Bank (6% and 2%), The IADB has a number of ongoing projects in Barbados with the goal of achieving sustainable growth that is less adversely affected by external shocks and commodity price changes.

Tourism, transport, energy and climate resilience remain high priorities. The World Bank has had 14 projects in Barbados, but these have now all ended, with the last project approval in 2008.

Paris Club and Bilateral Creditors

Barbados has never had a Paris Club agreement. There have been no modern debt restructurings with bilateral creditors prior to 2018, but bilateral creditors have not been excluded in the new government's debt restructuring. However, bilateral debt is a small part of Barbados's central government external debt, at just 8%, and represents just 2% of GDP. Current bilaterals include China, Canada, the UK and other European countries. Trinidad and Tobago was a bilateral creditor until 2012.

Sovereign Commercial Debt

Until 2018, Barbados had no modern history of default or rescheduling its sovereign commercial debt. But it is now in default on its three sovereign bonds, and other commercial loans, following Mottley's announcement on 1 June 2018 that the government intended to seek a comprehensive restructuring of its public debt, including its foreign commercial debt.

Barbados has three USD bonds outstanding with a total nominal amount of US$540mn (39% of central government external debt but just 6.5% of total public debt)—all of which are now in default. These bonds are the US$150mn 7.25% 2021 issued in 2001, the US$200mn 7% 2022 issued in 2010, and the US$190mn 6.625% 30-year bond (2035 maturity) issued in 2005. Debt service on the bonds is only US$41mn a year (interest only, until 2021). Barbados issued its first international government bonds in 1994, with US$20mn 10.5% issued in June and US$30mn 11.625% issued December, maturing in 1997 and 1999, respectively. Subsequent issues saw issued amounts and maturities increase, and annual coupon rates fall. These were followed by another issue in 2000 (matured 2010). A description of each of its outstanding bonds is given below.

In March 2017, Moody's downgraded Barbados to Caa3 from Caa1 based on a continued increase in government debt with sufficient fiscal reform deemed unlikely, leading to rising debt, both domestic and external, and unsustainable future debt servicing requirements, with a larger risk to short-term debt service, following an increase in the short-term debt stock. Moody's reported that short term issuance had been relied upon as commercial banks reduced their exposure to sovereign debt. Moody's rating was investment grade over 2000–2009, and was downgraded to sub-investment grade (Ba1) in December 2012. The rating had descended to B3 by June 2014 and was cut again to Caa1 in April 2016. S&P, also in March 2017, downgraded Barbados to CCC+ from B– citing its limited financing alternatives and low international reserves. S&P issued a negative outlook for the island, while warning that the sustainability of the Barbados dollar had become an additional challenge, as the government continued to rely on the central bank for deficit financing. S&P's rating was also investment grade over 2004–2010, downgraded to sub-investment grade (BB+) in July 2012.

The new Mottley government announced on 1 June 2018, soon after she took office, its intention to pursue a debt restructuring covering most of its public debt, and with that, the immediate suspension of payments on Barbados external commercial debt. The restructuring is intended to include domestic and external debt, including the three international bonds. Only official multilateral debt and certain domestic debt and savings instruments will be excluded. The government noted that it intended to pay interest on domestic debt while forcibly rolling over principal payments until a restructuring agreement is reached. Since the moratorium, it missed the interest payment on 5 June on the 6.625% 2035, on 15 June on the 7.25% 2021, and on 4 August on the 7% 2022. Payments were not made before the end of their 15-day grace periods. All three bonds are governed by English law and have collective action-type terms and the fact that they are small and concentrated may help to facilitate negotiations. A creditor committee, advised by Newstate Partners, has been formed. The government appointed White Oak Advisory Ltd as financial adviser and Cleary Gottlieb Steen & Hamilton LLP as external legal adviser.

The restructuring announcement came as a surprise, more due to the timing, than any shock about the weakened ability to pay (high debt burden and low reserves). Indeed, the BLP's election manifesto had set out its intention to deal with the debt. However, while public debt is high, bonded debt was only 7% of total public debt, suggesting that what Barbados needed was a Jamaica-style domestic debt restructuring as restructuring the bonds would not lead to significant cash flow savings. However, besides the eurobonds, there is also other (more expensive) commercial debt outstanding, which was not fully known before the government disclosed it after the restructuring announcement, meaning that while commercial debt was only 10% of public debt, it accounted for c70% of overall debt service over the next five years. In particular, scheduled debt service amounting to 25% of reserves in June 2018 alone was a key factor behind the decision to suspend payments (debt service of US$50mn compared with reserves of US$220mn). June's debt service included US$12mn in interest payments on two of its three eurobonds (namely, US$6.3mn on the 2035s due on 5 June and US$5.4mn on the 2021s due on 15 June) and US$30mn–40mn due on a Credit Suisse loan the same month. The Credit Suisse loan (originally for US$150mn in 2013, increased to US$225mn in 2014), amortised over 2015–2018 but was extended by one year in 2016 (to 2019). At end-2017, outstanding principal on the Credit Suisse loan was US$92.125mn. The interest rate on the loan had also rocketed to, from 7.34% in 2013 to 11.735% at end-2017 (and now 12.5%, according to government figures). In addition to the onerous debt service, large arrears had also accumulated under the previous government, and were also a factor in the decision to restructure. The existence of the arrears was known, but their magnitude was not, with the new government reporting them at 17% of GDP in its mini budget on 11 June 2018. Finally, restructuring may have been a prior action for any IMF programme given the Fund's lending rules and its finding in the 2017 Article IV that debt was unsustainable.

At the time of writing, the government launched its domestic debt exchange.

Barbados bond—in default
Barbados 7.25% 2021
Bloomberg ticker: BARBAD

Borrower	Government of Barbados
Issue date	10 December 2001
Form	Eurobond
ISIN	USP48864AC94
Issued amount	US$150mn
Currency	US dollar
Denomination	US$1000 and US$1000 thereafter
Amortisation	Bullet
Maturity date	15 December 2021
Coupon/interest	7.25% per annum, paid semi-annually June and December
Day count	30/360
Method of transfer	Euroclear/Clearstream
Settlement period	T + 2
Governing law	English
Exchange	Dusseldorf, Luxembourg, Stuttgart
Lead manager	Bear Stearns

Source: Bloomberg

Barbados bond—in default
Barbados 7% 2022
Bloomberg ticker: BARBAD

Borrower	Government of Barbados
Issue date	4 August 2010
Form	Eurobond
ISIN	USP48864AD77
Issued amount	US$200mn
Currency	US dollar
Denomination	US$100,000 and US$1000 thereafter
Amortisation	Bullet
Maturity date	4 August 2022
Coupon/interest	7% per annum, paid semi-annually February and August
Day count	30/360
Method of transfer	Euroclear/Clearstream, FED FUNDS, DTC
Settlement period	T + 2
Governing law	English
Exchange	Berlin, Frankfurt, Luxembourg, Stuttgart
Lead managers	Deutsche Bank

Source: Bloomberg

Barbados bond—in default
Barbados 6.625% 2035
Bloomberg ticker: BARBAD

Borrower	Government of Barbados
Issue date	5 December 2005
Form	Eurobond
ISIN	USP48864AF26
Issued amount	US$190mn
Currency	US dollar
Denomination	US$100,000 and US$1000 thereafter
Amortisation	Bullet
Maturity date	5 December 2035
Coupon/interest	6.625% per annum, paid semi-annually June and December
Day count	30/360
Method of transfer	Euroclear/Clearstream, FED FUNDS
Settlement period	T + 2
Governing law	English
Exchange	Euro MFT, Luxembourg, Frankfurt
Joint lead managers	Deutsche Bank

Source: Bloomberg

Corporate Bond Markets

The Barbados international corporate bond market is very limited. Its first corporate bond was issued in March 2003 by the University of the West Indies, with maturity March 2015, coupon of 7.75% and issue size US$10.5mn. There have been mainly small issues since, of which 11 USD-denominated issues are still outstanding. The amount of USD bonds outstanding in Jan. 2018 was US$1.1bn, according to Bloomberg. Most issues are small, but two are worth mentioning: a US$600mn 6.35% 2036 bullet bond was issued by Barrick International Barbados Corp (ABXCN) in October 2006, and a US$320mn 8.875% 2022 bond issued by Sagicor in August 2015. Sagicor had previously issued a US$150mn 7.5% 10-year bond in May 2006 that matured in May 2016. Details of the Barrick and Sagicor bonds follow.

Barrick International bond
Barrick International Corp 2036
Bloomberg ticker: ABXCN

Borrower	Barrick International Barbados Corp
Issue date	12 October 2006
Form	Eurobond
ISIN	USP1619PAB42
Issue size	US$600mn
Amount outstanding	US$600mn
Currency	US dollar
Denomination	US$100,000 minimum, increments of US$1000 thereafter
Amortisation	Bullet
Final maturity date	15 October 2036
Coupon/interest	6.35% per annum, paid semi-annually
Day count	30/360
Method of transfer	Euroclear, Clearstream, DTC
Settlement period	T + 2 business days
Joint lead managers	Morgan Stanley, UBS Securities, Deutsche Bank, Merrill Lynch, Scotia Capital, JP Morgan, Goldman Sachs, HSBC, Bank of Montreal

Source: Bloomberg

Sagicor bond
Sagicor Finance Corp 2022
Bloomberg ticker: SFCBA

Borrower	Sagicor Finance 2015 Ltd	
Issue date	11 August 2015	
Form	Eurobond	
ISIN	USG7776BAA38	
Issue size	US$320mn	
Amount outstanding	US$320mn	
Currency	US dollar	
Denomination	US$200,000 minimum, increments of US$1000 thereafter	
Amortisation	Callable (callable on and any time after dates shown in the schedule below)	
Call schedule	11/8/2019	104.438
	11/8/2020	102.219
	11/8/2021	100.000
Final maturity date	11 August 2022	
Coupon/interest	8.875% per annum, paid semi-annually	
Day count	30/360	
Method of transfer	Euroclear, Clearstream	
Exchange	Berlin	
Settlement period	T + 2 business days	
Joint lead managers	JP Morgan, Scotiabank	

Source: Bloomberg

Belarus

Nominal GDP (US$mn, 2018)[a]		56,934
Population (thousand, 2018)[a]		9457
GDP per capita (USD, 2018)[a]		6020
Credit ratings (long-term foreign currency)[b]	Fitch	B
	Moody's	B3
	S&P	B

[a]IMF WEO October 2018
[b]As at end-September 2018

Country Summary

- Since being elected in 1994, President Alexander Lukashenko has increasingly concentrated political power in his own hands. Belarus has poor country rankings for governance and corruption, with the US and EU having long-standing sanctions relating to human rights abuses and disappearances of opposition leaders, and arms embargos imposed on the country.
- The economy has recovered from a period of protracted stagnation, after it fell into deep recession over 2015–2016 owing to domestic structural weaknesses and weaker growth in Russia, its main trading partner. The Belarusian ruble has lost over 40% of its value against USD since 2014, in part reflecting a shift to a more flexible exchange rate regime in 2015, triggered by the Russian ruble's devaluation.

Exotix Capital, *Exotix Developing Markets Guide*,
https://doi.org/10.1007/978-3-030-05867-8_7

Growth recovered in 2017 and is projected at close to 3% in 2018. Financial conditions are weak, however, with banking profitability low, amid rising NPLs and currency mismatches.

- The public debt burden has risen sharply due to increased borrowing and currency devaluation, increasing to 55% of GDP in 2017 on IMF figures. After its debut issues in 2010 and 2011 (both since repaid at maturity), Belarus placed two tranches of eurobonds totalling US$1.4bn in June 2017 and returned to the market in February 2018 with another issue. However, Russia is by far the single biggest public sector external creditor (accounting for 70% of bilateral debt and 41% of public external debt). A key macro vulnerability stems from its high gross financing needs, driven by private sector external indebtedness.

Economic data	*Avg*[a]	*2014*	*2015*	*2016*	*2017 (e)*	*2018 (f)*	*2019 (f)*
Real GDP growth	3.7	1.7	−3.8	−2.5	2.4	4.0	3.1
Inflation (annual average)	20.5	18.1	13.5	11.8	6.0	5.5	5.5
Current account (% of GDP)	−7.2	−6.6	−3.3	−3.5	−1.7	−2.5	−4.2
Reserves (US$mn, end-period)[b]	5207	5059	4176	4927	7315	6831[c]	–
Reserves/imports (months)[d]	1.5	1.3	1.4	1.8	2.2	–	–
Overall fiscal balance (% of GDP)[e]	−4.2	0.1	−3.0	−1.7	−0.3	−2.4	−4.3
Currency (ticker)	Belarusian ruble (BYN)						
FX regime	De jure managed float with crawling band. Moved in 2015 from a de jure crawling peg against USD that had been maintained over the preceding 20 years, which was accompanied by a sharp (20%) initial devaluation.						
Key exports	Fuels (29%), chemicals (16%), animal products (10%), metals (6.5%), machinery and electronics (6.3%). Services exports came to US$7.8bn and remittances were US$2.3bn in 2017, compared with goods of US$29bn.						

Source: IMF WEO Database, IMF 2017 country report

[a]10y average to 2016 unless otherwise stated

[b]Total international reserves

[c]Latest figure, June 2018

[d]Months of imports of the current year's imports of goods services and primary income debits

[e]Overall government net lending

Key figures		*Party*	*Since*
President	Alexandr Lukashenko	Independent	1994
Prime minister	Andrei Kobyakov	Independent	Dec. 2014
Minister of finance	Vladimir Amarin	Independent	Nov. 2016
Key opposition figure	Tatsiana Karatkevich	Social Democratic	2015
Central bank chairman	Pavel Kallaur	–	Dec. 2014

Politics

Executive power

The president is head of government and responsible for the appointment of the prime minister, deputy prime ministers and cabinet. Although the executive model is constitutionally based on the Republican model, the power of the president in Belarus is central within the government structure. Often referred to as Europe's last dictator, president Lukashenko, who has won every presidential election since the country's independence in 1991, has been heavily criticised for suppressing democracy and free speech, violating human rights, and denying the opposition access to state media. The president is elected by absolute majority vote through a two-round system to serve a 5-year term; half of all registered voters must turn out for the result to be valid.

Presidential term: Five years **Parliamentary term:** Four years

Legislature

The Natsionalnoye Sobraniye (National Assembly) is bicameral and consists of: (1) the *Soviet Respubliki* (Council of the Republic) composed of 64 seats, of which 56 are elected by regional governing councils and eight are appointed by the president directly; and (2) the Palata Predstaviteley (House of Representatives) with 110 members elected by popular vote in a first-past-the-post electoral system.

Elections

Next due *Legislative: September 2020* *Presidential: October 2020*

Last legislative election[a] *(September 2016)*	*Seats*	*Last presidential (October 2015)*	*% of vote*
Communist Party of Belarus	8	Alexander Lukashenko (Independent)	83.5
Republican Party of Labor and Justice	3	Tatsiana Karatkevich (People's Referendum)	4.4

(*continued*)

(continued)

Elections			
Next due *Legislative: September 2020*		*Presidential: October 2020*	
Last legislative election[a] *(September 2016)*	*Seats*	*Last presidential (October 2015)*	*% of vote*
The Belarusian Patriotic Party (BPP)	3	Sergei Gaidukevich (LDP)	3.3
The Liberal Democratic Party (LDP)	1	Nikolai Ulakhovich (BPP)	1.7
United Civic Party	1	Did not support any of the candidates	6.3
Independents	94	Invalid	0.8
Total	**110**	**Total**	**100.0**

[a]House of Representatives

People

Belarus gained independence from Russia in 1991. Its population is primarily composed of Eastern Orthodox Belarusians at just over 80%. Russians make up a further 8.3% with Polish and Ukrainians constituting the majority of the remaining share. The official languages are Belarusian and Russian with the greater proportion (70%) speaking Russian. The country is officially secular and net migration is low (0.7 per 1000).

Debt

	2012	*2017*
External debt ratios (%)		
Total external debt/GDP[a]	51.4	73.3
Public external debt/GDP	19.8	33.7
Private external debt[a]/GDP	31.6	39.6
Total external debt/exports of goods and services	65.1	109.5
External debt service ratio (public)	2.8	4.7
Public debt ratios (%)		
Public domestic debt/GDP	8.8	11.8
Public debt (incl. guarantees)[b]/GDP	29.6	46.5

Source: Eurobond prospectus (2018), Haver, National Bank of Belarus, Ministry of Finance, IMF, Exotix calculations

[a]Including intercompany lending
[b]PED and PDD do not sum to public debt due to the use of different sources

Belarus began incurring external public debt in 1992 after its independence and has never defaulted since. Owing to tightly managed public finances, public and external debt remained relatively modest up until the global financial crisis of 2007–2008. But the recessionary environment and rapidly depreciating currency that followed—BYN lost more than 40% of its value against USD in 2014–2016—put debt on an upward trajectory.

Belarus's total external debt was US$40bn at end-2017, based on official figures on a BPM6 basis from Haver. This comprised cUS$18bn in public debt (46% of the total)—general government plus central bank—and US$22bn in private debt (54% of the total)—including intercompany lending. The total has increased from US$34bn in 2012, with most of the rise coming from general government debt, due largely to an increase in long-term securities, as private debt was largely unchanged. As a share of GDP, total external debt increased to 73% from 51% over this period (nominal GDP in USD terms has fallen by 17% due to currency depreciation). Total external debt as a share of exports of goods and services has nearly doubled from 65% to 110%, with exports of goods (which accounts for 80% of G&S) having fallen by nearly 40% since 2012. Meanwhile, the public external debt service ratio has increased to 4.7%, although this understates liquidity risk as it omits private sector external debt service (no figures available). Private external debt service would be expected to be much larger because it is a bigger share of external debt and likely to be on less favourable terms than government borrowing. As an alternative measure of liquidity risk, IMF figures show a persistently high gross external financing requirement. This was estimated at US$17.4bn in 2017 (32.7% of GDP) and is projected to average 27% of GDP over 2018–2022.

For the creditor composition of public external debt, Exotix has adapted this from the 2018 bond prospectus as a creditor breakdown is not available under BPM6 (however, the two sources give slightly different totals). The bond prospectus showed public and publicly guaranteed (PPG) external debt of US$18.9bn at end-2017 (compared with US$18.4bn on a BPM6 basis), comprising US$16.7bn in direct debt and US$2.1bn in publicly guaranteed debt. As of end-2017, Belarus had US$2.2bn of eurobonds outstanding, having placed two new issuances totalling US$1.4bn in June 2017, along with the existing US$800mn 8.95% bond maturing in January 2018. Exotix has included the US$600mn bond issued in February 2018, and taken out the January maturity, to give a more representative breakdown of public external debt. On that basis, public external debt is estimated at US$16.5bn and PPG external debt is US$18.7bn. Eurobonds accounted for 10.7% of the PPG external debt and 5% of total external debt. Bilaterals are, however, the main public sector creditor group. Nearly 60% of PPG external debt, and 27% of total external debt is owed to bilateral creditors, primarily Russia. Loans extended by the Russian government and Russian banks account for 70% of bilateral debt and 41% of the public sector's external debt portfolio (and 19% of total external debt); indeed, Russia is Belarus's single biggest creditor by far. Nearly all the remaining 30% of bilateral debt is owed to China. 54% of the external debt portfolio is issued by the private sector (as per BPM6), although the IMF estimates that around one-third of that is publicly guaranteed or in private corporations in which the share of state ownership is 50% of more.

Public debt has been on a rising trend since 2012 despite running headline fiscal surpluses. Total public debt (including guarantees) increased from 30% of GDP in 2012 to 47% of GDP in 2017, based on figures from the 2018 eurobond prospectus. Most public debt is public external debt, although public domestic debt has also been rising as a share of GDP. Public domestic debt was 8.8% of GDP in 2012, rising to 11.8% of GDP in 2017. Guarantees amounted to 7.2% of GDP in 2017. IMF data, however, show public debt (gross public and publicly guaranteed debt) is even higher, as it includes a higher figure for guarantees (11.2% of GDP in 2017) and a wider level of government (other domestic debt and local government). On this basis, the IMF estimated public debt was 55.3% of GDP in 2017, compared with 36.9% of GDP in 2012. The higher debt burden has been driven by the sharp currency depreciation and quasi-fiscal operations, including bank recapitalisations and called guarantees. The IMF projects public debt to peak at 59% in 2020 as quasi-fiscal liabilities are realised, with gross financing needs remaining high at 15% of GDP (and forecast to peak at over 16.5% in 2019). In January 2017, Belarus approved a pension reform which will see a gradual increase in retirement ages. The IMF expects these measures to maintain fiscal balance of the pension system by 2022.

Composition of external debt

External debt by creditor (Feb. 2018 estimate)	*Nominal amount outstanding (US$mn)*	*Share of total (%)*
Public and publicly guaranteed (PPG) external debt	18,664	46.4
o/w Public sector external debt	16,527	41.1
Official multilateral	3725	9.3
IBRD	822	2.0

(*continued*)

(continued)

External debt by creditor (Feb. 2018 estimate)	*Nominal amount outstanding (US$mn)*	*Share of total (%)*
EBRD	67	0.2
EFSD[a]	2836	7.1
Official bilateral	10,802	26.9
Russia	7602	18.9
USA	23	0.1
China	3177	7.9
Eurobonds	2000	5.0
Private sector external debt[b]	21,557	53.6
Total external debt	**40,221**	**100.0**

Source: Eurobond prospectus (2018), Haver, Exotix calculations. PPG data is for end-2017 to which we have added the US$600mn eurobond issued in February 2018 and removed the US$800mn maturity in January 2018

[a]EFSD = Eurasian Fund for Stabilisation and Development
[b]Private sector external debt for end-2017, including intercompany lending (BPM6 basis)

Rescheduling History

Belarus has never rescheduled public debt.

Relations with Multilateral Creditors

Belarus has had two IMF programmes since becoming a member in 1992 (see table below). In January 2009, the IMF agreed its most recent programme, a US$2.5bn 15-month SBA. At 419% of quota, the SBA entailed exceptional access. The programme was increased to US$3.4bn in June 2009. The programme came after Belarus was hit hard by the global financial crisis, which led to adverse terms of trade and slowing export demand, while a contraction in accessing trade and other external finance led to a decline in its official reserves. The economy, which had been growing strongly for the preceding several years, was also showing signs of overheating. The main challenge for the programme was to stabilise current account vulnerabilities; hence, the build-up in external debt. The last of five tranches was disbursed in March 2010 on the conclusion of the fourth review. There was some discussion about a possible successor programme in June 2011 following a regular staff visit to the country, although this did not lead to anything. Belarus was however subjected to post-programme monitoring after the conclusion of the SBA, with the first review being conducted by the IMF Board in August 2011. The fifth and final post-programme monitoring discussion concluded in December 2013.

The World Bank has funded various projects since 1992. Since 2013, its active portfolio in Belarus has almost doubled from US$457mn to US$973mn (as of April 2017), split across a total of nine IBRD loans, most of them in transport infrastructure. The EBRD has been operating in Belarus since 1994 and currently has 59 active projects totalling nearly EUR500mn, almost all of which are in the industry, commerce and agriculture businesses. In May 2017, the EIB and Belarus signed its first agreement on cooperation. The EIB plans to invest up to EUR200mn in Belarusian projects by late 2017.

IMF programmes

Date	*Arrangements*	*Comments*
1995–1996	SBA	12-month SBA worth SDR196.2mn (US$293mn) with the aim of stabilising inflation, achieving a sustainable balance of payments and establish a sustainable market economy. Only SDR50mn was drawn.
2009–2010	SBA	In January 2009, a 15-month programme of SDR1.62bn (US$2.46bn, 419% of quota) was approved, which was augmented in June 2009 to SDR2.27bn (US$3.44bn). Nearly US$800mn was available immediately. In the third review, performance criteria on international reserves and net domestic assets were modified for December 2009 as well as remaining structural benchmarks. Expired March 2010. The programme was fully drawn and fully repaid in March 2015.

Source: IMF

Paris Club History and Bilateral Creditors

Belarus has not entered into any agreements with the Paris Club.

Russia is Belarus's main trading partner and bilateral creditor. According to the 2018 eurobond prospectus, in November 2008, Russia provided a 15-year loan facility of USD1 billion to Belarus which was extended in March 2009 by a further USD500 million. Belarus received two loans under the facility to the tune of USD2 billion from the Russian

Government in 2014 and two loans amounting to USD870 million in 2015. In September 2017 the Russian Government granted a loan of USD700 million to Belarus for refinancing its external public debt in the amount of USD700 million. The construction of the Belarusian nuclear power plant (NPP) has also been financed by loans received from Russia, through a USD10 billion credit line from the Russian Government (with USD2.7 billion utilised as at end-2017) and a USD500 million credit line from Vnesheconombank (USD290 million utilised as at end-2017).

Sovereign Commercial Debt

Belarus has no history of restructuring its commercial debt. Its first bond issue came in 2010.

Belarus now has three sovereign eurobonds outstanding (maturing in 2023, 2027 and 2030), totalling US$2bn, all having been issued since June 2017, and it has successfully repaid at maturity its two previous issues. Belarus issued its first eurobond in 2010. The five-year bond had a coupon of 8.75% and was priced at 99.011 (with a spread at issue of 727bps). The US$600mn issue was subsequently topped up to US$1bn. It was repaid in full and on time at maturity on 3 August 2015. In 2011, Belarus issued its second eurobond, a US$800mn seven-year issue with a coupon of 8.95% issued at par (the spread at issue was 627bps). The bond was also repaid in full and on time at maturity on 26 January 2018. In preparation for the maturing 2018 eurobond, Belarus placed two tranches of eurobonds totalling US$1.4bn in June 2017. The first, for US$800mn, matures in 2023 and has a coupon of 6.875% (it was issued at 98.864); and the second, for US$600mn, matures in 2027 and has a coupon of 7.625% (issued at par). The bonds were nearly twice oversubscribed with over 110 international investors, the majority being from the US, the UK and Germany. In February 2018, Belarus returned to the market with another US$600mn issue, a 12-year bond (2030 maturity) with a 6.2% coupon (also issued at par). Details of this bond are shown below.

Belarus Bond
Republic of Belarus 6.2% 2030
Bloomberg ticker: BELRUS

Borrower	Republic of Belarus
Issue date	28 February 2018
Form	Eurobond
ISIN	XS1760804184
Issue size	US$600mn
Currency	US dollar
Denomination	Minimum of US$200,000 and US$1000 thereafter
Amortisation	Bullet
Final maturity date	28 February 2030
Coupon/interest	6.2% paid semi-annually, February and August
Day count	30/360
Method of transfer	Euroclear/Clearstream
Settlement period	T + 3 business days
Governing law	English
Joint lead managers	Citigroup, Raiffeisen Bank International

Source: Bloomberg

Corporate Bonds

The Belarusian international corporate bond market is limited. Companies first started issuing bonds in 2006–2007, with Belagroprombank OAO (BELGRO) issuing the first EUR-denominated bond issued in December 2006 and the first USD bonds in 2008, although these were all very small issues (EUR70mn and US$3mn, respectively). Belagroprombank issued the first sizeable USD instrument, US$100mn with a 9.5% coupon (issued at par) in an LPN structure, in November 2010, which was repaid on maturity in November 2013. Other small issuers have included BTA Bank of Belarus (BTABY) and Belgazprom Bank (BELGAZ), but they no longer have any instruments outstanding. To date, 178 corporate bonds have been issued, mostly in local currency, of which 51 have been USD-denominated. 11 are still active, of which six are USD-denominated, three are EUR-denominated and two are BYN-denominated. With the exception of the Eurotorg bond below, all of these issues are quite small.

Eurotorg, a retail store owner and operator, issued Belarus's biggest international issue in October 2017. Issued in an LPN structure through a special purpose entity, Eurotorg LLC Via Bonitron DAC (EUROTG), the five-year

US$350mn issue had an 8.75% coupon (issued at par) and amortises over its last four payments until it matures in October 2022. The Group is the largest food retailer in Belarus, with a market share of 19% and 460 stores in Belarus as at end-June 2017. The Group has a diversified selection of store types, from local convenience stores to large supermarkets and focusses on high turnover, highly demanded products. The details of the issue are shown below.

Eurotorg LLC Via Bonitron DAC Bond
Eurotorg 8.75% 2022
Bloomberg ticker: EUROTG

Borrower	Eurotorg LLC Via Bonitron DAC	
Issue date	30 October 2017	
Form	Loan participation note	
ISIN	XS1577952010	
Issue size	US$350mn	
Amount outstanding	US$350mn	
Currency	US dollar	
Denomination	Minimum of US$200,000 and US$1000 thereafter	
Amortisation	Sinkable:	
	30 April 2021	US$50mn
	30 October 2021	US$50mn
	30 April 2022	US$125mn
	30 October 2022	US$125mn
Final maturity date	30 October 2022	
Coupon/interest	8.75% paid semi-annually April and October	
Day count	30/360	
Method of transfer	Euroclear/Clearstream	
Settlement period	T + 2 business days	
Governing law	English	
Joint lead managers	JP Morgan, Renaissance Capital Holdings, Sberbank CIB	
Exchange	Dublin	

Source: Bloomberg

Belize

Nominal GDP (US$mn, 2018)[a]		1912
Population (thousand, 2018)[a]		396
GDP per capita (USD, 2018)[a]		4830
Credit ratings (long-term foreign currency)[b]	Fitch	NR
	Moody's	B3
	S&P	B−

[a]IMF WEO October 2018
[b]As at end-September 2018

Country Summary

- Generally stable political conditions since self-government began over 50 years ago. Power has alternated between the two dominant political parties although, ideologically, there is little difference between them. Rising crime is now an issue, with the country having one of the world's highest murder rates.
- Belize is a small, open economy in Central America, but is widely considered a part of the Caribbean. Tourism is the top foreign exchange earner, but shrimp farming and agriculture (bananas, sugar and citrus), and garment re-exports are also important. Oil was discovered in 2005, although oil revenues remain low. Belize has benefited from FDI inflows, although reduced aid from Venezuela, vulnerability to external (climatic) shocks—which adversely affect

Exotix Capital, *Exotix Developing Markets Guide*,
https://doi.org/10.1007/978-3-030-05867-8_8

agriculture—and rising unemployment pose additional risks to the economy. The macroeconomic outlook remains weak, according to the IMF.

- A high public debt burden (100% of GDP) and historically low reserve coverage in the context of a fixed exchange rate regime pose ongoing challenges to policymakers, and the country has seen three bond restructurings over the past decade; the two most recent essentially being strategic bond defaults by Prime Minister Barrow. The most recent exchange provided significant cash flow relief, and a 20% NPV loss for bondholders, but was supported by a commitment to fiscal consolidation. However, further structural reforms are needed to boost growth and put the economy on a sounder footing.

Economic data	*Avg*[a]	*2014*	*2015*	*2016*	*2017 (e)*	*2018 (f)*	*2019 (f)*
Real GDP growth	2.4	4.0	3.8	−0.5	0.8	1.8	2.0
Inflation (annual average)	1.6	1.2	−0.9	0.7	1.1	1.3	1.9
Current account (% of GDP)	−5.1	−7.8	−9.8	−9.0	−7.7	−6.0	−5.8
Reserves (US$mn, end-period)[b]	286	487	437	376	312	305[c]	–
Reserves/imports (months)[d]	–	4.5	4.1	3.7	3.0	–	–
Overall fiscal balance (% of GDP)[e]	−2.1	−2.4	−7.4	−3.8	−4.1	−1.5	−1.6
Currency (ticker)	Belize dollar (BZD)						
FX regime	Peg to the US dollar (BZD2:USD1) since 1976.						
Key exports	Sugar (21%), fruit juice (18%), marine products (8.2%), oil (7.2%). Tourism is also a significant foreign exchange earner. Goods exports were US$440mn in 2016, while services were US$525mn (of which, tourism earnings were US$390mn).						

Source: IMF WEO Database, IMF country reports, Central Bank of Belize, OEC

[a]10-year average to 2016 unless otherwise stated

[b]Gross official international reserves, from CBB

[c]Latest figure, May 2018

[d]Months of imports of goods, services and income debits (Exotix calculation)

[e]IMF general government net lending

Key figures		*Party*	*Since*
Prime minister (and minister of finance)	Dean Barrow	UDP	Feb. 2008
Deputy prime minister	Patrick Faber	UDP	Jun. 2016
Key opposition figure	Johnny Briceno	PUP	Feb. 2016[a]
Central bank governor	Audrey Joy Grant	–	Oct. 2016

Note: Belize is a member of the Commonwealth. Queen Elizabeth II (UK) remains Monarch, represented by Governor General Sir Coleville Young

[a]Briceno replaced Francis Fonseca who was leader of the PUP in the 2015 general election. Briceno had previously been leader of the PUP during 2008–2011, after Said Musa resigned following the PUP's defeat in the 2008 election

Politics

Executive power

Concentrated around the prime minister and cabinet. Queen Elizabeth II remains chief of state, while the prime minister is head of government.

Parliamentary term: Five years

Legislature

Bicameral legislature, the National Assembly, consisting of the Senate (upper house) and House of Representatives (lower house). Both houses are elected by popular vote (prior to February 2008, the Senate comprised political and institutional appointments). General elections take place every five years, although the prime minister is chosen by the governor general on behalf of the Queen, usually from the winning party. The cabinet is subsequently recommended to the governor by the prime minister. The Senate, which acts primarily as a review and approval body, must stand down at each election to be reinitiated after the next government is formed.

Senate: 12 seats **House of Representatives:** 31 seats

Elections

Next legislative: 2021[a]

Last general election (November 2015)	*Seats*[b]	*% of valid vote*
United Democratic Party (UDP)	19	50.5
Peoples United Party (PUP)	12	47.8
Other	0	1.7
Total (directly elected)	**31**	**100.0**

(*continued*)

(continued)

[a]The last Belize election was held on 4 November 2015. Under the constitution, parliament must be dissolved within five years from when the two Houses first met. This means that the next election must be held on or before 13 February 2021, although recent elections have been called early, and both the UDP and PUP have considered changing the constitution to four-year terms
[b]House of Representatives

People

Migration continues to transform the demography as immigration of Central Americans and emigration to the US, Canada and Mexico of Belizeans leaves Mestizo (mixed race indigenous) at 52.9% of the population, followed by Creole at 25.9%, Maya 11.3%, Garifuna 6.1%. Around 75% of the population is thought to be Christian, with Catholicism the largest doctrine.

Formerly British Honduras, the country was renamed in 1973. Full internal self-government under a ministerial system was granted in January 1964 and full independence from Britain followed in 1981. The centre-left PUP ruled unbroken from 1964 until 1984, when the centre-right UDP finally achieved prominence. Since 1984, power has alternated between the two main parties.

The country has generally seen stability throughout this period although unrest broke out in 2005. This came after the PUP, under prime minister Said Musa, elected in 1998 and re-elected in 2003, pursued a high-growth strategy through highly expansionary fiscal and monetary policies, financed by external borrowing and a build-up of public debt. An unsustainable fiscal position forced much-needed budget tightening from 2005 onwards, which proved unpopular. The Musa government faced mounting pressure over corruption, the misappropriation of public funds and poor economic management. This ultimately led to riots in April in Belize City. These problems proved decisive in the 2008 general election, as the opposition UDP led by Dean Barrow defeated the incumbent PUP by 25 seats to six; the PUP under Prime Minister Barrow has been in office ever since.

Newly appointed as prime minister, Barrow received a strong mandate and, in 2009, after building political consensus, implemented his own fiscal austerity measures in response to the global financial crisis and country's high debt burden. Elections were called a year early, in 2012, and during a successful campaign, Barrow proposed renegotiating the terms of the 2029 "Superbond", which was born out of a previous restructuring under Musa in 2006. Popular policies from opposition leader Francis Fonseca focused on growth, oil drilling, job creation and lower living costs, and led to a narrowing of Barrow's majority (17-14 seats). This was partially reversed in 2015, as elections were called early again, which saw Barrow win an unprecedented third consecutive term.

Low oil prices threatened Venezuela's aid to Belize, US$150mn of which Barrow had recently spent on infrastructure projects, and was cited by some as the reason for the early election.

Belize's next election should take place by February 2021. Barrow has said he will step down by May 2019 (due to ill health). The Deputy PM may continue the term or, given the common practice of calling elections early, a general election could be held in 2019.

Crime has also emerged in recent years as a key social issue, with the country ranked among the highest in the world in terms of homicide rates (record at 44.7 homicides per 100,000 population, compared with a global average of 6.2, in a UN study in 2013).

Debt

	2012	*2017*
External debt ratios (%)		
Total external debt/GDP	75.5	75.1
Public external debt/GDP	64.4	67.7
Private external debt/GDP	11.0	7.5
Total external debt/exports of goods and services	123.5	138.6
External debt service ratio (public)	8.2	8.5
Public debt ratios (%)		
Public domestic debt/GDP	12.4	29.4
Public debt/GDP	76.8	97.1

Source: Central Bank of Belize, IMF, Exotix

Belize's total external debt stood at US$1.4bn at end-2017, according to central bank figures (75.1% of GDP, based on IMF WEO GDP). 90% of this was owed by the public sector. Public external debt was US$1.25bn (68% of GDP). This mostly comprised central government debt (96% of the total), with most of the remainder being owed by the financial public sector, while the non-financial public sector comprised a very small amount. Commercial creditors were the largest public sector external creditor group, solely comprising Belize's only international bond (the restructured "superbond"). This one bond (now 4.9375% 2034) accounted for 42% of PPG external debt and 38% of Belize's entire external debt. Official data show there is no other commercial debt (eg owed to banks). The remaining public sector external debt was divided roughly evenly between multilateral and bilateral creditors. The main multilateral creditor was the Caribbean Development Bank (CDB) followed by the Inter-American Development Bank (IADB), at c12% and 9% of public external debt, respectively. The main bilateral creditors were Venezuela followed by the Republic of China (Taiwan), at 17% and 12% of public external debt, respectively. Private external debt was another US$139mn (7.5% of GDP). According to the central bank's detailed sectoral breakdown, private external debt was mostly owed in the fishing and agricultural sectors, although private debt has been on a declining trend, both in absolute terms and as a share of GDP, over recent years (falling by nearly half in USD terms since 2010, when central bank figures began).

Total external debt, as a share of GDP, has remained relatively unchanged since 2012. The fall in private debt has been offset by the rise in public debt. Public external debt in USD terms was relatively unchanged over 2006–2012 (at cUS$1bn), but began to increase in late 2013 and over 2014–2017. The increase was almost entirely driven by "other" bilateral lending (which was probably mainly Venezuela; CDB and OPEC debt also increased, while ROC debt fell). During 2012–2017, public external debt increased by 24% in nominal terms, while debt owed to "other bilaterals" increased 11-fold. Total external debt increased modestly as a share of exports of goods and exports over 2012–2017, from 123.5% to 138.6%, as exports of goods and services were relatively unchanged (2017 data are based on the four quarters to Q3 17). Exports of goods and services were cUS$1bn in the four quarters to Q3 17, comprising goods exports of US$450mn and services of US$550mn (80% of services were tourism earnings). The total of exports of goods and services was about the same in 2012 although. Compositionally, goods accounted for two-thirds of goods and services earnings and one-third back then. Services now account for 55% of goods and services earnings. Meanwhile, the public sector external debt service ratio has been relatively unchanged at c8%. Debt service in 2017 was US$86mn, divided fairly evenly between principal and interest payments.

Total public debt in 2017 was US$1.8bn, amounting to 97% of GDP, up from 77% in 2012. Of this, 70% was external debt and 30% was domestic debt. Central government domestic debt amounted to US$0.5bn (29.4% of GDP). Domestic debt was only 12% of GDP in 2012. Domestic debt has increased by more than 2.5 times since 2012 in USD terms, after being relatively constant since 2007. The increase began noticeably in 2015, when it rose by 30%, and it rose by another 50% in 2016 and 40% in 2017. The increase was mainly driven by central bank issuance of T-bills and notes, and note issuance to domestic banks. Most of this increased issuance during 2016 and 2017 was to fund the BTL settlement and the recognition of another liability in November 2017, according to central bank reports.

Composition of external debt

External debt by creditor (Dec. 2017)	*Nominal amount outstanding (US$mn)*	*Share of total (%)*
Public sector external debt	**1254.4**	**90.0**
o/w Official multilateral	358.2	25.7
CDB	152.6	11.0
IADB	113.7	8.2
OPEC Fund	34.9	2.5

(*continued*)

(continued)

External debt by creditor (Dec. 2017)	*Nominal amount outstanding (US$mn)*	*Share of total (%)*
World Bank	16.1	1.2
CABEI	10.7	0.8
IMF (SDR allocation)	25.5	1.8
Other	4.7	0.3
Official bilateral	369.7	26.5
Venezuela	209.7	15.1
Republic of China (Taiwan)	145.8	10.5
Kuwait	12.7	0.9
Other	1.5	0.1
Commercial creditors	526.5	37.8
Bonds	526.5	37.8
Private sector external debt	**138.8**	**10.0**
Total external debt	**1393.2**	**100.0**

Source: Central Bank of Belize, Exotix

Rescheduling History

Belize has now had three commercial debt (bond) restructurings in the past decade (2007–2017), despite previously having no modern history of debt rescheduling, of either its official or commercial debt. This is some kind of a record. Moreover, the two most recent bond restructurings resembled strategic defaults (reflecting weak willingness to pay) as opposed to ability to pay.

Belize's recent restructurings may be traced back to the late 1990s, and a combination of a rising public debt burden and weak liquidity conditions. Public external debt nearly tripled in USD terms over 1999–2003, after having nearly doubled over 1993–1998, as governments pursued expansionary policies to boost growth, resorting to external sources to finance a wider budget deficit (mostly on commercial terms), while debt rose further in 1999 as the government assumed contingent liabilities. The budget deficit averaged nearly 9% of GDP over the period 1999–2004, with a primary deficit averaging 6.3% of GDP over 1999–2001. This itself reflected a history of poor fiscal management; especially capital expenditure financed externally, due to post-hurricane reconstruction efforts, and the expanded lending activities of the Development Finance Corporation (DFC). Securitisation operations during 1999–2000 by the DFC and the Social

Security Board increased the contingent liabilities on the public sector. By selling securities to a foreign bank (US$102.2mn) and pledging the income stream from a specific domestic portfolio of mortgages and other collateralised loans for repayment, the public sector had to assume the credit, liquidity and exchange rate risks of this operation in order to obtain financing. The collapse of the DFC from insolvency in 2003 added some 18% of GDP to public external debt. Total public sector debt soared to 107% of GDP in 2003 (WEO data), reaching US$1bn, with 86% owed to external creditors, from only 50% of GDP in 1999. Liquidity concerns surfaced when gross official reserves fell to only US$40mn by end-2004, forcing the government to embark on liability management operations to roll over maturing debt. But these were at ever higher commercial rates of interest, in operations that also required high up-front fees. After a series of refinancing operations had failed to alleviate cash-flow constraints, the PUP government of Said Musa announced in August 2006 an intention to restructure all its public external debt, including its commercial debt. A market-friendly restructuring was concluded in 2007, with various commercial loans and small bonds consolidated into one single bond, the Superbond, which amounted to US$547mn in size (over 40% of GDP). There was no principal reduction. The coupon was initially set at 4.25% over 2007–2009, before stepping up. The resulting cash-flow relief eased the near-term financing position while tighter fiscal policies helped to reduce the public debt burden to 82% of GDP by 2011, notwithstanding a temporary rise in 2009 during the global financial crisis. The budget deficit averaged just 0.8% of GDP over 2007–2011, and the primary balance moved into surplus.

However, the change in government to the DUP's Dean Barrow in 2008 led to its questioning the inheritance of the Superbond. Barrow made restructuring the bond a manifesto commitment in early elections he called for 2012, when the bond still accounted for around one-third of GDP, and which coincidentally came at the time of a scheduled step-up in the coupon on the Superbond from 6% over 2010–2011 to 8.5% from 2012. A market-friendly restructuring followed in February 2013, which involved a small (10%) principal reduction. The decision also followed the government's decision to nationalise Belize Electricity Limited (BEL), the country's sole electricity transmission and retail distribution company, in June 2011 (which itself followed the nationalisation of the telecoms company BTL), and led some investors to question the government's commitment to contracts. The restructuring proved short-lived as Barrow pledged again in a

State of the Union address in September 2016 to "do something about the bond", especially as this time around the government was confronted with paying massive compensation payments to the former owners of the nationalised companies following arbitration awards in the former owners' favour. A third restructuring was announced in October 2016, which this time took place through a consent solicitation approach to change the bonds' terms, again providing significant cashflow relief. There was no principal reduction.

Relations with Multilateral Creditors

Belize has had only one IMF programme, in the 1980s (a standby agreement over 1984–1986). It has not sought a programme since, although does engage with the IMF through the Article IV process and Technical Assistance. However, particularly over the past several years (arguably until 2017), despite its high public debt burden (averaging 80% of GDP over 2011–2015, and increasing to near 100% in 2017), it has generally rejected IMF advice for a bigger, up-front fiscal adjustment to improve its debt sustainability. Indeed, unusually during its three commercial debt restructurings over the past decade, Belize did not seek an IMF programme either before or during the exchange process, and did not receive specific multilateral support from other IFIs. However, as part of its most recent bond restructuring concluded in 2017, bondholders were successful in negotiating a greater role for IMF oversight (see "Sovereign Commercial Debt" section below). Still, in its 2017 Article IV, published in September 2017, the IMF described Belize's medium-term outlook as weak, citing average medium-term growth of just under 2% per annum, partly due to declining productivity and structural weaknesses.

IMF programmes

Date	*Arrangements*	*Comments*
1984–1986	SBA	

Source: IMF. Belize joined the IMF in 1977

Belize is a member of the World Bank Group, which has projects in Belize focused around sustainability and developing infrastructure resistant to adverse weather. However, the World Bank is only a minor creditor, accounting for only around one-tenth of Belize's debt to the CDB and

IADB, its biggest multilateral creditors and most active lenders. The World Bank was however expected to launch a new Country Partnership Framework (CPF) in the summer of 2017 to guide its support to Belize over 2017–2022. The CPF will carry forward the existing portfolio which is focused on infrastructure resilience to climate change and sustainable natural resource management, and enhance Bank support for Belize's financial inclusion and social resilience efforts. The CDB approved a new country strategy for Belize in October 2016. As of May 2017, the CDB had 20 active loans, with most of its portfolio focused on critical transport and water infrastructure. The CDB also provides support for private sector development through lines of credit managed by the Development Finance Corporation (DFC), which on-lends the funds to the agriculture, industry, housing and education sectors. The IADB aims to improve public expenditure efficiency, promote private sector development and develop sustainable export-led growth in four priority areas (education, tourism, transport and trade & tax policy). In February 2009, Belize requested emergency assistance from the IMF following significant flood damage in 2008, estimated to have caused US$66mn in total economic losses. The Executive Board approved financing of SDR4.7mn (cUS$6.9mn). Some infrastructure loans were also received by the IADB and CDB, in addition to humanitarian aid and technical assistance from the UN and international aid groups.

Paris Club and Bilateral Creditors

Belize has never had a Paris Club restructuring agreement.

Total bilateral debt increased significantly during 2013, and now stands at over double its end-2012 level. The main increases are categorised as 'other' in central bank statistics, but a large portion of this is owed to Venezuela, reported by local media to be the largest bilateral lender since 2015.

Belize has retained diplomatic ties with the Republic of China (Taiwan) since 1989, and is now just one of 19 countries to do so. Belize receives technical and financial assistance across various economic sectors, and the relationship includes bilateral cooperation in various areas and official visits. The Republic of China (Taiwan) was Belize's second biggest bilateral creditor, after Venezuela, in 2017, accounting for nearly 12% of its public external debt.

Sovereign Commercial Debt

Belize has undertaken three restructurings of its commercial debt over the past decade.

Commercial debt agreements

Date	*Details*
2006–2007	Restructuring of US$516mn of commercial debt, including two small bonds, into a new US$543.8mn bond (the Superbond) in an exchange offer which was completed in February 2007. The Superbond had a 2029 maturity, step-up coupons, amortising from 2019 and no principal haircut. The exchange implied an NPV loss of 24% according to IMF research.
2012–2013	Restructuring of US$543.8mn Superbond in an exchange offer which closed in March 2013. The new bond had a 2038 maturity, step-up coupons, amortising from 2019 and a 10% principal haircut. Total capitalised interest amounted to 7.083% of the principal, comprising the unpaid half of the August 2012 coupon on the Superbond plus the February coupon and subsequent accrued interest at a rate of 8.5%. The new bond amounted to US$529.9mn in size. The exchange implied an NPV loss of 29% according to IMF research.
2016–2017	Consent solicitation to change the payment terms of the 2038 bond which closed in March 2017. It involved: a shortening in the final maturity date of the bond by four years, to 20 February 2034 from 20 February 2038; a new principal amortisation schedule, over 2030–2034; and an interest rate of 4.9375%. There was no principal haircut. The exchange implied an NPV loss of 20%, according to IMF research.

Source: Exotix

The 2006–2007 Restructuring

Belize embarked on its first commercial debt restructuring in 2006, when the government announced on 3 August its intention to pursue a "market friendly" restructuring of its total US$960mn in public external debt. Over half the debt was owed to private creditors (bondholders and banks)—this included two large bond issues (US$125mn 9.5% 2012 and US$100mn 9.75% 2015). The authorities also approached official creditors. The intention came as no real surprise. After all, the IMF, in its annual Article IV survey in August 2005, projected financing gaps for 2016 of US$28mn (2.5% of GDP). However, the precise timing of any announcement on the debt was uncertain. The crunch point came with a worsening in the balance of payments and rising debt service costs, which put international reserves under pressure. Usable reserves were dangerously low, projected at year-end to be US$30mn (less than one month's worth of imports).

The authorities launched a cooperative debt exchange on 18 December 2006, which was completed on 20 February 2007. The terms of the offer covered over 90% of outstanding external commercial debt. The authorities had tested market appetite with three different new bonds in its proposal to creditors, depending on the coupon profile, whether there was a principal haircut or not, and whether it was a bullet or amortising. In the event, creditors holding eligible debt were offered a new 22-year bond (maturing in 2029) with step-up coupons (starting at 4.25% over February 2007–February 2010, then 6% from February 2010–February 2012, and 8.5% thereafter), amortising from August 2019 in 20 equal semi-annual instalments, and with no principal haircut. The exchange implied an NPV loss of 24%, according to the IMF, based on a comparing the PV of the old debt with the PV of the new debt at the same discount rate. Participation reached 98% of creditors. The new bond (the 2029 Superbond) amounted to US$543.8mn (becoming 55% of public external debt and 42% of GDP).

The restructuring presented maturity relief across all outstanding securities and eliminated financing gaps into the medium term. It (would have) reduced the government's cash outflow in aggregate by US$481.5mn to 2015. Crucially, although the exchange slashed debt service payments, the debt burden itself was unchanged in nominal terms. In anticipation of the exchange, S&P cut its rating in 2005 and again in 2006, through CCC to Selective Default. It subsequently raised its rating to B in February 2007 after the exchange was completed.

Eligible claims in the 2007 exchange included:

Description	*Date of issue*	*Maturity*	*Amount (as of Nov. 2006)*
Bonds			
Bear Stearns 9.5% note	2002	2012	US$125mn
Bear Stearns 9.75% note	2003	2015	US$100mn
RBTT 9.95%	2004	2014	US$76.1mn
Royal Merchant Bank and Finance 9.50%	2000	2010	US$25.6mn
Citicorp Merchant Bank 8.95%	2003	2013	US$17.5mn
Citicorp Merchant Bank 9.75%	1998	2008	US$2.6mn
Citicorp Merchant Bank 9.75%	1997	2007	US$1.4mn
Bank facilities			
International Bank of Miami 10% promissory note	2002	2012	US$18mn
International Bank of Miami 9.25% promissory note	2004	2011	US$12mn

(*continued*)

(continued)

Description	*Date of issue*	*Maturity*	*Amount (as of Nov. 2006)*
International Bank of Miami Tranche A promissory note	2003	2010	US$12mn
International Bank of Miami Tranche A yield compensation note	2003	2010	US$0.6mn
International Bank of Miami Tranche A interest notes	Series of 7 notes issued from 2003–2006	2010	US$7.0mn
International Bank of Miami promissory note tranches B and C	2003	B: 2010 C: 2008	US$3mn
Insured loans			
Belize Sovereign Investments I	2005	2015	US$65.2mn
Belize Sovereign Investments I	2005	2010	US$50.0mn

Source: Belize Offering Memorandum, 18 December 2006

Before the 2007 exchange, the government had refinanced a number of loans and arranged new financing in 2004–2005. In 2004, the government was able to restructure two large commercial bank loans, totalling US$150mn, both of which were scheduled to mature in the final quarter. Royal Merchant Bank of Trinidad and Tobago (RMBTT) rolled over three payments totalling US$65.5mn, due between October–January 2005, with a new note for an amount of US$75.6mn at a rate of 9.95%. The 10-year bullet maturity had a yield of 13% and a put option, at the request of RMBTT, exercisable after three years. The put option effectively imposed a buyback clause on Belize (as liquidity concerns increased, the likelihood of the put being called grew, which would have stretched debt service capacity in 2007 and added further pressure to already very low reserves). The deal involved up-front fees amounting to 1.2% of GDP. Similar terms were sought by International Bank of Miami (IBOM) when, in November 2006, it rolled over a total of US$79mn. The loan had seven years to maturity, a yield of 11% and included put options exercisable by bondholders in November 2005. Fees amounted to 0.3% of GDP. Increased credit risk was best typified by two failed attempts at a new international bond issue in 2004 and two insured loans arranged through private placements in March 2005 by Bear Stearns. The bonds totalled US$137mn in five- and 10-year maturities, with a yield of 13%. The issues had up-front fees and payments of 1.2% of GDP. A debt service reserve account was held in escrow to cover future debt service payments and 90% of the principal was guaranteed by the Zurich Insurance Company.

Exotix understands Belize's partial use of collective action clauses (CACs) in its 2007 exchange made it the first country to use CACs on the basis of US law instruments (prior to this, Ukraine (2000), Moldova (2002) and Uruguay (2003) had used CACs, according to IMF research, but the former was under Luxembourg/German law and the latter two English law). Of the two outstanding Eurobonds Belize had at the time, the 2015s contained a CAC while the 2012s did not. While the exchange removed all the 2015 bond, there remained a small rump left of the 2012 bond (less than US$3mn). The absence of a CAC in the 2012 bond made it harder to capture all creditors. Exotix understands that non-participating creditors were not deliberate holdouts but rather were unable or forgot to tender. The authorities did allow such creditors to come in again, by exchanging the old bond for the new one, on an informal basis for a year afterwards, out of goodwill. The bond was not serviced however. The new 2029 Superbond contained a CAC with a 75% threshold to change certain payment terms under Reserve Matters.

The 2012–2013 Restructuring

Belize embarked on its second commercial debt restructuring in 2012, after Prime Minister Barrow's successful re-election in March of that year, an election he had called early and one in which seeking a restructuring of the Superbond was a manifesto commitment. A cooperative debt exchange was finally launched in February 2013.

The government published its long-awaited proposals for restructuring the Superbond on 8 August 2012, in its Indicative Restructuring Scenarios. The proposals were worse than the market expected, although were discounted by investors as a low-ball starting point to the negotiations. There were three scenarios: (1) a par bond with no principal reduction, final maturity in 2062, with equal semi-annual principal payments after 15 years grace and a 2% fixed coupon; (2) a discount bond with 45% principal reduction, final maturity in 2042 with equal semi-annual principal payments and no grace period, and a step up coupon of 1% through to 2019, 2% through to 2026, and 4% through to 2042; and (3) a discount bond with 45% principal reduction, final maturity in 2042, and level repayments of principal and interest after a five-year grace period, with a 3.5% fixed coupon. The offer was valued at around 20 cents on the dollar at a 12% exit yield, excluding the August coupon.

Lengthy discussions with bondholders followed, many of whom were grouped under the Coordinating Committee. The initial proposals threatened an adversarial negotiation, compounded by the government's decision shortly after to miss the August coupon. In the event, the government made a partial payment on the August coupon at the end of the grace period. The government's decision was seen as being one to facilitate continued good-faith discussions and to reduce the risk from creditors of accelerating the bond. A limited non-disclosure agreement between the government and the creditor committee was reached in early October. The creditor committee presented a counter-proposal to the government on 21 October, which did not involve a nominal haircut, unlike two of Belize's initial restructuring proposals, and included temporary coupon reduction, maturity extension and proposals for state-contingent liabilities. Although Belize said the counter proposal provided some short-term cash flow relief, it dismissed it as "wholly incompatible" with its objectives and estimated that it was NPV neutral.

The government presented improved terms on 29 November 2012, which were NPV enhancing compared with the previous proposals presented on 8 August. The new indicative proposal had two options: (1) a par bond, with a higher step up coupon profile and shorter maturity. The bond had a 40-year final maturity, with 10 years' grace, and a 2.75% coupon for the first five years, and 4.5% thereafter; and (2) a discount bond, with 33% principal reduction compared with 45% in the previous proposal, higher coupons but the same maturity. It still had a 30-year final maturity, with five years' grace, and with a 4.5% coupon for the first five years, and 6.75% thereafter. The proposal was more creditor-friendly than the previous one, and nearly doubled the value of the offer. The need to improve the offer likely reflected the bond's 75% CAC threshold.

The Belize government presented the final terms for a restructuring of the Superbond on 12 February 2013. This followed an announcement by Barrow on 21 December that a deal with creditors had been reached and a subsequent statement on 22 January that terms would be disclosed in two weeks. The final terms marked a clear victory for creditors (at least for a time). They represented a further improvement on the November indicative proposal and were a far cry from the August scenarios. The offer, which was valued in the mid-50s at a 12% exit yield, was NPV positive for creditors compared with the November scenario, with slightly higher coupons, a minimal amount of debt reduction that was in any case clawed back with capitalised interest and a shorter maturity than the previous proposal (albeit much longer than the superbond). The offer therefore marked a significant concession by the government and, in fact, it is difficult to think of other restructurings in which the final terms have differed so far from the initial proposals.

The government finally launched its exchange offer for the Superbond later that month, which closed in late March 2013. 86.2% of bondholders agreed to new terms, well above the bond's 75% CAC threshold, which enabled the government to roll in non-participating creditors. The restructuring entailed an exchange offer for the 2029 Superbond into a new 25-year bond (2038 maturity—perhaps Superbond 2.0?). The new bond had a lower step up (the coupon was reduced in the first 4.5 years to 5% from the 8.5% on the Superbond, rising to 6.767% thereafter) and maturity extension. It was nine years longer than the 2029 Superbond, and amortised from 2019, at the same time as the Superbond was due to. The offer involved a 10% haircut on the principal of the Superbond (the Superbond was US$543.8mn), although this was effectively clawed back through adding capitalised interest, which was not subject to a haircut, for past due and accrued but unpaid interest through 19 March 2013. This included half the August 2012 coupon plus the February coupon and subsequent accrued interest at a rate of 8.5%. Total capitalised interest amounted to 7.083% of the principal of the 2029 Superbond (cUS$38.5mn). Hence, the effective nominal haircut was only c3% and the new bond had a nominal amount outstanding of US$529.928mn. Expenses of US$1.7mn were deducted from the first coupon payment to cover certain expenses of the creditor committee. The new 2038 bond contained a CAC with a 75% threshold to change certain payment terms under Reserve Matters.

The exchange implied an NPV loss of c29%, according to the IMF. The restructuring helped the government to achieve its prime objective, that of debt service relief and in particular to address the 2019 debt servicing hump when the Superbond was due to amortise. However, the restructuring did nothing to reduce the public debt burden, despite a 10% haircut. The new bond was only 2.6% smaller in size than the Superbond, after including capitalised interest. As a result, the difference in the public debt/GDP ratio was negligible.

The 2016–2017 Restructuring

Belize embarked on its third commercial debt restructuring in 2016, after Barrow had seemed to set out his stall to undertake such a restructuring in his Independence Day address on 21 September. A consent solicitation to change the payment terms of the 2038 bond was concluded in March 2017.

The government motivated the restructuring by stating that it faced serious economic and financial challenges, ahead of the bond's coupon step up from 5% to 6.767% in February 2018 and amortisation payments that were scheduled to start from August 2019. However, bondholders were less sympathetic as weak policy discipline and implementation was also a factor. In particular, the government did not deliver on the promises made to bondholders in its previous restructuring in 2013 (which created the 2038 bond) in which it committed to a 2% of GDP primary surplus. In the event, the primary balance went in the opposite direction and the window of opportunity provided by the cashflow relief in the 2013 restructuring was wasted.

The Belize government announced on 9 November 2016 that it intended to start restructuring discussions with holders of the 2038 sovereign bond. The government stated that it intended to meet bondholders before the end of November and aimed to conclude a restructuring in early 2017. The bond had US$530mn nominal outstanding (c45% of public external debt). The next coupon was due on 20 February 2017 (for an amount of US$13.3mn).

Creditor engagement was an important aspect of the restructuring. The formation of a bondholder committee was announced on 16 November. Not only did bondholders organise quickly, in this case, the bond's representative committee clause made it important from a public policy point of view for bondholders to be seen to fulfil an obligation that they sought in the existing bonds' terms. Under the clause, bondholders had the right to appoint a bondholder committee and the authorities had to (take reasonable steps to) recognise such a committee, negotiate with it in good faith, and provide information that is reasonably requested by it promptly. The committee did not have to wait for a default to happen to form; a public announcement of an intention to restructure was sufficient. Exotix understands this was the first time creditor engagement clauses were used in a sovereign restructuring.

The government published on 6 December 2016 a set of possible restructuring structures for the sovereign bond for consultation. Three possible repayment structures were: (1) to reduce the outstanding principal, while keeping coupon rates and the amortisation schedule unchanged; (2) to amend the amortisation schedule and coupon rates, eg reducing the coupon and/or turning the amortisation schedule into a "soft bullet" which, for instance, sees the principal amortise in semi-annual instalments over the past three years (presumably but not necessarily equally). The final maturity date would remain unchanged and there would be no reduction in principal; and (3) to extend the bond's final maturity and amend the amortisation schedule and coupon rates.

The government also proposed a consent solicitation approach to changing the existing terms of the 2038 bond, which would change some repayment terms under the existing bond and avoid the need to issue a new instrument in exchange. Under the bond's modification clause (CAC), the changes would require support of not less than 75% of existing bondholders to become binding on all holders. The government said that it hoped to send the consent solicitation statement to holders in early January, obtain responses by mid-February and to have necessary amendments take effect not later than 20 February 2017 (ie by the date of the next coupon). Another incentive for the government to reach a quick deal was the 2038 bonds' principal reinstatement clause. This provided that in the event of any unpaid principal or interest (before the bonds' 10th anniversary), the government had to issue to holders an additional amount of 2038 bonds equal to 11.11% of the original principal amount within five days; which amounted to cUS$59mn. This gave bondholders the incentive to wait for an actual default to increase the size of their claim.

The government presented its consent solicitation on 12 January 2017 in order to change certain terms of the existing 2038 bond. It sought a reduced coupon (4% fixed over the remaining life of the bond instead of the step-up) and a soft bullet (amortising in the last three years, ie 2036, 2037 and 2038, instead of from 2019). There was no maturity extension and no principal reduction. The offer was due to expire on 26 January. The bondholder committee, which represented a significant amount of the bond, flatly rejected the consent solicitation in a statement issued on 17 January. It had two concerns: (1) the process, with little, if any, substantive negotiation; and (2) the terms. The offer was valued in the low 40s at a 12% exit yield and thereby implied a significant reduction in value (in present value terms) from the existing bond, which bondholders clearly resisted. The deadline was subsequently extended as discussions continued.

After Belize missed a US$13mn interest payment on 20 February, the government announced on 3 March materially improved terms in its consent solicitation offer to holders of the 2038 bond compared with its original offer on 12 January. The key changes to the financial terms were:

(1) a shortening in the final maturity date of the bond by four years, to 20 February 2034 from 20 February 2038; (2) a new principal amortisation schedule, which saw five equal annual instalments commencing on 20 February 2030 through to 20 February 2034, instead of three equal annual instalments over 2036–2038 proposed in the original consent solicitation. The existing bond on the other hand saw 38 equal semi-annual instalments commencing in August 2019 through February 2038; (3) an interest rate of 4.9375%, commencing 20 February 2017, rather than the 4% rate that had been proposed. The coupon on the existing bond was 5% but this was due to step up to 6.767% from August 2017; and (4) no principal reduction. The offer was due to expire at 5pm (NY time) on 10 March, but was extended on that day to 15 March in order to allow sufficient time for the process to be completed. The authorities finally announced on 15 March that more than 87% of bondholders had consented to the amendments, well above the bond's 75% CAC threshold, which enabled the government to roll in non-participating creditors. However, a condition precedent for closing the deal was payment of the February coupon (and payment of the bondholders' committee's fees and expenses). The coupon, which was due on 20 February, was by this time in its 30-day grace period after it went unpaid as the government went through its consent solicitation exercise. The government stated that it expected all conditions precedent to be met no later than 21 March 2017. On 21 March, the government announced that over 88% of holders had consented to the proposed amendments and that all conditions precedent had been satisfied so that the terms of the bond were amended with immediate effect.

The new terms were a marked improvement from the original offer and were accepted by bondholders. The offer was valued in the mid-50s at a 12% exit yield, which implied an estimated 29% PV gain from the original consent solicitation. However, the improved final terms still entailed a PV reduction compared with the existing 2038 bond, estimated at c25% when comparing the PV on the new terms with the PV of the existing bond at the same exit yield (12%). However, the new bond was initially indicated in the mid-60s, which implied a c10% exit yield and meant an NPV loss of closer to 20% when comparing the PV on the new bond with the PV of the old bond at the same 10% discount rate. The exchange implied an NPV loss of c20%, according to the IMF. But the bondholder committee was not only able to improve the financial terms of the offer. It also secured important commitments from the government regarding fiscal adjustment and its continued adherence to fiscal discipline over the next four years. This was an important objective for bondholders, to avoid merely kicking the can down the road (as in the 2013 exercise). Under these commitments, Belize undertook to: (1) implement a fiscal consolidation equal to at least 3.0% of GDP in its forthcoming fiscal year 2017/18 budget, and (2) achieve a primary surplus target of at least 2.0% of GDP in each of the subsequent three fiscal years, namely 2018/19, 2019/20 and 2020/21. Belize enacted a Statutory Instrument to incorporate these targets into law and undertook to cooperate with the IMF in the preparation of its annual Article IV consultation, and to approve their publication, and to publish its fiscal outlooks and mid-year reviews. If Belize failed to meet the 2% primary surplus target in any of these years, (1) interest payments on the new bonds for the subsequent fiscal year will be payable quarterly rather than semi-annually, and (2) Belize shall submit a report to the National Assembly explaining the reasons why, and in addition, seek technical assistance from the IMF in analysing the reasons for the failure to meet the primary surplus target and seek IMF recommendations regarding appropriate remedial measures. The IMF's assessment and recommendations will be made publicly available.

Once again, the restructuring delivered significant cash flow savings for the government. Amortisations, due to start in 2019 under the existing bond, were pushed back, with no amortisations on the new bond until 2030. Debt service on the new bond, comprising interest only, amounted to just US$26mn per year until then; it was a little higher in the first year, because of the 5% coupon rate paid in February and the consent solicitation fee. Cumulative debt service over 2017–2029 thus amounted to US$342mn, compared with US$651mn under the bond's old terms (given the impending step up to a higher coupon and amortisation payments), on an undiscounted basis. However, debt service increases in the past five years of the new bond, with payments averaging US$120mn per year over 2030–2034 (undiscounted). However, once again, the restructuring did nothing to reduce the public debt burden. The bond still makes up 42% of public external debt.

Belize bond
Government of Belize 4.9375% 2034
Bloomberg ticker: BELIZE

Borrower	Republic of Belize	
Restructuring	Issued in exchange for 8.5% 2029 (ISIN USP16394AF89) on 20 March 2013 Terms changed with effect from 21 March 2017 through consent solicitation	
Issue date	20 March 2013 (revised on 21 March 2017)	
Form	Eurobond	
ISIN	USP16394AF62	
Issue size	US$529,928,000	
Amount outstanding	US$526,502,100	
Currency	US dollar	
Denomination	Minimum of US$100 and increments thereof	
Amortisation	Five equal annual instalments 2030–2034 Changed from 38 equal semi-annual instalments commencing August 2019	
Final maturity date	20 February 2034 Changed from 20 February 2038	
Coupon/interest	Step down, paid semi-annually, February and August	
	Feb. 2017	5%
	Aug. 2017–Feb. 2034	4.9375% (changed from 6.767% over 2017–2038)
Day count	30/360	
Method of transfer	Euroclear/Clearstream	
Settlement period	T + 2 business days	
Governing law	New York	
Exchange agent	Bank of New York	

Source: Bloomberg

Bosnia and Herzegovina

Nominal GDP (US$mn, 2018)[a]		19,984
Population (thousand, 2018)[a]		3504
GDP per capita (US$, 2018)[a]		5704
Credit ratings (long-term foreign currency)[b]	Fitch	NR
	Moody's	B3
	S&P	B

[a]IMF WEO October 2018
[b]As at end-September 2018

Country Summary

- The 1995 Dayton Peace Agreement divided the country into two entities, the Bosniak-Croat Federation of Bosnia and Herzegovina and the Serb-dominated Republika Srpska, under a central state level government. Devolved structures and ethnic rivalries have historically hindered reform attempts and the 2018 elections reaffirmed a divided but stable political landscape. In February 2016, the country submitted its application to join the EU.
- The economy has emerged out of an extended period of meagre growth after falling into a four-year-long recession in the aftermath of the global financial crisis. Growth began to pick up in 2015, and is projected to rise to 4% by 2022, according to the IMF; however,

Exotix Capital, *Exotix Developing Markets Guide*,
https://doi.org/10.1007/978-3-030-05867-8_9

the unemployment rate remains high (stuck at over 25%) and per capita incomes are around one-quarter of the average EU income level. The country is under an IMF programme, which is intended to support its domestic reform agenda, although the first review was only completed in February 2018 after a delay of over a year. However, the programme now looks to be getting back on track.

- Bosnia has a fairly low public debt ratio relative to its European peers (41% of GDP in 2017). Around two-thirds is external and 80% of this is borrowing from multilateral creditors through concessional lending. The country has not borrowed from international capital markets since post-independence restructurings in 1992, although Republika Srpska issued its own small international bond in June 2018. High gross external financing needs (c10–12% of GDP a year) present a key macro vulnerability.

Economic data	*Avg*[a]	*2014*	*2015*	*2016*	*2017 (e)*	*2018 (f)*	*2019 (f)*
Real GDP growth	2.5	1.2	3.1	3.2	3.0	3.2	3.5
Inflation (annual average)	1.3	−0.9	−1.0	−1.1	1.2	1.4	1.6
Current account (% of GDP)	−7.7	−7.4	−5.4	−4.9	−4.8	−6.0	−6.6
Reserves (US$mn, end-period)[b]	4573	4858	4791	5137	6473	6530[c]	–
Reserves/imports (months)[d]	5.5	5.8	6.5	6.9	6.9	–	–
Overall fiscal balance (% of GDP)[e]	−1.9	−2.9	−0.2	0.3	2.1	1.5	0.2
Currency (ticker)	Bosnian convertible mark (BAM)						
FX regime	De jure exchange rate is a currency board. The convertible marka is pegged to the euro at EUR1:KM1.95583.						
Key exports	Metals (17%), machinery (12%), minerals (8%).						

Source: IMF WEO Database, Haver, Central Bank of Bosnia, OEC

[a]10-year average to 2016 unless otherwise stated

[b]Total foreign reserve assets

[c]Latest figure, May 2018

[d]In months of the current year's imports of goods, services and primary income debits

[e]Overall government net lending

Key figures: State level		*Party*	*Since*
Shared presidency	Milorad Dodik (Serb)	SNSD	Oct. 2018
	Zeljko Komsic (Croat)	DF	Oct. 2018
	Sefik Dzaferovic (Bosniak)	SDA	Oct. 2018

(*continued*)

(continued)

Key figures: State level		*Party*	*Since*
Chairman, Council of Ministers	Denis Zvizdic	SDA	Mar. 2015
Minister of finance	Vjekoslav Bevanda	HDZ BiH	Mar. 2015
Central bank governor	Senad Softic	–	Aug. 2015
High representative of the international community	Valentin Inzko	–	Mar. 2009

Key figures: Federation of BiH (FBiH)		*Party*	*Since*
Entity president	Marinko Cavara	HDZ BiH	Feb. 2015
Prime minister	Fadil Novalic	SDA	Mar. 2015
Deputy PM/minister of finance	Jelka Milicevic	SDA	Mar. 2015

Key figures: Republika Srpska (RS)		*Party*	*Since*
Entity president	Milorad Dodik	SNSD	Nov. 2010
Prime minister	Zeljka Cvijanovic	SNSD	Mar. 2013
Minister of finance	Zoran Tegeltija	SNSD	Dec. 2010

Politics

State executive power

Bosnia and Herzegovina (BiH) has a complex constitutional framework with a central government (the Institutions of Bosnia and Herzegovina), two regional entities with a high degree of autonomy (the Federation of Bosnia and Herzegovina, FBiH; and the Republika Srpska, RS) and a small district, Brcko.

The presidency is shared between three presidents on a rotating basis every eight months. Each president is elected by popular vote, with the Croat and Bosniak members directly elected from the FBiH and the Serb member directly elected from RS. The responsibilities of the presidency lie largely in international affairs and in executing law, although considerable power is devolved to the cabinet.

The state-level executive is the Council of Ministers, with the chairman (also known as the prime minister) serving as head of government. The prime minister is chosen by the presidents and approved by the parliament. The chairman nominates the other ministers, who also need to be approved by the legislature. Two-thirds of the ministers are required to come from FBiH and one-third from RS. The position of High Representative, which is combined with the position of EU Special Representative, retains significant executive power.

Presidential term: Four years (two-term consecutive limit; break enables re-election)

Parliamentary term: Four years

State legislature

BiH is a democracy with a bicameral parliament, consisting of the Dom Naroda (House of Peoples—upper house) and Predstavnicki Dom (House of Representatives—lower house). Members of the House of Representatives are elected by popular vote to serve four-year terms, based on proportional representation, with allocation split two-thirds FBiH and one-third RS. Members of the House of Peoples are decided indirectly, by the Federation and Republic parliaments. Each house serves four-year terms. As well as elections for the presidency (state level), the House of Representative and House of Peoples (state level), there are elections to Parliamentary Assemblies in the entities, as well as municipal elections.

House of Peoples (15 seats)	**House of Representatives** (42 seats)
Five seats each allocated to Bosniak, Serb and Croat, elected at the entity level.	28 seats reserved for Federation of BiH candidates. 14 seats reserved for Republika Srpska candidates.

Elections

Next due *Presidential and legislative: October 2022*

Last legislative election (October 2014)[a]	*Seats*	*Last presidential (October 2018)*	*% of vote*
Party of Democratic Action	10	***Serb seat***	***(% of Serb vote)***
Alliance of Independent Social Democrats	6	Milorad Dodik (Alliance of Independent Social Democrats)	53.8
Serb Democratic Party	5	Mladen Ivanic (Party of Democratic Progress)	43.0
Democratic Front	5	Mirjana Popovic (Serb Progressive Party)	1.7
Union for a Better Future of BiH	4	Gojko Klickovic (First Serb Democratic Party)	1.5
HDZ-HSS-HKDU-HSP-AS BiH-HSP HB	4	***Croat seat***	***(% of Croat vote)***
Social Democratic Party	3	Zeljko Komsic (Democratic Front)	53.9
PDP-NDP	1	Dragan Covic (HDZ BiH)	34.8
HDZ 1990	1	Diana Zelenika (HDZ 1990)	6.0
BiH Patriotic Party	1	Other	5.3
Democratic People's Alliance	1	***Bosniak seat***	***(% of Bosniak vote)***
Party of Democratic Activity	1	Sefik Dzaferovic (Party of Democratic Action)	36.6
		Denis Becirovic (Social Democratic Party)	33.6

(*continued*)

(continued)

Elections

Next due	*Presidential and legislative: October 2022*		
Last legislative election (October 2014)[a]	*Seats*	*Last presidential (October 2018)*	*% of vote*
		Fahrudin Radoncic (SBB BiH)	13.0
		Other	16.8
Total	**42**	**Total**	**100.0**

[a]Legislative elections were held on 7 October 2018, but final results were not available at the time of writing

People

BiH gained independence in 1992 following the dissolution of Yugoslavia. The three main ethnic groups of BiH are referred to as Bosniak (Bosnian Muslim), Croat and Serb. Part of the Austro-Hungarian Empire from 1878, having previously been the northwestern-most boundary of the Ottoman Empire, its collapse following the First World War saw BiH incorporated into the Kingdom of the Serbs, Croats and Slovenes (which became known as Yugoslavia in 1929) under The Treaty of Versailles. After the Second World War, the Kingdom formed the Socialist Federal Republic of Yugoslavia, under communist rule, with BiH one of its six constituent republics until the fall of communism. After the collapse of Yugoslavia, the border of Bosnia and Herzegovina was established in the 1995 Dayton Peace Agreement. This divided the country into two entities of roughly similar size. Muslims (40%) and Croats (14%) came together to form the Federation BiH in 1994 and Republika Srpska, which is predominantly Serb (almost two-fifths of Bosnia's population), was created after hostilities ended in 1995. Christianity is practiced by over half the population and Islam by 40%. Bosnia and Herzegovina was identified as a potential candidate for EU membership in June 2003 and submitted its application to join the EU in February 2016. It has yet to become recognised as an official candidate for membership, at which time formal membership negotiations would begin. This would require the country meeting the conditions for joining, known as the accession criteria.

Debt

	2012	*2017e*
External debt ratios (%)		
Total external debt/GDP	62.7	61.8
Public external debt/GDP	29.0	27.9
Private external debt/GDP	33.7	33.9

(*continued*)

(continued)

	2012	*2017e*
Total external debt/exports of goods and services	193.4	157.5
External debt service ratio	11.8	19.9
Public debt ratios (%)		
Public domestic debt/GDP	15.5	13.3
Public debt/GDP	44.5	41.2

Source: Central Bank of Bosnia and Herzegovina, IMF, Exotix

Total external debt was cUS$11bn in 2017, standing at an estimated 62% of GDP (according to Exotix estimates based on central bank and IMF data), and has remained fairly constant in a range of 62–64% of GDP since 2012. This was split c45% in terms of public external debt and 55% as private external debt. Public external debt, according to central bank data for September 2017, amounted to US$5bn (based on the prevailing BAM/USD exchange rate), or 27.9% of GDP (it was 27.2% on recent IMF data). Almost 80% of public external debt (US$4.0bn) was owed to multilateral creditors. The World Bank's IDA was the single largest individual creditor (amounting to US$1.13bn, 22.4% of public external debt), and with IBRD lending a further 9% of public external debt, the World Bank Group overall accounted for 32% of the total. The next biggest individual multilateral creditor was the European Investment Bank (EIB), amounting to US$1.10bn (21.9% of public external debt), with the EBRD a further 11%. Together with the EC and EDB, European institutions were collectively the largest creditor group, owed c36% of public external debt. Around US$526mn (10.4% of public external debt) is "old" debt contracted before and during the country's independence, and is composed of debts owed to the Paris Club and London Club. Bilaterals comprised just 17% of public external debt, nearly half of which was owed to the Paris Club. Commercial creditors made up the remaining 3.8% of public external debt, and comprised just 1.7% of total external debt. This consisted mainly of US$110mn of London Club debt (the Bosnia A's and B's). By end-September 2017, after the June amortisation payments on both instruments, the A's amounted to just US$11mn and the B's US$99mn. With the maturing of the A's in December 2017 and another amortisation payment on the B's, the London Club debt would have fallen to just US$89mn by year-end. Private external debt was a further 33.9% of GDP, according to IMF figures, which equated to cUS$6bn, although there is little information on its composition.

Total external debt was 158% of exports of goods and services, according to the IMF, showing a decline from 193% in 2012, due to the increase in exports. The ratio is not especially high according to standard metrics. However, the external debt service ratio has shown a steady increase since 2012, to stand at 20% in 2017, according to the IMF. Much of this would seem to relate to private external debt, given the large share of public external debt that is owed to multilaterals and is therefore likely to be on concessional terms. Central bank figures suggest public external debt service in 2017 amounted to US$590mn (c8% of exports of goods and services). Gross external financing needs are also high (cUS$2bn a year over 2018–2020, according to the IMF, c10–12% of GDP per year), reflecting high import demand and debt amortisation, which poses a key macro vulnerability.

Meanwhile, total public debt was 41.2% of GDP on Exotix estimates (40.5% according to the IMF, in its first review of the EFF in February 2018). Public domestic debt was c13% of GDP in 2017, according to the IMF. Overall public debt doubled relative to GDP over the period 2007–2009, from its historical low of 19% to 35%, but has remained at around the 40–45% of GDP level since then, which is still fairly low relative to the country's eastern European peers. Indeed, the public debt ratio has shown a slight decline since 2012 (and more so since 2014–2015, when it was 45%) and is projected to decline to below 40% of GDP by the IMF in 2018, and to fall to 34% by 2023 due to the stronger primary balance and higher GDP growth. However, public sector debt statistics cover only the general government. Debt contracted by SOEs is not included and therefore could present a potential contingent liability to the government.

Composition of external debt

External debt by creditor (Sep. 2017)	*Nominal amount outstanding (US$mn)*	*Share of total (%)*
Public sector external debt[a]	**5040.8**	**45.2**
o/w Official multilateral	3992.0	35.8
IDA	1128.4	10.1
IBRD	470.5	4.2
EIB	1102.3	9.9
EBRD	534.1	4.8
IMF	456.1	4.1
EC	132.4	1.2
EDB	58.5	0.5

(*continued*)

(continued)

External debt by creditor (Sep. 2017)	Nominal amount outstanding (US$mn)	Share of total (%)
IFAD	45.0	0.4
Others	64.8	0.6
Official bilateral and government	855.2	7.7
Paris Club	415.6	3.7
Saudi Development Fund	54.8	0.5
Japan	52.5	0.5
Kuwait	19.2	0.2
Others	313.1	2.8
Private creditors	193.6	1.7
London Club	110.0	1.0
Others	83.6	0.7
Private sector external debt[b]	6122.6	54.8
Total external debt	**11,163.4**	**100.0**

Source: Central Bank of Bosnia and Herzegovina, IMF, Exotix

[a]End-September 2017 data from central bank converted using BAM/USD at 1.6549 (end-September rate from Bloomberg)

[b]IMF 2017 projection

Rescheduling History

Bosnia's rescheduling history relates to resolving debt following the country's separation from the Socialist Federal Republic of Yugoslavia (SFRY) under which it restructured both official bilateral and commercial claims. A London Club rescheduling was completed in 1997, culminating in the issuance of two international bonds, referred to as Bosnia 'A' bonds (which matured in December 2017) and performance warrants known as the Bosnia 'B' bonds (which mature in December 2021), both described in detail in the sovereign commercial debt section. BiH, like the other former republics of Yugoslavia, provided a joint guarantee to the former Yugoslav commercial creditors under the 1988 New Financing Agreement. As a successor to Yugoslavia, it became liable for a portion of these debts, as well as those to the IMF, other multilateral organisations and bilateral creditors. BiH assumed 10.6% of the NFA liability, compared with its IMF quota of 13.2%. In addition, the commercial banks agreed to write off the overdue interest, and much of the principal was forgiven in the form of a generous performance bond.

Relations with Multilateral Creditors

Bosnia and Herzegovina joined the IMF and World Bank in December 1992 although membership was only made possible after clearing outstanding arrears from the SFRY by a bridging loan from the Dutch central bank. It is now on its fifth arrangement since membership, an Extended Fund Facility (EFF). Bosnia has completed four SBAs (1998–2001, 2002–2004, 2009–2012, and 2012–2015). The last SBA was agreed in order to address structural weaknesses, improve deteriorating external conditions and meet urgent balance of payment needs caused by a flood in May 2014. The SBA succeeded in supporting the external environment, but progress in addressing domestic weaknesses was weak.

The IMF approved its current arrangement, a three-year EFF of SDR443mn (EUR553mn, 167% of quota), in September 2016 to support a domestic reform agenda, with the aim of lowering employment taxes and privatising several state enterprises, in order to raise BiH's potential growth rate while maintaining macroeconomic stability. As of December 2017, BiH had drawn SDR63.4mn, which was the initial disbursement on programme approval. Staff-level agreement on the first review was reached in November 2016, with the review expected at the time to go to the Board in Q1 2017, although this was delayed as the authorities needed more time to complete a number of remaining prior actions. These included, inter alia, an increase in fuel excises, amendments to the deposit insurance scheme, and amendments to the banking agency law. The first review of the EFF, along with the long overdue Article IV (the 2017 Article IV), was finally approved by the IMF Board in February 2018. The previous Article IV was in 2013 and Bosnia is on a 12-month cycle. Completion of the first review of the current EFF made available another SDR63.4mn. Staff-level approval of the second review was reached in May 2018. By the time the EFF is finished, in 2019, if it remains on track, Bosnia will have been under an IMF programme every year for the past decade.

The World Bank, BiH's biggest creditor, engaged early and extensively in the post-war reconstruction of the country. Over the past 20 years since the end of the conflict, the World Bank has approved 71 projects in the total amount of roughly US$1.9bn. Most of the projects have been earmarked to improve governance, create an environment for private sector-led growth and to foster 'social sustainability'. In per capita terms, the World Bank's assistance programs to BiH, including IDA concessional loans, have been the largest in the history of the organisation for any post-conflict country. BiH graduated to IBRD-only status in 2014.

IMF programmes

Date	*Arrangements*	*Comments*
1998–2001	SBA	To support Bosnia's 1998–1999 economic programme in the post-Dayton period.
2002–2004	SBA	A successor SBA was approved in August 2002 to support the economic programme from August 2002 to November 2003. An extension was agreed in December 2003, taking the SBA to February 2004 (600% of quota).
2009–2012	SBA	SDR1015mn (US$1.57bn, 600% of quota) approved in July 2009 in response to the global financial crisis with the aim of shoring up the country's fiscal position and maintaining long-term economic growth. SDR338mn was drawn.
2012–2015	SBA	A two-year SBA worth SDR338mn (US$521mn, 200% of quota) approved in September 2012, later extended by nine months and topped up to SDR558mn, to address structural weaknesses, to improve deteriorating external conditions, and to meet urgent balance of payment needs caused by floods in May 2014. BiH drew SDR443mn. Full repayment is expected by 2019.
2016–2019	EFF	A three-year EFF of SDR443 million (167% of quota) approved in September 2016 to support a domestic reform agenda. Repayment will begin in 2021 and is expected to be completed by 2026. The first review was approved in February 2018 after a lengthy delay. Waivers were granted for non-observance of the end-June 2017 performance criteria on net lending for the Institutions of Bosnia and Herzegovina (IBiH) and the Federation (FBiH) central government. Several prior actions for the first review were completed and there was progress with implementing structural benchmarks, although several were delayed because of technical or capacity reasons. As of completion of the first review, SDR126.8 million has been drawn in all.

Source: IMF. Bosnia & Herzegovina joined the IMF in 1992

Paris Club and Bilateral Creditors

Bosnia's two Paris Club rescheduling agreements, as an independent country, remain active. As of 2016, BiH held US$403mn in Paris Club debt, from the 1998 and 2000 agreements.

Paris Club agreements

Date	*Terms*	*Status*	*Details*
1984	Classic	Fully repaid	Agreements under Federal Republic of Yugoslavia.
1985	Classic	Fully repaid	Agreements under Federal Republic of Yugoslavia.
1986	Classic	Fully repaid	Agreements under Federal Republic of Yugoslavia.
1988	Classic	Fully repaid	Agreements under Federal Republic of Yugoslavia.
1998	Naples	Active	US$588mn treated covering arrears as of end-June 1998 and maturities falling due from July 1998 to April 1999. Non-ODA credits repaid over 23 years, six years' grace, with cancellation to 67%, and ODA credits over 40 years with 16 years' grace.
2000	Naples	Active	US$9mn treated under similar terms to the 1998 treatment.

Source: Paris Club

London Club Debt

In December 1997, Bosnia reached an agreement with the London Club to restructure US$1.3bn of debt (principal and interest) owed to commercial banks. In so doing, 85.8% of commercial debt was written off, with the remainder rescheduled. The total amount treated comprised of US$0.7bn of past due interest, which was written off completely, while eligible principal of US$0.6bn was exchanged into US$400mn of bonds, denominated in Deutschemarks.

The DEM700mn (EUR357mn) in bonds comprised two instruments. The Bosnia 'A' Bonds, some DEM262mn (EUR134mn), was a floating rate note, to be paid over 20 years with a seven-year grace period on (amortising) principal payments. Stepped-up interest rates rose from 2% to LIBOR + 13/16%. The first principal repayment was made in November 2005. The bond matured in December 2017.

The country became liable for the remaining DEM437mn, issued in the form of the Bosnia 'B' Warrants, when performance triggers were met: ie when GDP per capita reached the inflation-adjusted equivalent of US$2800 and remained at that level for two consecutive years over the period 2004–2017. The country was exempt from making any payments for the first 10 years. At the time of the London Club restructuring, the likelihood of triggering payments under the performance bonds was seen as remote. Per capita income in 1997 was estimated at US$1079, having collapsed after the devastation of the war. Subsequently, however, there was strong growth in the Bosnian economy, with a strong marka against the dollar and statistical revisions by BHAS and the World Bank (mainly to population) increasing GNI per capita to a value above the warrant's trigger. In July 2009, the fiscal agent accepted that the trigger would be activated in December 2009, and the warrants converted into a simple FRN-structure similar to the A's. Payments commenced in June 2010. The bond matures in December 2021, and began amortising in June 2010. By end-2017, the amount outstanding on the Bs was DEM145.5mn (cUS$89.3mn equivalent). This had fallen to just DEM127.3mn after the June 2018 amortisation payment.

In contrast to the other republics, a portion of the country's API, or Exit Bond, was also written down. This is unrestructured debt of the former Yugoslavia, for which all former republics retain their original liabilities. Because the World Bank is more actively engaged in countries with lower per capita GDP, BiH now has a higher share of post-FYR debt. Reflecting its economy (real GDP fell to 14% of its 1980s peak at one stage), its status as a post-conflict economy and its unusually high financing needs, the World Bank granted exceptional forbearance and organised additional official financial assistance.

Bosnia 'B' notes emanating from triggered performance warrants
Bosnia FRN 2021
Bloomberg ticker: BOSNIA

Borrower	Bosnia and Herzegovina (BiH)
Issue date	Fiscal agent accepted trigger would be activated in December 2009 and the first payments were made in June 2010
Form	Registered
ISIN	XS0082227546
Bonds	DEM436.524mn worth of new Performance Bonds paying LIBOR +13/16% and amortising in equal semi-annual instalments in 24 periods after the Performance-Addition Date
Amount outstanding	DEM127.32mn (as of end-June 2018)
Coupon	LIBOR + 13/16% (currently, 0.5%)
Currency	DEM
Denomination	DEM1000 minimum and increments of DEM1000 thereafter

(*continued*)

(continued)

Bosnia 'B' notes emanating from triggered performance warrants *Bosnia FRN 2021* *Bloomberg ticker: BOSNIA*	
Performance trigger:	Subject to the GDP per capita of issuer BiH reaching US$2800 (further subject to indexation) for two consecutive years during 2004–2017, as calculated by the Fiscal Agent. The Notes would have expired worthless if trigger had not been met by 11 December 2017. The Performance-Addition Date could not have occurred before 11 December 2007. The calculation referee was the IBRD.
Final maturity date	20 December 2021
Maturity profile	24 equal semi-annual instalments, the first six months after interest payment date on the 'A' bonds immediately succeeding the date the GDP target has been met for two consecutive years (Performance-Addition Date).
Day count	ACT/360
Method of transfer	Euroclear/Clearstream
Settlement period	T + 2 business days
Governing law	US

Source: Bloomberg

Sub-sovereign Debt

Republika Srpska (RS) became the first Bosnian entity to issue a eurobond, following the placement of a EUR168mn issue on 20 June 2018. The five-year bond had a 4.75% coupon and was issued at par. The entity's finance minister had spoken about plans for a EUR200mn issue in mid-May, as it sought to increase its long-term funding amid limited capacity in the domestic market, although limited investor interest resulted in a smaller amount being issued. Prevailing media reports of financial strains and RS's leadership instability may have discouraged some investors, although the ministry expressed satisfaction with its debut issue. RS had previously tried to access international capital markets in 2015 with help from the World Bank. Details of the RS bond are shown below.

Previously, the city of Banja Luka in RS raised EUR3.2mn from the sale of a seven-year bond in April 2018. The coupon was 4.5%, paid semi-annually, with the proceeds used to fund five capital projects in the city. The sale took place through the Banja Luka stock exchange.

Republika Srpska bond
Republika Srpska 4.75% 2023
Bloomberg ticker: REPSBN

Borrower	Republika Srpska
Issue date	20 June 2018
Form	Eurobond
ISIN	AT0000A21PN2
Issued amount	EUR168mn
Currency	Euro
Denomination	EUR100,000 and then EUR100,000 thereafter
Amortisation	Bullet
Maturity date	28 June 2023
Coupon/interest	4.75% per annum, paid semi-annually June and December
Day count	ACT/ACT
Method of transfer	OKB
Lead manager	BM Intelligence Ltd
Exchange	Vienna
Governing law	Republic of Austria

Source: Bloomberg

Cameroon

Nominal GDP (US$mn, 2018)[a]		38,445
Population (thousand, 2018)[a]		24,884
GDP per capita (USD, 2018)[a]		1545
Credit ratings (long-term foreign currency)[b]	Fitch	B
	Moody's	B2
	S&P	B

[a]IMF WEO October 2018
[b]As at end-September 2018

Country Summary

- Cameroon has enjoyed a long period of political stability, dominated by one man, President Paul Biya, who has been in power since 1982 and is now Africa's second longest-serving leader. He has successfully contrived this tenure through a balancing act appeasing ethnicities and opposition with a series of appointments to the government. In April 2008, the constitution was amended to remove term limits on the presidency, and his party (RDPC) maintains a dominant position. However, this exposes Cameroon to key-man risk. Biya is in his 80s and, when he does leave office, future stability could be in doubt. The country also faces a secessionist threat from the Anglophone regions.

Exotix Capital, *Exotix Developing Markets Guide*,
https://doi.org/10.1007/978-3-030-05867-8_10

- Cameroon is the biggest of the six members of the CEMAC region, accounting for 40% of the region's GDP. It is a commodity exporter, although arguably diversified across a range of primary products. It is a small non-OPEC oil exporter, producing c90,000 barrels per day, although oil revenues have been a significant source of FX earnings. Oil reserves are, however, depleting. The country is also rich in other commodity resources, including cocoa, coffee, cotton and timber. Agriculture is the mainstay of the economy and remains the largest employer.
- Public debt is still fairly low, at c34% of GDP, but is rising again, over a decade after Cameroon benefitted from an HIPC debt reduction in 2006, which resulted in a commercial debt buyback. The country debuted in the eurobond market in 2015, but China is now its single biggest creditor (some one-third of public external debt). The oil price crash in 2014 hurt the region, potentially putting the CFA peg at risk, and forcing Cameroon and the rest of CEMAC to turn to the IMF, although Cameroon had been less badly hit than the other members.

Economic data	*Avg*[a]	*2014*	*2015*	*2016*	*2017 (e)*	*2018 (f)*	*2019 (f)*
Real GDP growth	4.3	5.9	5.7	4.6	3.5	3.8	4.4
Inflation (annual average)	2.6	1.9	2.7	0.9	0.6	1.0	1.1
Current account (% of GDP)	−2.2	−4.0	−3.8	−3.2	−2.7	−3.2	−3.0
Reserves (US$mn, end-period)[b]	3229	3204	3568	2260	3235	–	–
Reserves/imports (months)[c]	–	4.2	5.4	3.9	4.3	–	–
Overall fiscal balance (% of GDP)[d]	1.2	−4.2	−4.4	−6.1	−4.9	−2.6	−2.1
Currency (ticker)	Member of the CFA franc zone (XAF).						
FX regime	The CFA franc is pegged to the euro at a rate of CFAF655.957 per euro. The CFA franc floats freely against other currencies.						
Key exports	Crude petroleum (35%), wood (17%), cocoa (12%), bananas (6.5%).						

Source: IMF WEO Database, IMF country reports, BEAC, OEC (exports)

[a]10-year average to 2016 unless otherwise stated

[b]Net external assets

[c]In months of the current year's imports of goods, services and transfer outflows

[d]IMF general government net lending

Key figures		*Party*	*Since*
President	Paul Biya	RDPC	Nov. 1982
Prime minister	Philemon Yang	RDPC	Jun. 2009
Minister of finance	Louis Paul Motaze	RDPC	Mar. 2018
Key opposition figure	John Fru Ndi	SDF	May 1992
Central bank governor	Abbas Mahamat Tolli (Governor of BEAC)	n/a	Mar. 2017

Note: Cameroon is a member of the Commonwealth, joining in 1995

POLITICS

Executive power

Although the National Assembly is the constitutional lawmaker, legislative power is also centred on the president, who has the power to reject bills, direct policy and change the length of term of any Assembly. The president is also responsible for the appointment of the prime minister and all ministerial government roles, upon recommendation of the prime minister. Therefore, despite being the head of government, the prime ministership remains largely a powerless, ceremonial role. The President is elected by plurality vote to serve a seven-year term.

Presidential term: Unlimited seven-year terms

Parliamentary term: Five years

Legislature

Bicameral since 2013. There had previously been only the National Assembly (Chamber of Deputies, lower house), although a constitutional amendment in 1996 contained a provision for the creation of a bicameral legislature with an upper house, the Senate. The Senate was formed following elections in April 2013, after the President signed a decree in February.

Senate (100 seats)
The Senate is presided over by its own president and committee. There are 10 senators per region, serving five-year terms. Per region; seven senators are indirectly elected by electors from regional governing councils while three are decided by the president. Therefore, 70 members are chosen by electors and the 30 remaining senators are appointed by the President.

National Assembly (180 seats)
Elected by popular vote to serve five-year terms. 34 members are elected by plurality vote in single-member constituencies and 146 members are elected by plurality vote in multi-member constituencies. The president has the power to determine a legislative term.

Elections

Next due *Presidential: 2025; legislative: 2019*

Last legislative election[a] *(Sep. 2013)*	*Seats*	*Last presidential (Oct. 2018)*	*% of vote*
Cameroon People's Democratic Movement (RDPC)	148	Paul Biya (RDPC)	71.3
Social Democratic Front (SDF)	18	Maurice Kamto (MRC)	14.2
National Union for Democracy and Progress (UNDP)	5	Cabral Libii (Univers)	6.3
Other	9	Other	8.2
Total	**180**	**Total**	**100.0**

[a]Results shown for the National Assembly. In the Senate, the RDPC received 56 seats compared with the SDF's 14. The 2018 legislative election was delayed until October 2019

People

Cameroon has an estimated 240 different tribal/ethnic groups, speaking c230 languages and divided between three religions (Christianity, Islam and animism), whose distinctness has waned as citizens have settled in five main regions; the Central Highlands, Western Highlands, Coastal Tropics, Southern Tropics and the northern Islamic region of the Sahel. This has provided for a relatively peaceful society, and Cameroon has been one of the more stable countries in Africa, although there have been instances of violence. Most recently, a secessionist movement has emerged in the two Anglophone regions (the North West and South West), which has led to the deaths of a dozen members of the security forces since late 2016, as the government seeks to quash it. In March 2018, President Biya announced changes to the government that saw the creation of a new ministry (the Ministry of Decentralisation and Local Development), and the appointment of two new ministers from the Anglophone regions in order to appease the secessionist threat. In October 2017, at least 17 people were killed in violent anti-government protests in Yaounde, which had started as transport strikes, while in September 2010, senior security officials were sacked following rumours of an attempted coup. Since 2013, Cameroon has also suffered from militant attacks and kidnappings from Boko Haram, and the authorities were accused by Amnesty International of torturing and killing suspected members in July 2017. Christianity is the largest religion, with all Christian denominations making up almost 70% of the population. Islam is the next largest (21%). French Cameroon achieved independence from France in January 1960. A year later, one-third of British Cameroon elected to form the Federal Republic of Cameroon with their ex-French counterparts. Over 1961–1982, President Ahmadou Ahidjo centralised power; creating a one-party state in 1966 and replacing the Federation with a unified constitution of the Republic in 1970. Paul Biya became President in 1982, having ascended from the premiership upon Ahidjo's resignation. Previously endorsed by Ahidjo, Biya's relationship with his predecessor quickly deteriorated and Ahidjo's supporters staged a failed coup in 1984. Over 1984–1990, the political environment stabilised, with multiparty democracy reinstalled in 1990. In several elections since, the main opposition parties boycotted, and Cameroon began to cement democracy, with the RDPC remaining the firm party of choice. An independent electoral commission only emerged in December 2006 and, in April 2008, the legislative approved a constitutional amendment removing term limits on the presidency. Biya's opponents alleged fraud in the 2011 presidential election. Corruption has also become an issue, illustrated by the conviction of a former finance minister (Polycarpe Abah Abah) for embezzlement, although Biya's anti-corruption crackdown in recent years may also be seen as an attempt to remove potential rivals. Cameroon is the biggest of the six members of the Central African Economic and Monetary Community (CEMAC), which also comprises Gabon, CAR, Chad, the Republic of Congo, and Equatorial Guinea, accounting for 40% of its GDP and 50% of its population.

Debt

	2012	*2017 Q2*
External debt ratios (%)		
Total external debt/GDP	14.0	24.8
Public (PPG) external debt/GDP	12.6	22.2
Private external debt/GDP	1.4	2.6
Total external debt/exports of goods and services	48.8	116.1
External debt service ratio (PPG)	1.7	5.6
Public debt ratios (%)		
Public domestic debt/GDP	5.7	5.8
Public debt/GDP	18.3	27.9

Source: Autonomous Sinking Fund of Cameroon, IMF, World Bank, Exotix

Cameroon's total public debt was US$9.5bn in Q2 17, based on figures from state institution, the Autonomous Sinking Fund of Cameroon (CAA). This was c28% of GDP (based on 2017 estimated GDP in the IMF WEO)—although public debt is higher on IMF data, estimated at 34% of GDP in 2017 according to the WEO. Its level in 2005 was c52% of GDP, which continued to fall following the HIPC completion point, to below 10% in 2008. It has risen every year since, although new debt is mostly on concessional terms: 81% of external debt was concessional in 2014, before falling after the eurobond issue in 2015 to 67% in 2016. Of the total public debt, public and publicly guaranteed (PPG) external debt in Q2 17 was US$7.5bn, 22.2% of GDP, of which US$6.9bn was non-guaranteed and US$611mn was external debt guaranteed by the central government, issued by public enterprises and the private sector. Bilaterals were the largest creditor group, accounting for nearly half of public external debt. China has overtaken France as the single largest bilateral creditor, owed almost US$2.4bn (about one-third of public external debt), while France was owed US$939mn. Other significant bilateral creditors were Japan and South Korea. Multilaterals were the next largest creditor group, owed almost US$2bn, just over one-quarter of public external debt. The main multilateral creditors were the World Bank (owed around half all multilateral debt), the African Development Bank (AfDB/AfDF) and the Islamic Development Bank (IsDB). In 2012, before the eurobond issue, commercial creditors were owed US$181mn. This rose to US$1.4bn in Q2 17. The eurobond has US$750mn outstanding and starts to amortise in November 2023. Other commercial creditors were owed US$661mn. Public domestic debt, which amounted to the remaining

US$1.9bn, c5.8% of GDP, comprised c31% domestic bonds, 21% BEAC statutory advances, 40% structured debt and 8% unstructured debt. Some recent increases have been due to construction efforts for the African Nations Cup in 2019.

Exotix estimates total external debt at US$8.4bn, as of Q2 17, comprising public external debt as above and private external debt of cUS$0.9bn for the same period, according to the World Bank's GDDS data (private external debt was about the same in Q4, on the most recent World Bank statistics, but we stick with Q2 data to match the timing of the public debt stock). As a result, total external debt was c25% of GDP, comprising public external debt of 22% of GDP and private external debt of 3% of GDP. As a percentage of exports of goods, services and remittances, as provided by the IMF, total external debt was 116% in 2017, although this figure is lower (95.3%) if only central government external debt is included (and not government guaranteed). This is significantly higher than its 2012 ratio of 48.8%, reflecting much higher public external debt and a fall in exports since 2012, in part due to lower commodity prices and oil revenues. A lower proportion of external debt on concessional terms has also forced the external debt service ratio higher, from 1.7% in 2012 to 5.6% in 2017, based on IMF data.

Composition of external debt

External debt by creditor (Q2 2017)	*Nominal amount outstanding (US$mn)*	*Share of total (%)*
Public and publicly guaranteed external debt	**7533**	**89.4**
o/w Publicly guaranteed	611	7.3
o/w Official multilateral	1994	23.7
World Bank	1029	12.2
AfDB/AfDF	545	6.5
IDB	95	1.1
IMF	72	0.9
EU	71	0.8
Official bilateral	3517	41.7
China	2380	28.2
France	939	11.1
Commercial creditors	1411	16.7
Eurobond	750	8.9
Banks and other	661	7.8
Private sector external debt[a]	**896**	**10.6**
Total external debt	**8429**	**100.0**

Source: CAA

[a]Private sector non-guaranteed from the World Bank (as of 2016)

Rescheduling History

Cameroon has a fairly modest history of debt restructuring, with the most recent operations coming in the context of HIPC debt relief after the emergence of an unsustainable debt burden during the 1980s and 1990s. Cameroon benefitted from HIPC debt relief in 2006, becoming the 19th country to do so. Prior to this, it received a number of Paris Club restructuring agreements, mostly during the 1990s, and a commercial restructuring of its bank debt in 2002, but has not had any payment issues since then as far as Exotix is aware.

Cameroon's debt problems emerged after over-borrowing during the oil boom years of the early 1980s. The country's debt burden became unsustainable, however, later that decade as a result of a severe terms-of-trade shock and an overvalued exchange rate (the CFA franc was pegged to the French franc). Its terms of trade fell by 50% between 1984 and 1986 and the real exchange rate appreciated by 60%. These external shocks were combined with economic mismanagement and expansionary fiscal policy, financed by external borrowing. A decade-long recession lasted until 1994, while the debt burden and debt servicing problems were aggravated by the devaluation of the CFA franc (external debt/GDP doubled after the devaluation). Arrears accumulated over the course of the 1990s. An economic reform programme began in 1997 under a new government. Reforms had begun in 1988, but were not implemented consistently. By the mid-1990s, the country was saddled with an unsustainable debt and large external and domestic arrears. A restructuring of official and commercial claims was essential. Inability to pay saw five restructuring deals made with Paris Club creditors on various terms, pre-2000, although these never completely solved Cameroon's external debt burden, which stood at 90.2% of GDP in FY 99/00 (US$6.3bn). In 1997, external debt service was c30% of exports.

Cameroon became eligible for debt relief under the HIPC initiative, and an improvement in policy performance after 1996 offered some hope that it would qualify. Agreement on a flow rescheduling, as a prelude to a stock treatment, was reached with the Paris Club in 1997. As Cameroon reached decision point under HIPC in October 2000, the authorities turned to a new round of talks with bilateral and commercial creditors, with the latter paving the way for a London Club agreement in 2002 on debt and arrears with commercial bank creditors. After a six-year wait, the IMF and World Bank concluded that Cameroon had made sufficient progress on policy reforms under its PRGF facility, agreed in October 2005, to grant HIPC completion-point status in April 2006. Cameroon benefited from debt relief on Cologne terms ("90%"), with a common reduction factor (CRF) of 27%, while further debt relief was granted, amounting to 100% on eligible debt, under the Multilateral Debt Relief Initiative (MDRI). For example, France, Cameroon's largest bilateral creditor at the time, agreed to a 100% write-off, with the residual from HIPC transferred to a C2D development contract. Regarding the multilaterals, which mainly comprised the IDA, AfDB/AfDF and IMF, following MDRI implementation, NPV relief amounted to 78% in total. As a result of debt reduction, external debt in NPV terms fell to 16% of exports in 2007 from 130% in 2005 (after traditional relief, but before HIPC relief) and to 22% of government revenues from 194%. Public debt fell from a peak of 86% of GDP in 2000 to 10% in 2008, as a result of debt relief, and remained fairly low for the next few years, rising only slightly to 15% in 2012 (IMF WEO figures). However public debt has since risen more sharply to 36% of GDP in 2017 following the oil price crash that began in 2014, a shock that ultimately caused liquidity problems across the CEMAC zone, forcing its members to turn to the IMF for help.

Relations with Multilateral Creditors

Cameroon has had eight financial programmes with the IMF, including the one currently underway. Prior to the current ECF, the programmes mainly supported Cameroon's path to HIPC debt relief, with two back-to-back ECFs around decision point and another ECF approved in 2005 before the granting of completion point. Successful performance under these programmes was in contrast to some of Cameroon's previous programmes during the 1990s, under which policy performance was not satisfactory. SBAs went off track and IDA disbursements were suspended. Performance began to improve after the appointment of a new government in September 1996, which subsequently secured a three-year ESAF (later renamed PRGF) from the IMF in August 1997, which was accompanied by a three-year Paris Club rescheduling. Generally satisfactory performance under IMF programmes followed, although fiscal slippages in 2004 derailed progress temporarily and led to the PRGF being suspended. After debt relief and the conclusion of the related ECF in 2009, Cameroon did not have another IMF programme for eight years, until 2017.

The IMF approved Cameroon's current programme, a three-year ECF, in June 2017. It amounted to US$666mn (175% of quota). The programme came after the IMF announced in March 2017 that discussions on a Fund-supported programme were underway, a move that was a direct response to the wider regional initiative to address imbalances in the CEMAC zone. This followed a statement of support by the IMF's MD Lagarde on 23 December 2016 after a meeting with CEMAC Heads of State. The first review of the new programme was concluded in December 2017. The second review of the programme was approved in July 2018, taking total disbursements under the arrangement to about US$366mn.

IMF programmes

Date	*Arrangements*	*Comments*
1988–1990	SBA	Agreed for SDR61.8mn, SDR38.6mn drawn. Went off track in 1989.
1991–1992	SBA	Agreed for SDR28mn, SDR8mn drawn. Went off track in 1992.
1994–1995	SBA	Agreed for SDR81.1mn, SDR21.9mn drawn. Programme adopted after the devaluation of the CFA franc. Performance went off track.
1995–1996	SBA	Agreed for SDR67.6mn, SDR28.2mn drawn. Performance went off track.
1997–2000	ECF	Originally an ESAF, then known as a PRGF, approved to support the new government's medium-term strategy, amounting to SDR162.12mn, which was fully drawn. Programme completed in October 2000 with substantial progress being made. PRGFs are now known as Extended Credit Facilities (ECFs).
2000–2004	ECF	Approved in December 2000 for SDR111.4mn and SDR79.6 was drawn. The programme continued the adjustment effort and targeted second-generation reforms. The fourth review was concluded in December 2003 and extended by one year, but no further reviews were completed because of deterioration in the public finances. The programme lapsed in December 2004. Suspension followed loss of budgetary control in 2004, which also saw delays in implementing structural reforms, notably privatisation.
2005	SMP	A new staff-monitored programme (SMP) was approved to re-establish a track record of policy implementation after the previous arrangement went off track. The SMP covered H1 2005. Performance was broadly satisfactory.

(*continued*)

(continued)

Date	*Arrangements*	*Comments*
2005–2009	ECF	Approved in October 2005. Due to expire in October 2008, but extended to January 2009. Performance was satisfactory. The agreed amount was SDR18.57mn, which was fully drawn.
2017–2020	ECF	A three-year ECF for SDR483mn (US$666mn, 175% of quota) was approved in June 2017. SDR124.2 (US$171mn) was immediately disbursed. The first review was concluded in December 2017, and allowed a further disbursement of SDR82.8mn (US$117mn). The second review was approved in July 2018 and allowed a disbursement of SDR55.2mn (US$78mn).

Source: IMF. Cameroon joined the IMF in 1963

The World Bank/IDA continues to be an active lender, with the World Bank Group having 21 active projects at end-H1, with another six in the pipeline. The AfDB also has 17 ongoing projects, with a wide variety of objectives.

Paris Club and Bilateral Creditors

Cameroon has had seven Paris Club agreements, the last one of which was a HIPC exit treatment on 17 June 2006. In October 1997, Cameroon received a three-year flow rescheduling from the Paris Club after agreement was reached earlier that year on an IMF ESAF. That was on Naples terms, although debt service reduction was 50% on NPV terms rather than the usual 67% that most HIPC countries have received. The decision point treatment in 2001 was on Cologne terms.

Paris Club agreements

Date	*Terms*	*Status*	*Details*
1989	Classic	Fully repaid	The deal covered US$435mn in principle, interest and arrears.
1992	Houston	Fully repaid	US$922mn, split evenly between principle and interest, rescheduled.

(*continued*)

(continued)

Date	Terms	Status	Details
1994	London	Fully repaid	Agreement followed CFA franc devaluation as external debt/GDP doubled. US$1258mn treated, of which US$534mn cancelled. Repayment of non-ODA credits over 23 years with six years' grace, after cancellation to a rate of 50%, and ODA credits over 30 years with 12 years' grace.
1995	Naples (50%)	Fully repaid	US$1348mn treated with repayment of non-ODA credits over 23 years with six years, grace, after cancellation to a rate of 50%, and ODA credits over 40 years with 16 years, grace.
1997	Naples (50%)	Fully repaid	New deal in October followed IMF ESAF agreement in August. US$1270mn treated with repayment of non-ODA credits over 23 years with six years, grace, after cancellation to a rate of 50%, and ODA credits over 40 years with 16 years, grace. Treatment of arrears as of September 1997 and maturities falling due between October 1997 and December 2000.
2001	Cologne	Fully repaid	US$1300mn treated, of which US$900mn cancelled and US$400mn rescheduled, with repayment of non-ODA credits over 23 years with six years' grace, after cancellation to a rate of 90%, and ODA credits over 40 years with 16 years' grace. Treatment of arrears as of December. 2000 and maturities falling due between January 2001 and March 2006. Total Paris Club debt of US$5400mn as of June 1999, out of total external debt of US$7800mn.
2006	HIPC initiative exit	Active	US$1829mn treated, of which US$1090mn cancelled and US$739mn rescheduled, with repayment under HIPC exit terms. Treatment of arrears as of March 2006 and stock as of April 2006. Total Paris Club debt of US$4198mn as of April 2006, out of total external debt of US$6200mn.

Source: Paris Club

China is Cameroon's biggest bilateral creditor, accounting for 68% of its bilateral debt. China is also Cameroon's single-biggest creditor overall, accounting for 32% of public (PPG) external debt, twice that of the next single-biggest creditor, the World Bank. In August 2010, the Cameroonian finance minister and the Chinese Ambassador agreed to cancel XAF21mn of Cameroon's debt to China. This was a relatively small amount, given that Chinese debt has risen to XAF1.4tn, as of June 2017. China is supporting a number of projects in Cameroon, such as an agreement in January 2016 for a US$303mn loan to Cameroon to finance the construction of the Bini Hydroelectric dam from the International and Commercial Bank of China.

London Club History and Commercial Debt

Cameroon has undertaken one commercial debt restructuring. This was in May 2002 and took the form of a buyback of London Club debt at a deep discount. Creditors agreed a buyback of commercial bank debt, amounting to US$600mn (including interest arrears), which had been in arrears since 1985. The buyback was financed by the World Bank, under the IDA's Debt Reduction Facility (DRF), and other official bilateral creditors. Creditors were offered 14.5% of the principal amount due (all interest arrears were written off). Principal accounted for US$294mn, implying a reduction in London Club debt of US$557mn. Although precise estimates are unavailable, Exotix believes that the government bought 80% of the London Club debt by the time the deal closed in August 2003. Exotix is not aware of any remaining London Club debt.

Commercial debt agreements

Date	*Details*
2002 May	Buyback at 14.5% of principal amount due of US$600mn (including interest arrears) of commercial bank debt, which had been in arrears since 1985.

Source: World Bank GDF

Under certain loan agreements, creditors have sought recompense through litigation. There were 22 non-participating creditors ("holdouts") when the London Club offer closed, holding US$240mn of claims (including US$78mn in principal). This was c20% of the total debt to private creditors. According to the IMF, five of these creditors pursued litigation to recover the claim in full, including seizure of Cameroonian assets abroad. In 2005, Winslow Bank seized US$50mn of deposits in France held by SNH, the state oil company, following a suit pursued in the French courts. Del Favero was able to freeze the account of the Cameroonian embassy in the UK under a similar action. Negotiations with other creditors at the time was ongoing. Cameroon is said to have offered terms comparable with HIPC, but some commercial creditors were reluctant to accept them, demanding full repayment of principal and costs, although conceding to forgo accrued interest and penalties. In 2009 and again in 2010, the IMF noted in its reports that agreements were finalised with most London Club commercial creditors, whereby the debt stock was reduced to US$1.24mn in 2009. The IMF reported that the authorities had made every effort to settle the remaining amount, but difficulties arose because creditors either did not respond or no longer existed as ongoing commercial entities. As there were 22 syndicated loan agreements with very different terms, there is no standard form of London Club loan.

Cameroon issued its debut (and to date, only) eurobond in November 2015. The 10-year US$750mn bond had a coupon of 9.5%, but was priced to yield 9.767% (the issue price was 98.426). The spread at issue was 743bps. The yield was relatively high—IPT was 9.75%—coming after bond yields across Africa/frontier rose sharply in Q4 because of the impact of the fall in oil prices and general market disruptions. Still, the order book totalled US$1.3bn. The bond includes a EUR500mn partial credit guarantee from the African Development Bank (AfDB) to cover the payment obligations of the Republic of Cameroon related to the cross-currency swaps executed with commercial banks to hedge the proceeds of the USD-denominated Eurobond, although its precise details remain sketchy. Besides the bond, the market occasionally sees trade in bank loans (primary and secondary market), although these tend to be irregular and small in size.

Cameroon bond
Cameroon 9.5% 2025
Bloomberg ticker: REPCAM

Borrower	Republic of Cameroon
Issue date	19 November 2015
Form	Eurobond
ISIN	XS1313779081
Issued amount	US$750mn
Issue price	98.426
Currency	USD
Denomination	US$200,000 and US$1000 thereafter
Amortisation	Amortises in three equal instalments in November of 2023, 2024 and 2025
Final maturity date	19 November 2025
Coupon/interest	9.5% per annum, paid semi-annually May and November
Collateral/guarantor	AfDB partial guarantee for EUR500mn through a cross currency swap to ensure dollar availability for servicing
Day count	30/360
Method of transfer	Euroclear/Clearstream
Settlement period	T + 2
Governing law	English
Listing	Dublin
Joint lead managers	Société Générale, Standard Chartered Bank

Source: Bloomberg

Congo, Republic of

Nominal GDP (US$mn, 2018)[a]		11,460
Population (thousand, 2018)[a]		4456
GDP per capita (USD, 2018)[a]		2572
Credit ratings (long-term foreign currency)[b]	Fitch	CC
	Moody's	Caa2
	S&P	B–

[a]IMF WEO October 2018
[b]As at end-September 2018

Country Summary

- Republic of Congo (Congo Brazzaville), hereon Congo, saw two decades of one-party rule end in the early 1990s only to lead to civil war (1997 and 1998–1999). Sassou Nguesso emerged victorious and has been president since 1997, most recently being re-elected in 2016.
- The economy is dominated by oil, mostly located offshore, accounting for 60% of GDP, 85% of government revenue and 90% of exports. Congo is Sub-Saharan Africa's (SSA) fourth-largest oil producer (behind Nigeria, Angola and Equatorial Guinea). New investment has reversed the production declines seen in the last decade, as old oil fields matured, and production increased further with the coming on stream of the Moho Bilondo offshore block in December 2015. The government targets an increase in production in 2018 to 350,000 barrels per

Exotix Capital, *Exotix Developing Markets Guide*,
https://doi.org/10.1007/978-3-030-05867-8_11

day (bpd) from c300,000bpd currently. Although rich in other natural resources (wood, lead, zinc, uranium, diamonds), other industries are at a nascent stage of development, and infrastructure is poor, after the civil war in the 1990s.

- Congo is in debt distress, less than 10 years after reaching HIPC completion point in January 2010, with public debt now standing at 110% of GDP (IMF WEO projection for 2018). The fall in the oil price during 2014–2016 eroded fiscal and external buffers, and created liquidity problems and a rising debt burden, resulting in the need for IMF financial assistance as part of the CEMAC's wider regional response to the crisis (at the time of writing, Board approval of a programme was still pending), The government also announced in October 2017 its intention to restructure its debt, later confirming its sole international bond would be excluded (at the time of writing, no further details were available). However, the likely participation of China, probably Congo's biggest creditor, could be an important test case of a sovereign debt restructuring in the presence of such a large non-traditional bilateral creditor.

Economic data	*Avg*[a]	*2014*	*2015*	*2016*	*2017 (e)*	*2018 (f)*	*2019 (f)*
Real GDP growth	4.0	6.8	2.6	−2.8	−3.1	2.0	3.7
Inflation (annual average)	3.2	0.9	3.2	3.2	0.5	1.2	2.0
Current account (% of GDP)	−8.5	1.4	−54.1	−73.6	−12.9	9.1	12.4
Reserves (US$mn, end-period)[b]	3901	4994	2291	835	506	417[c]	–
Reserves/imports (months)[d]	6.6	6.0	3.3	1.6	1.2	–	–
Overall fiscal balance (% of GDP)[e]	3.6	−13.6	−24.8	−20.4	−7.6	9.0	10.5
Currency (ticker)	Member of the CFA Franc Zone (XAF)						
FX regime	The CFA franc is pegged to the euro at a rate of CFAF655.957 per euro. The CFA franc floats freely against other currencies.						
Key exports	Oil (90%), timber (5%)						

Source: IMF WEO Database, IMF Country Report, World Bank, Haver, OEC, Exotix

[a]10-year average to 2016 unless otherwise stated

[b]Reserves from BEAC, converted into USD from CFA Franc using EOP exchange rate from Haver

[c]Latest figure, February 2018

[d]Exotix calculation. Imports of goods and services from World Bank WDI database

[e]Overall government net lending

Key figures		*Party*	*Since*
President	Denis Sassou Nguesso	PCT	1997
Prime minister	Clément Mouamba	PCT	2016
Minister of finance and budget	Calixte Nganongo	–	Apr. 2016
Key opposition figure	Guy Brice Kolélas	MCDDI	–
Central bank governor	Abbas Mahamat Tolli (Governor of BEAC)	n/a	Mar. 2017

Politics

Executive power

The 2002 constitution provides for a strong executive president. In 2015 a referendum on a constitution change regarding the length of a presidential term and the age limit, proposed by Sassou Nguesso's PCT party, took place. The age limit of 70 years for candidates was eliminated, the minimum age requirement for candidates fell from 40 to 30 years, the length of presidential terms was reduced from seven to five years and the term limit went up to three terms. The referendum also re-established the post of prime minister as head of government rather than the president.

Presidential term: Five years (three-term limit; consecutive allowed)

Parliamentary term: Five/six years

Legislature

Bicameral, consisting of a 72-seat Senate (upper house) elected every six years by indirect vote and a 151-seat National Assembly (lower house), elected by popular vote to serve five-year terms. The statutory number of members of the National Assembly increased from 139 to 151 following amendments to the electoral law in April 2017, which created new constituencies in several departments.

Senate: 72 seats

National Assembly: 151 seats

Elections

Next due	*Presidential: May 2020*		*Legislative: Senate 2019; Assembly 2022*	
Last legislative election[a] (July 2017[b])		*Seats*	*Last presidential (March 2016)*	*% of vote*
Congolese Labour Party (PCT)		96	Denis Sassou Nguesso (PCT)	60.4
Pan-African Union for Social Democracy (UPADS)		8	Guy Brice Kolélas (MCDDI)	15.1

(*continued*)

(continued)

Elections

Next due	*Presidential: May 2020*	*Legislative: Senate 2019; Assembly 2022*	
Last legislative election[a] *(July 2017*[b]*)*	*Seats*	*Last presidential (March 2016)*	*% of vote*
Congolese Movement for Democracy & Integral Development (MCDDI)	4	Jean-Marie Mokoko (Independent)	13.9
Other	23	Other	11.0
Independents	20		
Total	**151**	**Total**	**100.0**

[a]National Assembly elections
[b]Legislative election held on 16 July 2017, with a second round on 30 July in constituencies where no candidate secured a majority. These are the final results

People

Bantu are the ethnic majority and divide into 15 principal groups. The four major ones are Kongo (48% of the population), Sangha (20%), Teke (15%) and M'Bochi (12%). There is a small population (100,000) of Pygmies. Congo is highly urbanised, one of the most urbanised countries in Africa, with 70% of the population living in urban centres in the southwest, mainly Brazzaville and Pointe-Noire and along the connecting railway. Much of the north, which is covered with rainforest, is virtually uninhabited. Some 66% of the workforce, which is only 40% of the population, works in agriculture. The state is also a significant employer. Around two-thirds of the population still live in poverty.
Congo came under French sovereignty in the 1880s and, as Middle Congo, as it was then known, was one of a group of colonies known collectively as French Equatorial Africa (AEF), which included Gabon, Chad and the Central African Republic. The AEF was dissolved in 1958 and autonomy was granted to the four territories.
After Congo gained independence from France in 1960, a period of instability followed leading to a coup in 1968 and a military government that pursed Marxist-Leninist ideology and imposed one-party rule, which lasted until 1992. Following pressure on the president, an agenda for transition to multiparty democracy was laid out in the National Conference of 1991, leading to presidential elections in August 1992.
A power struggle subsequently ensued between the then democratically elected President Pascal Lissouba, representing the south, and Col. Denis Sassou-Nguesso, a military leader from the north. This took the country into civil war in 1997 and again in 1998–1999, in which some 700,000 were displaced from the south. Sassou-Nguesso, with Angolan backing, emerged victorious over this period (Pascal Lissouba subsequently sought exile in Paris in 2004, where he remains). He has been president since 1997, although it was not until elections in 2002 that his leadership was legitimised. He won virtually unopposed with 89% of the vote. He has won two presidential elections since.
His position was further strengthened with his victory in 2009s presidential election (although the elections were boycotted by the opposition), and the ruling party's success in the 2007 legislative elections, in which it won 90% of seats. The legislative elections were viewed as disorganised and with irregularities. They were boycotted by 40 parties and voter turnout was low. Sassou-Nguesso also won the most recent presidential election in 2016.
A fragile peace agreement was signed in 1999 with most rebel groups and completed in March 2003, since when the country has remained calm.
The Republic of Congo is one of the smaller members of the Central African Economic and Monetary Community (CEMAC), which also comprises Cameroon, the Central African Republic, Chad, Equatorial Guinea and Gabon, being the fifth biggest by GDP (accounting for 10% of the region's GDP) and the fourth biggest by population (9% of the region's population). The Republic of Congo joined OPEC on 22 June 2018.

Debt

	2012	2016
External debt ratios (%)		
Total external debt/GDP	24.9	77.4
Public external debt/GDP	24.9	77.4
Private external debt/GDP	0.0	0.0
Total external debt/exports of goods and services	33.5	151.5
External debt service ratio (public)	1.6	3.5
Public debt ratios (%)		
Public domestic debt/GDP	3.7	37.2
Public debt/GDP	28.6	114.6

Source: BEAC 2016 Annual Report, IMF, World Bank IDS, Exotix

Congo's debt position has deteriorated sharply in the past few years, since the fall in the oil price in 2014, and although it is considered "high" (over 100% of GDP), there is a lack of clarity as to its actual level and composition, with no detailed or up to date figures. According to media reports in August 2017, Congo's total external debt was estimated at CFAF4300bn (cUS$7.7bn), which would have put it at c93% of GDP. China was said to account for c40% of this (CFAF1776bn). The regional central bank (BEAC) has some data on public external debt for 2016 and the World Bank IDS has a creditor breakdown for 2016, although both differ on its amount. The IDS showed public external debt (MLT) at US$3.5bn, while the BEAC data implies public external debt of US$6.25bn. The IMF's last country report was the 2015 Article IV published in September 2015 and the rise in public debt has been well documented since. An IMF statement in October 2017 estimated total public and publicly-guaranteed debt as of end-July 2017 at CFAF5329bn (cUS$9.14bn), 110% of GDP. This figure excluded domestic arrears accumulated since 2014 and debt under litigation. The IMF's October 2017 WEO showed overall public debt at 115% of GDP in 2017, while the April 2018 WEO showed it reaching 119% of GDP in 2017, up slightly from 114.6% of GDP in 2016, and easing slightly to 110% of GDP in 2018. The WEO shows public debt was just 48% of GDP in 2014. However, the IMF's CEMAC regional review shows a higher figure for public debt, putting it at 126.6% of GDP in 2017 in its report published in July 2018, unchanged from 126.5% in 2016, but falling to 110% in 2018. To decompose this into external and domestic debt, BEAC data showed public external debt was 77% of GDP in 2016, which suggests public domestic debt was 37% of GDP, taking the WEO figure for total public debt for that year.

Crucially, the public debt ratio has seen a four-fold increase since 2012 (based on WEO data). The sharp increase since then is due to a rise in the nominal debt burden, due to wider budget deficits, and the fall in nominal GDP (due to lower oil prices). For instance, BEAC data imply public external debt rose by 111% over 2012–2016 in CFA franc terms (and by 80% in USD terms, from US$3.45bn to US$6.25bn), while IMF WEO data show that overall public debt rose by 170% in local currency terms. Meanwhile, nominal GDP fell by 33% in local currency terms (CFA franc), and 42% in USD terms. Both public external and public domestic debt saw similar increases. External debt to exports of goods and services also saw a sharp increase, rising from 34% in 2012 to 152% in 2016, in part due to the 53% fall in export values. Debt service in nominal terms remained low and relatively unchanged, although the DSR ratio also increased due to the fall in the denominator. That said, the debt service ratio remained low due to the extent of concessional borrowing.

The creditor composition of external debt according to IDS data for 2016 is shown below. As noted, this seems markedly to underestimate the true level of debt. Hence, inferences are difficult to draw. It shows most external debt is public medium and long term (PPG MLT) and most of this is owed to bilateral creditors—some 62%, and most of this is on concessional terms. Commercial creditors make up 30% of PPG MLT external debt, with the REPCON 2029 bond representing around one-third of commercial debt. The 2029 bond has amortised even further since then, while disbursements of new external debt have probably been limited (given the emerging debt problems over 2017 will have discouraged new lending from most creditors, with the possible exception of non-traditional bilateral lenders). However, the data may underestimate bilateral debt (in particular, debt owed to China) and it is not clear if the commercial debt figures include the cUS$2bn of debt reportedly owed to oil traders, including Glencore and Trafigura.

Composition of external debt

External debt by creditor (end-2016)	*Nominal amount outstanding (US$mn)*	*Share of total (%)*
Public sector external debt (PPG MLT[a])	**3518.8**	**91.7**
o/w Official multilateral	242.5	6.3
o/w Concessional	202.8	5.3

(*continued*)

(continued)

External debt by creditor (end-2016)	*Nominal amount outstanding (US$mn)*	*Share of total (%)*
Official bilateral	2214.6	57.7
o/w Concessional	2109.1	55.0
Commercial creditors	1061.7	27.7
o/w Bonds	376.7	9.8
Banks	561.3	14.6
Other	123.7	3.2
Private non-guaranteed (PNG)	**0.0**	**0.0**
Short term external debt	**202.4**	**5.3**
Use of IMF credit	**115.6**	**3.0**
Total external debt	**3836.8**	**100.0**

Source: World Bank IDS

[a]Public and publicly guaranteed (PPG) medium and long-term (MLT) debt

Rescheduling History

Congo has historically been something of a serial rescheduler, eventually benefitting from highly indebted poor countries (HIPC) debt reduction after its debt became unsustainable during the 1980s–1990s, and now, a decade on from securing HIPC debt relief, liquidity and solvency problems have returned following the fall in the oil price in 2014. Coupons on its only international bond (which came out of a restructuring of commercial claims under HIPC in 2007) were paid late in 2015–2016 (and again in 2017, when legal action froze the payment at the trustee). With the debt officially becoming unsustainable again (according to the IMF), as the debt burden climbed to 119% of GDP in 2017 (IMF WEO figures) and reserves fell to just two months of import cover by early 2017, the IMF announced in March 2017 that it had initiated discussions with the Congo authorities on a possible IMF programme, as a requirement of the coordinated response to the balance of payments pressure that had surfaced in the region. The government later announced on 5 October 2017 that it would initiate discussions with its "main" creditors in order to reprofile or finance its debt, likely a direct result of the need for an IMF programme, given the Fund cannot lend into an unsustainable situation. The authorities later clarified the territory of its debt restructuring in a statement on 18 April 2018, noting that multilateral creditors and certain commercial debt (the international bond and a domestic CFA issue) would be excluded. Bilateral debt and other commercial debt (eg commodity traders debt) would be included, with potentially far-reaching implications for the modern international financial architecture and the future of sovereign debt restructurings, given the presence of such a large non-traditional bilateral (non-Paris Club) creditor (ie China). No further details were available at the time of writing.

Congo was deemed eligible for debt reduction under the IMF/World Bank HIPC debt relief initiative given its unsustainable debt burden, and reached decision point in March 2006. Public external debt was US$9.2bn (nominal) at end-2004 (213% of GDP, 252% of exports, and debt/revenue an even higher 661%), even after the implementation of Paris Club debt relief that year. As such, Congo qualified under the fiscal window (under which the debt/revenue threshold is 250%). Unusually for a HIPC country, multilateral debt (eg World Bank and African Development Bank) was low, comprising only 12% of the total, reflecting the fact that much of Congo's debt was contracted on commercial terms in the 1970s and 1980s (hence, the PV of its external debt was not that much lower than its nominal amount). This was a period when debt rose sharply to finance domestic investment projects as rising oil production encouraged pro-cyclical fiscal policy. This led to the highest debt burden in Africa by the mid-1990s, peaking at over 250% of GDP, while its debt per capita was one of the highest in the world. The oil boom, however, came to an end with the decline in oil prices in the late 1980s, which prompted a series of reschedulings of both Paris Club and commercial debt before its HIPC treatment.

Progress towards HIPC, however, was slow due to weak policy performance. Congo quickly went off track with its IMF programme, a three-year poverty reduction and growth facility (PRGF) agreed in December 2004 (and due to expire in December 2007). The IMF was able to conclude satisfactorily the first and second reviews of Congo's PRGF, in August 2005 and July 2006, respectively (the second review was delayed due to governance and transparency concerns). However, the third review in October 2006 could not be concluded because of substantial fiscal slippages and delays in structural reforms. The performance criterion on the primary fiscal balance was missed (by 2.7% of GDP) and cumulative spending overruns amounted to 5% of GDP. Congo's PRGF programme was subsequently suspended by the IMF. As part of the process to get the country back on track towards obtaining HIPC debt relief, Congo requested a staff-monitored programme (SMP) for April–September 2007. Satisfactory performance against the SMP was seen as enabling Congo to resume discussions on a (possibly new) PRGF programme. The

IMF's review of the SMP in September 2007 noted that there had been some positive developments, but that slippages had occurred—further fiscal slippages occurred in H1 2007 as well as delays on structural reform—forcing the SMP off-track. The SMP could therefore not be concluded. A new SMP was agreed for H1 2008, under which performance was satisfactory. Yet, even while Congo was off track with its IMF programme over 2006, shortly after it reached HIPC decision point in March of that year, it was—unusually—able to complete a London Club restructuring in December 2007 (it had defaulted on its London Club debt in 1984). This saw debt forgiveness of c80%. HIPC completion point was finally reached in January 2010, with a common reduction factor of 31.1%.

HIPC debt reduction saw a significant reduction in Congo's outstanding public external debt and transformed its debt ratios (at least temporarily). Ministry of Finance figures show that, in nominal terms, debt fell from US$5.7bn at end-2008 to US$1.9bn in June 2010. The biggest contributor to the decline was the fall in debt owed to Paris Club creditors, who agreed a final HIPC exit treatment (and, hence, stock reduction) in March 2010. Paris Club debt fell by US$3.25bn from end-2008 to June 2010. There was also a fall of US$269mn in multilateral debt over this period. As a result, Congo's main external creditors became non-Paris Club bilateral creditors (36% of the total) and commercial creditors (49% of the total). The latter included the eurobond issued in December 2007, which came out of the London Club's agreement to restructure eligible commercial claims on comparability terms. The combination of debt relief and increasing export revenues saw the debt burden restored to a sustainable level. Public external debt fell to 16% of GDP in June 2010 from 53% in 2008, and public debt/exports of goods and services was also very low, at 20% in June 2010, compared with 68% in 2008. With domestic public debt just 4% of GDP in 2010, total public debt was just US$2.4bn in June 2010, just 20% of GDP, compared with US$6.7bn in 2008 (62% of GDP). There was little sizeable financing need expected over the medium term and, thanks to higher oil prices over 2010–2014, Congo was able to accumulate significant foreign reserves (amounting to as much as 40% of GDP in 2012), thus becoming a net external creditor. However, underlying fiscal sustainability—judged by the non-oil primary balance to non-oil GDP (a deficit of at 34% in 2010)—and weak governance illustrate a continued vulnerability to oil prices and production, which was exposed when oil prices fell in 2014, resulting in its current debt problems and calling for another restructuring of part of its debt.

Relations with Multilateral Creditors

Congo's relationship with the IMF/World Bank group was historically defined by the country's HIPC status. After debt reduction was achieved, attention turned to whether the government continued policy and reform orthodoxy, although for most of the immediate post-HIPC period (until 2014), the country built up a sizeable external buffer (reserves and savings), along with low debt, that meant that it didn't need an IMF programme. This may however have contributed to some policy complacency, as revealed by the subsequent oil price crash.

Congo does have a long relationship with the IMF, with a series of programmes through the 1980s and 1990s and eight programmes in all (and ten arrangements altogether if policy monitoring arrangements are included). This relationship was mostly positive although performance weakened in 2006–2007 in the run up to debt relief being granted. As a result, the 2004–2008 PRGF that Congo was under at the time was suspended in 2006 as Congo went off track. Weakness in capacity resulted in uneven performance under this arrangement. This delayed progress towards securing HIPC debt relief. Policy performance eventually got back on track after the country followed SMPs, paving the way for the approval of an ECF (formerly PRGF) arrangement in December 2008. Satisfactory performance under this arrangement led to completion point being approved in January 2010. Congo had no further IMF programmes (and no need for one) for several years after the 2008 ECF expired in 2011.

On 9 March 2017, an IMF mission to conduct the 2017 Article IV announced that it had initiated discussions with the Congo authorities on a possible IMF-supported financial arrangement. The announcement came at the same time as similar announcements were made about possible Fund programmes for other CEMAC members, namely Gabon (28 February) and Cameroon (7 March), and can be seen as part of coordinated regional response to the balance of payments pressure that had surfaced in the region. The response followed IMF Managing Director Christine Lagarde's meetings with CEMAC Heads of State in December 2016, which noted that the Fund stood ready to support the region. Crucially, the response came after the region's foreign currency reserves at BEAC had fallen by 52% in June 2014–May 2016. The IMF statement on 9 March noted that Congo's public debt had increased to 77% of GDP and that the country's imputed international reserves had fallen to two months of imports.

Discussions on an IMF programme for Congo, however, seemingly stalled for a period as IMF staff awaited more information on the debt situation and progress on governance reforms. After media reports in the summer of 2017 that the debt burden was even higher than expected, an IMF technical mission in October 2017 sought to reassess the country's debt, discuss cash management with the authorities, and scope out a diagnostic study on governance issues in the country. The accompanying statement put public and publicly guaranteed debt at 110% of GDP (cUS$9.14bn), rather than the 77% the Fund had reported previously. On 5 October 2017, the government announced that it would initiate discussions with its "main" creditors in order to reprofile or finance its debt, a move that might be viewed as a prior action to any IMF programme given the country's high debt burden. The IMF announced on 20 December 2017, after another staff visit to discuss the authorities' economic programme and possible IMF support, that progress had been made on the formulation of medium-term macroeconomic and structural policies that could be supported by the IMF, and took note of the authorities' planned measures to restore medium-term debt sustainability. The mission welcomed the draft 2018 budget and encouraged the authorities to finalise the appointment of financial and legal advisors to help with the restructuring. Another IMF technical mission was scheduled for the first half of April 2018, with the Fund reportedly seeking more details on what the country owed to bilateral and commercial creditors.

An IMF press statement on 19 April 2018 at the end of the programme negotiation mission stated that staff had reached a broad understanding with the authorities on policies that could be supported by an IMF programme (a three-year programme according to the authorities). The agreement came just over a year after programme discussions had been initiated. The press statement reiterated that debt was unsustainable, but did not provide updated figures for the debt situation. Policy actions in a possible programme include the 2018 budget and the fiscal framework, governance reform (including an asset declaration register for high level officials, an anti-corruption body and stronger oversight of large investment projects and state-owned enterprises, especially the public oil company—SNPC), enhancing transparency in the oil sector and financing assurances from creditors (eg restructuring), although details remain limited. At the timing of writing, the request for a programme had still not gone to the IMF Executive Board although, curiously, a meeting had appeared on the Board schedule a few times, for the end of July/beginning of August 2018, only to be subsequently removed. The timing of the Board is still not certain.

IMF programmes

Date	*Arrangements*	*Comments*
1970s–1990s	Various	1977 SBA, 1979–1980 SBA, 1986–1988 SBA, 1990–1992 SBA, 1994–1995 SBA.
1996–1999	ECF	SDR69.5mn PRGF (now known as ECF) approved in June 1996.
2004–2008	ECF	SDR55.0mn PRGF (now known as ECF) approved in December 2004. Programme was suspended in 2006 before the completion of the third review because of substantial fiscal slippages and delays in structural reforms. Congo moved to an SMP to get back on track.
2007	SMP	April–September 2007. Not completed.
2008	SMP	January–June 2008.
2008–2011	ECF	A three-year ECF arrangement was approved in December 2008 for an amount of SDR8.5mn (US$12.5mn). The programme expired in December 2011. The first review was completed in June 2009, with four waivers. The second review was competed in November 2009 and the third in September 2010.

Source: IMF. Congo joined the IMF in 1963

Paris Club and Bilateral Creditors

Congo has had eight Paris Club agreements, the last of which was the HIPC exit treatment in March 2010, after it reached completion point in January 2010. The agreements have led to various debt reschedulings and, more recently, debt reduction. The 2004 agreement was on Naples terms (67% debt reduction) for maturities between 2004 and 2007. The last phase of the 2006 agreement was not enacted as it was contingent on implementation of the then suspended IMF PRGF arrangement. Congo was able to get back on track with the IMF, which led to the 2008 agreement.

Paris Club agreements

Date	*Terms*	*Status*	*Details*
1986	Classic	Fully repaid	
1990	Classic	Fully repaid	
1994	Houston	Active	Amount treated: US$1.175bn.

(*continued*)

(continued)

Date	*Terms*	*Status*	*Details*
1996	Naples	Active	Amount treated: US$1.758bn; of maturities falling due from July 1996 to June 1999. Repayment of non-ODA credits over 23 years with six years' grace, after cancellation of 67%. ODA credits repaid over 40 years with 16 years grace.
2004	Naples	Active	Amount treated: US$3.016bn (out of total Paris Club debt of US$4.694bn) of which US$1.68bn cancelled and US$1.336bn rescheduled on Naples terms. Maturities falling due between October 2004 and September 2007 treated. Repayment of non-ODA credits over 23 years with six years' grace, after cancellation of 67%. ODA credits repaid over 40 years with 16 years' grace.
2006 Mar.	Cologne	Active	Treated of maturities falling due between March 2006 and September 2007. Cancellation rate of 90%. Agreement was suspended.
2008 Dec.	Cologne	Active	Treatment of arrears as of June 2008, treatment of maturities falling due from July 2008 up to June 2011. Cancellation rate of 90%. Repayment of non-ODA credits over 23 years, with 6 years of grace. Repayment of ODA credits over 40 years with 16 years of grace. US$961mn was treated with US$806mn cancelled and US$155mn rescheduled.
2010 Mar.	HIPC Initiative Exit	Active	US$2.474bn treated, of which US$981mn cancelled and US$1.493bn rescheduled. Creditor nations of the Paris Club also expressed their intention to grant additional debt relief to 100% on a bilateral basis for an amount of US$1.4bn, implying total debt relief of US$2.4bn.

Source: Paris Club

China has become one of Republic of Congo's most significant creditors, and its main bilateral creditor. Congo's bilateral debt to China was CFAF1.4tn (cUS$2.5bn) as of October 2017, according to Reuters citing figures provided in a speech by the prime minister. If correct, that is c25% of Congo's public debt. Since reaching HIPC completion point in January 2010, external debt doubled within four years, notably from large bilateral loan disbursements from China, contracted in 2006–2014. These loans were on concessional terms (20-year maturity, five-year grace period and 0.25% interest rate). By end-2014, China accounted for 90% of all bilateral debt of the Congo, and 64% of all external debt. In May 2017, in one of

China's biggest collaborative projects in Sub-Saharan Africa was announced: a new parliament building in Congo, to be constructed by a Chinese firm over three years. Valued at over CFAF34bn (cUS$58mn), China was expected to fund this project entirely as a gift, hoping to strengthen bilateral ties.

China looks likely to have to participate in Congo's debt restructuring, as one its biggest creditors and biggest bilateral creditor, and its role could pose a challenge to the established world order on sovereign debt restructuring. The inclusion of bilateral debt in Congo's debt restructuring, as signalled in the authorities' statement on 18 April 2018, would strongly suggest China will be involved; as one of its largest creditors (if not the largest), China needs to be part of the solution. But, as at the time of writing, its involvement has not been officially confirmed nor has what such a bilateral restructuring would look like, especially in the context of an IMF programme. The full extent of China's debt, the terms of its lending, and who it was lent by, is not known publicly and will likely require an effort at debt reconciliation as well as coordination within China and with the IMF, while the necessary financing assurances for an IMF programme to be approved will also require a degree of transparency hitherto seldom seen in Chinese bilateral lending. Aside from Russia's treatment of Soviet-era debts, the presence of such a large non-traditional bilateral creditor as China in a sovereign debt restructuring is probably unprecedented in the modern international financial architecture and could prove a test case for future workouts.

Sovereign Commercial Debt

Congo undertook a London Club restructuring of its commercial debt in 2007, as part of its wider HIPC treatment. Unusually, the agreement with London Club commercial creditors occurred before the final implementation of HIPC completion point and Paris Club debt relief.

Congo's London Club debt amounted to US$2.284bn (as at June 2006, based on information in Congo's exchange information memorandum), comprising US$300mn principle and the remainder as past-due interest. The country had been in default on its London Club debt since 1984. BNP Paris was the co-ordinator for Congo's London Club debt. An agreement on commercial bank debt restructuring was reached in 1986, but was never implemented. It would have restructured maturities due over 1986–1988, valued at some US$200mn, repayable over nine years with three years' grace and interest of LIBOR+2.785%, and provided US$60mn in new money. Between 1997 and 2004, little progress was made in the commercial debt negotiations, largely because of the political upheavals.

Congo reached an agreement with its commercial creditors in June 2007 on restructuring its old defaulted London Club debt. Subsequently, the government issued a dollar-denominated eurobond (REPCON) on 7 December 2007 in an exchange for most of the old commercial debt. In the exchange, the government recognised CFAF288bn as eligible debt (US$644mn at the prevailing exchange rate). The size of the bond issue arising out of the exchange was US$477.79mn (5% of the principal was paid in cash immediately on issue). The bond amortised from 2012, maturing on 30 June 2029, with low step-up coupons. The implied debt reduction is officially reported as 80%, although academic estimates suggest it was higher (90.8% in NPV terms, according to the Cruces and Trebesch database) and is said to be consistent with HIPC debt relief. Participation in the exchange was over 92%.

Congo has suffered from a number of late payments on its REPCON bond in the past two years, albeit the causes were for slightly different reasons, but it is now current. The fall in the oil price that began in H2 14, and the lack of policy adjustment, hit the economy hard, eroding the country's fiscal and external buffers, leading to a sharp decline in its imputed reserves at the regional central bank and the accumulation of (mainly domestic) arrears. In fact, three of the last six payments (up to and including the June 2018 payment) on the REPCON bond were paid late: the December 2015 payment was paid in January 2016, but within the 30-day grace period; the June 2016 payment was paid after the 30-day grace period expired; and the June 2017 payment was paid several weeks' late. But, in all cases, bondholders did not accelerate the bonds. The authorities attributed the late June 2016 payment to an administrative error, but two successive late payments looked like the government was running out of money. The late June 2017 payment, however, occurred after the bond's trustee was unexpectedly served with a restraining notice in relation to a long-running legal dispute to prevent payment. In the dispute, the judgment creditor, Commissions Import Export SA ("Commisimpex"), was awarded two default judgements in the US District Court of Columbia for debts owed to it by the Republic of Congo, the judgement debtor. The debts related to public works done in the country by Commisimpex, as a contractor, in the 1980s, which had been unpaid since 1992. Two judgements were granted in 2013 and 2015 for a total amount of US$961mn as per court filings. In order to seek to collect on its default judgements, Commisimpex issued two restraining notices on the trustee of the REPCON bond, the Delaware Trust Company, in June 2017. Thereafter, the trustee submitted a request to vacate the restraining notices, arguing that it neither owed any debt to the Republic of Congo nor possessed any property in which the Republic had an interest. The NY District Court judge lifted the restraining notice on the trustee, which allowed the Republic to satisfy debt payments of cUS$21mn (comprising interest and amortisation) on 29 August 2017 instead of 30 June. However, the non-payment forced the Republic of Congo into selective default. S&P downgraded the country to CCC from B– (with a negative credit watch) on 7 July after the trustee of the REPCON 2029 bonds froze the payment and downgraded again to SD on 1 August. Its rating was subsequently upgraded to CCC+ on 5 September 2017. The other agencies took similar actions. Congo has since been current on its bond, with the two payments since then (December 2017 and June 2018) being made on time.

The government announced on 5 October 2017 that it will initiate discussions with its "main" creditors in order to reprofile or refinance its debt, consistent with its requirements in seeking an IMF programme. It was not clear at the time whether this was intended to include the REPCON bond or not, but the authorities later clarified the territory of its debt restructuring in a statement on 18 April 2018. It noted, guided by international principles, that it will exclude multilateral creditors with preferred creditor status and, taking into account previous forgiveness provided in the HIPC initiative, that the REPCON 2029 bond will also be excluded. It will also exclude the regional CFA bond issued in December 2016 (2021 maturity). Bilateral debt and other commercial debt (eg commodity traders debt) would be included. No further details were available at the time of writing.

Republic of Congo bond
Republic of Congo 6% 2029
Bloomberg ticker: REPCON

Borrower	Republic of Congo
Issue date	7 December 2007
Form	Registered
ISIN	XS0334989000
Issue size	US$477,790,000
Amount outstanding	US$335,886,370 (after June 2018 payment)
Currency	US dollar
Denomination	US$1000 minimum and increments thereof
Amortisation	First amortisation of 5% on the Closing Date. Amortises from December 2012 in 34 semi-annual instalments (after deduction of the first amortisation of 5%): 1–2 1% 3–8 2% 9–26 3% 27–34 4%
Final maturity date	30 June 2029
Coupon/interest	Paid semi-annually, in June and December, beginning 31 December 2007 Step-up, according to semi-annual periods as described below: 1–3 2.5% 4–12 3.0% 13–16 3.5% 17–20 4.0% 21– 6.0%
Day count	30/360
Method of transfer	Euroclear/Clearstream
Settlement period	T + 2 business days
Governing law	State of New York

Source: Bloomberg

Cote d'Ivoire

Nominal GDP (US$mn, 2018)[a]		45,875
Population (thousand, 2018)[a]		25,609
GDP per capita (USD, 2018)[a]		1791
Credit ratings (long-term foreign currency)[b]	Fitch	B+
	Moody's	Ba3
	S&P	NR

[a]IMF WEO October 2018
[b]As at end-September 2018

Country Summary

- Cote d'Ivoire has had a turbulent, and often violent, past, but after the conflict that followed the 2010–11 political crisis, President Ouattara has overseen a period of greater stability. The next presidential election in 2020, in which Ouattara cannot stand because of term limits, will be a key test of the country's political maturity.
- Cote d'Ivoire's economy is mainly based on primary products. It is the world's largest cocoa producer, consistently producing 40% of global output, while oil has also emerged as a significant export, with production running at c60,000 barrels per day. Economic recovery after the political crisis and debt relief helped the country grow by an

Exotix Capital, *Exotix Developing Markets Guide*,
https://doi.org/10.1007/978-3-030-05867-8_12

average of 8.9% over 2012–17, the fourth-fastest rate in the world (on WEO figures). But it still ranks low on the Doing Business survey (139th in 2018 out of 190).

- Cote d'Ivoire's long history of sovereign default, on both its official and commercial debt, seemingly looks behind it. This included most recently 2010–11 when it missed coupon payments on its restructured London Club debt. It is now a post-HIPC country, after reaching completion point in 2012, and returned to the international capital markets soon after, with gross bond issuance over 2014–18 of US$5.8bn. It has remained current on is external debt ever since. Sovereign eurobonds now account for 60% of public external debt, while total public debt has increased from 34% in 2012 to 46% of GDP in 2017.

Economic data	*Avg*[a]	*2014*	*2015*	*2016*	*2017 (e)*	*2018 (f)*	*2019 (f)*
Real GDP growth	4.7	8.8	8.8	8.3	7.8	7.4	7.0
Inflation (annual average)	2.2	0.4	1.2	0.7	0.8	1.7	2.0
Current account (% of GDP)	1.8	1.4	−0.6	−1.1	−4.6	−4.6	−4.2
Reserves (US$bn, end-period)[b]	–	13.0	12.4	10.4	13.0	17.6[c]	–
Reserves/imports (months)[d]	–	4.8	5.0	3.9	4.2	–	–
Overall fiscal balance (% of GDP)[e]	−2.2	−2.2	−2.8	−3.9	−4.2	−3.8	−3.0
Currency (ticker)	Member of the CFA Franc Zone (XOF)						
FX regime	The CFA franc is pegged against the euro at a rate of CFAF655.957 per euro. The CFA franc floats freely against other currencies.						
Key exports	Cocoa and oil historically two main exports, but relative shares have shifted since 2012, with decline in oil and increase in cocoa. Oil was main export over most of 2006–12; cocoa has replaced it since then. Five products (cocoa, petroleum, cashew nuts, gold, rubber) make up three-quarters of goods' exports (2016 data): cocoa (43%), petroleum (13.5%), cashews (8%), gold (7.5%) and rubber (5%). Goods' exports in 2016 were US$11bn.						

Source: IMF WEO Database, IMF country reports, Haver, Bloomberg, OEC, Exotix

[a]10-year avg. to 2016 unless otherwise stated

[b]WAEMU gross official reserves from IMF reports

[c]Latest figure, April 2018

[d]Months of WAEMU imports of GNFS from IMF reports

[e]General government net lending (IMF WEO)

Key figures		*Party*	*Since*
President	Alassane Ouattara	RDR	May 2011[a]
Vice president	Daniel Kablan Duncan[b]	PDCI-RDA	Jan. 2017
Prime minister	Amadou Gon Coulibaly	RDR	Jan. 2017
Minister of economy and finance	Adama Koné	–	Jan. 2016
Main opposition figure	Armand Georges Ouegnin	EDS	Apr. 2017[c]
Central bank governor	Tiémoko Meyliet Koné (Governor of BCEAO)	n/a	Sep. 2011

[a]Alassane Ouattara became president in May 2011 following the disputed run-off elections in November 2010, after which Ouattara and incumbent President Gbagbo had both sworn in parallel governments. Ouattara was re-elected for another five-year presidential term in 2015

[b]Prime minister in 2012–17

[c]Ouegnin headed the new Together for Democracy and Sovereignty (EDS) coalition in April 2017, which united various opposition parties, including the FPI

Politics

Executive power

The president, who is chief of state, has retained a strong executive position with wide powers, being able to appoint the prime minister (head of government), appoint members of the government and submit legislation to government, where approval is often a given. The president is elected by popular vote for a five-year term, renewable once. A second round is required if an absolute majority is not achieved in the first round. A two-term limit for the president was approved in a constitutional referendum in October 2016, along with several other amendments. These included that presidential candidates should have one natural-born Ivorian parent (previously both), removed the age limit of 75 for presidential candidates and created the position of vice president.

Presidential term: Five years (two-term limit; consecutive allowed) **Parliamentary term:** Five years

Legislature

Cote d'Ivoire moved to a bicameral Parliament following a constitutional change approved by a referendum in October 2016. Since November 2016, the National Assembly, is the lower house of the Parliament, the 255 members of which are elected by popular vote to serve a five-year term. The Senate, the upper house, will first sit in 2017 after the first elections in history. The Senate will have 120 seats, of which 80 will be elected and 40 appointed by the president. It was created to represent the regions. The last parliamentary elections were held in December 2016.

Elections

Next due	*Presidential: 2020*	*Legislative: 2021 (tentatively)*	
Last legislative election (Dec. 2016)	*Seats*	*Last presidential (Oct. 2015)*	*% of vote*
Rally of Houphouëtists for Democracy and Peace (RHDP)[a]	167	Alassane Ouattara (Rally of the Republicans, RDR)	83.7
Independents	76	Pascal Affi N'Guessan (Ivorian Popular Front, FPI)	9.3
Ivorian Popular Front (FPI)	3	Kouadio Konan Bertin (Independent)	3.9
Others (UDPCI, UPCI)	9	Other	3.2
Total	**255**	**Total**	**100.0**

[a]Coalition formed in 2005 including the Rally of the Republicans (RDR), the Democratic Party of Côte d'Ivoire (PDCI), the Union for Democracy and Peace in Côte d'Ivoire (UDPCI), the Movement of the Forces of the Future (MFA) and the Union for Ivory Coast (UPCI). The Ivorian Workers' Party (PIT) joined the coalition in 2016

People

Cote d'Ivoire is by far the biggest of the eight countries that make up the West Africa Economic and Monetary Union (WAEMU), which also includes Benin, Burkina Faso, Guinea-Bissau, Mali, Niger, Senegal and Togo, comprising nearly 40% of its GDP and 20% of its population. There are thought to be around 60 ethnic groups living in Cote d'Ivoire, roughly split between five main regions. The Akan dominate East and Central regions, accounting for c40% of Cote d'Ivoire's population. The Krou (South-west) at 12%, Northern and Southern Mandes' located in the West and North-West and at around 10% and 15%, respectively, and the Senofu and Lobi constituting the Gur group around the North and North-East at over 15%. Considerable number of Ghanaians, Burkinabé, Lebanese and French also live in the country. Christians and Muslims are predominant and roughly equal in number. Cote d'Ivoire has had a turbulent, and often violent past. The country fell into civil war in 2002 after ethnic and regional tensions between the mainly Christian South and the mainly Muslim North, and an undercurrent of discontent between Ivorians and non-Ivorians, emerged during the 1990s and the country divided into two. The war came after the country had earned a reputation as one of West Africa's most stable and prosperous nations after its independence from France in 1960 under Felix Houphouet-Boigny (PDCI-RDA) who ruled from independence until his death in 1993. He was succeeded by Henri Bedie (1993–2000), but several years of economic malaise followed, along with corruption and a rise in nationalist sentiment between Ivorians (natural) and Ivoirite (foreign nationals), stirred by politicians. Ahead of elections in 2000, Alassane Ouattara (said to be from Burkina Faso, not Ivory Coast) returned from the US to challenge Bedie, dividing the country while, in December 1999, General Robert Guei led a bloodless coup against President Bedie. The 2000 elections ended in turmoil. Guei instituted a newly ratified constitution with secondary rights for non-Ivorians, who mainly inhabit the north and are Muslim. A puppet Supreme Court disqualified major opposition candidates (including Ouattara) ahead of October's elections and, when polls suggested Laurent Gbagbo of the FPI may win, Guei declared himself victor. Supporters and militia loyal to Gbagbo staged an uprising and Guei fled. Gbagbo was declared president. Fighting broke out between Gbagbo's southern Christian supporters and Ouattara's mostly Muslim followers in the north before leaders accepted the decision. Yet in September 2002, Guei and conspirators launched a three-pronged coup to oust President Gbagbo that proved unsuccessful. Guei was killed and the country divided. The south was controlled by the government (and pro-government militia) and the central, western and north of the country was occupied by rebel forces (becoming the Forces Nouvelles). Overall, some 1.2mn were displaced. A France-brokered peace deal, the Linas Marcoussis Accord (LMA), was signed on 23 January 2003 in Paris between the government and New Force rebels.

(*continued*)

(continued)

People
The situation stabilised by 2003–04, with a government of national reconciliation appointed in March 2003, with Gbagbo as president, supported by the deployment of ECOWAS, French and later UN troops, and the task of disarmament, demobilisation and reintegration (DDR) a precondition for holding new elections. The 2005 Pretoria agreements set a deadline for elections by end-October 2005, with President Gbagbo's mandate extended by the African Union (AU) when it became clear this date would be missed. As the election process stalled, further impetus to the peace process was provided with the creation of the transitional unity government in April 2007 to work towards fresh elections in February 2008. However, this—and subsequent—dates were missed amid repeated delays to the election timetable. The election process itself was logistically challenging, requiring identification records and nearly 6mn voting cards. Conflict returned after disputed elections in November 2010 saw Cote d'Ivoire fall into another political crisis. The long-delayed presidential election finally took place in October 2010, in which President Laurent Gbagbo faced long-time opposition leader Alassane Ouattara. Gbagbo gained 38% of the vote compared with Ouattara's 32%, which forced a second-round run-off on 28 November. In December, the IEC released results showing that Ouattara had won the run-off with c54% of the vote. However, the president of the constitutional council declared the results invalid and announced Gbagbo as the winner. Gbagbo and Ouattara both claimed victory, and the ensuing political crisis led to a short-lived but bloody conflict, which exposed the country's regional and ethnic divisions, a source of the civil war in 2002, but it probably also reflected the reluctance of Gbagbo (who derived most of his support from the south) to give up power to the internationally recognised winner of the election, Ouattara (from the north). After months of negotiation, and regional mediation led by the AU and ECOWAS, and fighting between Gbagbo's militias and security forces and Ouattara's supporters, the conflict ultimately came to a quick conclusion after a military operation began on 4 April, in which Ouattara's forces were backed by an authorised UN force, UN Operations in Cote d'Ivoire (UNOCI), and the French military. Gbagbo was arrested on 11 April and extradited to the International Criminal Court (ICC) in the Hague in November 2011, becoming the first head of state to be taken into the court's custody, where he faced charges of crimes against humanity. The ICC trial began on 28 January 2016. 1500 people are thought to have died during the fighting and 500,000 displaced. Ouattara took office in May 2011 and established a truth and reconciliation commission to investigate human rights violations and to help heal the deep divisions in the country. He was re-elected by a large margin in 2015. Ouattara is not eligible to stand again in the next presidential election, due in 2020, which could prompt concerns over political stability in the run up to, during, and after the election. It has already exposed disagreement on election strategy in the ruling RHDP coalition whereby, despite its alliance, each party has in the past put forward its own presidential candidate. In July 2018, the PDCI of former president Bedie rejected plans to merge with Ouattara's Rally of the Republicans (RDR) before the election and field a single candidate.

Debt

	2012	*2017*
External debt ratios (%)		
Total external debt/GDP	36.3	38.7
Public external debt/GDP	17.5	26.2

(*continued*)

(continued)

	2012	2017
Private external debt/GDP	18.8	12.5
Total external debt/exports of goods and services	75.9	124.2
External debt service ratio	9.8	10.8
Public debt ratios (%)		
Public domestic debt/GDP	16.7	19.4
Public debt/GDP	34.2	45.6

Source: Eurobond prospectuses (2030/48 and 2028 bond issues), IMF

Cote d'Ivoire's public external debt was CFAF5,770bn (US$10.6bn) at end-2017 (26.2% of GDP, as per GDP from the IMF WEO), according to the eurobond prospectus for the 2030/2048 bond issues in March 2018. Just over half (51.5%) of this (some US$5.4bn) was owed to commercial creditors, mainly in the form of eurobonds. At end-2017, Cote d'Ivoire had five sovereign eurobonds outstanding. Of the remaining debt, which was owed to official creditors, 27% was owed to multilaterals (with c45% of this owed to the IMF), and 21% was owed to bilaterals. Nearly all bilateral debt (91%) was owed to non-Paris Club creditors, chiefly China. Indeed, China accounted for 75% of all bilateral debt and 16% of all public external debt. Cote d'Ivoire, however, returned to the market in March 2018 with more eurobond issues (EUR850mn each in two maturities), amounting to cUS$2.1bn (equivalent) altogether. As a result, Exotix adds this to the end-2017 debt stock to give a more representative picture of the overall public external debt and its composition, as of end-March 2018, with other items unchanged from their end-2017 position. This shows that total public external debt rose to US$12.7bn (26.4% of 2018 projected WEO GDP), with eurobonds accounting for nearly 60% of the debt stock and China's share falling to 13%. The creditor composition shown on this adjusted basis is presented below.

Exotix estimates that total external debt at end-2017 was US$15.6bn, c38.7% of GDP, comprising public external debt of US$10.6bn as above (26.2% of GDP) and private external debt of US$5.1bn (12.5% of GDP). Private external debt has been derived from the IMF's 2018 Article IV from June 2018. Total external debt has increased from US$10bn in 2012, although remains largely unchanged as a share of GDP over this period, given nominal GDP's 50% rise (in USD terms). And total external debt would have increased further to an estimated US$18bn in Q1 18 with the 2018 eurobond issuance included (still c37% of 2018 projected WEO

GDP). The composition has, however, changed. Public external debt has increased both in USD terms and as a share of GDP, rising from just US$5bn at end-2012 (after its final HIPC debt relief treatment)—just 17.5% of GDP—to US$10.6bn (26.2% of GDP) in 2017, while private external debt has decreased as a share of GDP (it has remained unchanged in USD terms). Total external debt has increased as a share of exports of goods and services from 76% to 124%. Exports of goods and services, derived from IMF figures, were relatively unchanged over this period (standing at cUS$13bn). Meanwhile, public external debt alone increased from just 37% of exports of goods and services in 2012 to 84% in 2017. The external debt service ratio, based on IMF figures, was c10.8% in 2017 overall, little changed from 2012, and was 5.3% for PPG external debt alone, up from just 1.8% in 2012—due to the increase in commercial debt (bonds).

Exotix estimates total public debt was 45.6% of GDP in 2017, up from 34.2% in 2012. Public domestic debt was cUS$7.8bn (equivalent) in 2017 (c19.4% of GDP), up from US$4.6bn in 2012 (16.7% of GDP), so that total public debt in 2017 stood at US$18.4bn. Since Cote d'Ivoire's completion point under the HIPC initiative in 2012, the government has used the borrowing space provided to finance investment plans, such as large investments in the energy and infrastructure sectors, as well as to access the eurobond market with issues in 2014, 2015, 2017 and 2018 (see Commercial debt section below). Cote d'Ivoire's domestic public debt is denominated in local currency (CFA franc), and is mostly held by regional banks, and includes significant treasury bill issuance. Domestic issuance in WAEMU is now centralised through a separate debt management agency called Agence UMOA-Titres. According to the IMF, Cote d'Ivoire is the main issuer on the regional market, accounting for 28% of outstanding securities in WAEMU.

Composition of external debt

External debt by creditor (Mar. 2018)	*Nominal amount outstanding (US$mn)*	*Share of total (%)*
Public sector external debt[a]	**12,671**	**71.5**
o/w Official multilateral	2900	16.4
IMF	1298	7.3
World Bank	781	4.4
IsDB	287	1.5
BOAD	200	1.1
AfDB	192	1.1

(*continued*)

(continued)

External debt by creditor (Mar. 2018)	*Nominal amount outstanding (US$mn)*	*Share of total (%)*
BADEA	49	0.3
Official bilateral	2230	12.6
Paris Club	208	1.2
France	205	1.1
Non-Paris Club	2022	11.4
China	1714	9.7
Commercial creditors	7540	42.5
Eurobonds[b]	7506	42.3
Private sector external debt[c]	**5063**	**28.5**
Total external debt	**17,733**	**100.0**

Source: Eurobond prospectus (2030/2048 issue, March 2018), IMF, Exotix

[a]All components of public external debt taken from eurobond prospectus as at end-2017, with eurobonds adjusted

[b]End-2017 eurobond stock from eurobond prospectus plus the 2018 issuance

[c]Derived from IMF 2018 Article IV (June 2018)

Rescheduling History

Cote d'Ivoire has had numerous debt treatments and restructurings in the past, on both its official and commercial debt. It has had 12 Paris Club agreements and five commercial restructurings. Its debt problems ultimately led it to being eligible for HIPC debt relief, with completion point finally being reached in June 2012 following numerous delays, after having reached decision point under the original framework in March 1998.

The country's historical debt overhang resulted from excessive borrowing during the 1980s, when lenders were attracted by the booming cocoa and coffee sectors, and relative political stability. The debt burden was exacerbated by the 50% devaluation of the CFA franc in 1994 and peaked in the mid-1990s when it was in excess of 200% of GDP (external debt was US$19.5bn in 1996), with much of the external debt (and even some domestic debt) in arrears. Arrears began accumulating especially from 2000 with the onset of the events that led to civil war in 2002.

Although the country had been seen as eligible for debt relief under the HIPC initiative for some time before, it only reached decision point under the enhanced framework in April 2009 after facing a number of obstacles along the way. Delays were due to continuing arrears to multilateral agencies (notably the World Bank and the African Development Bank—AfDB), the need to establish a track record under an IMF programme and lack of political progress. Arrears to the World Bank Group were cleared in April 2008. Even so, by end-2008, external arrears were nearly 40% of the external debt (the vast bulk was owed to the Paris Club). Arrears to the AfDB were subsequently cleared in early 2009 through a bridge loan provided by a bilateral donor. Cote d'Ivoire used the proceeds of a development policy loan to repay the bridge finance. The IMF confirmed in December 2008 Cote d'Ivoire's eligibility for HIPC assistance, given the actual and expected progress on arrears clearance, and satisfactory performance under its post-conflict financial arrangements. By end-2008, total public debt was estimated at 72% of GDP, of which 35% was in arrears, according to IMF figures. Decision point was approved four months later, by which time external debt (PPG) was estimated by the IMF at US$14.3bn as of end-2007, which was US$12.8bn in NPV terms after assuming the full application of traditional debt relief mechanisms. By end-2009, virtually all of its external arrears had been eliminated.

Still, despite reaching decision point, public external debt remained relatively high and stable in nominal terms, at cCFAF6bn-6.5bn over 2007–09 (equivalent to US$13.3bn at end-2009), which was mostly owed to Paris Club creditors (50% of the total), multilaterals (24%) and commercial creditors (25%). Yet, given steady improvement in GDP and exports, its external debt ratios were improving—raising concerns that the longer it took to reach HIPC decision point, it may no longer qualify for debt relief. Cote d'Ivoire qualified for debt relief under the fiscal window, with a debt (NPV basis)/revenue ratio of 327% after traditional debt relief mechanisms, compared with the HIPC threshold of 250%, while its debt/exports ratio under the HIPC definition was already close to or below the 150% threshold. Cote d'Ivoire's common reduction factor (CRF) at decision point was 23.6%, implying total debt relief in NPV terms across all creditors after traditional debt relief mechanisms of 74.8%. Unusually, the London Club of commercial creditors announced the terms of the deal for the defaulted Brady bonds in September 2009, before completion point, and an exchange offer for the defaulted Brady bonds was finally launched in March 2010. The new 2032 bond was issued in April 2010.

Cote d'Ivoire finally reached HIPC completion point in June 2012, itself delayed by the onset of the 2010–11 political crisis and resulting conflict, although by this time the IMF/World Bank recognised that Cote d'Ivoire had already received 55% of estimated debt relief in its Brady deal (1998), Paris Club restructurings (1998 and 2002) and arrears-clearance operations on concessional terms. The IMF and World Bank announced in June 2012 more than US$4bn in debt relief under HIPC, helping drastically to transform the economy's fortunes.

Relations with Multilateral Creditors

Cote d'Ivoire has a long, and mostly constructive, relationship with the IMF and other multilaterals, with 14 IMF programmes and 18 arrangements overall if other emergency facilities or non-financed monitoring arrangements are included. Most of these were geared towards achieving HIPC debt relief, although the period of political turmoil leading up to—and since—the civil war interrupted progress. Decision point had in fact been reached in 1998, although this was suspended as the country fell into arrears with most creditors, including with multilateral institutions, in the run up to civil war. The World Bank suspended its lending operations in October 2000 due to arrears. By end-2007, arrears to both the World Bank and AfDB were estimated at US$450mn (Cote d'Ivoire was current on payments to the IMF).

A strategy for clearing arrears to multilaterals was central to resuming the HIPC process. Clearance of World Bank arrears was planned in 2007 and those to the AfDB in early 2008. This schedule was missed, however, as Cote d'Ivoire was unable to obtain the necessary bridging finance. Greater progress was made during 2008. Cote d'Ivoire repaid its share (half) of World Bank arrears by end-February 2008. The other half was paid by the World Bank in April 2008 as expected, after it approved an arrears clearance grant for Cote d'Ivoire of US$308mn. Cote d'Ivoire was expected to clear its share (one-third) of AfDB arrears by end-April 2008, with the remaining portion provided by the AfDB through its new fragile states facility. But this was delayed. At end-September 2008, arrears to the AfDB were estimated at CFAF150bn (US$326mn), for which Cote d'Ivoire was trying to secure a loan from western and African banks. AfDB arrears were eventually cleared in early 2009.

After tackling its multilateral arrears and showing a track record of performance under two funded IMF arrangements, the IMF/World Bank finally granted decision point for Cote d'Ivoire in April 2009. At about the same time, the IMF also approved a three-year ECF (formerly PRGF) to support the HIPC process and the government's economic programme, although this later went off track due to the political crisis in 2010 and the arrangement was cancelled. A new ECF was approved in November 2011 to see the country through completion point, which was finally achieved in June 2012. The ECF was initially for three years, but was extended, and finished successfully in December 2015.

Now a post-HIPC country, Cote d'Ivoire remains engaged with the multilaterals and the IMF approved its first post-HIPC programme(s) in December 2016—in fact, this was a parallel three-year ECF and EFF programme, amounting to a combined total of cUS$659mn at the time (75% of quota), which was later augmented to a combined total of US$899mn (100% of quota). Both programmes are due to finish in December 2019. The latest review, the third review of the combined ECF/EFF, was approved in June 2018.

IMF programmes

Date	*Arrangements*	*Comments*
1980s–90s	SBA	Various: 1981–84, 1984–85, 1985–86, 1986–88, 1988–89, 1989–91, 1991–92.
1994–97	ECF	Originally approved as ESAF, later known as a PRGF (now ECF). Performance under this three-year arrangement, which expired in June 1997, was satisfactory.
1998–01	ECF	Originally approved as ESAF in March 1998, later known as a PRGF (now ECF). Cote d'Ivoire met decision point under the original HIPC framework in March 1998. The PRGF agreed in 1998 went off track after the first year.
2001	SMP	SMP agreed for period July–December 2001 to pave way for new PRGF after previous arrangement went off-track.
2002–05	ECF	Formerly known as PRGF. The programme was interrupted in 2002 and expired un-concluded in March 2005.
2007	EPCA	Emergency post-conflict assistance (EPCA) approved in August 2007, a funded programme to support post-conflict recovery and seen as a precursor to a PRGF arrangement, which normally accompanies HIPC candidates. The programme amounted to US$62.2mn and expired at end-December 2007. Performance was broadly satisfactory.
2008	EPCA	Successor post-conflict programme approved in April 2008 designed to continue the efforts that commenced under the initial EPCA-supported programme. It came with an immediate dispersal of US$66.2mn. Performance was broadly satisfactory. The IMF anticipated that a track record of solid performance under the EPCA would pave the way for reaching HIPC decision point, although timing of this was then uncertain. It had been suggested a PRGF might be in place by end-2008.
2009–11	ECF	Formerly known as PRGF. Three-year programme approved in March 2009 for SDR374mn (cUS$566mn), with US$241mn available immediately. Programme designed to support the authorities' economic programme and followed the broadly satisfactory track record of performance under the two EPCA programmes. The first review was completed in November 2009 allowing a further disbursement of US$57mn. Two waivers were granted for non-observance of the performance criteria on the overall fiscal balance and non-accumulation of new external payment arrears. The second review was completed in July 2010. It enabled a further disbursement of US$54mn. Waivers were granted for the non-observance of the same criteria as occurred in the first review. No further reviews were completed because of the onset of the 2010 political crisis and the programme was later cancelled in July 2011. Total disbursements equivalent to SDR230.9mn (US$345.4mn) were made.

(*continued*)

(continued)

Date	*Arrangements*	*Comments*
2011	RCF	The IMF Board approved an immediate US$129mn disbursement (25% of quota) under the rapid credit facility (RCF) in July 2011 in order to support the country's post-crisis recovery. A staff-level agreement on an economic recovery programme that could be supported by the IMF's RCF had been reached in May 2011 after President Ouattara had been sworn in earlier that month. At the same time as approving the RCF, the authorities formally requested the cancellation of the 2009 ECF, which went off track during the country's political crisis. The IMF noted at the time that the authorities expressed their intention to request a new arrangement under the ECF later in 2011 once they were in a position to formulate a medium-term economic programme.
2011–15	ECF	An initial three-year ECF for SDR390.24mn (cUS$615.9mn, 120% of quota) was approved in November 2011 to support key structural and social reforms, including the areas of public financial management, debt management and governance and the coffee and cocoa sector, alongside a national poverty reduction strategy. In June 2014, at the time of the fifth review, the programme was extended from 3 November 2014 to end-December 2014 in order to allow time to complete the last review (sixth review). The sixth review was completed in December 2014 and, at the same time, the IMF Board approved a 12-month extension of the programme and augmented access by SDR130mn (cUS$190mn, 40% of quota), bringing the total size to SDR520mn (160% of quota). The eighth and final review was completed in December 2015, with the IMF noting that economic performance over the course of the programme was impressive and that programme implementation was strong. However, progress on structural reforms was mixed, with only four of the seven structural benchmarks under the eighth review being met while the other three were subject to minor delays, which the authorities were taking steps to address. The full amount was drawn (cUS$722mn).
2016–19	ECF+EFF	A parallel three-year arrangement under both the ECF and the EFF, for a combined total of SDR488mn (cUS$659mn, 75% of quota), was approved in December 2016 to further support Côte d'Ivoire's economic and financial reform programmes. The programmes aimed to achieve a sustainable balance of payments position, inclusive growth, and poverty reduction by investing in infrastructure and priority social projects. It also focused on containing current spending, catalysing official and private financing, and building resilience to future economic shocks. Total access was augmented by SDR162.6mn (US$225mn, 25% of quota) at the conclusion of the first review in June 2017, taking the total size of the two arrangements to SDR650mn (US$899mn, 100% of quota), split as SDR433.6mn under the EFF and US$216.8mn under the ECF. The second review under the combined arrangements was approved in December 2017. The third review under the combined arrangements was approved in June 2018. As of end-June 2018, 55% of the total amount approved had been drawn, comprising SDR240mn of the EFF and SDR120mn of the ECF.

Source: IMF. Cote d'Ivoire joined the IMF in 1963

Paris Club and Bilateral Creditors

Cote d'Ivoire has had 12 Paris Club agreements since the mid-1980s, with the most recent being its final HIPC exit treatment in June 2012.

Paris Club agreements

Date	*Terms*	*Status*	*Details*
1980s	Classic	Fully repaid	Five agreements: 1984, 1985, 1986, 1987 and 1989.
1991	Houston	Active	US$724mn treated.
1994	London	Active	US$1.849bn treated, with ODA credits repaid over 23 years (six years' grace) and non-ODA credits over 30 years (12 years' grace) after cancellation to a rate of 50%.
1998	Lyon	Active	Treatment of US$1.402bn of maturities falling due between April 1998 and March 2001. ODA credits repaid over 40 years (16 years' grace) and non-ODA credits over 23 years (six years' grace) after cancellation to a rate of 80%.
2002	Lyon	Active	Treatment of US$1.822bn out of Paris Club debt of US$4.16bn (NPV basis). Of which, US$911mn was cancelled and US$911mn rescheduled. ODA credits repaid over 40 years (16 years' grace) and non-ODA credits over 23 years (six years' grace) after cancellation to a rate of 80%. Treatment of arrears as of end-March 2002 and maturities falling due between April 2002 and December 2004. Creditors agreed to top up the debt reduction to Cologne terms (90%) when the country reached HIPC decision point. However, the 2002 agreement was not implemented in full due to the onset of the civil war. Rescheduled payments were not made after September 2002.
May 2009	Cologne	Active	Treatment following decision point of US$4.69bn, of which US$845mn cancelled and US$3.845bn rescheduled. Treatment of arrears as of March 2009, treatment of maturities falling due from April 2009 to March 2012. Repayment of non-ODA credits over 23 years with six years' grace, ODA credits over 40 years with 16 years' grace. On an exceptional basis, creditors also agreed to defer the repayment of arrears on post-cut-off date debts, maturities falling due during the consolidation period under the post-cut-off date debts and moratorium interest due during the consolidation period on rescheduled and deferred amounts. The repayment of post-cut-off date debt and deferred payments becomes due from April 2012.

(*continued*)

(continued)

Date	*Terms*	*Status*	*Details*
Nov 2011	Cologne	Active	Creditors agreed to alleviate the external public debt of the Republic of Cote d'Ivoire, following the IMF's approval of a new three-year ECF. Participating creditors also agreed on an exceptional basis to defer and reschedule over a 10-year period the repayment of maturities on short-term and post-cut-off date debts and over an eight-year period the arrears on those claims. Interest due on the amounts treated were deferred. Debt service due between 1 July 2011 and 30 June 2014 was reduced by more than 78%, corresponding to US$1,822mn, of which US$$397mn was cancelled.
June 2012	HIPC Initiative exit	Active	Paris Club creditors agreed to cancel US$1,772mn under the HIPC initiative. Paris Club creditors also confirmed their willingness to provide additional debt relief on a bilateral basis. These efforts led to a 99.5% reduction in the debt owed to Paris Club creditors.

Source: Paris Club

Sovereign Commercial Debt

Cote d'Ivoire has had two major restructurings of its commercial debt in the past 20 years, consisting of a Brady deal in 1998 and a restructuring of its by then defaulted Brady bonds in 2010. Prior to this, Cote d'Ivoire saw three bank debt restructurings in the 1980s which ultimately resulted in an agreement in May 1997 with its London Club creditors on a Brady deal. However, the Brady bonds quickly went into default following the then conflict. It took a long time, given persistent delays in the HIPC process, but the defaulted Brady bonds were finally restructured in another London Club bond exchange in March 2010. The authorities paid the first coupon on the 2032 bond that came out of the exchange in June 2010, but the bond subsequently went into default following the 2010 disputed election and ensuing conflict in early 2011. The 31 December 2010 coupon, which amounted to US$29mn, was missed and was not paid in the 30-day grace period. However, bondholders did not accelerate and the resolution of the conflict soon led to a repayment plan for the missed coupons. Cote d'Ivoire has remained current on the bond ever since, and even returned to the market in 2014 for its debut eurobond issue. It has issued regularly ever since, in both USD and EUR denominations.

Cote d'Ivoire's Brady deal closed in March 1998. Eligible claims (principal and past-due interest—PDI) amounting to US$6.5bn were restructured into three Brady bonds (each in two currencies, the US dollar and French franc). The deal involved a 62.8% haircut in NPV terms according to the Cruces and Trebesch database. However, the Brady bonds soon went into default. Payments ceased in 2000 after the military regime in 1999 announced that external debt payments had been stopped in order to pay civil servants' salaries. At first it was unclear whether this temporary suspension was applicable to Brady bonds or to debt owed to bilateral creditors—in fact, it applied to Paris Club debt in the short term and London Club debt in the medium term. In April 2000, a US$20mn interest payment on the front-loaded interest reduction bonds (FLIRBs) was missed on due date, just days after scrambling to find funds to pay a modest amortisation on the PDI bonds. By September, Cote d'Ivoire was said to be in default on coupon payments on its FLIRBs and discounts and on coupons and principal of the PDI bonds (the authorities subsequently recognised September 2000 as the default date on its Brady bonds). A creditors' steering committee was formed and a handful of meetings were held with Ivorian officials. The steering committee was expected to hold a formal meeting in October 2002, but the resumption in political violence intervened and no further meetings were held. Interest arrears on the Brady bonds accumulated over the next 10 years. The authorities did, however, sign a tolling agreement on 24 March 2006 to recognise all amounts due under the existing Brady bonds and waive the statute of limitations.

After years of inactivity, talks on a restructuring of the Brady bonds, and other private sector claims, gained momentum in 2008. Crucially, none of the Brady bonds contained collective action clauses or CACs (their issuance pre-dated their general inclusion in NY law bonds) and they were issued under a fiscal agency agreement, so that a comprehensive solution required a good faith approach on all sides. Several months of behind-the-scenes discussions resulted in the private creditors coordinating committee (London Club), chaired by BNP Paribas, being announced on 8 October 2008. The government was advised by Lazard Frères and its legal advisers were Cleary Gottlieb Steen & Hamilton LLP. But it was not until the IMF confirmed Cote d'Ivoire's eligibility for HIPC debt relief in December 2008, and subsequently published its preliminary HIPC document in January 2009, that the broad parameters of Cote d'Ivoire's debt treatment were officially defined. This finally gave greater clarity over what the official sector would demand in terms of comparability of treatment, although, in the run up to this announcement, there had been fervent market speculation over what a potential deal might look like, which drove secondary market trading in the defaulted bonds. The chairman of the London Club creditors committee subsequently shed further light on the terms in a Reuters interview on 26 August 2009. The main highlights were that the debt would be most likely rescheduled over 20 years, there might only be one or two instruments and that it might be possible to reach an agreement before year-end.

The London Club finally announced the terms for an exchange of the defaulted Brady bonds on 28 September 2009 and an exchange offer for them was launched on 15 March 2010. The exchange offer closed on 16 April 2010. The terms of the London Club deal were as follows. Holders of the defaulted Brady bonds would be invited to exchange their bonds for a single new amortising USD-denominated bond with a step-up coupon. There were six eligible bonds consisting of discount bonds due 2028 denominated in both US dollars and French francs, FLIRBs due 2018 denominated in both US dollars and French francs, and PDI bonds due 2018 denominated in both US dollars and French francs. The new bond would have a 23-year term (maturing in 2032) and a six-year grace period on principal. The new bond also included a 75% CAC and was under New York law. There had been some prior market discussion over whether there would be one or two bonds, in different currencies, but creditor feedback pointed towards one single USD bond so as not to fragment the issue and reduce liquidity in the bond. Crucially, September's London Club announcement also confirmed the accrued unpaid interest on the defaulted bonds. The full claim was recognised, amounting to US$3.1bn. However, the deal also involved a 20% discount on the exchangeable debt (total claim). This was despite the IMF, in its preliminary HIPC document, acknowledging previous debt reduction delivered by London Club creditors and that the common reduction factor itself suggested there was no need for any additional debt relief beyond that already implied in the Brady deal (ie no further debt reduction—or topping up—was seen as necessary). The discount came as a late development and was largely for presentational purposes. In any case, creditors were able to claw back this discount in NPV terms through the new bond's faster step-up coupon. The deal involved a 55.2% haircut in NPV terms according to the Cruces and Trebesch database. The London Club announcement in September also said the exchange would take place no later than 31 March 2010 and, in any case, interest would accrue from 31 December 2009 (so creditors had some protection from delays). In the event, Cote d'Ivoire's political crisis in February 2010 pushed back the date of the exchange offer, albeit by just a few weeks. The new 2032 bond, when it was finally issued in April 2010, had a nominal amount outstanding of US$2.3bn. The first coupon was paid on 30 June 2010. The second coupon was not paid because of the ensuing political crisis that followed the disputed result of the presidential election run-off in November 2010. Therefore, in over 12 years, following the Brady deal in 1998, Cote d'Ivoire had only made five coupon payment dates.

Cote d'Ivoire missed three payments on its restructured 2032 bond in total because of the political crisis that followed the disputed 2010 election. The coupon due on 31 December 2010 was not paid on time and subsequently was not paid at the end of the 30-day grace period (31 January 2011). The coupon amounted to some US$29.15mn (the coupon rate was 2.5% on principal of US$2.332bn). Despite reports at the time that the central bank had sufficient funds, there was a problem with the authorisation within the Ministry of Finance given there were, at this stage, two competing governments. Payment problems continued after the resolution of the political crisis in April 2011, given the resulting dislocation in the economy. The next two coupon payments went unpaid, those due on 30 June 2011 and 31 December 2011. Exotix calculates that the total missed coupons amounted to cUS$87.5mn, excluding late interest and penalties.

Cote d'Ivoire eventually repaid the interest arrears on its 2032 bond after seeking the requisite support to approve a new repayment schedule through consent solicitation. The authorities announced on 14 June 2012 that they would resume contractual coupon payments that month and, in a gesture of goodwill, make a payment equal to 2.4% of the total coupon arrears. Holders were paid the US$43.728mn due on 30 June and a good faith payment of US$2.099mn, with payments being made on 2 July. On 5 July 2012, the authorities announced that they will make a reimbursement proposal on the remaining coupon arrears consistent with its repayment capacity, which would be assessed in an IMF mission scheduled for September. Investor meetings were held in October and consent solicitation seeking to approve a revised calendar for the unpaid interest payments and waive any event of default associated with the rescheduled interest payments was launched on 18 October. It also allowed the issuance of additional bonds of the same series in exchange for certain of the Republic's other existing bonds. At the same time, the government announced that an agreement in principle had been reached on claims held by Sphynx creditors and Standard Bank. The consent solicitation, which received 85.5% support (well above the required 75%), expired on 6 November. The revised calendar, presented on 12 November, allowed for repayment of the remaining missed coupons over a two-year period (December 2012–December 2014) on a semi-annual basis (ie in five payments), with repayments in the form of additional payments to scheduled coupon payments over this period. A first payment of US$10,477,664 was made on 31 December 2012 (which amounted to US$4.49 per US$1000 of principal) and, of the remaining balance, 40% was repaid in two equal amounts in 2013 (each payment being US$6.75 per US$1000 of principal) and 60% was repaid in two equal amounts in 2014 (each payment being US$10.12 per US$1000 of principal).

On 13 November 2012, the government also announced the issuance of an additional amount of US$186.755mn of 2032 bonds in respect of settlement of the claims held by Sphynx creditors and Standard Bank. The government had invited creditors of its other commercial debts to confirm their positions, a few days after the terms of the London Club deal were presented in September 2009, in order to facilitate restructuring proposals for these instruments. They included the Sphynx 10.25% 2007–10, Sphynx 10% 2008–11 and BNI securitisations. Restructuring of the Sphynx deals in particular on comparable terms, as required under HIPC, was seen by market participants as more contentious given their origin and that they were CFA franc issues sold initially to local investors. The official sector, however, insisted that the debts were external and were therefore caught up in the debt reduction initiative. Creditors eventually accepted a debt reduction of 74.8% in NPV terms, consistent with Paris Club comparability, according to government figures. As a result of the settlement for its other commercial debt, the aggregate principal amount of the 2032 bonds increased from US$2332.149mn to US$2518.904mn.

Commercial debt agreements

Date	*Details*
1985	Bank debt restructurings. The last agreement was suspended because interest arrears were not cleared.
1986	Bank debt restructurings. The last agreement was suspended because interest arrears were not cleared.
1988	Bank debt restructurings. The last agreement was suspended because interest arrears were not cleared.

(*continued*)

(continued)

Date	*Details*
1998 Mar.	Brady deal. US$6.5bn of principal and PDI was restructured. Eligible principal amounted to US$2.3bn, with US$4.2bn in PDI. The deal was structured as follows: For principal claims, amounting to US$2.272bn, creditors agreed to: 1. exchange US$159mn for discount bonds (DISC) at a 50% discount; 2. exchange US$1.431bn for FLIRBs; 3. buyback US$682mn at 24 cents per dollar. The total amount of principal written off was US$597mn. The new bonds had collateral. Principal was collateralised with a 30-year US zero coupon Treasury bond for the discount bonds, but not for the FLIRBs. A six-month rolling interest guarantee (RIG) was required for the FLIRBs, but not for the discount bonds. For past-due interest, amounting to US$4.19bn, US$30mn was settled in cash, US$867mn was exchanged for a 20-year amortising bonds (with six months' grace) and US$3.293bn was written off. There was no collateral on the PDIs for either principal or interest Different figures circulate regarding the size of the NPV haircut in the Brady deal. Reports around the time give a haircut of 77%, while market estimates were c80% or more. The IMF reported a NPV haircut of 75.86% in its preliminary HIPC document published in January 2009. The NPV haircut was 62.8% according to the Cruces and Trebesch database.
2010 Mar.	Exchange offer opened for the defaulted Brady bonds. The offer closed on 16 April 2010. A total claim of US$3.1bn was exchanged for a new amortising bond with step-up coupon maturing in 2032. The exchange involved a 20% discount on exchangeable debt. The size of the new bond was cUS$2.3bn. The NPV haircut was 55.2%, according to the Cruces and Trebesch database.
2012 Nov.	Agreement on revised schedule for the repayment of the missed coupons on the 2032 bond following the 31 December 2010 coupon default. Three missed coupons to be repaid over a two-year period (December 2012–December 2014) on a semi-annual basis after consent solicitation was approved by 85.5% of bondholders. The repayments amounted to some US$89mn in total.

Source: Exotix, World Bank GDF

Cote d'Ivoire now has seven sovereign eurobonds outstanding (excluding Brady bonds), denominated in both USD and EUR, with all but one having been issued since 2014. Just three years after its 2010–11 default on the restructured 2032s, and after having spent most of the preceding 15 years in default, a revitalised Cote d'Ivoire under President Ouattara returned to the bond market in July 2014 with a new 10-year sovereign eurobond issue. The US$750mn 2024 bullet bond had a coupon of 5.375%. It was priced to yield 5.625% (issue price 98.108) with a spread of 308.9 bps. The offer was over six times oversubscribed with an order book reported at US$4.75bn.

Cote d'Ivoire has subsequently returned to the market three more times. It issued a US$1bn 2028 bond in March 2015. The bond had a coupon of 6.375% and was priced to yield 6.625% (issue price 97.955). The bond amortises annually in equal amounts over its last three years. In June 2017, it came with a dual tranche USD and EUR issue, a US$1.25bn long 15-year (2033) bond and a EUR625mn eight-year (2025) bond (cUS$700mn equivalent). The USD bond amortises annually in equal amounts over its last three years with a coupon of 6.125% and was priced to yield 6.25% (issue price 98.747). The EUR bullet bond was priced at par with a coupon of 5.125%.

At the same time, a tender offer was launched for the cash purchase of up to US$250mn of the 2024s, which saw its size reduced to US$500mn, and up to US$500mn of the 2032s, which is now down to US$1.97bn (after amortisations and the tender). Cote d'Ivoire's most recent issuance came in March 2018 with another dual tranche offer, although both were EUR-denominated this time around, with a EUR850mn 12-year bond (2030 maturity) and a EUR850mn 30-year bond (2048 maturity), cUS$1.05bn equivalent each (so cUS$2.1bn in total). Both bonds amortise annually in equal amounts over the last three years and were issued at par. The combined order book had totalled EUR4.8bn before final guidance of 5.375% plus or minus 12.5 bps and 6.75% plus or minus 12.5 bps, respectively, was given and finished at EUR4.2bn (two and a half times oversubscribed), split evenly between the two tranches, with final pricing at the tighter end of the pricing guidance at 5.25% and 6.625%, respectively, both well inside initial pricing guidance.

As a result of this issuance and liability management operations, Cote d'Ivoire's outstanding stock of eurobonds stood at US$7.5bn (equivalent) at end-Q1, and, excluding the restructured 2032 bond, gross issuance over the four-year period 2014–18 was US$5.8bn.

Cote d'Ivoire's outstanding eurobonds are summarised in the table below and details of the 2032 bond are also given.

Cote d'Ivoire's outstanding eurobonds[a]

Description	*Amount issued*	*Amount outstanding*	*Maturity type*	*Issue date*
USD 5.375% due 2024	US$750mn	US$500mn[b]	Bullet	Jul. 2014
EUR 5.125% due 2025	EUR625mn	EUR625mn	Bullet	Jun. 2017
USD 6.375% due 2028	US$1000mn	US$1000mn	Sinkable	Mar. 2015
EUR 5.25% due 2030	EUR850mn	EUR850mn	Sinkable	Mar. 2018

(*continued*)

(continued)

Description	*Amount issued*	*Amount outstanding*	*Maturity type*	*Issue date*
USD 5.75% due 2032	US$2,519mn[c]	US$1,969mn[d]	Call/sink	Apr. 2010
USD 6.125% due 2033	US$1,250mn	US$1,250mn	Sinkable	Jun. 2017
EUR 6.625% due 2048	EUR850mn	EUR850mn	Sinkable	Mar. 2018

Source: Bloomberg

[a]Excludes residual amounts of defaulted Brady bonds
[b]A tender offer in June 2017 for the 2024 bond reduced its size by US$250mn
[c]Original issue size was US$2332mn, which was increased to US$2519mn after Sphynx settlement in October 2012
[d]A tender offer in June 2017 for the 2032 bond reduced its size by US$500mn

Cote d'Ivoire bond
Cote d'Ivoire 5.75% 2032
Bloomberg ticker: IVYCST

Borrower	Republic of Cote d'Ivoire	
Restructuring	Issued in exchange for defaulted Brady bonds	
Issue date	16 April 2010	
Form	Eurobond	
ISIN	XS0496488395	
Issued amount	US$2332.149mn (increased to US$2519.048mn)	
Amount outstanding	US$1968.668mn	
Currency	US dollar	
Denomination	US$100,000 and US$1000 thereafter	
Amortisation	34 semi-annual instalments commencing 30 June 2016:	
	Instalment	*% of original principal amount*
	1–2	1.00%
	3	1.50%
	4–6	2.00%
	7–12	2.50%
	13–22	3.00%
	23–26	3.50%
	27–28	3.75%
	29–34	4.00%
Maturity date	31 December 2032	
Coupon/interest	Step up, paid semi-annually June and December	
	To 31/12/2011	2.50%
	To 31/12/2012	3.75%
	To 31/12/2032	5.75%
Day count	30/360	

(*continued*)

(continued)

Cote d'Ivoire bond *Cote d'Ivoire 5.75% 2032* *Bloomberg ticker: IVYCST*	
Method of transfer	Euroclear/Clearstream
Settlement period	T + 2
Governing law	New York
Exchange	Berlin, EuroNext-Paris, Frankfurt, Luxembourg, Stuttgart
Joint lead managers	BNP Paribas, JP Morgan, Deutsche Bank, Natixis, Standard Chartered
Governing law	New York law

Source: Bloomberg

Cuba

Nominal GDP (US$mn, 2017)[a]		93,204
Population (thousand, 2017)[a]		11,466
GDP per capita (USD, 2017)[b]		8129
Credit ratings (long-term foreign currency)[c]	Fitch	NR
	Moody's	Caa2
	S&P	NR

[a]UN estimates
[b]Exotix calculation
[c]As at end-September 2018

Country Summary

- Fifty-nine years of Castro rule came to an end in 2018. Raul Castro, who formally took over from Fidel Castro in February 2008, stepped down as president after elections for the National Assembly on 11 March 2018. Former First Vice President Miguel Diaz-Canel succeeded Raul, but the latter will remain influential as leader of the Communist Party until at least 2021, reducing doubts over future political stability, policy and the direction of international relations, while at the same time not presaging significant economic and political change either.
- A process of rapprochement between the US and Cuba, which began in November 2014, has largely stalled under President Trump.

Exotix Capital, *Exotix Developing Markets Guide*,
https://doi.org/10.1007/978-3-030-05867-8_13

President Obama eased a number of sanctions, raising optimism over Cuba's investment potential, but the Trump administration has re-imposed various restrictions. The US's 1962 trade embargo remains intact. Meanwhile, a process of economic liberalisation begun under Raul has been disappointing so far and the economy has struggled recently in the wake of lower commodity prices, the Venezuela crisis and hurricanes.

- Cuba stopped servicing bank debt and bilateral claims of western governments in 1986 after announcing a moratorium, but has started to acknowledge and restructure various bilateral debts. Cuba agreed to restructure its Paris Club debt in 2015, although there has been little progress on restructuring its commercial (London Club) debt.

Economic data	*Avg*[a]	*2014*	*2015*	*2016*	*2017 (e)*	*2018 (f)*	*2019 (f)*
Real GDP growth	2.2	1.0	4.4	−0.9	1.6	1.8	2.1
Inflation (annual average)[b]	5.2	5.3	4.6	4.5	5.5	6.9	4.8
Current account (% of GDP)	2.7	3.9	2.2	2.8	2.7	2.2	2.2
Reserves (US$mn, end-period)[c]	10,783	11,103	11,803	12,003	11,353	11,553	11,003
Reserves/ imports (months)[d]	10.4	10.2	12.1	14.0	12.4	12.1	11.1
Overall fiscal balance (% of GDP)	−3.7	−2.0	−6.0	−6.9	−10.5	−10.1	−7.7
Currency (ticker)	Dual: Cuban peso (CUP), Cuban convertible peso (CUC)						

(*continued*)

(continued)

Economic data	*Avg*[a]	*2014*	*2015*	*2016*	*2017 (e)*	*2018 (f)*	*2019 (f)*
FX regime	The CUC is for international transactions (incl. tourism), and forms the official exchange rate (fixed at CUC1 per US$1). The CUP is for domestic transactions only (CUP24 per US$1). There are various rates between the two currencies, the two main ones being the official CUP1:CUC1 in the state sector, and an unofficial CUP24:CUC1 used for personal transactions and in the non-state sector. Some other sectors use rates of CUP10:CUC1 or CUP11:CUC1. The government announced its intention to unify the two currencies in 2013, eliminating the CUC, but no timing for this has been given. The dual currency system makes economic measurement difficult and inaccurate.						
Key exports	Minerals (mostly nickel) (28%), sugar (27%), tobacco (15%). Goods exports in 2016 were US$3.6bn. Services exports were US$11.4bn (2015), with tourism (US$1.2bn in 2016) a significant source of income.						

Source: Cuba Office for National Statistics (ONE), Economist Intelligence Unit (EIU), Exotix. Real GDP, inflation and fiscal balance: historicals from ONE, figures for 2012–19 from EIU Country Reports (latest February 2018)

[a]Seven-year avg. to 2016 unless otherwise stated
[b]Five-year avg. only
[c]Net international reserves, five-year avg. only
[d]In months of imports of goods only

Key figures		*Party*	*Since*
President of the councils of state and ministers	Miguel Diaz-Canel Bermudez	PCC	Apr. 2018
First Secretary of the Politburo and Communist Party	Raúl Castro	PCC	Apr. 2018[a]
First vice president of the councils of state and ministers	Salvador Valdés Mesa	PCC	Feb. 2013
Minister of economy and planning	Ricardo Cabrisas Ruíz	PCC	Jul. 2016
Minister of finance and prices	Lina Olinda Pedraza Rodríguez	PCC	Mar. 2009
Central bank governor	Irma Martinez Castrillon	–	Jun. 2017

[a]Raul Castro formally became president in February 2008. He had assumed power on a temporary basis on 31 July 2006, after his brother President Fidel Castro stepped aside due to ill health. At the time, Raul, was first vice president of the council of state. Fidel Castro remained first secretary of the politburo of the central committee of the Communist Party of Cuba (PCC; ie communist party leader) until April 2011. In April 2018, Raul stepped down as president, but he remains in control of the PCC

Politics

Executive power

The president is both chief of state and head of government, although the Council of Ministers (cabinet) is vested with a shared executive power. The first vice president is the de factor prime minister. Under the constitution, the National Assembly is responsible for law-making but, under the communist regime, is effectively directed by the executive. Appointments to the Council of Ministers are recommended by the Politburo, although the majority of ministers are not on the Politburo, and approved by the Assembly; effectively deciding Council members before their legislative election.
The president is appointed by the Assembly. Elections for the national and provincial assemblies are held every five years and the last one took place on 11 March 2018. Members of the National Assembly in turn selected the president when that body met on 19 April. Raul Castro, who formally became President on 24 February 2008 after being elected unanimously by the National Assembly as President of the Council of State (thus, Head of State) and Council of Ministers (thus, Head of Government) after Fidel stepped down, did not seek a third term in 2018, and he was succeeded by Vice President Miguel Diaz-Canel. Raul Castro will remain influential as leader of the Communist Party until the next party congress in 2021.

Presidential term: Officially, five years (no limits)

Parliamentary term: Officially, five years

Legislature

Unicameral, the 605-member (based on population) National Assembly of People's Power, whose members are elected by absolute majority vote to serve five-year terms. Under Cuba's one-party system, the PCC is the only legal political party. In theory, candidates do not have to be members of the PCC (independents are permitted), but all are vetted by the Candidacy Commission before being listed, to consider their worthiness as Cuban citizens (effectively, whether their actions are those of an ardent socialist, or not). In practice, this produces PCC candidates or those in favour of the PCC regime who are often unchallenged when going to popular poll, although voter turnout remains high. There is a 31-member Council of State that rules in the Assembly's place when not in session. Many members hail from the Council of Ministers, including all senior roles, such as the president and vice presidents. This body is elected by assembly members, although the president and vice presidents are permanent appointments.

Elections

Next legislative election: May 2023.
Last legislative election: 11 March 2018. The PCC unsurprisingly won all seats.

People

64% of the population is white, 27% mixed race (Mulatto) and 9% black. Unlike other communist countries, religion is not banned and Christianity is predominant, mostly Roman Catholic. The population has been ageing rapidly, as a result of improving health care and net outward migration. Only around one-quarter of the workforce is employed by the private sector (especially tourism). Unemployment is fairly low, at the cost of a high state wage bill.
Before the Cuban revolution, the country was dominated by Fulgencio (General) Batista, who ruled for 17 years over a 25-year period. He came to power in a coup in 1933 and ruled until 1944, seizing power again in 1952 after a period of civilian rule. The US maintained significant influence, although its military aid was withdrawn by 1958. After a failed coup in 1953 and a return to Cuba from exile in 1956, Fidel Castro finally took control of the country after the Cuban Revolution in 1959. US businesses were nationalised in 1960 without recompense. In 1961, the US-sponsored Bay of Pigs invasion failed. Castro declared Cuba a communist state in December and allied it with the USSR. The US imposed a trade embargo on Cuba. In 1972, Cuba became a member of the Soviet-based Council for Mutual Economic Assistance (COMECON, or CMEA).
1990–94 was known as the "Special Period". It marked the decline of the Cuban economy following the collapse of the USSR, which destroyed Cuba's export markets and ended the massive Soviet subsidies to Cuba. Severe austerity measures were implemented and market reforms were undertaken in 1993 in order to try and stem the deterioration of the economy, including the legalisation of the US dollar and transformation of many state-owned farms to semi-autonomous co-operatives as well as limited private enterprise. The US Congress passed the Helms-Burton Act in 1996 and permitted food and agricultural exports to Cuba in 2000. In 2004, the Bush administration in the US tightened the embargo relating to remittances and travel restrictions, although these were subsequently relaxed for Cuban-Americans under the Obama administration in April 2009.
Fifty years of rule by Fidel Castro came to an end in 2006 with the handing over of power to his younger brother Raul Castro due to illness, which was formalised in February 2008. The transition from Fidel to Raul was smooth, and marked a watershed in leadership style and personality; but came as a disappointment to those observers who hoped it would expose a vacuum and cause the regime to collapse. The regime's focus, especially under Raul, was on gradual economic, rather than political, reform aimed at producing a better-functioning state model. After Raul took over, a number of measures were announced, especially over the course of 2008, which aimed to reform and liberalise certain areas of the economy and reduce state subsidies. Reform announcements picked up again after the global financial crisis, although implementation has been slow. For instance, the government announced in September 2010 that it would lay-off half a million state workers while opening new opportunities for citizens to start private businesses as the leadership attempts to overhaul the ailing economy. Nearly 60 years of Castro family rule finally ended in April 2018 following elections to the National Assembly in March. Raul, having said in advance that he would step down, was replaced as president by Miguel Diaz-Canel, Raul's first vice president. The economy has struggled in recent years. Real growth slowed sharply in 2016, and the economy entered recession in 2016–17, according to some forecasts, suffering from the low commodity prices, the ongoing crisis in its main trading partner, Venezuela, the tightening of economic sanctions US President Trump, and the impact of Hurricane Irma in September 2017. Tourism, and strong performances by agriculture and construction, have helped to support growth.

Debt

	2012e	*2016e*
External debt ratios (%)		
Total external debt/GDP	79.2	33.2
Public external debt/GDP	79.2	33.2
Private external debt/GDP	n/a	n/a
Total external debt/exports of goods and services	310.6	222.4
External debt service ratio[a]	n/a	n/a
Public debt ratios (%)		
Public domestic debt/GDP	n/a	n/a
Public debt/GDP[b]	n/a	43.5

Source: Office for National Statistics (ONE), UN, EIU, Exotix

[a]There are no figures on debt service payments, and Cuba remains on default on its commercial debt
[b]Net public debt (EIU estimate)

There are no official up-to-date and comprehensive external debt figures, either published by Cuba or multilateral agencies. Cuba's Office for National Statistics (ONE) does publish external debt figures for what it calls its active (new) debt, although its most recent figures are only up to 2014. Active debt is debt issued since the banking reforms of the mid-1990s and which Cuba says it has remained current on (although strictly, this may not have always been the case). However, Cuba's figures exclude its old defaulted debt (what Cuba has called "immobilised" debt) so understates the true debt position, although the full extent of defaulted debt is not publicly known. It is also not clear if Cuba's own figures include other previous restructurings, mainly bilateral, and if so, on what basis. Hence, Exotix attempts to estimate the debt position by combining the ONE figures, rolling them over to 2016, with other estimates, to try to provide a more realistic current view. Exotix estimated creditor composition is shown in the table below. The figures are only illustrative.

Exotix estimates Cuba's total external debt at US$30.5bn in 2016, c33% of GDP (dollar GDP based on UN ECLAC figures)—this relates to public sector debt only, as there is no private external debt as far as Exotix is aware. Cuba's ONE figures showed external public debt of US$15.2bn in 2014. Most of this was owed to official creditors (cUS$11bn), but it is unclear what this includes (one might assume it includes Venezuela and China, even if this has been restructured), while banks and suppliers were owed a further

US$2.1bn each. The figures showed that most of the debt (83%) was MLT debt, with the remainder being short term, and most of the MLT debt (82%) was owed to official creditors. Some 65% of the bank debt was MLT while 60% of supplier debt was short term. The figures showed that external public debt had increased by US$2.7bn since 2012, from US$12.5bn, mainly due to a US$3.5bn increase in official debt (mainly MLT) while bank debt and suppliers fell. However, the active debt ignores defaulted debt. Until 2015, this would have included defaulted Paris Club debt and commercial debt (including London Club), but the 2015 agreement with the Paris Club's Group of Creditors of Cuba should mean that the restructured amount should be consolidated into ONE's figures going forward. Paris Club figures showed that its debt to Cuba was US$35.1bn in 2012, falling to US$5.8bn in 2016. London Club debt is cEUR1bn (principal). Exotix assumes London Club debt in 2016 was cUS$6.4bn (equivalent) in claim (principal, interest and penalties, on a compound basis), based on figures previously released by creditors in 2015. There might be other defaulted commercial debt (based on figures provided by research from The Association for the Study of the Cuban Economy [ASCE]). On a comparable basis, Exotix therefore estimates that Cuba's external debt was US$58bn in 2012, comprising active debt of US$12.5bn and cUS$45bn in defaulted debt (Paris Club and London Club), amounting overall to 79% of GDP.

Hence, on the surface, Cuba's debt/GDP ratio does not suggest insolvency problems, as they appear to be below standard thresholds; although Cuba is clearly in debt distress because of debt still in default and persistent repayment problems. On official figures, Cuba's active debt is only 17.3% of GDP, and this increases only to 33% when including its defaulted or newly restructured debt. But there are some grounds for being cautious over drawing conclusions from these figures.

First, the numerator (debt) in these ratios may be understated for the reasons mentioned above.

Second, the figure for GDP may be overstated or in dispute given methodological differences (although the World Bank and UN ECLAC appear to have accepted Cuba's GDP revisions). Moreover, GDP and other variables have been converted at the overvalued official CUC exchange rate. The debt burden (as a share of GDP) would be much higher at a significantly more depreciated exchange rate.

Third, the debt situation looks much worse relative to FX earnings. As a share of goods' exports, Cuba's debt is very high, estimated at 1200% in 2016, up from 980% in 2012, based on ONE export figures. These showed that Cuba's goods' exports more than halved over this period, falling from US$5.9bn in 2012 to US$2.5bn in 2016. However, Cuba's services exports have become a much more significant revenue earner (especially tourism), such that services exports only fell slightly according to ONE figures, from US$12.8bn in 2012 to US$11.1bn in 2016. As a result, as a share of exports of goods and services, Cuba's external debt fell from 311% in 2012 to 222% in 2016. This excludes remittances which are also an important source of FX inflows.

Fourth, there are no official figures for debt service payments, and historically, Cuba has only paid a small amount of its overall debt because it was in default on most of it. And even on its active debt, it has not been clear what debt Cuba has paid. However, debt service payments may have gone up since 2015 (other things equal), due to repayments under new bilateral agreements, especially with the Paris Club repayment agreement under which payments resumed in 2016.

Composition of external debt

External debt by creditor (end-2016e)	*Nominal amount outstanding (US$bn)*	*Share of total (%)*
Public sector external debt	**30.466**	**100.0**
o/w Active debt[a]	15.229	50.0
Official creditors	10.998	36.1
Bank debt	2.119	7.0
Suppliers	2.112	6.9
o/w Restructured and defaulted ("immobilised") debt[b]	15.237	50.0
Paris Club[c]	5.811	19.1
London Club (claim)[d]	6.426	21.1
Other commercial debt[e]	3.000	9.8
Private sector external debt[f]	**n/a**	**n/a**
Total external debt	**30.466**	**100.0**

Source: Cuba Office for National Statistics (ONE), BIS, Paris Club, ASCE, Exotix

[a]Figures from ONE for 2014

[b]Exotix estimates

[c]Paris Club figure

[d]Exotix estimate of claim

[e]Exotix estimate of face value derived from ASCE figures

[f]Exotix is not aware of any privately issued external debt

Rescheduling History

Until recently, Cuba's payment experience has been (at best) chequered ever since it announced a moratorium on its external debts to commercial banks and western governments in 1986. The 1986 payments moratorium was declared by the Banco Nacional de Cuba (BNC), then Cuba's central bank and also a commercial bank, and covered debt contracted by the state and BNC. Cuba's external debt was mainly contracted in the late 1970s and early 1980s as it began to finance development projects with loans from non-US western banks. This was complemented by aid and subsidies from the USSR. However, as interest rates in the developed world increased in the early 1980s, Cuba was unable to service its debts to the banks, estimated at US$3.5bn. Various attempts at reschedulings with the Paris Club and commercial creditors followed, culminating in the 1986 debt moratorium. Part of this debt was rescheduled although most remained in default and, under Decree Law Number 172 of 1997, is required to be managed by BNC. Cuba contended that Banco Central de Cuba (BCC), the 'new' central bank, was not responsible for this debt. It has been Cuba's policy to segregate completely the old defaulted debt from debt incurred since the moratorium (ie 'new' debt). Since 2010, Cuba has incrementally acknowledged and successfully restructured on favourable terms, large stocks of defaulted or previously unrecognised debt. Bilateral deals have been struck (notably with Russia, Mexico and Japan) and Cuba has been able to secure new money, although it is not entirely clear this has been done on commercial terms. Most prominently, this led to a bilateral debt agreement with a subset of Paris Club creditors in 2015 although, to date, there has been little progress on restructuring its London Club or other commercial debt, despite the efforts of the London Club to do so.

Cuba has, however, been able to access new financing on a limited basis. Given the long-standing default to (mainly) Western creditors (bilateral and commercial), and the presence of US sanctions, Cuba turned mainly to non-Paris Club bilaterals such as China and Venezuela for new credit, and some non-Western commercial creditors. Cuba's access to multilateral debt is also very low, since US sanctions prevent Cuban membership of many international organisations.

Still, Cuba's payment experience remains patchy. Although Cuba has stated categorically that it had not defaulted on any new debt, Exotix thinks this is debateable. Cuba reports that BCC has never defaulted on any debt incurred by it and, since 1994, when the banking system was restructured, that no other Cuban commercial bank has defaulted on any of its domestic or external borrowings. Notwithstanding the fact that Cuba saw a period of a seemingly improving track record on debt repayment, at least on new loans, in 2004–08, there were still persistent suggestions of failed, or at least delayed, trade finance transactions and, after the global financial crisis hit, further defaults were reported during 2009 and 2010; even new borrowing either went into default or payments were deferred. But the situation reportedly improved at least for some trade finance creditors. Although the extent to which payments may have resumed is not clear, Exotix understands that Cuba is making selective payments, with repayment rationed and dependent on priorities. Repayment of trade finance also prioritises creditors who continue to discount letters of credit.

Relations with Multilateral Creditors

Cuba is not a member of the Bretton Woods institutions (the IMF and World Bank), and membership is prevented by US sanctions. A US trade embargo has existed since the 1960s, administered by OFAC, and remains largely in place today, despite the rapprochement seen under Obama, which led to some easing in certain restrictions, although some of these have been reversed under Trump. Economic sanctions were tightened by the Helms Burton Act in 1996 and preclude Cuba while under a Castro regime from membership of—and thereby receiving financing from—international financial organisations in which the US is a member. To date, even with the change in the Cuban leadership in April 2018, this situation has not changed.

Cuba has recently seen more engagement with other multilateral development agencies. In September 2016, the Andean Development Corporation (CAF) signed its first agreement with Cuba to establish a joint working agenda, aiming to boost Cuban economic and social development, and work towards Cuba potentially becoming a shareholder with the CAF. In April 2017, Cuba was accepted as an extra-regional partner of the Central American Bank for Economic Integration (CABEI), which became the first multilateral to accept Cuba as a member, and making it eligible for financing, especially for infrastructure projects. Following the recent Paris Club agreement, access to other bilateral creditors may improve, and Cuba may have options to join the CDB or IADB, although future US-Cuba relations may determine progress. From the start of November 2017, Cuba entered into the Political Dialogue and Cooperation Agreement with the EU, aiming to promote dialogue, trade and sustainable development.

Paris Club and Bilateral Creditors

Cuba was in default to most of the Paris Club since 1986 until it reached an agreement with its bilateral creditors in December 2015. Four rescheduling agreements were reached in the early 1980s although no official deal was concluded. Talks between the Cuban authorities and the Inter Creditor Group (an informal gathering of Paris Club creditors) had been on and off since the default. Official talks were reported to have stopped in 1989, resuming on an informal basis in 1995. Talks resumed again in 2000–01, but were subsequently broken off, reportedly as the Cubans refused to provide basic data, such as the country's FX reserves. Exotix believes that, while some reconciliation of loans took place, there were no substantive negotiations with the Paris Club from 2001 until around 2014.

Instead of a comprehensive deal, Cuba pursued bilateral deals with some governments and export credit agencies with some success, picking off creditors one by one, and thereby weakening their collective bargaining position. Bilateral agreements had been reported with several creditors over the years, although it is thought these mainly related to short-term debt. This is despite the Paris Club common position that demands all its creditor members are treated equally. Maintaining this unified position became increasingly difficult as each creditor sought its own deal. Agreements with Cuba were also often on the basis that Cuba will service bilateral debts in return for provision of new credit, therefore requiring creditors to maintain exposure levels, which was unacceptable to some creditors. Medium-term export cover was, however, available on a case-by-case basis, reflecting individual circumstances.

Most notably, since around 2010, Cuba restructured official debts on a bilateral basis with Japan, Russia, China and Mexico. China restructured US$6bn in debt in 2010. This covered both official and commercial debt, with principal deferred until 2015. A settlement with Japan came in 2012 as it forgave 80% of its debt of US$1.4bn, with the remainder to be repaid over 20 years. Russia agreed in October 2013 to write off 90% of its US$32bn debt. Media reports suggested this consisted of US$20bn in principal. The agreement saw Cuba repay the remaining US$3.2bn over 10 years. The first payment was due in October 2014. It is not known if this payment was made. Also in 2013, Mexico forgave 70% of its US$478mn owed by Cuba, with Cuba agreeing to repay US$146mn over 10 years. This appeared to be a re-restructuring after an original US$400mn restructuring agreement was reached in 2008.

Prior to this, a number of bilateral deals were seen in the 2000s. The German export credit agency (Hermes) is believed to have reached a bilateral deal to settle Cuba's DEM240mn debt to the former GDR and, as a result, resumed guarantees in the summer of 2001. Details of the agreement were not made public. Agreements with France and Spain were signed during 2000, although it is believed that these agreements were not put into effect. Similarly, an agreement with Italy was not implemented. It is understood that arrears to Spain and Italy continued to mount and their provision of trade cover was suspended for some time. The UK agreed a memorandum of understanding with Cuba in 1999. A better-known bilateral rescheduling was the agreement with Japanese commercial creditors in April 1998. This agreement, which restructured US$769mn equivalent of debts over 20 years with a five-year grace period, facilitated increased bilateral trade. Cuba started defaulting on this agreement in October 2002, but appeared to be current, although late on payments as of end-04. The details of this debt rescheduling are outlined below.

A "Paris Club" deal finally, and unexpectedly, came in late 2015. Representatives of the Group of Creditors of Cuba, under the guise of the Paris Club, announced on 12 December 2015 that it had met with the Cuban government and agreed to waive US$8.5bn of Cuba's total outstanding stock of Paris Club debt of US$11.1bn, including late interest, due as of 31 October 2015, with a plan to clear the remaining US$2.6bn in arrears over an 18-year period. The remainder was repayable annually on 31 October each year, with no grace period on principal, so that repayment commenced in October 2016, amounting to 1.6% of the rescheduled debt, rising to 8.9% in 2033 (the full path was not provided). In addition to the write-off, repayments were kept low over the first five years, matching Cuba's limited debt service capacity. There was five years' grace on interest, with interest on the rescheduled debt fixed at 1.5% per annum. Past due interest and penalties were forgiven. A large part will be converted into development assistance funds, which strengthen diplomatic ties and often come with private equity opportunities on the island. In October 2016, the first payment for US$40mn was made (paid five days early, confirmed by the French ambassador to Cuba) and the second payment for US$60mn was made in October 2017 (paid 14 days early). The deal implied a nominal debt reduction of 76.6%, on Exotix's calculations, although the lack of details casts uncertainty over this figure.

The Paris Club deal, however, is not officially called a Paris Club deal; in fact, the Paris Club goes to great lengths to say it is not a Paris Club deal (thus, it is a non-Paris Club Paris Club deal, if you will). The agreement saw 14 Paris Club members participate (out of 19 bilateral creditors). The US did not participate, hence the reluctance of the Paris Club to call it a Paris Club deal. The Group of Creditors of Cuba includes Australia, Austria, Belgium, Canada, Denmark, Finland, France, Italy, Japan, the Netherlands, Spain, Sweden, Switzerland and the UK. The government representatives also described progress made towards the normalisation of relations with creditors and the international community. The clearance of arrears is an important step towards normalising relations. The Paris Club deal came at a similar time to the EU removing sanctions against development assistance to Cuba. In April 2016, the UK agreed a restructuring of Cuba's medium- and long-term debt. Cuba will now pay US$82.5mn in principal and interest between 2016 and 2033, in return for the UK forgiving US$183mn in late interest. Any missed payment (45-day grace period) will see a sharp increase in interest from the agreed 1.5% to 9%. Meanwhile, France, Cuba's main bilateral Paris Club creditor, is involved in the renovation of Cuba's largest airport. The French Development Agency (AFD) opened an office in Cuba in October 2016 to boost cooperation. Various agreements have been signed in recent years between France and Cuba for economic and tourism development. The AFD signed its first credit agreement with Cuba in November 2017, worth EUR25mn, for a project to support livestock development. France, Spain, Japan and Italy were Cuba's main bilateral creditors as of December 2015.

Russia agreed a deal with Cuba over its outstanding COMECON-era debts in 2013. US$32bn was owed to Russia, from immobilised debt to the former Soviet Union, although Cuba had not previously included it in its debt figures, on the grounds that it was in overvalued convertible rubles and that the country had endured damage following the Soviet Union's collapse as various contracts were broken. A deal was agreed between Cuba and Russia over outstanding debt in March 2013 and signed in October 2013, reportedly without the knowledge of other Paris Club members. Russia forgave 90% of the US$32bn (reported US$20bn of principal) owed, with 10 years to repay the remaining amount.

Paris Club agreements

Date	*Terms*	*Status*	*Details*
1983	Classic	Fully repaid	Cut-off date 1 September 1982. US$426mn consolidated.
1984	Classic	Fully repaid	Cut-off date 1 September 1982. US$204mn consolidated.
1985	Classic	Active	Cut-off date 1 September 1982. US$156mn consolidated.
1986	Classic	Active	Cut-off date 1 September 1982. Amount not available.
Dec. 2015	–	Active	Rescheduling agreement with the Group of Creditors of Cuba (the deal was signed in early-2016). Of the US$11.1bn outstanding stock owed to the Group, US$8.5 was forgiven with the remainder to be repaid over 18 years to 2033. No grace period on principal, with repayments commencing in October 2016. Fixed 1.5% interest starts after the first five years. The first payment of US$40mn was received early in October 2016, and the second instalment of US$60mn was received early in October 2017.

Source: World Bank GDF, Paris Club, Exotix

Non-Paris Club bilateral lending was the greatest source of new financing for Cuba during the 2000s and the early part of this decade. Cuba maintained strong relations with Venezuela under President Hugo Chavez, and his successor Nicolas Maduro, becoming key bilateral partners. An economic pact between the two countries since 2000 grew in significance, and became worth billions of dollars a year to the Cuban economy. Central to this relationship was a trade arrangement under which Venezuela provided petroleum products to Cuba on preferential terms, supplying nearly 100,000 barrels of oil per day, which Cuba paid for partly through the export of Cuban doctors and medical services to Venezuela. However, Venezuela failed to meet these arrangements after oil prices fell sharply from mid-2014 and trade between the two countries fell by c70% between mid-2014 and mid-2017, reflected in Cuban overall export growth of –15% and import growth of –7% in 2016.

China has become Cuba's second-biggest trading partner, after Venezuela, and probably its biggest creditor, having provided billions in loans in recent years. Indeed, Chinese lending to Cuba dates back at least until 2004, when China agreed a US$400mn loan, according to media reports. But even China has been forced to restructure its Cuban debt, according to a Reuters report. US$6bn of official and commercial debt was restructured with China in 2010. Restructuring agreements reached during 2010 were said to have covered both government and commercial debts, with principal repayments deferred until after 2015 and repayments on soft terms (not given). China had reportedly (as had other creditors) been frustrated by late payments and repeated requests for rescheduling, although it agreed to provide new credit.

Cuba remains subject to US sanctions, codified in various pieces of legislation, notably including the Cuban Liberty and Democratic Solidarity (Libertad) Act (1996), also known as Helms Burton, OFAC sanctions, and other Executive Orders. The surprise US-Cuba rapprochement announced on 17 December 2014 by Obama saw a gradual easing in certain sanctions. This included an easing in US travel and banking restrictions. Cuba was also removed from the US list as a state sponsor of terrorism in May 2015 after a State Department review. Diplomatic relations were re-established on 20 July 2015 with the reopening of the US embassy in Havana. Indeed, President Obama had already begun to loosen travel and other restrictions in 2009, including family travel, remittances and gifts, as well as authorising expanded telecommunication services between the two countries. Further measures to ease travel and other restrictions were announced in 2011. A US congressional delegation even visited Cuba in 2012 to discuss bilateral relations. Further amendments to sanctions' regulations were announced on 26 January 2016. But, even by then, most Americans could still not travel to and trade freely with Cuba. However, the easing of sanctions was reversed by Trump after his election in October 2016, including US tourism restrictions. The thawing in the rapprochement, and subsequently, the alleged sonic attacks on the US embassy in Havana, which led to the removal of the majority of US staff, has led to a worsening of US-Cuba relations.

Sovereign Commercial Debt

US investors should be aware that US-owned and -domiciled entities are under OFAC restrictions regarding trading and holdings of Cuban debt.

Cuba has been in default on most of its (old) commercial debt since the 1980s. At the same time as Cuba reached various Paris Club agreements in the 1980s, it also reached agreements on rescheduling its bank debt. These agreements dated in December 1983, December 1984 and July 1985, each on similar terms, and rescheduled just US$0.1bn of maturities over two-year periods and maintained short-term credit lines (US$0.5bn). A moratorium was, however, placed on bank debt in 1986. There have been no payments since.

The precise principal amount of Cuba's outstanding commercial debt is unclear. Its commercial debt consists of restructured medium- and short-term Credit Lyonnais loans as well as other unrestructured debt and old Letters of Credit. The Credit Lyonnais loans have historically been the only tradable debt, their origins relating to Western syndicated bank loans from the 1960s and 1970s that have been in default since 1986, and it is these that currently form the basis of Cuba's London Club debt (Cuba's Tokyo Club debt is separate). London Club debt covered four medium-term (DEM, JPY, CHF and CAD) and short-term loans for which Exotix has details; there are likely to be other loans, particularly short term. Exotix estimates that Cuba's London Club debt (Credit Lyonnais loans) amounts in total to cEUR1.15bn (equivalent) face, cUS$1.3bn, comprising EUR452mn in medium-term and EUR695mn in short-term loans (at prevailing exchange rates). However, total commercial debt could be much higher, due to other unrestructured debt and LCs, although Exotix understands Cuba may have bought back some of this paper over time. The total claim is higher still. Default interest has been accruing for nearly 30 years. By end-2018, Exotix estimates that PDI on the medium-term DEM loans averaged c176% of principal on a simple basis with no penalty interest, and 204% on a simple basis with penalty. PDI is significantly higher on a compound basis, rising to 480–660% of principal without and with penalty, respectively. PDI is slightly lower on medium-term CHF loans. PDI is much lower on short-term loans. Hence, total claim (on medium-term DEM loans, simple interest basis) was nearly 300%.

There has been very little progress on resolving the London Club debt, and most of the effort has come from the creditor side. A small group of creditors formed a creditor committee in early 2015 to be ready to negotiate a restructuring of Cuba's London Club debt, when the time came. According to a Reuters report on 8 April 2015, the committee consisted of three funds reportedly holding almost 50% of the commercial debt. The committee later submitted a restructuring proposal to Cuba in January 2018 that involved very significant debt relief, according to reports from CNBC and Reuters, by which time the committee was reported to have grown with the addition of a commercial bank and represented at least 50% of the commercial debt. The committee retained Cleary Gottlieb Steen & Hamilton LLP as its legal adviser. The committee's formation came at a time of growing excitement over the possible opening up of Cuba to foreign investors, following the rapprochement under Obama, while the committee's efforts picked up after the Paris Club agreement in December 2015. The restructuring proposal was sent shortly before the Cuban National Assembly elections and change of leadership, and was intended to be open for a limited period of time. According to the committee, as per reports in April 2015, Cuba owed commercial creditors at least EUR1bn (equivalent) in principal and EUR5bn in PDI, presumably on a compound basis with penalty interest, implying a total claim of EUR6bn. This implied PDI of 500%. Although the details of the offer were not released, the creditors claimed their offer was even more generous than that agreed by the Paris Club, with longer repayment times and the future possibility of converting debt into equity investments. However, there has been little indication that a comprehensive restructuring of Cuba's London Club debt is a priority for the regime. There were signs that some of this non-performing debt has—in the past and over time—been renegotiated. Cuba has pursued bilateral negotiations with some commercial creditors, on a case-by-case basis, although often these agreements are tied to the provision of new credits in exchange for the servicing of interest and gradual debt reduction and are never implemented. Subsequently, it was reported on 4 April 2018 that the government failed to respond to the restructuring proposal and the offer was withdrawn.

Meanwhile, Cuba, through the BCC, has sought to secure new money on an ad hoc basis. The BCC issued three bonds in the 2000s: a EUR400mn 7% one-year bond on 30 March 2006 that was repaid in full on maturity on 14 February 2007; a EUR150mn 9% and a EUR50mn 8.5%, both two-year bonds issued on 3 May 2007 and maturing on 3 May 2009. Both bonds were listed on the London Stock Exchange. Although the issues allowed Cuba to access international credit—a prior transaction was the Humming Bird deal in October 2005—Exotix believes the bonds were tightly placed among certain creditors. It is likely Venezuelan banks bought much of these issues and, as such, pricing did not reflect adequately country risk. Details are hard to come by, but Exotix understands that Cuba paid the interest on the 9% 2009 bond and that, upon its maturity, holders were offered a new bond. Creditors accepting the new bond were paid one-third of the principal in cash and two-thirds in the new short-maturity bond. It is not clear what happened to creditors who did not accept the new bond. Exotix understands that the interest on the new bond was also paid and that holders were again offered another bond at its maturity. It is not clear what happened to creditors who did not accept this new bond either.

A number of Cuban state-owned entities and banks have been accessing short-term trade-finance facilities from European and other international banks since the mid-2000s, generally at double-digit yields, although the payment experience has varied over time and by borrower. Until the global financial crisis, such borrowing was to the tune of cUS$1bn per annum, although it has fallen since then. It seems that these credits were paid promptly on due dates for some time and there were no reports of defaults—supporting Cuba's assertion that there were no defaults on its new debts—although Exotix believes the payment experience deteriorated sharply in 2009, as the global financial crisis hit Cuba hard following the fall in export earnings (export revenue fell by 20% in 2009), lower nickel prices and lower tourism revenue. Availability of financing became restricted and portions of the performing debt were said to have gone into default. Even new borrowing, and trade finance paper, either went into default in 2009 and 2010 or payments were deferred. But it probably also was a result of Cuba simply over-extending itself in previous years as it took advantage of new, and more abundant, sources of credit. Some of the commercial debt could have been restructured, although there are few details. The situation deteriorated again after 2014, with the fall in commodity prices and Venezuela's economic crisis. Moreover, Exotix understands that, since the Paris Club agreement in December 2015, new trade finance paper has suffered from payment delays as the government seemingly prioritises on repaying its Paris Club commitments. However, the situation still varies, according to the borrowing entity. Banco Financiero Internacional (BFI), regarded by observers as the strongest Cuban bank, has not seen any payment delays as far as Exotix is aware, while other well-regarded banks have not seen delays of more than a week. Banks such as BNC and BICSA have reportedly seen delays of up to six months.

Cuba-Tokyo 1998 Refinancing Agreement

The Republic of Cuba and various Japanese institutions agreed a refinancing whereby Cuba's obligations were restructured into two tranches. This restructuring was a watershed for Cuba's relationship with foreign creditors, even though negotiations were secretive and final terms remained uncertain throughout 1998. International creditors became optimistic that this would herald further restructurings. However, hopes were dashed when it became clear this pact was motivated by Havana's desire to secure new money from Tokyo and was highly politicised. The LTPR coupon fixing occurs three months before the start of the interest period and so far (as far as Exotix knows) all interest is current, although it is often paid 10 to 14 days late. The Japanese are very secretive over terms, but Exotix believes the original terms were amended in 2003 and repayments of interest and principal reduced further to levels detailed below.

Cuba "Tokyo Club" debt
Tranche 1
First rescheduling agreement

Issuer	Banco Nacional de Cuba
Restructuring date	March 1998, effective April 1998
Form	Bilateral loan agreements incorporating the term of memorandum between Japan-Cuba Economic Conference and Banco Nacional de Cuba, dated January 23, 1998
Amount outstanding	Approximately JPY50bn
Currency	JPY
Maturity	1 October 2012
Amortisation	20 equal semi-annual instalments commencing April 1, 2003.
Coupon	LTPR + 0.9% (LTPR capped at 6.5%), 1% of principal amortising semi-annually (April 1 and October 1), the balance is capitalised into Tranche 2. Subsequently amended to LPTR + 0.2%, with 0.5% of principal amortising semi-annually.
Method of transfer	By assignment to another Japanese resident company only. It is still not clear whether Banco Nacional de Cuba will consent to assignment to non-resident Japanese or non-Japanese entities.

Cuba "Tokyo Club" debt
Tranche 2
Second rescheduling agreement

Issuer	Banco Nacional de Cuba
restructuring date	March 1998
Form	Bilateral loan agreements incorporating the term of Memorandum between Japan-Cuba Economic Conference and Banco Nacional de Cuba, dated January 23, 1998
Amount outstanding	Approximately JPY50bn
Currency	JPY
Maturity	1 October 2017
Amortisation	20 equal semi-annual instalments commencing April 1, 2003
Coupon	LTPR + 0.9% (LTPR capped at 6.5%), margin to be reviewed by mutual agreement every five years. Subsequently amended to LPTR + 0.2%, with 0.5% of principal amortising semi-annually.
Method of transfer	By assignment to another Japanese resident company only. It is still not clear whether Banco Nacional de Cuba will consent to assignment to non-resident Japanese or non-Japanese entities.

The Secondary Market for Cuban Debt

Historically, the only Cuban debts that had traded with any degree of regularity were the rescheduled loans: the medium-term (MT) Credit Lyonnais loans and the short-term non-trade (STNT) loans. Both have guarantees from the Republic of Cuba, but the MT loans have the advantage of an official agent (Credit Lyonnais).

When Cuba first defaulted in the early 1980s, the MT and the STNT loans used to trade as a package. Within a few years, the loans started to trade separately. This continues to be the case.

Cuban loan settlement became far more onerous from the start of 2010. Although assignment using standard EMTA documents has not changed, BNC now requires all notices of assignments and incumbency certificates to be submitted in both English and Spanish. Furthermore, these documents have to be notarised and apostilled by both the Cuban consulate and the UK Foreign Office. Estimated settlement time is now two-to-three months for all document preparation prior to submission to BNC in Cuba, with a further one month for approval and re-registration in Cuba.

MT Credit Lyonnais

1983 refinancing agreement

Issuer	Banco Nacional de Cuba
Guarantor	The Republic of Cuba
Form	Registered Loan
issue date	Refinancing Agreement dated 30 December 1983
Amounts outstanding and issued	DEM179mn JPY LTPR 1.378bn JPY Fixed 4.129bn CHF26.4mn CAD12.0mn
Currency	DEM, CAD, JPY and CHF
Amortisation	5 January 1986 and the dates falling six, 12, 18, 24, 30, 42, 48 and 54 months thereafter.
Maturity	7 June 1989
Interest	Six-month LIBOR + 2.25%, principal and interest have not been serviced since 1986. PDI for DEM to end 2018 estimated by Exotix at 185% on a simple basis, without penalty interest, and 216% on a simple basis, with penalty interest, but currently trades for free.
Restrictions	Under the terms of US sanctions, the US Treasury Office for Foreign Assets Control (OFAC) states that US entities cannot buy or sell any Cuba assets, including debt, without the explicit written authorisation of OFAC itself. This also applies to persons and entities controlled by US entities.
Agent	Credit Lyonnais

1984 refinancing agreement

Issuer	Banco Nacional de Cuba
Guarantor	The Republic of Cuba
Form	Registered Loan
issue date	Refinancing Agreement dated 13 December 1984
Amount and currency issued	DEM170mn JPY LTPR 1.155bn JPY Fixed 4.168bn CHF10.3mn CAD2.5mn
Currency	DEM, CAD, JPY and CHF
Amortisation	5 August 1989 and the dates falling six, 12, 18, 24, 30, 36, 42 and 48 months thereafter.
Maturity	7 June 1989
Interest	Six-month LIBOR + 1.875% or six-month CD + 1.625%, principal and interest have not been serviced since 1986. PDI for DEM to end-2018 estimated by Exotix at 181% on a simple basis, without penalty interest, and 209% on a simple basis, with penalty interest, but currently trades for free.
Restrictions	Under the terms of US sanctions, the US Treasury Office for Foreign Assets Control (OFAC) states that US entities cannot buy or sell any Cuba assets, including debt, without the explicit written authorisation of OFAC itself. This also applies to persons and entities controlled by US entities.
Agent	Credit Lyonnais

1985 refinancing agreement

Issuer	Banco Nacional de Cuba
Guarantor	The Republic of Cuba
Form	Registered Loan
Issue date	Refinancing Agreement dated 16 September 1985
Amount and currency issued	DEM156.8mn JPY LTPR 1.149bn JPY Fixed 4.267bn
Currency	DEM, JPY
Amortisation	5 September 1991 and the dates falling six, 12, 18, 24, 30, 36, 42 and 48 months thereafter.
Maturity	1 July 1995
Interest	Six-month LIBOR + 1.5% or six-month CD + 1.25%, principal and interest have not been serviced since 1986. PDI for DEM to end-2018 estimated by Exotix at 162% on a simple basis, without penalty interest, and 188% on a simple basis, with penalty interest, but currently trades for free.

(*continued*)

(continued)

Restrictions	Under the terms of US sanctions, the US Treasury Office for Foreign Assets Control (OFAC) states that US entities cannot buy or sell any Cuba assets, including debt, without the explicit written authorisation of OFAC itself. This also applies to persons and entities controlled by US entities.
Agent	Credit Lyonnais

Short-Term Non-trade Bilateral Loans

There is no official agent for the STNT, although Credit Lyonnais does unofficially act as registrar. Participants trading the STNT have no obligation to inform Credit Lyonnais of assignments but, if they do, then Credit Lyonnais will adjust their records. Credit Lyonnais does not calculate accrued interest and has no obligation to safeguard the Statute of Limitations for the STNT but, to date, this has not been necessary as both Banco Nacional de Cuba and the Government of Cuba telex Credit Lyonnais to acknowledge both their Cuba medium- and short-term obligations on a quarterly basis.

Issuer	Banco Nacional de Cuba
Guarantor	The Republic of Cuba
Issue date	From 1983–85
Amount and currency issued	DEM538mn CHF411mn CAD11.6mn PAB4mn JPY unknown
Original creditors	Numerous
Interest	Various. Exotix estimates PDI to end-Sep. 18 at 148% (DEM), 113% (CHF), and 89% (JPY) without penalty and 181% (DEM), 145% (CHF), and 122% (JPY) with penalty.
Settlement considerations	These are assignable loans to financial institutions with the consent of the borrower not to be unreasonably withheld. Please note, it is important to check that all the documents including the guarantees (separate documents attached to the loan documents) are present and have the same dates.
Restrictions	Under the terms of US sanctions, the US Treasury Office for Foreign Assets Control (OFAC) states that US entities cannot buy or sell any Cuba assets, including debt, without the explicit written authorisation of OFAC itself. This also applies to persons and entities controlled by US entities.

Other Cuba structured and unrestructured debt[a]

Borrower	Banco Nacional de Cuba
Issue date	Various
Form	Loans, deposits, trade paper, interbank lines
Amount outstanding	Unknown
Currency	DEM, JPY, CHF and GBP
Settlement considerations	Case-by-case basis
Restrictions	Under the terms of US sanctions, the US Treasury Office for Foreign Assets Control (OFAC) states that US entities cannot buy or sell any Cuba assets, including debt, without the explicit written authorisation of OFAC itself. This also applies to persons and entities controlled by US entities.

[a]These include the 1986 and 1987 maturities of pre-1983 syndicated loans, plus numerous bilateral trade finance agreements and the unguaranteed portion of European export credits, which have never been restructured

Letters of Credit

There are a number of pre-1996 letters of credit and syndicated trade finance facilities that trade from time to time in the market. Available documentation varies in quality and these are very illiquid.

CDR Limited

CDR Limited was created as a limited liability company in Jersey for the purpose of issuing Cuban loan pass-through certificates. In September 2005 Cuban medium- and short-term non-trade bilateral loans were placed in separate series (according to loan type and currency) and euroclearable notes were issued to reflect holder's rights to any distributions made on the underlying loans. Only loans with an acceptable quality of paperwork have been accepted into these series. Each series can be re-opened and enlarged as and when further holders of loans wish to 'convert' their loans into euroclearable notes, the benefits being easier settlement, an enlarged potential investor base and historically higher pricing.

Standard Terms for Each Series

Issuer	CDR Limited
Form	Securities in bearer form to be represented by a Permanent Global Bearer Security, which is exchangeable for securities in definitive form only upon exchange event.
1st issue date	September 2005
2nd issue date	November 2006
Maturity	29 September 2025
Interest	No interest as underlying loans are non-performing
Past due interest	For the account of the holder
Currencies	EUR, CHF and JPY
Settlement	Euroclear and Clearstream
Listing	Channel Islands (CISX)
Issuing and payment agent	HSBC Bank Plc
Trustee	Capital Trust Company Limited, London
Servicer and dealer	Exotix Ltd

Series

Series A (XS0229182737)

Underlying assets:	DEM Short Term Non-Trade Related Indebtedness
Issue size (9 Dec 2008):	EUR48,362,708.60
Minimum denomination:	EUR250,000
Minimum incremental:	EUR1.00

Series B (XS0229182497)

Underlying assets:	CHF Cuba Short Term Bank Non-Trade Related Indebtedness
Issue size (9 Dec 2008):	CHF36,325,000
Minimum denomination:	CHF500,000
Minimum incremental:	CHF1.00

Series C (XS0229181846)

Underlying assets:	JPY Cuba unrestructured loans
Issue size (9 Dec 2008)	JPY5,475,210,830
Minimum denomination:	JPY35,000,000
Minimum incremental:	JPY1.00

Series D (XS0229182067)

Underlying assets:	DEM Cuba Medium Term Loans
Issue size (9 Dec 2008):	EUR49,692,376.00
Minimum denomination:	EUR250,000
Minimum incremental:	EUR1.00

Series E (XS0229181689)

Underlying assets:	JPY Cuba Medium Term Loan
Issue size (9 Dec 2008):	JPY2,018,897,452
Minimum denominator:	JPY35,000,000
Minimum incremental:	JPY1.00

Series F (XS0229181507)

Underlying assets:	DEM Cuba unrestructured loans
Issue size (9 Dec 2008):	EUR1,866,908.02
Minimum denomination:	EUR250,000
Minimum incremental:	EUR1.00

Series G (XS08229181333)

Underlying assets:	JPY Cuba unrestructured loans
Issue size (9 Dec 2008):	JPY4,508,888,763
Minimum denomination:	JPY35,000,000
Minimum incremental:	JPY1.00

Dominican Republic

Nominal GDP (US$mn, 2018)[a]		81,103
Population (thousand, 2018)[a]		10,278
GDP per capita (USD, 2018)[a]		7891
Credit ratings (long-term foreign currency)[b]	Fitch	BB−
	Moody's	Ba3
	S&P	BB−

[a]IMF WEO October 2018
[b]As at end-September 2018

Country Summary

- Politically stable over the past 15 years, the Dominican Republic has a volatile history, with successive governments facing problems of corruption, social inequality and election irregularities. Several elections since 1996 have been more peaceful, although President Medina's re-election in 2016 sparked violent protests.
- The fastest-growing economy in the Caribbean, the Dominican Republic has enjoyed strong GDP growth in the past five years, averaging c6% over 2013–17 (the fastest in Central America-Caribbean), buoyed by diversified manufacturing activity, mining (nickel, gold and bauxite), tourism and remittances. The country is susceptible to climatic shocks and, in 2017, Hurricanes Irma and Maria caused severe damage, including widespread power outages and flooding.

Exotix Capital, *Exotix Developing Markets Guide*,
https://doi.org/10.1007/978-3-030-05867-8_14

- Solvency indicators appear solid (with public debt at c40% of GDP) although the liquidity cushion is low (just three months import cover). Dominican Republic has undergone various commercial debt restructurings in the past, but its most recent (in 2005) is now well behind it. The country has been an active borrower in the international bond market, with 11 USD sovereign bonds now outstanding, amounting to a total of US$13bn (17% of GDP). A persistent fiscal primary deficit is expected to move into a small surplus in 2018 (0.4% of GDP), and remain there over the medium term, according to IMF projections.

Economic data	*Avg*[a]	*2014*	*2015*	*2016*	*2017 (e)*	*2018 (f)*	*2019 (f)*
Real GDP growth	5.6	7.6	7.0	6.6	4.6	6.4	5.0
Inflation (annual average)	5.0	3.0	0.8	1.6	3.3	4.3	4.2
Current account (% of GDP)	−4.9	−3.3	−1.9	−1.1	−0.2	−1.6	−2.1
Reserves (US$mn, end-period)[b]	3714	4862	5266	6047	6781	6598[c]	–
Reserves/ imports (months)[d]	2.1	2.4	2.7	3.0	3.2	–	–
Overall fiscal balance (% of GDP)[e]	−2.6	−2.9	−0.2	−2.8	−3.2	−3.0	−3.2
Currency (ticker)	Dominican peso (DOP)						
FX regime	De jure floating but with intervention, although the actual path of the exchange rate over the past decade shows a gradual depreciation against the US dollar annually. The IMF classifies the regime as a crawl-like arrangement.						
Key exports	Gold and jewellery (23.5%), medical equipment (11%) and rolled tobacco (7.5%). Goods exports were US$10bn in 2017. Services (mainly tourism), at nearly US$9bn in 2017, and remittances worth US$6bn are also significant FX earners.						

Source: IMF WEO Database, Haver, OEC

[a]10-year average to 2016 unless otherwise stated
[b]Gross international reserves
[c]Latest figure, June 2018
[d]Months of the current year's imports of goods, services and income debits
[e]Overall government net lending

Key figures		*Party*	*Since*
President	Danilo Medina Sánchez	PLD	Aug. 2012
Vice president	Margarita Cedeño de Fernández	PLD	Aug. 2012
Minister of finance	Simón Lizardo	PLD	Aug. 2012
Key opposition figure	Luis Rodolfo Abinader Corona	PRM	–
Central bank governor	Héctor Valdez Albizu	–	Aug. 2004

Politics

Executive power

The president is chief of state and head of government executing legislation passed by the Chamber of Deputies. They are also responsible for appointing cabinet members. The president is directly elected for a renewable four-year term by absolute majority in two rounds if needed. A second consecutive term was allowed in the 2015 constitution.

Presidential term: Four years (two-term limit; consecutive allowed)

Parliamentary term: Four years

Legislature

Bicameral, the National Congress, consisting of the Senate (upper house) and Chamber of Deputies (lower house). Each house, and the position of president and vice president (voted for on the same ticket), are elected by popular vote. The country comprises 31 provinces plus a federal district. After legislative elections in 2010, terms for both houses ran for six years, returning to four years in 2016, so that they can run concurrently with presidential elections. Also in 2010, the number of seats in the Chamber of Deputies was increased to 190, with 178 representing provincial districts, five elected by nationwide votes and seven new deputies to represent Dominicans abroad.

Senate: 32 seats

Chamber of Deputies: 190 seats

Elections

Next due *Presidential and legislative: May 2020*

Last legislative election[a] *(May 2016)*	*Seats*	*Last presidential (May 2016)*	*% of vote*
Dominican Liberation Party (PLD)	106	Danilo Medina Sánchez (PLD)	61.7
Modern Revolutionary Party (PRM)	42	Luis Rodolfo Abinader Corona (PRM)	35.0

(*continued*)

(continued)

Elections

Next due *Presidential and legislative: May 2020*

Last legislative election[a] *(May 2016)*	*Seats*	*Last presidential (May 2016)*	*% of vote*
Social Christian Reformist Party (PRSC)	18	Other	3.3
Dominican Revolutionary Party (PRD)	16		
Liberal Reformist Party (PRL)	3		
Others	5		
Total	**190**	**Total**	**100.0**

[a]Results shown for Chamber of Deputies, in which the PLD increased its majority from 105 to 106 seats. In the Senate, the PLD won 26 seats, the PRM won 2 seats and PRSC, the PLR, the BIS and the PRD each won one seat

People

The Dominican Republic shares the island of Hispaniola with Haiti, declaring its independence from Haiti in 1844. Around 70% of the population is mixed race, with black and white accounting for about 16% and 14%, respectively. Haitians form the bulk of foreign nationals; however, border immigration is tightly controlled. Catholicism is the overwhelming religion of choice. After various power struggles before its independence, the country's modern history has also been volatile, with the US often playing an active role in events. Commander of the National Guard Rafael Leonidas Trujillo, elected in May 1930, ruled under a dictatorship until his CIA-backed assassination in 1961. His rule oversaw economic decline, mismanagement and corruption. A period of transition ensued, including coups, counter-coups and a US military invasion in 1965 as the country fell into near civil war, until Joaquin Balaguer (PRSC) (1966–78) oversaw a period of rapid economic growth, built on economic reform and opening the country, although with rising income inequality. Balaguer was defeated in the 1978 election by Antonio Guzman Fernandez (PRD) (1978–82), marking the country's first peaceful transfer of power from one elected president to another, after Balaguer, disputing the result, was eventually forced to step down under US pressure. It also marked the beginning of a period of frequent changes of government, being followed by Salvador Jorge Blanco (also PRD) (1982–86), Balaguer again (1986–96), who was accused of electoral fraud in the 1994 elections and, under pressure from the US, held new elections in 1996 in which he did not run, Leonel Fernandez Reyna (PLD) (1996–2000 and again from 2004–12) and Hipolito Mejia (PRD) (2000–04). Danilo Medina (PLD) won in 2012 and was re-elected with a large majority in 2016; his main opponent, Luis Abinader, accepted defeat, but accused Medina of misusing state resources to win re-election. The Dominican Republic is a signatory of the Central America Free Trade Agreement (CAFTA-DR), a free trade agreement with the US, which came into force over 2006–09. The other regional members are Costa Rica, El Salvador, Guatemala, Honduras and Nicaragua.

DEBT

	2012	*2017*
External debt ratios (%)		
Total external debt/GDP	33.1	35.0
Public external debt/GDP	21.2	25.1
Private external debt/GDP	11.9	9.9
Total external debt/exports of goods and services	134.3	138.7
External debt service ratio	16.5	20.9[a]
Public debt ratios (%)		
Public domestic debt/GDP	10.9	14.3
Public debt/GDP	32.1	39.4

Source: Ministry of Finance Public Credit Office, Central Bank, IMF, World Bank, Exotix

[a]Figure is for 2016 (latest)

The Dominican Republic's public external debt (PED) was US$20.5bn as of February 2018, on Ministry of Finance figures. This included the two international bonds issued during the month. In USD terms, PED has risen sharply since 2012, when it stood at US$12.8bn, with most of the change reflecting just two events: (1) a surge in eurobond issues, with outstanding bonds increasing from US$2.5bn to US$13.3bn; and (2) the virtual elimination of its Venezuela bilateral debt through a buyback in 2015 of its PetroCaribe debt (Venezuela debt in 2012 was US$3.1bn). Now, 65% of public external debt is owed in bonds (and 46% of total external debt), with 22% owed to multilaterals (of which, two-thirds is owed to the Inter-American Development Bank, IADB), and 12% to bilaterals (60% of which is owed to just three countries, France, Brazil and Spain). The IMF is no longer a creditor of the Dominican Republic, with the latter repaying all its IMF loans by 2012 (IMF debt stood at US$845mn in 2012). Meanwhile, Exotix calculates that private external debt was US$8.6bn (figure for 2017), based on IMF data, although the authorities do not provide details. As a result, total external debt was cUS$29bn.

At end-2017, total external debt was 35% of GDP and 139% of exports. Public external debt was 25.1% of GDP (amounting to US$18.8bn at end-2017—the difference of US$1.65bn compared with the February 2018 figure being due mainly to the eurobond issues), while private external debt was 10% of GDP. The debt/GDP and debt/

exports ratios are largely unchanged from 2012, despite the 23% rise in USD GDP over this period, and the 26% rise in current account earnings (services and remittances grew by 46% each over 2012–17, while goods exports rose by just 13%). The latest available figures on external debt service, provided by the World Bank, show that this was 20.9% of exports in 2016, from 16.5% in 2012. The IMF's DSA in 2017 reported that the Dominican Republic's debt profile was able to withstand a number of shocks, although the debt ratio increased in 2016 as a large fiscal deficit outweighed the effects of strong growth. The CAFTA-Dominican Republic agreement has led to an increase in exports and a large proportion of trade is now under this agreement; however, there is a risk of change to the terms, such as changes to effective tariffs. The overall contribution of exports to economic growth has been limited, though, partly due to a Haitian overland import ban, while remittances and tourism are rebounding in line with the global economy. The payoff from significant foreign direct investment in the mining industry has boosted exports.

Public debt remains low, at just 39% of GDP in 2017 (40% of GDP on official figures, using a different figure for GDP), with public domestic debt of 14% of GDP (US$10.7bn). Total public debt was therefore US$29.5bn. However, although low, the government debt ratio is at its highest level on IMF WEO data since the series began in 1997 (with general government debt at 37.7% in 2017 in the WEO). It has fractionally surpassed its previous peak of 36% in 2003, following its banking crisis at the time, which caused the government to assume contingent liabilities and also led to a widening in the budget deficit (general government debt was only 17% of GDP in 2002, so the debt ratio doubled in one year). The government debt burden subsequently declined to a low of 17% of GDP in 2007, but has been on a gradual upward trajectory since, passing 30% in 2012, despite the country's strong real GDP growth rates, due to the presence of a persistent primary deficit. The Dominican Republic has posted a primary deficit each year since 2008, except in 2015–16 when it was positive due to one-off factors, but the IMF WEO projects a shift into a small primary surplus in 2018 (0.4% of GDP), and for it to remain at modest levels (c0.5%) over the medium term. The IMF projects general government debt to increase above 40% of GDP in 2022.

Composition of external debt

External debt by creditor (Feb. 2018)	*Nominal amount outstanding (US$mn)*	*Share of total (%)*
Public sector external debt	**20,475**	**70.4**
o/w Multilateral creditors	4417	15.2
IADB	2938	10.1
World Bank	922	3.2
CAF	196	0.7
Bilateral creditors	2382	8.2
France	594	2.0
Brazil	456	1.6
Spain	429	1.5
Venezuela	239	0.8
o/w PetroCaribe agreement	78	0.3
Japan	26	0.1
US	18	0.1
Commercial creditors	13,676	47.1
Banks	353	1.2
Bonds	13,318	45.8
Other (including suppliers)	6	0.0
Private sector external debt	**8591**	**29.6**
Total external debt	**29,067**	**100.0**

Source: Ministry of Finance Public Credit Office, IMF, Exotix

Rescheduling History

The Dominican Republic has had a history of rescheduling its official and commercial debts in modern times, although has not undertaken any kind of rescheduling or suffered external payment problems over the past decade. Previous episodes of rescheduling have tended to reflect a temporary build-up of arrears and short-term liquidity concerns, rather than insolvency, as, historically, public and external debt ratios have tended to be low. Public debt averaged only c15% of GDP annually over 1997–2001, reflecting generally only modest fiscal deficits (averaging 1.2% of GDP), and strong real GDP growth (averaging nearly 6%). With a relatively low debt burden, which on most metrics would have been considered safe, the poor payment experience was therefore illustrative of a weak credit and payment culture and institutions, which, until early the 2000s, had perhaps been masked by historically high rates of GDP growth. It also reflects the traditionally very low level of international reserves, averaging between one and two months between 1999 and 2002. Such a poor liquidity cushion left the country vulnerable to a crisis of confidence, as occurred during the 2003 banking crisis.

The country's most recent rescheduling, a comprehensive treatment of both Paris Club and commercial debt, followed from the 2003 banking and subsequent financial crisis. But what started as a liquidity shock threatened to undermine solvency. In particular, the cost of the government's bail out for the banking sector was significant, as it guaranteed deposits of three banks. While few could have predicted a massive banking fraud most infamously uncovered at Baninter, the low level of reserves left the country vulnerable to exogenous shocks, which manifested in a loss of confidence—downward pressure on the currency, loss of reserves and higher inflation. Perhaps significantly, the resulting financial crisis was more to do with the weak policy response of the authorities rather than the fraud itself. The Dominican peso fell by over 40% in the first seven months of 2003 and inflation rose to 30% yoy. Reserves at end-2003 fell to US$347mn, just 0.9 months of imports. The crisis also resulted in a sharp increase in domestic, and hence total, public debt (in part to bail out the banks) and added to quasi-fiscal losses at the central bank (the weak electricity sector posed a further contingent liability on the government, and public debt also rose as the government nationalised two electricity companies). The fiscal deficit rose to 6% of GDP in 2003 while the historically low (total) public debt/GDP ratio doubled, rising from 26.8% of GDP in 2002 to 54.3% in 2003 (meanwhile, general government debt rose from 17% of GDP to 36%). Faced with exhaustion of central bank reserves and the accumulation of external arrears to US$330mn (1% of GDP) by September 2004, the authorities were forced to seek debt service relief. One bond interest payment was missed in January 2004, but this was paid within the 30-day grace period. Subsequent late payments ended when the authorities sought a debt exchange in April 2005, in which holders of the 2006 and 2013 sovereign eurobonds accepted a five-year lengthening, with the same coupons and some capitalised interest payments, to grant short-term debt service relief.

Relations with Multilateral Creditors

The Dominican Republic has had seven IMF programmes, mostly standby credits, since the early 1980s (and nine programmes in all, including two in the 1960s). Its last programme was for the period 2009–12 and was concluded satisfactorily. There has been no programme since, although the authorities continue engagement with the Fund through regular Article IV consultations and technical assistance. The most recent Article IV, the 2018 Article IV, was concluded in April 2018 (the Board paper has not been published). The accompanying press release noted that the economy continued to perform well. Real GDP growth was expected to accelerate to 5.5% in 2018, employment and real wages continued to recover, the unemployment rate had fallen to 5.1%, near historical lows, and inflation was projected to remain in line with the central bank's inflation target over the forecast horizon. The main domestic concerns centred on fiscal policy and structural reform. On the former, staff note that meaningful fiscal consolidation measures are needed to address structural fiscal weaknesses and a stronger fiscal policy framework would support efforts to improve the fiscal position.

A two-year SBA was approved in August 2003, as the government was forced to turn to the IMF for assistance in an attempt to restore confidence after the banking crisis. But the programme quickly went off track. This was mainly due to ongoing problems in the electricity sector that led the government to nationalise two electricity companies in October, putting further strain on the public finances. Controversially the government repurchased two electricity distribution units of Spain's Union Fenosa in September 2003 (at a cost of US$187mn). The IMF's first review of the SBA in February 2004 (delayed from October in part due to the problems in the electricity sector) was approved (after modifications), but in the face of significant concerns among some Board members. Although recognising the policy effort in the early part of the year (for example, in the 2004 budget), concerns focused on the failure to bring the fiscal situation under control, governance problems in the banking sector, interference in the FX market and the nationalisation of the two electricity companies. More widely, Board members were concerned about the continued poor track record of programme implementation. Arrears built up with suppliers and bilateral creditors (standing at US$195mn by end-2003). The second review was delayed in early spring 2004 and the programme was suspended pending the arrival of a new government. The government was eventually forced to approach the Paris Club for rescheduling.

The combination of weak implementation of the 2003 programme and arrival of a new government led quickly to negotiations on a new SBA. Confidence returned in 2004, largely stemming from the election of Fernandez, who moved quickly to implement corrective policies. Monetary policy was tightened and a fiscal package was approved by Congress, aimed at revenue raising and spending cuts. The 2004 and 2005 budgets announced fiscal reforms including the raising of VAT from 12% to 16%, a reduction in the government payroll by a hiring freeze and improving the performance of the non-financial public sector, which moved to a 1.2% of GDP surplus a year after the election. This compared with a 3.3% deficit in 2004, with the overall fiscal deficit falling 0.8% to –7.3%. The peso appreciated 16.5% against the US dollar on improving sentiment. Concessionary loans of a combined US$341.5mn from the World Bank and IDB were also approved. Subsequently, the SBA was renegotiated and the initial funds of US$670mn procured in 2003 were re-instigated in January 2005. Still, despite the new austerity measures, a financing gap of US$327mn was projected in 2005, which forced the country to undergo a bond restructuring. The government was also able to significantly restructure other external debt commitments, with public sector external debt service as a percentage of GDP falling to 2.7%, from 6.8% in 2003. By year-end, the overall fiscal deficit had improved by 4.2ppts to 3.1% of GDP, with a primary surplus of 1.5%. The SBA expired in January 2008. Performance under the programme was much improved, leading the IMF to report on the conclusion of the arrangement that "recovery from the 2002–04 financial crisis has been impressive". In August 2008, the IMF announced that it expected the Dominican Republic to engage in post-programme monitoring following the completion of the SBA. However, the authorities did not take up such an arrangement until the onset of the global financial crisis forced the authorities to return to the IMF in 2009.

The IMF approved a 28-month SBA, the country's last IMF programme, in November 2009 for US$1.7bn (500% of quota). The authorities requested a programme in order to pursue short-term counter-cyclical policies (the consolidated public sector deficit widened from 1.7% of GDP in 2007 to 4.6% in 2008 and 4.5% in 2009), while strengthening medium-term sustainability, reducing vulnerabilities exposed during the global financial crisis, and laying the foundation for a gradual recovery and sustained growth. A key part of the programme was the shift from an expansionary fiscal stance in H1 2010 to consolidation in H2, while fiscal reform objectives included control of current spending, elimination of tax exemptions and strengthened tax administration; a key IMF recommendation was to widen the tax base. Tax revenues were seen as relatively low compared with peers. Widening the tax base could be a relatively easy solution to government finances—streamlining tax incentives were seen as saving some 6–7% of GDP and solving the fiscal deficit problem (and ensuring fiscal sustainability), with minimal adverse effects. The IMF completed its final reviews, the fifth and sixth, in July 2011, concluding that stability had been maintained and conditions remained favourable.

IMF programmes

Date	*Arrange-ments*	*Comments*
1980s–90s	Various	EFF 1983–85; SBA 1985–86; SBA 1991–93; SBA 1993–94.
2003–05	SBA	Two-year SDR437.8mn (US$600mn, 200% of quota) programme approved in August 2003 in response to the banking crisis. It was due to expire in August 2005. The first review, scheduled for October 2003, was delayed. Agreement on the main elements of the review was reached in December 2003. These included the need to control the fiscal deficit and public debt, to strengthen confidence in the banking system and address problems in the electricity sector. Most of the targets for the December 2003 review were missed and the programme was revised. The first review was finally completed in February 2004. However, the election of new President Fernandez in May 2004, who took office in August, led to negotiations on a new SBA programme and the 2003 agreement was subsequently cancelled in January 2005. Only SDR131mn was drawn.
2005–08	SBA	A new three-year SDR437.8mn (US$695mn, 200% of quota) agreement was approved in January 2005 and the 2003 programme was cancelled. The new programme was supported by the new government's commitment to corrective policies, evidenced by the passing of a revenue-raising package in Congress in October 2004. Initial and subsequent performance exceeded expectations. At the conclusion of the fifth and sixth reviews in February 2007, the original programme, which was for 28 months, lasting until May 2007, was extended to January 2008. The eighth and final review was concluded satisfactorily in January. The programme was fully drawn.
2009–12	SBA	A 28-month programme was approved November 2009 for SDR1.1bn (cUS$1.7bn) or 500% of quota. The programme was scheduled to expire in March 2012. The first review was completed in April 2010 when modifications to a number of performance criteria the rest of the year were approved. The second and third reviews were completed together in October 2010, after the second review was postponed as the authorities needed additional time to articulate policies for H2 10. A waiver was approved for the non-observance of end-September performance criterion for public sector arrears to electricity generators (subsequently corrected). The board also approved additional performance criteria for 2011 and structural benchmarks for 2010 and 2011. The fourth review was completed in December 2010, and the fifth and sixth reviews (the last reviews to be completed) were completed together in July 2011, unlocking final disbursements. SDR766mn was drawn in total.

Source: IMF. Dominican Republic joined the IMF in 1945

Electricity reform, viewed as also crucial to securing medium-term fiscal sustainability, also formed part of the 2009 IMF programme and the sector continues to be an issue. Electricity losses and untargeted electricity subsidies continued to be a drain on the government's finances and acted as a constraint on growth. A change in the management of the electricity distribution companies and increased electricity tariffs in December 2010 were seen as important first steps in this process, but continued tariff reform in 2011, toward a flexible regime, was also important. Electricity transfers in 2016 amounted to some 1.5% of GDP, cUS$1bn a year. Subsequently, President Danilo Medina (2012–present) sought to address the deep-seated energy sector problems through an electricity pact (*pacto electrico*), a process of national consultation aimed at finding "a definitive solution to the problems of the electricity sector". The sector's problems are well documented: half of households not metered, poor infrastructure, technical losses and electricity theft through illegal connections. There has been some progress with technical losses falling over the past few years, increased metering and improvements in the legal framework (electricity theft is now a criminal act). According to the World Bank, the economic future will depend on policies to improve the electricity sector.

The World Bank has a number of active projects in the Dominican Republic, with objectives including modernising the electricity grid and improving water and sanitation in tourist areas. The most recently approved project was in September 2017; new in 2017 were projects to develop extractive industries with transparency and to develop the capacity to produce and use quality education statistics. Low education levels remain a problem for growth as the services sector expands. Education spending has increased to 4% of GDP. The IADB is the biggest multilateral creditor, though.

Paris Club and Bilateral Creditors

The Dominican Republic has had four Paris Club agreements. Its two most recent agreements were concluded in April 2004 and October 2005 and followed as a result of the country's banking and financial crisis of 2003, which had impaired debt service ability. Flow rescheduling was agreed. The 2004 agreement followed after approval of an IMF SBA in August 2003 and required, as a pre-condition to further relief, that the authorities seek comparable treatment from private creditors. The 2004

Paris Club agreement amounted to debt service relief of cUS$200mn, reducing debt service to the Paris Club over 2004 from US$479mn to US$293mn. The authorities subsequently sought a bond exchange, although this took time to implement, knowing that a successful operation would unlock further Paris Club relief. After the successful conclusion of commercial debt negotiations, a further Paris Club deal in October 2005 saw debt service relief of US$137mn due in 2005, on 2004 equivalent Classic terms, reducing Paris Club servicing costs by 38% in 2005/06.

Paris Club agreements

Date	*Terms*	*Status*	*Details*
1985	Classic	Fully repaid	Treated US$280mn under Classic terms.
1991	Houston	Fully repaid	Treated US$771mn under Houston terms, with the possibility to conduct debt swaps.
2004 Apr.	Classic	Active	Treated US$193mn (comprising US$155mn in maturities due in 2004 and US$38mn in arrears) out of Paris Club debt of US$1561mn as of 1 January 2004. Treatment of arrears as of end-2003 and maturities falling due from January 2004 to December 2004. Repayment of both ODA and non-ODA credits over 12 years with five years grace. Comparability from private creditors was sought.
2005 Oct.	Classic	Active	Treated US$137mn out of Paris Club debt of US$2047mn as of 1 January 2005. Total external debt was US$6414mn (54% of GDP) as at end-2004. Treatment of maturities falling due from January 2005 to December 2005. Repayment of both ODA and non-ODA credits over 12 years with five years grace. Comparability from private creditors was sought.

Source: Paris Club

Venezuela and Spain have traditionally been among the Dominican Republic's main bilateral creditors, and international relationships, although Brazil and France have emerged as its single biggest bilateral creditors over 2015–17. Venezuela was the biggest bilateral lender by far in 2014 (owed US$4.2bn), mostly through its PetroCaribe arrangement, and accounted for over 60% of bilateral debt. The repayment of Dominican

Republic's PetroCaribe debt in January 2015 saw its Venezuelan debt fall to US$230mn, a level around which it has remained since (c10% of bilateral debt). The Dominican Republic bought back its PetroCaribe debt with Venezuelan state oil company PDVSA at a 52% discount on the US$4bn that it owed (only US$1.93bn was paid to satisfy the debt). The operation was financed by some of the proceeds from the sovereign bond sales that year. Total bilateral debt as of December 2017 stood at US$2.4bn (c12% of public external debt).

Sovereign Commercial Debt

The Dominican Republic completed a bond restructuring in July 2005 and concluded a rescheduling agreement with commercial banks that October. The country had previously seen two commercial debt agreements in the 1980s and a Brady deal in 1994. None of the Brady bonds remain outstanding now, after the FRN 08/2024 (XS0052684601) was called on 30 November 2017.

The government was able to return to the international capital markets seven years after its Brady deal with a five-year US$500mn eurobond in September 2001. This was followed by a 10-year US$600mn eurobond in January 2003. However, the impact of the banking crisis that emerged that year tested the country's repayment capacity, given its low level of reserves, and led to a build-up of arrears with official (Paris Club) and commercial creditors. The Dominican Republic missed a coupon payment in January 2004, which was cured within the 30-day grace period, and further late payments occurred thereafter. A Paris Club agreement in 2004 sought comparable treatment from private creditors and, in April 2005, a debt exchange was proposed. An added incentive for a commercial restructuring was to avoid the looming 2006 maturity of the US$500mn eurobond that was issued in 2001, which represented 37% of net reserves at the time of the eventual exchange. Subsequently, in February 2005, S&P downgraded Dominican Republic to SD from CC in anticipation of a debt exchange (marking the end of a rapid descent in the country rating, which was BB– in May 2003). Moody's viewed the exchange as a distressed exchange, because the maturity extension and interest deferral were needed to avoid default, and dated the default as April 2005.

Commercial debt agreements

Date	*Details*
1983	Bank debt restructurings.
1986	Bank debt restructurings.
1994	Brady deal. US$1.2bn of principal and past-due interest (PDI) was restructured. The menu comprised: (1) buyback of US$0.4bn; (2) US$0.5bn in discount exchange bonds with a 35% discount repaid in 30 years as a bullet maturity with interest of LIBOR+13/16 per cent; and (3) PDI bonds (US$171mn) with 15-year maturity, with three years' grace, and interest at LIBOR+13/16 per cent. Agreement also included a write-off of US$112mn of PDI and US$52mn paid in cash at closing.
2005 Jul.	Bond exchange. Maturity extension of two bonds, one issued in 2001 (US$500mn, 9.5% coupon and five-year maturity) and 2003 (US$600mn, 9.04% coupon and 10-year maturity). Combined principal amount US$1.1bn. Maturities extended by five years, from 2006 into 2011 and from 2013 into 2018. Coupons unchanged. NPV haircut was negligible (less than 5%). Participation was 94%.
2005 Oct.	Commercial bank debt restructuring.

Source: Exotix, World Bank GDF

The 2005 exchange offer was a success. It covered the outstanding US$1.1bn in external sovereign bonds, which had been issued in 2001 and 2003. The exchange sought five-year maturity extension, with no nominal principal reduction, which implied little NPV loss to bondholders. It comprised a new 9.50% amortising bond due 2011 for the outstanding US$500mn 9.50% bond due 2006 and a new 9.04% amortising bond due 2018 for the US$600mn 9.04% bond due 2013. The new bonds provided repayments of principal in 10 equal semi-annual instalments over their final five years. Half of the new coupons were capitalised for 2005–06, consistent with the flow relief provided by the Paris Club over the same period. The exchange offer closed on 11 May 2005 and was conditional on receiving at least an 85% acceptance rate. In the event, 93.7% of bondholders participated in the exchange; neither of the exited bonds had CACs (the two new bonds did) and so exit consents were used, although their use here (the third time, after Ecuador in 2000 and Uruguay in 2003) was seen as more investor-friendly than in the case of Ecuador, where their use was seen by some market participants at the time as especially egregious. In the Dominican Republic's case, tendering holders were deemed to consent to a number of changes to non-payment terms, including a waiver of sovereign immunity provisions, subject to a few provisos, deleting the cross default and cross acceleration provisions of an event of default, deleting the event of default provision triggered by unsatisfied or discharged judgments in the existing bond, and removing the existing bonds' negative pledge covenants. A reopening in July captured a further 4% of principal outstanding. A small portion of the original 2013 bond, US$13.5mn, remained in circulation. The government had feared that, should the restructuring not be accepted, confidence in the currency would again fall. With capital outflows, its ability to meet obligations could be pressured further. In the event, debt service obligations fell by US$50.9mn in 2005. An agreement was also reached with external commercial banks and suppliers to restructure US$550mn. Obligations to external commercial banks due across 2005/06 were rescheduled in October 2005 as a total of US$147mn in payments were postponed to 2007, amortising in six equal semi-annual instalments thereafter. Combined with the Paris Club treatments, the debt service scheduled was greatly alleviated. S&P restored its B rating in June 2005 shortly after the bond exchange. Both the new 2011 bond and 2018 bond were subsequently repaid on schedule.

Demonstrating the improved performance of the country, the sovereign was soon able to re-access the international capital markets after its commercial debt exchange. It returned with a 20-year eurobond issue in March 2006. The US$300mn bond had an 8.625% coupon and matures in April 2027. Proceeds from the sale were used to buy back its debt to Union Fenosa, the Spanish gas and electricity company. The bond issue was the third since 2001, although both the previous two bonds were subject to the 2005 debt exchange. Then, in May 2010, the government issued a new 10-year eurobond. The 7.5% 2021 had an issue size of US$750mn (it has since been increased to US$1.5bn). Dominican Republic has been a regular issuer since then, returning to the market on an annual basis since 2012. The government even issued a 30-year bond in April 2014 (US$1.25bn 7.45% 2044 bond) and another 30-year in January 2015 (US$1.5bn 6.85% 2045 bond), the latter in a dual tranche issue with a 10-year (US$1bn 5.5% 2025). Both 2015 issues were tapped by an additional US$500mn each in May 2015, partly to finance the repayment of the Venezuelan PetroCaribe energy agreement.

The Dominican Republic now has 12 USD sovereign bonds outstanding, amounting to a total of US$14.3bn (18% of GDP). The country's latest issuance came in July 2018 with a US$1.3bn 10-year issue. Prior to that, it issued in February 2018 a dual tranche 30-year US$ bond (US$1bn with a 6.5% coupon) and a five-year DOP dual currency bond (DOP40bn, US$816mn equivalent, with an 8.9% coupon). The DOP-denominated issue was its first non-dollar eurobond, issued outside a GDN programme, with all payments made in US dollars. The bond was issued under NY law. All the outstanding USD-denominated bonds are listed in the table below. Details for the DOP dual-currency bond issued in February 2018 are also given.

Dominican Republic's outstanding sovereign USD bonds

Description	*Size*	*Maturity type*	*Issue date*
USD 9.04% due 2018	NOW MATURED	Sinkable	May 2005
USD 7.5% due 2021	US$1500mn	Sinkable	May 2010
USD 7% due 2023	US$500mn	Bullet	Jul. 2012
USD 6.6% due 2024	US$500mn	Bullet	Oct. 2013
USD 5.875% due 2024	US$1000mn	Sinkable	Apr. 2013
USD 5.5% due 2025	US$1500mn[a]	Bullet	Jan. 2015
USD 6.875% due 2026	US$1500mn[b]	Bullet	Jan. 2016
USD 5.95% due 2027	US$1700mn[c]	Bullet	Jan. 2017
USD 8.625% due 2027	US$300mn	Sinkable	Mar. 2006
USD 6.0% due 2028	US$1300mn	Bullet	Jul. 2018
USD 7.45% due 2044	US$1500mn[d]	Bullet	Apr. 2014
USD 6.85% due 2045	US$2000mn[a]	Bullet	Jan. 2015
USD 6.5% due 2048	US$1000mn	Bullet	Feb. 2018

Source: Bloomberg

[a]Both original US$1bn 10y and US$1.5bn 30y issues tapped by US$0.5bn in May 2015
[b]Original US$1bn issue tapped by US$0.5bn in August 2016
[c]Original US$1.2bn issue tapped by US$0.5bn in July 2017
[d]Original US$1.25bn issue tapped by US$250mn in August 2014

Dominican Republic bond
Dominican Republic 8.9% 2023
Bloomberg ticker: DOMREP

Borrower	Dominican Republic
Issue date	15 February 2018
Form	Euro non-dollar dual currency
ISIN	USP3579EBZ99
Issue size	DOP40bn
Outstanding amount	DOP40bn
Currency	Dominican peso (all amounts in respect of principal and interest will be paid in USD, as calculated by the calculation agent)
Denomination	DOP8,000,000 minimum and DOP50,000 thereafter
Amortisation	Bullet
Final maturity date	15 February 2023
Coupon/interest	8.9%, paid semi-annually February and August
Day count	30/360

(*continued*)

(continued)

Dominican Republic bond *Dominican Republic 8.9% 2023* *Bloomberg ticker: DOMREP*	
Method of transfer	Euroclear/Clearstream
Settlement period	T + 2
Book runner	Citi, JP Morgan
Calculation agent, paying agent and trustee	BONY
Listing	Luxembourg
Governing law	New York

Source: Bloomberg

Corporate Bond Markets

The Dominican Republic's international corporate bond market is fairly limited. There have been a number of issuers in the past, but the two main outstanding USD issues of any size are now from Aeropuertos Dominicanos (AERDOS), the airport maintenance service provider, with a US$317mn 6.75% 2029 bond issued in January 2017 under Aeropuertos Dominicanos Siglo XXI SA, and Banco de Reservas de la Republica Dominicana (BRSVDR) with a US$300mn 7% 2023 bond issued in 2013. AERDOS also had a US$550mn bond issued in 2012, which was called in February 2017 ahead of its November 2019 maturity. Other issuers have included Cap Cana (CAPCAN), a recreation and resort company, whose biggest issue was its US$250mn 2013 bond issued in 2006, which defaulted in June 2009; Tricom SA, a wireless telecoms company, which issued a US$200mn bond in 1997 which was due to mature in 2004. It was defaulted on and the company went into bankruptcy in March 2008; Empresa Generadora de Electricidad Haina (EGEHAI) whose biggest bond was US$175mn issued in 2007 and which matured in April 2017; and Consorcio Remix CxA (CONSRE) with a US$2bn bond that matured in September 2018. In November 2010, a bond (USG0111KAA28) for a combined US$284mn was issued by AES Andres Dominican (receiving US$167.5mn) and Dominican Itabo (receiving US$116.5mn) with a 9.5% annual coupon and a 10y maturity. It was the largest private offer ever by Dominican corporates. This bond was called in December 2015 when AES Andres redeemed the notes in full with the proceeds of a bridge loan; AES Andres paid a premium of US$8.8mn for the early redemption.

Other domestic corporate bond issuers include Cia de Electricidad de Puerto Plata SA, Consorcio Energetico Punta Cana-Macao SA, and Dominican Power Partners.

Details for the AERDOS bond and the BRSVDR bond are shown below.

Aeropuertos Dominicanos bond
Aeropuertos Dominicanos 6.75% 2029
Bloomberg ticker: AERDOS

Borrower	Aeropuertos Dominicanos Siglo XXI SA
Issue date	20 January 2017
Form	Eurobond
ISIN	USP0100VAB91
Issue size	US$317mn
Amount outstanding	US$317mn
Currency	US dollar
Denomination	US$200,000 minimum, increments of US$1000 thereafter
Amortisation	Call/sink
Final maturity date	30 March 2029
Coupon/interest	6.75% per annum, paid quarterly
Day count	30/360
Method of transfer	Euroclear, Clearstream
Exchange	EUROMFT, Luxembourg
Settlement period	T + 2 business days
Joint lead managers	JP Morgan, Scotia Capital USD Inc

Source: Bloomberg

Banco de Reservas de la Republica Dominicana bond
Banco de Reservas de la Republica Dominicana 7% 2023
Bloomberg ticker: BRSVDR

Borrower	Banco de Reservas de la Republica Dominicana
Issue date	1 February 2013
Form	Eurobond
ISIN	USP10475AA22
Issue size	US$300mn
Amount outstanding	US$300mn
Currency	US dollar
Denomination	US$150,000 minimum, increments of US$1000 thereafter
Amortisation	Bullet

(*continued*)

(continued)

Banco de Reservas de la Republica Dominicana bond *Banco de Reservas de la Republica Dominicana 7% 2023* *Bloomberg ticker: BRSVDR*	
Final maturity date	1 February 2023
Coupon/interest	7% per annum, paid semi-annually
Day count	30/360
Method of transfer	Euroclear, Clearstream, DTC
Exchange	Luxembourg
Settlement period	T + 2 business days
Managers	Citi

Source: Bloomberg

Ecuador

Nominal GDP (US$mn, 2018)[a]		107,266
Population (thousand, 2018)[a]		17,023
GDP per capita (USD, 2018)[a]		6301
Credit ratings (long-term foreign currency)[b]	Fitch	B–
	Moody's	B3
	S&P	B–

[a]IMF WEO October 2018
[b]As at end-September 2018

Country Summary

- President Lenin Moreno took office in May 2017, after the decade-long rule of Rafael Correa. Correa, known for his 2008/09 bond default, leftist populist model and autocratic style, stood down and picked Moreno as the ruling party's candidate. But, in an unexpected twist, Moreno has since tried to distance himself from Correa's policies, although their broken relationship could threaten governability. The new president also inherited a weak economy.
- Ecuador has been hit hard by the oil price drop that began in mid-2014, with oil accounting for 50% of exports at the time. Without the luxury of being able to devalue, and amid tighter financing conditions, contractionary fiscal policy saw Ecuador quickly fall into recession.

Exotix Capital, *Exotix Developing Markets Guide*,
https://doi.org/10.1007/978-3-030-05867-8_15

Growth has been anaemic since. Ecuador subsequently embarked on a borrowing spree over 2015–17 from the international bond market and China, to try to offset the impact of lower oil revenues, while the 2017 election cycle also led to a sharp widening in the budget deficit. Public debt has doubled since 2012 to 46% of GDP.

- Ecuador has been a serial defaulter and rescheduler, with two bond defaults in the 2000s (2000 and 2008), the latter being among the worst cases of opportunistic default. Given tighter financing conditions, the government announced on 3 April 2018 that it will seek to renegotiate bilateral loan terms with China, although little has been heard on this since, while Moreno has also sought to improve ties with multilateral creditors and bondholders. China has become a significant creditor (owed c22% of public external debt), while Ecuador issued cUS$14.75bn in eurobonds over 2014–18.

Economic data	*Avg*[a]	*2014*	*2015*	*2016*	*2017 (e)*	*2018 (f)*	*2019 (f)*
Real GDP growth	3.5	3.8	0.1	−1.2	2.4	1.1	0.7
Inflation (annual average)	4.0	3.6	4.0	1.7	0.4	−0.2	0.5
Current account (% of GDP)	0.5	−0.5	−2.1	1.4	−0.3	−0.5	0.7
Reserves (US$mn, end-period)[b]	3963	3949	2496	4259	2451	3128[c]	–
Reserves/ imports (months)[d]	2.0	1.5	1.2	2.4	1.2	–	–
Overall fiscal balance (% of GDP)[e]	−2.2	−5.2	−6.1	−8.2	−4.5	−2.7	−2.3
Currency (ticker)	US dollar (USD)						
FX regime	Ecuador was dollarised in 2000 and has no separate legal tender.						
Key exports	Oil and oil products (31%), fruit, vegetables and cut flowers (23%), fish and seafood (17%), other foodstuffs (14%). Oil was 55% of exports in 2013.						

Source: IMF WEO Database, IMF Country Reports, Haver, OEC

[a]10-year average to 2016 unless otherwise stated

[b]Total foreign reserves

[c]Latest figure, August 2018

[d]In months of the current year's imports of goods, services and income debit, Exotix calculation

[e]Overall government net lending

Key figures		*Party*	*Since*
President	Lenin Moreno	PAIS	May 2017
Vice president	Maria Alejandra Vicuña	PAIS	Jan. 2018[a]
Minister of finance	Richard Martinez	PAIS	May 2018
Key opposition figure	Guillermo Lasso	CREO	Feb. 2013
Central bank governor	Veronica Artola Jarrin	–	Jun. 2017

[a]Vicuña replaced Jorge Glas in January 2018, after already performing the role of vice president in the temporary absence of Jorge Glas, who faced legal proceedings, and was convicted in December 2017, over corruption involving the Brazilian construction firm Odebrecht

Politics

Executive power

The president, who is chief of state and head of government, maintains strong executive power. The president heads the cabinet and is elected by popular vote every four years in a two-round run-off system. To win in the first round, a candidate needs at least 40% of the vote and to gain a 10-point advantage over the closest rival. Presidential powers increased considerably after changes to the constitution were agreed in a referendum in September 2008 under President Correa. This included permission for the president to run for immediate re-election for a second four-year term (previously, the constitution allowed multiple non-consecutive terms). In February 2018, President Moreno held a constitutional referendum in which voters were faced with seven questions, the main one being whether to reintroduce term limits for elected officials, limiting them to a single re-election to the same office, in effect reversing the amendment to allow indefinite re-election approved in 2008. Crucially, this will limit presidents to two terms and, applied retrospectively, will have the effect of banning Correa from running again. Other questions included whether to ban officials convicted of corruption from running for office, whether an election should be held to replace current members of the National Council for Citizen Participation and Social Control (a body set up by Correa in 2008, which has the power to appoint heads of various entities that oversee the government, including the attorney general, office of the comptroller general and the public defender), and whether to prohibit metal mining in protected areas. Results showed those in favour (a Yes vote) ranged from 63–74% of the vote, depending on the question (with 65% voting Yes for question 2).

Presidential term: Four years (immediate re-election allowed)

Parliamentary term: Four years (immediate re-election allowed)

Legislature

Unicameral: the National Assembly, which replaced Congress under the 2008 constitution. Previously, Congress comprised 100 members elected through a party-list proportional representation system to serve four-year terms in office. The Assembly, now made up of 137 members serving four-year terms, has the power to pass laws, while the Judicial Council appoints judges. 116 members of the Assembly are elected by popular vote by simple majority (based on provincial constituencies), 15 members are directly elected from a national list by proportional representation and six are elected representatives of the emigrant community.

Elections

Next due *Presidential and legislative: February 2021*

Last legislative election (Feb. 2017)	*Seats*	*Last presidential (Feb./Apr. 2017)*	*% of vote*
Movimiento Alianza Pais (PAIS)	74	*First round (February 2017)*	
Creating Opportunities Movement (CREO-SUMA)	34	Lenin Moreno (PAIS)	39.4
Social Christian Party (PSC)	15	Guillermo Lasso (CREO)	28.1
PACHAKUTIK (MUPP)	4	Cynthia Viteri	16.3
Democratic Left (ID)	4	Other	16.2
Patriotic Society Party (PSP)	2	*Second round (April 2017)*	
Other	4	Lenin Moreno	51.2
		Guillermo Lasso	48.8
Total	**137**	**Total**	**100.0**

People

16mn people in total, comprising 72% mestizo, 7% montubio, 7% Amerindian, 6% black and 8% others. Spanish is the official language, but Amerindian languages, especially Quechua, are common. 74% of the population are Roman Catholic.

Ecuador gained independence from Spain in 1822 and was predominantly an agrarian economy until the discovery of oil in 1972, which led to a military overthrow and rapid industrialisation, although over-reliance on oil has led Ecuador to become susceptible to external shocks. As the oil boom waned, the military ceded power in 1979. A new constitution was signed, marking a return to democracy.

Despite weak legislative support, governments have generally pursued free-market reforms and crackdowns on drug crime and terrorism. A state of emergency was declared after oil prices fell in 1982. Broad political stability over the past decade under President Correa came after a volatile period. Between 1997 and 2007, Ecuador had eight presidents, three of whom were overthrown during periods of political unrest (2000 saw a banking crisis and default that led to dollarisation).

Although popular, and delivering macro-stability and increased social spending, Correa was criticised for being increasingly authoritarian, in particular for clamping down on the free press. He decided to step down in the country's 2017 elections, and nominated Lenin Moreno, his vice president in his first term, as the PAIS presidential candidate. The election gave voters a choice of continuity of Correa's policies under his deputy, Lenin Moreno, or economic liberalism under right-winger Guillermo Lasso, with the threat of harsh austerity. Moreno narrowly missed out on victory in the first round, but went on to win the second round in April 2017. In a contested result, Lasso's campaign expressed concern over the four-day delay to the vote count in the first-round election and later alleged fraud when it became clear that Lasso had lost the second round.

Since taking power, Moreno, a moderate leftist, has distanced himself from the policies of Correa, cracked down on corruption, appeared more conciliatory and implemented more market-friendly policies, leading to a rift between the two. Moreno's own plans for constitutional changes were passed in a referendum in February 2018. Correa announced in January 2018 that he had split from PAIS to form his own party.

Ecuador is currently a member of OPEC after re-joining in 2007 (having left in 1992).

Debt

	2012	2017
External debt ratios (%)		
Total external debt/GDP	18.1	38.6
Public external debt/GDP	12.4	31.0
Private external debt/GDP	5.7	7.6
Total external debt/exports of goods, services and remittances	55.3	159.3
External debt service ratio (public)	21.5	35.9
Public debt ratios (%)		
Public domestic debt[a]/GDP	8.8	14.5
Public debt/GDP	21.2	45.5

Source: Central Bank of Ecuador, Ministry of Finance, IMF, Haver, Exotix

[a]Aggregated method

Ecuador's total external debt was US$41.9bn at end-March 2018, according to central bank figures, which included the government's US$3bn bond issue in January 2018. Of the total, over four-fifths (82%) was owed by the public sector (cUS$34.6bn) and 18% was owed by the private sector (US$7.3bn). Ministry of Finance figures showed that the majority of public external debt was commercial debt owed to banks and bondholders (54% of the total, cUS$18.7bn). Eurobonds, including the January 2018 issue, amounted to US$14.75bn (43% of public external debt and 35% of total external debt), across eight issues, all of which had been issued since 2014 (following the 2015 maturity). Other bonds, comprising defaulted Brady and Global 2012/2030 bonds, and Petroamazonas bonds, were another 4% of public external debt. Commercial loans, including those from China, were US$2.5bn (7% of public external debt). 24% of public external debt was owed to multilateral creditors. Two creditors (IADB and CAF) made up 94% of multilateral debt. The IADB owed 56% of all multilateral debt and 14% of public external debt and CAF owed 39% of multilateral debt and 9% of public external debt. Most of the remaining multilateral debt was owed to the World Bank. Bilateral debt was 21% of public external debt (US$7.1bn) with most of it (98%) owed to non-Paris Club creditors (although official figures include new debt owed to Paris Club members in non-Paris Club debt). Most bilateral debt was owed to China. Official figures show that China was owed US$7.3bn in total, comprising official debt and commercial bank loans (that is, China was owed 21% of all public external debt)—c76% of the US$9.7bn in bilateral debt and commercial loans. Brazil is also a bilateral creditor (3% of bilateral debt). Of the very small amount of Paris Club debt (just US$121mn), Italy was the largest creditor, with the next largest being Israel, France and Japan.

Total external debt amounted to 39% of GDP in 2017, about double what it was in 2012, with most of the growth coming from public external debt. Public external debt as a share of GDP rose c2.5 times, from 12% of GDP to 31% of GDP, while private external debt was 8% of GDP. In absolute terms, public external debt virtually tripled to US$31.7bn in 2017 from just US$10.9bn in 2012 (a level around which it had hovered since 2005), suggesting that most of the increase that occurred between end-2017 and March 2018 was due to the eurobond issue in January 2018. Most of the increase in public external debt since 2012 has been due to commercial banks and bondholders, rising from US$1bn (10% of PED) in 2012 to US$15.5bn (49% of PED) at end-2017. Bilateral debt also saw a significant increase, rising from US$3.9bn in 2012 to US$7.4bn in 2017, mostly due to Chinese debt. Multilateral debt rose from US$5.9bn in 2012 to US$8.5bn in 2017, mostly from the IADB. As a share of exports of goods and services, total external debt rose 55% in 2012 to 160% in 2017 (based on official current account statistics for the full year 2017, from Haver). This also reflected the 14% fall in current account earnings, which is in part due to the period of low oil prices since 2014. Exports of goods, services and remittances were US$24.8bn in 2017, compared with US$28.8bn in 2012. Goods exports (which made up 80–85% of total current account earnings) fell by 20% to US$19.6bn, while remittances rose by 15% to US$2.8bn and services rose by 27% to 2.3bn. The overall external debt service ratio (the ratio of public and private external debt service to exports of goods, services and remittances) is also high. It rose from 22% in 2012 to 36% in 2017, as overall external debt service rose from US$6.2bn to US$8.9bn. Whereas private external debt service comprised the majority of total external debt service in 2012 (c70% of the total and almost all of it being principal payments), its share in the total in 2017 had declined, given the rise in public sector debt service (more debt, and bonds being on more expensive terms), to c50:50. The public external debt service ratio rose from 6.6% to 18.7%. In 2017, principal repayments on public external debt were US$2.9bn (up from US$1.2bn in 2012), and interest payments rose to US$1.7bn from US$0.7bn.

Ecuador's total public debt has shown a sharp increase over the past several years, although it should be noted that Ecuador presents domestic public debt under two methodologies—the consolidated method, which nets out intra-public sector debt (consistent with IMF methodology), all of which is domestic debt, and the aggregated method, which includes intra-public sector debt. The government adopted the consolidated method in

October 2016, a move that was seen at the time as a way to provide more borrowing space under the government's self-imposed 40% debt ceiling, although it switched back to the aggregated method in May 2018, after the appointment of the new finance minister Richard Martinez to replace Maria Elsa Viteri. Martinez has been more open about the debt situation. As a result of a shift to the aggregated method, Ecuador's total public debt is now reported as higher than it was, although it has risen under both approaches, in part due to the increase in public external debt. Under the aggregated method, total public debt has doubled as a share of GDP since 2012. Public domestic debt was US$14.8bn in 2017 (14.5% of GDP), up from US$7.8bn in 2012 (8.8% of GDP), so that total public debt was 45.5% of GDP in 2017 (US$46.5bn), up from 21.2% in 2012 (US$18.7bn), with external debt c70% of the total. Under the consolidated method, total public debt has tripled as a share of GDP since 2012. Public domestic debt (on a net basis) was just US$0.9bn in 2017 (0.9% of GDP), up slightly from US$0.7bn in 2012 (0.7% of GDP), so that total public debt was 31.9% of GDP in 2017 (US$32.6bn), up from 13.1% in 2012 (US$11.5bn), with external debt about 95% of the total.

The new government of President Moreno announced the formation of a debt audit in July 2017. The independent audit committee, under the Office of the Comptroller General, will review the sources and uses of all internal and external debt of the Republic incurred between January 2012 and May 2017. Amid reports public debt could be much higher than official figures show, the audit was expected to be concluded in April 2018.

Composition of external debt

External debt by creditor (Mar. 2018)	*Nominal amount outstanding (US$mn)*	*Share of total (%)*
Public sector external debt	**34,566.9**	**82.5**
o/w Official multilateral	8419.3	20.1
IADB	4706.7	11.2
CAF	3259.4	7.8
World Bank	409.5	1.0
Official bilateral	7140.5	17.0
Paris Club	120.7	0.3
Non-Paris Club	7019.8	16.8
Commercial creditors	18,690.0	44.6
Sovereign eurobonds	14,750.0	35.2
Other bonds	1400.1	3.3

(*continued*)

(continued)

External debt by creditor (Mar. 2018)	*Nominal amount outstanding (US$mn)*	*Share of total (%)*
Loans	2539.9	6.1
Suppliers' Credit	317.1	0.8
Private sector external debt	**7338.8**	**17.5**
Total external debt	**41,905.7**	**100.0**
Memo: China[a]	*7317.0*	*17.5*

Source: Ministry of Finance, Central Bank of Ecuador, Exotix

[a]Ministry of Finance figure, bilateral lending and commercial loans

Rescheduling History

Ecuador has been a serial rescheduler, with a history of defaulting and restructuring its debt obligations, with eight Paris Club agreements and six commercial debt rescheduling agreements or defaults since the 1980s. Public debt ballooned in the mid-1970s in the oil boom Junta years, resulting in a build-up of unsustainable obligations and sought debt reduction under the Brady plan, in common with much of Latin America. Ecuador's 1995 Brady plan implied a 45% haircut, after a series of bank debt reschedulings in the 1980s. Its two most recent bond defaults occurred in 1999–2000 and 2008–09.

Ecuador defaulted on its Brady bonds in 1999–2000, suffering a severe financial crisis in 1999 that included a banking crisis and debt default. An export crisis due to depressed world oil prices and an unusually long El Nino effect that decimated the agricultural sector, combined with a tightening in emerging market financing conditions, had resulted in the economy deteriorating sharply over 1997–98. The decision in December 1998 of President Mahaud, elected in August 1998, to mediate in the troubled banking sector led to bank-runs and the closure of or state intervention in 16 commercial banks. A deposit freeze was ordered in March 1999. The decision to float the currency in February 1999 in the wake of capital outflows and low reserves saw the currency fall by 51% against the US dollar in 1999 alone. Public debt was 85% of GDP in 1999, according to Moody's. The economy contracted severely, with real GDP falling by over 6% in 1999 while inflation rose to 96% in 2000. Ecuador defaulted on its Brady bonds in late 1999 and early 2000, and other bonds it had outstanding, and a restructuring saw a 40% haircut. Dollarisation followed in

January 2000, under Mahuad, who was later deposed. It was unpopular at first, it but proved essential to stabilise the economy. Bank deposits began to be unfrozen in March 2000. The economy subsequently performed reasonably well between 2001 and 2009, notwithstanding political turmoil along the way. The external anchor helped inflation fall to below 3% by 2004. Productivity growth, higher investment and tighter fiscal policy, aided by rising oil prices, saw the economy achieve annual average real GDP growth of over 5% across 2000–05 and a primary surplus average of c4% of GDP. High oil revenues did, however, mask structural and institutional inadequacies.

Ecuador defaulted again in 2008–09 on certain of its bonds under President Correa. Ecuador's willingness to pay had already been doubted, not least because Correa's External Debt Commission, which reported in September 2008, found evidence in its audit of both illegal and illegitimate public debt, as widely expected, specifically in regard to two bonds (the 2012 Global and 2030 Global bonds). Both had been issued in the 2000 debt exchange for defaulted Brady bonds, and amounted to US$3.2bn in principal. The Commission's findings were used in November to justify not paying a forthcoming eurobond coupon (the 2012 Global bond) on the due date (15 November), despite acknowledging the money was available, while the government evaluated its options during the grace period. The government then defaulted on the 2030 Global bond in February 2009. A repurchase offer for the two defaulted bonds was subsequently made in April 2009.

The then Minister of Economy and Finance Maria Elsa Viteri, who had only been appointed in March 2018, announced on 3 April 2018 that Ecuador will to seek to renegotiate bilateral loan terms with China. It followed the presentation of the president's economic plan on 2 April that said the authorities would seek a review of loan terms from creditors and which proposed US$1bn in spending cuts aimed at reducing the budget deficit from a targeted 5.64% of GDP in 2018 to 2.47% in 2021. It suggested no action would be taken on the bonds, although markets were cautious as Viteri had been finance minister under Correa during the 2008–09 default. Viteri was subsequently replaced by Richard Martinez in May 2018, who immediately adopted a more open and transparent approach on the debt situation and established dialogue with the multilaterals and bondholders. At the time of writing, no further details were available on discussions over Ecuador's Chinese debt.

Relations with Multilateral Creditors

Ecuador has sought to re-engage with the IFIs (and IMF in particular) since 2014, first under President Correa and continued under Moreno, after a decade in which ties had gradually been severed, ironically a process that began under Correa during his first term in office. Ecuador has had 18 IMF programmes in all, dating back to the 1960s, although just two in the 1990s and two in the 2000s. It has not had a programme since 2004, and while Ecuador submitted itself to Article IV reviews in 2004, and again in 2006 and 2008, even these ceased under President Correa. All IMF balances were cleared in 2007. Ecuador was on poor terms with the majority of the international community due to the default on foreign debt in 1998 and again on US$3.2bn of international bonds in 2008, deemed to be "illegal" by President Correa, after which it followed a more isolated approach, and became more dependent on Venezuela and China. But a desire to diversify funding sources away from China, and find new sources to fund large infrastructure spending plans, subsequently encouraged Correa to re-engage with the IMF as a deliberate strategy to rebuild market confidence ahead of a return to the bond market. After a six-year break, an Article IV consultation was concluded in July 2014, albeit with discussions taking place outside the country and over video conference. The 2015 Article IV was completed in September 2015, which did involve a country visit. In July 2016, the IMF concluded its 2016 Article IV—the last one to have been undertaken—along with financial support under its rapid financing instrument (RFI) to support the country's post-earthquake reconstruction after the earthquake that hit in April 2016. However, there was no Article IV in 2017, as the authorities' engagement with the IMF was interrupted over the year and into 2018 by the country's political changes, first due to the election and change of government, and second due to the constitutional referendum, probably at just the wrong time given the country's emerging liquidity problems. A staff visit in November 2017, after the new president took office in May, said the next Article IV would be in "early 2018", although this was postponed because of the change in the minister of finance in early March. Hence, the last real engagement was the RFI agreed in September 2016.

On 11 June 2018, IMF staff met with Ecuador ministers to discuss macroeconomic issues and areas of cooperation with the Fund, including the Article IV consultation. An IMF mission to the capital, Quito, subsequently took place over late June-early July, with a Fund press statement published on 5 July noting that the new government had taken important steps to strengthen fiscal institutions (including improvements in the fiscal policy framework and increasing fiscal transparency) and to re-establish a competitive private-sector driven economy. However, the IMF noted that addressing fiscal imbalances remained an important policy priority. The non-financial public sector deficit was reported at 4.8% of GDP in 2017, down from 8.4% of GDP in 2016. The external position needed to be strengthened, including building an adequate reserve cushion, while the real effective exchange rate was overvalued. At the time of writing, there was no date for the IMF board review.

IMF programmes

Date	*Arrangements*	*Comments*
1980s–90s	Various SBAs	1983–84, 1985–86, 1986–87, 1988–89, 1989–91, 1991–92, 1994–95.
2000–2001	SBA	A 12-month SDR226.7mn (US$304mn, 75% of quota) credit approved in April 2000 to support the government's economic programme for 2000, centred on dollarisation; a new government took office in January 2000. At the first review, completed in August, the IMF reported better than expected fiscal performance. In May 2001, the programme was extended to end-2001. The programme was fully drawn.
2003–2004	SBA	A 13-month SDR151mn (US$205mn, 50% of quota) credit was approved in March 2003. In approving the SBA, the IMF noted although a recovery had begun after dollarisation, policy slippages were seen in 2002. In particular, rapid public sector wage increases undermined the fiscal position. Structural reforms in some areas had also been suspended. The IMF noted that the new government elected in November 2002 had shown strong leadership in dealing with the economic situation and had acted quickly to reverse policy slippages in 2002. The IMF said in its first review in August 2003 that, despite the government's ambitious fiscal and structural reform agenda, performance in H1 had been uneven. This was due in part to political and institutional challenges. The programme finished in April 2004 and was only partly drawn.
July 2016	RFI	The IMF approved a request for purchase under the RFI in July 2016 amounting to US$364mn. The financial support was intended to help the country meet an urgent balance of payments need due to the April 2016 earthquake.

Source: IMF. Ecuador joined the IMF in 1945

Ecuador changed the focus of its external creditors beginning in 2007 under Correa. It shifted away from commercial sources and traditional multilateral lenders (Bretton Woods institutions) and bilaterals, and towards Latin American-based multilateral entities and new bilateral partners, such as China. In Latin America, Ecuador strengthened ties with the Inter-American Development Bank (IADB), Corporación Andina de Fomento (CAF), and Fondo Latinoamericano de Reservas (FLAR). The IADB is Ecuador's biggest multilateral creditor, owed US$4.7bn on latest figures (56% of multilateral debt). Aiming to promote inclusive and sustainable growth and help the country to overcome constraints and structural barriers to growth, the IADB has many active projects, focused on fiscal management, urban sustainability and rural development. The energy sector is the largest recipient of IADB loans. CAF is owed US$3.3bn (39% of multilateral debt). It also has a role in infrastructure development in Ecuador. CAF and FLAR both provided new loans in 2017. For example, Ecuador entered into a US$200mn two-year loan with CAF in March 2017 to partially finance projects relating to the generation, distribution and transmission of electricity while FLAR approved a three-year loan of US$637.8mn in October 2017. Meanwhile, the World Bank has eight active projects in Ecuador, the latest of which was approved in November 2016. The projects are varied but focus on improving infrastructure. Educational support is also a large ongoing project.

Paris Club and Bilateral Creditors

Ecuador has been a frequent rescheduler in the Paris Club, seeing eight treatments since the early 1980s. Its last agreement was in 2003 although the last four agreements remain active. Terms have been on a flow rescheduling basis rather than debt cancellation. In the last agreement in 2003, although on a small scale, participating creditors included most of the major countries, including Canada, France, Germany, Israel, Italy, Japan, Norway, Spain, the UK and the US.

Paris Club agreements

Date	*Terms*	*Status*	*Details*
1983	Classic	Fully repaid	US$169mn treated, rescheduled on a case-by-case basis.
1985	Classic	Fully repaid	US$330mn treated.
1988	Classic	Fully repaid	US$277mn treated.

(*continued*)

(continued)

Date	*Terms*	*Status*	*Details*
1989	Classic	Fully repaid	US$393mn treated.
1992	Houston	Active	US$339mn treated. Houston terms, adopted in 1990, enhanced Classic terms. Non-ODA repayment lengthened to 15 years or beyond and ODA repayments lengthened up to 20 years with maximum 10-year grace. ODA credits rescheduled at a concessional rate.
1994	Houston	Active	US$292mn treated.
2000	Houston	Active	Agreement in September 2000 treated US$880mn out of US$2511mn due to the Paris Club as of April 2000. Treatment of arrears as of April 2000 and maturities falling due from May 2000 to April 2001. The IMF enabling programme was the SBA agreed in April 2000.
2003	Houston	Active	June 2003, following the IMF SBA agreed in March 2003. The agreement treated US$81mn out of US$2730mn due to the Paris Club as of January 2003. Total external debt was US$11.4bn as at end-2002. The agreement treated maturities falling due from March 2003 to March 2004. Repayment of non-ODA credits over 18 years, three years' grace. Repayment of ODA credits over 20 years, 10 years' grace. Debt service due to the Paris Club was reduced by an estimated US$272mn over 2003–04.

Source: Paris Club

Ecuador turned to non-traditional bilateral creditors after its 2009 strategic default, having lost access to the international bond market (until its return in 2014) and suffering from strains with the main multilateral creditors. Over 2009–13, non-Paris Club bilateral debt increased from US$672mn (compared with US$680mn in Paris Club debt) to US$5.3bn (compared with Paris Club debt of US$0.4bn). Non-Paris Club debt now stands at over 10 times its end-2009 level. Ecuador has executed several loan agreements with China in the past seven years and continues to collaborate with long-time partners, such as Spain and Brazil.

China has become Ecuador's largest bilateral creditor, although, as noted above, the government announced on 3 April 2018 that it will to seek to renegotiate its Chinese loans: bilateral debt to the Chinese government and debt to Chinese banks combined was US$7.3bn in March 2018 (21% of public external debt), according to Ministry of Finance figures. According to the 2028 bond prospectus, Ecuador entered into three separate loan agreements with the China Development Bank (CDB) totalling

US$5bn over 2010–14, in which loan amounts were to be invested in specific infrastructure projects or programmes in return for crude oil delivery contracts with PetroChina and Unipec. The first loan agreement was signed in 2010 for US$1bn and was repaid in full at the end of its original four-year term. The second loan agreement was signed in 2011 for US$2bn, with an eight-year term. The third loan agreement was signed in 2012 for US$1bn, also with an eight-year term. In January 2015, in response to lower oil prices, Ecuador entered into a memorandum of understanding (MOU) with the CDB for a loan of up to US$1.5bn. Ecuador entered into a fourth loan agreement with the CDB, under the MOU, in April 2016 for US$2bn (more than the amount initially contemplated), with a maturity of eight years. The agreement was related to a multi-party contractual structure involving a crude oil delivery contract entered into with PetroChina. On 7 January 2015, Ecuador also entered into a framework agreement for future cooperation with the Export Import Bank of China. Under the agreement, the Ministry of Finance was able to submit priority lists of projects which it proposed to be financed by China Exim Bank within three years of the date of the agreement. The initial priority list included six projects to be financed at a total cost of US$5.3bn. In February 2016, Ecuador entered into a US$198mn loan agreement with China Exim Bank, to finance the first phase of Yachay as part of the framework agreement for future cooperation agreed in January 2015. The concessional loan agreement has a 3% interest rate and a 20-year term.

Various other bilateral Chinese loans occurred over 2016–17, with some examples as follows. In January 2016, Petroecuador, the state-owned oil company, entered into a credit agreement for a facility of up to US$970mn from a consortium of Chinese banks led by Industrial and Commercial Bank of China, China Exim Bank and China Minsheng Banking Corporation. The facility relates to a multi-party contractual structure involving a crude oil delivery contract entered into with PetroChina. The credit has a term of five years, with an interest rate of LIBOR + 6.2%, and has a Ministry of Finance guarantee. The first tranche of US$820mn was disbursed in February 2016. The second tranche of US$150mn was disbursed in November 2017. In October 2017, the Development Bank of Ecuador (DBE) entered into an eight-year US$200mn facility agreement with the CDB with a ministry of finance guarantee.

In July 2016, Ecuador and the Instituto de Crédito Oficial (the Official Credit Institute of Spain), acting for Spain, entered into a US$183.6mn credit agreement for the financing of the supply of rolling stock, auxiliary vehicles, workshop tools and equipment and parts for Quito's first metro line.

Sovereign Commercial Debt

Ecuador has seen a number of commercial debt restructuring agreements and defaults, with its most recent incident—a decade ago—relating to Correa's strategic default in 2008–09. This followed a bond default in 2000 (which included default on its Brady bonds and followed the country's 1999 crisis), and its Brady deal in 1995 (following earlier bank debt reschedulings of the 1980s).

The government reached an agreement with its commercial bank creditors to restructure its MLT commercial bank debt under the Brady Plan in May 1994. Ecuador's Brady deal offered creditors to exchange existing principal for either a 30-year par bond with a 3% coupon, rising to 5% 10 years later, or a 30-year discount bond at 55% of face value at Libor + 13/16. Both bonds were collateralised against US Treasuries; the principal of the par bonds and discount bonds was fully collateralised by 20-year UST bonds and interest on both notes was collateralised on a 12-month rolling basis. Accrued and unpaid interest to that point was issued in two separate Brady-backed instruments, being nine- and 20-year maturities, both paying Libor + 13/16, termed the interest equalisation (IE) and past due interest (PDI) bonds respectively. The Republic issued US$1.9bn, US$1.4bn and US$2.4bn of par notes, discount notes and PDI notes, respectively, in February 1995. It had issued US$191mn of IE notes in December 1994 and also agreed to make certain additional cash payments in respect of overdue interest. The Brady deal implied a c40% NPV haircut.

The government defaulted on its Brady bonds in 1999–2000, as well as on two eurobonds it had issued in 1997. Public debt was already high (85% of GDP), and with just over US$1bn of servicing split equally between domestic and external obligations falling due in that year and total reserves of US$1.6bn, the Mahaud administration began defaulting on all its bonds by end-1999. It defaulted on its discount bonds in August 1999, which were subsequently accelerated in October 1999, and then defaulted on US$500mn worth of eurobonds also in October (US$350mn 11.25% 2002 and US$150mn FRN 2004 that had been issued in April 1997). Defaults on the par bonds, IE bonds, and finally PDI bonds followed in November and December 1999, and February 2000, respectively. Although pre-default attempts to consolidate obligations with creditors failed, by August 2000, an exchange offer had been launched with commercial debts consolidated into new 2012 and 2030 dollar-denominated global bonds as well as cash payments. The 12% 2012 bond had US$1250mn outstanding while the step-up 2030 bond had US$2687mn outstanding. The former bond incorporated accrued interest from the time of each instrument's default, whilst the 2030 issue restructured all aforementioned bonds with an option to exchange into the 2012 at increased loss to the holder. The new 2030 issues also had a feature whereby if a payment was missed in 10 years from issue, the holders would get extra bonds on a sliding factor scale of 1.3, 1.2, 1.1 dependent on how soon the event horizon was. The Brady collateral-backed discount and par bonds realised 51.3% and 42.6% of original value, respectively, resulting in haircuts at the exit yield of 27.1% and 18.9%. Liquidated collateral enabled 55% of the discount restructure's final value to be paid in cash, with 65% for the par bond. Cash payments were also received on the US$500mn 2002 and 2004 eurobonds for past due principal and interest, as was the case on the PDI and IE issues to varying degrees, each witnessing a present value haircut ranging between 28.9% and 47.2%, based on IMF research. There is now a very small residual amount of unswapped Brady bonds left (cUS$60mn or less in each bond, according to Bloomberg), and secondary market trading in them is very limited.

The 2000 exchange of its defaulted Brady (and other) bonds was highly successful with a 98% acceptance rate (according to Moody's). The exchange offer was preceded by an IMF stand-by arrangement (SBA) in April 2000, which also secured cUS$900mn from multilaterals over the following year. Ecuador also secured a seventh Paris Club treatment on US$880mn by September of that year, repayable over 18 years with three years' grace. With successive administrations continuing a hawkish fiscal stance, the IMF approved a further 13-month SBA in March 2003, the country's last IMF financing facility.

The use of exit consents by Ecuador in its 2000 exchange was also seen as a big factor in its success, driving high participation. The 2000 exchange marked the first time exit consents were used in restructuring a sovereign bond under New York law, although their use was seen by some market participants at the time as especially egregious. Specifically, tendering holders were instructed to waive certain rights and delete various terms in the outgoing bonds, which made them less desirable to hold. According to the IMF, consents sought, inter alia, to delete the requirement that all payment defaults must be cured as a condition to annul any acceleration, removing the provision restricting Ecuador from purchasing any Brady bond while the default was continuing, removing the negative pledge clause and removing the requirement to maintain the listing of the defaulted bonds on the Luxembourg Stock Exchange.

Yet, within five years of its default, Ecuador was able to return to the market and issued US$650mn in a new 9.375% 2015 bond in December 2005. Proceeds were used in part to buy back some of the 2012 bonds. The 2015 bond was successfully repaid in full and on time in December 2015; reported, with some amusement, as Ecuador's first bond repayment in 180 years (according to Bloomberg).

If the 2000 default reflected weakened ability to pay, the subsequent 2009 default under Correa resembled a classic case of unwillingness to pay (a strategic default). At the time, Ecuador had three bonds outstanding, the 12% 2012 Global bond (US$510mn nominal) and the 10% 2030 Global bond (US$2.7bn), both of which came out of the 2000 restructuring, and the 9.375% 2015 Global bond (US$650mn) issued in 2005. Ostensibly due to the impact of the global financial crisis and the fall in the oil price in 2008, Correa argued that withholding of debt service payments (with interest more than 5% of GDP) was necessary to maintain the high levels of social spending that the government had developed after the oil price spike had produced a revenue windfall. Yet, public debt was only 23% of GDP (according to Moody's). Default (specifically on the 2012 and 2030 bonds) followed the findings of the government's Commission on Integral Audit of Public Credit, published in November 2008. The commission found evidence of illegitimacy and illegality in the process of the 2012 and 2030 bond issues, and their high coupons were also a factor. Although the commission provided the moral case for default, the selective non-payment of the 2012s and 2030s was ultimately seen by the market as politically motivated by a solvent and (at the time) liquid sovereign (for example, the 2015 eurobond and rump of Brady's were not included in the default). Ecuador missed a US$30.6mn coupon payment on 15 November 2008 on the 2012s, which was not cured during the 30-day grace period, and a US$135mn coupon payment on 15 February 2009 on the 2030s, which was also not cured during its 30-day grace period. So, by mid-March 2009, Ecuador was in default on an aggregate amount of US$157mn in interest on both bonds, with a combined principal of US$3.2bn (according to government figures). Holders of the 2012 bond subsequently demanded acceleration of the bond. However, Correa's administration remained current on the 2015 Global bonds, issued in December 2005, when he was finance minister (it was repaid on due date).

The government announced a take it or leave cash buyback for the two defaulted Global bonds on 20 April 2009. It launched a cash tender offer at

35 cents on the dollar on the face value of the bonds and resulted in in NPV haircut of around 70%. PDI was not recognised. The offer closed on 15 May although the tender was reopened in November 2009. A one-way conference call for bondholders was given on 5 May by the then Minister of Finance Maria Viteri, in an attempt to explain the Republic's thinking and address bondholder questions, but there was no negotiation with bondholders. The government claimed the offer was not coercive, and that participation was voluntary but, amid suggestions that the government had also embarked on a secondary market buyback after the default, bondholders feared that after the offer, the government (and its nominees) could control a simple majority and then be able to force through certain amendments to the bonds' terms, to the detriment of remaining holders. Despite the poor terms and unilateral nature of the process, c93.22% of the bonds were tendered in all (according to government figures), and the government had paid only US$900mn for US$2.9bn in bonds. By end-2009, on Ministry of Finance figures, US$84mn of the 2012s remained and US$167mn of the 2030s. Ecuador has since also successfully repurchased additional amounts of the 2012 and 2030 bonds from remaining holders, often in off-market bilateral transactions. By November 2017, according to the 2028 bond prospectus, the total aggregate amount of outstanding principal on the 2012 and 2030 bonds was just US$52.1mn, representing just 1.6% of the original aggregate principal amount of the two bonds (although Bloomberg shows outstandings of US$68.05mn and US$149.63mn for the 2012s and 2030s, respectively). A few legal proceedings from remaining holders of the 2030 bonds have been seen, although these motions have been withdrawn or dismissed. Exotix is not aware of any active trading in the residual amount of the 2012 and 2030 bonds.

Commercial debt agreements

Date	*Details*
1983	Bank debt restructuring in October covering US$2.8bn of maturities over November 1982–December 1983. New long-term money of US$0.4bn and maintenance of short-term credit lines (US$0.7bn).
1985	Multi-year restructuring agreement of bank debt in December covering US$4.2bn of maturities over January 1985–January 2000. New long-term money of US$0.2bn and maintenance of short-term credit lines (US$0.7bn).
1987	Replaced the 1985 agreement.

(continued)

(continued)

Date	*Details*
1995 Feb.	Brady deal. Restructuring of US$7.8bn in principal and PDI. For principal: exchange US$2.6bn for discount bonds (45% haircut) yielding LIBOR+ 13/16% and US$1.9bn for par reduced-interest rate bonds. Both bonds had a 30-year (2025) bullet maturity, collateralised principal and twelve-month rolling interest guarantee. For PDI: US$75mn settled in cash at closing, US$2.3bn exchanged for 20-year amortising (PDI) bonds, US$191mn exchanged for nine-year IE bonds and US$582mn written off. The NPV haircut was 42.2%, according to the Cruces and Trebesch database.
2000 Aug.	Exchange of US$6.1bn (principal) in existing defaulted bonds (comprising US$5.6bn in Brady bonds and US$0.5bn in its two new eurobonds) for US$3.9bn in two new global bonds. A new 12-year bond had a fixed 12% coupon. A new 30-year bond had a step-up coupon, set at an initial 4%, rising annually by 1 ppt each year, to 10% annually after six years. The operation saw a 40% reduction in principal for bondholders. US$5.8bn in total was tendered. The NPV loss amounted to 38%, according to the IMF.
2009 May	Cash buy back following default on its 2012 and 2030 bonds in November 2008 and February 2009, respectively. The two bonds comprised US$3.2bn in principal. The government subsequently bought back 93% of the defaulted bonds at 35 cents on the dollar, although some holders sought alternative arrangements. The NPV loss amounted to 68%, according to IMF research.

Source: GDF, Ecuador bond prospectuses, Exotix

Ecuador returned to the market in 2014 with a new eurobond issue, after a five-year break following its 2009 default, and when it had just one bond outstanding at the time (the 2015 maturity), and has issued a number of other bonds since then. A return had been signalled as early as 2011, in order to finance its reported more than US$7.5bn in infrastructure and energy projects, but it is likely that the sequence of issuance depended on re-engagement with the IMF first, which had occurred by 2014. The US$2bn 10-year bond (2024 maturity), at 7.95%, was issued in June 2014. Despite dividing opinion, the bond was oversubscribed. It was quickly followed by a US$750mn five-year bond (2020 maturity) in March 2015 at a coupon of 10.5%, in the process inverting its curve and sending a negative signal to markets, although the curve later disinverted. The 2020s were tapped for another US$750mn in May 2015. Ecuador issued two bonds in 2016, a US$1bn long five-year bond in July (2022 maturity), again with a high coupon (10.75%), which was tapped for another US$1bn in September, and a new US$750mn 10-year in December (2026 maturity), with a still high coupon (9.65%), which was tapped for another US$1bn in January 2017. Ecuador returned to the market in June 2017, after the presidential transition, with a US$2bn dual tranche issue in a six-year and 10-year, and issued again in October 2017 (a new US$2.5bn 10-year). Ecuador's most recent foray came in January 2018 with a bumper US$3bn new 10-year (2028 bond) issue at 7.875%. In the meantime, it also repaid its 2015 bond. All outstanding bonds are listed in the table below.

In the space of the four years since returning to the market, Ecuador has issued a total of eight new bonds (by January 2018) for an aggregate nominal amount of (currently) US$14.75bn (about 14% of projected 2018 GDP). Ecuador's aggressive borrowing on the international markets which has often been at high cost, since it resumed access in 2014, coincided with a funding gap created by lower oil revenues following the oil price declines over the same period.

Ecuador's outstanding eurobonds

Description	*Issued amount*	*Amount outstanding*	*Issue date*
USD 10.5% due 2020	US$750mn	US$1500mn[a]	24 Mar. 2015
USD 10.75% due 2022	US$1000mn	US$2378mn[b]	28 Jul. 2016
USD 8.75% due 2023	US$1000mn	US$1187mn[c]	2 Jun. 2017
USD 7.95% due 2024	US$2000mn	US$2000mn	20 Jun. 2014
USD 9.65% due 2026	US$750mn	US$1791mn[d]	13 Dec. 2016
USD 9.625% due 2027	US$1000mn	US$1000mn	2 Jun. 2017
USD 8.875% due 2027	US$2500mn	US$2500mn	23 Oct. 2017
USD 7.875% due 2028	US$3000mn	US$3000mn	23 Jan. 2018

Source: Bloomberg

[a]2020s were tapped by US$750mn in May 2015

[b]2022s were tapped by US$1bn in September 2016 and another US$378mn, in the context of the GSI loan, in October 2017

[c]2023s were tapped by US$187mn, in the context of the GSI loan, in October 2017

[d]2026s were tapped by US$1bn in January 2017 and another US$41mn, in the context of the GSI loan, in October 2017

Ecuador has also entered into other commercial borrowings through Petroamazonas and a GSI loan facility, according to its 2028 bond prospectus. Petroamazonas, the state-owned oil company involved in the exploration and exploitation of hydrocarbon resources, issued two tranches of notes guaranteed by Ecuador in February 2017, the PAM 2019 Notes and the PAM First Remarketing Notes, totalling US$671mn. Holders of the PAM First Remarketing Notes sold them in the international capital markets in May 2017. Petroamazonas subsequently issued US$300mn of its 4.625% notes due 2020 in November 2017, also guaranteed by Ecuador, and later remarketed those notes in December 2017 (the "PAM Second Remarketing Notes"). The PAM First and Second Remarketing Notes are both listed on Bloomberg as REGS/144A issues (under the ticker PTROAM), a US$315mn 4.625% February 2020 and US$300mn 4.625% November 2020, issued in February 2017 and November 2017, respectively. The PAM notes are, however, very illiquid, and secondary market trading in them is limited. In October 2017, Ecuador, through its central bank, entered into a US$500mn 35-month loan facility with Goldman Sachs International (the GSI loan facility) governed by Ecuador law, which involved a simultaneous three-year gold derivative transaction and three-year bond derivative transaction.

Ecuador bond
Republic of Ecuador 7.875% 2028
Bloomberg ticker: ECUA

Borrower	Republic of Ecuador
Issue date	23 January 2018
Form	Eurobond
ISIN	XS1755429732
Issue size	US$3000mn
Issue outstanding	US$3000mn
Currency	US dollar
Denomination	US$200,000 and US$1000 thereafter
Amortisation	Bullet
Final maturity date	23 January 2028
Coupon/interest	7.875% per annum, paid semi-annually January and July
Day count	30/360
Method of transfer	Euroclear/Clearstream
Settlement period	T + 2
Managers	CS, DB, JP Morgan

Source: Bloomberg

Corporate Bond Markets

The Ecuador international corporate bond market is very limited. Although Ecuador corporates have issued a number of bonds (over 200), these tend to be domestic issues, and there are only three international issues currently outstanding in any size (totalling almost US$800mn). These are issued by the state-owned Petroamazonas EP (PTROAM), as noted above, and EP Petroecuador, issued through Noble Sovereign Funding (NBLSOV). Details for the NBLSOV bond are given below.

EP PetroEcuador (Noble) bond
EP PetroEcuador (Noble) FRN 2019
Bloomberg ticker: NBLSOV

Borrower	EP PetroEcuador via Noble Sovereign Funding I Ltd
Issue date	24 September 2014
Form	Eurobond
ISIN	XS1111082779
Issue size	US$1000mn
Amount outstanding	US$263.2mn (after June 2018 payment)
Currency	US dollar
Denomination	US$250,000 minimum, increments of US$1000 thereafter
Amortisation	Sinkable (5.2632% of par every quarter, commencing 24 March 2015)
Final maturity date	24 September 2019
Coupon/interest	FRN: US LIBOR + 563bps (currently 7.92%) paid quarterly
Day count	ACT/360
Method of transfer	Euroclear/Clearstream
Exchange	Berlin
Joint lead managers	Bank of America Merrill Lynch, JP Morgan

Source: Bloomberg

El Salvador

Nominal GDP (US$mn, 2018)[a]		25,855
Population (thousand, 2018)[a]		6398
GDP per capita (USD, 2018)[a]		4041
Credit ratings (long-term foreign currency)[b]	Fitch	B−
	Moody's	B3
	S&P	CCC+

[a]IMF WEO October 2018
[b]As at end-September 2018

Country Summary

- El Salvador is the smallest (by area), but the most densely populated, of the seven Central American countries and the fourth largest by GDP (behind Guatemala, Costa Rica and Panama). Since the end of a 12-year guerrilla war in 1992, the country has been stable, although social challenges remain (crime, gangs, drugs, poverty and income distribution).
- El Salvador is heavily dependent on the US economy and is vulnerable to natural disasters. The US accounts for half of its exports, although workers' remittances from the US are now the main FX earner (worth 18% of GDP), which is at risk if the US follows through with its intention to deport certain Salvadorans living in the US. Hurricane Mitch struck in 1998 (although El Salvador suffered

Exotix Capital, *Exotix Developing Markets Guide*,
https://doi.org/10.1007/978-3-030-05867-8_16

less than Honduras and Nicaragua) and earthquakes in 2001 left more than 1200 people dead and over 1mn homeless.

- The main economic challenge is raising its lacklustre GDP growth rate in the context of limited policy flexibility because of dollarisation and a high debt burden. Indeed, the IMF's recent 2018 Article IV, approved in May 2018, called the medium-term outlook tepid. Weak growth might also put debt sustainability at risk, while a short-lived local payment default in April 2017 led to rating downgrades and raised liquidity concerns. A subsequent pension reform, however, provides some near-term cashflow savings. High gross external financing requirements present another key vulnerability, especially with a US$800mn sovereign eurobond maturity in December 2019.

Economic data	*Avg*[a]	*2014*	*2015*	*2016*	*2017 (e)*	*2018 (f)*	*2019 (f)*
Real GDP growth	2.2	2.0	2.4	2.6	2.3	2.5	2.3
Inflation (annual average)	2.4	1.1	−0.7	0.6	1.0	1.2	1.8
Current account (% of GDP)	−4.9	−5.4	−3.2	−2.1	−2.0	−3.9	−4.3
Reserves (US$mn, end-period)[b]	2683	2661	2670	2923	3273	–	–
Reserves/imports (months)[c]	3.1	2.6	2.6	2.9	3.0	–	–
Overall fiscal balance (% of GDP)[d]	−3.9	−3.7	−3.6	−3.0	−2.3	−2.1	−2.6
Currency (ticker)	Salvadorean Colón (SVC) although the US dollar is also legal tender in El Salvador and circulates freely. Payments may be made in either dollars or colones.						
FX regime	Dollarised (since 1 January 2001). The central bank, the Central Reserve Bank of El Salvador (BCR), is obligated to exchange colones for US dollars on request from banks at the fixed and unalterable rate of SVC8.75 per US dollar.						
Key exports	Non-traditional (74%), maquila (22%, mainly comprising textiles & apparel), traditional (4%, comprising coffee 2% & sugar 2%). Workers' remittances worth US$5bn in 2017 (18% of GDP), compared with goods exports of US$4.7bn and services of US$2.6bn.						

Source: IMF WEO Database, Haver, IMF Country Reports, OEC

[a]10-year average to 2016 unless otherwise stated

[b]Net international reserves

[c]In months of the current year's imports of goods, services and primary income debit

[d]Overall government net lending

Key figures		*Party*	*Since*
President	Salvador Sanchez Ceren	FMLN	Jun. 2014
Vice president	Oscar Ortiz	FMLN	Jun. 2014
Minister of finance	Carlos Caceres	FMLN	Jun. 2009
Key opposition figure	Mauricio Interiano	ARENA	Aug. 2016
Central bank president	Oscar Cabrera	–	Jun. 2014

Politics

Executive power

President is both chief of state and head of government. The executive is vested in the president, vice president and 15 cabinet ministers. Cabinet ministers are appointed, and can be dismissed, by the president. The president may propose legislation to the legislative assembly and has veto power over legislation, which can be over-ridden by a two-thirds vote of the assembly. President and vice president are elected on the same ticket by popular vote for a single five-year term.

Presidential term: Five years (no re-election permitted) **Parliamentary term:** Three years

Legislature

Unicameral, the Legislative Assembly (Asamblea Legislativa) with 84 members. Members, elected on a party list system with proportional distribution of seats, serve three-year terms.

Elections

Next due *Presidential: March 2019; Legislative: March 2021*

Last legislative election (March 2018)	*Seats*	*Presidential election (Feb/Mar 2014)*	*% of vote*
Nationalist Republican Alliance (ARENA)	37	*First round*	
Farabundo Marti National Liberation Front (FMLN)	23	Salvador Sanchez Ceren (FMLN)	48.9
Grand Alliance for National Unity (GANA)	11	Norman Quijano (ARENA)	39.0
National Coalition Party (PCN)	8	Antonio Saca (GANA)	11.4
Christian Democratic Party	3	Others	0.7
Other	2	*Second round*	
		Salvador Sanchez Ceren (FMLN)	50.1
		Norman Quijano (ARENA)	49.9
Total	**84**	**Total**	**100.0**

People

Mestizo makes up 86% of the population, with whites making up 13%. 50% of the population are Roman Catholic and 36% are Protestant. 26% of the population are below age 15. Crime, gangs, drugs and poverty present social challenges and the homicide rate is said to be one of the highest in the world (in January 2017, police said that 24 hours had passed without a reported murder, for the first time in two years). El Salvador is a signatory of the Central America Free Trade Agreement (CAFTA-DR), a free trade agreement with the US, which came into force over 2006–09. The other regional members are Costa Rica, the Dominican Republic, Guatemala, Honduras and Nicaragua. The country has enjoyed political stability over the past two decades, but had a troubled past. From 1932 to 1979, El Salvador was ruled by a succession of military leaders. A revolutionary junta, comprising civilians and military, assumed control of the country in 1979 and, after the PDC joined the junta in 1980, imposed a programme of land redistribution and nationalisation of key coffee and sugar sectors, and the banking system. Several left-wing guerrilla organisations emerged during this time, unifying into the FMLN, opposed to what they saw as a ruling elite that dominated the economy and the government, while the majority of the population lived and continue to live in poverty. A 12-year-long guerrilla war followed (1979–92), which ravaged the country and caused the loss of 75,000 lives, until the then ARENA government (backed by the US) and the FMLN (recognised by France and Mexico) signed a Peace Accord on 16 January 1992, brokered by the UN. ARENA was the dominant party until 2009s election, holding the presidency from 1994–2009. The FMLN has held the presidency since. President Mauricio Funes in 2009 became the first president from the FMLN group since the end of the civil war. Salvador Sanchez Ceren of the FMLN then won a very narrow majority in the 2014 presidential election, after serving as vice president under President Mauricio Funes since June 2009. The legislature has alternated between the two leading parties, although neither party has been able to command a majority. In the most recent legislative elections, held in March 2018, the opposition ARENA gained five seats while the ruling FMLN lost eight seats. In January 2018, US President Trump announced the intention to terminate the provisional residency permits of about 200,000 Salvadorans who have lived in the US since at least 2001, leaving them to face deportation.

Debt

	2012	*2017*
External debt ratios (%)		
Total external debt/GDP	56.1	57.1
Public external debt/GDP	32.1	33.6
Private external debt/GDP	24.0	23.5
Total external debt/exports of goods, services and remittances	133.6	130.6
External debt service ratio[a] (public)	5.8	6.8
Public debt ratios (%)		
Public domestic debt/GDP	28.8	31.9
Public debt/GDP	60.9	65.5

Sources: Central bank, Ministry of Finance, IMF, Haver, Exotix

[a]Ratio to exports of goods, services and remittances

El Salvador's total external debt was US$16.0bn at the end of 2017, according to the central bank (following a BPM6 methodology). This represented c57% of GDP. The USD amount has increased modestly from US$13bn in 2012, but, as a share of GDP, has remained relatively unchanged. Of the total, c60% was public debt (general government and central bank)—amounting to 33.6% of GDP in 2017—and 40% was private (including intercompany lending)—amounting to 23.5% of GDP in 2017. These relative shares have also remained largely unchanged since 2012. In US dollar terms, public external debt was US$9.4bn at end-2017, comprising US$8.7bn in general government external debt and US$0.7bn from the central bank. Private external debt was US$6.6bn at end-2017, including intercompany lending (which amounted to a fairly low US$0.8bn, and which has averaged about US$0.9bn over the last five years). The total external debt/exports ratio (comprising goods, services and remittances) has also been largely stable, in the 130–140% range over this period, and ended 2017 at 131%. This ratio rises to 215–240% over this period based on exports of goods and services only (ie excluding remittances), and ended 2017 at 222%. Exports of goods and services were US$7.2bn in 2017, while remittances were another US$5bn.

For the creditor composition, separate figures for a breakdown of public external debt by creditor are provided by the ministry of finance and give a broadly similar total to the central bank's BPM6 figures. We present the most recent creditor composition for public external debt as of May 2018, the most recent available. It shows public external debt was US$9.7bn in May 2018 (note, the central bank's data show US$9.3bn at end-Q1). The bulk of public external debt is owed to private creditors, primarily in the form of eurobonds. Sovereign eurobonds outstanding amounted to US$6.4bn (nominal), c66% of public external debt (and 39% of total external debt). Around US$3.1bn was owed to multilateral creditors, which accounted for 32% of public external debt and 19% of total external debt. The main multilateral creditor was the Inter-American Development Bank (IADB), c56% of all multilateral debt, followed by the World Bank and CABEI. Bilateral debt is relatively low, amounting to just US$232mn, comprising just 2% of the total public external debt. The main bilateral creditor is Germany's KfW. For private external debt, including intercompany lending, we have used central bank figures for Q1, the most recent available, which show a small increase to US$6.7bn from US$6.6bn at end-2017 (the increase was due to an increase in intercompany lending from US$0.8bn to US$1bn over the quarter). A large proportion of private external debt is owed by the non-financial sector, and some companies in the Republic have accessed the international bond market. The figure for private external debt is broadly in line with that contained in the last published IMF Article IV, the 2016 Article IV, in July 2016, which projected it at 22.5% of GDP in 2017 (cUS$6.3bn). Splicing the MOF and central bank figures together gives the most representative up-to-date breakdown by creditor of total external debt, with a total of cUS$16.4bn by Q2 2018.

Total public debt in 2017, meanwhile, is estimated at 66% of GDP, an increase of 5ppts since 2012. Public debt is split relatively evenly between external and domestic debt. Public domestic debt was 32% of GDP. Public sector debt service is quite high. Based on IMF debt service figures, the projected (public) external debt service ratio in 2017 was 11.7% of exports of goods and services, although this falls to 6.8% of exports of goods, services and remittances. However, the public external DSR will increase in 2019 with the maturity of the 2019 eurobond (US$800mn). Moreover, overall external debt service will be much higher if private debt is included, although figures on private external debt servicing are not readily available. As a proxy, IMF projections for gross external financing requirements (GEFR)—current account deficit plus MLT debt amortisations—amounted to cUS$4.2bn in 2017 (15% of GDP).

The authorities published revised GDP statistics in early 2018. The IMF noted in its 2018 Article IV in May that a downward adjustment of nominal GDP had increased the 2017 debt/GDP ratio from 63 to 71%. Exotix's calculations use WEO GDP and, thus, do not currently reflect the recent GDP revisions.

Composition of external debt

External debt by creditor (May 2018)	*Nominal amount outstanding (US$mn)*	*Share of total (%)*
Public sector external debt	**9682**	**59.0**
o/w Official multilateral	3089	18.8
Inter-American Development Bank	1744	10.6
World Bank IBRD/IDA	894	5.4
CABEI	373	2.3
IFAD	64	0.4
OPEC	14	0.1
Official bilateral	232	1.4
Germany (KfW)	108	0.7
USA (USAD-CCC[a])	49	0.3

(*continued*)

(continued)

External debt by creditor (May 2018)	*Nominal amount outstanding (US$mn)*	*Share of total (%)*
Japan (JICA[b])	37	0.2
Spain (ICO[c])	35	0.2
China	3	0.0
Private creditors (bonds)	6361	38.7
Private sector external debt[d]	**6738**	**41.0**
Total external debt	**16,420**	**100.0**

Source: Central bank, Ministry of Finance, Bloomberg, Exotix

[a]US Department of Agriculture Commodity Credit Corporation

[b]Japan International Cooperation Agency

[c]Spain Institute of Official Credit

[d]As of Q1 2018, central bank BPM6 figures on Haver (including intercompany lending)

Rescheduling History

El Salvador has not rescheduled any of its external loans or defaulted on its debts since 1993, following the end of the civil war in 1992. Its debt service ability was severely eroded by the long civil war and El Salvador was unable to service a portion of its international debt during this period. Between 1990 and 1993, El Salvador successfully negotiated the rescheduling of certain bilateral and multilateral loans and received forgiveness of certain other obligations with some of its international creditors. A few bilateral deals with governments have also taken place since. It has had only one Paris Club treatment, though, which was in 1990. There has been no rescheduling of sovereign external commercial debt.

The government missed a series of payments for pension certificates (CIP bonds) held by public and private sector pension funds from 7 April 2017. Later that month, it was able to resolve financial obligations of US$56.5mn through a budget reallocation approved by Congress. The incident illustrated the fractious political situation in the divided Congress, although the government may have misjudged the negative fallout. This was the government's first missed debt payment and liquidity concerns led to a lowering of the S&P rating in April to selective default from CCC–. The rating had already been lowered to B– in December 2016. It was then revised up to CC in May, following the budget reallocation. In September 2017, Congress passed a pension reform, which was seen as a bit of a mixed bag. It helped to solidify the current system, with an increase in the contribution rate (from 13% to 15%—paid into a longevity fund), widened the coverage and provided some cashflow relief through restructuring of the CIP bonds, which extended payments from 25 to 30 years, with a grace period and modified interest rates. But the main bottleneck to sustainability is the low retirement age and this was not increased. However, the optics were seen as important in showing that a political compromise has been possible. S&P downgraded El Salvador again, temporarily, to selective default, upon the CIP restructuring, but its rating was subsequently lifted to CCC+ the next day after it was completed.

Relations with Multilateral Creditors

El Salvador has had 21 IMF programmes since becoming a member in 1946, with nearly as many taking place since 1980 (10) as before 1980 (11), when many dated back to the 1960s and before. In modern times, after a gap in engagement between 1983 and 1990, El Salvador was in an IMF programme (SBA) in every year during the 1990s. There was then another break of nearly a decade before the country returned to the Fund in the wake of the global financial crisis and possible uncertainty surrounding the country's 2009 election schedule, which saw legislative elections in January and a presidential election in March.

A 14.5-month SBA, amounting to 300% of quota, was approved in January 2009. It was treated as precautionary (and went undrawn) as El Salvador was not seen to be facing any immediate balance of payments need. Its main goal was to provide liquidity in light of the global financial crisis, which hit the economy hard and tipped it into recession, but also to protect from uncertainty in the run-up to the elections and in the first few months of a new administration. El Salvador also secured loans from the World Bank and the IADB to the tune of US$950mn. After the scheduled presidential election in March 2009, the new government of president Mauricio Funes (which took office in June 2009) continued the programme, while undertaking discussions on a new arrangement. A staff-level agreement on a new three-year SBA was reached in September 2009. The new three-year SBA, again worth 300% of quota, was approved by the IMF's executive board in March 2010. The authorities stated their intention to treat it as precautionary, and it again went undrawn.

El Salvador has not had an IMF programme since the 2010 SBA expired in 2013. In December 2016, an IMF team met with a variety of politicians in San Salvador, and reported cross-party support for a new IMF programme to support economic reform, public enterprise transparency and fiscal consolidation, while protecting vulnerable citizens. However, political disagreements in a divided Congress and changing priorities meant that no subsequent IMF programme materialised; there has been no more progress on this since. The 2018 Article IV was, however, concluded by the IMF Board in May 2018.

In its latest Article IV, directors welcomed the continued economic recovery, with growth expected to remain above potential at 2.3% over 2018–19, reflecting the temporary acceleration of US growth, along with the recent improvement in public debt dynamics, supported by fiscal discipline and savings from the pension reform plan. The authorities' fiscal adjustment had improved the fiscal balance since 2014 and stabilised public debt, through higher revenues and spending restraint. This produced a primary surplus of 0.9% of GDP in 2017, although the overall deficit was 2.5% of GDP due to the interest bill. The overall deficit was expected to narrow to 2.2% in 2018. However, public debt had increased in 2017 from 63% to 71% due to the authorities' GDP revisions. But directors noted that potential growth continued to be lower than desirable, debt levels remained high and large financing gaps are projected for 2019 and beyond. This called for further fiscal consolidation, a strengthening of the financial sector and the implementation of far-reaching structural reforms to improve the business environment and support formal employment.

IMF programmes

Date	*Arrangements*	*Comments*
1980s–90s	Various SBAs	1980–81, 1982–83, 1990–91, 1992–93, 1993–94, 1995–96, 1997–98, 1998–2000
2009–10	SBA	14.5-month programme of SDR513.9mn (US$800mn, 300% quota) approved in January 2009 through to end-March 2010. It was treated as precautionary and went undrawn.
2010–13	SBA	Three-year programme of SDR513.9mn (US$790mn, 300% quota) approved in March 2010 under the new government. The programme expired in March 2013 and went undrawn.

Source: IMF. El Salvador joined the IMF in 1946

Multilateral lending increased during the 2000s, mainly related to loan disbursements for reconstruction, other infrastructure and policy-based loans. The World Bank has two active projects in El Salvador: Strengthening the public healthcare system and improving education quality, with large loans to the country, including significant concessional amounts, totalling US$921mn in 2015. The IADB has a number of ongoing projects and others that are still in preparation. Loans total US$800mn, and strategies aim to create future economic growth, improve infrastructure and strengthen public finance over 2015–19. Transport is currently the most significant project category, with US$210mn of allocated finance.

Paris Club and Bilateral Creditors

El Salvador has only had one Paris Club agreement. This came in 1990 and was on Houston (rescheduling) terms. Participating creditors were the US, Canada, Japan, France and Spain.

Paris Club agreements

Date	*Terms*	*Status*	*Details*
1985	Classic	Fully repaid	Treated US$280mn under Classic terms.

Source: Paris Club

A series of bilateral reschedulings took place during the 1990s after the end of the civil war. In 1993, US AID forgave (of its own accord) US$464mn of the Republic's outstanding debt and Canada converted CAD8.1mn of outstanding debt to an obligation of the government to use amounts that would have been applied to service this debt for environmental projects. In addition, El Salvador rescheduled certain other loans between 1990–93 for an amount of US$383mn. In 1999, France, on its own initiative, forgave FRF133mn of the country's outstanding debt, enabling the funds previously allocated to repay El Salvador's outstanding debt to France to be reallocated to establish the Fondo Franco-Salvadoreño, a fund that provides financing for infrastructure projects. In 2006, with the government of Spain, US$10mn of outstanding debt was reallocated to finance projects in the education sector.

Sovereign Commercial Debt

El Salvador has no modern history of rescheduling its sovereign commercial debt. Indeed, even after the civil war, access to commercial funding was limited and most of the external debt incurred by the Republic was with multilateral organisations, with the proceeds used mainly for reconstruction and developing infrastructure. This changed, however, by end-1999 and into the 2000s, when the Republic issued a series of eurobonds, and it has since become a regular issuer over the past two decades.

El Salvador's debut in the international bond market came in 1999 with a US$150mn issue that matured in 2006. This was followed by another issue in July 2001, a US$353.5mn 10-year bond, into which a US$300mn additional issue in July 2002 was fully fungible. Four more issues were seen over 2002–05, all of which are still outstanding, with the increase in commercial borrowing over this period in particular related to post-2001 earthquake reconstruction, financing the pension system and other capital expenditure. This included its first 30-year bond (2032 maturity) issued in April 2002 and a long 20-year bond (2023 maturity) in October 2002. A break in issuance lasted until a December 2009 issue and, after another pause, El Salvador retuned to the market in February 2011. It has been issuing regularly, typically annually, until recently.

El Salvador had nine sovereign eurobonds outstanding, as of February 2018, for a combined amount of US$6.24bn. This includes its most recent issue, the 2029 bond issued in February 2017, the sale of which occurred before the (short-lived) default on domestic pension bonds, since when market access may have become more restricted. Prior to that, its previous issue was in 2014. Details for its outstanding bonds are shown in the table below. As well as the maturity in December 2019 of the 2009 bond issue, the put option on the 2034 bond also becomes exercisable in 2019. The put option gives holders of the 2034 bond, which is US$286.5mn in size, the right to force the Republic to redeem the bond at par in September 2019 (as of 30 June, the bond was trading above par). A description for the 2034 putable bond is also given below.

El Salvador's outstanding eurobonds

Description	*Size*	*Maturity type*	*Issue date*
USD 7.375% due 2019	US$800mn	Bullet	Dec. 2009
USD 7.75% due 2023	US$800mn[a]	Putable	Oct. 2002
USD 5.875% due 2025	US$800mn	Bullet	Dec. 2012
USD 6.375% due 2027	US$800mn	Bullet	Sep. 2014
USD 8.625% due 2029	US$601.1mn	Bullet	Feb. 2017
USD 8.25% due 2032	US$500mn	Bullet	Apr. 2002
USD 7.625% due 2034	US$286.5mn	Putable	Sep. 2004
USD 7.65% due 2035	US$1000mn[b]	Bullet	Jun. 2005
USD 7.625% due 2041	US$653.5mn	Bullet	Jan. 2011

Source: Bloomberg

[a]Original issue was US$451.5mn, increased in March 2003 by US$348.5mn

[b]Original issue was US$375mn, increased in April 2006 by US$400mn and again in July 2006 by US$225mn

El Salvador bond
El Salvador 7.625% 2034
Bloomberg ticker: ELSALV

Borrower	Republic of El Salvador
Issue date	21 September 2004
Form	Eurobond
ISIN	USP01012AM84
Issued amount	US$286.458mn
Currency	US dollar
Denomination	US$10,000 and US$1000 thereafter
Amortisation	Bullet (putable)
Final maturity date	21 September 2034
Other features	Putable (on 21 September 2019 at 100%). Holders must elect to redeem the notes between 21 July 2019 and 21 August 2019. The bond also contains Collective Action Clauses under which certain amendments can be made with the consent of 75% of holders of the outstanding amount.
Coupon/interest	7.625% per annum, paid semi-annually March and September
Day count	30/360
Method of transfer	Euroclear/Clearstream
Settlement period	T + 2
Governing law	State of New York
Joint lead managers	Citi

Source: Bloomberg

Corporate Bond Markets

There are currently three main corporate eurobonds outstanding in El Salvador, amounting to nearly US$1bn. Details are shown below. Many other issues, typically much smaller (less than US$100mn), exist. The first non-sovereign issue came when the Coffee Emergency Fund issued zero coupon notes, with a guarantee from the Republic, maturing from 2001 to 2010. One current issuer, AES El Salvador Trust, issued a 10-year US$300mn bond in 2006 which was called at par in April 2013.

Grupo Unicomer Co Ltd 7.875% 2024
Bloomberg ticker: UNICMR

Borrower	Grupo Unicomer Co Ltd
Issue date	27 March 2017
Form	Eurobond
ISIN	USG42037AA25
Issue size	US$350mn
Currency	US dollar
Denomination	US$200,000 and US$1000 thereafter
Amortisation	Callable
Call schedule	1 April 2021 at 103.938; 1 April 2022 at 101.969; 1 April 2023 at 100.000
Final maturity date	1 April 2024
Coupon/interest	7.875%, paid semi-annually in April and October
Collateralisation	Senior unsecured
Day count	30/360

Source: Bloomberg

AES 6.75% 2023
Bloomberg ticker: AES

Borrower	AES El Salvador Trust II
Issue date	28 March 2013
Form	Eurobond
ISIN	USP06076AA49
Issue size	US$310mn
Currency	US dollar
Denomination	US$200,000 and US$1000 thereafter
Amortisation	Callable
Call schedule	28 March 2018 at 103.375; 28 March 2019 at 102.250; 28 March 2020 at 101.125; 28 March 2021 at 100.000
Final maturity date	28 March 2023
Coupon/interest	6.75%, paid semi-annually in March and September
Collateralisation	Senior unsecured
Day count	30/360

Source: Bloomberg

Banco Agricola 6.75% 2020
Bloomberg ticker: BACEL

Borrower	Agricola Senior Trust
Issue date	18 June 2015
Form	Eurobond
ISIN	USG4109CAA65
Issue size	US$300mn
Currency	US dollar
Denomination	US$150,000 and US$1000 thereafter
Amortisation	Bullet
Final maturity date	18 June 2020
Coupon/interest	6.75%, paid semi-annually in June and December
Collateralisation	Senior unsecured
Day count	30/360

Source: Bloomberg

Ethiopia

Nominal GDP (US$mn, 2018)[a]		83,836
Population (thousand, 2018)[a]		94,138
GDP per capita (USD, 2018)[a]		891
Credit ratings (long-term foreign currency)[b]	Fitch	B
	Moody's	(p)B1
	S&P	B

[a]IMF WEO October 2018
[b]As at end-September 2018

Country Summary

- Ethiopia is a land-locked country in Sub-Saharan Africa. A significant amount of international trade relies upon access to the Port of Djibouti. 2017 IMF forecasts suggest a two-tier Africa, with many economies slowing to 2.5% annual growth, and six countries, including Ethiopia, growing at above 6%. Following recovery from the 2016 drought, Ethiopia's economy is forecast to show the continent's second-fastest growth rate in 2018 (after Ghana).
- Fiscal policy has been cautious with rises in spending matched with rises in revenues. Although Ethiopia's competitiveness and export diversification have historically lagged those of its competitors, recent government policies have led to some improvements. The government continues to tackle corruption with multiple high-profile arrests in 2017.

Exotix Capital, *Exotix Developing Markets Guide*,
https://doi.org/10.1007/978-3-030-05867-8_17

- Public debt has been on the rise since its low of 38% of GDP in 2009, following HIPC debt relief and before an expansionary fiscal response to the global financial crisis. Despite a large eurobond issue in 2014, much of the country's external debt is still on concessional terms, as official creditors help to finance state-led infrastructure development that, in addition to PPPs, is helping to develop the private sector.

Economic data	*Avg*[a]	*2014*	*2015*	*2016*	*2017 (e)*	*2018 (f)*	*2019 (f)*
Real GDP growth	10.3	10.3	10.4	8.0	10.9	7.5	8.5
Inflation (annual average)	16.5	7.4	10.1	7.3	9.9	12.7	9.5
Current account (% of GDP)	−6.5	−6.4	−10.2	−9.0	−8.1	−6.2	−6.2
Reserves (US$mn, end-period)[b]	2289	2496	3248	3402	3197	–	–
Reserves/imports (months)[c]	2.0	1.5	1.9	2.1	1.9	–	–
Overall fiscal balance (% of GDP)[d]	−2.2	−2.6	−1.9	−2.3	−3.3	−3.7	−3.5
Currency (ticker)	Ethiopia birr (ETB)						
FX regime	The birr has been a managed float since 1992, described by the IMF as a crawl-like arrangement. It has been devalued three times, most recently by 15% against USD in October 2017.						
Key exports	Coffee (41%), dried legumes (15%), gold (7.5%), meats (6%), clothing and fabrics (5%) in 2016						

Source: IMF WEO Database, IMF Country Reports, OEC

[a]Ten-year average to 2016 unless otherwise stated
[b]Gross official reserves for end of the fiscal year (July)
[c]In months of the next year's imports of goods and services
[d]IMF general government net lending

Key figures		*Party*	*Since*
President	Sahle-Work Zewde	Independent	Oct. 2018
Prime minister	Abiy Ahmed Ali[a]	ODP	Apr. 2018
Minister of finance	Ahmed Shide	ESPDP	Oct. 2018
Key opposition figure	Merera Gudina[b]	OPC	–
Central bank governor	Yinager Dessie	–	Jun. 2018

[a]Abiy Ahmed Ali succeeded Hailemariam Desalegn on 2 April 2018 following his resignation
[b]Gudina was arrested on 30 November 2016 for meeting with an Ethiopian organisation in Europe that the government considered to be 'terrorists' but he pled not guilty. In May 2017, the European Parliament called for his release, but the government refused. He was released in January 2018, shortly after the government announced the general release of political prisoners

Politics

Executive power

The president is the head of state and the role is largely ceremonial. The president is elected by the House of People's Representatives. Under the 1995 Constitution, the president retains various powers, including calling and dissolving parliament and overseeing parliamentary decisions. The prime minister is the head of government and has most administrative power. The prime minister is nominated by the president, on the advice of party leaders and is head of the Council of Ministers.

Presidential term: Six years, two-term limit **Parliamentary term:** Five years

Legislature

Bicameral comprising of the House of Federation (upper house) with 112 members, at least one member for each feature of Ethiopia's demography, as in Constitution Article 61:2, and the House of People's Representatives (lower house), with 547 seats elected in single-seat constituencies, of which 22 seats are reserved for the representation of minority groups. Elections are on a first-past-the-post basis.

Elections

Next due *Legislative: May 2019* *Presidential: 2019*

Last legislative election (May 2015)	*Seats*	*Last presidential (October 2013)*	*% of vote*
Ethiopian People's Revolutionary Democratic Front	501	Mulatu Teshome (ODP)	100.0
Somali People's Democratic Front	24		
Benishangul Gumuz People's Democratic Party	9		
Afar National Democratic Party	8		
Other	5		
Total	**547**	**Total**	**100.0**

People

Ethiopia was historically a Christian country, after Coptic Christianity was introduced from Egypt, but it became more diversified in the 1530s when Muslim leader Ahmad Gran conquered much of the country. Today 63% of the population is Christian and another 34% are Muslim. Around 80% of the population live in rural areas. The median age in 2017 was just 17.9 years; infant, child, and maternity mortality remain high but have fallen over the past decade. Almost 65% of the population is under 25 and life expectancy at birth is now 63. Literacy levels remain low and over 70% of the population work in agriculture, much of which is part of the informal sector.

In 1868, a British expeditionary force defeated Emperor Tewodros II and, following the battle of Assem and defeat of rebellions, Tigrayan chieftain Yohannes IV became Emperor of Ethiopia in 1872, until he was killed fighting Mahdist forces in 1889 and was succeeded by the King of Shoa, who became Emperor Menelik II. Ethiopia signed a friendship agreement with Italy in 1889, although six years later, Italy invaded. The following year, after Italy's defeat, it recognised Ethiopia's independence, but retained control of Eritrea under the moniker Italian Eritrea. Hereditary ruler Zewditu died in 1930 and her regent Ras Tafari Makonnen became Emperor Haile Selassie.

In 1935, Italy invaded Ethiopia again, marking the start of the Second Italo-Ethiopian War, and instilled Italian King, Victor Emmanuel III the Ethiopian Emperor. Together with Italian Somaliland, Ethiopia and Eritrea now collectively formed Italian East Africa. The Italians were defeated by local resistance and British and Commonwealth troops in 1941, and Ethiopia was ruled by the Commonwealth until the UN federated Eritrea with Ethiopia in 1952. A decade later, Ethiopia annexed Eritrea and it became an Ethiopian province.

Somaliland was occupied by the British in 1941. Haile Selassie regained control in 1942 until being overthrown in a military coup in 1974 and General Teferi Benti became head of state. Three years later he was killed and replaced by Colonel Mengistu Haile Mariam, under whom thousands of government opponents were killed during Qey Shibir, or the 'Red Terror'. Following a 1977 Somalian invasion, Somali forces were defeated with help from the Soviet Union and Cuba. A new constitution in 1987 saw Mengistu elected president, although he was forced to flee the country in 1991 when the Ethiopian People's Revolutionary Democratic Front (EPRDF) captured Addis Ababa, establishing a provisional government. The Soviet Union also supported the Ethiopian government during the 1980s to push back Eritrean forces fighting for independence, but this support ceased in the late 1980s. Eritrean forces captured the Eritrean capital Asmara in 1991 and aided Ethiopian rebels to topple Mengistu Haile Mariam in Ethiopia.

(*continued*)

(continued)

People

Following a vote in 1993, Eritrea became independent and in 1994, a new Ethiopian constitution was introduced with Negasso Gidada becoming president and Meles Zenawi assuming the role of prime minister in 1995. Over 1998–99, border clashes with Eritrea led to a full-scale war until a peace accord was signed in 2000. The 2005 elections were disputed leading to violent protests lasting months. Over 30 seats were subjected to re-elections and the EPRDF emerged with a majority. Ethiopian troops entered Somalia in 2006 to engage in fighting with Islamists, until formally withdrawing forces in January 2009. Heavy fighting in 2009 led to rebel members of Ogaden National Liberation Front (ONLF) claiming capture of several towns. The ruling EPRDF won the 2010 legislative election with a large majority. Tensions built with Eritrea again in 2011, in April of that year the government openly supported rebel groups attempting to overthrow the Eritrean president. ONLF rebels attacked an army convoy in June 2012, leading to 168 Ethiopian troop deaths. In August, Prime Minister Meles Zenawi died following illness and was succeeded by Hailemariam Desalegn. The ruling EPRDF won a huge majority in the 2015 election. Anti-government protests began in July 2016 and violence led to a six-month state of emergency declared in October. In January 2018, Desalegn announced the release of all political prisoners, in what many see as a hopeful sign of enhanced democracy and free speech. Following political unrest, Desalegn resigned in March 2018 and was succeeded by Abiy Ahmed Ali in April. Abiy has since replaced the finance minister and reduced cabinet posts to 20 from 28 by merging some ministries.

Debt

	2012	*Q3 17*
External debt ratios (%)		
Total external debt/GDP	22.8	31.5
Public external debt/GDP	20.5	30.0
Private external debt/GDP	2.3	1.6
Total external debt/exports of goods and services	166.1	409.5
External debt service ratio (total)	6.6	19.6
Public debt ratios (%)		
Public domestic debt/GDP	10.2	13.3
Public debt/GDP	30.7	43.2

Source: National Bank of Ethiopia, Haver, IMF, Exotix

Public sector external debt was US$24.2bn (30% of GDP) in September 2017, based on figures from the Ministry of Finance and Economic Cooperation. Separate figures from the IMF indicate that private sector external debt was an additional US$1.28bn (1.6% of GDP). As a result, total external debt was US$25.5bn, more than double its level in June 2012 (end of fiscal year). This was 32% of GDP and 410% of exports in Q3 17.

The largest external creditor group of the public sector was multilaterals, owed 37% of total external debt, the largest of whom was the World Bank IDA, owed US$6.8bn. Others include the African Development Bank/Fund, the International Fund for Agricultural Development, the International Monetary Fund, the OPEC Fund for International Development, the Arab Bank for Economic Development in Africa and the European Investment Bank. Bilateral creditors were the second-largest creditor group, owed US$8.2bn. Following the various agreements detailed below, Paris Club creditors were owed just 1.7% of the total, while other bilaterals, especially China, were owed the remaining US$7.8bn. Ethiopia issued its first sovereign eurobond in December 2014 for US$1bn. This bond has a bullet maturity in 2024, and amounted to 3.9% of external debt in 2017, with foreign suppliers and commercial banks owed the remaining commercial debt. The proportion of external debt that is on concessional terms peaked at 76.3% in 2008, according to World Bank IDS figures, and has since fallen, to 68.6% in 2016.

Total public (external and domestic) debt was US$35bn (43.2% of GDP), including US$10.7bn (13.3% of GDP) in domestic debt. The external debt service ratio (all debtors) increased from 6.6% of exports in June 2012 to 19.6% in September 2017. These figures include debt service for publicly guaranteed external debt as well as central government external debt, much of which is concessional. Only 45% of public domestic debt was owed by central government and 55% is owed by state-owned enterprises, a proportion that has remained constant in recent years. 88% of total public domestic debt was owed to banks.

Composition of external debt

External debt by creditor (Sep. 2017)	*Nominal amount outstanding (US$mn)*	*Share of total (%)*
Public sector external debt	**24,226**	**95.0**
o/w Official multilateral	9451	37.0
World Bank IDA	6830	26.8
AfDB/AfDF	1907	7.5
UN IFAD	278	1.1
IMF	155	0.6
OFID	94	0.4
BADEA	86	0.3
EIB	73	0.3

(*continued*)

(continued)

External debt by creditor (Sep. 2017)	*Nominal amount outstanding (US$mn)*	*Share of total (%)*
Official bilateral	8202	32.2
Paris Club	419	1.7
Non-Paris Club	7783	30.5
Private creditors	6573	25.8
Eurobond	1000	3.9
Commercial banks	2672	10.5
Suppliers	2901	11.4
Private non-guaranteed external debt	**1276**	**5.0**
Total external debt	**25,502**	**100.0**

Source: Ministry of Finance and Economic Cooperation, Haver, IMF

Rescheduling History

Public external debt increased quickly during the 1980s and 1990s, reaching 155% of GDP in 1994. Paris Club agreements in 1992 and 1997 treated US$441mn with a 50% cancellation rate and US$183mn with a 67% cancellation rate, respectively, and there was a donor-funded debt buyback of US$226mn in January 1996. Despite this, in November 2001, the IMF and the World Bank agreed on decision point for Ethiopia under the HIPC initiative, which then reached completion point in April 2004. Subsequent Paris Club agreements in 2001, 2002, and 2004 were part of HIPC debt relief, implemented in stages and with some additional bilateral agreements in the following years, bringing public debt down from almost 113% of GDP in 2003, to 78% in 2005 and 38% in 2009.

Ethiopia has benefitted from high growth and low debt servicing cost, with 68.6% of total external debt on concessional terms in 2016. Despite the most recent IMF programme reporting progress on building foreign reserves, the latest Article IV shows less than two months of import cover, only forecast to increase slowly to 2.2 months by 2020–21. The weak institutional framework is another vulnerability, although the government appears committed to its anti-corruption stance, with high-profile arrests in 2017. Central government debt is low relative to its peers. Debt has increased due to the financing of large capital projects, and large-scale infrastructure projects. The birr was devalued by 15% in October 2017, which can provide gains in the external trade sector, and controlling inflation is an important objective as it reached double figures again in 2015;

food and import prices have been key contributors. Additionally, the interest rate on deposits was raised to 7% from 5%.

As an importer and exporter of commodities, Ethiopia is exposed to commodity price changes, especially of coffee and gold. Foreign trade mostly goes through the Port of Djibouti, making Ethiopia dependent on the port and transport infrastructure, this necessitates that diplomatic ties with Djibouti are maintained. Ethiopia has renewable energy sources, but the economy remains dependent on oil imports and commodity exports.

In October 2015, Ethiopia's authorities launched the second five-year Growth and Transformation Plan (GTP II), following much success under the first, setting medium-term economic and social policy priorities. The focus is on competitiveness, private sector development and FDI, with the new legal and regulatory framework supporting further PPPs and small and medium-sized enterprises (SMEs) development, aiding private sector activity and limiting public sector expenditure. The informal sector is significant and leads to inaccuracy in national statistics, inefficient tax collection, and inability to monitor and regulate some activities. An historical lack of coordination between ministries and agencies has led to inconsistencies and lower reliability of national statistics.

Ethiopia is subject to global conditions, but recently the economy coped well amid a weaker global environment. Despite a major drought in 2017, growth remained strong and is forecast to remain over 8% per annum until 2019. This reflects improved resilience of the agriculture sector, helped by infrastructure projects and development projects funded by multilateral donors, though the economy and food security are still subject to weather conditions. Continued growth relies upon successful implementation of policies relating to infrastructure development and economic reforms to continue yielding the growth already attributed to them. Infrastructure helps to promote private sector activity, which should drive exporting industries in particular and could help to improve the current account over the medium to long term. Although the current account has been in deficit every year since 2001, WEO forecasts show a gradual improvement, following a short-term worsening.

Fiscal policy helped to minimise the social impact of the drought and a careful expansionary policy was implemented from 2009 to minimise the effects of the global financial crisis. Increases in expenditure were matched with increases in revenue, however the overall budget has been in deficit every year since the earliest WEO figure in 1980, and the budget deficit is expected to exceed 2% of GDP each year to 2023. The IMF has recommended that until more infrastructure projects start to provide export and government revenues, policies must focus on controlling the external debt stock, which may require putting the brakes on new development projects, since social needs remain large. Previous IMF advice was followed with some success in policy implementation.

Relations with Multilateral Creditors

Since joining the IMF in 1945, Ethiopia has had five programmes, the most recent expiring in 2010, although SDR81.6mn (about US$114.3mn) remains outstanding from the 2009–10 ESF. Before 1996, there had been two programmes as detailed in the table below, which were fully drawn. The 1996–99 poverty reduction and growth facility (PRGF, now called an extended credit facility, ECF), had been agreed for SDR88.5mn (about US$127mn) and the first disbursement of SDR29.5mn was immediately disbursed. Before the midterm review could be completed, weather impacts on agriculture and transportation led to crop shortfalls, higher food imports, food price inflation, and a monetary policy response aimed at non-food price inflation, which was successful at containing overall inflation. However, the ECF programme expired with only SDR29.5mn drawn.

In March 2001, the Executive Board approved a three-year PRGF for SDR87mn (cUS$112mn) to support the government's economic reforms. The first and second reviews were completed in August 2001 and March 2002, after which the Board approved an SDR13.37mn augmentation, as the 9/11 attacks led to a balance of payments deterioration. After the fourth review in August 2003, the Board approved additional interim HIPC assistance for SDR2.1mn (cUS$2.9mn). The sixth and final review in September 2004, allowed for full disbursements and satisfactory performance throughout. In November 2001, the IMF and the World Bank's IDA agreed on decision point for Ethiopia under the HIPC initiative.

In August 2009, the Board approved a 14-month exogenous shocks facility (ESF) for SDR153.8mn (cUS$241mn) to provide balance of payments support following the global financial crisis. The ESF programme aims to provide policy support and financial assistance on concessional terms to countries facing temporary exogenous shocks. Both reviews were completed and reported the successful implementation of policies to reduce inflation and rebuild reserves. At the end of 2009, consumer inflation had declined to below 10% and reserves exceeded two months' import cover. The IMF highlighted tax reforms as a future focus, while the authorities plan for ambitious public investment.

IMF programmes

Date	*Arrangements*	*Comments*
1981–82	SBA	Stand-by arrangement with SDR67.5mn, which was fully drawn.
1992–95	SAFC	Structural adjustment facility commitment with SDR49.42mn, which was fully drawn.
1996–99	PRGF	Previously referred to as an enhanced structural adjustment facility and a PRGF (now ECF). In October 1996, a three-year loan under the ECF was approved for SDR88.5mn (about US$127mn) disbursed in annual instalments, the first immediately for SDR29.5mn. However adverse weather caused economic consequences that prevented the mid-term review being completed and the programme expired with only SDR29.5mn drawn.
2001–04	PRGF	In March 2001, the Executive Board approved a three-year PRGF for SDR87mn (cUS$112mn) to support the government's economic reforms. The first and second reviews were completed in August 2001 and March 2002, after which the Board approved an SDR13.37mn augmentation, as the 9/11 attacks led to a balance of payments deterioration. The IMF commended Ethiopia's performance. The sixth and final review in September 2004 allowed for full disbursements.
2009–10	ESF	In August 2009, the Board approved a 14-month ESF for SDR153.8mn (cUS$241mn) to reduce the effects of the global recession on the balance of payments. The programme aimed to provide policy support and financial assistance on concessional terms, in the face of temporary exogenous shocks. The first review was completed in June 2010 and reported the successful implementation of policies to reduce inflation and rebuild reserves. At end-09, consumer inflation had declined to below 10% and reserves exceeded two months' import cover. All performance criteria for December 2009 were met. The second and final review was completed in November 2010, allowing full disbursements, of which SDR81.6mn (about US$114.3mn) remains outstanding. Continued policy implementation had further led to reduced inflation and improving reserves, although tax reforms were cited as a key policy implementation for the future.

Source: IMF. Ethiopia joined the IMF in 1945

In mid-2018, the World Bank had 49 active projects in Ethiopia, with a broad range of development and infrastructure objectives. The World Bank's IDA remains Ethiopia's largest multilateral creditor. Debt owed to the IDA has increased since the figures presented above, as various new projects and loans were approved throughout 2017 and H1 18. These notably include a US$600mn commitment to an urban development project and a US$170mn loan for the development of the livestock and fisheries sector. The African Development Bank is Ethiopia's second-largest multilateral creditor and has various projects in the country, especially focused on power, water and sanitation development. UN IFAD also describes its partnership with Ethiopia as effective for rural development.

Paris Club and Bilateral Creditors

Ethiopia has had five Paris Club agreements, as detailed in the table below, the most recent three being as part of HIPC debt relief. Ethiopia's decision point under the enhanced HIPC initiative was November 2001 and completion point was reached in April 2004. Participating creditors in the 2004 HIPC initiative exit agreement were Australia, Austria, Belgium, Finland, France, Germany, Italy, Japan, the Netherlands, Russia, Sweden, the UK and the US.

Paris Club agreements

Date	*Terms*	*Status*	*Details*
1992 Dec.	London	Fully repaid	Treated US$441mn, with a cancellation rate of 50% under London terms. Non-ODA credits repayable over 23 years, with six years of grace, after 50% cancellation, and ODA credits repayable over 30 years with 12 years of grace. Possibility to conduct debt swaps.
1997 Jan.	Naples	Fully repaid	Treated US$183mn of arrears and maturities falling due between January 1997 and October 1999, with a cancellation rate of 67% under Naples terms. Non-ODA credits repayable over 23 years, with six years of grace, after 67% cancellation, and ODA credits repayable over 40 years with 16 years of grace. Possibility to conduct debt swaps. Intended to be implemented over three stages, although the third stage was never implemented.
2001 Apr.	Naples	Active	Treated US$432mn of arrears and maturities, with US$130mn cancelled and US$302mn rescheduled. Non-ODA credits repayable over 23 years, with six years of grace, after 48.6% cancellation, and ODA credits repayable over 40 years with 16 years of grace. Possibility to conduct debt swaps. Implemented over three stages.
2002 Apr.	Cologne	Active	US$8mn was cancelled from maturities due between November 2001 and March
2004 May	HIPC initiative exit	Active	Of the US$1899mn due to the Paris Club, US$1487mn was treated (US$1296mn cancelled and US$191mn rescheduled). Possibility to conduct debt swaps.

Source: Paris Club

On 2016 figures, Paris Club creditors were owed just 1.5% of total external debt. Official figures do not provide a complete bilateral creditor breakdown, although the single largest bilateral creditor by 2016 disbursements was China (government and Exim Bank). Others include Poland, Exim Bank of India and Exim Bank of Korea.

Further to the agreed 90% debt cancellation as part of the Paris Club, Italy cancelled 100% of Ethiopia's Italian debt in November 2014. The US$462.4mn of cancelled Italian debt to contribute to solving the debt sustainability problem, and the finance minister said this could allow resources to be used for new development projects and support poverty reduction. In May 2007, China agreed debt relief of US$18.5mn for Ethiopia, which could then be used to finance the poverty reduction programme.

Sovereign Commercial Debt

Ethiopia's public external debt from commercial creditors is relatively high, at 27% of total public external debt, although only a small part of this relates to eurobond issuance. Historically, Ethiopia has borrowed from commercial banks and this saw one commercial debt agreement (a small debt buyback operation) in 1996.

Commercial debt agreements

Date	*Details*
1996 Jan	Buyback of US$226mn of debt owed to commercial banks at 8 cents on the US dollar. Funded by the World Bank's DRF.

Source: World Bank GDF

Ethiopia issued its first (and still only, to date) sovereign eurobond in 2014, the details of which are shown in the table below. The US$1bn fixed rate bullet bond, with a coupon of 6.625%, was issued in December 2014 and had a 10-year maturity. Total demand was reported at US$2.6bn. Proceeds were to be used to fund planned government capital expenditure in priority areas including industrial zone development and the development of the sugar and energy industries. Ethiopia was assigned a single B rating from both Fitch and S&P in May 2014, ahead of the planned bond issue. Moody's assigned a B1 rating in December 2014. There have been reports that Ethiopia will issue another eurobond, possibly larger than the first, but no other bond has been issued, as of August 2018.

Ethiopia bond
Ethiopia 6.625% 2024
Bloomberg ticker: ETHOPI

Borrower	Federal Democratic Republic of Ethiopia
Issue date	11 December 2014
Form	Eurobond
ISIN	XS1151974877
Issued amount	US$1000mn
Currency	US dollar
Denomination	US$200,00 and US$1000 thereafter
Amortisation	Bullet
Maturity date	11 December 2024
Coupon/interest	6.623% per annum, paid semi-annually June and December
Day count	30/360
Method of transfer	Euroclear/Clearstream
Settlement period	T + 2
Governing law	English
Joint lead managers	DB, JPM

Source: Bloomberg

Corporate Bond Markets

According to Bloomberg, no Ethiopian corporate has ever issued a eurobond.

Ethiopian Railways Corporation (ERC) is the national railway operator of Ethiopia, providing rail passenger and freight transport services, and also offering some railway infrastructure development services. Established in 2007, it is a quasi-public corporation, which receives government subsidies, but also operates for profit. Chinese financing (US$2–3 billion from ExIm Bank of China) and a term loan were used to construct the Addis Ababa-Djibouti railway over 2011–16. In 2014, the government closed an US$865 million financing package to fund various railway development projects. Included in the 2014 financing was a US$450 million syndicated commercial loan, detailed below. In addition, there was a US$415 million 13 year loan backed by the Swedish Export Credit

Guarantee Board (EKN), Eksport Kredit Fonden (EKF) and Swiss Export Risk Insurance (SERV).

Financial trouble in 2017 followed delays in establishing connecting infrastructure. While the rail connection was inaugurated in October 2016, rail operations did not commence until the start of 2018. Chinese loan repayments were made over the interim period. In September 2018, returning from the China-Africa Forum for Cooperation, Prime Minister Abiy Ahmed announced that a reprofiling with China had extended the repayment of the Chinese railway debt by 20 years.

Ethiopian railways loan

Borrower	Ethiopian Railways Corporation
Loan type	Commercial Loan Facility
Issue date	7 July 2014
Issue size	US$450mn
Amortisation	Seven equal semi-annual instalments over 7 July 2018 to 2 August 2021
Final maturity date	2 August 2021
Interest basis and rate	Six-month LIBOR + 3 ¾% Margin
Guarantor	Ministry of Finance and Economic Development, FDR Ethiopia

Source: Bloomberg

Gabon

Nominal GDP (US$mn, 2018)[a]		17,212
Population (thousand, 2018)[a]		2053
GDP per capita (USD, 2018)[a]		8385
Credit ratings (long-term foreign currency)[b]	Fitch	B
	Moody's	Caa1
	S&P	NR

[a]IMF WEO October 2018
[b]As at end-September 2018

Country Summary

- Gabon has only had three heads of state since independence in 1960. Together with the ruling PDG party dominating government since multi-party politics was introduced in 1990, such continuity has provided peace for over fifty years, although initial protests followed the past two presidential elections and the 2016 presidential election result was disputed. Hence the parliamentary elections, which were delayed from December 2016 due to a lack of funds, will be keenly watched when they eventually take place (they had been rearranged for April 2018, but this was later cancelled).
- Hydrocarbons have dominated the economy, contributing four-fifths of exports and amounting to half of GDP, before the oil price fall in 2014 (Gabon is an OPEC member, and produces c190k bpd).

Exotix Capital, *Exotix Developing Markets Guide*,
https://doi.org/10.1007/978-3-030-05867-8_18

Lower oil prices since then have hit the economy hard, causing growth to weaken and leading to weaker fiscal and external balances, and a significant rise in the debt burden (having quadrupled in five years to over 60% of GDP). The country was eventually forced to turn to the IMF for financial support, as part of a wider regional CEMAC initiative, and a three-year Fund programme was approved in June 2017. Performance has been weak however, and continuing arrears (domestic and external) remain a problem, as reflected in Moody's low rating (downgraded to Caa1 in June 2018), with arrears clearance a key structural benchmark for the programme.

- Economic diversification is needed to provide non-oil revenue and also for when oil runs out. Other resources include considerable quantities of timber, iron ore and manganese. But resource wealth has not brought wider benefits. Corruption is still a concern with the recent example of former minister, Magloire Ngambia, prosecuted for corruption and embezzlement in 2017. There has been much needed investment in infrastructure in recent years.

Economic data	*Avg*[a]	*2014*	*2015*	*2016*	*2017 (e)*	*2018 (f)*	*2019 (f)*
Real GDP growth	3.5	4.4	3.9	2.1	0.5	2.0	3.4
Inflation (annual average)	1.5	4.5	−0.1	2.1	2.7	2.8	2.5
Current account (% of GDP)	10.3	7.6	−5.6	−9.9	−4.9	−1.6	−0.5
Reserves (US$mn, end-period)[b]	1942	2494	1877	804	982	–	–
Reserves/imports (months)[c]	4.6	4.4	4.1	2.1	2.2	–	–
Overall fiscal balance (% of GDP)[d]	3.8	6.0	−1.1	−4.7	−1.7	1.3	0.7
Currency (ticker)	Member of the CFA franc zone (XAF)						
FX regime	The CFA franc is pegged to the euro at a rate of CFAF655.957 per euro. The CFA franc floats freely against other currencies.						
Key exports	Crude petroleum (70%), manganese ore (13%), wood and wood products (7.7%)						

Source: IMF WEO Database, IMF country reports, BEAC, OEC (exports)

[a]10-year average to 2016 unless otherwise stated

[b]Net external assets

[c]In months of the current year's imports of goods and services

[d]IMF general government net lending

Key figures		*Party*	*Since*
President	Ali Ben Bongo Ondimba	PDG	Oct. 2009[a]
Vice President	Pierre Claver Maganga Moussavou	PSD	Aug. 2017
Prime minister	Emmanuel Issoze-Ngondet	PDG	Sep. 2016
Minister of economy	Regis Immongault Tatangani	PDG	Oct. 2014
Minister of budget	Jean-Fidele Otandault	PDG	Aug. 2017
Key Opposition Figure	Jean Ping	UFC	–
Central Bank Governor	Abbas Mahamat Tolli (Governor of BEAC)	n/a	Mar. 2017

[a]Ali Bongo, previously defence minister, and son of Omar Bongo, was elected president after securing the PDG nomination following the death of his father in June 2009. In accordance with the constitution, the Senate President Rose Francine Rogombe assumed the interim presidency until the holding of elections, required within three months. Elections were held on 30 August. He was inaugurated on 16 October after the Constitutional Court confirmed a recount of Ali's victory on 12 October. He was re-elected in August 2016

Politics

Executive power

The president is chief of state, and although the prime minister remains head of government, the president effectively dominates all public institutions. The president is elected by popular vote and is responsible for appointing the prime minister, although the latter in consultation with the president appoints the cabinet (Council of Ministers). The president has the power to dismiss the legislature up to two times, per seven-year office period.

Presidential term: Seven years (term extended and limits removed in 2003)

Parliamentary term: Five/six years

Legislature

Bicameral consisting of the Senate (upper house) and the National Assembly (lower house). A multi-party parliamentary system was established under the 1991 constitution (subsequently revised in 1997). All members of the Senate are indirectly elected by provincial councillors. It is presently controlled by the PDG with 81 seats. In the Assembly, 111 seats are elected by popular vote and nine are reserved for presidential appointments. The Assembly serves for five years, whilst Senate members are appointed for six.

Senate (102 seats, from 91 before January 2009)

National Assembly (120 seats)

Elections			
Next due	*Legislative: n/a—rearranged to April 2018, but subsequently cancelled, after being postponed from December 2016*	*Presidential: 2023*	

Last legislative election (December 2011)	*Seats*	*Last presidential (August 2016)*	*% of vote*
Gabonese Democratic Party (PDG)	113	Ali Bongo Ondimba (PDG)	49.8
Rally for Gabon (RPG—PDG ally)	3	Jean Ping (UFC)	48.2
Other PDG allies	3	Other	2.0
Union for the New Republic (UPNR—opposition)	1		
Gabonese Peoples Union (UPG—previously the main opposition)	0		
Total	**120**	**Total**	**100.0**

People

Gabon has now seen fifty years of dynastic family rule. Long-time president El Hadj Omar Bongo died in June 2009 aged 73, one of the world's longest serving heads of state. As expected, he was succeeded by his son Ali Ben Bongo who won the 2009 presidential election. The results were contested, with most violence seen in the opposition stronghold of Port Gentil. Ali Ben Bongo was re-elected in the 2016 presidential elections, albeit on a narrow margin of victory that translated into just 5594 votes, and the result was disputed by opposition Jean Ping's representatives, who believed that he had beaten Bongo by a large margin. Both candidates claimed victory but the Constitutional Court upheld Bongo's narrow victory.

A constitutional amendment was however approved by parliament in January 2018, to extend presidential elections to two rounds, which was a priority for the opposition. Other changes, including the exact role of the president in policy making, were criticised by the opposition as being a power grab. The last parliamentary election was in 2011, when Bongo's ruling PDG party took 95% of seats (parliamentary elections were meant to be held in December 2016, but the disputed presidential election result meant they were delayed, and have still not taken place). The main opposition Gabonese Peoples Party (UPG) lost all eight of its seats.

Independence from France was declared in August 1960. Leon Mba (BDG) was elected president in 1961. He was overthrown by the military in 1964 in Gabon's only successful coup, but subsequently reinstalled by the French. In November 1967, President Leon Mba died, succeeded by his Vice President Albert (later Omar) Bongo. President Bongo declared Gabon a one-party state, which it remained until 1990, turning the BDG into the current PDG. Over two decades of centralised power followed, although Gabon remained relatively stable. Bongo was re-elected under the one-party system in 1973, 1979 and 1986. A national conference in 1990 established a multi-party system, resulting in a new constitution in 1991 and elections in 1993 which Bongo won. He was re-elected for a second time in 1998 and a third time in 2005.

(*continued*)

(continued)

People
Almost all the peoples of Gabon are of Bantu origin, with around 40 ethnic/tribal divides therein and distinct languages and cultures. However, ethnic origins are of lesser importance in Gabon than other parts of Africa. There are four main ethnic groups: Fang, Bapounou, Nzebi and Obamba. Other ethnicities include Myene, Eschira and Bandjabi. A small proportion of the population is European, mainly French. Christianity is the predominant religion. French is the official language, although in 2010, President Bongo said that France was no longer its exclusive partner and in 2012 introduced plans to promote the English language. Gabon is one of the least densely populated countries in Africa and over 60% of the population is under 25. Gabon has upper-middle income status but much of the country lives in poverty, due to unemployment and income inequality. Gabon's ranking on the World Bank's Doing Business Indicators has fallen from 156 in 2010 to 167 in 2018, continuing a trend. Various reforms aimed at economic diversification and public-sector transparency are being introduced. Gabon is the second biggest by GDP of the six members of the Central African Economic and Monetary Community (CEMAC), which also comprises Cameroon, CAR, Chad, the Republic of Congo, and Equatorial Guinea, accounting for 19% of its GDP, but is the second smallest by population, accounting for just 4% of the region.

Debt

	2012	*2016*
External debt ratios (%)		
Total external debt/GDP	16.3	37.4
Public external debt/GDP	16.3	37.4
Private external debt/GDP	n/a	n/a
Total external debt/exports of goods and services	23.8	103.4
External debt service ratio (public)	4.3	12.5
Public debt ratios (%)		
Public domestic debt/GDP	0.7	26.8
Public debt/GDP	16.9	64.2

Source: Eurobond prospectus for the 2025 tap (August 2017), IMF, Exotix

Public external debt was US$4.9bn at the end of 2016, according to the official figures provided in the eurobond prospectus for the 2025 tap in August 2017 (the tap left net debt largely unchanged as the US$200mn proceeds went to retiring the remaining outstanding of the 2017s). The creditor composition shows that bondholders are the single largest creditor group, accounting for 43% of public external debt (cUS$2.1bn), and that commercial creditors, comprising both banks and bonds, accounted for 64% of the debt. Bonds—at the time (end 2016)—comprised the residual amount of the 8.2% 2017 (cUS$160mn), and the 6.375% 2024 (US$1500mn) and 6.95% 2025 (US$500mn at the end of 2016, pre-tap). Bilaterals accounted for 24% of public external debt, of which almost all (97%) was owed to non-Paris Club creditors, and most of this was owed to China (China accounted for 78% of bilateral debt—some US$1bn—and c19% of public external debt). Multilaterals accounted for the remaining 12% of public external debt, owed mostly to the AFDB, IsDB and EBRD, as well as some to the World Bank. The debt stock figures also predate the 2017 IMF ECF under which cUS$204mn has been drawn to date (end June 2018).

The creditor profile has changed rapidly over recent years, following a Paris Club debt buyback in 2007, subsequent eurobond issues and the growing role of Chinese lending. Indeed, external public debt has more than doubled in nominal CFA terms since 2012 (and nearly doubled in US$ terms, up 72%), after having been fairly constant over 2009–12. The biggest rise has been in bonds (up 2.5 times), followed by non Paris Club bilaterals (up 2.0 times). Whereas private creditors now comprise 64% of public external debt, 11 years ago, nearly three quarters of its debt was owed to official creditors, with the Paris Club being the biggest creditor group.

Public external debt has therefore risen to 37% of GDP in 2016, just over twice its level in 2012. Because there is no official data for private sector external debt, and no figures from the IMF or World Bank, total external debt is the same. Total external debt amounted to 103.4% of exports of goods and services. This is up significantly (more than fourfold) from 2012, due in part to higher debt, but also due to the sharp fall in goods' exports. Exports of goods and services fell by 50% over this period, from US$11.7bn to US$5.1bn, due to lower oil prices. The external debt service ratio (public only) has similarly seen a sharp increase, rising to 12.5% from 4.3%.

Total public sector debt in 2016 was equivalent to US$8.5bn based on official figures. This was 64.2% of GDP, almost four times the ratio in 2012, and is back to levels last seen in 2003–04. This reflects not only the sharp rise in public external debt, but also a substantial rise in public domestic debt, up from just 0.7% of GDP (CFAF57bn) in 2012 to 26.8%

of GDP (CFAF2228bn) in 2016. The main contributors to the increase are banks, including statutory advances from the regional central bank (BEAC) in 2016, VAT reimbursements in 2016 and domestic arrears since 2014. Domestic debt has been low historically due to the shallow domestic debt market and limited credit supply within CEMAC.

In its most recent statement in June 2018, following a staff visit to conduct the second review of the ECF, the IMF noted that public debt (including domestic arrears) was 63% of GDP. The IMF, in the past, attributed the rapid accumulation of debt over the past ten years to pronounced investment expenditure, in particular related to three major events. First, large investment activity related to the government's strategic plan for economic diversification (PSGE). Second, capital spending in the run-up to the two soccer African Cup of Nations in 2012 and 2016. Third, government borrowing increased to dampen the recent oil price shock. The incorporation of domestic arrears (7.5% of GDP) as well as statutory advances from BEAC are also factors in explaining the much higher public debt ratio now seen in 2016/17 compared to previous estimates. Gabon's debt was however still judged by the IMF to be sustainable in its DSA from July 2017 for the approval of the ECF programme.

Composition of external debt

External debt by creditor (end-2016)	*Nominal amount outstanding (US$mn)*	*Share of total (%)*
Public sector external debt[a]	**4932.5**	**100.0**
o/w Official multilateral	598.2	12.1
World Bank IBRD	67.2	1.3
Official bilateral	1179.2	23.9
Paris Club	38.6	0.8
Non-Paris Club	1140.7	23.1
o/w China	919.8	18.6
Private creditors	3155.1	64.0
Commercial banks	1018.3	20.6
International capital markets (bonds)	2136.8	43.3
Private sector external debt	**n/a**	**n/a**
Total external debt	**4932.5**	**100.0**

Source: Eurobond prospectus for the 2025 tap, World Bank WDI. Figures in CFA Franc converted in to US$ at the end-2016 exchange rate from Bloomberg

[a]Excludes arrears

Rescheduling History

Gabon has a long history of rescheduling both its official Paris Club debt and its commercial debt, although it was not eligible for HIPC debt relief because of its middle-income status. Its impaired payment history stemmed largely from high borrowing on the back of oil revenues in the 1980s, to fund large infrastructure projects such as the Transgabonais railway and to establish public companies, as well as the failure to save oil windfalls and a pro-cyclical fiscal policy in which governments have been unable to respond to economic downturns.

Gabon did not always meet its repayment obligations in the early 1990s, due to adverse macroeconomic conditions and severe monetary and financial instability, particularly the 50% devaluation of the CFA franc in 1994, which doubled the debt burden in local currency terms. This saw Gabon resort to numerous rescheduling agreements. However, indicating improving liquidity conditions and policy performance, in part on the back of an oil windfall, the Paris Club agreed in July 2007 to accept Gabon's request to buy back most of its Paris Club debt. The operation was financed in part by Gabon's first eurobond, which was issued in December 2007.

Gabon's debt situation has quickly deteriorated since 2013 however, due to higher borrowing and the lower oil price, and it accumulated significant domestic and external arrears. Nevertheless, Gabon remains current on its now two outstanding eurobonds.

Relations with Multilateral Creditors

Gabon has had a number of arrangements with the IMF since the mid-1980s, mostly in the form of standby credit facilities, although performance has historically been mixed. The 2004 agreement unlocked the eighth and most recent Paris Club treatment. Its last SBA expired in May 2010 with three reviews completed. Gabon expressed a desire to continue its collaboration with the IMF but until 2017, no further programme was agreed. The interim relationship facilitated Article IV missions, technical assistance and annual meetings between Gabon and the IMF and World Bank.

Gabon entered another IMF arrangement, a three year EFF, which was approved in June 2017. The SDR464.4mn programme (cUS$642mn), or 215% quota, was in support of the authorities' medium-term recovery program after the country was hit hard by lower oil prices since 2014 with the key objectives of balanced fiscal consolidation, structural reforms, financial sector stability and economic diversification. While the initial impact of lower oil prices was mild, it caused growth to slow, led to a weaker fiscal and external balance, and put severe pressure on the regional central bank's (BCEAO) reserves. The country was eventually forced to turn to the IMF for financial support, as part of a wider regional CEMAC initiative, which the IMF MD Lagarde signalled in December 2016 at a regional Heads of Government meeting. An arrears clearance strategy was also central to the programme. Total arrears amounted to 9.7% of GDP at end-2016, of which 2 ppt were external arrears. Gabon had payments in arrears with about 10 bilateral creditors and to 21 commercial creditors in 18 countries. The first review of the programme, which was scheduled to be completed by end-year, was approved on 21 December 2017. A key performance criterion for the first review, and essentially a prior action for the programme's approval, was the clearance of external arrears due to official creditors, multilateral and bilateral (mainly Paris Club and China), prior to the first review. This was done by the authorities. However, the IMF's accompanying DSA (at the time the programme was approved) also noted that while Gabon's debt was high, public debt was sustainable, and the DSA showed that with a Fund-supported programme, debt may be put on a sustainable trajectory, with public debt of less than 50% of GDP by 2022.

An IMF mission to conduct the second review of the EFF took place in June 2018. It noted that programme performance was weak, with substantial fiscal slippages and slow progress on structural reforms. While the overall fiscal deficit (cash basis) declined by c3% of GDP, in line with programme projections, staff noted the composition of the adjustment was less than optimal, relying on cuts in public investment. There was also insufficient progress to contain current spending and weak non-oil revenue collections. Progress to clear domestic and external arrears was also slower than expected, and many important structural reforms had been delayed or not implemented as planned. The authorities agreed to take strong corrective action. Discussions continued on a package of measures and reforms that could lead to approval of the second review by the IMF Board by end-July.

IMF programmes

Date	*Arrangements*	*Comments*
1980s–90s	Various SBAs	1986–88, 1989–91, 1991–93, 1994–95
1995–99	EFF	EFF agreed to support the government's economic programme over 1995–98 as sizeable financing gaps, although declining, were projected over this period. Gaps were expected to be covered by additional Paris Club reschedulings and by other creditors.
2000–02	SBA	Eighteen-month programme agreed in October 2000. Performance was mixed with only the first two reviews completed.
2003	SMP	A SMP for Sept.–Dec. 2003 was agreed to strengthen the track record before requesting a new fund-supported programme. This was in view of policy slippages in both the 2000 SBA and the 1995 EFF. Performance under the SMP was satisfactory.
2004–05	SBA	A 14-month SBA was requested in May 2004 after the SMP was completed.
2007–10	SBA	A three-year US$117mn programme was agreed in May 2007, which the authorities intended to keep precautionary. The first review was completed in December 2007, with two waivers. The second and third reviews were completed together in March 2009 with waivers. The programme expired undrawn in May 2010.
2017–20	EFF	A three-year SDR464.4mn (cUS$642mn, 215% of quota) programme to help ensure macroeconomic stability and sustainable growth was approved in June 2017. The first review was completed on schedule in December 2017. Performance was broadly satisfactory. The review enabled the disbursement of another SDR71.43mn (US$101.1mn), bringing total disbursements to SDR142.86 mn (US$202.3mn), with the remaining amount disbursed gradually, subject to semi-annual reviews. The expected end date is June 2020.

Source: IMF. Gabon joined the IMF in 1963

Gabon's main multilateral creditors are the African Development Bank, the Islamic Development Bank, the European Bank for Reconstruction and Development and the Development Bank of the Central African States. The World Bank's IBRD is also a creditor and has 12 active projects in Gabon, the largest by commitment amount being for fiscal consolidation and growth, workforce skills and various infrastructure projects.

Paris Club and Bilateral Creditors

Gabon has had a total of eight agreements since the mid-1980s, all on Classic ("flow") rescheduling terms. Only the most recent is still active. By 2004, the last rescheduling agreement, there was acknowledgement amongst international creditors that Gabon would require further relief. Constituents included Brazil, Canada, France, the UK and US; although, members remained resolute in maintaining that any further rescheduling would involve substantial improvements in public governance. Hence the Paris Club agreement, reached in June 2004, only followed the approval of a Standby Agreement with the IMF in May of that year. The deal was expected to reduce debt service payments over the period from US$953mn to US$270mn.

The principle of an early repayment by Gabon of certain of its Paris Club debts was agreed by the Paris Club on 18 July 2007. The agreement was for a debt buyback of non-ODA debt at market value (a 15% discount to net present value). Creditors were allowed to decide themselves whether to participate or not in the early repayment operation: creditors were Austria, Belgium, Brazil, Canada, France, Germany, Italy, Japan, the Netherlands, Spain, Switzerland, the UK and the US. The buyback was to be financed from a combination of reserves, a local bond issue and a sovereign eurobond issue. Paris Club creditors agreed to the buyback to help improve Gabon's debt service profile. 86% of holders of the US$2.3bn of eligible claims were expected to participate. The operation was completed in April 2008. The only Paris Club debt that still remained outstanding at end-2016 was cUS$41mn, from the June 2004 agreement.

Paris Club agreements

Date	*Terms*	*Status*	*Details*
Various	Classic	Fully repaid	4 agreements: 1987, 1988, 1989 and 1991
1994	Classic	Fully repaid	Treated US$1359mn.
1995	Classic	Fully repaid	Treated US$1031mn. Maturities falling due between December 1995 and November 1998.
2000	Classic	Fully repaid	Treated US$532mn. Treatment of arrears as at September 2000. Repayment of non-ODA credits over 12 years with three years of grace.
2004	Classic	Active	Treated US$716mn (out of a stock of Paris Club debt of US$2460). Treatment of arrears as of April 2004 (US$456mn) and maturities falling due between May 2004 and June 2005 (US$261mn); repayment of non-ODA credits over 14 years with three years' grace and ODA credits repaid over 14 years with three years' grace.
2007 Jul.	Buyback	–	Agreement in principle to accept Gabon's offer of an early repayment (at market value) of non-ODA debt rescheduled under the 1994, 1995, 2000 and 2004 agreements. Debt eligible for the debt buyback was US$2.182bn (face value), to be paid until 2019, out of a total Paris Club debt of US$2.334bn (face value) as of 1 July 2007.

Source: Paris Club

China is now a much larger creditor than the Paris Club, owed cUS$978mn at end-2016 (about a fifth of public external debt). Many Chinese loans have been for specific infrastructure projects, such as major roads, and some are on concessional terms.

Sovereign Commercial Debt

After two previous restructuring episodes, London Club obligations were the subject of a post-devaluation rescheduling agreement on 26 May 1994. Effectively accounting for all the government's commercial borrowings (bilateral and syndicated loans), amounting to cUS$30mn (in various currencies) the 1994 restructuring agreement arranged for loans to be repaid over ten years commencing in January 1997. Interest was paid at LIBOR + 7/8% and the final maturity was April 2004. However, temporary budget problems, owing to lower oil prices in 1998, along with the low level of reserves, soon prompted payment difficulties. A technical default on the restructured payments occurred in 1999. Payment delays continued. However, on 8 March 2000, Gabon made a payment of US$14.3mn to London Club creditors. The disbursement covered all overdue principal, interest and interest on interest.

Gabon stayed current until its April 2002 payment, when it returned to a state of default on principal and interest from 2002 until October 2005, at which time the outstanding debt was rescheduled with a new maturity of August 2007. The agreement, in August 2005, was negotiated by Standard Bank as agent for the small group of remaining creditors and included 20% "conditional" principal forgiveness to be deducted from the final payment but no forgiveness of interest. London Club debt was successfully cleared by this agreement. The London Club's back-loaded debt forgiveness mechanism was consistent with the Paris Club's comparability requirement in its 2004 treatment.

Commercial debt agreements

Date	*Details*
1987	Bank debt restructurings
1991	Bank debt restructurings
1994 May	Rescheduling of US$187mn of bank debt maturities. Principle due through 1994 on debt contracted prior to 20 September 1986 (debt covered by the 1991 agreement but not implemented) was rescheduled with a ten-year maturity including 2.5 years' grace at LIBOR + 7/8 percent.

(*continued*)

(continued)

Date	*Details*
1999 Jan.	Missed principal payment, applicable to the September 1998 maturity, as well as interest. This triggered a technical default, which was eventually cleared.
2002 Apr.	Default on the remainder of bank loans restructured in 1994 (cUS$30mn); failure to make further principle and interest payments under the 1994 restructuring agreement (although these sums were subsequently cleared in the 2005 agreement).
2004 Apr.	Missed final payment of the 1994 restructured loan. The sum due comprised US$33.1mn of principal and US$1.1mn of interest payments, as well as US$1.6mn of past due interest (PDI) and a small charge relating to the missed amortisation (US$1.6mn).
2005 Aug.	Subsequent to the 2004 default, an Amendment Agreement was reached to clear interest and all PDI by October 2005, the effective date. Principal was amortised until 2007 in 15 equal quarterly instalments, of which four were overdue by and paid on effective date (to make up for delays in negotiation). Interest was charged at Libor + 13/16. The final three payments were due on 1 August 2007 when principal and interest was to be forgiven, provided the authorities remained current to the repayment schedule as occurred at August 2007.

Source: Exotix, World Bank GDF

Gabon issued a maiden US$1bn dollar-denominated sovereign eurobond on 12 December 2007, becoming the second plain vanilla benchmark bond issue in SSA (ex SA) after Ghana just a few months before. The groundwork for the bond issue was supported by the IMF's SBA and the assignment of a BB– long-term foreign currency rating from Fitch in October 2007 and S&P in November. The ten-year (2017) maturity, with an 8.2% coupon, was almost two and a half times oversubscribed and had a spread at issue of 426 basis points. Part of the proceeds of the bond were to fund the Paris Club buyback. The eurobond had a sinking fund feature whereby the Gabonese authorities regularly funded an investment management account, held in escrow at the World Bank, to amortise the bond prior to final maturity. Liability operations meant that the principal had been reduced to US$775mn by November 2011. The outstanding amount was further reduced to US$185mn in December 2013 with the proceeds from a liability management exercise in which the issue of a new US$1.5bn ten year (2024) bond was combined with a tender and exchange offer for the 2017s, in order to extend the debt maturity profile. The residual amount was repaid on due date on 12 December 2017, with the help of another liability management operation in August 2017.

Gabon now has only two US dollar bonds outstanding after the 2017s' maturity, for a combined amount of US$2.2bn. Gabon issued two more eurobonds after its 2007 debut. It returned to the market in December 2013 with a US$1.5bn ten-year issue (2024 maturity), and a coupon of 6.375%, which was at the lower end of initial price expectations. About US$610mn was used for partial repayment of the US$1bn bond maturing in 2017; the bond was planned in conjunction with a tender and exchange offer for the 2017s. Although the maturity date was 2024, the weighted average life was ten years. The most recent issue was in June 2015, a new ten-year (2025) for US$500mn at a coupon of 6.95%. The bond was tapped by US$200mn in August 2017, the proceeds of which were for refinancing the remaining amount of the 2017 bond. Details for the 2025 bond are shown below.

Gabon bond
Gabonese Republic 6.95% 2025
Bloomberg ticker: GABON

Borrower	Gabonese Republic
Issue date	16 June 2015
Form	Eurobond
ISIN	XS1245960684
Amount issued	US$500mn
Amount outstanding	US$700mn (following US$200mn tap on 11 August 2017)
Currency	US dollar
Denomination	Minimum US$200,000; increments of US$1000 thereafter
Amortisation	Bullet
Final maturity date	16 June 2025
Coupon/interest	6.95%, payable semi-annually, June and December
Day count	30/360
Method of transfer	Euroclear/Clearstream
Settlement period	T + 2 business days
Governing law	English
Listing	Irish Stock Exchange
Lead managers	Deutsche Bank, JP Morgan, Standard Chartered

Source: Bloomberg

Georgia

Nominal GDP (US$mn, 2018)[a]		16,716
Population (thousand, 2018)[a]		3710
GDP per capita (USD, 2018)[a]		4506
Credit ratings (long-term foreign currency)[b]	Fitch	BB–
	Moody's	Ba2
	S&P	BB–

[a]IMF WEO October 2018
[b]As at end-September 2018

Country Summary

- Generally politically stable, although Russia still illegally occupies South Ossetia and Abkhazia a decade after a Russian-backed separatist driven war in the territory, and, politically, there are domestic concerns over the concentration of power. But economic policy is one of orthodoxy and the country is open to foreign investment. Georgia consistently ranks highly in the global ranking on the ease of doing business (ninth in 2018) and regularly features amongst the survey's top reformers.
- The economy finally picked up in 2017 after a period of subdued growth following the 2014 drop in oil prices, due to low demand from its major trading partners. Its currency (GEL) depreciated more than 30% against the US$ in the period 2014–17, harming domestic

Exotix Capital, *Exotix Developing Markets Guide*,
https://doi.org/10.1007/978-3-030-05867-8_19

balance sheets as a substantial part of total borrowing was in foreign currency. The country also suffers from an external imbalance, with a large current account deficit (10% of GDP projected in 2018) reflecting the country's narrow export base, low savings rate, and lack of domestic investment vehicles, although these have primarily been FDI-financed (FDI amounted to 10.5% of GDP in 2017).

- Total external debt has risen sharply and is now at elevated levels (100% of GDP, excluding intercompany loans), although most of this is owed by the private sector, while public external debt is mostly owed to multilaterals on concessional terms. Georgia has one eurobond outstanding (it issued its first eurobond in 2008, which has since matured). Total public debt is low (just 45% of GDP). The IMF approved a US$285mn (100% of quota) loan to meet the country's balance of payments needs in April 2017. Georgia has been in an active IMF programme pretty much every year since the turn of the century.

Economic data	*Avg*[a]	*2014*	*2015*	*2016*	*2017 (e)*	*2018 (f)*	*2019 (f)*
Real GDP growth	4.9	4.6	2.9	2.8	5.0	5.5	4.8
Inflation (annual average)	4.9	3.1	4.0	2.1	6.0	2.8	2.7
Current account (% of GDP)	−13.0	−10.7	−12.0	−12.8	−8.9	−10.5	−10.2
Reserves (US$mn, end-period)[b]	2301	2699	2521	2756	3039	3005[c]	–
Reserves/imports (months)[d]	3.2	2.9	3.1	3.3	3.2	–	–
Overall fiscal balance (% of GDP)[e]	−1.5	−1.9	−1.3	−1.6	−0.5	−1.6	−1.6
Currency (ticker)	Georgian lari (GEL)						
FX regime	De jure floating arrangement, and de facto classified as floating by the IMF.						
Key exports	Minerals (19%), foodstuffs (17%), metals (12%).						

Source: IMF WEO Database, Haver, OEC

[a]10-year average to 2016 unless otherwise stated

[b]Official reserve assets

[c]Latest figure, June 2018

[d]In months of the current year's imports of goods, services and primary income debit

[e]Overall government net lending

Key figures		*Party*	*Since*
President	Giorgi Margvelashvili	Independent	Nov 2013
Prime minister	Mamuka Bakhtadze	Georgian Dream	Jun 2018
First vice prime minister and minister of economy and sustainable development	Dimitri Kumsishvili	Georgian Dream	Nov 2017[a]
Minister of finance	Ivane Matchavariani	Georgian Dream	Jul 2018
Key opposition figure	David Bakradze	Movement to Liberty	Oct 2016
Central bank president	Koba Gvenetadze	–	Mar 2016

[a]Kumsishvili was initially appointed minister of economy and sustainable development in September 2015, and vice prime minister in December 2015. After becoming first vice prime minister in June 2016, he became minister of finance in November 2016, before returning as minister of economy and sustainable development in November 2017

Politics

Executive power

Georgia has been a democratic republic since a constitutional referendum in October 1995. The president, who is chief of state, is elected by popular vote and is limited to two five-year terms. A run-off between the top two contenders is required if the leading candidate does not obtain 50% of the vote. The presidential appointment of the prime minister, who is head of government, and who has to be confirmed through a vote of confidence in parliament, allows for strong unity between the two offices and enables the head of state to forge a dominant control over the political establishment. The prime minister heads an 18-member cabinet and holds the position of senior minister of the parliament. Controversial constitutional amendments were signed into law in October 2017 and pushed through parliament by the ruling Georgian Dream party (which has a significant majority), in the face of opposition from across the political spectrum and the president himself. The changes are seen as shifting power from the presidency to the prime minister. The amendments included holding the parliamentary election due in 2020 under a fully proportional system, rather than the current mixed majoritarian-proportional system, and changing the way the president is elected (via parliament rather than directly).

Presidential term: Five years (maximum of two consecutive terms)

Parliamentary term: Four years

Legislature

The parliament (known as Supreme Council or Umaghlesi) consists of 150 directly elected seats; 77 members elected by proportional representation and 73 members elected by majority vote in single-member constituencies. All members serve four-year terms. The constitution stipulates that the parliament will become bicameral after Georgia regains full control over its breakaway republics of Abkhazia and South Ossetia.

Elections

Next due	*Legislative: October 2020*		*Presidential: November 2018*[a]	
Last legislative election[b] *(Oct 2016)*		*Seats*	*Last presidential (Oct 2013)*	*% of vote*
Georgian Dream Coalition		115	Giorgi Margvelashvili (Independent[c])	62.1
Movement to Liberty-European Georgia (MLEG)		21	David Bakradze (MLEG)	21.7
United National Movement (ENM)		6	Nino Burjanadze (Democratic Movement)	10.2
Alliance of Patriots of Georgia		6	Shalva Natelashvili (Labour)	2.9
Industry Will Save Georgia		1	Giorgi Targamadze (Christian-Democratic)	1.1
Independent		1	Other	2.0
Total		**150**	**Total**	**100.0**

[a]At the time of writing, results were not available
[b]Position after two rounds. Elections were held on 8 October. A second round was held on 30 October to determine the 50 seats that were undecided in the first round
[c]Giorgi Margvelashvili was named as the presidential candidate for the Georgian Dream coalition, although he is not a member of any political party

People

The population is comprised of 87% Georgians, 6% Azeri, 5% Armenian, 1% Russian and 1% other. 83% are Orthodox Christian, 11% Muslim and 3% Armenian Apostolic. Georgia has recently experienced a rapid decline in its population due to mass emigration following the country's recent period of economic weakness. In 2014–17, the population contracted by almost 20%, from 4.5mn to 3.7mn.

Prior to its independence in 1991, Georgia was part of the Soviet Union, except for a brief period between the 1917 declaration of independence and its reabsorbing in 1921. Poor relations with Russia have simmered since the election of Putin in 2000 and the pro-Western change of power in Georgia in 2003. This reached its height in the costly 2008 war over South Ossetia and Abkhazia, during which Ossetian separatists began shelling Georgian villages and artillery attacks by pro-Russian separatists broke a 1992 ceasefire agreement. The Georgian Army was sent to the conflict zone to restore order, however Russia had already illicitly advanced into the South Ossetian conflict zone. A ceasefire agreement between both parties was again negotiated shortly afterwards. However, a decade on, Russian forces still illegally occupy South Ossetia and Abkhazia (which together account for 20% of Georgia's internationally recognised territory) in violation of the ceasefire agreement of August 2008.

(*continued*)

(continued)

People
Long-time leader Eduard Shevardnadze resigned in November 2003 after the bloodless Rose Revolution. He served as president from 1995 until 2003 (and had ruled Georgia prior to its independence from Russia as its Soviet-era Communist Party boss), when he resigned in November in his second term during the bloodless Rose Revolution led by Mikheil Saakashvili and his allies. According to the BBC, tens of thousands of demonstrators took to the streets to protest against the flawed results of a parliamentary election demanding Shevardnadze's resignation. Shevardnadze deployed soldiers on the capital's streets, but they laid down their guns after student demonstrators gave them red roses. After an interim period, he was succeeded by Mikheil Saakashvili of the United National Movement (UNM) as president over 2004–13. Saakashvili pursued a strong reformist agenda, and was regarded as pro-West and pro-NATO, but also introduced amendments concentrating power in the hands of the executive. His UNM party was defeated by Georgian Dream in parliamentary elections in October 2012 and he was constitutionally barred from seeking a third term in the 2013 presidential elections, which his party's candidate lost to Georgian Dream. Soon after the election, he left the country to pursue a political career in Ukraine, where he was governor of Odessa Oblast briefly over 2015–16, although he is wanted by Georgia's government on multiple criminal charges. The Georgian Dream alliance, the ruling centre-left coalition, have controlled Parliament since their victory in the October 2012 parliamentary elections, when they defeated the party of ex-president Mikheil Saakashvili, leader of the 2003 Rose Revolution. Georgian Dream—Democratic Georgia, its leading party, was formed in 2011 by Bidzina Ivanishvili, Georgia's richest person, to oppose the then ruling party United National Movement (ENM). In the 2016 legislative elections, Georgian Dream won a clear majority (77%) in an election with a low voter turnout (51.7%). Ever since, the concentration of power has raised international concerns, as the government has proposed constitutional changes that will allow the ruling coalition to govern unchecked. UNM dissolved in January 2017. Many of its prominent members broke away to set up Movement to Liberty-European Georgia, which now serves as the main opposition party. Prime Minister Giorgi Kvirikashvili resigned on 13 June 2018, reportedly due to a disagreement with Bidzina Ivanishvili. In July 2018, new Prime Minister Mamuka Bakhtadze (who was previously finance minister) vowed to press ahead with the country's NATO membership ambitions.

Debt

	2012	*2017*
External debt ratios (%)		
Total external debt[a]/GDP	67.0	96.8
Public external debt[b]/GDP	30.5	36.9
Private external debt[c]/GDP	36.5	59.9

(*continued*)

(continued)

	2012	*2017*
Total external debt[a]/exports of goods and services	176.4	193.9
External debt service ratio[d]	n/a	20.2
Public debt ratios (%)		
Public domestic debt/GDP	4.7	7.6
Public debt/GDP	35.2	44.5

Source: National Bank of Georgia, Ministry of Finance of Georgia, IMF WEO, Exotix calculations

[a]BPM6 basis

[b]Includes external debt of the central bank

[c]Excludes intercompany lending

[d]IMF figures

Total external debt has risen sharply in recent years, with the external debt ratio (excluding intercompany lending) standing at 97% of GDP in 2017 (US$14.7bn), up from 67% of GDP in 2012 (US$10.6bn), on a BPM6 basis according to central bank figures and using IMF WEO GDP; IMF external debt ratios are similar. However, c60% is owed by the private sector. Nominal borrowing increased by all sectors, but most of the growth was caused by a sharp depreciation of the local currency (GEL) against the US$, with lacklustre output growth acting as a drag on the debt ratios too. Private external debt (excluding intercompany lending) increased from 37% to 60% of GDP over 2012–17. Most of that growth has taken place in the non-financial sector, with corporates choosing to borrow externally in light of the country's low domestic savings rate and lack of domestic investment vehicles. Non-financial corporates now account for 59% of total private external debt, with the banking sector making up for the remaining 41%, respectively. Intercompany lending represented another 17% of GDP in 2017 (US$2.6bn), and has been fairly steady around this level over this period, so that total external debt including intercompany lending was 114% of GDP in 2017 (US$17.3bn), up from 85% in 2012 (US$13.4bn). Public external debt (BPM6 basis—general government and central bank) has however been fairly steady as a share of GDP, at c30–35% of GDP, rising only slightly in US$ terms from US$4.8bn in 2012 to US$5.6bn in 2017.

Total external debt rose as a share of exports of goods and services to 194% in 2017, up from 176% in 2012 (excluding intercompany lending). Exports of goods and services grew by 25% over this period, from US$6.0bn to US$7.6bn, although goods exports remained relatively flat (at US$3.5bn) and services grew by 55% to US$4bn. Including intercompany lending, total external debt as a share of exports of goods and services was in a range of 190–260%, ending 2017 at 229%. Meanwhile, public external debt was only 74% of exports of goods and services. The external debt service ratio is elevated, mainly due to the high share of private external debt, and was 20.2% in 2017 on IMF figures (debt service on medium/long-term debt as a percentage of exports of goods and services). The public external debt service ratio however was just 3.7% in 2017 on IMF figures, as much of Georgia's public external debt is owed to multilaterals on concessional terms.

Exotix estimates total public debt was 44.5% of GDP in 2017, based on public external debt of 36.9% of GDP (BPM6 basis) and public domestic debt of 7.6% of GDP (ministry of finance figures). The public debt ratio has increased from 35% in 2012 on this basis, as the government ran persistent, albeit small, fiscal deficits over this period (averaging about 1.2% of GDP). The IMF expects the budget deficit to widen in the short term, to 1.7% of GDP in 2020, as the government aims to put in place a large infrastructure programme to promote trade and tourism.

Note that separate ministry of finance (MOF) figures put public external debt at US$5.2bn (35% of GDP) in 2017, slightly lower than the US$5.6bn shown on a BPM6 basis—this might be because the MOF figures are central government (including guarantees) and central bank while the BPM6 figures are at a wider general government level and the central bank. The difference is cUS$410mn. However, BPM6 does not provide a creditor breakdown of general government debt, whereas the MOF figures do, so Exotix uses the latter in the creditor composition table below (despite the small difference in the two totals). This shows that most of its public sector external debt (73%) is owed to multilateral creditors—hence the low public external debt service ratio. The single biggest multilateral creditor, and biggest overall public sector creditor, is the World Bank's IDA (31% of multilateral debt and 22% of public external debt). This is followed by the Asian Development Bank (28% of multilateral debt and 21% of public external debt). However, when debt owed to the World Bank (23% of multilateral debt and 17% of public external debt) is added to IDA debt, the World Bank Group becomes the single biggest creditor by far, accounting for 54% of multilateral debt and 39% of public external debt. Bilaterals accounted for just 16% of public external debt, with Germany and Japan the biggest single bilateral creditors. Georgia's only outstanding eurobond (US$500mn 6.875% 2021, issued in 2011) accounted for 10% of public external debt. Although Georgia issues its first eurobond in 2008 (since matured), it has not been a frequent issuer, and multilaterals remain the public sector's most significant creditor.

Composition of external debt

External debt by creditor (Dec. 2017)	*Nominal amount outstanding (US$mn)*	*Share of total (%)*
Public sector external debt	**5177**	**36.3**
Central government (including guarantees)	5092	35.7
o/w Official multilateral	3765	26.4
IDA	1162	8.2
ADB	1059	7.4
IBRD	858	6.0
EIB	379	2.7
IMF	107	0.8
EBRD	134	0.9
Other	67	0.5
Official bilateral	827	5.8
Germany (KfW)[a]	288	2.0
Japan	210	1.5
France	139	1.0
Russia	71	0.5
Commercial (bonds)	500	3.5
Central bank	85	0.6
Private sector external debt[b]	**9067**	**63.7**
Total external debt	**14,244**	**100.0**

Source: Ministry of Finance of Georgia, National Bank of Georgia, Exotix calculations

[a]Includes US$2mn of guaranteed debt

[b]Excludes intercompany lending

Rescheduling History

Georgia's limited experience with debt restructuring came after its independence from the USSR. It had two Paris Club rescheduling agreements but no commercial debt treatments. In December 2000, then-President Shevardnadze accepted Moscow's 'Zero Option', a strategy that nullified all Soviet era debt in return for the rescinding of claims to Soviet era assets. The debt at the time of nullification ran to US$179mn.

Relations with Multilateral Creditors

Georgia has had nine IMF programmes since joining the Fund in 1992. Its most recent programme, a 3-year US$285mn (100% of quota) Extended Fund Facility (EFF), was approved in April 2017. It is scheduled to finish in 2020. The loan responded to the balance of payments needs that were caused by the large current account deficit and a depreciating currency. The latest programme review, the second, was completed in June 2018, in which directors commended Georgia's strong economic performance under the EFF programme, supported by favourable external conditions and prudent economic policies, which has enhanced confidence and improved growth. Directors welcomed the authorities' commitment to prudent fiscal policies to preserve fiscal sustainability and strengthen fiscal credibility. However, they noted Georgia remained vulnerable to external shocks, including market volatility in major trading partners. Previously, Georgia undertook three Poverty Reduction and Growth Facility (PRGF) arrangements over the period 1996–2007 and three SBA arrangements over the period 2008–17. Indeed, by the end of its current programme, Georgia will have spent all the preceding 20 years (the whole of this century) in an IMF programme of one sort or another, and nearly every year in the preceding 25 years bar two in one (since 1994). Georgia has a strong track record in repayments to the Fund as indicated in timely repurchases to date. Exposure to the IMF is expected to peak at 1.6% of GDP in 2020, before declining to 1.3% of GDP by 2022.

The World Bank Group (IBRD and IDA) and the Asian Development Bank (ADB) have been Georgia's key development partners since 1992 and 2007, respectively. Most of their loans have been on concessional terms, with infrastructure and services being the key engagement areas. In 2014, Georgia graduated from the IDA to become an IBRD-only borrower. And in 2017, Georgia's country classification as a middle-income country excluded it from further access to concessional loans from the ADB. As of April 2018, the IBRD/IDA portfolio comprised 11 investment projects with a total commitment of US$699mn, of which US$381mn was undisbursed. Of these commitments, 60% were concentrated in the ongoing East-West Highway and secondary roads projects, 18% was in urban development and 22% covered energy, land management and irrigation, and innovation ecosystems. By end 2017, the ADB has approved cUS$2.8bn in lending to Georgia, with US$2.4bn in sovereign loans and US$330mn in non-sovereign lending. European institutions are also a key partner, mainly through the EBRD and EIB. The EBRD supports Georgia's transformation toward a market economy. As of May 2018, its cumulative investments reached EUR2.9bn with 215 projects, with an outstanding portfolio of EUR781mn and 78 active projects. In its current investment portfolio, 34% was in the power and energy sector, 30% was in the corporate sector, 29% was in the financial institutions sector, and 8% was in infrastructure. The EBRD's overall investments in 2017 reached EUR271mn with 20 projects, a record number of investments for the Bank in Georgia. The EIB has so far supported 21 projects with a total loan volume of over EUR1.5bn. In 2016–17, the EIB financed local projects with a total loan volume of EUR897mn.

IMF programmes

Date	*Arrangements*	*Comments*
1994	STF	Approved in December 1994, the Systemic Transformation Facility (STF) was a temporary financing window to provide assistance to members facing balance of payments problems. The STF was created in 1993 and lapsed in April 1995.
1995–1996	SBA	SDR72 million programme approved in June 1995, expired in February 1996.
1996–1999	ECF	Formerly a PRGF. SDR172 million programme approved in February 1996. It sought to reduce overall government deficit by 3% of GDP by 1996 from 6% in 1995.
2001–2004	ECF	Formerly a PRGF. Under the SDR108mn facility, targeted a reduced fiscal deficit from 4.5% of GDP in 2000 to 1.75% of GDP in 2001, real-GDP was expected to rise 3.75% for the year 2001 compared with 1.25% for 2000.
2004–2007	ECF	Formerly a PRGF. SDR98mn to support the economic reform program expired in September 2007. The programme facilitated Paris Club rescheduling. Tax reforms were undertaken in order to bolster private sector growth.
2008–2011	SBA	Agreement in principal on a SDR477.1mn (US$750mn), later extended to a total of SDR747.1mn (US$1.1bn) in 2009, programme was reached after the Georgian authorities requested IMF assistance. The SBA was designed to cover part of an expected financing gap and to help to replenish international reserves and support investor confidence.
2012–2014	SBA & SCF	SDR250mn (US$386mn, 119% of quota) two-year programme approved in April 2012, split evenly across an SBA and SCF arrangement, as a precautionary measure to balance the unsettling environment in Europe. No money was drawn.
2014–2017	SBA	SDR100mn (US$154mn, 47% of quota) 36-month SBA programme approved in July 2014, aimed at reducing the twin deficit and other macroeconomic vulnerabilities. Georgia drew SDR80mn in the first year. The loan is expected to be fully repaid by 2019.
2017–2020	EFF	In April 2017, the IMF approved a 3-year arrangement under the EFF for SDR210.4mn (US$285mn, 100% of quota), responding to weak economic activity. Georgia immediately drew SDR30mn. A further SDR30mn was drawn after the first review which was approved in December 2017. The second review was concluded in June 2018, with another SDR30mn disbursed. Repayment will begin in 2021.

Source: IMF

Paris Club and Bilateral Creditors

Georgia has undertaken two Paris Club agreements, both involving flow rescheduling. The 2001 agreement followed a Letter of Intent with the IMF in December 2000, while the 2004 agreement followed approval of the IMF's PRGF in June 2004. The more recent agreement contained a provision whereby, if Georgia: (1) fulfilled its criteria under the agreement; (2) established a track record under the 2004 minute; (3) made all payments on due date; and (4) concluded a follow up IMF programme, then Paris Club creditors would be willing to consider a debt treatment for Georgia under the Evian Approach. This allowed for flexible repayments with the intention of reducing unsustainable payments and allowance for the redistribution of finance for the support of IMF development programs. Georgia was admitted to the Paris Club's 'Evian' approach at the end of 2007.

Paris Club agreements

Date	*Terms*	*Status*	*Details*
Mar. 2001	Ad hoc	Active	US$58mn treated out of Paris Club debt of US$482mn at end-1999. Total external debt was US$1700mn. Treatment of maturities falling due between January 2001 and December 2002. Repayment profile was on ad hoc terms. Repayment of ODA credits over 20 years with 10 years of grace. Repayment of non-ODA credits over 20 years with 3 years grace.
Jul. 2004	Houston	Active	US$161mn treated out of Paris Club debt of US$525mn at June 2004. Total external debt was US$1950mn. Treatment of arrears as of May 2004 and maturities falling due between June 2004 and December 2006. Repayment profile on Houston terms. Repayment of ODA credits over 20 years with 10 years grace. Repayment of non-ODA credits over 20 years with 5 years grace.

Source: Paris Club

Sovereign Commercial Debt

Georgia has not previously restructured its commercial debt, probably because it didn't inherit much after its independence from the USSR. Georgia has issued two eurobonds, one of which is still outstanding. The first issue (US$500mn, five-year bullet maturity, coupon of 7.5%)

was sold in April 2008 to boost foreign exchange reserves and matured in 2013. Georgia issued its second bond (US$500mn, ten-year bullet maturity, coupon of 6.875%, maturing in April 2021) in April 2011 and in parallel redeemed US$417mn of its then existing eurobond due in 2013. The 2021 bond was issued below par at 98.233, priced to yield 7.125%, and broadened the investor base (RegS/144A in 2011 vs RegS in 2008) and extended the maturity profile of Georgia's debt portfolio.

Georgia bond
Georgia 6.875% 2021
Bloomberg ticker: GEORG

Borrower	Republic of Georgia
Issue date	12 April 2011
Form	Global
ISIN	XS0617134092
Issue size	US$500mn
Currency	US dollar
Denomination	Minimum US$200,000; increments of US$1000 thereafter
Amortisation	Bullet
Final maturity date	12 April 2021
Coupon/interest	6.875% paid semi-annually, April and October
Day count	30/360
Method of transfer	Euroclear/Clearstream
Settlement period	T + 2 business days
Governing law	Dusseldorf, Frankfurt, London, Munich
Listing	English
Joint lead managers	Goldman Sachs and JP Morgan

Source: Bloomberg

Corporate Bond Markets

The Georgian international corporate bond market began about a decade ago, although it remains underdeveloped with only five eurobond issues of any size (from three issuers). The most notable are listed below. Various corporates have issued US$-, GEL-, ILS-, and EUR-denominated bonds since.

The first eurobond to be issued by a Georgian corporate came in 2007 from Bank of Georgia, a privately owned bank, which has since established itself as a well-known name in the market. The US$200mn five-year bullet, with a coupon of 9%, was issued in February 2007 through a LPN structure. Unusually, at least for a sub-investment grade country, the issue came before a sovereign eurobond (the first sovereign eurobond was issued fourteen months later, and Georgia was rated B+ by S&P at the time of Bank of Georgia's issue). Parts of the bond were repurchased through various tenders in 2011. The bank issued a second bond in July 2012, a US$250mn five-year note due 2017, which was increased by a further US$150mn in November 2013. The bond had a 7.75% coupon. On 30 June 2016, the bank invited holders of the US$400mn 2017 notes to tender any or all of the bond for purchase by the bank for cash, and to approve an exit consent that, inter alia, provided for the bond's mandatory early redemption. The notes were redeemed in August 2016 ahead of their maturity in July 2017. The bank also issued a US$350mn seven-year bullet bond, maturing in 2023, through its holding company (BGEO Group), in July 2016. The bond had a 6% coupon and was priced at 99.297. Up to US$250mn of the proceeds of the 2023 bond were to be used to fund the acquisition of the 2017 notes. This bond was moved to the bank, as part of a demerger of banking and investment activities. In June 2017, Bank of Georgia issued an international bond denominated in local currency (Georgian lari), showing the development of the market. The three-year bullet bond with an 11% coupon was GEL500mn in size (equivalent to cUS$208mn at the prevailing exchange rate), with payments in US$. Lastly, in March 2018 Georgia Capital issued a six-year bullet bond. The amount issued was US$300mn, and the coupon was 6.125%. The bond was priced to yield 6.375%, with an issue price of 98.77. IPT was 6.625%. This new issue was placed ahead of its demerger from the bank, which was effective on 29 May 2018.

Two state-owned companies have also issued in the international market. Georgian Railway JSC, the state-owned railway monopoly, launched its first sizeable issue in July 2010 with a US$250mn, five-year eurobond and a coupon of 9.875%. The bond matured in 2015. The company returned to the international market in July 2012 with a US$500mn, 10-year eurobond which had a 7.75% coupon and bullet maturity. The bond was priced at 99.998 at issue. The state owned Georgian Oil and Gas Corporation JSC issued its first bond in May 2012, a US$250mn five-year bullet bond with a coupon of 6.875%. The bond was priced at 98.694. It matured in May 2017. In April 2016, the company returned to the international market with another US$250mn, five-year bullet bond with a 6.75% coupon and maturing in 2021. The bond was priced at 98.96.

Georgia corporate eurobonds

Issuer	*Ticker*	*Size*	*Coupon*	*Maturity date*	*Issue date*
Bank of Georgia JSC	GEBGG	GEL500mn	11%	Jun. 2020	Jun. 2017
Georgian Oil and Gas Corp JSC	GEOROG	US$250mn	6.75%	Apr. 2021	Apr. 2016
Georgian Railway JSC	GRAIL	US$500mn	7.75%	Jul. 2022	Jul. 2012
BGEO Group JSC	GEBGG	US$350mn	6%	Jul. 2023	Jul. 2016
Georgia Capital	GEOCAP	US$300mn	6.125%	Sep. 2024	Mar. 2018

Source: Bloomberg

Georgian Oil and Gas bond
Georgian Oil and Cos Corporation 6.75% 2021
Bloomberg ticker: GEOROG

Borrower	Georgian Oil and Gas Corporation
Issue date	19 April 2016
Form	Global
ISIN	XS1319820384
Issue size	US$250mn
Currency	US dollar
Denomination	Minimum US$200,000; increments of US$1000 thereafter
Amortisation	Bullet
Final maturity date	26 April 2021
Coupon/interest	6.75% paid semi-annually
Day count	30/360
Method of transfer	Euroclear/Clearstream
Settlement period	T + 2 business days
Joint lead managers	Barclays, JP Morgan

Source: Bloomberg

Georgian Railway bond
Georgian Railway 7.75% 2022
Bloomberg ticker: GRAIL

Borrower	Georgian Railway JSC
Issue date	26 June 2012
Form	Global
ISIN	XS0800346362
Issue size	US$500mn

(*continued*)

(continued)

Georgian Railway bond *Georgian Railway 7.75% 2022* *Bloomberg ticker: GRAIL*	
Currency	US dollar
Denomination	Minimum US$200,000; increments of US$1000 thereafter
Amortisation	Bullet
Final maturity date	11 July 2022
Coupon/interest	7.75% paid semi-annually
Day count	30/360
Method of transfer	Euroclear/Clearstream
Settlement period	T + 2 business days
Joint lead managers	Goldman Sachs, JP Morgan, Bank of America Merrill Lynch

Source: Bloomberg

Bank of Georgia bond *BGEO Group 6% 2023* *Bloomberg ticker: GEBGG*	
Borrower	BGEO Group JSC
Issue date	26 July 2016
Form	Global
ISIN	XS1405775880
Issue size	US$350mn
Currency	US dollar
Denomination	Minimum US$200,000; increments of US$1000 thereafter
Amortisation	Bullet
Final maturity date	26 July 2023
Coupon/interest	6% paid semi-annually January and July
Day count	30/360
Method of transfer	FED FUNDS/DTC
Settlement period	T + 2 business days
Joint lead managers	JP Morgan, Bank of America Merrill Lynch, Galt & Taggart Brokerage

Source: Bloomberg

Bank of Georgia bond
Bank of Georgia 11% 2020
Bloomberg ticker: GEBGG

Borrower	Bank of Georgia JSC
Issue date	1 June 2017
Form	Euro Non-Dollar Dual Currency
ISIN	XS1577958488
Issue size	GEL500mn
Currency	GEL
Denomination	Minimum GEL500,000; increments of GEL5000 thereafter
Amortisation	Bullet
Final maturity date	1 June 2020
Coupon/interest	11% paid semi-annually
Day count	30/360
Method of transfer	Euroclear/Clearstream
Settlement period	T + 2 business days
Joint lead managers	JP Morgan, Renaissance Capital, Galt & Taggart Brokerage

Source: Bloomberg

Georgia Capital bond
Georgia Capital 6.125% 2024
Bloomberg ticker: GEOCAP

Borrower	Georgia Capital JSC
Issue date	9 March 2018
Form	Eurobond
ISIN	XS1778929478
Issue size	US$300mn
Currency	US dollar
Denomination	Minimum US$200,000; increments of US$1000 thereafter
Amortisation	Bullet
Final maturity date	9 March 2024
Coupon/interest	6.125% paid semi-annually
Day count	30/360
Method of transfer	Clearstream
Settlement period	T + 2 business days
Joint lead managers	Citi, JP Morgan, Renaissance Capital, Galt & Taggart Brokerage

Source: Bloomberg

Ghana

Nominal GDP (US$mn, 2018)[a]		51,815
Population (thousand, 2018)[a]		29,001
GDP per capita (USD, 2018)[a]		1787
Credit ratings (long-term foreign currency)[b]	Fitch	B
	Moody's	B3
	S&P	B

[a]IMF WEO October 2018
[b]As at end-September 2018

Country Summary

- Ghana has established itself as largely politically stable after a number of democratic transitions since multiparty democracy returned in 1992. Power has alternated between the two main parties over the past two and a half decades, with the NPP (under Nana Akufo Addo) returning to office following the 2016 elections, after eight years in opposition. Little really separates the parties with regards macroeconomic policy, although Ghana has suffered from marked fiscal weakness in election periods.
- Ghana is a commodity exporter, although exports are fairly well diversified across gold, oil and cocoa. Gold is the biggest export (nearly half of all goods' exports), with Ghana the second-largest producer in Africa, after South Africa. Cocoa has traditionally been

Exotix Capital, *Exotix Developing Markets Guide*,
https://doi.org/10.1007/978-3-030-05867-8_20

its second-biggest export, with Ghana the world's second-largest cocoa producer, after Cote d'Ivoire. But oil has seen the most growth in recent years, since production started in 2010, with oil exports overtaking cocoa in 2017. Oil production, which amounts to nearly 200,000 barrels per day, has helped to transform the economy, although it has been a mixed blessing.

- Ghana's public debt burden has risen sharply in the past five years and is back to levels last seen at the time of HIPC debt relief about 15 years ago (80% of GDP on Exotix estimates). Despite fiscal consolidation under successive governments and implementation of an IMF programme since 2015 (which is due to end in April 2019), the debt burden has been fairly sticky. Eurobonds are now the biggest creditor group, accounting for nearly 30% of central government external debt.

Economic data	*Avg*[a]	*2014*	*2015*	*2016*	*2017 (e)*	*2018 (f)*	*2019 (f)*
Real GDP growth	6.8	4.0	3.8	3.7	8.4	6.3	7.6
Inflation (annual average)	12.3	15.5	17.2	17.5	12.4	9.5	8.0
Current account (% of GDP)	−9.0	−9.5	−7.7	−6.7	−4.5	−4.1	−4.0
Reserves (US$mn, end-period)[b]	2423	3199	3094	3431	4522	3871[c]	–
Reserves/imports (months)[d]	1.7	1.8	1.7	1.9	2.2	–	–
Overall fiscal balance (% of GDP)[e]	−8.5	−10.9	−5.4	−8.9	−5.1	−6.0	−3.9
Currency (ticker)	Ghana cedi (GHS)						
FX regime	Officially independent free float, but de facto managed float.						
Key exports	Gold (42%), crude petroleum (22%), cocoa beans (14%). Exports of goods were US$13.8bn in 2017, while services were US$6.6bn. Remittances came to nearly 5% of GDP in 2016.						

Source: IMF WEO Database, Haver, IMF Country Reports, OEC

[a]10-year average to 2016, unless otherwise stated

[b]Net international reserves

[c]Latest figure, April 2018

[d]In months of the current year's imports of goods, services and income debit (Exotix calculation)

[e]Overall central government balance excluding financial sector-related costs from 2014, average based on IMF general government net lending

Key figures		*Party*	*Since*
President	Nana Akufo Addo	NPP	Jan. 2017
Vice president	Mahamudu Bawumia	NPP	Jan. 2017
Minister of finance	Ken Ofori-Atta	NPP	Jan. 2017
Key opposition figure	John Dramani Mahama[a]	NDC	Jan. 2017
Central bank governor	Dr Ernest Addison	–	Apr. 2017

Notes: Ghana is a member of The Commonwealth. It gained independence from Britain in 1957

[a]After serving as president for one term (2012–16), Mahama remains the NDC leader

Politics

Executive power

The President as chief of state and head of government enjoys significant power, with the ability to make law and veto bills passed by the legislature, except when a bill is 'urgent'. The President is elected by popular vote, co-running with the Vice President on the same ticket, and requires over 50% of the vote in the first round to avoid a second round. The President appoints the cabinet (Council of State) and only half of its members must be drawn from the legislature.

Presidential term: Four years (two-term limit; consecutive allowed)

Parliamentary term: Four years

Legislature

The 275-seat unicameral Parliament is heavily dependent on the President's role. Each member is elected by popular vote to serve a four-year term, using a simple vote. The seat number increased from 230 in 2012.

Elections

Next due *Presidential and legislative: December 2020*

Last legislative election (Dec. 2016)	*Seats*	*Last presidential (Dec. 2016)*	*% of vote*
New Patriotic Party (NPP)	171	Nana Akufu Addo (NPP)	53.9
National Democratic Congress (NDC)	104	John Dramani Mahama (NDC)	44.4
		Paa Kwesi Nduom (PPP)	1.0
		Other	0.7
Total	**275**	**Total**	**100.0**

People

Ghana has a recent modern history of social stability, holding democratic multi-party elections and seeing changes of government. Stable democracy returned in 1992, after authoritarian socialist rule followed independence from the UK in 1957, which gave way to a period of instability, with power alternating between military rule, weak elected governments and coups, eventually leading to the former head of government and coup leader Jerry Rawlings being elected president.

Rawlings served until 2000, after being re-elected in 1996 under the NDC ticket. He was followed by John Kufuor (NPP) over 2000–08, John Atta Mills (NDC) over 2008–12 and John Dramani Mahama (NDC) over 2012–16.

Economic growth and government policies since 2000 helped to sustain poverty reduction and life expectancy at birth is now 67 years. Ghana's official language is English, but many other languages and dialects are also spoken. Just under half of Ghanaians are classed as Akans, common to the coastal (Fantis) and forest (Ashantis) regions. The Mole-Dagbon (17%) and Ewe (14%) of the North and South, respectively, are also large in number. Christianity is thought to be practiced by c70% of the population; Islam is the second-largest religion (18%).

55% of the population live in urban areas and the population is concentrated in the southern half of the country, especially near to the coast. Electricity is generated from hydropower, fossil fuels and renewable energy sources. Industrialisation has put its productive capacity under pressure and years of power shortages have already held back economic growth. Ghana became a Portuguese trading settlement in 1482, and the Gold Coast became a British Crown colony in 1874.

Debt

	2012	*2017*
External debt ratios (%)		
Total external debt/GDP	34.1	51.0
Public external debt/GDP	28.9	47.0
Private external debt/GDP	5.2	4.0
Total external debt/exports of goods and services	85.1	117.4
External debt service ratio (PPG)[a]	5.8	17.0
Public debt ratios (%)		
Public domestic debt/GDP	23.5	32.1
Public debt/GDP	52.4	79.1

Source: Ministry of Finance, IMF, Haver, Exotix

Note: GDP figures taken from October 2018 IMF WEO, which do not incorporate the authorities' GDP revisions. Hence, our ratios would be overstated

[a]Publicly and publicly guaranteed, taken from IMF DSAs

Exotix estimates Ghana's total external debt was 51% of GDP in 2017, most of which was owed by the public sector. Public and publicly guaranteed (PPG) external debt was 47% of GDP, while private sector external debt was just 4% of GDP. These ratios are in line with the IMF's DSA contained in the fifth and sixth review of the ECF from April 2018. The external debt/GDP ratio has increased from 34% in 2012, driven by the increase in PPG external debt/GDP over this period (private external debt/GDP went down slightly). In absolute US dollar terms, total external debt increased from US$14.3bn in 2012 to US$24.0bn, with PPG external debt rising from US$12.1bn to US$22.1bn, while nominal GDP rose 12%. Total external debt rose from 85% of exports of goods and services to 117%, despite the rise in the denominator over this period. Exports of goods and services rose by 22% from US$16.8bn to US$20.4bn, with all the rise accounted for by an increase in service exports (doubling) as goods exports remained largely unchanged. The external debt service ratio (PPG only) rose significantly over this period, as nominal debt increased, most of which was on non-concessional terms, to stand at 17% in 2017, according to the IMF.

Exotix estimates Ghana's total public debt was 79% of GDP in 2017, with PPG external debt of 47% of GDP and domestic debt of 32% of GDP. The public debt ratio increased from 52% of GDP in 2012. Of this, central government external debt, as per Ministry of Finance data, rose from 21.8% of GDP (US$9.2bn) to 36.5% of GDP (US$17.2bn). The remaining amount, consisting of broader public sector external debt and guarantees, rose from 7.1% of GDP (US$3bn) to 10.5% of GDP (US$4.9bn), as derived from IMF figures. Ministry of Finance figures showed that domestic debt (central government) rose by nearly three-fold in local currency terms, from GHS18.5bn to GHS66.5bn, as sizeable fiscal deficits were increasingly financed domestically. Nearly all domestic debt is the form of marketable securities (T-bills and bonds), with over half issued in the form of medium-term instruments (two- to 10-year notes). Around 38% of domestic debt was held by non-residents at end-2017. Note that IMF figures for Ghana's public debt are lower than Exotix estimates. The IMF puts overall public debt at 72.3% of GDP in 2017, in the public debt DSA in the fifth and sixth review of the ECF, comprising PPG external debt of 47% of GDP and, hence, domestic debt (central government) of 25.3% of GDP (compared with Exotix's estimate of 32.1% of GDP based on Ministry of Finance figures), while central government debt was 71.8% of GDP, comprising external debt of 37.0% of GDP and domestic debt of 34.8% of GDP.

The Ministry of Finance provides the composition of public external debt (central government actually) by creditor at end-2017. It showed public external debt was US$17.16bn in total, comprising US$6.4bn owed to multilaterals (of which US$3.9bn was owed to the World Bank IDA, the biggest multilateral creditor and biggest single creditor overall), just US$1.2bn owed to bilaterals, and US$9.5bn owed to "other creditors", which included commercial creditors (including sovereign eurobonds). Indeed, eurobonds (which Exotix calculated as US$3.75bn (nominal) at end-2017) were the second-biggest creditor, after the World Bank. That is, the World Bank and eurobonds accounted for 40% of central government external debt. China Development Bank (CDB) accounted for just 3% of central government external debt. The remaining debt owed to "other creditors" was split between banks, export credits and other concessional lending. The purely commercial debt, according to Ministry of Finance figures, comprising eurobonds, CDB and banks, amounted to 36% of central government external debt (cUS$6.2bn). Ghana, however, issued US$2bn of eurobonds in May 2018, with a tender for the 2022s at the same time, so that net issuance was cUS$1.3bn. Outstanding eurobonds at end-May 2018 therefore rose to US$5.048bn, as per Bloomberg. This operation thus changed the debt stock and its composition. Consequently, Exotix has added this eurobond issuance to the end-2017 debt stock (other creditors unchanged) in order to provide a more representative (current) creditor composition, which is summarised below. This shows central government external debt increasing to US$18.5bn, of which 27% is owed in the form of eurobonds. To complete the breakdown of total external debt, other public and publicly guaranteed external debt and private external debt have been included, as at end-2017, both derived from IMF figures. Total external debt is therefore currently estimated at cUS$25.3bn.

The rise in Ghana's public indebtedness is notable, coming some 15 years after the delivery of HIPC and MDRI debt relief. This had reduced public external debt sharply. According to IMF WEO figures, public debt fell from 82% of GDP in 2002 to just 26% in 2006, although it rose above 50% again in 2013, and above 70% the following year. The rise in the debt burden over this period (2012–14) reflected persistently wide fiscal deficits (over 10% of GDP) and the impact of currency weakness as the fiscal laxity hit investor confidence. Despite attempts at fiscal consolidation under successive governments and implementation of an

IMF programme since 2015, the debt burden has been fairly sticky at this elevated level since then. The IMF's latest DSA (April 2018) showed that Ghana remains at high risk of external debt distress, as it has done since 2015. This is because of the high total public debt/GDP ratio, and four of five external debt indicators breached the thresholds under the baseline scenario. It noted that maintaining fiscal discipline and building buffers, supported by appropriate debt and cash management, will be the key to locking in a downward debt path, particularly as Ghana is buffeted by the realisation of significant contingent liabilities from the energy and financial sectors.

Composition of external debt

External debt by creditor (est May 2018[a])	*Nominal amount outstanding (US$mn)*	*Share of total (%)*
Public and publicly guaranteed external debt	**23,467**	**92.6**
Central government external debt[b]	18,530	73.1
o/w Official multilateral	6437	25.4
World Bank IDA	3922	15.5
AfDB	1200	4.7
IMF	958	3.8
Official bilateral	1211	4.8
Paris Club	746	2.9
Non-Paris Club	464	1.8
Commercial creditors	7622	30.1
Eurobonds[c]	5048	19.9
CDB	515	2.0
Commercial banks and other	2059	8.1
Other	3261	12.9
Export credits	1544	6.1
Other concessional	1716	6.8
Other public and guaranteed external debt[d]	4937	19.5
Private sector external debt[d]	**1881**	**7.4**
Total external debt	**25,347**	**100.0**

Source: Ghana Ministry of Finance, IMF, Bloomberg, Exotix

[a]External debt as of end-2017 plus net Eurobond issuance in May 2018

[b]Ministry of Finance Quarterly Public Debt Statistics Bulletin, Q4 2017. Note, some of the items do not match with the subtotals

[c]Includes US$2bn eurobonds issued in May 2018 and tender for 2022 bond

[d]IMF report for fifth and sixth review of the ECF, May 2018

Rescheduling History

Ghana has been a major beneficiary of debt relief, first under HIPC and then under MDRI, which helped to transform the country's balance sheet (at least until the global financial crisis struck and, since then, the emergence of wide and persistent fiscal deficits). Ghana reached decision point under enhanced HIPC in February 2002 and completion point two years later in July 2004. Ghana has had four Paris Club agreements, the three most recent involving debt reductions, but has not previously rescheduled any commercial debt.

Ghana's debt burden was only considered to be unsustainable as late as 1999. In 1996, external public debt was c80% of GDP and on a declining trend. The debt/exports ratio had fallen to c200% by 1998 and debt/revenue had hovered at c400%. Ghana's debt built up during the 1970s and 1980s (rising by 300%), although the scaling up of lending by multilaterals was not offset by a corresponding increase in exports. Exports only rose by 20% in US dollar terms over this period. In particular, between 1980 and 1983, the debt burden increased markedly (from 120% to 360% of exports—where it remained until the mid-1990s) as cocoa prices fell (cocoa accounted for 60% of export earnings).

By 2000 Ghana's debt had become unsustainable. Several factors accounted for the change including fiscal slippages and quasi-fiscal losses leading to increasing budget deficits, partly financed by commercial external borrowing; the low rate of return on public investment; weaker real GDP growth; and sharp depreciation of the cedi in 2000. Spending overruns in the run-up to the 2000 presidential election, weaker-than-projected privatisation revenue and slower donor disbursements were also factors. External debt had risen to 120% of GDP (in nominal terms) in 2000. Although debt/exports remained fairly constant at 250%, the application of a lower threshold under the HIPC sustainability framework indicated the debt was unsustainable. Ghana's external debt (PPG basis) was US$6bn in nominal terms at end-2000, US$3.9bn on an NPV basis (given the high degree of concessionality in the debt), c157% of exports of goods and non-factor services and 570% of central government revenues. The World Bank was the largest creditor, accounting for 52% of the nominal debt stock, while the Paris Club accounted for 26.5% and commercial creditors just 6%. At decision point, the common reduction factor was 56.2%, implying NPV reduction after traditional debt relief mechanisms of 85.5%. HIPC debt relief from all creditors was worth US$3.7bn (nominal), equivalent to US$2.186bn in NPV terms. After debt relief, public external debt, which had reached 99% of GDP in 2003, had fallen to 17% by 2006.

Relations with Multilateral Creditors

Ghana has had a series of programmes with the IMF since the early 1980s (11 programmes in all) and has generally had a positive relationship since the mid-1990s when multilateral engagement was characterised by Ghana's status as a HIPC country. The corresponding IMF programme whilst under HIPC was completed in October 2006. This allowed Ghana to graduate from IMF resources—for a period—although it was reported to be considering a policy support instrument (PSI) to support its policy implementation, but this failed to materialise. However, a change of government in 2009, which inherited a weak fiscal position, and the onset of the global financial crisis, forced Ghana back to the IMF and it secured a three-year ECF in July 2009. Performance was satisfactory, although following non-observance of performance criteria waivers, criteria were modified to allow for non-concessional borrowing for development projects. The results were better than expected, as there was widespread scepticism that the authorities could achieve a big front-loaded adjustment.

Ghana is currently under another IMF programme, which was approved in 2015, when it turned, somewhat belatedly, to the Fund after another bout of fiscal weakness and the failure of the government's own homegrown economic plan. In early 2013, the central bank reported that the budget deficit rose to 12% of GDP in 2012 (an election year), almost double the government's revised target of 6.7% of GDP, set in its July supplementary budget, and compared with the original 2012 budget target of 4.8% of GDP. The deterioration in the fiscal position reflected mainly higher-than-budgeted expenditure (particularly a 34% increase in wages and salaries) rather than significantly lower revenues. The negative fiscal surprise undermined policy credibility. The exchange rate fell sharply (depreciating by 15% against USD in 2013 and a further 30% in 2014, according to Haver) and inflation accelerated (rising from 10.1% yoy in January 2013 to a peak of 19.2% in March 2016), with the central bank generally behind the curve. The significant currency depreciation also contributed to the worsening of debt/GDP ratios, as public debt rose from 48% of GDP in 2012 to 70% in 2014 (WEO figures). The authorities initially sought their own homegrown adjustment plan, but it proved insufficient, and they had little choice but to go back to the IMF in order to restore policy credibility and satisfy investors. News in August 2014 that Ghana would seek some form of assistance from the IMF came as a positive shock and marked a policy U-turn for the government. An ECF, initially for three years, was approved in April 2015 for SDR664.2mn (cUS$918mn and 180% of quota) to support medium-term economic reform, achieve high growth and job creation and debt sustainability. Although performance in the first year was strong, the 2016 election saw more fiscal slippage and the new government, which took office in January 2017, inherited a 2016 fiscal deficit of close to 9% of GDP. The programme's 2017 fiscal target of 3.8% of GDP (revised from the original target of 3.5%)—the last full year before the programme was due to expire in April 2018—became unobtainable (neither feasible or desirable) and the programme risked going off track. The new government's lukewarm attitude to the Fund programme, rather than agree to a one-year extension as sought by Staff, also did not inspire confidence. The extension would allow the programme to get back on track and allow more time to reach the fiscal target. In the end, the authorities conceded.

A one-year extension (to April 2019) to the current ECF was approved by the Fund Board on completion of the fourth review at end-August 2017. The revised programme targeted a fiscal deficit in 2017 of 6.3% of GDP, falling to 3.8% in 2018. In the fourth review, the IMF reported on some positive steps taken by the authorities and signs of economic recovery, although further reforms, especially in efficient tax collection and fiscal consolidation, were needed. It noted that energy sector inefficiencies remain, including the management of state-owned enterprises (SOEs). Real GDP growth declined to just 3.5% in 2016 (revised to 3.7%) but was forecast to rise to almost 9% in 2018 due to new oil and gas production coming on stream (subsequently, oil and gas came on stream earlier, boosting 2017 growth to 8.5% so that 2018 growth projections were lowered to 6.3%). After a further delay, the combined fifth and sixth review of the ECF was approved in April 2018, with some adjustments and waivers. The IMF noted that programme implementation had significantly improved in 2017. Growth rebounded, the fiscal deficit declined, with a primary surplus for the first time in 15 years, and the external position strengthened. Key steps had been taken to address financial sector weakness. The Fund noted that the government should continue to implement its fiscal consolidation programme, with the emphasis on domestic revenue mobilisation.

IMF programmes

Date	*Arrangements*	*Comments*
1980s	Various	SBA 1983–84, SBA 1984–85, SBA 1986–87, ESAF+EFF in parallel 1987–88.
1988–92	PRGF	Originally approved as ESAF loans, the programme expired in March 1992. The first multi-party elections in 1992, under the new constitution, however led to serious difficulties in implementing economic reform and the programme went off track. Subsequent efforts to bring the situation under control was met with mixed success.
1995–99	PRGF	Originally approved as ESAF loans. SDR137mn was drawn of SDR164.4mn agreed.
1999–02	PRGF	SDR176.2mn was drawn of SDR228.8mn agreed.
2003–06	ECF	Formerly known as PRGF. The programme supported Ghana's progress towards HIPC completion point. Ghana graduated from IMF resources after the final review was completed in October 2006. The programme (SDR184.5mn) was fully drawn.
2009–12	ECF	Three-year programme approved in July 2009 amounting to SDR387.5mn (US$602.6mn, 105% of quota). It was designed to support the new government's economic programme and re-establish macroeconomic stability after the budget deficit widened to 14.5% of GDP in 2008 and balance of payments pressures emerged after the global financial crisis. First and second reviews completed in June 2010, with waivers for the contracting of non-concessional debt and the overall budget deficit. The third and fourth reviews were completed in May 2011, also with waivers for the non-observance of performance criteria, but with further disbursements approved. On completion of the fifth review in December 2011, performance criteria were modified to allow for non-concessional borrowing for infrastructure projects. Total disbursements were approved in July 2012, on completion of the sixth and seventh reviews.
2015–19	ECF	A three-year programme, originally to April 2018, was approved in April 2015 for SDR664.2mn (US$918mn, 180% of quota), to help the authorities boost growth, employment and stability. Performance in the first year was strong. The first and second reviews were completed with waivers for the non-observance of some performance criteria. The third review was completed in October 2016, also with waivers. However, fiscal slippage in 2016 under the out-going NDC government delayed completion of the fourth review. The IMF approved the fourth review in August 2017 along with a one-year extension of the programme to April 2019. US$94.2mn was disbursed. The combined fifth and sixth review was completed in April 2018. US$191mn was disbursed. Total disbursements under the programme as of June 2018 were SDR531.4mn (about US$764mn).

Source: IMF. Ghana joined the IMF in 1957

The World Bank currently has 44 active projects in Ghana with five more in the pipeline. By commitment amount, the Sankofa Gas project, macroeconomic stability, poverty reduction and transport sector development are priorities. The African Development Bank's projects in Ghana include rural enterprise and sustainable agriculture development. Ghana benefits from the third-largest IFAD programme in West and Central Africa, focusing on poverty reduction and natural resource management. IFAD began operations in Ghana in 1980 and has since approved 17 projects and US$271.5mn of loans and grants.

Paris Club and Bilateral Creditors

Ghana has had four Paris Club agreements. The most recent agreement in July 2004 came after Ghana reached HIPC completion point. It remains active.

Paris Club agreements

Date	*Terms*	*Status*	*Details*
1996	Classic	Fully repaid	Amount treated US$93mn.
2001	Naples	Fully repaid	Treated US$199mn out of Paris Club debt of US$1.893bn as at end-December 2003. Total external debt put at US$5.918bn, 119% of GDP. US$27mn was cancelled and US$172mn rescheduled.
2002	Cologne	Fully repaid	Treated US$163mn out of Paris Club debt of US$1.8bn as at February 2002. Total external debt put at US$6.0bn. US$91mn was cancelled and US$72mn rescheduled.
2004 Jul.	HIPC Initiative exit	Active	Treated US$1.560bn out of Paris Club debt of US$1.942bn as at June 2004. Total external debt put at US$7.5bn at end-2003. US$823mn cancelled, US$737mn rescheduled under HIPC exit terms. Treatment of arrears as of May 2004, treatment of stock as of June 2004.

Source: Paris Club

Ghana's non-Paris Club creditors include China, Kuwait, South Korea, Saudi Arabia and India. According to the Ministry of Finance, debt to China increased to US$235mn in 2012 and then US$381mn in 2013, a level where it remained over the next two years. Subsequent deals, such as the 2017 US$10bn memorandum of understanding (MOU) to develop the bauxite industry have pushed liabilities higher. Ghana has also signed various deals with Chinese private investors and the Exim Bank of China. Some loans from the Chinese government have been interest free, including for construction projects.

Sovereign Commercial Debt

Ghana has had no commercial debt restructurings. It earned a glowing reputation in the international capital market after becoming the first country in Sub-Saharan Africa (excluding South Africa) and the first post-HIPC debtor to access the international capital market with a plain vanilla benchmark-sized issue in 2007 (Seychelles had issued a much smaller bond in 2006, and some other African sovereigns had Brady bonds outstanding at the time after previous debt restructurings). Exotix believes it was also—at the time—the poorest country to issue a debut eurobond, with income per head of just US$680 (a figure that has since been revised up significantly), and, even now, remains one of the poorest to have issued (surpassed only by Ethiopia in 2014, and similar to Tanzania and Mozambique in 2013). Combined with sound economic policies, Ghana became the poster child of the international financial community. However, its reputation was tarnished over 2012–14—and since—due to recurring fiscal weakness that resulted in a rise in the public debt burden to 70% of GDP, a level around which it still remains, despite efforts aimed at fiscal consolidation.

Ghana's maiden international sovereign bond was issued on 4 October 2007. The US$750mn B+ rated issue was at the upper end of expectations due to strong demand, being nearly four times oversubscribed. Bids totalled nearly US$3bn, almost 25% of Ghana's GDP. It was priced at a spread of 387bps above US Treasuries. Proceeds of the bond issue were intended for use on infrastructure investment, particularly in the energy sector and roads. On 26 July 2013, the government announced an exchange offer for the 2017 bonds, in which the Republic accepted US$219.5mn in principal in exchange for US$250mn in new 2023 bonds. The government later embarked on a series of liability management operations to reduce the outstanding ahead of its maturity and alleviate fears over rollover risks, which became especially important in light of volatile market conditions and Ghana's own fiscal weakness. The government launched a cash tender offer in July 2016 for the 2017 bond. They were purchased by the Republic at a price of 103% (plus accrued), and the government accepted US$100mn. This reduced the outstanding principal to US$400.6mn, from the US$500.6mn that remained before the tender was launched. A further tender offer was launched on 8 September

2016, in tandem with the new 2022 bond issue (see below), in which the government purchased US$201.6mn in bonds at 103.625% (plus accrued). This left just US$199.013mn in aggregate outstanding, and the remaining amount was subsequently repaid on due date.

Ghana has since issued six other eurobonds to date (end-June 2018), all of which are still outstanding, with its most recent issuance coming in May 2018. The total amount now outstanding is cUS$5bn. Ghana returned to the market in August 2013 with a US$1bn 10-year issue (comprising US$750mn in new money and US$250mn from an exchange offer for the 2017s) and again in September 2014 with another US$1bn 12-year issue. In October 2015, Ghana issued another US$1bn in a 15-year bond, as part of the World Bank IDA's inaugural guarantee programme. The guarantee comprised a US$400mn rolling guarantee on interest and principal. The bond was heralded as a further example of Ghana's part in the development of bond market innovation, but arguably Ghana's fiscal problems at the time meant it was unable to issue without a guarantee anyway. Moreover, even with the guarantee, Ghana ended up paying a very high 10.75% coupon (the spread at issue was 868bps). Ghana returned again to the market in September 2016 with a US$750mn six-year bond (2022 maturity), part of the proceeds of which were used to pay back some of the 2017 maturity. The bond had a coupon of 9.25% (issued at par). With an order book of US$4.1bn, it was more than five times oversubscribed, attracting 288 accounts, 45% of which were US and 41% UK, and 85% asset managers. The sale was initially planned for early August 2016, but was postponed because of rising costs, forcing the government to return in September with a shorter maturity.

The most recent issuance was a dual tranche offering in May 2018, for a combined US$2bn, split between a US$1bn long 10-year (2029) and US$1bn 30-year (2049). Both bonds were issued at par. The Ministry of Finance reported that the offer was four times oversubscribed with orders over US$8bn. Both bonds amortise by one-third in each of the final three years. The government also launched a tender offer for the shorter maturities (2022 and 2023) but, in the event, due to general market turbulence, it decided to proceed only with the repurchase of the higher-priced 2022 bond, omitting the 2023 bond. It accepted US$702mn of the 2022s at a price of 115.125%. The government therefore decided to issue only US$1.5bn (US$750mn to repay the 2022 euro bonds and US$750mn of new debt for the budget), despite parliamentary approval to issue more (up to US$2.5bn, with up to US$1.5bn for liability management), although strong demand meant the government was able to scale up the amount to be issued to US$2bn. The government was therefore able to reduce refinancing risks at the front end, lengthen the maturity of its curve (extending it to 30 years) and achieve the lowest rate on a 10-year bond since its debut eurobond issue in 2007.

All the outstanding sovereign bonds are listed in the table below. Details for the World Bank guaranteed 2030 bond are also shown.

Ghana's outstanding eurobonds

Description	*Amount outstanding*	*Maturity type*	*Issue date*
USD 9.25% due 2022	US$48.0mn[a]	Sinkable	Sep. 2016
USD 7.875% due 2023	US$1000mn[b]	Bullet	Aug. 2013
USD 8.125% due 2026	US$1000mn	Sinkable	Sep. 2014
USD 7.625% due 2029	US$1000mn	Sinkable	May 2018
USD 10.75% due 2030	US$1000mn	Sinkable	Oct. 2015
USD 8.627% due 2049	US$1000mn	Sinkable	May 2018

Source: Bloomberg

[a]Issue size was US$750mn. US$702mn was repurchased in a tender offer in May 2018
[b]Issue comprised US$750mn in new money and US$250mn from an exchange of the 2017s

Ghana bond
Republic of Ghana 10.75% 2030
Bloomberg ticker: GHANA

Borrower	Republic of Ghana
Issue date	7 October 2015
Form	Eurobond
ISIN	XS1297557412
Issue size	US$1000mn
Currency	US dollar
Denomination	Minimum of US$200,000 and US$1000 thereafter
Amortisation	Amortises in three equal annual instalments over 2028–30
Final maturity date	14 October 2030
Coupon/interest	10.75% paid semi-annually, April and October
Collateral/guarantor	World Bank IDA partial guarantee up to US$400mn (US$400 per US$1000 face)
Day count	30/360
Method of transfer	Euroclear/Clearstream
Settlement period	T + 2 business days
Joint lead managers	Barclays, Deutsche Bank, Standard Chartered Bank
Governing law	English

Source: Bloomberg

Another commercial instrument that trades like Ghana sovereign debt was issued by Saderea Limited (ticker SDEREA), an SPV formed for the purpose of purchasing promissory notes issued by the Republic of Ghana (Saderea promissory notes). The issuance relates to borrowing by the Republic from Euroget (the lender), an Egyptian firm, to finance the construction of military, regional and district hospitals in Ghana in November 2008. The Republic issued transferrable promissory notes to Euroget in support of its repayment obligations to Euroget, which included the Saderea promissory notes, while Saderea Limited (the issuer) issued a USD bond to international investors. The proceeds of the USD bond sale were to allow for the purchase of the Saderea Promissory Notes from Euroget. The Saderea bond is therefore collateralised by the promissory notes issued by the Republic. The Saderea bond issue was for US$253.2mn, in the form of 12.5% senior secured amortising notes due in 2026, which were issued in November 2014.

Saderea bond
Saderea 12.5% 2026
Bloomberg ticker: SDEREA

Borrower	Saderea
Issue date	21 November 2014
Form	Euro MTN
ISIN	XS1136935506
Issue size	US$253.190mn
Amount outstanding	US$205.536mn
Currency	US dollar
Denomination	Minimum of US$200,000 and US$1000 thereafter
Amortisation	Sinkable: amortises semi-annually by continually increasing amounts, starting at US$5.3mn, a factor of 2.1%, to US$17.5mn, the remaining principle outstanding on the maturity date
Final maturity date	30 November 2026
Coupon/interest	12.5% paid semi-annually May and November
Day count	ACT/365
Method of transfer	Euroclear/Clearstream
Settlement period	T + 2 business days
Joint lead managers	Barclays, Citi
Exchange	Dublin
Governing law	English

Source: Bloomberg

Corporate Bonds

Ghana has a very limited domestic corporate bond market and no domestically issued USD corporate bonds. However, two Western oil companies that operate in the country have bond issues that figure in the Ghana constituent of the CEMBI corporate bond index. Kosmos Energy (a US-based E&P company) has one bond outstanding, the US$300mn 7.875% 2021s, which is callable. The bond was issued in a private placement in August 2014. Tullow Oil (the UK-based E&P company that operates the Jubilee field) has three bonds outstanding, the US$650mn 6.25% 2022 (issued in April 2014) and US$800mn 7% 2025 (issued in March 2018), and the US$300mn 6.625% 2021 convertible bond (issued in July 2016). The 2022s and 2025s are both callable. Its other issue, the US$650mn 6% 2020 was called on 23 March 2018. Asset descriptions are provided below for the Kosmos bond and Tullow Oil convertible.

Kosmos Energy bond
Kosmos Energy 7.875% 2021
Bloomberg ticker: KOS

Borrower	Kosmos Energy Ltd
Issue date	1 August 2014
Form	Private placement
ISIN	USG5315BAA55 (RegS)/US500688AA48 (144a)
Issue size	US$300mn
Currency	US dollar
Denomination	Minimum of US$200,000 and US$1000 thereafter
Amortisation	Callable (next call 1 August 2019 at 100.00)
Final maturity date	1 August 2021
Coupon/interest	7.875% paid semi-annually
Day count	30/360
Method of transfer	FED FUNDS, DTC
Settlement period	T + 2 business days
Joint lead managers	Bank of America Merrill Lynch, Barclays, BNP Paribas, Credit Agricole, HSBC, Société Générale, Standard Chartered, Standard Bank
Exchange	EuroMFT, Luxembourg
Governing law	New York

Source: Bloomberg

Tullow Oil convertible bond
Tullow Oil 6.625% 2021
Bloomberg ticker: TLWLN

Borrower	Tullow Oil Jersey Ltd
Issue date	12 July 2016
Form	Eurobond
ISIN	XS1443221343
Issue size	US$300mn
Currency	US dollar
Denomination	Minimum of US$200,000 and US$200,000 thereafter
Amortisation	Convertible
Final maturity date	12 July 2021
Coupon/interest	6.25% paid semi-annually
Method of transfer	Euroclear/Clearstream
Settlement period	T + 2 business days
Joint lead managers	Barclays, BNP Paribas, Credit Agricole, JP Morgan, Société Générale
Exchange	Channel Islands
Governing law	English

Source: Bloomberg

Greece

Nominal GDP (US$mn, 2018)[a]		218,057
Population (thousand, 2018)[a]		10,736
GDP per capita (USD, 2018)[a]		20,311
Credit ratings (long-term foreign currency)[b]	Fitch	BB–
	Moody's	B3
	S&P	B+

[a]IMF WEO October 2018
[b]As at end-September 2018

Country Summary

- Greece is exiting its deep public debt crisis that began in 2010 but the debt burden remains high and achieving debt sustainability remains a challenge. The economy experienced one of the world's longest recessions in modern times, lasting nine years (over 2008–2016) while nominal GDP fell 28%. Greece benefited from three rounds of international rescue packages, involving European creditors and initially the IMF (approving its biggest ever programme in 2010, on an access basis, at 3212% of quota), amounting to total disbursements of EUR290bn, an unprecedented bailout in modern history.

Exotix Capital, *Exotix Developing Markets Guide*,
https://doi.org/10.1007/978-3-030-05867-8_21

- Greece undertook the biggest sovereign debt exchange in history in 2012, as part of its bailout, covering EUR206bn in debt and involving a 53.5% nominal debt reduction. Greece returned to the market in 2014, just two years after its sovereign debt restructuring, and has issued nine bonds in all since then, in five operations. Bonds now comprise about 15.5% of total government debt. Official sector creditors are now, unsurprisingly, Greece's largest creditors accounting for about 75% of Greek debt, comprised mainly of European rescue funds (EFSF/ESM/GLF).
- Greece completed successfully its third and most recent bailout programme, under the European ESM, in August 2018. But Greece's total public debt remains high, at about 189% of 2018 projected GDP (standing at EUR345.4bn in June 2018), and sustainability will depend on maintaining fiscal discipline, delivery of recently agreed official sector commitments to debt relief and boosting growth. But the bailout programmes also imposed significant austerity on the Greek people and changed the political landscape in the country.

Economic data	*Avg*[a]	*2014*	*2015*	*2016*	*2017 (e)*	*2018 (f)*	*2019 (f)*
Real GDP growth	−2.6	0.7	−0.3	−0.2	1.4	2.0	2.4
Inflation (annual average)	1.4	−1.4	−1.1	0.0	1.1	0.7	1.2
Current account (% of GDP)	−7.3	−1.6	−0.2	−1.1	−0.8	−0.8	−0.4
Reserves (US$mn, end-period)[b]	4489	5117	5535	6539	6509	6317[c]	–
Reserves/ imports (months)[d]	0.79	0.89	1.11	1.38	1.24	–	–
Overall fiscal balance (% of GDP)[e]	−7.0	−4.0	−2.8	0.7	1.1	0.5	0.0
Currency (ticker)	Euro (EUR)						
FX regime	Fixed within currency union. Floating vis-à-vis other currencies.						
Key exports	Minerals (30%), metals (11%), foodstuffs (9%).						

Source: IMF WEO Database, Central Bank of Greece, OEC

[a]10-year arithmetic average to 2016 unless otherwise stated
[b]Gross official reserve assets
[c]Latest figure, July 2018
[d]Months of imports of the current year's goods, services and primary income debits
[e]General government net lending (IMF WEO)

Key figures		*Party*	*Since*
President	Prokopis Pavlopoulos	New Democracy	Mar. 2015
Prime minister	Alexis Tsipras	Syriza	Jan. 2015
Minister of finance	Euclid Tsakalotos	Syriza	Jul. 2015
Key opposition figure	Kyriakos Mitsotakis	New Democracy	Jan. 2016
Central bank governor	Yannis Stournaras	–	Jun. 2014

POLITICS

Executive power

The president serves as head of state and is elected by the parliament for a five-year term. Although the president performs some executive and legislative functions, the role is largely ceremonial, with the cabinet and prime minister instead playing the central role in the political process. The president appoints the prime minister but is obliged to select the candidate proposed by the party with the largest number of seats in the parliament. The president subsequently appoints the cabinet on recommendation of the prime minister.

Presidential term: Five years (maximum two terms) **Parliamentary term:** Four years

Legislature

Legislative power is vested in both the cabinet and the 'Hellenic' parliament. The parliament comprises 300 MPs who serve four-year terms. 250 MPs are elected through a proportional representation system and 50 MPs are allocated for the party that wins the plurality of votes.

Elections

Next due *Legislative: Oct 2019* *Presidential: Feb 2020*

Last legislative election (September 2015)	*Seats*	*Last presidential (February 2015)*	*# of votes*
Syriza Unionist Social Front	145	Prokopis Pavlopoulos	233
New Democracy	75	Niko Alivizatos	30
Golden Dawn	18		
PASOK	17		
Communist Party of Greece	15		
The River	11		
Independent Greeks	10		
Union of Centrists	9		
Total	**300**	**Total**	**300**[a]

[a]32 MPs voted 'present' and 5 MPs were absent

People

Independent from the Ottoman empire in 1829, Greece has historically played a strategic geopolitical role given its political and geographical proximity to Europe, Asia, Africa, and the Middle East. Its 10.8 million population is ethnically diverse, with one-third living in and around Athens, and with almost everyone (98%) belonging to the Greek Orthodox Church. Greece joined NATO in 1952, the EU in 1981 and adopted the euro in 2001. Since the onset of the debt crisis, the country has suffered from social unrest with frequent demonstrations against the austerity measures that have been implemented as a condition for the bail-out assistance. The socio-political problems have recently been compounded by the large wave of refugees fleeing to Greece from Syria. Syriza, a left-wing party led by prime minister Alexis Tsipras, has been in power since a snap election in 2015.

Debt

	2012	*2017*
External debt ratios (%)		
Total external debt/GDP	233.5	227.9
Public external debt/GDP[a]	183.6	192.7
Private external debt/GDP	49.9	35.2
Total external debt/exports of goods and services	911.1	720.6
External debt service ratio (PPG)	n/a	n/a
Public debt ratios (%)		
Public domestic debt/GDP	n/a	46.0
Public debt/GDP[b]	159.6	184.9

Sources: PDMA Public Debt Bulletin June 2018, IMF Country Reports, IMF WEO, Exotix

[a]Includes external debt of the central bank

[b]Excludes debt of the central bank

Greece's total public debt stood at EUR345.4bn in June 2018, according to the Greek debt management agency (PDMA); which Exotix estimates is about 189% of 2018 projected WEO GDP. Official sector creditors are now Greece's largest creditors (and have been since the PSI deal), accounting for about EUR260bn of Greek debt (75% of the total). The EFSF is the largest of Greece's creditors, owed EUR130.9bn (38% of the total), followed by the ESM (EUR44.9bn. 13% of the total) and GLF (EUR52.9bn, 15% of the total). The EFSF/ESM together held 51% of Greek public debt (EUR176bn). These are followed by the IMF (3.0%), SMP/ANFA (3.7%) and EIB (2.3%). Bonds comprised another EUR53bn (about 15.5% of total government debt). This is mostly domestically issued bonds (GGBs), although some of these are held externally, and include the PSI bonds, with about three quarters of this (about EUR38.3bn according to Exotix' calculations) being marketable bonds (remaining PSI bonds, and new issues since 2014). Since the debt restructuring deal in 2012, Greece has issued four domestic bonds (EUR3bn in April 2014, EUR1.5bn in July 2014, EUR3bn in August 2017 and EUR3bn in February 2015) and no international bonds. It also includes non-marketable bonds held by other national central banks. External bonds are only EUR1.7bn. The rest of Greek government debt is comprised of mainly short-term notes (T-bills), about 4.3% of the total, and Repos, about 6.8% of the total. Of the total, public external debt (excluding debt owed by the central bank) was about EUR253bn (comprising mainly the EFSF/ESM/IMF, bilateral loans from the EIB, and foreign bonds), about 138% of GDP. That implied public domestic debt was 51% of GDP.

Nominal government debt has edged up from EUR328.7bn at end 2017 (185% of GDP; 182% in the IMF's latest 2018 Article IV and the WEO) and EUR305.1bn in 2012 (160% of GDP). Curiously, the 53.5% face value reduction in some EUR200bn of bonded debt in the PSI deal in 2012 does not seem to have reduced the overall debt level as it has been largely replaced by official sector debt, albeit on more concessional terms. In less than a year, from early 2012 to late 2012, the outstanding value of privately held sovereign bonds collapsed from EUR206bn to EUR30bn, following the PSI deal and subsequent buyback, while loans from the IMF and euro-area bilateral creditors soared from EUR73bn to EUR183bn.

Indeed, public debt/GDP hovered around the 180% level for five years over the period 2013–2017 and is expected to increase in 2018 (the IMF projected 188%). Public debt has risen from 160% of GDP in 2012 and 146% in 2010 (IMF WEO figures); it was about 100% over most of the 2000s. In 2017, public external debt (excluding debt owed by the central bank) was about 139% of GDP (EUR247bn), with public domestic debt of 46% of GDP. Meanwhile, total external debt in 2017 was 228% of GDP and 721% of exports of goods and services, according to the IMF's DSA in its 2018 Article IV in July 2018. Greece's stock of external debt has remained broadly constant in nominal terms since 2012, although on an increasing path relative to GDP, and remains as one of the highest among European economies, having doubled from 97% of GDP in 2004 to 185% of GDP in 2010 as Greece financed growing domestic demand through large current account deficits (which averaged 12% of GDP in 2004–10). In 2017, about 80% of total external borrowing was by the public sector (including the central bank), with the composition of external debt having modestly shifted away from private banks to the central bank in 2015 when it provided emergency liquidity assistance amid rapid deposit outflows. Banks have been hit especially hard by the crisis and have required three rounds of recapitalizations since 2010 to shore up capital ratios. The NPL ratio stood at 49% in March 2017, the highest among euro area countries.

Public sector debt service, especially external, since 2012 is unclear. Some payments on foreign law bonds were likely made in early 2012, before the PSI exchange was concluded, although it is not clear what payments to official creditors were made at the time. Thereafter, following PSI, and the consolidation of domestic and foreign law bonds into a single series of PSI bonds (EUR denominated, English law), bond payments should have been very low for two reasons. First, they would have been in part limited to the few unswapped foreign law bonds (holdouts). There were scheduled maturities of holdout bonds over 2012–2017 but it is not clear what payments were made. Second, payments on the new PSI bonds were designed to be low for the first several years. The new PSI bonds had an annual coupon, commencing in February 2013 at 2% (implying interest of about EUR1.2bn on the stock of PSI bonds) but maturities do no commence until 2023. So, there was no debt service on these bonds in 2012 itself. Moreover, it is not clear what payments on the new PSI bonds would constitute external or domestic, which should depend on residency of holder, which is unclear. Similar uncertainties relate to the new issues of GGBs since 2014, which should mean debt interest would have increased (one 2014 issue matured in 2017), although the increase may have been swamped by the reduction in PSI bonds following the buyback, but it is not clear either how much of these is held domestically rather than abroad. Moreover, following PSI, the composition of public debt shifted from private creditors to official creditors, and while some big repayments were made to the IMF, the vast majority of Greece's new borrowing was from the European rescue funds (ESM/EFSF) which typically had long grace periods and low interest rates, and full details on the debt service schedule is not available.

Greece faces a heavy principal repayment schedule in 2019 with about EUR11.8bn coming due. This mainly comprises bonds and loans, including ECB held bonds under the SMP programme. It also includes the EUR2.5bn remaining maturity of the five year GGB (4.75% 2019) issued in 2014. Repayments fall sharply over 2020–2021 (to EUR5bn per year), before picking up again in 2022–2023 (to EUR9.8bn and EUR12.2bn respectively). However, this excludes the some EUR38bn in T-bills and Repos which need to be rolled over every year.

Composition of Greek public debt

Public debt by category (June 2018)	*Nominal amount outstanding*		*Share of total (%)*
	EUR million	*US$mn (equivalent)*[a]	
Bonds	53,410	62,381	15.5
o/w Issued domestically	51,683	60,363	15.0
Issued internationally	1728	2018	0.5
Securitization issued abroad	30	35	0.0
Short-term notes	14,698	17,166	4.3
Loans	277,241	323,804	80.3
Bank of Greece	2379	2778	0.7
Other domestic loans	240	280	0.1
Special purpose and bilateral loans (EIB)	7846	9164	2.3
Financial Support Mechanism (FSM) loans	239,080	279,234	69.2
o/w EFSF	130,900	152,885	37.9
ESM	44,900	52,441	13.0
GLF	52,900	61,785	15.3
IMF	10,400	12,147	3.0
Other external loans	4246	4959	1.2
Repos	23,451	27,389	6.8
Total debt	**345,379**	**403,386**	**100.0**

Source: Ministry of Finance Public Debt Bulletin June 2018

[a]Converted at rate of US$/EUR1.168 from Haver

Rescheduling History

Since its independence in 1829, Greece has defaulted or rescheduled its debt six times (1826, 1843, 1860, 1893, 1932, 2012) and has spent more than half of the years in a state of default or rescheduling (with the 1826 default, for instance, shutting the country out from international capital markets for 53 consecutive years), more than any country in the world. The most recent rescheduling, of its commercial debt in 2012, followed the Greek debt crisis and is the largest restructuring deal in the history of sovereign defaults, wiping out EUR107bn in face value of Greece's debt stock (see section '*Sovereign commercial debt*'). Greece also benefitted from generous official sector lending over 2010–2018 during the Greek debt crisis, much of which has also been subject to various debt relief measures and rescheduling, although without any principal reduction.

Greece's modern debt crisis began in 2010, but as usual, its origins dated further back. A number of factors were to blame, including euro-accession (as the adoption of the euro and loose credit conditions fuelled an economic boom), pro-cyclical fiscal policy, a deterioration in the current account (due to the economic boom, lack of structural adjustment and real exchange rate overvaluation), and concerns over the quality of Greek deficit and debt statistics. A new government took office in October 2009, under PASOK Prime Minster George Papandreou, and announced that the fiscal position had been significantly understated. According to the IMF, the projected budget deficit for 2009 was revised up from 4% to 12.5% of GDP (the final deficit was 15.5%). Public debt was also revised higher. Public debt stood at 127% of GDP in 2009, up from 109% in 2008. Fitch downgraded Greece's sovereign rating from A– to BBB+. Investor sentiment, post the global financial crisis, was also fragile after the events in Iceland, Latvia and Dubai. The government responded by agreeing a fiscal consolidation plan with the EC (the IMF was explicitly ruled out as part of the solution) and was able to issue EUR5bn on two occasions in March 2010.

In fact, while Greece fell into only a mild recession during the global financial crisis (real GDP fell by just 0.3% in 2008), it soon became deeper and more protracted. Real GDP fell by 4.3% in 2009, 5.5% in 2010 and 9.1% in 2011. After a modest recovery in 2014, recession returned over 2015 and 2016, such that Greece endured one of the longest recessions in modern times, lasting nine years, with real GDP growth averaging –3.3% over 2008–2016. Nominal GDP fell 28% from a peak of EUR242bn in 2008 to EUR174bn in 2016.

Responding to the debt crisis, the IMF and euro area (in various guises) provided financial assistance through three bail-out packages (2010–12, 2012–15, 2015–2018, see section '*Relations with multilateral creditors*'). Discussions on a rescue plan for Greece first began in April 2010, with the Troika (the EC, ECB and IMF), culminating in a EUR110bn financing package being announced in early May. The IMF provided EUR30bn in a three year SBA. The remaining financing was in the form of bilateral loans from euro area countries to be pooled by the EC under the Greek Loan Facility (GLF). The programme was described at the time as one of "shock and awe", designed to outsize expectations and reassure markets, and a process of building a firewall began to limit contagion from Greece to other euro area periphery countries (although ultimately it wasn't enough). In early May 2010, agreement was reached to set up the European Financial Stability Facility (EFSF) with EUR500bn in financing, which could be supplemented by an additional EUR250bn in lending from the Fund provided on a country by country basis. Additional assistance came from the ECB which created the Securities Markets Program (SMP) in May 2010 to purchase public debt securities in secondary markets.

The first rescue programme met with some initial success. It saw encouraging fiscal performance under the IMF programme, although privatisation revenues disappointed and public debt overshot projections, in part as real GDP fell by more than expected. The cumulative improvement in the primary fiscal balance over 2010–2011 was about 7% of GDP, but the primary fiscal balance remained in deficit, the overall fiscal deficit was more than 10% of GDP in 2011, and debt was still on an unsustainable path. The fiscal adjustment was mainly revenue based. The IMF's ex post assessment of the 2010 SBA noted that at the outset of the programme, debt was projected to peak at 154–156% of GDP in 2013 but by the fourth review in July 2011, it was projected at 170%. Moreover, crucially, from the perspective of the official sector, private creditors were able to reduce their exposure. This prompted questions about programme design, and whether a more gradual fiscal adjustment should have been targeted, whether the adjustment path should have been more flexible, whether structural reforms were strong enough (structural reforms started to face significant opposition from vested interests), whether there was sufficient ownership of the reform programme by the then PASOK government, and whether debt restructuring (PSI) should have been attempted sooner. That it wasn't was in part due to official sector concerns about the impact on Greek banks and the risk of contagion, although by and large, markets had begun to anticipate that some form of sovereign debt restructuring was inevitable. The official sector appeared to put debt restructuring firmly on the agenda in the Deauville Summit in October 2010.

The first bailout programme started to veer off track by early 2011. The IMF's second review of the SBA was completed in December 2010, but problems in programme implementation were becoming apparent by the time of the third review in February 2011. Efforts were made to bring the programme back on track during 2011, including ambitious privatization plans. The need for PSI was acknowledged by the fourth review in July 2011. Faced with rising discontent, and fears over Grexit, PM Papandreou announced in October 2011 a referendum on the rescue package he had negotiated with the Troika to test the views of the Greek people. The plan for a referendum was withdrawn a month later but the government resigned and was replaced in November 2011 by a technocratic coalition government of PASOK and New Democracy, under PM Lucas Papademos, which appeared to forge a political consensus for reforms in support of Greece's choice to remain in the euro area. The SBA was cancelled in March 2012 (a year early) and a second bailout package was approved. The IMF approved a new EUR28bn EFF in March 2012, which contained PSI as a prior action, with EUR130bn coming from Europe through the EFSF. The EFF aimed to reduce the stock of public debt to 120% of GDP by 2020. Sentiment subsequently turned more positive after the bond exchange and ECB President Draghi's comments in May 2012 ("whatever it takes").

The second bailout package had some success, despite ongoing political uncertainty. The IMF's ex post assessment of the EFF noted that programme implementation was poor during a tumultuous 2012 with two parliamentary elections and intense Grexit fears. Papademos stepped down in May 2012 and PM Antonis Samaras emerged as PM. As a result of the turmoil, the assumed confidence effects did not take hold. However, a period of relative stability ensued during early 2013–early 2014 with stronger programme implementation reflected in over-performance on fiscal targets. Green shoots of recovery became visible by mid 2014 and investor confidence had improved. The IMF board completed the long-overdue fifth review of Greece's EFF programme on 30 May 2014. Approval allowed the disbursement of USD4.6bn (combining two disbursements because of delays to the review). The IMF's statement recognised the significant progress in consolidating the fiscal position and that the primary fiscal position was in surplus ahead of schedule. However additional fiscal adjustment through high quality and durable measures was necessary to ensure debt sustainability. Attention also turned to official sector debt relief (OSI). The Greek government was demanding that its European partners honour a commitment made in November 2012 to grant further debt relief after Eurostat confirmed in April that the country ran a primary surplus in 2013. Indeed, the situation had eased so much that Greece was able to return to the debt markets. In April 2014 it issued its first bond since 2010. Another bond was issued in July 2014.

However, the second bailout programme also began to go off-track by late 2014. Popular discontent was never far away after a deeper-than-expected 5-year recession and a 30-percent fall in real disposable incomes. As a result, the parties opposing the agreed adjustment programme gained ground throughout this period, hindering programme implementation and unnerving investors. Bond yields began to rise by the autumn of 2014 with the yield on the new 5 year (2019 GGB) breaching the psychologically important 7%

threshold in October 2014. Grexit concerns resurfaced. The EFF programme was by now irretrievably off track, after having already encountered significant delays during March 2012–June 2014. Support for the traditional political parties collapsed, and the failure of the Greek parliament to elect a new president on 29 December 2014, resulted in early legislative elections, held in January 2015, which saw the radical left-wing anti-austerity party Syriza assume power under new PM Alexis Tsipras. Its first months in office were marked by the controversial Finance Minister Yanis Varoufakis who resigned after five months. The new government announced a major policy shift, halting the previous reform agenda, and further EU-imposed austerity was rejected by Greek voters in a popular referendum on 5 July 2015. A proposed EU rescue programme was rejected by Greek voters in a July 2015 referendum, bringing renewed fears over Grexit. This resulted in the temporary closure of banks and the imposition of deposit withdrawal limits and capital controls. By then, the IMF published an updated DSA in July 2015 that concluded that public debt was unsustainable.

A third bailout programme, led by the European Institutions, and without IMF involvement, was agreed in August 2015. The new ESM programme (EUR86bn) covered the three year period to August 2018. Greece exited the ESM programme successfully in August 2018 having secured commitment from Europe to additional medium term debt relief measures.

PSI and OSI (thus far) were exceptionally large by international comparisons. The haircut to private bondholders of EUR107bn was the highest in modern history according to Zettelmeyer et al. But, according to the IMF ex post assessment of the EFF, they achieved a relatively modest immediate decline in the stock of public debt. Public debt declined to EUR305bn (160% of GDP) at end-2012 from EUR356bn (172% of GDP) at end-2011. This was explained by a number of factors, including the fact that Greek bond holdings by EU institutions were excluded from the restructuring, constraints on OSI related to certain EU loans, that the commercial bond exchange had to be attractive enough to ensure participation, and lower nominal GDP. In fact, the IMF argued that debt relief wasn't sufficient, but more should have come from OSI not more PSI.

Relations with Multilateral Creditors

Greece has had three bailout packages. Until the Greek crisis began, Greece had never had an IMF programme but had two massive Fund programmes during the crisis over a seven year period. Each IMF programme, the first in 2010 and the second in 2012, was part of a wider bailout package under the 'Troika' (European Commission, the ECB, and the IMF) and were back to back. The IMF declined to participate at the outset of the third European bailout package in 2015.

The first bail-out package, approved in May 2010, was a three-year EUR110bn loan (subsequently reduced by EUR2.7bn when loans were also extended to Ireland and Portugal), split across EUR80bn in bilateral loans from euro area Member States (with Germany being the single biggest creditor at EUR22bn) through the 'Greek Loan Facility (GLF)' and an EUR30bn SBA programme from the IMF. Access under the 2010 SBA was the largest in Fund history at 3212% of quota and required that the IMF amend its lending criteria for exceptional access. In particular, Staff could not argue that public debt was sustainable with high probability (Criteria 2) although contagion risks led to the "systemic exemption" so that the programme could go forward. The package responded to Greece's unsustainable fiscal situation with ever-increasing borrowing costs and rising public debt, and was conditional on the implementation of austerity measures and structural reforms. The programme was cancelled in March 2012 ahead of the second bail-out package, about one year before the original end date. By the end of the first bailout programme, the euro area countries and the IMF had disbursed EUR53bn and EUR20bn, respectively, leaving EUR34bn in undisbursed credit.

The second bail-out package was approved in March 2012, with the euro area members (via the EFSF) and the IMF committing a total of EUR164bn in loans through 2014. This consisted of EUR130bn in new credit under the second programme plus EUR34bn in undisbursed amounts from the first bail-out programme. The IMF committed EUR28bn through a four-year EFF programme (of which EUR20bn was expected to be disbursed by the end of 2014). Access under the 2012 EFF was also very high at 2159% of quota. The IMF loan was conditional on a significant debt restructuring of Greece's privately held sovereign bonds (see section '*Sovereign commercial debt*'). In December 2012, the Troika provided further financial assistance through: (1) retroactively lowering the interest rate on the GLF and EFSF lending (but no face value reduction); (2) committing to returning the profits that the ECB would make in its purchases on Greek bonds to Greece; and (3) a partial buyback of Greece's debt, retiring EUR32bn of sovereign bonds. The second bail-out package was extended twice in the first half of 2015 but was finally terminated in June 2015 due to lack of progress and waning political ownership (although the IMF's

EFF wasn't formally cancelled until January 2016), as the Europeans approved a new bailout in August 2015. The EFF encountered significant delays during March 2012–June 2014, after which it went irretrievably off track, with only five out of 16 scheduled reviews completed by the time it was cancelled. The EFSF and IMF had disbursed a total of EUR142bn and EUR12bn (SDR10.2bn), respectively. At the end of the programme (and three days after a referendum that rejected further austerity measures imposed by the Troika), Greece missed payments totalling EUR1.6bn to the IMF, becoming the first developed country to fail to make an IMF loan repayment. At the same time, Greece imposed capital controls on banks, preventing a bank run, and temporarily closed the Athens stock exchange. It subsequently repaid its IMF arrears in July 2015 thanks to a EUR7bn bridge financing loan from the EFSF. Despite the referendum rejecting further austerity measures, the Greek parliament passed an austerity bill in July 2015, freeing up further financial assistance from the ESM in the form of the third bail-out package. However, by then, the Fund was having severe doubts about providing further financial assistance (lending into an unsustainable situation), as an updated DSA published in July 2015 showed that Greece's public debt had become unsustainable.

The IMF approved a total of SDR50.2bn (EUR60.3bn) across both programmes, with SDR27.8bn (EUR33.3bn) being drawn in all (comprising two thirds of the SBA and 43% of the EFF). However, Greece has repaid most of its IMF borrowings. The SBA had been fully repaid. As of August 2018, SDR8.6bn (EUR10.3bn) of EFF borrowings remained outstanding.

The IMF did not participate in the third European bailout package in 2015, demanding as a condition of its involvement further debt relief and structural reforms. But in July 2017, the Executive Board announced an Agreement in Principle (AIP) on a 14-month SDR1.3bn (EUR1.6bn, 55% of quota) SBA. The programme was to become effective only after the IMF received specific assurances from Greece's European partners to ensure debt sustainability. However, the SBA-AIP was not implemented by the time the ESM expired in August 2018 and so the IMF ended up not disbursing any money to Greece in parallel with the European programme. Ironically, the IMF concluded in its 2018 Article IV in July that it expected many of the SBA-AIP benchmarks to be completed by the end of August 2018. The SBA-AIP, while never implemented, set out 21 structural benchmarks which were closely tied to the ESM programme objectives. Various quantitative performance targets were also on track.

The IMF Board concluded the 2018 Article IV for Greece in July 2018 in which it recommended the initiation of post-programme monitoring (PPM).

Greece met the Fund's criteria for PPM given the IMF's exposure. The first PPM Board discussion was expected to take place in early 2019. In the Article IV, Staff concluded that the envisaged level of official sector debt relief will mitigate refinancing risks over the medium term, but cautioned that longer term prospects remained uncertain.

IMF programmes

Date	*Arrangements*	*Comments*
2010–12 (cancelled early)	SBA	A three-year SDR26.4bn (EUR30bn, 3212% of quota) SBA programme approved in May 2010 as part of a joint EU-IMF EUR110bn (subsequently reduced to EUR107bn) financing package. Commonly referred to as the 'first bail-out package', the loan responded to the country's debt crisis and ordered significant fiscal consolidation though higher taxes and spending cuts. Greece drew SDR17.5bn (EUR20bn). The programme was cancelled early, in March 2012 (one year prior to the original end date) at the start of the new 2012 EFF programme.
2012–16 (cancelled early)	EFF	A four-year SDR23.8bn (EUR28bn, 2159% of quota) EFF programme approved in March 2012 as part of a joint EU-IMF EUR164bn financing package. Greece drew SDR10.2bn (EUR12bn). Greece missed an IMF payment in June 2015, which it subsequently repaid one month later. The last review to be completed was the fifth in May 2014. In February 2015, the IMF MD signalled support for the new Greek government's measures and hoped to conclude the sixth review as soon as possible. However, delays continued and Greece fell into arrears to the Fund on 30 June 2015 after failing to make a SDR1.2bn (EUR1.5bn) repayment. This meant that Greece could only receive IMF financing once the arrears were cleared. Another repayment, for SDR360mn, was missed on 13 July 2015. The arrears were later cleared on 20 July 2015. The IMF also published an updated DSA in July 2015 which concluded that Greece's debt had become highly unsustainable, spelling the end of the programme (and signalling the Fund's unwillingness to participate in the third bailout programme approved in August 2015). The EFF was cancelled a few months early, in January 2016.
2017 July (not implemented)	SBA-AIP	Agreement in Principle (AIP) on a 14-month Standby Arrangement for SDR1.3bn (EUR1.6bn, 55% of quota), effective once European partners can provide assurances on debt sustainability.

Source: IMF

Paris Club and Bilateral Creditors

Greece has not entered any rescheduling agreement with the Paris Club.

The euro area Member States, along with other European institutions, provided three bailout programmes for Greece. The first European bailout programme was approved in May 2010 and the second bailout was approved in February 2012. Both these programmes had IMF participation. The third European bailout, under the ESM programme, which was approved in May 2015, was agreed on the expectation of future IMF participation but in the event the IMF kept out and did not disburse any money to Greece in parallel with the ESM programme. The ESM programme expired successfully in August 2018, with Greece becoming the fifth country after Ireland, Spain, Portugal, and Cyprus to exit an EFSF or an ESM programme.

In total, the three European bailout programmes lent EUR256.6bn to Greece. This comprised EUR52.9bn in bilateral loans Greece received over 2010–2012 out of a total commitment of EUR80bn under the so-called Greek Loan Facility (GLF) from euro area Member States in the first programme, and total disbursements of EUR203.8bn under the EFSF/ESM rescue funds from its second and third bailout programmes, an unprecedented amount in modern history. Greece received EUR141.8bn in loans from the EFSF between 2012 and 2015 (out of a total commitment of EUR144.7bn; of which EUR130.9bn is outstanding) and EUR61.9bn from the ESM over 2015–2018 (out of a total commitment of EUR86bn). The EFSF/ESM loans have long maturities (over 30 years on average) and very favourable interest rates. The EFSF and ESM are Greece's largest creditors, holding over 55% of total Greek government debt, according to ESM data (slightly lower on PDMA figures).

The ESM programme had risked going off track in early 2017 because of stalling on the second review. The situation took a negative turn towards the end of 2016. First, a war of words developed between Greece, Brussels and the IMF soon after the Eurogroup statement on 5 December which had seemingly looked like a positive step as it welcomed the progress towards reaching a staff level agreement (SLA) on the second review of the ESM programme. Greece said the IMF was pushing for more austerity, an accusation the Fund vehemently rejected in a blog post on 12 December. Then, on 15 December, European lenders froze the short-term debt relief measures that were agreed on 5 December as a result of government fiscal measures that the Europeans were unaware of. These consisted of one-off payments to low-income pensioners and postponed

VAT increases for refugee-hit islands. However, a Eurogroup meeting on 7 April 2017 signalled progress on at least the first of the two conditions for completing the second review of the ESM bailout programme (ie the fiscal side, concerning pensions and personal income tax, rather than structural reforms, on the financial sector, labour market and product market). Creditors announced on 2 May 2017 that they had concluded discussions on elements of the second review which followed an agreement in principle on these matters at the 7 April Eurogroup. The second review was concluded soon after and ultimately the rest of the ESM programme proceeded without incident. The ESM bailout programme finished on schedule in August 2018 although the European Institutions, along with the IMF, maintain a monitoring process under the enhanced surveillance framework.

Official sector involvement (OSI) by the Europeans was an on-going issue of contention during the ESM programme. The IMF concluded in a DSA in July 2015 that Greece's debt was unsustainable and couldn't therefore agree to participate in the new ESM programme unless there was a commitment to debt relief from the European side, by then Greece's biggest creditor. But the Europeans resisted debt relief, partly for political reasons (the European election calendar and in particular Germany's own election in 2017) and for reasons of moral hazard (and outright German resistance to haircuts, and concern that member states needed to see measures implemented and some sort of track record before rewarding Greece with debt relief). But Europe, and in particular Germany, wanted IMF participation in the bailout programme to give it some amount of independent credibility in the face of a sceptical electorate. It was hoped that the IMF would find a way to participate after completion of the second review of the ESM, which was expected by end 2016 (the review was delayed). The Eurogroup did agree on 5 December 2016 only to short-term debt measures to be implemented immediately—extending repayments and freezing of an interest rate step up—although discussion on full OSI was deferred and maturity extension was left until 2018, with Germany unwilling to provide debt relief to Greece before then. The IMF's delay reflected its concern that the Greek commitment to a 3.5% primary surplus target in the ESM programme, a target supported by Europe, was neither credible nor realistic; the difference in opinion in part reflected differing views about long-run growth and fiscal effort. The IMF thought adjustment measures in the ESM programme would be enough to deliver a surplus of only 1.5% of GDP in 2018, and even this needed to be accompanied by two pillars of structural reform and significant debt relief. The IMF did finally agree a programme on an in principle basis in July 2017, but it always looked like the timing would be such that it was unlikely to come into effect before the ESM expired. In the end, it was a compromise that kept the IMF out (but engaged), the Europeans in and the German parliament on-side.

Greece's European partners agreed at the 22 June 2018 Eurogroup meeting to provide further debt relief through a number of medium term measures. This consisted of: (1) a 10-year weighted average maturity (WAM) extension of certain EFSF loans (amounting to EUR96.9bn) and 10-year deferral of interest payments (the WAM has increased to 42.5 years, as per the IMF); (2) a EUR3.3bn additional disbursement, aimed at mitigating refinancing risks, increasing the state government cash buffer to about EUR24bn; (3) abolishing the step-up interest rate margin on the EFSF debt buy-back tranche for 2018 onwards; and (4) restoration of ECB profits from 2014 and 2017 onwards for a total amount of EUR5.8bn to be distributed over 2018–2022. The interest extension and deferral (item (1)) was an immediate and unconditional measure, whereas (3) and (4) were conditional on compliance with a set of European benchmarks. The Eurogroup also agreed to a "rendez-vous clause" to another review in 2032 should the debt dynamics not be deemed satisfactory and require implementation of longer-term measures. With these measures, according to PDMA's September 2018 Investor Presentation, the debt/GDP ratio is expected to decline to 128% in 2032 against 134% previously while Gross Financing Needs over the period 2018–2032 period have been reduced by 2.7ppts of GDP on average to an average of 10.6% of GDP. Additionally, the EUR24.1bn cash buffer at the end of the programme is equivalent to 2 years of gross financing needs (over 4 years of debt maturities assuming T-Bills are rolled over).

European bailout programmes

Date	*Lenders*	*Comments*
May 2010	Euro area and IMF	A three-year joint programme between the euro area Member States and the IMF, the euro area contributed EUR80bn out of a total financing package of EUR110bn, of which up to EUR30bn was available in the first year. The IMF SBA provided the remaining EUR30bn. The first European disbursement was to be made available before the payment obligations of the Greek government fall due on 19 May. In total, EUR52.9bn in bilateral loans was provided under the auspices of the Greek Loan Facility (GLF).

(*continued*)

(continued)

Date	*Lenders*	*Comments*
Feb. 2012	EFSF and IMF	An initial two-year joint programme between the euro area Member States and the IMF, with the euro area, acting through the EFSF, providing EUR130bn. The IMF was expected to make a significant contribution, and subsequently agreed a EUR28bn EFF. Approval of the second European bailout programme followed agreement reached with the Greek government on a policy package and its approval by the Greek parliament, identification of additional measures to close the 2012 financing gap and a political agreement on programme implementation. It also came after the common understanding was reached on PSI. In November, interest payments were reduced and deferred, and loan maturities on Greek debt were extended. The EFSF programme expired in June 2015. It was originally due to end on 31 December 2014, but was extended twice upon request of the Greek government. In the context of the programme, the EFSF disbursed EUR141.8bn to Greece, including EUR48.2bn to cover the costs of bank resolution and recapitalisation. Of this amount, EUR10.9bn in EFSF notes was not needed and was later returned to the EFSF. Accordingly, the outstanding loan amount was EUR130.9bn at the end of the EFSF programme.
Aug. 2015	ESM	Euro area Member States, acting through the ESM, agreed to provide up to EUR86bn over three years. The IMF was expected to take a decision on its participation in the third European bailout following the completion of the first ESM programme review (but in the event, the IMF did not provide any financing during the ESM programme). EUR13bn was disbursed by the ESM upon programme approval and a total of EUR21.4bn was disbursed during 2015. In December 2015, the ESM provided a EUR5.4bn loan for the recapitalization of two banks (Piraeus and NBG). The first review of the ESM programme was completed in May 2016, leading to the disbursement of the second tranche of EUR10.3bn, in two stages. The Eurogroup also agreed a number of debt relief measures for OSI, which were later endorsed at a Eurogroup meeting on 5 December 2016. Short-term debt relief measures were approved in January 2017. EUR8.5bn was disbursed in 2017, after the second review was completed in June 2017. More disbursements were made during 2018, in March and June, concluding with a final tranche of EUR15bn on 6 August 2018. The ESM programme was concluded on 20 August 2018. Total disbursements under the ESM programme were EUR61.9bn. The first amortisation payments from ESM borrowings do not commence until 2034.

Source: ESM

Sovereign Commercial Debt

Greece has undertaken one commercial debt restructuring in modern times, in 2012, albeit the biggest sovereign debt exchange (default) in history. However, Greece avoided payment default on its bonds (domestic and foreign law), and even repaid maturities on its foreign law sovereign bonds right up until its exchange was launched (before the exchange in March 2012, its most recent maturity was April 2011). According to the IMF, amortization payments to the private sector amounted to about EUR50bn during 2010–early 2012 (before PSI). However, two of the ratings agencies declared default in advance of the 2012 exchange. S&P moved to Selective Default on 27 February 2012 (its rating had been downgraded to CCC in June 2011) while Fitch moved to Restricted Default on 9 March 2012 (it too had downgraded its rating to CCC in July 2011). Moody's however avoided a default rating, lowering its rating to C on 2 March 2012. CDS were also triggered on 9 March 2012. The settlement price was 31.5%.

Initially dismissed by the official sector in the first bailout programme in May 2010, the possibility of a commercial debt restructuring had increasing inevitability as the 2010 SBA began to go off-track. The possibility of debt haircuts became more real after the Deauville Summit of October 2010, which envisaged that future crisis resolution would require an "adequate participation of private creditors." The official sector first pushed for private sector involvement (PSI) in Greece in June 2011, although an initial French proposal was seen as too mild. The IIF, representing major banks and investors, subsequently outlined the basis of a voluntary exchange in July 2011. It consisted of four options depending on the maturity of the new bond and face reduction (up to 20%), and was estimated to imply a 21% NPV loss (at an assumed 9% discount rate). The proposal also targeted only bonds with less than nine years to maturity, which raised questions about inter-creditor equity. However, the IIF proposal was not implemented as secondary market yields continued to widen, raising concerns over participation, and the offer had to be recalibrated in part because of the deepening recession. A Euro Summit in October 2011 subsequently demanded that concerned parties develop a voluntary bond exchange with a nominal 50% reduction, which formed the basis of the final PSI offer, whose terms were announced in February 2012. This raised questions about how voluntary it could be, but Europe maintained the pretence that such an exchange would avoid the stigma of default. Completion of a debt exchange became a prior action for the IMF's EFF programme that was approved in March 2012.

Greece reached an agreement with its private creditors on a debt restructuring, Private Sector Involvement (PSI), in March 2012. Creditors were led by a steering group of 12 banks and asset managers. Greece's financial adviser was Lazard Frères and its legal adviser as to English law was Cleary Gottlieb Steen and Hamilton LLP. The restructuring was a condition for the second bail-out package from the IMF and EFSF. In the rescheduling offer, private holders of Greek debt were offered a take-it-or-leave-it package composed of three elements: (1) short-term notes issued by the EFSF for a value of 15% of the old debt's principal amount, plus accrued interest (eg short-term notes with no credit risk, akin to a cash component); (2) 20 new bonds (GGBs) issued under English law maturing annually between 2023 and 2042 (the PSI Strip) for a value of 31.5% of the old debt's principal amount, with an annual step up coupon starting at 2% escalating over time to 4.3% and an average coupon of 3.4%; and (3) a detachable GDP warrant which could provide an extra payment stream of up to 1% of the outstanding new bonds if GDP exceeded certain official projections. In effect, the deal deferred principal repayments by 11 years (no amortisation payments until 2023) and kept interest payments low in the first few years.

A key difference with the IIF proposal was that the restructured covered more debt (about EUR50bn more, according to Zettelmeyer et al.). The restructuring covered EUR205.6bn of its sovereign and state-enterprise debt, including guaranteed bonds, consisting of 117 bonds in all, marking the biggest restructuring deal in the history of sovereign defaults. It comprised EUR195.8bn in government bonds and EUR9.8bn in bonds and sovereign-guaranteed bonds issued by public enterprises. According to the main exchange prospectus, covering 88 bonds issued under Greek law and English law amounting to some EUR197.2bn, designated instruments consisted of EUR177.3bn in sovereign bonds under domestic law (89.9% of designated securities and 86.2% of all eligible debt) and EUR19.9bn equivalent of foreign law (English law) bonds. Most of the English law bonds were sovereign issues (Exotix estimates EUR16.9bn), but there were also EUR3bn in some Helenic Railways guaranteed bonds and foreign law bonds issued by Athens Urban Transport. Of the English law issues, 88% was EUR-denominated, with one USD-denominated bond under English law and four JPY-denominated bonds under English law. However, according to other research (Zettelmeyer et al. in July 2013), the bond exchange also included additional debt of EUR8.4bn. This consisted of EUR1.74bn (equivalent) in bonds issued under Italian, Japanese and Swiss law (comprising EUR1.57bn equivalent in five sovereign bonds and EUR176mn equivalent in two Helenic Railways bonds), and EUR6.7bn in guaranteed bonds under Greek law (from Helenic Railways, Helenic Defense Systems and Athens Urban Transport). As a result, according to Exotix calculations, foreign law sovereign bonds amounted to EUR18.5bn (equivalent) in 28 issues with maturities ranging from May 2012 to July 2057. The offer excluded Greek T-bills (EUR15bn) and debt owed to the ECB (EUR42.7bn), national central banks (EUR13.5bn) and the EIB (EUR315mn), which instead were swapped to newly-issued debt with an identical payment profile. The ECB subsequently (in December 2012) committed to remitting the profits on its Greek bond holdings to the Greek government.

The exchange saw high overall participation and the issuance of EUR62.4bn in 20 new PSI bonds as per Bloomberg (as well as the issuance of EUR29.7bn in short term EFSF notes, according to Zettelmeyer et al.). While some of the foreign (English law) bonds had CACs, many didn't, including its domestic law bonds, which made up most of the offer (86% of eligible debt). However, while restructuring domestic law bonds would ordinarily have required the unanimous consent of all holders, they were issued under Greek law and so the government took the highly unusual step (with the tacit support of the official sector) of change the law. The government passed legislation in February 2012, just before launching the exchange, to allow the restructuring of the Greek law bonds with the consent of a qualified majority across the totality of all Greek law sovereign bonds outstanding, rather than bond-by-bond (a retrofit aggregated CAC). A 90% minimum participation threshold was set. In the event, according to Zettelmeyer et al., 82.5% of the EUR177.3bn in sovereign bonds issued under domestic law accepted the exchange offer. Participation among the foreign-law bondholders was lower, at around 61%, and the deadline was extended twice (to early April); the final participation rate among foreign law bondholders was 71%. But, combined, it was enough to ensure the exchange could go forward. By the end, total participation reached EUR199.2bn, or 96.9% of eligible principal. Hence, according to Zettelmeyer et al., the face value of Greece's debt declined by about EUR107bn as the result of the exchange, or 52% of the eligible debt (and about 56% of GDP).

There were holdouts however, and holdouts all got paid in full on scheduled maturity. According to Zettelmeyer et al., holders amounted to EUR6.4bn in face value, comprising 25 bonds, of which 24 were foreign law. According to Exotix estimates, based on Zettelmeyer et al. and Bloomberg data, by end-2017, 21 of the foreign law holdout bonds had reached their scheduled maturity (and been repaid) leaving only 3 remaining holdout bonds (all of which are sovereign bonds), with maturities in March 2019 (EUR35.6mn outstanding Italian law bond), April 2028 (EUR200mn English law bond) and July 2034 (EUR313.9mn outstanding English law bond). That said, the status of the July 2057 HICP bond, with EUR1bn outstanding on Bloomberg, is unclear.

Furthermore, the authorities undertook a partial buyback of its PSI bonds in December 2012 which saw the outstanding amount fall by around half, to about USD30bn. The buyback was funded by the EFSF. At the time, the PSI bonds were still trading at a significant discount. According to Zettelmeyer et al., the buyback used EUR11.3bn in EFSF financing to retire EUR31.9bn of Greek bonds, reducing the face value of Greece's debt by EUR20.6bn.

Commercial debt agreements

Date	*Details*
Mar. 2012	Agreement to restructure EUR206bn in government and government-guaranteed bonds. The main offer covered EUR197bn in domestic law and English law bonds. For each EUR1000 face amount tendered, holders were offered: 1. EUR315 face amount of New Bonds, with maturities ranging from 2023–2042; 2. EUR315 notional amount of GDP linked securities (GDP warrants); 3. EUR150 face of PSI Payment Notes. Principal was divided across 20 new bonds maturing annually over 2023–2042 (a principal strip). For each EUR315 aggregate face amount of new bonds, the face amount was divided as follows: EUR15 face for the first five maturity dates (11th–15th anniversaries, ie 2023–2027), and EUR16 for the remaining 15 maturity dates (16th–30th anniversaries, ie 2028–2042). Interest on the new bonds was paid annually, commencing February 2013. All the new PSI bonds had step up coupons on the same schedule, commencing at 2% until February 2015, rising to 3% until 2020, 3.65% until 2021, and 4.3% thereafter. EUR62.4bn in new PSI bonds were issued. The face value reduction (excluding the GDP warrants) was 53.5% (=1000 – (315 + 150)). The NPV haircut was 64.6% according to the Cruces and Trebesch database. The NPV haircut ranged from 59–65% according to Zettelmeyer et al., depending on the exit yield and curve assumptions, which ascribed little value to the GDP warrants.

Source: Exotix

Greece returned to the market, twice, in 2014 for its first issues in four years and just two years after the biggest sovereign default in history. A new five year GGB (2019 maturity) was issued in April. The bond had a 4.75% coupon and was priced at 99.133 for a yield at issue of 4.95%. EUR3bn was issued, with demand exceeding EUR20bn. The bond was tapped for an additional EUR1.03bn in September 2014, taking the overall issue to EUR4.03bn. A second bond was issued in July 2014, this time a three year GGB (2017 maturity). The bond had a 3.375% coupon and was priced at 99.65 for a yield at issue of 3.5%. EUR1.5bn was issued although it was later increased in September 2014 by EUR589.1mn taking the outstanding to EUR2.089bn. The bond was repaid on maturity.

The government returned to the market again in 2017 after a three year break. In July 2017, the authorities launched a cash tender offer for the 4.75% 2019 bond and issued a new note. It repurchased EUR1.574bn, reducing the stock from EUR4.03bn to EUR2.46bn. A new five year GGB (2022 maturity) was priced on 25 July 2017, for settlement on 1 August, for EUR3bn. The new bond had a coupon of 4.375% and a yield at issue of 4.625%, below the initial guidance (the issue price was 98.906). Demand for the new 2022 bond exceeded EUR6.25bn.

In November 2017, the authorities launched a voluntary exchange of its PSI bonds, with a nominal value of EUR29.5bn, for five new bonds. The maturities of the new bonds were 2023, 2028, 2033, 2037 and 2042, with coupons ranging from 3.5% to 4.2%. The total amount of new bonds issued was EUR25.8bn, resulting in a participation rate of 86.3%. The swap consolidated a series of small bonds, with an average outstanding of EUR1.5bn each, into fewer, bigger benchmark bonds, enhancing their liquidity. The new series of bonds had an average outstanding amount of EUR5.1bn each. As a result, following the buyback and exchange, the amount outstanding of the PSI bonds has fallen to just EUR4.04bn in total, as per Bloomberg, compared to the original issuance of EUR62.4bn. The exchange settled on 5 December.

In February 2018, the authorities issued a new seven year GGB (2025 maturity) for EUR3bn. The bond had a coupon of 3.375% and was issued at a price of 99.236 to yield 3.5%. Demand was EUR6.5bn. At the time, media reported that two more bonds, a three-year bond and a ten-year bond, were expected to be issued by August. The government repeated its intention in July 2018 to return to the market, in part to help refinance 2019 debt maturities amounting to EUR10-11bn.

As a result of this issuance and liability management operations, Exotix calculates that the outstanding stock of GGBs amounted to EUR38.3bn at time of writing. Together with about EUR550mn in remaining foreign law holdout bonds, and EUR11bn in non-marketable GGBs held by the ECB/EIB (series CBE on Bloomberg), the total stock of Greek domestic and foreign law bonds is estimated at about EUR49.8bn.

The outstanding Greek government bonds issued since the 2012 exchange are shown below (ie excluding PSI bonds and the maturity of the 2017 bond issued in 2014). Descriptions of the latest issue (2025) and the GDP warrants are also given.

Greece's outstanding GGB bonds (bonds issued since the 2012 exchange)[a]

Description	*Issue size*	*Amount outstanding*	*Issue date*
EUR 4.75% due 2019	EUR 4.03bn	EUR 2.46bn	Apr. 2014
EUR 4.375% due 2022	EUR 3.00bn	EUR 3.00bn	Aug. 2017
EUR 3.5% due 2023	EUR 4.36bn	EUR 4.36bn	Dec. 2017
EUR 3.375% due 2025	EUR 3.00bn	EUR 3.00bn	Feb. 2018
EUR 3.75% due 2028	EUR 5.96bn	EUR 5.96bn	Dec. 2017
EUR 3.9% due 2033	EUR 6.09bn	EUR 6.09bn	Dec. 2017
EUR 4% due 2037	EUR 4.81bn	EUR 4.81bn	Dec. 2017
EUR 4.2% due 2042	EUR 4.60bn	EUR 4.60bn	Dec. 2017

Source: Bloomberg

[a]Excluding the remaining amounts of the PSI strip

Greece government bond
Hellenic Republic 3.375% 2025
Bloomberg ticker: GGB

Borrower	Hellenic Republic
Issue date	15 February 2018
Form	Euro zone
ISIN	GR0118017657
Issue size	EUR 3000mn
Currency	Euro
Denomination	EUR 1000 and EUR 1000 thereafter
Amortisation	Bullet
Final maturity date	15 February 2025
Coupon/interest	3.375% per annum, paid semi-annually
Day count	ACT/ACT
Method of transfer	Euroclear/Clearstream
Settlement period	T + 2
Joint lead managers	Barclays, BNP Paribas, Citi, JP Morgan, Nomura
Exchange	All German SE, Athens, EuroTLX, MTS Greece
Governing law	English

Source: Bloomberg

Greece GDP warrants
Hellenic Republic 0% 2042
Bloomberg ticker: GGB

Borrower	Hellenic Republic
Issue date	12 March 2012
Form	GDP-linked security
ISIN	GRR000000010
Issue size	EUR 62.383bn
Amount outstanding	EUR 62.383bn
Payment currency	Euro
Denomination	Minimum of EUR 100 and EUR 100 thereafter
Payments	Variable rate subject to a payment formula
Final maturity date	15 October 2042
First payment date	15 October 2015, for the reference year 2014
Final payment date	15 October 2042, for the reference year 2041
Payment trigger	Nominal GDP must exceed the Reference Nominal GDP, as set out prior to issuance
Payment amount	Rounded down to the nearest EUR0.01 for each security, equal to the GDP Index Percentage (1.5 multiplied by 'the real GDP growth rate less the reference real GDP growth rate', subject to conditions) for the reference year multiplied by the notional amount (a fraction of the original notional amount, as set out prior to issuance), provided that the Payment Amount for any Reference Year will be zero if Nominal GDP did not exceed the Reference Nominal GDP in the Reference Year

Reference nominal GDP	Reference year	Reference nominal GDP (EUR billion)
	2014	210.1014
	2015	217.9036
	2016	226.3532
	2017	235.7155
	2018	245.4696
	2019	255.8822
	2020–2041	266.4703

Reference real GDP growth rate	Reference year	Reference real GDP growth rate (%)
	2014	2.345
	2015	2.896
	2016	2.845
	2017	2.797
	2018	2.597
	2019	2.497
	2020	2.247
	2021–2041	2.000

(*continued*)

(continued)

Greece GDP warrants *Hellenic Republic 0% 2042* *Bloomberg ticker: GGB*				
Notional amount	Payment date	Fraction of original notional	Payment date	Fraction of original notional
	15 Oct 2023	315/315	15 Oct 2033	160/315
	15 Oct 2024	300/315	15 Oct 2034	144/315
	15 Oct 2025	285/315	15 Oct 2035	128/315
	15 Oct 2026	270/315	15 Oct 2036	112/315
	15 Oct 2027	255/315	15 Oct 2037	96/315
	15 Oct 2028	240/315	15 Oct 2038	80/315
	15 Oct 2029	224/315	15 Oct 2039	64/315
	15 Oct 2030	208/315	15 Oct 2040	48/315
	15 Oct 2031	192/315	15 Oct 2041	32/315
	15 Oct 2032	176/315	15 Oct 2042	16/315
Calculation date	For any reference year, a day no later than the fifth business day following 30 September of the calendar year following that reference year			
Calculation currency	Euro			
Other features	Issuer call option			
Day count	30/360			
Method of transfer	Euroclear/Clearstream			
Governing law	English			
Listing	All German SE, Athens			

Corporate Bond Markets

There have been numerous international bonds issued by Greek banks and corporates over the years. Following the Greek debt crisis, some went into default although corporate issuance largely resumed in 2014 and the banks after 2016. We provide only a short and selective summary of activity here.

On 30 June 2015, S&P downgraded the Greek banks Alpha Bank (ALPHA), Eurobank (EUROB), National Bank of Greece (ETEGA) and Piraeus Bank (TPEIR) to selective default (SD) following the government's imposition of capital controls and limits to deposit withdrawals on 29 June. The combined amount of debt covered EUR4.8bn. Following this, each bank launched tender offers (S&P classified each as a distressed exchange and downgraded them from SD to D) and secured new capital, with Piraeus and Alpha Bank launching tender offers in October 2015 and completing a EUR4.9bn and a EUR2.6bn capital raise respectively, and Eurobank and National Bank of Greece launching tender offers in November 2015 and completing a EUR2.0bn and EUR4.5bn capital raise respectively.

The Greek banks generally returned to the markets over 2016–2018 with a number of covered bond issues. Eurobank and National Bank of Greece were the first banks to issue bonds since 2015 with their three year covered bond issues in 2016 (May and October respectively). National Bank of Greece also issued a three year covered bond for EUR750mn in October 2017, with the 2.7% 2020 bond priced to yield 2.921% at issue. A EUR200mn five year covered bond followed in July 2018 and a EUR600mn one year covered bond in August 2018. Alpha Bank issued a EUR1bn two year covered bond in December 2017 and two covered bonds in 2018, a EUR500mn five year covered bond in February 2018 and a EUR1bn one year covered bond in May 2018. Eurobank issued a EUR500mn three year covered bond in November 2017, and two small one year covered bonds in 2018. The bank also issued a EUR950mn ten year Tier 2 subordinated bond in January 2018, with a 6.41% coupon. The bond was issued to the Greek state and used, along with cash, to redeem preference shares which had been subscribed to and paid for by Greek state. Piraeus issued five covered bonds over 2017–2018, including a EUR500mn five year covered bond in October 2017 at par with a 2.18% coupon.

In the corporate space, Yioula Glassworks was downgraded to selective default by S&P in February 2013. Yioula undertook a number of refinancings in 2012–2013, but was later able to issue EUR185mn 8.5% senior secured notes due 2019 in May 2014. Proceeds were used to fund the redemption of the outstanding EUR140mn 9% senior notes due 2015 and other obligations. The Notes were senior obligations of Glasstank and were subsequently called in October 2016 with the sale of part of the company's business.

Today, Exotix estimates outstanding Greek corporate issuance of EUR5.7bn across nine issuers (see table below).

Greek companies seemingly returned to the market en masse in 2014 with five issues amounting to EUR2.1bn. A flurry of deals in the early summer saw Titan Cement, Hellenic Petroleum, OTE and Folli Follie Group all issue bonds in July, with a EUR300mn five year bond from Titan Cement, a EUR325mn five year bond Hellenic Petroleum, a EUR700mn six year bond from OTE, and a EUR250mn five year bond from Folli Follie, after PPC had issued a EUR500mn five year bond in May.

Activity picked up again in 2016–2017. After a muted 2015, with saw only OTE's EUR350mn four year bond being issued in November, the following two years saw issues from Hellenic Petroleum, Titan Cement, Motor Oil, Frigoglass, Crystal Almond, Folli Follie and Intralot. Issuance amounted to EUR1.3bn in 2016 and EUR1.4bn in 2017.

2018 has seen only modest issuance, with just EUR490mn combined from two issues, OTE (EUR400mn four year bond in July) and Motor Oil's Coral AE (EUR90mn five year in May).

As we went to press, most Greek corporate bonds were trading at or around par, but two were at more distressed levels. Folli Follie Group, a Greek retail company, was trading below 20 on both its bonds, while Intralot, a Greek gambling company, was trading at around 70–80 for its two bonds as investors grew concerned about the currency impact from its Turkish operations.

Selected Greek corporate bonds outstanding

Company	*Ticker*	*Coupon (%)*	*Maturity date*	*Issue date*	*Issued amount (million)*	*Amount outstanding (million)*	*CCY*
OTE PLC	HTOGA	4.375	02/12/2019	02/12/2015	350	350	EUR
OTE PLC	HTOGA	3.5	09/07/2020	10/07/2014	700	700	EUR
OTE PLC	HTOGA	2.375	18/07/2022	18/07/2018	400	400	EUR
Hellenic Petroleum Finance PLC	ELPEGA	5.25	04/07/2019	04/07/2014	325	325	EUR
Hellenic Petroleum Finance PLC	ELPEGA	4.875	14/10/2021	14/10/2016	450	450	EUR
Titan Global Finance PLC	TITKGA	4.25	10/07/2019	10/07/2014	300	161	EUR
Titan Global Finance PLC	TITKGA	3.5	17/06/2021	17/06/2016	300	300	EUR
Titan Global Finance PLC	TITKGA	2.375	16/11/2024	16/11/2017	350	350	EUR
Public Power Corp Finance PLC	PPCGA	5.5	01/05/2019	08/05/2014	500	350	EUR
Motor Oil Finance PLC	MOHGA	3.25	01/04/2022	10/04/2017	350	350	EUR
Coral AE Oil & Chemicals Co	MOHGA	3	11/05/2023	11/05/2018	90	90	EUR
Frigoglass Finance BV	FRIGOG	7	31/03/2022	23/10/2017	99	99	EUR
Crystal Almond SARL	CRYALM	10	01/11/2021	04/11/2016	345	345	EUR
FF Group Finance Lux. SA	FFGRPG	1.75	03/07/2019	03/07/2014	250	250	EUR
FF Group Finance Lux. II SA	FFGRPG	3.25	02/11/2021	02/11/2017	150	150	CHF
Intralot Capital Luxembourg SA	INLOTG	6.75	15/09/2021	23/09/2016	250	250	EUR
Intralot Capital Luxembourg SA	INLOTG	5.25	15/09/2024	20/09/2017	500	500	EUR

Source: Bloomberg

Grenada

Nominal GDP (US$mn, 2018)[a]		1192
Population (thousand, 2018)[a]		108
GDP per capita (USD, 2018)[a]		11,032
Credit ratings (long-term foreign currency)[b]	Fitch	NR
	Moody's	NR
	S&P	NR

[a]IMF WEO October 2018
[b]As at end-September 2018

Country Summary

- The southernmost of the Caribbean Windward Islands, Grenada, known as the "Spice Island" because of its production of nutmeg and mace crops, has become dependent on tourism and travel as the main sources of foreign exchange. It was the world's second-largest exporter of nutmeg and mace (after Indonesia) until the devastation of Hurricane Ivan in 2004. Construction and manufacturing, together with an offshore banking industry, have also contributed to growth.
- The country remains susceptible to natural disasters and adverse weather, which have dictated the island's volatile growth performance in recent years. This is illustrated by Hurricanes Lili (2002)

Exotix Capital, *Exotix Developing Markets Guide*,
https://doi.org/10.1007/978-3-030-05867-8_22

and Ivan (2004), one of the strongest storms ever in the Caribbean, and which caused widespread devastation, and Emily (2005), although it avoided Irma (2017).

- Grenada has historically (over the past 20 years) suffered from a high debt burden, from which it is now only just beginning to recover. Volatile growth and climatic vulnerability, together with lax fiscal policy, resulted in a rapid rise in the public debt burden in the early 2000s. Public debt peaked at 108% of GDP in 2013 (IMF WEO), the second-highest level in the Latin America/Caribbean region. It resulted in two commercial debt restructurings over this period, in 2005 and 2015, with the latter operation involving 50% nominal debt reduction, tied to the country's successful performance under an IMF programme, on nearly 30% of its total public debt. But even after this, public debt remains high (still c80% of GDP on Exotix estimates) and the economy will require ongoing fiscal discipline and structural reforms in order to restore debt sustainability.

Economic data	*Avg*[a]	*2014*	*2015*	*2016*	*2017 (e)*	*2018 (f)*	*2019 (f)*
Real GDP growth	1.4	7.3	6.4	3.7	5.1	3.6	3.6
Inflation (annual average)	2.3	−1.0	−0.6	1.7	0.9	2.6	1.8
Current account (% of GDP)	−3.8	−4.4	−3.8	−3.2	−6.8	−7.5	−7.5
Reserves (US$mn, end-period)[b]	130.5	158.3	188.5	201.4	194.9	202.4	208.8
Reserves/imports (months)[c]	3.2	3.4	4.1	3.9	3.5	3.4	3.4
Overall fiscal balance (% of GDP)[d]	−4.3	−4.7	−1.2	2.3	3.0	3.4	3.3
Currency (ticker)	Eastern Caribbean dollar (XCD)						
FX regime	Fixed to USD at USD1:XCD2.70						
Key exports	Nutmeg (25%), fish (16.5%), copper and other minerals (14%), cocoa beans (10%). Goods exports were US$38mn in 2016, compared with services revenue of US$554mn (most of which was tourism—cUS$510mn, 50% of GDP). Net (inward) remittances were US$29mn.						

Source: IMF WEO Database, IMF Country Reports, ECCB, OEC

[a]Ten-year average to 2016 unless otherwise stated

[b]Net imputed international reserves, incl. projections, from IMF (July 2018)

[c]Months of imports of goods and services (from IMF)

[d]Overall government net lending

Key figures		*Party*	*Since*
Prime minister	Keith Mitchell	NNP	Feb. 2013
Minister of Finance and Energy	Keith Mitchell	NNP	Feb. 2013
Permanent Secretary, Ministry of Finance and Energy	Wayne Sandiford	–	Apr. 2017
Key opposition figure	Nazim Burke	NDC	Feb. 2014
Central bank governor (ECCB)	Timothy Antoine	–	Feb. 2016

Note: Grenada is a member of the Commonwealth. It gained independence from Britain in 1974. Queen Elizabeth II (UK) remains Monarch, represented by the governor general, Her Excellency Cécile La Grenade (since May 2013)

Politics

Executive power

Grenada's constitution provides that Queen Elizabeth II remains chief of state with the governor general executing legislation on her behalf. In practice, this has become a formality, suggesting the prime minister is a de facto executive. The prime minister is head of government and appointed by the governor general from the ruling party. The prime minister heads the cabinet.

Parliamentary term: Five years

Legislature

Bicameral legislature comprising the Senate (upper house) and House of Representatives (lower house). Senate members act as a review body and are appointed by the Governor General under the advisement of both the prime minister and the leading opposition figure. The House of Representatives is decided by popular vote.

Senate: 13 seats
10 seats under the advisement of the prime minister. Three seats on the advice of the main opposition leader.

House of Representatives: 15 seats
Directly elected.

Elections

Next due *General election: 2023*

Last general election[a] *(March 2018)*	*% of the vote*	*Seats*
New National Party (NNP)	58.9	15
National Democratic Congress (NDC)	40.5	0
Others	0.6	0
Total	**100.0**	**15**

[a]Results shown for the House of Representatives

People

Grenada's population is predominantly Afro-Caribbean, at over four-fifths. Mixed race and Caucasian are thought to comprise a further 15% and fewer than 5% are of Indian descent. Christianity is the main religion of the island, covering almost all the population, and Catholicism is the largest branch thereof.

Grenada became a self-governing state in 1967 and gained full independence from Britain in 1974. Maurice Bishop led a successful Marxist/Leninist coup against the elected government in 1979, installing himself as the head of government and forming the People's Revolutionary Government (PRG). A bloody mutiny in October 1983 supported by members of the armed forces broke out among the ranks of the PRG. Bishop and several cabinet members were executed, along with dozens of civilians. In the same month, the US sent a joint-Caribbean invasion force, quickly defeating the conspirators.

After a transitional government, Grenada returned to parliamentary democracy in December 1984. It has enjoyed relatively peaceful rule since then. Keith Mitchell has been the Prime Minister (and finance minister) since his centre-right New National Party (NNP) won all 15 seats in the House of Representatives in the 2013 election, defeating the incumbent prime minister, Tillman Thomas, of the centre-left NDC.

Mitchell was previously prime minister from 1995–2008, making him the longest serving prime minister in the country's history. His rule was broken by the NDC's brief one term in power, in which Tillman Thomas won the 2008 election. Mitchell congratulated Thomas, saying that "people voted for change". However, after his defeat in the 2013 general election, Thomas stepped down and was replaced as party leader by Nazim Burke. Now, after 28 years as NNP leader, Mitchell says that he is unable to find a successor. The prime minister's term limit and six other issues were put to public vote in the country's only referendum in November 2016. Voters did not back any of the seven constitutional changes. In March 2018, Mitchell's NNP again won all 15 seats in the House of Representatives.

Grenada is highly susceptible to adverse weather conditions. Hurricane Ivan in September 2004, the worst storm in 49 years, left 90% of the island's buildings and infrastructure devastated. Damage was estimated at US$900mn (almost 200% of GDP), two-thirds of which was housing stock. Damage also extended to nutmeg plantations and tourist resorts. The international community responded quickly with a donor conference in October. Grenada avoided the worst of the damage following the regional devastation caused by Hurricane Irma and Maria in September 2017.

Grenada is one of eight members of the Eastern Caribbean Currency Union (ECCU), overseen by the regional central bank, the Eastern Caribbean Central Bank (ECCB). The other members are Anguilla, Antigua and Barbuda, Dominica, Montserrat, St Kitts and Nevis, St Lucia, and St Vincent and the Grenadines. In terms of size, Grenada is the third biggest by GDP (behind St Lucia and Antigua), and the second biggest by population (behind St Lucia).

Debt

	2012	*2017*
External debt ratios (%)		
Total external debt/GDP	141.8	129.2
Public external debt/GDP	68.4[a]	60.1
Private external debt/GDP	73.4	69.1
Total external debt/exports of goods and services	n/a	229.8
External debt service ratio	n/a	10.6[b]
Public debt ratios (%)		
Public domestic debt/GDP	34.9	21.0
Public debt/GDP	103.3	81.1

Source: Ministry of Finance, IMF, Exotix

[a]Central government only (excludes other public sector external debt)
[b]IMF 2018 Article IV (July 2018)

Grenada's public and publicly guaranteed (PPG) external debt was US$670mn at end-2017, according to figures from the Ministry of Finance. Most of this was central government (CG) external debt, amounting to US$519mn, or US$532mn including guarantees on external debt. Other public sector external debt (US$138mn) made up the remainder. Within central government debt (excluding guarantees), multilaterals were the largest creditor group, accounting for 57% of the total (Exotix has added debt owed to the Caricom Development Fund—cUS$2.5mn—to the multilateral debt (US$291mn), as per Ministry of Finance figures).

Ministry of Finance figures do not give a more detailed breakdown of multilateral debt, but separate IMF figures showed that, for 2016, the Caribbean Development Bank (CDB) was the largest single multilateral creditor, followed by the World Bank/IDA and IMF. Other multilateral creditors include OPEC and IFAD.

Debt owed to commercial creditors accounted for 26.5% of central government debt (excluding guarantees). This amounted to US$137mn on Ministry of Finance figures and mainly consisted of the restructured GRENAD 7% 2030 USD Global bond (although Exotix understands the principal on the 2030 bond had fallen to US$112.3mn in November 2017 after the second tranche of debt reduction and amortisation). Before the second tranche of debt reduction on the bond in November 2017, as per the restructuring agreement, bondholders were the single biggest creditor, although that operation means they are now likely to have been surpassed by the CDB.

Bilateral creditors comprised just 17% of CG external debt, which was mostly owed to non-Paris Club governments. These include Kuwait, Trinidad, China Exim Bank, Taiwan and Venezuela. Paris Club creditors are relatively minor, with the main creditor countries being France, the UK and the US.

Exotix estimates total external debt was US$1.4bn in 2017, some 129% of GDP, split roughly evenly between public and private debt (Note: the new IMF Article IV from July 2018 showed 116.4% of GDP, with PPG external debt of 48% of GDP, although this appears to exclude 12% of GDP due to "other public sector external debt" as per official figures). Exotix estimates that PPG external debt amounted to 60% of GDP in 2017, comprising CG external debt (including guarantees) of 47.8% of GDP and other public sector external debt of 12.4% of GDP. Historical comparisons are made difficult by data availability. Exotix estimates that CG external debt (including guarantees) was 68.4% of GDP in 2012, although this excludes other public sector debt, so that PPG external debt was likely higher. Exotix estimates that private external debt was a further US$771mn (69.1% of GDP) in 2017, derived from IMF data, and which showed a 30% increase in USD terms from 2012. Notwithstanding Grenada's 2015 debt restructuring, which involved a significant haircut on about 30% of its public external debt, Exotix estimates that total external debt fell as a share of GDP over 2012–17 from 142% to 129%, in part also due to a 40% rise in nominal GDP. As a share of exports of goods and services, total external debt was 230% in 2017, while the PPG external debt/exports ratio was 107%. This is based on projected 2017 exports of goods and services of US$627mn from the IMF (2018 Article IV, July 2018)—which reveal significant revisions to balance of payments data, as reflected in official (ECCB) figures, which appear to make goods and services exports around twice as high as previously reported (for instance, the IMF projections for 2017 exports of goods and services in May 2017 was US$307mn). However, pre-2014 balance of payments figures on the revised basis are not available. As per IMF figures (July 2018), the external debt service ratio was 10.6% in 2017, while the external debt service ratio for PPG debt alone was 10.3%. The same ratios from the IMF in May 2017 showed a sharp increase over 2012–17 from 7.2% to 20.5% and 6.4% to 19.8%, respectively.

Exotix estimates total public and publicly guaranteed debt at 81% of GDP at end-2017 based on Ministry of Finance figures, with external debt comprising about three-quarters of the total and domestic debt about one-quarter (Note: the new IMF Article IV from July 2018 showed 70.8% of GDP, with PPG external debt of 48% of GDP, although this appears to exclude 12% of GDP due to "other public sector external debt" as per official figures).

This comprised PPG external debt of 60% of GDP and domestic debt (central government including guarantees) of 21% of GDP. Domestic debt (excluding guarantees) amounted to cUS$220mn (19.8% of GDP), while domestic guarantees were US$13mn (1.2% of GDP). Most of the domestic debt (excluding guarantees) was in the form of restructured domestic bonds (51% of the total) and Treasury bills (35% of the total), while most was held by non-bank financial institutions (37% of the total), followed by other public sector holders (19%) and commercial banks (7%). The debt/GDP ratio was down from 103% in 2012, due to the combination of debt reduction and nominal GDP growth, although it may in fact underestimate the extent of the decline as the 2012 figure relates only to CG debt including guarantees and excludes other public sector debt. On a like-for-like basis (CG domestic and external debt including guarantees), Exotix estimates that the debt ratio fell from 103.3% to 68.8% of GDP.

Composition of external debt

External debt by creditor (Dec. 2017)	*Nominal amount outstanding (US$mn)*	*Share of total (%)*
Public and publicly guaranteed external debt	**670.2**	**46.5**
Central government	519.0	36.0
Official multilateral[a]	293.9	20.4
Incl. CDB[b]	141.3	9.8
World Bank[b]	92.3	6.4
IMF[b]	28.9	2.0
Official bilateral	87.8	6.1
Paris Club	8.2	0.6
Non-Paris Club	79.6	5.5
Commercial creditors	137.4	9.5
Bonds	137.0	9.5
Commercial banks	0.3	0.0
Guarantees	13.3	0.9
Other public sector external debt	137.8	9.6
Private sector external debt[c]	**770.9**	**53.5**
Total external debt	**1441.0**	**100.0**

Source: Ministry of Finance, IMF

[a]Multilaterals plus Caricom Development Fund
[b]IMF figures for end-2016, from IMF ECF sixth review (May 2017)
[c]Derived from IMF ECF sixth review (May 2017)

Rescheduling History

Grenada has undertaken two commercial debt restructurings in the past 15 years, one completed in 2005 and another completed in 2015. It also undertook, in tandem, two Paris Club restructurings.

The authorities embarked on a debt restructuring in 2004 after recognising that the debt situation had become unsustainable in the aftermath of Hurricane Ivan, although past fiscal imbalances were also partly to blame. Hurricane Ivan, one of the strongest storms ever recorded in the Caribbean, resulted in damage estimated at US$900mn, equivalent to 200% of GDP. Public debt peaked at 131% of GDP in 2004, although this has subsequently been revised down to 95%. An IMF mission provided a debt sustainability assessment and cash flow analysis, concluding that fiscal efforts alone could not achieve debt sustainability. This resulted in a commercial debt exchange in 2005 followed by a Paris Club agreement in 2006; both of which provided sizeable debt servicing relief, easing the near-term financing position (through to end-2008), although there was no principal reduction. The authorities also undertook fiscal consolidation in a bid to reduce the sizeable debt burden to a target of 60% of GDP by 2020, aiming at primary surpluses of 2.5% of GDP.

However, problems soon resurfaced following a weaker-than-expected recovery post-Ivan amid severe fiscal slippage in 2006 and 2007 caused by spending overruns. Needs for government spending on post-hurricane infrastructure projects and expansionary policies following the global financial crisis led to primary deficits, when the 2006 short-term aims had been surpluses. The average annual primary deficit was 4.9% between 2006 and 2015. Meanwhile, adverse shocks led to lower growth than expected, with a decline in the tourism and construction industries following the global financial crisis. Lower growth and worsening fiscal deficits led to new debt problems and it was realised that the first restructuring did not provide enough space for fiscal slippages. It achieved a decline in short-term debt service as average maturity was increased, but there was no nominal haircut; public debt remained high at 112% of GDP in 2007, according to IMF figures in 2009 (subsequently revised down to 89%). Negative real GDP growth in 2009 and 2010 left public debt projected at 119% of GDP in 2010 (subsequently given as 96%). Partly due to the global financial crisis and restructurings in other countries, such as Belize, the government had limited external financing options. The government did not have the funds to make debt service payments; the unsustainable debt burden had led to solvency concerns, not just a liquidity problem. By 2012, Grenada was suffering from acute cash flow difficulties. After weak or negative real GDP growth since the global financial crisis and running a primary deficit every year since 2006, public debt had reached an unsustainable 103% of GDP at end-2012, on the revised data series (up from 84% in 2008). The government just managed to avoid a default on its 2025 USD bond, paying the September 2012 coupon late, by securing a short-term bridging loan, but by the time of the March 2013 coupon (due 15 March), the government said that it did not have the funds to pay it and announced its intention to seek a "comprehensive and collaborative" restructuring of its commercial and bilateral debt, domestic and external. Debt issued on the regional securities market (RGSM) and multilateral debt were to be excluded.

The government embarked on a second debt restructuring in 2013. In particular, the debt problem was recognised as one of solvency and the creditor composition in Grenada meant that a comprehensive solution would require other creditors' participation; while commercial creditors (mostly the bondholders) made up around half of public external debt, multilaterals (CDB, World Bank) and bilaterals held a large portion of the external debt, which was well above the ECCU's own public debt target of 60% of GDP. Although multilateral debt was not restructured, the Paris Club treated US$8mn of the US$11mn owed, including US$6mn of arrears, in a November 2015 agreement on Classic terms (see below). The EXIM Bank of Taiwan agreed to a 50% haircut on outstanding principal, with the remaining principal repayable over 15 years. Bilateral arrears with other creditors, including Trinidad & Tobago, Algeria and Libya remain outstanding, based on a May 2017 IMF report. Various smaller agreements with domestic creditors have been completed since. Regarding commercial creditors, holders of USD 2025 bonds accepted the exchange offer of new 2030 bonds, amortising from March 2016, with 50% nominal debt reduction tied to successful completion of the IMF programme. The government announced in November 2015 that overwhelming support had been received for the exchange offer launched the previous month. The bilateral and commercial agreements included a novel 'hurricane clause' to defer debt service in the event of future natural disasters.

Relations with Multilateral Creditors

After a long period without the need for IMF support, Grenada was buffeted by climatic shocks in the early 2000s that necessitated emergency IMF assistance. Indeed, thereafter until 2018, Grenada had been under IMF tutelage pretty much for all but one year in the past 15 years. A donor conference was held in October 2004 following Hurricane Ivan. Since Ivan, Grenada has had three largely back to back ECFs, with its most recent programme being approved in 2014 to support its debt restructuring. The programme was completed after the sixth and final review in May 2017. The IMF noted that Grenada successfully met its original reform programme targets, which included fiscal adjustment and debt reduction amid strong growth, reflecting strong construction activity and steady external demand for tourism services. The overall fiscal balance shifted from a 4.7% of GDP deficit in 2014 to a 2.4% of GDP surplus in 2016, with the primary balance going from a 1.1% deficit to a 5.3% surplus (an adjustment of nearly 6.5ppts in two years), while the medium-term projections over 2018–20 (ie outside an IMF programme) showed the primary surplus being maintained at c4.3%. The programme saw the debt-to-GDP ratio decline to 83.4% at end-2016, from 108% in 2013, and this was projected to fall further to 71.8% in 2017, 65.8% in 2018 and 54.9% by 2020. There are no plans for a successor arrangement.

Grenada continues to engage with the IMF through the regular Article IV consultation, with its latest review (the 2018 Article IV) being completed in July 2018. This concluded that the country had made important strides under its last ECF programme, achieving an impressive debt reduction amounting to 37% of GDP since 2013, upgrading its fiscal policy framework, strengthening the financial system, improving governance and creating a better business environment. Real GDP growth had picked up to 4.5% in 2017, driven by the construction, tourism and education sectors. The primary surplus increased to 5.75% of GDP, while public debt fell from 82% of GDP in 2016 to 71% in 2017. However, Staff noted public debt was still relatively high, although it was projected to fall below 55% of GDP by 2020. More work was needed on job creation and strengthening institutional capacity.

IMF programmes

Date	*Arrangements*	*Comments*
1970s–80s	Various	SBA 1975–76, 1976, 1979–80, 1981–82, EFF 1983–84
2003 Jan.	Emergency assistance	Approved after tropical storm Lili in September 2002.
2004 Nov.	Emergency assistance	Approved after Hurricane Ivan in September 2004.

(*continued*)

(continued)

Date	*Arrangements*	*Comments*
2006–10	ECF	In April 2006, the Executive Board approved a PRGF arrangement (now known as an ECF) for 90% of quota (SDR10.53mn) to support the government's medium-term economic programme. The first review was completed in November 2008. It was delayed because of fiscal slippages, time needed to address an unregulated bank and slow pace of reforms. The programme was originally due to expire in April 2009 but a one-year extension to 2010 was requested with augmented access: The Board augmented access to 102.5% of quota in July 2008 (first review) and to 140% of quota in June 2009 (third review). The total amount approved (SDR16.38mn) was fully drawn. The programme expired in April 2010.
2010–13	ECF	Approved in April 2010, this ECF came with access to SDR8.775mn (US$13.3mn, 75% of quota) to support economic reforms, boost growth and reduce poverty. It came immediately after successful completion of the final review of the preceding programme, with a missed performance criteria waiver. Shortly after the first review in November 2010, the programme went off track as poor economic performance, an approaching election and considerations of a debt restructuring led to policy loosening. Expired in April 2013 with only SDR2.5mn drawn.
2014–17	ECF	A SDR14.04mn (US$21.7mn, 120% of quota) ECF was approved by the Board in June 2014, to improve competitiveness and medium-term growth and support the authorities' debt restructuring efforts. Successfully completed in May 2017 with the sixth and final review, the programme was fully disbursed. The IMF reported original target success, including fiscal consolidation and debt reduction.

Source: IMF. Grenada joined the IMF in 1975

Grenada is a member of the World Bank Group. The World Bank has three active projects in Grenada and various others in the Caribbean community, with the aims of improving the investment climate, improving resource management and enhancing resilience against natural disasters. Grenada is also a member of the CDB, receiving a soft-financing package in 2005, worth US$25mn, for a number of reconstruction projects after Hurricane Ivan, including infrastructure and natural disaster management. Grenada was removed in 2004 from the Financial Action Task Force (FATF) list of non-cooperative countries.

Paris Club and Bilateral Creditors

Grenada has received two Paris Club treatments, both of which remain active.

The Paris Club agreed a debt rescheduling for Grenada on Classic terms in May 2006. The agreement followed IMF approval of a PRGF (now ECF) for Grenada on 17 April 2006 and came as comparable debt relief to that provided by commercial creditors was sought from official creditors. The agreement saw debt service to Paris Club creditors fall by over 90% through to end-2008. The Paris Club creditors were Belgium, France, Russia, UK and US. However, Grenada's PC debt, at US$17mn, was quite small in relation to its overall debt.

In November 2015, the Paris Club agreed to another rescheduling following IMF approval of an ECF in June 2014, and the assurance by Paris Club creditors to contribute to its financing. The Paris Club treatment covered US$7.7mn under Classic terms, following an agreement with bondholders to restructure the 2025 USD bond the previous April. The Paris Club creditors were France, Russia, UK and US, and the restructuring was completed with a bilateral agreement with Russia in March 2017, although Paris Club debt was only 1.2% of Grenada's total debt in 2015. Consistent with the agreement for bondholders, the deal for bilateral creditors included a two-stage nominal haircut of 50% and contained a Hurricane Clause.

Paris Club agreements

Date	*Terms*	*Status*	*Details*
May 2006	Classic	Active	Treated US$16mn out of Paris Club debt of US$17mn and total external debt of US$437mn as at end-2005. Treatment of arrears as at December 2005, treatment of maturities falling due between January 2006 to December 2009. Repayment of ODA and non-ODA credits over 12 years with five years of grace.
Nov. 2015	Classic	Active	Treated US$8mn out of Paris Club debt of US$11mn and total external debt of US$610mn as at end-2014. Treatment of arrears as at October 2005, treatment of maturities falling due between November 2015 to June 2017. Consistent with the commercial (bonds) agreement, the deal included a two-stage nominal haircut of 50%, the first part in 2015 and the second part in 2017. Repayment of ODA credits over 20 years including seven years of grace and a 7% interest rate, and non-ODA credits over 15 years including eight years of grace and a 7% interest rate. A hurricane clause was also included.

Source: Paris Club

Progress with non-Paris Club bilateral creditors continues. The IMF reports discussions with Algeria in particular. Following a decade-long dispute with the Export Import Bank of Taiwan Province of China (EXIM Bank), a solution was reached regarding the US$28mn debt. The original loan was for infrastructure projects, but was complicated by diplomatic problems relating to Taiwan. In 2005, Grenada dropped Taiwan and recognised Beijing, which responded with generous post-hurricane support. In 2007, the EXIM Bank won a court ruling including Grenada paying legal fees; however, in 2012, a US judge freed Grenada of this ruling, preventing Taiwan from seizing tourism-related revenues essential to the Grenadian economy. Finally, in January 2014, Grenada officials announced that a deal had been reached: it involved a 50% up-front principal reduction and the remaining loan balance would be payable over 15 years, including a three-year grace period, at an interest rate of 7%, also with a Hurricane Clause.

Sovereign Commercial Debt

Grenada has now undertaken two commercial debt restructurings in the past 15 years.

Commercial debt agreements

Date	*Details*
Nov. 2005	Restructuring of US$190mn in external commercial debt, including US$100mn 2012 global bond, at par into a new 20-year bond, with a 2025 maturity, step-up coupons, and bullet maturity. No principal haircut. PDI was capitalised. The new bond was US$193.5mn in size. The exchange implied an NPV loss of 40% according to IMF research.
Nov. 2015	Restructuring of the US$193.5mn 2025 global bond into a new 15-year bond, with a 2030 maturity, fixed 7% coupon, amortising in 29 ESIA from March 2016. A 50% nominal haircut on principal was agreed, to be delivered in two tranches, with half up-front and half conditional upon the successful completion of the IMF programme (expected March 2017). The second tranche of nominal debt reduction was subsequently delivered on 11 November 2017. PDI was capitalised. The new bond was, initially, US$179mn in size. The exchange implied an NPV loss of 49%, according to IMF research.

Source: Exotix

Grenada opened its 2005 commercial exchange offer in September, which closed on 15 November. The authorities had stated their intention to seek a cooperative solution to their debt problem in October 2004, after saying they would not be able to service their debt following Hurricane Ivan, which struck the island on 7 September 2004. A donor's conference that November saw significant financial support for the country, to help with reconstruction and also to plug the sizeable financing gaps that were expected to emerge. Shortly afterwards, the government defaulted on a coupon payment on its only outstanding international bond at the time (the 9.375% 2012 Global bond, which had been issued in June 2002, in part to finance works for St George's General Hospital, hotel projects and road construction). The 30 December 2004 coupon payment was missed and was not paid by the end of the 30-day grace period which expired on 29 January 2005. The exchange offer involved swapping eligible external commercial debt, covering about half the total public sector debt, into a single new bond issue (a domestic offer also took place). Eligible external debt amounted to US$190mn, which included the defaulted US$100mn 9.375% 2012 global bond and cUS$90mn in other external bonded debt and loans (including two RBTT loans, one worth US$41.5mn contracted in 2004, two UTC loans, a Citibank loan and two Wachovia loans). The new bond, with an outstanding size of US$193.5mn, had a step-up coupon, starting at 1% for the first three years, rising to 9%, and maturing in 2025. There was no principal reduction and past-due interest was capitalised. Overall participation was high, at 91% of eligible claims with 93% of external creditors and 86% of domestic creditors. The exchange resulted in an NPV reduction of c40%, according to the IMF, when comparing the PV of the new bond with the PV of the old bond at the same discount rate (8.9%), although in nominal terms public debt was unaffected.

All eligible external claims were swapped, except cUS$5.6mn of the 2012 bond, which was untendered and therefore remained outstanding, although in default. There was no collective action clause (CAC) in the 2012 bond issue (which was issued under NY law). Exotix understands, however, that the authorities did embark on off-market buy backs for the 2012 bond on a case-by-case basis.

Cash-flow relief was significant. The exchange reformed 44% of external claims and reduced commercial debt service costs by 83% through to 2008 (IMF figures). The interest cost was cut by more than half, while postponing the maturity of c45% of total government debt until 2025.

A second default occurred in 2013, leading to an eventual restructuring in 2015. The government announced on 8 March 2013 that it would not make the upcoming coupon payments on the USD and EC$ 2025 bonds that were due on 15 March and simultaneously announced its intention to seek a comprehensive restructuring of its public debt, including its USD and EC$ bonds. These comprised the USD 2025 bond (US$193.5mn) and the EC$ 2025 bond (EC$185mn, cUS$68.5mn equivalent), which amounted to US$262mn in aggregate (EC$707.4mn)—the USD bond represented c32% of Grenada's public external debt, while the two bonds were 28% of its total public debt. The intention to default came after the government had faced increasing difficulties making debt service payments, and a default on the 2025 USD bond was only avoided on the September 2012 coupon after the government managed to secure a short-term bridging loan (US$4.4mn) on seemingly expensive terms; the payment was not made on the due date, but was paid during the 30-day grace period. Interest on the 2025 USD bond had stepped up to 4.5% in March 2012, from 2.5%, and was due to step up again to 6% in March 2014. After the default, interest arrears began to accumulate on debt to commercial creditors and treasury bill holders. The need for a restructuring was also motivated by the economy's underperformance relative to the expectations held at the time of the previous restructuring in 2005. The government noted that real GDP contracted by an average 1.2% a year over 2008–12, compared with the 4.7% per annum growth assumption that had underpinned the 2005 restructuring. The restructuring excluded multilaterals and Treasury Bills registered on the Regional Government Securities Market (RGSM).

A bondholder group, comprising a steering committee and ad-hoc committee, was formed relatively quickly, in April 2013. According to the IMF, the steering committee consisted of six of the largest bondholders (with exposure reported of cUS$168mn). The ad-hoc committee represented a broader group of bondholders (with cUS$32mn of exposure). Together they held just over 75% of the outstanding USD and EC$ 2025 bonds. The bondholder's group controlled almost 90% of the USD 2025 bond.

After a relatively slow start in restructuring negotiations, an agreement in principle with creditors of the USD bond was finally announced 9 April 2015. Prior to this, Grenada had published two indicative debt restructuring proposals in April 2014. Option one involved a 60% face-value haircut, no grace period, a 15-year maturity and a 6.5% coupon. Option two involved a 50% face-value haircut, two years' grace, a 20-year maturity and 5% coupon.

They differed slightly on the amortisation profile and treatment of interest arrears. As it was, delays to agreeing the final terms meant that the exchange took place in November 2015. Eligible debt in the USD exchange consisted of US$193.5mn. Creditors agreed to a 50% nominal reduction on the new USD bond, in recognition of Grenada's unsustainable debt burden, but in order to ensure ongoing commitment to strong policies, the authorities agreed for this to be delivered in two tranches, half up front and half (the Second Principal Reduction) automatically upon the successful completion of the IMF's sixth and final review of the ECF (which occurred in May 2017). Past Due Interest (PDI), which amounted to c17.58 points, was capitalised but not subject to any haircut. Hence, the principal amount of the new bond was equal to 92.58075% of the old notional. The new USD bond had a 2030 maturity, with a fixed 7% coupon (after the reduction of fees from the first coupon, which was paid in May 2016), and began to amortise at the first payment date (ie no grace period on amortisation). Amortisation was due to be paid in 29 equal semi-annual payments. With the steering committee representing, directly and indirectly, over 75% of outstanding bonds, high participation was virtually guaranteed and triggering the 2025 USD bonds' 75% CAC threshold ensured that any holdouts were swept into the exchange. Debt service was reduced in both the short term and notably from 2021 onwards, as higher coupon step-ups and amortisations were avoided. The implied NPV haircut was estimated at 49% by the IMF, based on computing the PV of the new debt with the PV of the old debt at the same discount rate (13.9%).

The original amount of the new 7% 2030 USD bond was US$179.1785mn after the first 25% tranche of debt reduction was applied up front and with recognition of PDI. The second tranche of nominal debt reduction on the new 2030 USD bond was subsequently delivered on 11 November 2017, the second haircut being 25.277% of the exchanged amount to make up for the impact of delay until a coupon date rather than when the programme was completed. The delivery of the second tranche however was effected through an automatic exchange through DTC/Euroclear into a new bond with a new ISIN. Together with four amortisation payments, delivery of the second haircut saw the amount outstanding fall to US$112.2914mn. Details of the 2030 bond are summarised in the table below.

The new Grenada bond also contained a couple of other innovative features. First, a hurricane clause was included that provided some relief to the authorities on debt payments in the event of any future natural disaster. The clause enables the authorities to defer bond payments following the occurrence of any Caribbean Tropical Cyclone Event, as defined in the Caribbean Catastrophe Risk Insurance Facility (CCRIF) Policy, if inter alia, the modelled loss to Grenada is greater than US$15mn. Deferred payments shall continue to be payable and shall continue to accrue interest. Second, bondholders were also offered a capped portion of revenues generated by Grenada's citizenship-by-investment (CBI) programme, an enhancement loosely termed "passport warrants" (although they are not detachable instruments). Under the scheme, bondholders receive an additional amount (the CBI Payment Amount) according to a formula, depending on the lesser of an uncapped amount and a capped payment, multiplied by the CBI Payment Ratio, provided eligible CBI revenues in the reference year exceed US$15mn. The uncapped payment is calculated as 25% of eligible revenues between US$15mn and US$50mn and 35% of eligible revenues over US$50mn. Overall payments are subject to a cumulative cap, such that the NPV of cumulative payments cannot exceed 35% of the face value of the 2030 bond. The CBI Payment Amount, following the relevant reference year, is determined by the CBI Calculation Agent on the Calculation Date preceding the relevant Payment Date. The Calculation Date, for any Reference Year, is 15 May of the calendar year following the relevant reference year, and commencing 15 May 2018.

Grenada bond
Government of Grenada 7% 2030
Bloomberg ticker: GRENAD

Borrower	Government of Grenada
Restructuring	Issued in exchange for 8.5% 2025 (ISIN USP48863AC12) on 12 November 2015 Amended on 12 November 2017 to effect the Second Principal Reduction as per the creditor agreement, which involved re-issuing with a new ISIN
Issue date	12 November 2015 (amended on 12 November 2017)
Form	Eurobond
ISIN	USP48863AE77 after second principal reduction (originally issued as USP48863AD94)
Issue size	US$179,179,200 (original issue size) US$112,291,390 (after second principal reduction)
Amount outstanding	US$107,799,720 (after May 2018 amortisation)
Currency	US dollar
Denomination	US$100 minimum, US$100 thereafter
Amortisation	Amortising, 25 remaining equal semi-annual payments
Final maturity date	12 May 2030

(continued)

(continued)

Grenada bond *Government of Grenada 7% 2030* *Bloomberg ticker: GRENAD*	
Coupon/interest	7% paid semi-annually, May and November
Day count	30/360
Method of transfer	Euroclear/Clearstream
Settlement period	T + 2 business days
Governing law	State of New York
Listing	Not listed
Main agent	BONY

Source: Bloomberg

Iraq

Nominal GDP (US$mn, 2018)[a]		220,911
Population (thousand, 2018)[a]		39,857
GDP per capita (USD, 2018)[a]		5793
Credit ratings (long-term foreign currency)[b]	Fitch	B–
	Moody's	Caa1
	S&P	B–

[a]MF WEO October 2018
[b]As at end-September 2018

Country Summary

- Iraq's security situation has remained fragile since Saddam Hussein's government was toppled in 2003; its recovery since has shown uneven improvement and been frequently delayed. Iraq currently ranks in the 9th percentile of government effectiveness, according to the World Bank, indicating that weak governance and lack of institutions severely hamper development.
- Since 2014, large pockets of northern Iraq have been controlled by the Islamic State (IS or ISIS) militant group, which grew out of the power vacuum that was created when international military forces began large-scale draw downs in 2011, leading to a worsened security situation. Recent victories over IS forces, in particular the reclaiming of Mosul, are viewed by some as a sign of IS's defeat.

Exotix Capital, *Exotix Developing Markets Guide*,
https://doi.org/10.1007/978-3-030-05867-8_23

- Iraq's government revenues were severely hurt as a result of oil price declines beginning in 2014, leading to its fourth IMF programme in the post-Saddam era. Oil production numbers have shown consistent increases since the invasion-related low in 2003. Oil accounts for 95% of government (non-grant) revenue and 93% of exports. Annual production increased by less than 25% in 2007–2010 (to 2.4mbpd), but is likely to grow steadily over coming years.
- In September 2017, a referendum was held to vote for the independence of Kurdistan, the semi-autonomous region of north-western Iraq. The referendum was passed with 93% of the vote, which prompted widespread celebrations across Kurdish regions. Before independence was formally announced, Iraqi forces took control of the Kurdish city of Kirkuk, leading to the resignation of Masoud Barzani, the then president of Iraqi Kurdistan.

Economic data	*Avg*[a]	*2014*	*2015*	*2016*	*2017 (e)*	*2018 (f)*	*2019 (f)*
Real GDP growth	6.5	0.7	2.5	13.1	−2.1	1.5	6.5
Inflation (annual average)	9.5	2.2	1.4	0.5	0.1	2.0	2.0
Current account (% of GDP)	0.7	2.6	−6.5	−7.8	2.3	6.9	3.1
Reserves (US$bn, end-period)[b]	52.6	66.3	53.1	44.5	48.4	54.5[c]	–
Reserves/imports (months)[d]	10.8	9.2	8.7	7.6	8.1	–	–
Overall fiscal balance (% of GDP)[e]	−2.7	−5.6	−12.8	−14.3	−1.6	5.6	3.8
Currency (ticker)	Iraq dinar (IQD)						
FX regime	Floating exchange rate by law, which has until recently operated as a crawling peg. Since January 2009, the rate of crawl has been zero, so in effect it has been fixed.						
Key exports	Crude petroleum (93%), gold (5.4%).						

Source: IMF WEO Database, WDI, Haver, OEC

[a]10-year average to 2016 unless otherwise stated
[b]Gross foreign assets of central bank
[c]Latest figure, June 2018
[d]In months of imports of goods and services
[e]Overall government net lending

Key figures		*Party*	*Since*
President	Barham Salih	PUK	Oct. 2018
Vice president	Nouri al-Maliki	IDP	Oct. 2014
Vice president	Osama al-Nujaifi	Muttahidoon	Oct. 2014
Vice president	Ayad Allawai	INA	Oct. 2014
Prime minister	Adel Abdul-Mahdi	ISCI	Oct. 2018
Minister of finance	Hoshyar Zebari	–	Oct. 2014
Central bank governor	Ali Mohsen Ismail Al-Alaq	–	Sep. 2014

Note: At the time of writing, Iraq's prime minister is expected to present a new cabinet shortly. Some roles are currently unchanged since the election in May 2018

Politics

Executive power

The president acts as head of state in what is a federal republic. However, the president and presidency council (and vice presidents) are effectively ceremonial roles. The president is elected by the Council of Representatives by a two-thirds majority. This makes the legislative and cabinet (Council of Ministers) a particularly powerful body. The prime minister is head of government and chairs the cabinet.

Presidential term: Four years (two-term limit; consecutive allowed) **Parliamentary term**: Four years

Legislature

Unicameral—The Council of Representatives (CoR) is elected by popular vote to serve four-year terms. There is one directly elected seat for every 100,000 head of population and nine seats that are reserved for minority groups (one more was added for the 2018 election)—This amounts to a current total of 329. The CoR elects the presidency council and the largest bloc within the CoR is responsible for nominating the prime minister (the nomination then requires CoR assent). The prime minister selects the Council of Ministers, which also requires the approval of the CoR. The constitution also provides for a Federal Council (at the federal not central level).

Council of Representatives: 329 seats

Elections

Next due *Presidential and legislative: May 2022*

Last legislative election (May 2018)	*Seats*
Alliance Towards Reforms (Forward)	54
Conquest Alliance	47
Victory Coalition	42
Kurdistan Democratic Party	25
State of Law Coalition	25
National Coalition	21
National Wisdom Movement	19
Patriotic Union of Kurdistan	18
Arab Decision Alliance	14
Other parties	62
Independents	2
Total	329

Note: The president is indirectly elected by two-thirds majority by the Council of Representatives

People

Almost four-fifths of Iraqis are thought to be of Arab descent and nearly one-fifth of the population are Kurdish. 97% of the population follow Islam, with Shi'a being dominant in number, at c60%, and Sunni below that, at 40%. The balance of power has shifted since the fall of Saddam Hussein. Sunni Arabs were the politically dominant group under Hussein, although the religious minority, and, within the Sunnis, the ruling Ba'athist party enjoyed special privileges.

Sunnis occupy most of the Centre of the country, an area without substantial oil resources. The majority Shi'a, occupying mainly the south of the country, were oppressed by Hussein's Sunni regime. The political landscape now sees the Shi'a as the dominant political group, being the main group in government, leaving the Sunnis feeling marginalised since the 2003 invasion.

The Kurdish Regional Government (KRG) controls the northern territory of Iraq, having enjoyed virtual autonomy since 1991.

Kurds want to annex the city of Kirkuk (which is outside the KRG territory), although their claim is disputed by ethnic Turkmen and Arabs. Turkey fears Kurdish attempts to annex Kirkuk will lead to calls for an independent Kurdish state, which would threaten the breakup of Turkey, home to 12mn Kurds. A referendum on Kurdish independence was held in September 2017; however, before independence was officially declared, the city of Kirkuk was retaken by Iraqi forces, effectively ending the immediate hopes of an independent Kurdistan.

Regional powers also play out their own proxy wars in Iraq. Sunni Arab states such as Saudi Arabia, Egypt and Jordan support Iraqi Sunnis, concerned about the emergence of a Shi'a Iraq regional rival backed by Shi'a Iran. Syria is said to support former Ba'athists.

Debt

	2012	*2017*
External debt ratios (%)		
Total external debt/GDP	27.3	33.0
Total external debt/exports of goods and services	61.6	85.5
External debt service ratio	4.2	4.0
Public debt ratios (%)		
Public domestic debt/GDP	7.1	25.7
Public debt/GDP	34.4	58.7

Source: Ministry of Finance, IMF, WDI, Exotix

Iraq is nearly at the end of its long and bumpy (post-Saddam Hussein) path to public and external debt sustainability. The 2004 Paris Club agreement was a defining moment that put Iraqi public finances back on track. Before debt reduction, Iraq's external debt was 552% of GDP. Non-Paris Club creditors were the biggest creditor group, accounting for half of the outstanding debt, followed by Paris Club creditors. By end-2007, after Paris Club and commercial debt reductions, Iraq's external debt was US$102bn (a still sizeable 162% of GDP). With the third and final stage of Paris Club debt reduction and assuming comparable treatment by non-Paris Club creditors, debt was projected to fall by end-2008 to US$33bn (36% of GDP). Private creditors comprised US$21bn of the total debt. Agreement on the official debt came in November 2004 with a Paris Club deal. A commercial debt deal followed in 2005. These resulted in significant debt reduction (80% on a NPV basis on official Paris Club debt and 90% on commercial debt). But, even as this led to a sharp decline in Iraq's external debt burden, by end-2007 it was still some 162% of GDP.

Up-to-date debt stock figures are hard to come by. The IMF has published its estimates for total public and external debt, but other figures are largely absent. Of the US$136.5bn external debt outstanding in 2009, the Paris Club was owed US$9.4bn. Even these figures are unreliable because some of the Paris Club debt has now been traded on the secondary market with private creditors.

Debt restructuring has been much more protracted than is the case in most other countries. First, because Paris Club creditors imposed three stages of debt forgiveness, each of which was dependent on achieving key IMF benchmarks, originally attended for completion only by end-2008. Second, finalising agreements on non-Paris Club debt has been slower than expected.

By end-2007 total debt was still US$102bn, some 162% of GDP. In 2008, negotiations with Greece, Morocco, Tunisia, and the UAE were concluded, and, in 2010 Iraq reached a rescheduling with the People's Republic of China, providing 80% debt relief in line with Paris Club agreements. Even by late 2010, further debt restructuring remained to be completed with some creditors in the Gulf. The IMF reiterated in 2010 its view that Iraq had been negotiating in good faith to resolve the remaining arrears to private creditors, consistent with the Fund's policy on lending into arrears. However, as of 2018, this final-stage debt reduction has not been completed, leaving an addition US$41bn in outstanding arrears. Once debt restructuring is complete, Iraq's total external debt is expected to fall to US$22.6bn.

Liquidity risks, meanwhile, have also greatly diminished. Gross international reserves were US$54bn at October 2009, covering c10.5 months of goods' imports. Reserves have risen strongly since end-2004, when they were US$8bn, due to rising oil revenues and large current account surpluses.

Iraq's public external debt was cUS$22.6bn in Q3 17, based on figures provided in the 2017 eurobond prospectus, plus the US$1bn bond subsequently issued in August. This proxy includes US$10.8bn of renegotiated claims, of which US$7.7bn was owed to bilateral creditors (mostly, Paris Club members), and new debt incurred since 2003, including debt owed to the IMF (RFI and SBA disbursements), two World Bank loans totalling US$2.6bn, a bilateral loan from the US for Ministry of Defence financing and the 2022 notes, which are guaranteed by USAID (principal and interest). A further US$41bn was in arrears, taking public external debt to US$63.6bn, 33% of GDP and 86% of exports of goods and services. The IMF estimated that 2017 public domestic debt came to US$49.5bn, 25.7% of GDP, which takes total public debt to US$113bn, 59% of GDP. Public external debt service has declined since 2012 to 4% of exports in 2017, despite a fall in exports over this period, based on WDI data.

Composition of external debt

External debt by creditor (end-Q3 2017)	*Nominal amount outstanding (US$bn)*	*Share of total (%)*	
Renegotiated claims	**10.8**	**47.8**	**(17.0)**
o/w official bilateral	7.7	34.1	(12.1)
Paris club	5.8	25.7	(9.1)
Non-Paris Club	1.9	8.4	(3.0)
Commercial creditors	2.9	12.8	(4.6)
Other	0.2	0.9	(0.3)

(*continued*)

(continued)

External debt by creditor (end-Q3 2017)	*Nominal amount outstanding (US$bn)*	*Share of total (%)*	
New debt since 2003	**11.8**	**52.2**	**(18.6)**
IMF	2.5	11.1	(3.9)
World Bank	2.6	11.5	(4.1)
US	2.7	11.9	(4.2)
2022 notes	1.0	4.4	(1.6)
Eurobond[a]	1.0	4.4	(1.6)
Other	2.0	8.8	(3.1)
Total external debt (excl. arrears)	**22.6**	**100.0**	**(35.5)**
Arrears	41.0	–	(64.5)
Total external debt (incl. arrears)	**63.6**	–	**(100.0)**

Source: Iraq Debt Management Office, Bloomberg

Note: Figures in () show % of total incl. outstanding arrears

[a]US$1bn eurobond issued August 2017

Rescheduling History

Over 1975–1980 Iraq was a donor and creditor country with estimated foreign currency reserves of US$36bn. Indebtedness built up over the 1980s, over the period of the 1981/1985 Development Plan, when Iraq made large scale infrastructure and import commitments just as oil exports and prices collapsed, shifting the country into large trade deficits. This financial reversal was so sudden that by 1982–1983 Iraq was forced to arrange new external financing (1982 UBAF US$500mn syndicated loan) and the deferment of contractually due payments, and this availability of financing serviced the growing debt burden. By the time of the First Gulf War in 1990, Iraq did not have enough funds to meet all debt obligations so only selectively made payments, favouring some creditors over others. Over this period, Iraq entered into a long list of agreements, protocols and arrangements with nearly all of its trade creditors. UN sanctions following the First Gulf War not only prevented the Iraqis from making payments, but also restricted the country's foreign currency earning capacity (aside from 'oil-for-food' arrangements) so that it could not service debt. This period was characterised by accumulating past due interest claims. By the end of the Second Gulf War in 2003, Iraq's debt was estimated at US$119bn (principal and past due interest).

After the Second Gulf War, attention turned to debt forgiveness for Iraq. Various advisers were appointed: in March 2004, Ernst & Young were appointed by Iraq's Coalition Provisional Authority as manager of the

Government of Iraq Debt Reconciliation Office; Clearly Gottlieb was selected by the Interim Government of Iraq in July 2004 as Iraq's International Legal Advisor in the Restructuring of External debt; Citigroup Global Markets & J.P. Morgan Securities were appointed in January 2005 to act as Iraq's joint global co-ordinators in the restructuring of the claims of private commercial creditors (including financial institution creditors) against Iraq; also in January 2005, Lazards were appointed as advisor on debt talks with Iraq's 17 Paris Club creditors and Houlihan Lokey Howard & Zukin were appointed to assist in talks with other creditors. Crucially, in order to facilitate a restructuring of various diverse commercial claims and avoid expensive litigation, a UN Security Council Resolution was passed in 2003 to prevent creditors attaching oil shipments.

Although creditors agreed that a level of 'sustainable' debt was their target, even among Paris Club creditors estimates of the actual level of forgiveness needed to achieve this level ranged from 50% of face (France) to 100% (US). Political considerations as well as debt sustainability parameters influenced these views. By the time of the announcement of a commercial debt settlement offer in July 2005, the total amount of Saddam-era claims held by commercial and bilateral creditors was estimated at more than US$125bn. Commercial creditors were estimated to hold claims totalling cUS$20bn. At the first Iraqi creditors' meeting on 3 May 2005, organised by Citigroup, the most important conclusion was that all the different types of claims would be dealt with in the same way.

Milestones on Road to Iraqi Debt Restructuring

May 2003	UN resolution 1483 precluding creditors from resolving their debt claims through litigation or attempting to attach liens on Iraq's energy resources until December 2007.
Apr. 2004	Initial IMF debt sustainability analysis (not published).
Sep. 2004	IMF debt sustainability analysis update (not published).
Sep. 2004	Ernst & Young starts to contact sovereign creditors and asks them to 'register' their Iraq claims.
Sep. 2004	IMF agrees emergency post-conflict assistance with Iraq.
21 Nov. 2004	Paris Club agreement to "cancel 80% of Iraq's debt" in NPV terms, to be delivered in three stages (details below). Comparability was sought from other external creditors.
Dec. 2004	Ernst & Young contacts commercial creditors and requests they "register" their claims with Ernst & Young by 15 February 2005, subsequently extended to April 2005.

26 Jul. 2005	Iraq announces terms of its commercial debt settlement offer, to settle outstanding Saddam-era commercial claims (details below). The offer comprised a cash buyback for small aggregate claims. Large claims were eligible to receive the debt-for-debt exchange offer with a choice of two new debt instruments, a new loan and a new note.
16 Nov. 2005	Iraq opens its commercial debt exchange
23 Jan. 2006	Iraq closes the debt-for-debt exchange, resulting in the issue of US$2.7bn (principal) of the new note and cUS$177mn (initial principal amount) in a multicurrency loan. Approximately US$14bn in eligible commercial claims were tendered. The exchange offer therefore resulted in a new reduction of debt equal to US$11bn.
30 Jan. 2008	Iraq announces it will re-open the cash buyback offer for outstanding claims, at a price of 10.25%. Claims had to be registered by 15 March and the offer was scheduled to close around 28 August 2008. The third and final tranche of this debt relief was granted following the completion of the last review under the second SBA in December 2008. Out of a total of US$37.2bn due to Paris Club creditors, US$29.7bn was cancelled, and the remaining US$7.4bn has been rescheduled.
2010	Rescheduling agreement reached with China, providing 80% debt relief. IMF states Iraq making best efforts to reach bilateral agreements on its arrears to official non-Paris Club creditors and that the authorities have been negotiating in good faith to resolve the remaining arrears to private creditors. By 2010, 12 non-Paris Club official creditor claims already signed and were being implemented. The UAE announced the full cancellation of Iraq's debt and substantial progress was made with Morocco and Egypt.

Relations with Multilateral Creditors

Iraq secured post-conflict assistance from the IMF in September 2004 after it settled overdue obligations to the IMF amounting to US$81mn. An SBA agreement was subsequently approved in December 2005. The arrangement was cancelled in December 2007, as it expired, and a successor arrangement was implemented. The same month, Iraq repaid all its drawings in full to the IMF made under EPCA, some two years ahead of schedule (repayment was due in 2009). In 2010 a two-year SBA of SDR2.28bn (US$3.6bn), equivalent to 200% of Iraq's quota, was approved. A first purchase of SDR297.1mn (25% of quota) was made. The SBA aimed to ensure macroeconomic stability during the political transition after the March elections, and to provide a framework for advancing structural reforms. Performance under the program through 2010 was broadly satisfactory.

IMF programmes

Date	*Arrangements*	*Comments*
2004	EPCA	Approved 29 September 2004.
2005–2007	SBA	Cancelled on 18 December 2007, just a few weeks before the expiry date. Two extensions to the programme were made, in March 2007 (to end-September) and August 2007 (to December). The programme was treated as precautionary. No purchases were made. The programme remained on track despite a difficult security situation.
2007–2009	SBA	Agreed on 19 December 2007. Expired 18 March 2009. The authorities treated the programme as precautionary. The SBA was 40% of quota (SDR475mn).
2010–2013	SBA	Agreed on 24 February 2010. Expired 23 February 2013.
2016–2019	SBA	Agreed on 7 July 2016. Expires on 6 July 2019. First review completed in December 2016, second review completed in August 2017; both required waivers for non-observance of applicable performance criteria.

Source: IMF. Iraq joined the IMF in 1945

Paris Club and Bilateral Creditors

Paris Club creditors reached an agreement on debt reduction for Iraq on 21 November 2004. The agreement covered all its outstanding Iraqi debt, amounting to US$37bn, for which creditors agreed to cancel 80% in NPV terms. Comparability was sought from other external creditors. Debt cancellation was to be delivered in three stages, as detailed in the table below. Paris Club creditors were given the option of debt reduction or debt service reduction, which would lead to the same overall NPV forgiveness. The debt reduction option is to be repaid over a 23-year period with six years' grace on principal repayments. All 18 of Iraq's Paris Club creditors have signed bilateral agreements. The final country to sign was Russia in February 2008.

Paris Club agreements

Date	*Terms*	*Status*	*Details*
2004 Nov.	Ad hoc	Active	Treated all US$37.158bn of its Paris Club debt as at 1 January 2004. Total Iraqi external debt put at US$120.2bn. US$29.727bn was cancelled and US$7.431bn rescheduled. Treatment of arrears as of end-2004, treatment of stock as of 1 January 2005. Creditor governments have the ability to conduct debt swaps, such as debt for nature swaps, although some restrictions exist for non-ODA loans. Debt cancellation occurred in three phases: 1. Cancellation of 30% of the debt stock as of the date of the agreement. 2. Cancellation of 30% of the initial debt stock as soon as an agreement with the IMF in the upper credit tranches was approved, implemented on 22 December 2005. 3. Cancellation of 20% of the initial debt stock as soon as the last IMF programme review was approved, implemented on 22 December 2008. Then the payment of non-consolidated amounts before 1 June 2005.

Source: Paris Club

The Paris Club agreed on 21 November 2004 to a debt reduction for Iraq, equivalent to 80% in NPV terms, and to be achieved in three stages. The first and second stages, each comprising a 30% debt reduction in NPV terms, went into effect in November 2004 and in December 2005 (following approval of the first SBA), respectively. The third and final tranche of this debt relief was granted following the completion of the last review under the second SBA in December 2008. Out of a total of US$37.2bn due to Paris Club creditors, US$29.7bn was cancelled, and the remaining US$7.4bn has been rescheduled.

To deliver the 30% debt reduction in NPV linked to the approval of the initial standard IMF programme, Paris Club creditors were able to choose between a debt reduction option and a debt service reduction option. The debt reduction option resulted in a rescheduling over a 23-year period from 2005, with six years' grace on principal repayments. The latter option resulted in a longer rescheduling profile of 33 years, including a grace period of six years. The two amortisation schedules of each are shown below. There is no public information on which countries chose which option, although the IMF indicated in 2005 that Japan and Russia chose the second option.

Sovereign Commercial Debt

Iraq closed its debt for debt exchange on 23 January 2006. The offer settled nearly all outstanding Saddam-era commercial claims, the terms of which were announced on 26 July 2005. The commercial debt exchange had opened on 16 November 2005. The commercial debt buyback involved an 89.75% write off in NPV terms.

The offer comprised:

1. Cash buyback if the aggregate amount of a claimant's outstanding registered claims as of 6 August 1990 was US$35mn or less (or its equivalent in other currencies). The cash-purchase price for reconciled eligible claims for the cash buy-back was 10.25% of the reconciled outstanding amount of those claims (including principal and accrued interest);
2. Claimants with aggregate registered claims above the threshold (as of 6 August 1990) were eligible to receive the debt-for-debt exchange offer. Claimants were able to exchange eligible claims (principal plus calculated interest accrued through the date of exchange) for two new debt instruments: a syndicated multi-currency loan ("new loan") or a privately placed bond (5.8% 2028 ("new note"), with an exchange ratio of 20%).

The exchange resulted in the issue of US$2.7bn (principal) of the new note, which is shown below, and cUS$177mn (initial principal amount) in a multi-currency loan. Approximately US$14bn in eligible commercial claims were tendered. The exchange offer therefore resulted in a net reduction of debt equal to US$11bn.

On 30 January 2008, Iraq announced it was reopening the cash buy-back for outstanding claims. The price was set at 10.25%. Claims had to be registered by 15 March and the offer was scheduled to close around 28 August 2008. Nearly all private claims (c96%) were settled by 2008.

Iraq eurobond *Iraq 5.8% 2028* *Bloomberg ticker: IRAQ*	
Borrower	Republic of Iraq
Issue date	19 January 2006
Form	Eurobond
ISIN	XS0240295575
Issue size	US$2.7bn
Currency	USD
Denomination	Min. US$250,000/increments on US$1000
Amortisation	Sinkable
Final maturity date	15 January 2028
Coupon/interest	5.8%, paid semi-annually
Method of transfer	Euroclear/Clearstream
Day count	30/360
Settlement period	T + 2
Joint lead managers	Citi, JP Morgan
Exchange	Berlin, Frankfurt, Stuttgart

Source: Bloomberg

Iraq issued a US$1bn bond in January 2017, which was guaranteed in full by the US government, paying interest of just 2.1%. In contrast, in August 2017, Iraq issued another US$1bn bond (shown below) with no guarantee and interest of 6.752%. The bond was seven times oversubscribed. In late 2017, the governor of the Central Bank of Iraq told the media that the government intended to issue another bond, for US$2bn in 2018.

Iraq eurobond *Iraq 6.752% 2023* *Bloomberg ticker: IRAQ*	
Borrower	Republic of Iraq
Issue date	9 August 2017
ISIN	XS1662407862
Issue size	US$1bn
Currency	USD
Denomination	Min. US$200,000/increments on US$1000
Amortisation	Bullet
Final maturity date	9 March 2023
Coupon/interest	6.752%, paid semi-annually

(*continued*)

(continued)

Iraq eurobond *Iraq 6.752% 2023* *Bloomberg ticker: IRAQ*	
Method of transfer	Euroclear/Clearstream
Day count	30/360
Settlement period	T + 2
Joint lead managers	Citi, Deutsche Bank, JP Morgan
Exchange	Berlin, Dublin, Frankfurt, Stuttgart
Governing law	New York

Source: Bloomberg

Corporate Bond Markets

With its sizable oil and gas reserves, Iraq is an area or particular interest for international oil companies. In 2014–2016, a number of exploration and production firms operating in Iraq under PSA agreements were caught between a rock and a hard place when the Islamic State militant group invaded Iraq and seized control over parts of the country including oil and gas infrastructure. At the same time crude oil prices started their decline from US$100/bbl in summer 2014 to US$30/bbl and lower in winter 2016. Oil and gas companies operating in the region accumulated substantial receivables from the government but were paid very little. Liquidity problems, production disruptions and in some cases operating challenges and legal disputes led Gulf Keystone, Dana Gas and Genel into restructuring of their eurobonds. Although none of the issues below represent financial obligations of Iraqi companies, all of them are highly exposed to the region.

Oilflow SPV 12% 2022 *Bloomberg ticker: OILFLO*	
Borrower	Oilflow SPV 1 DAC
Issue date	13 January 2017
Form	Eurobond
ISIN	XS1539823093
Issue size	US$500mn
Currency	US dollar
Denomination	US$200,000 and US$1000 thereafter
Amortisation	Sinkable
Final maturity date	13 January 2022 (expected)

(*continued*)

(continued)

Oilflow SPV 12% 2022 *Bloomberg ticker: OILFLO*	
Coupon/interest	12%, paid monthly
Collateralisation	Secured
Day count	ACT/360

Source: Bloomberg

Gulf Keystone 10% 2023 *Bloomberg ticker: GULFKY*	
Borrower	Gulf Keystone Petroleum Ltd
Issue date	25 July 2018
Form	Eurobond
ISIN	NO0010828106
Issue size	US$100mn
Currency	US dollar
Denomination	US$200,000 and US$1 thereafter
Amortisation	Callable
Final maturity date	25 July 2023
Coupon/interest	10%, paid semi-annually
Collateralisation	Senior unsecured
Day count	ACT/365

Source: Bloomberg

Kuwait Energy 9.5% 2019 *Bloomberg ticker: KUWAIE*	
Borrower	Kuwait Energy PLC
Issue date	4 August 2014
Form	Eurobond
ISIN	XS1086694111
Issue size	US$250mn
Currency	US dollar
Denomination	US$200,000 and US$1000 thereafter
Amortisation	Call 12 April 2018 @ 104.75
Final maturity date	4 August 2019
Coupon/interest	9.5%, paid semi-annually February and August
Collateralisation	Senior unsecured
Day count	30/360

Source: Bloomberg

DNO ASA 8.75% 2020
Bloomberg ticker: DNONO

Borrower	DNO ASA
Issue date	18 June 2015
Form	Eurobond
ISIN	NO0010740392
Issue size	US$400mn
Amount outstanding	US$200mn
Currency	US dollar
Denomination	US$200,000 and US$100,000 thereafter
Amortisation	Call 12 April 2018 @ 105
Final maturity date	18 June 2020
Coupon/interest	8.75%, paid semi-annually
Collateralisation	Senior unsecured
Day count	ACT/365

Source: Bloomberg

DNO ASA 8.75% 2023
Bloomberg ticker: DNONO

Borrower	DNO ASA
Issue date	31 May 2018
Form	Eurobond
ISIN	NO0010740392
Issue size	US$400mn
Currency	US dollar
Denomination	US$100,000 and US$100,000 thereafter
Amortisation	Call 31 May 2023 @ 103.5
Final maturity date	31 May 2023
Coupon/interest	8.75%, paid quarterly
Collateralisation	Senior unsecured
Day count	ACT/365

Source: Bloomberg

Genel Energy Finance 2 Ltd 10% 2022
Bloomberg ticker: GENLLN

Borrower	Genel Energy Finance 2 Ltd
Issue date	14 May 2014
Form	Eurobond
ISIN	NO0010710882
Issue size	US$300mn
Currency	US dollar

(*continued*)

(continued)

Genel Energy Finance 2 Ltd 10% 2022 *Bloomberg ticker: GENLLN*	
Denomination	US$1 and US$1 thereafter
Amortisation	Callable
Final maturity date	22 December 2022
Coupon/interest	10%, paid quarterly
Collateralisation	Senior unsecured
Day count	ACT/365

Source: Bloomberg

Shamaran Petroleum 12% 2023 *Bloomberg ticker: SNMCN*	
Borrower	Shamaran Petroleum
Issue date	5 July 2018
Form	Eurobond
ISIN	NO0010826456
Issue size	US$240mn
Currency	US dollar
Denomination	US$1 and US$1 thereafter
Amortisation	Call 5 July 2023 @ 107.2
Final maturity date	5 July 2023
Coupon/interest	12%, paid semi-annually
Collateralisation	Senior unsecured
Day count	ACT/365

Source: Bloomberg

Nile Delta Sukuk Ltd 4% 2020 *Bloomberg ticker: DANAGS*	
Borrower	Nile Delta Sukuk Ltd
Issue date	13 August 2020
Form	Eurobond
ISIN	XS1857667569
Issue size	US$530.4mn
Amount outstanding	US$530.4mn
Currency	US dollar
Denomination	US$36,000 and US$1 thereafter
Amortisation	Callable
Final maturity date	31 October 2020
Coupon/interest	4%, paid quarterly
Collateralisation	Secured

Source: Bloomberg

Jamaica

Nominal GDP (US$mn, 2018)[a]		15,424
Population (thousand, 2018)[a]		2860
GDP per capita (USD, 2018)[a]		5393
Credit ratings (long-term foreign currency)[b]	Fitch	B
	Moody's	B3
	S&P	B

[a]IMF WEO October 2018
[b]As at end-September 2018

Country Summary

- Historically, Jamaica has been one of the Caribbean's slowest-growing economies (real GDP growth has averaged just 0.5% over the past 20 years, the sixth slowest rate in the world, and has been flat over the past decade, ahead of the Bahamas and behind Barbados). This reflects the country's vulnerability to external economic shocks and adverse weather, especially hurricanes and flooding, as well as its sizeable debt burden, which not only constrains economic growth but also limits fiscal flexibility, and social challenges (such as a high crime rate). However, real GDP growth has picked up since 2014 and is forecast to exceed 2% annually from 2020, according to the IMF.
- Traditionally, the economy is agriculture-based (mainly sugar and coffee), and alumina and bauxite are the main goods exports. A light

Exotix Capital, *Exotix Developing Markets Guide*,
https://doi.org/10.1007/978-3-030-05867-8_24

manufacturing base also exists. But the economy is now more dependent on services, such that tourism and sizeable private remittances provide most current account receipts.

- Despite a sizeable public debt burden (estimated at 112% of GDP in 2017), it is declining and Jamaica has remained current on external debt and committed to multi-year fiscal consolidation. Two domestic debt exchanges have occurred (in 2010 and 2013), which has provided some fiscal space through a reduction in interest rates and extension of maturities—both were prior actions in the context of separate IMF programmes. Programme implementation has been good. Jamaica's current arrangement is due to expire in 2019, after nearly a decade under IMF supervision.

Economic data	*Avg*[a]	*2014*	*2015*	*2016*	*2017 (e)*	*2018 (f)*	*2019 (f)*
Real GDP growth	0.2	0.6	0.9	1.5	0.7	1.2	1.5
Inflation (annual average)	9.1	8.3	3.7	2.3	4.4	3.4	4.2
Current account (% of GDP)	−9.8	−7.5	−3.2	−2.7	−4.6	−4.9	−4.2
Reserves (US$mn, end-period)[b]	1894	2001	2437	2719	3208	3135[c]	–
Reserves/imports (months)[d]	2.8	3.0	4.0	4.5	4.7	–	–
Overall fiscal balance (% of GDP)[e]	−4.1	−0.5	−0.3	−0.2	0.5	−0.1	0.8
Currency (ticker)	Jamaican dollar (JMD)						
FX regime	De jure floating, although the IMF classifies the regime as a de facto stabilised arrangement, which has exhibited a crawling peg-like depreciation almost annually over the past 20 years.						
Key exports	Chemicals and chemical products (38%), fuels (14%), aluminium ore (7.7%). Tourism and remittances earnings are more significant than goods, worth US$3.5bn and US$2.6bn, respectively, in 2017, compared with goods' exports worth US$1.3bn.						

Source: IMF WEO Database, Haver, IMF Country Reports, OEC

[a]10-year average to 2016 unless otherwise stated

[b]Net international reserves

[c]Latest figure, June 2018

[d]Months of the current year's imports of goods, services and primary income debits

[e]Overall government net lending from WEO (same as central government balance)

Key figures		*Party*	*Since*
Prime minister	Andrew Holness	JLP	Mar. 2016[a]
Minister of finance and public service	Nigel Clarke	JLP	Mar. 2018
Key opposition figure	Peter Phillips	PNP	Apr. 2017[b]
Central bank governor	Bryan Wynter	–	Nov. 2009

Notes: Jamaica is a member of the Commonwealth. It gained independence from Britain in 1962. Queen Elizabeth II (UK) remains Monarch, represented by the governor general, The Most Hon Sir Patrick Allen (since February 2009)

[a]Previously PM from Oct. 2011 to Jan. 2012 after the resignation of Bruce Golding

[b]Peter Phillips became leader of the PNP after Portia Simpson-Miller stepped down as leader following the party's defeat in the 2016 general election

Politics

Executive power

Under the constitution, power is concentrated around the prime minister and cabinet, with the Senate acting primarily as a review body. Queen Elizabeth II remains chief of state, while the prime minister is head of the government. Although the governor general provides assent to legislation, for and on behalf of the monarch who is executive, this is essentially a formality. The governor general appoints the prime minister, usually from the ruling party.

Parliamentary term: Five years

Legislature

Bicameral comprising of Senate (upper house) and the House of Representatives (lower house). Senate members are directly appointed by the governor general under the advisement of both the PM and leading opposition member, while the House of Representatives is decided by popular vote. The close results in the 2007 elections led to an increase in House of Representatives seats from 60 to 63 (not an even number).

Senate (21 seats)

13 seats under the advisement of the prime minister, usually on his/her party's consensus.
Eight seats on the advice of the main opposition leader, usually on his/her party's consensus.

House of Representatives (63 seats)
Directly elected.

Elections

Next due 2021

Last legislative election[a] *(February 2016)*	*Seats*
Jamaica Labour Party (JLP)	32
People's National Party (PNP)	31
Total	63

[a]Results shown for House of Representatives

People

Over 90% of Jamaica's population is black, with c6% mixed race. A lack of opportunities has produced a migratory culture. Over the past 10 years, population growth has slowed as it reaches 3mn, with negative net migration as a key contributor. The predominant religion is Christianity.

Originally a Spanish colony, the country fell to Britain in 1655 and the island became a major producer of sugar and coffee based on slave labour. Jamaica gained some political self-control in the 1940s and, in 1958, joined nine other UK territories in the Federation of the West Indies. It subsequently withdrew in 1961 after voters rejected membership. Independence from the UK was granted the next year, although Jamaica remains a member of the Commonwealth.

Power has alternated between the two dominant parties since, albeit after some extended periods, and the country has generally enjoyed a stable political environment, despite a reputation for a violent gang culture, crime, drugs, poverty and high unemployment. The JLP (centre-right) were in power at independence until 1972. Michael Manley (1972–1980) became the first PNP (centre-left) prime minister and pursued a socialist agenda, forging closer relations with Cuba. Edward Seaga (1980–1989) of the JLP reversed Manley's policies, embarking on a privatisation programme and seeking closer ties with the US. An extended period of PNP rule followed (1989–2007), with four consecutive terms in office. Manley returned as prime minister in 1989 although this time he followed a more moderate course, continuing the policies of his predecessor. Manley retired for health reasons in 1992, succeeded by Percival Patterson.

The PNP went on to win re-election in 1993, 1998 and 2002. Portia Simpson-Miller, Jamaica's first female prime minister, succeeded Patterson following his retirement on 30 March 2006. The JLP (2007–2011) won elections in 2007, with its victory seen as a time for change. Its leader Bruce Golding became prime minister, despite a campaign financing scandal. The election period also saw several outbreaks of politically motivated violence. Further violence was seen in May 2010 after the government yielded to pressure from the US authorities and attempted to extradite an alleged gang leader. The government imposed a state of emergency (lifted in July). The death toll was reported to have exceeded 70. Andrew Holness succeeded Golding as prime minister in October 2011 after Golding announced he would not seek re-election, and subsequently went to the polls early in December 2011, promising economic growth and a reduction in crime, and accusing the opposition PNP of failing to achieve this during their 18 years in power to 2007.

(*continued*)

(continued)

People
However, the JLP lost badly and the PNP's Simpson-Miller returned as prime minister in 2012–2016, after winning a number of swing constituencies. There was speculation that she wanted to declare Jamaica a Republic and remove Queen Elizabeth II as chief of state. The JLP returned under Holness following its narrow victory in the 2016 elections. After the PNP's defeat in 2016, Simpson-Miller stepped down as its leader and was replaced by Peter Phillips who, as finance minister in 2013, signed the 2013 SBA with the IMF and oversaw the national debt exchange (NDX) operation (see below).

DEBT

	2012	*2017*
External debt ratios (%)		
Total external debt/GDP	98.5	100.5
Public external debt/GDP	55.9	70.4
Private external debt[a]/GDP	42.5	30.2
Total external debt/exports of goods, services and remittances	212.4	193.5
External debt service ratio (public)	14.8	17.1
Public debt ratios (%)		
Public domestic debt/GDP	72.5	41.2
Public debt/GDP	128.5	111.6

Source: Ministry of Finance Debt Management Unit, Bank of Jamaica, IMF, Exotix

[a]As of September 2017

Public and publicly guaranteed (PPG) external debt was US$10.1bn at end-2017, based on figures from the Ministry of Finance's debt management unit (c70% of GDP). Most debt (c62%) was owed to commercial creditors, mainly in the form of bonds, which amounted to US$6.1bn on official figures (61% of PPG external debt). Multilateral creditors were owed 31% of the total, with the Inter-American Development Bank (IADB) owed around half and the World Bank just under one-third. Bilateral creditors comprised the remaining 6.8% of PPG external debt, with 89% of this owed to non-OECD creditors and only 11% owed to OECD (typically Paris Club) creditors. According to central bank data, PPG debt comprises cUS$9.2bn in direct external debt and US$0.7bn in guaranteed debt, although the breakdown by creditor of direct external debt sums to US$9.9bn, resulting in overall PPG external debt of US$10.6bn rather than US$10.1bn. It is not clear why there is a discrepancy. Exotix uses MOF data and calculates debt ratios from this.

The composition of PPG external debt has not really changed much over the past several years, except for large bond issuance in 2015 and a fall in multilateral debt in 2017. Official data show that, in USD terms, PPG external debt has been fairly constant since July 2015, when it increased by nearly US$2bn, due to a dual tranche bond issue. Prior to then, it had been fairly steady in a range of US$8bn–9bn since late 2010. Multilateral debt had risen slowly since end-2010, when it was US$3bn, to peak at US$3.7bn in January 2017, but it fell by cUS$0.5bn in June 2017. Bilateral debt has trended down in the past few years. A breakdown of the maturity structure of all public external debt meanwhile shows a long average maturity at end-2017. The Ministry of Finance's debt management unit states that 72% of PPG external debt had a maturity of over 10 years, with a further 22% between five and 10 years. Since 2009, the average maturity has lengthened. Out of the bonds, less than 5% mature between one and five years.

Total external debt was cUS$14.4bn in 2017 (101% of GDP), little changed from 2012. This is based on PPG external debt, as above, plus private sector external debt, which amounted to US$4.3bn, according to the latest figures (as of September 2017) from the Bank of Jamaica, based on BPM6 methodology. Private external debt was therefore c30% of GDP. Hence, most of the external debt (70%) is owed by the public sector and, indeed, nine sovereign eurobonds now make up c40% of total external debt. As a share of goods and services, total external debt was c300% in 2017, although this ratio falls to 194% if private remittances are also included in the denominator. Earnings from services (mainly tourism) and remittances both dwarf goods' exports. Exports of goods were just US$1.3bn in 2017, while services' earnings amounted to US$3.5bn, and remittances were US$2.6bn; hence, exports of goods and services and remittances combined were US$7.5bn. External debt/exports has fallen modestly from 2012 (under both G&S, and G&S and remittances, formats), as goods, services and remittances' earnings rose by 9% over this period (goods exports actually fell by 25%, but services have risen by 28% and remittances by 12%). Exotix calculates the public external debt service ratio (based on exports of goods and services) at 26.7% in 2017, from 22.6% in 2012, or 17.1% and 14.8%, respectively, if remittances are included in the denominator.

Jamaica's total public debt burden (external and domestic) is, however, much more onerous, although it has been on a declining trend as a proportion of GDP in recent years. Overall public debt stood at 112% of GDP in 2017 (some US$16bn), albeit down from 128% of GDP in 2012, according to Exotix calculations. This compares with IMF figures, from April 2018, contained in the report for the third review of the EFF, that estimated public debt at end-FY 17/18 at 111.9% of GDP under the EFF definition and 104.1% under the fiscal responsibility law (FRL) definition (both down on their original programme targets of 113.9% and 107.1%, respectively). The main difference in the FRL definition, compared with the EFF definition, is the former excludes IMF debt held by the Bank of Jamaica. Public debt under the EFF definition had fallen from 140% of GDP in FY2014/2015, according to the IMF. Public domestic debt was 41.2% of GDP (J$760bn, cUS$6bn) in 2017 according to MOF data (note that central bank data give a lower figure of J$663bn, cUS$5.3bn, as it excludes post-JDX (Jamaica debt exchange) and NDX note issuance). Most domestic debt (c85%) was in the form of domestic notes that were issued in the two domestic debt exchanges in 2010 and 2013 that extended the maturity of domestic debt and consolidated it into fewer instruments. Domestic debt has fallen from 72.5% of GDP in 2012 since those exchanges, declining by 24% in Jamaican dollar terms from end-2013 (i.e. after the second exchange) to end-2017. This in part reflects ongoing fiscal adjustment, with a primary surplus of 7.0–7.5% and a reduced budget deficit. The domestic debt exchanges have also helped reduce vulnerabilities in the domestic debt stock, with a greater proportion at fixed rates rather than variable, and a longer average maturity. Only c10% of the debt falls due within a year, while over 60% falls due after five years. However, debt interest still accounts for 24% of fiscal revenue and 7% of GDP. Most of the debt is held locally. The IMF projects a public debt/GDP ratio (EFF definition) below 100% (at 98.6% of GDP) in FY 19/20, and down to 80.5% in FY 22/23.

Composition of external debt

External debt by creditor (Dec. 2017)	*Nominal amount outstanding (US$mn)*	*Share of total (%)*
Public and publicly guaranteed external debt	**10,103**	**70.0**
o/w Official multilateral	3121	21.6
Inter-American Development Bank	1622	11.2
World Bank	862	6.0
IMF	207	1.4
Other	431	3.0
Official bilateral	688	4.8
OECD	79	0.6
Non-OECD	609	4.2

(*continued*)

(continued)

External debt by creditor (Dec. 2017)	*Nominal amount outstanding (US$mn)*	*Share of total (%)*
Private creditors	6294	43.6
Commercial banks	143	1.0
Bonds	6142	42.5
Other	9	0.1
Private sector external debt[a]	**4334**	**30.0**
Total external debt	**14,437**	**100.0**

Source: Ministry of Finance Debt Management Unit, Bank of Jamaica, IMF, Exotix

[a]As of September 2017

Rescheduling History

Jamaica has undergone a number of debt rescheduling agreements in the past, in both the Paris Club and restructuring its bank debt, although it has not had such an agreement since 1993; at least for its external debt. Since January 2010, Jamaica has had two domestic debt exchanges (one in 2010, the other in 2013), seeking to reduce the interest bill and lengthen the maturity structure of its internal debt, in order to lower its high debt service and short-term debt (see section below). Both operations left external debt untouched.

Jamaica suffers from a classic debt overhang problem, which constrains fiscal policy and stunts economic growth; it has one of the highest debt burdens in the world. Its public debt burden reflects a combination of factors. Already high by the early 1990s, this was due to weak growth, high and volatile inflation, large budget deficits and a persistent current account deficit. Real GDP growth averaged just 0.9% per annum over the 1990s, to some degree the result of measures by previous governments to exert greater control over the economy in the 1970s and 1980s and adverse terms-of-trade shocks. Public debt, which stood at 80% of GDP in 1996, then rose rapidly in the second half of the 1990s due to a sharp increase in public domestic debt; rising from just 32% of GDP in 1996 to 58% in 1999. A significant part of this increase was the result of the 1995–1996 banking crisis, which cost 40% of GDP, as well as underlying poor debt dynamics, reflecting low growth and high interest rates. Fiscal slippages also occurred during the 1997 and 2002 elections. Most of the growth in the domestic debt, in absolute terms, came via domestic bond issues. Public debt reached 129% of GDP in 2003, according to the IMF WEO (previously reported as 143%). The authorities had some success in bringing the debt ratio down over 2005–2008, but the decline was not as fast as they had planned and went into reverse with the global financial crisis. This saw the public debt ratio set new highs, rising to 142% in 2009–2010, and reaching 145% in 2012, according to WEO data. Two separate domestic debt exchanges followed, both in the context of IMF support. These have had some success. Public debt has been on a declining trend since, and is projected to fall below 100% of GDP in FY 19/20 by the IMF (for the first time since 2000), helped by improved debt dynamics—a reduction in interest rates on domestic debt, higher real GDP growth (real GDP growth averaging 2.1% over 2020–2022, according to the WEO) and a continued primary surplus (6.5% of GDP in 2020–2021, down from 7% over 2017–2019, and an average of 7.5% over 2013–2016), consistently one of the highest in the world.

Relations with Multilateral Creditors

Jamaica has been under some form of IMF engagement, either through a formal programme or informal surveillance, for most of the past 30 years, barring a couple of breaks (notably, 1996–2000 and 2006–2010), and by the time its current three-year programme finishes in 2019, it will have been under a formal programme every year over the past decade. According to the IMF website, Jamaica has had 16 programmes, and that excludes engagement in the form of IS and staff-monitored programme (SMP) arrangements, which would take it to 21 altogether.

Jamaica received an IMF programme in 2010 after a 14-year break from a formal programme. The intervening period was, however, marked by ongoing but sporadic engagement through various unfunded surveillance and staff monitored programmes. After its EFF expired in 1996, Jamaica renewed its relationship with the fund in the 2000s. Two SMPs were agreed for the periods 2000–2002 and 2002–2003, although performance was mixed as they coincided with a combination of external shocks and weaker domestic performance. In 2004, the authorities requested regular monitoring of their economic programme by fund staff through "intensified surveillance" (which involved no money and a lower level of monitoring than required under a full executive board-approved programme). This arrangement lasted until 2006.

Jamaica turned to the IMF for financial support in 2010 in response to the pressures stemming from the global financial crisis, with its already weak fiscal flexibility, high public debt burden and low level of reserves. Its 27-month SBA approved in February 2010 had three pillars: (1) fiscal consolidation and institutional reform; (2) public debt restructuring; and (3) financial sector reform, including improving consolidated supervision and the regulation of non-banks. A domestic debt exchange, known as the Jamaica Debt Exchange (JDX), was a central part of the programme and formed a prior action in the government's memorandum of economic and financial policies (MEFP). The exchange was completed in January 2010. It was designed to reduce interest costs and extend maturities on domestic debt, which was mostly held by domestic banks. Initial performance under the programme was satisfactory, although it soon went off track and the third review in January 2011 was the last to be completed. The targeted fiscal consolidation that was critical to a sustained improvement in debt sustainability failed to materialise, beginning with slippages in wage costs. The IMF approved a follow-up arrangement in May 2013, this time a four-year EFF. The programme amounted to nearly US$1bn, c225% of quota, and formed part of a total funding package of cUS$2bn, with other money coming from the World Bank and IADB. A second domestic debt exchange, the National Debt Exchange (NDX), was a prior action and this operation was completed in February 2013. The programme also targeted a significant fiscal adjustment, aiming at a primary surplus of 7.5% of GDP over the medium term (FY 13/14-FY 16/17), compared with 5.2% in FY 12/13 and 3.2% the year before, and a reduction in public debt from 147% of GDP in FY 12/13 to 102% in FY 19/20. The government subsequently terminated the successful EFF ahead of time, in November 2016, and replaced it simultaneously with a new three-year SBA.

The new precautionary 36-month Standby Arrangement amounting to SDR1.2bn (cUS$1.64bn, 312% of quota) was approved in November 2016, and Jamaica is still under it (expiry date is November 2019). It aims to support continued reform amid potential exogenous shocks, which could lead to external pressures. Progress so far has been satisfactory. The first review was completed in April 2017 and the second in October 2017. The third review, along with the 2018 Article IV, was concluded in April 2018. The IMF noted that strong programme implementation continued to anchor macroeconomic stability. Fiscal consolidation is ongoing, with the primary surplus expected to be at least 7% of GDP in FY 17/18, with a similar target set in the FY 18/19 budget, while public debt (EFF definition) is projected to fall to under 100% of GDP in FY 19/20. However, real GDP growth remained weak. No drawings have yet been made under this arrangement.

IMF programmes

Date	*Arrangements*	*Comments*
1970s–1990s	Various	Including SBAs from 1984–1985, 1985–1986, 1987–1988, 1988–1990, 1990–1991, 1991–1992
1992–1996	EFF	
2000–2002	SMP	Running over FY 00/01 and 01/02 and ending March 2002, the programme aimed at reversing the debt build up and supporting growth prospects. It was supported by financial assistance from the World Bank, IADB and Caribbean Development Bank. It was on track in the first year, although targets for the second year were revised in December 2001 to take account of economic shocks (including 9/11 and flooding caused by Hurricane Michelle).
2002–2003	SMP	Lasting from April 2002 to March 2003, the programme aimed at fiscal consolidation, although the IMF noted it did not achieve its goals. Fiscal targets were missed and net international reserves fell more sharply than expected.
2004–2005	IS	Staff programme of "intensified surveillance" for the period April 2004 to March 2005. Targets were set during the 2004 Article IV consultation, presented to the IMF Board in August 2004. The "Interim Staff Report under Intensified Surveillance" was published in February 2005.
2005	IS	Interim report published June 2005.
2006	IS	Interim report published September 2006.
2010–2012	SBA	SDR820.5mn (US$1.27bn, 300% of quota) programme over a period of 27 months approved in February 2010. A domestic debt exchange (JDX) was a prior action for the programme. The programme was due to expire in May 2012, but was not completed. The first review was completed in June 2010. All quantitative performance targets and structural benchmarks for end-March were met and the country was on track to meet end-June targets. The second review was completed successfully in September, with only one performance target and one structural benchmark not achieved due to extenuating circumstances. The third review, in January 2011, was the last one to be concluded as the programme went off track because of fiscal slippage. SDR541.8mn was drawn and it has all been repaid.

(*continued*)

(continued)

Date	Arrangements	Comments
2013–2016	EFF	A four-year SDR615.4mn (US$932mn, 225% of quota) programme approved in May 2013 to restore economic stability, with a large first purchase of 50% of quota. The programme formed part of a total funding package of US$2bn from Jamaica's multilateral partners, including the World Bank and the IADB, each having preliminarily agreed to allocate US$510mn over the next four years. A second domestic debt exchange (NDX) was a prior action for the programme. It also required a large upfront and sustained fiscal adjustment, targeting an annual primary surplus of 7.5% of GDP. The 13th review was completed in September 2016, with domestic confidence indicators at an all-time high. Higher growth, job creation and living standards allowed further disbursements. In November, the authorities cancelled the EFF, ahead of time, replacing it with the 2016 SBA. SDR558.7mn was drawn, of which, SDR547mn remained outstanding as at end-2017.
2016–2019	SBA	36-month precautionary SBA approved in November 2016 with access to SDR1.2bn (US$1.64bn, 312% of quota). The first review was completed in April 2017 and the second in October 2017. The third review was concluded in April 2018, as programme implementation remained strong. To date, nothing has been drawn.

Source: IMF. Jamaica joined the IMF in 1963

The World Bank and IADB are Jamaica's other key multilateral creditors and both have been active in the country for many years. Both were significant contributors to the 2013 IMF-led financing package. Each agreed to provide US$510mn between April 2013 and March 2017. Around half of the World Bank's commitment was to be provided as development policy loans (DPLs) and the remainder through investment project financing (IPF). In June 2017, the World Bank board approved a US$70mn development policy loan to support efforts to improve the investment climate and sustain fiscal and public financial management. It will also help the government to ensure fiscal sustainability and builds on reforms supported by previous development policy loans. In addition, the IFC continues to support private sector development in Jamaica.

Paris Club and Bilateral Creditors

Jamaica had a series of debt rescheduling agreements with the Paris Club during the 1980s and early 1990s, although its last deal was in 1993. The timing of the agreements coincided with the country's various IMF standby credits at the time. All Paris Club agreements have now been fully repaid.

Paris Club agreements

Date	*Terms*	*Status*	*Details*
1984	Classic	Fully repaid	
1985	Classic	Fully repaid	
1987	Classic	Fully repaid	
1988	Classic	Fully repaid	
1990	Classic	Fully repaid	
1991	Houston	Fully repaid	Treated US$125mn.
1993	Houston	Fully repaid	Treated US$291mn of maturities falling due from 1992–1995. Implemented in three stages.

Source: Paris Club

Jamaica has enjoyed a long, close relationship with Venezuela. Hugo Chavez's first foreign trip as president was to Jamaica in 1999. Chavez founded the PetroCaribe alliance in June 2005, under which Jamaica and other Caribbean countries receive preferential pricing and payments on Venezuelan oil. While the oil is sold at market price, recipients only pay a certain percentage of the price up front (which depends on the international price), with 25 years to pay the remaining amount, at 1% interest. In July 2015, Jamaica issued two eurobonds totalling US$2bn and used US$1.5bn of the proceeds to repurchase US$3.2bn in debt owed by the PetroCaribe Development Fund to PDVSA (at 46 cents on the dollar), following the precedent set by the Dominican Republic in February 2015. The Ministry of Finance believed this would provide positive value, despite the higher interest when compared with the PetroCaribe rates.

More recently, an escalation in political and economic problems in Venezuela during 2017 has seen the supply of oil to Jamaica fall from the original quota of 23,000 barrels per day to 1300 barrels per day, according to the Minister of Foreign Affairs and Foreign Trade in April 2017. Not only does this leave a supply gap and a reduction in preferential pricing for Jamaica, but also leads to a lower inflow to the PetroCaribe Development Fund. The Government of Jamaica created the PetroCaribe Development

Fund in December 2006 to manage the proceeds of the PetroCaribe agreement. Its funds are used to service Jamaica's debt to Venezuela and to finance infrastructure projects; reduced inflows could affect projects in Jamaica. In February 2018, the Jamaican government announced its intention to buy Venezuela's stake in the Kingston oil refinery. PDVSA owns 49% of the Petrojam refinery, which the government wants to modernise to boost refining capacity to 50,000 barrels per day.

Sovereign Commercial Debt

Jamaica had a series of agreements to reschedule its foreign bank debt in the 1980s, coinciding with its various Paris Club deals (see table below). Yet, despite its significant (and ongoing) public debt burden, it has managed to avoid restructuring its sovereign external bonds, of which there are many, and they appear to have been given seniority over domestic public debt.

Commercial debt agreements

Date	*Details*
1981 Apr.	Rescheduling of US$126mn of bank debt maturities from 1979–1981.
1981 Jun.	Rescheduling of US$89mn of bank debt maturities from 1981–1983, with US$89mn in new long-term money.
1984	Rescheduling of US$164mn of bank debt maturities from 1983–1985.
1985	Rescheduling of US$359mn of bank debt maturities from 1985–1987.
1987	Rescheduling of US$366mn of bank debt maturities from 1987–1990 and reduced spreads on earlier rescheduling.
1990	Rescheduling of US$315mn of bank debt maturities from 1990–1991 and reduced spreads on earlier rescheduling.
2010	Domestic debt exchange (JDX)
2013	Domestic debt exchange (NDX)

Source: World Bank GDF, Exotix

Jamaica has been a very active borrower in the international capital markets over many years and has also seen a few liability management operations in recent years to consolidate its debt. It had 9 sovereign bonds outstanding as at end-June 2018, totalling US$5.7bn. Its first USD bond came in 1996, although it was small (at US$100mn). This was followed by fairly regular issuance over 1997–2006, although issued amounts remained small (of the order US$150mn–425mn), and included two small EUR-denominated bonds. Most of these issues have since matured. The 2007 issue (8% 2039) is now big, at over US$1.2bn, having been tapped twice. Jamaica's first biggest single issue came in 2008 with the US$750mn 8% 2019, which in terms of size was exceeded in 2014 by the US$800mn 7.625% 2025 bond. Jamaica's most recent issuance was a dual tranche 12-year (6.75% 2028 maturity) and 30-year (7.875% 2045 maturity) in July 2015, for a combined US$2bn, the proceeds of which were in large part used to buy-back its PetroCaribe debt (see above). Both bonds were tapped in an external liability management operation in August 2017 in order to finance a buy-back of US$758mn of bonds maturing between 2019 and 2025. The repurchase offer specifically targeted US$188mn in 8% 2019 notes, US$71mn in 8.5% 2021 notes, US$250mn in 11.625% 2022 notes, and US$250mn in 9.25% 2025 notes. The 6.75% 2028 was increased by US$505mn and the 7.875% 2045 was increased by US$364mn, a combined amount of US$870mn. A tap of the 2039 bond also took place in August 2016. The US$336mn 5.25% 2020 bond were also redeemed in September 2017, and this followed the scheduled repayment of the US$425mn 10.625% 2017 in June 2017 and US$300mn 9% 2015 in June 2015. Prior to these the previous redemption was in 2011. Details of its outstanding bonds are shown in the table.

Jamaica's outstanding eurobonds

Description	*Issue size*	*Outstanding size*	*Issue date*
USD 8% due 2019	US$750mn	US$88.7mn	Jun. 2008
USD 8.5% due 2021[a]	US$162mn	US$6.2mn	Aug. 2013
USD 11.625% due 2022	US$250mn	US$249mn	Dec. 2001
USD 7.625% due 2025	US$800mn	US$800mn	Jul. 2014
USD 9.25% due 2025	US$250mn	US$184mn	Oct. 2005
USD 6.75% due 2028[b]	US$1350mn	US$1850mn	Jul. 2015
USD 8.5% due 2036	US$250mn	US$250mn	Feb. 2006
USD 8.0% due 2039[c]	US$500mn	US$1243mn	Mar. 2007
USD 7.875% due 2045[d]	US$650mn	US$1000mn	Jul. 2015

Source: Bloomberg. As of end-June 2018

[a]Issued in exchange for Clarendon Aluminium Production 8.5% 2021

[b]Original issue size US$1350mn tapped for US$505mn in August 2017

[c]Original issue of US$350mn tapped for US$150mn in October 2007 and another US$743mn in August 2016

[d]Original issue size US$650mn tapped for US$364mn in August 2017

Jamaica bond
Jamaica 6.75% 2028
Bloomberg ticker: JAMAN

Borrower	Government of Jamaica
Issue date	28 July 2015
Form	Eurobond
ISIN	US470160CA80
Issued amount	US$1855mn (tapped in August 2017)
Amount outstanding	US$1850mn
Currency	US dollar
Denomination	US$200,000 and US$1000 thereafter
Amortisation	Sinkable
Maturity date	28 April 2028
Coupon/interest	6.75% per annum, paid semi-annually January and July
Day count	30/360
Method of transfer	Euroclear/clearstream
Settlement period	T + 2
Governing law	New York
Joint lead managers	B of A Merrill Lynch, Citi

Source: Bloomberg

Jamaica's Domestic Debt Exchanges

Jamaica has suffered two severe market shocks in the past 15 years, a (temporary) crisis in confidence in 2003 and the global financial crisis in 2008–2009. Even though access to international markets closed for a while during these periods of stress, the sovereign remained current on its sovereign external bonds on both occasions. Although both crisis episodes had different causes, the 2003 was domestic and the 2008 crisis external, they both exposed Jamaica's inherent vulnerabilities. Investor confidence was undermined in 2003 as fiscal slippages were revealed and the current account deficit worsened sharply. The budget deficit outturn for FY 02/03 was 8% of GDP compared with a deficit target of 4.4%, due to spending overruns in wages and the impact of flooding. Meanwhile, the current account deficit widened three percentage points to 12% of GDP. This hit investor confidence and the Jamaican dollar depreciated by 11%, domestic interest rates rose sharply and spreads on global bonds reached 950 bps. Rating downgrades from Moody's and S&P followed in May and July 2003 to B1 (from Ba3) and to B (from B+), respectively. Confidence did recover, however, and Jamaica was able to return to the international capital market in 2004, and a number of other issues followed. Subsequently, the global financial crisis led to recession, with real GDP falling by 1.6% in

2008/2009 and 3.5% in 2009/2010. The main driver was the collapse in bauxite and alumina production and exports, which fell by 60%, and a 33% fall in remittances. This saw the current account deficit widen, from 10% of GDP in 2006/2007 to 18% in 2007/2008, and gross reserves fall by US$1bn. The currency devalued in Q4 2008. The budget deficit also widened. Moody's and S&P both lowered their ratings in March 2009, to B2 and B–, respectively (both agencies downgraded their ratings to the CCC category later in the year).

However, despite a short respite, Jamaica was forced to undertake an exchange for its domestic bonds, twice, as pre-conditions for separate IMF programmes. The first exchange (JDX) was done in January 2010 but, because the IMF programme ultimately proved unsuccessful, a second exchange (NDX) was required just three years later, in January 2013, and this proved much more successful. Domestic securities have lower interest rates (averaging 9.5% after NDX, from 19% prior to JDX) and longer average maturities.

The 2010 "Jamaica Debt Exchange"

The government launched the JDX in January 2010, as a prior action for its US$1.27bn SBA from the IMF in February 2010. Following an over-reliance on short-term debt, the government sought to reduce interest rates and lengthen maturities, helping to lower near-term debt service payments. Interest accounted for 60% of fiscal revenue and 16% of GDP, and a significant bunching of maturities contributed to large gross borrowing needs. The two main fiscal objectives of the debt exchange were to achieve a reduction in the public interest bill of at least 3% of GDP in FY 10/11 and a three-quarters reduction in the rollover requirements of domestic bonds over the next three years, according to the IMF programme documentation. The debt operation aimed to extend domestically issued bonds for new bonds carrying a lower interest rate. The initial yield on domestic currency-denominated bonds was expected to average 12.5% across instruments and maturities, while the average rate on the bonds exchanged was 19%. The exchange covered US$7.8bn of domestic bonds. Participation of 99.2% exceeded the 80% envisaged by the IMF.

The JDX seemed, initially, successful. Local interest rates fell, the Jamaican dollar appreciated and Jamaica's EMBIG spread fell. It created some fiscal space and breathing space for fiscal reform, pushing back maturities by over two years, with lower interest (12% from 19%), and fiscal savings of 3.5% of

GDP. However, solutions to the debt overhang and high short-term debt stocks required sufficient fiscal consolidation, which did not occur—the ruling JLP government had gone off track with fiscal reform after only three IMF reviews and debt was not put on a sustainable path. The ambition of the JDX was criticised and, within three years, another exchange, the NDX, was needed to achieve the potential of the JDX, under a new government led by Simpson-Miller.

Jamaica's foreign currency long-term ratings were largely unaffected by the exchange, in part because they were already so low by end-2009. Upon the conclusion of the exchange, S&P lifted its rating to B– from CCC in February 2010 while Moody's raised its rating to B3 from Caa1 in March 2010.

The 2013 "National Debt Exchange"

The government launched the second debt restructuring operation in three years in February 2013 with the NDX, as a prior action for its US$2bn IMF-led bailout. The NDX covered US$9.1bn (nearly all) of the government's marketable domestic debt and half of the total government debt stock, with the aim of lowering debt service costs further, through longer maturities and lower interest. The exchange aimed at delivering gross savings equivalent to at least 8.5% of GDP by 2020. The bonds targeted by the exchange include local currency (including fixed, variable and CPI-indexed bonds), as well as locally issued US dollar-denominated bonds amounting to cJ$876bn, or 64% of GDP. The exchange did not include bonds issued in foreign jurisdictions or held by non-residents.

The NDX was considered a success, although that might have been as much due to a much stronger fiscal response and ownership of the new IMF programme than the mechanics of the swap itself. The government committed to, and delivered, a primary surplus averaging 7.5% of GDP over 2013–2016, compared with an average of just 4.4% over 2010–2012 (and 5.4% in 2012).

Ratings (foreign currency long-term) fell again ahead of the second exchange, and improved again on its successful conclusion. Moody's put a negative outlook on its B3 rating in February 2010, and downgraded its rating to Caa3 in March. Its rating was raised to Caa2 in May 2015 and to B3 in November 2016. S&P assigned Selective Default in February 2013, down from B–, and raised its rating to CCC+ in March 2013. S&P raised its rating again in September 2013 to B– and again to B in June 2015.

Corporate Bond Markets

There is a limited international corporate bond market in Jamaica, at least in terms of number of issuers if not total amount outstanding, which means, of the issuance there is, it is concentrated in one company. There have been five issuers of note in the past 15 years, but issuance has generally been small in size and infrequent. Air Jamaica (JAMAIR) was the first Jamaican company to access the international markets with a 10-year issue in July 2005. The US$200mn 2015 bond had a coupon of 9.375%. The company returned to the market with a second issue in June 2007, this time a 20-year bond. The 2027 was for an amount of US$125mn and had an 8.125% coupon; it is still outstanding. Both issues were guaranteed by the government. Other corporates have since issued international bonds, including Clarendon Aluminium Production (CAPJAM) 8.5% 2021 US$200mn issued in November 2006 (which was subsequently exchanged in August 2013 into the 8.5% 2021 USD sovereign bond), Development Bank of Jamaica (DBKJ) 7.5% 2026 EUR204mn issued in February 2007 (still outstanding), and National Commercial Bank of Jamaica (NCBJAM). NCB issued its first bond (US$100mn FRN 2013) in 2006, which has matured, and a second bond (US$125mn FRN 2021) in May 2013, which is still outstanding.

Digicel (DLLTD), the regional telecoms operator, is now the main issuer, with the most and the biggest corporate bonds outstanding. It first issued in July 2005, a seven-year US$450mn bond with a 9.25% coupon, and has issued 12 bonds since. Its last issue was in 2015. It currently has four bonds outstanding, maturing annually over 2020–2023, which total US$5.2bn. This means that over 90% of total outstanding USD corporate bonds has been issued by one company.

Digicel Group Limited (DGL) announced on 31 August 2018 a USD3 billion exchange offer and consent solicitation involving a two year maturity extension of its (1) USD2 billion 8.25% 2020 Notes issued by DGL into new USD2 billion 8.25% 2022 Senior Notes to be issued by Digicel Group One Limited, an indirect subsidiary of DGL, and (2) USD1 billion 7.125% 2022 Notes issued by DGL into new USD1 billion 8.25% 2024 Senior Cash Pay/PIK Notes to be issued by Digicel Group Two Limited, a direct subsidiary of DGL and parent of Digicel Group One Limited. Cash interest on the new 2024 Notes will accrue at a rate of 7.125% and PIK interest on them will accrue at a rate of 1.125%. The consent solicitation intended to eliminate substantially all of the restrictive covenants and events of default contained in each existing DGL Indenture. The early tender deadline was due on 14 September 2018 and the offer was due to expire on 28 September 2018. According to media reports, two groups of bondholders organised to seek better terms.

Details for the two bonds subject to the exchange offer are shown below.

Digicel's outstanding corporate bonds

Issue date	*Amount issued*	*Amount outstanding*	*Maturity*	*Coupon*
Sep. 2012	US$2000mn	US$2000mn	Sep. 2020 (callable)	8.25%
Mar. 2013	US$1300mn	US$1300mn	Apr. 2021 (callable)	6%
Apr. 2014	US$1000mn	US$1000mn	Apr. 2022 (callable)	7.125%
Mar. 2015	US$925mn	US$925mn	Mar. 2023 (callable)	6.75%

Source: Bloomberg

Digicel bond
Digicel Group Ltd 8.25% 2020
Bloomberg ticker: DLLTD

Borrower	Digicel Group Ltd	
Issue date	19 September 2012	
Form	Eurobond	
ISIN	USG27631AD56	
Issue size	US$2000mn	
Amount outstanding	US$2000mn	
Currency	US dollar	
Denomination	US$200,000 minimum, US$1000 thereafter	
Amortisation	Callable (callable on and any time after the dates shown on the schedule below)	
Call schedule	30/9/2016	104.125
	30/9/2017	102.063
	30/9/2018	100.00
Final maturity date	30 September 2020	
Coupon/interest	8.25% paid semi-annually	
Day count	30/360	
Method of transfer	Euroclear/Clearstream/DTC	
Settlement period	T + 2 business days	
Governing law	New York	
Exchange	Berlin	
Joint lead manager	Barclays, Citi, Credit Suisse, Davy, Deutsche Bank, JP Morgan	

Digicel bond
Digicel Group Ltd 7.125% 2022
Bloomberg ticker: DLLTD

Borrower	Digicel Group Ltd	
Issue date	2 April 2014	
Form	Eurobond	
ISIN	USG27631AF05	
Issue size	US$1000mn	
Amount outstanding	US$1000mn	
Currency	US dollar	
Denomination	US$200,000 minimum, US$1000 thereafter	
Amortisation	Callable (callable on and any time after the dates shown on the schedule below)	
Call schedule	1/4/2017	105.344
	1/4/2018	103.563
	1/4/2019	101.781
	1/4/2020	100.000
Final maturity date	1 April 2022	
Coupon/interest	7.125% paid semi-annually	
Day count	30/360	
Method of transfer	Euroclear/Clearstream	
Settlement period	T + 2 business days	
Governing law	New York	
Exchange	Berlin	
Joint lead manager	Barclays, Citi, Credit Suisse, Davy, Deutsche Bank, JP Morgan	

Source: Bloomberg

Kazakhstan

Nominal GDP (US$mn, 2018)[a]		184,209
Population (thousand, 2018)[a]		18,463
GDP per capita (USD, 2018)[a]		9977
Credit ratings (long-term foreign currency)[b]	Fitch	BBB
	Moody's	Baa3
	S&P	BBB–

[a]IMF WEO October 2018
[b]As at end-September 2018

Country Summary

- President Nazarbayev has been the country's sole ruler since its independence from the Soviet Union in 1991. This has enabled a long period of stability and gradual economic development, but there is limited political freedom and elections have not been considered free or fair. Corruption is also seen as high.
- The economy is mainly based on primary products. Oil has traditionally dominated, accounting for more than 50% of exports and more than 40% of government revenues. Hydrocarbons (mainly oil, but also coal and gas) and metals together comprise c80% of goods' exports. But the government is now trying to diversify the economy, and the country scores favourably in the Doing Business rankings (36th). The largest landlocked country in the world, and the world's

Exotix Capital, *Exotix Developing Markets Guide*,
https://doi.org/10.1007/978-3-030-05867-8_25

ninth-largest country by land mass, Kazakhstan is expected to gain significantly from China's Belt and Road Initiative, given its importance as a link between East and West.

- Public debt has nearly doubled as a share of GDP over the past five years, as the government responded to the 2014 oil price fall (and lower Russian rouble) through fiscal stimulus, currency devaluation and support for banks. But at 27% of GDP, public debt remains low and some of the risk from a higher debt burden is mitigated by assets in the sovereign wealth funds. There is no modern history of sovereign debt restructuring, but the banking system has seen two rounds of restructurings (2009–2010 and 2012–2014), which led to some defaults and forced consolidation. Private external debt, including intercompany loans, is high, amounting to some 100% of GDP.

Economic data	*Avg*[a]	*2014*	*2015*	*2016*	*2017 (e)*	*2018 (f)*	*2019 (f)*
Real GDP growth	5.1	4.3	1.2	1.1	4.0	3.7	3.1
Inflation (annual average)	8.9	6.7	6.7	14.6	7.4	6.4	5.6
Current account (% of GDP)	−0.8	2.8	−2.8	−6.5	−3.4	−0.2	0.2
Reserves (US$bn, end-period)[b]	26.4	29.2	27.9	29.7	30.7	30.6[c]	–
Reserves/imports (months)[d]	4.6	4.3	5.6	6.6	5.8	–	–
Overall fiscal balance (% of GDP)[d]	1.8	2.5	−6.3	−5.3	−6.4	1.4	1.4
Currency (ticker)	Kazakh tenge (KZT)						
FX regime	De jure free float according to the authorities since 20 August 2015 when the tenge saw an immediate 25% devaluation against USD, and a peak devaluation of 52% in early 2016. De facto free float since, albeit in a narrow band. Prior to the float, the rate was largely fixed but adjustable against USD, having devalued in 2008 and 2014.						
Key exports	Hydrocarbons are the biggest export (62% of exports in 2017), mostly crude oil and gas condensates (55% of exports), along with refined products, coal and natural gas. Metals (17%) are the next biggest. Total goods exports fell from US$80bn in 2014 to US$37bn in 2016, recovering to US$49bn in 2017. Services exports were US$6.4bn in 2017, relatively unchanged since 2014.						

Source: IMF WEO Database, Haver, IMF Country Reports, OEC

[a]10-year average to 2016 unless otherwise stated

[b]Gross international reserves

[c]Latest figure, June 2018

[d]In months of the current year's imports of goods, services and income debit

[e]Overall government net lending

Key figures		*Party*	*Since*
President	Nursultan Nazarbayev	Nur Otan	1991
Prime minister	Bakytzhan Sagintayev	Nur Otan	Sep. 2016
Minister of finance	Bakhyt Sultanov	Nur Otan	Nov. 2013
Key opposition figure	Zharmakhan Tuyakbay	OSDP	2005
Governor of National Bank	Daniyar Akishev	–	Nov. 2015

Kazakhstan is a member of the Commonwealth of Independent States (CIS) after gaining independence from the USSR in 1991.

POLITICS

Executive power

The president is elected by popular vote to serve a five-year term (shortened from seven years and reduced to a two-term limit by constitutional amendment in 2007, although the first president is excluded from this limit). The prime minister and deputy prime minister are both appointed by the president. Power officially rests with the president, who is the commander in chief of the armed forces and can veto any bill passed by parliament.

Presidential term: Five years

Parliamentary term: Five years lower house, six years upper house

Legislature

The bicameral parliament consists of the 47-member Senate (15 seats appointed by the president, 32 elected by local assemblies; members serve six-year terms) and the Mazhilis (lower house), formed of 107 seats (nine members appointed by a presidential advisory body, 98 popularly elected to serve five-year terms).

Elections

Next due Presidential and legislative (lower house): 2020

Last legislative election[a] *(2016)*	*Seats*	*Last presidential (2015)*	*% of vote*
Nur Otan	84	Nursultan Nazarbayev (Nur Otan)	97.8
Democratic Party of Kazakhstan (Ak Zhol)	7	Turgun Syzdykov (CPPK)	1.6
Communist People's Party (CPPK)	7	Abelgazi Kusainov (Independent)	0.6
Presidential appointment	9		
Total	107	Total	100

[a]Lower house elections

People

66% of the population is ethnic Kazakh, 22% Russian, 3% Uzbek, 1.8% Ukrainian and 7.2% other. 70% are registered as Muslim and 26% Christian. The official state language is Kazakh, but the business language is Russian. Ethnic Kazakhs (mix of Turkic and Mongol) migrated to the region by the thirteenth century.

The area was conquered by Russia in the eighteenth century and became a Soviet Republic in 1936. Between 1939 and 1945, large amounts of Soviet heavy industry were moved from Russia to Kazakhstan to place it out of reach of the threat of Nazi Germany. Between 1953 and 1965, the Virgin Lands Campaign attempted to convert grassland into productive agricultural land with mixed success, leading to large amounts of immigration into the region. In 1991, the breakup of the Soviet Union gave Kazakhstan independence; importantly, the country took control of large amounts of mineral wealth. In 2001, the oil pipeline between Tengiz oil field and the port of Novorossiysk opened, the major route for oil to be exported out of Kazakhstan and the only pipeline in Russian territory not wholly owned by the Russian government. The private ownership of land was allowed after a 2003 bill was passed. The Kazakhstan-China oil pipeline became China's first direct oil source from Central Asia when it was completed in December 2005.

Opposition figure Zamanbek Nurkadilov, outspoken critic of President Nazarbayev, was found dead at his home in 2005. The following year, opposition figure Altynbek Sarsenbaiuky, his bodyguard and driver were shot dead outside Almaty. In 2007, Parliament voted to allow President Nazarbayev to stay in office for an unlimited number of terms, and to limit the terms of future presidents. That year, he fired his son-in-law Rakhat Aliyev in an apparent power struggle. The following year, Aliyev was found guilty of plotting a coup and sentenced to 20 years in jail.

The 2007 elections handed President Nazarbayev's Nur-Otan party all the seats in the lower house of parliament, however, international observers noted that, although there was an improvement in the fairness of the elections, they still did not meet international standards.

In 2009, Kazakhstan signed deals with France worth US$6bn, mainly regarding energy. A natural gas pipeline to China opened in 2009. Kazakhstan became the first former Soviet state to take the chair of the Organisation of Security and Co-operation in Europe (OSCE), a regional security group and humanitarian agency, in 2010. This was despite widespread criticism of Kazakhstan's own democratic and rights record.

In May 2014, Kazakhstan entered the Eurasian Customs Union with Russia and Belarus (came into force in January 2015), to create a shared market and integrate economic policies. Possible succession planning was suspected when the president made his daughter Dariga deputy prime minister in September 2015; a year later she was instead appointed to the Senate. In March 2017, President Nazarbayev endorsed constitutional changes transferring presidential powers over to lawmakers and the cabinet.

Debt

	2012	*2017*
External debt ratios (%)		
Total external debt/GDP	65.8	104.1
Public external debt/GDP	2.6	8.1
Private external debt/GDP[a]	63.2	96.1
Total external debt/exports of goods and services	149.2	300.5
External debt service ratio (all)[b]	36.5	66.4[c]
Public debt ratios (%)		
Public domestic debt/GDP	10.1	17.3
Public debt/GDPd[d]	12.7	26.7

Source: Haver, National Bank, Ministry of Finance, IMF, World Bank IDS, Exotix

[a]Including intercompany lending

[b]IDS figures

[c]IDS figure is for 2016

[d]Note that public external and public domestic debt do not sum to total public debt due to differences in methodologies

Kazakhstan's total external debt was US$167.5bn at end-2017 (including intercompany lending), according to Haver (based on BPM6 methodology). Only c8% of this (just US$13bn) was owed by the public sector (defined in BPM6 as general government and the central bank), while 92% (US$154bn) was owed by the private sector (including intercompany lending and guarantees). In fact, intercompany lending itself amounted to US$104.5bn (c60% of the total), so that, excluding intercompany loans, private external debt was US$50bn and total external debt was just US$63bn. Total external debt (including intercompany lending) rose by 22% in US dollar terms since 2012 while nominal GDP also fell by 23% over the same period, due to currency devaluation, so that total external debt as a share of GDP rose from 66% in 2012 to 104% in 2017. Public external debt was 8% of GDP and private external debt (including intercompany lending) was 96% in 2017. Excluding intercompany lending, private external debt was more stable, at c30% of GDP, and total external debt rose from 33% of GDP in 2012 to 39% in 2017. Given the 40% fall in exports of goods and services over this period, led by the fall in goods (mainly oil) exports, total external debt as a share of exports of goods and services doubled over this period, standing at 300% in 2017. Public external debt alone, however, rose from just 6% of exports of goods and services in 2012 to 23% in 2017. The external debt service ratio rose from 37% to 66% (2016), although this is dominated by private sector debt service. The public external debt service ratio rose from only 0.4% in 2012 to just 1.5% in 2017.

The creditor composition of external debt as at end-2017 is summarised in the table below. The creditor breakdown of public external debt is based on public finance data rather than BPM6 methodology and, hence, the two approaches give slightly different totals, US$13.749bn on the former basis and US$12.994bn under BPM6. That difference notwithstanding, the breakdown of public external debt shows that commercial and multilateral creditors are the biggest creditor groups, together accounting for over 96% of the debt, and split roughly evenly between the two. Specifically, the eurobonds—with US$6.5bn outstanding at end-2017—are now the single biggest creditor group (around half of public external debt itself). This is followed by the World Bank (c30% of public external debt). Indeed, 80% of public external debt is now owed by just these two creditors. Most of the remaining multilateral debt is owed to the Asian Development Bank (ADB). Bilaterals accounted for just 4% of public external debt, and 96% of this is owed to the Japan Bank for International Cooperation (JBIC). Private external non-guaranteed debt was US$153.2bn. US$25.2bn of external debt (16% of GDP) was owed by state-owned enterprises in mid-2017, based on official figures.

Total public debt (government and state debt, including guarantees) was 26.7% of GDP in 2017 (cUS$43bn), based on public finance data from Haver and using IMF WEO GDP, around double the ratio in 2012. The increase was due to a sharp rise in the level of debt in local currency terms (up around 3.5 times). In USD terms, the debt was up 1.5 times, while nominal GDP also fell because of currency devaluation. The public debt/GDP ratio has risen over time (it averaged 7% of GDP over 2005–2008), partly due to fiscal stimulus following the global financial crisis, lower demand from trading partners, support for the banking sector and a lower oil price from mid-2014. The president initiated another domestic stimulus programme in November 2014, entitled Nurly Zhol (Bright Path), a US$9bn plan to help diversify the economy away from the oil sector and towards agribusiness, manufacturing, trade and logistics, tourism, information technology and finance, while also modernising infrastructure (roads, railways and ports). Most of the recent increase in the debt burden took place over 2014–2015, when most of the currency adjustment took place. The debt burden rose then from 15% in 2014 to 23% in 2015, and has risen more gradually since then. The figures imply public domestic debt rose from 10.1% of GDP in 2012 to 17.3% in 2017 (based on public external debt, including guarantees, under the public finance methodology rather than BPM6).

Kazakhstan also has considerable assets in two different sovereign wealth funds, in addition to its central bank reserves, which mitigates, to some extent, risks stemming from the rise in the gross public debt burden. The National Oil Fund (NOF; or, latterly, the National Fund for the Republic of Kazakhstan, NFRK) was established in 2000 as a stabilization fund and a savings fund. It receives all oil-related revenue. The government has accumulated considerable savings in the NFRK since 2005. Fund assets stood at US$58bn at end-June 2018 (according to Haver), some 32% of projected 2018 WEO GDP, up from US$40bn in 2011, although this is c25% below its peak in August 2014 before the decline in the oil price took hold. The limited accumulation over the past few years is probably due to lower oil revenues and drawdowns. The fund ensures that Kazakhstan's public sector, but not the country as a whole, is a net external creditor. Kazakhstan's other sovereign wealth fund is Samruk Kazyna (SK), a joint stock company, that was established in 2008. It is solely owned by the state (via the Ministry of Finance). The fund is one of the biggest shareholders in the country and is essentially a holding company for state-owned enterprises. It runs the national rail and postal service, the state oil and gas firm KazMunayGas and the state uranium company, among others. According to its website, its total assets amount to US$78bn, although Exotix believes their nature means it is unlikely they should be considered as liquid assets for reserves or net debt purposes.

Composition of external debt

External debt by creditor[a] (end-2017)	*Nominal amount outstanding (US$mn)*	*Share of total (%)*
Public and publicly guaranteed external debt	**14,308**	**8.5**
o/w Guarantees	1314	0.8
o/w Public sector external debt[b]	12,994	7.8
Multilateral creditors	6537	3.9
World Bank IBRD	4016	2.4
ADB	2164	1.3
EBRD	214	0.1
IsDB	143	0.1
Bilateral creditors	512	0.3
Japan (JBIC)	489	0.3
Germany (export credit agency)	12	0.0
Kuwait Fund for Arab Economic Development	6	0.0
Abu Dhabi Fund for Development	4	0.0

(*continued*)

(continued)

External debt by creditor[a] (end-2017)	*Nominal amount outstanding (US$mn)*	*Share of total (%)*
Saudi Arabia Fund for Development	1	0.0
Commercial creditors	6700	4.0
Eurobonds	6500	3.9
Banks	200	0.1
Private sector (non-guaranteed) external debt[c]	**153,177**	**91.5**
Total external debt	**167,485**	**100.0**

Source: Haver, Ministry of Finance, Exotix

[a]Totals based on BPM6 methodology

[b]Creditor composition of public external debt excluding guarantees is based on public finance data and not BPM6 methodology, so therefore totals do not match (total is US$13.748bn on the former basis and US$12.994bn on the latter)

[c]Including intercompany lending

Rescheduling History

Kazakhstan has not defaulted on any payment of its public external debt and there is no modern history of restructuring since its independence from the Soviet Union in 1991. This is in part because it started with little, or no, debt after Russia assumed all the former Soviet Union's assets and liabilities under a 1994 zero option agreement with the ex-Soviet Republics. Since then (until recently), there has been strong fiscal management, helped by extensive foreign asset positions, while large oil surpluses obviated the need to borrow. However, the economic downturn of 2008–2009 led to a full-scale domestic banking crisis. Four major banks, BTA, Alliance Bank, Temir Bank and Astana Finance all faced considerable liquidity and solvency issues as bonds and loans came to maturity, forcing them to restructure their liabilities in 2010 (see banks section below). Owing to the government's ample resources and low public debt, the authorities were able to respond swiftly to the crisis and the demand stimulus imparted by the government's "National Programme of Forced Industrial and Innovative Development of Kazakhstan for 2010–14" helped to boost economic activity, although problems for some banks resurfaced in 2012–2014, as pre-existing vulnerabilities were exposed, and the currency devaluation in early 2014 followed by the oil price fall later that year took their toll.

Relations with Multilateral Creditors

Kazakhstan has had only four IMF programmes, the last of which dates back nearly 20 years to 1999–2000 when it secured a US$453mn Extended Fund Facility (EFF) to support economic growth. The original three-year facility was completed early by May 2000 with the repayment of US$385mn in one instalment. In the same period, it was lent funds by the World Bank, European Bank for Reconstruction and Development (EBRD) and ADB. Kazakhstan has not had any programme or financial aid from the IMF since its 1999 EFF; however, the World Bank provided a US$1bn facility to Kazakhstan in response to the global financial crisis in 2008–2009, on top of outstanding loans. The IMF has provided technical assistance to Kazakhstan in all areas of economic policy since 1993, including monetary policy framework enhancement, public financial management and banking issues in recent years.

Kazakhstan continues to engage with the IMF through the Article IV process and is supposed to be on a regular 12-month cycle. The most recent Article IV (the 2017 Article IV) was concluded by the IMF Board in April 2017 and the staff report was published the following month. A staff mission to conduct the 2018 Article IV was concluded at end-June 2018. In the accompanying press release, the IMF noted that Kazakhstan needed to seize the opportunity provided by the strengthening economy and move decisively with reforms in order to transform the economy, support the development of the private sector, avoid reliance on state subsidies and pursue fiscal consolidation after several years of fiscal stimulus and significant support for the banking sector in 2017. At the time of writing, the Board review for the 2018 Article IV had not been taken place.

IMF programmes

Date	*Arrangements*	*Comments*
1994–1995	SBA	Stand-by agreement to support macroeconomic stabilisation. Overall budget balance however was not kept within the programme target of 4.6%, instead stretching to 7% of GDP.
1995–1996	SBA	12-month agreement of US$290mn to support economic reform programmes, mostly privatisation policies.
1996–1999	EFF	Three-year facility of US$446mn aimed at completing privatisation reforms, reform of the financial sector, overhauling state and public sector.
1999–2002 (completed May 2000)	EFF	Three-year facility of US$453mn in response to external shocks of 1998 and the need to maintain long term macroeconomic stability and growth. Went undrawn.

Source: IMF. Kazakhstan joined the IMF in 1992

Multilateral creditors include the International Bank for Reconstruction and Development (IBRD; owed US$6537mn), the ADB (owed US$2164mn), the EBRD (US$214mn) and the Islamic Development Bank (IsDB; owed US$143mn), as of end-2017. The World Bank has 13 active projects in the country, with total commitments of US$3.8bn. By commitment amount, the two largest projects (with a combined commitment of US$3.2bn) are both for the development of roads. Due to poor quality, the government announced plans in 2013 to improve 80% of all roads by 2020. The ADB's strategy in Kazakhstan until 2021 focuses on economic diversification, improving governance, regional integration and macroeconomic resilience. The ADB provided a US$500mn counter-cyclical loan to Kazakhstan following its sudden need for external financing in 2007–2008 during the global financial crisis. Another counter-cyclical loan for US$1bn was approved in 2015 following the oil price decline. The EBRD has also played a significant role in Kazakhstan, with a cumulative investment of EUR7.8bn across 246 projects, with the value of current projects amounting to EUR2.5bn. It has 122 active projects. The EBRD focuses on diversification, private sector development and sustainable energy.

Paris Club and Bilateral Creditors

Kazakhstan has undergone no Paris Club restructuring agreements.

Kazakhstan has benefited from various bilateral loans, with Japan its biggest single bilateral creditor; otherwise, such lending has tended to be small in size. Japan was owed US$489mn at end-2017, through the JBIC while Germany was owed US$12mn. Other bilateral creditors include sovereign development funds of Saudi Arabia (owed US$1mn), Kuwait (owed US$6mn), and UAE (Abu Dhabi, owed US$4mn). Kazakhstan has tended to be viewed favourably by bilateral creditors due to its strong levels of natural resources and its subsequent export capacity, although bilateral debt stocks have been declining, while multilateral and commercial debt stocks have increased.

China is not currently a significant bilateral creditor, according to official figures, although Kazakhstan, the largest landlocked country in the world, and the world's ninth largest country by land mass, is expected to gain significantly from China's Belt and Road Initiative, given its geographical importance as a link between East and West. China's land strategy runs through Kazakhstan and significant investments have been made to develop the country as a transit corridor. This includes the US$3.5bn Khorgos Gateway, a dry port on its eastern border with China, in which COSCO Shipping and Lianyungang Port Holding have acquired stakes, according to PwC.

Sovereign Commercial Debt

Kazakhstan has not defaulted or undertaken any kind of restructuring on its sovereign commercial debt in modern times. That is probably in part because it inherited low debt after its independence. Kazakhstan Exim Bank failed to make a payment on a loan facility that had been guaranteed by the government in 2000, although the government fulfilled the payment obligation under the guarantee. Its first eurobonds were issued for US$200mn in 1996, when the country had a BB– or equivalent rating, followed by US$350mn in 1997, US$300mn in 1999 and US$350mn in 2000, and each of these issues was repaid in full at maturity (1999, 2002, 2004 and 2007, respectively). Kazakhstan later gained investment grade status in 2004 from S&P and Fitch, which it still retains. Moody's awarded Kazakhstan investment grade in 2002, but this was withdrawn in 2007, although it reassigned a provisional investment grade rating in 2014.

Kazakhstan has six sovereign eurobonds outstanding, with four denominated in USD and two in EUR, amounting to a total of US$7.7bn nominal (equivalent) as of November 2018. After a 14-year break in issuance following the 2000 bond issue, Kazakhstan returned to the market in 2014. Kazakhstan issued a dual tranche US$1.5bn 10-year bullet bond (2024 maturity) with a 3.875% coupon and a US$1bn 30-year bullet bond (2044 maturity) with a 4.875% coupon in October 2014. The 10-year bond was priced at 98.387 to yield 4.07% (spread 165.5 bps) while the 30-year bond was priced at 96.324 to yield 5.12% (spread 200.6 bps). Despite the economic, export and fiscal dependency on oil, and a falling oil price at the time, the combined order book exceeded US$11bn. The authorities planned the issue to attract foreign capital and to lower the cost of borrowing. Kazakhstan returned nearly a year later, in July 2015, with another dual tranche sale, comprising a US$2.5bn 10-year bullet bond (2025 maturity) with a 5.125% coupon (priced at 98.976) and a US$1.5bn 30-year bullet bond (2045 maturity) with a 6.5% coupon (priced at 99.049). The combined order book reached almost US$10bn.

After a three-year break, Kazakhstan returned to the market in early November 2018 with a dual tranche EUR-denominated bond sale, a EUR525mn five-year bond (1.55% 2023) and EUR525mn 10-year bond (2.375% 2028). Both bonds were issued at par and have annual coupons. The authorities had intended to issue a single 10-year EUR bond, with initial price thoughts in the 2.625–2.75% area, with the additional five-year tranche generated by reverse enquiry. The combined order book had grown to cEUR4bn by the time of final guidance, before falling to EUR3.3bn when the transaction was launched on 5 November. The shorter tenor enjoyed significant participation from US investors. All six outstanding eurobonds are of the RegS/144A series and are summarised below. A full description of the 2025 maturity is also shown. The National Bank of Kazakhstan has also been looking into using blockchain technology to facilitate potential future security issues.

In April 2018, the government said it was planning a sovereign eurobond issue denominated in tenge this year, according to Bloomberg reports. EUR and CNY bonds were also being considered. The government was also reported in January 2018 to be working with Clearstream in order to give international investors access to local currency government debt. On 30 July, Clearstream announced that it had extended its clearing capability to include the tenge for Kazakh government bonds and National Bank notes, thereby offering easier access into the country for foreign investors.

Kazakhstan's outstanding international bonds

Description	*Size*	*Maturity type*	*Issue date*
EUR 1.55% due 2023	EUR525mn	Bullet	Nov. 2018
USD 3.875% due 2024	US$1500mn	Bullet	Oct. 2014
USD 5.125% due 2025	US$2500mn	Bullet	Jul. 2015
EUR 2.375% due 2028	EUR525mn	Bullet	Nov. 2018
USD 4.875% due 2044	US$1000mn	Bullet	Oct. 2014
USD 6.5% due 2045	US$1500mn	Bullet	Jul. 2015

Source: Bloomberg

Kazakhstan bond
Kazakhstan 5.125% 2025
Bloomberg ticker: KAZAKS

Borrower	Government of Kazakhstan
Issue date	21 July 2015
Form	Eurobond
ISIN	XS1263054519
Issue size	US$2500mn
Currency	US dollar
Denomination	US$200,000 and US$1000 thereafter
Amortisation	Bullet
Final maturity date	21 July 2025
Coupon/interest	5.125% per annum, paid semi-annually January and July
Day count	30/360
Method of transfer	Euroclear/Clearstream/LSE Reportable
Settlement period	T + 2

(*continued*)

(continued)

Kazakhstan bond *Kazakhstan 5.125% 2025* *Bloomberg ticker: KAZAKS*	
Governing law	English law
Managers	Citi, JP Morgan

Source: Bloomberg

Kazakhstan Banks

The banking sector has changed markedly over the past decade, with at least two rounds of debt restructurings and various consolidations through mergers following the 2009 banking crisis. Today, there are just a few outstanding USD bonds that trade, issued by Halyk Bank (which has assumed the liabilities of Kazkommertsbank, KKB), ForteBank (formerly Alliance Bank), ATF and Bank CenterCredit.

- Halyk Bank (HSBKKZ) has two USD bonds outstanding—a US$500mn 7.25% 2021 bond issued in January 2011 and a US$750mn 5.5% 2022 bond issued in December 2012. The 2022 bond was originally issued by Bank TuranAlem (BTA), a single USD bond it issued as part of its second restructuring in 2012. It was subsequently assumed by KKB, and then by Halyk. Halyk Savings Bank issued four other USD bonds, over 2004–2008, each of which has matured, with its most recent maturity in May 2017 of US$700mn. KKB had two USD bonds outstanding before being assumed by Halyk Bank. One of these bonds (a US$300mn bond issued in 2011) matured in May 2018. The other was the 2022 bond. KKB had issued a number of bonds in the past, being a regular issuer, albeit in US$100mn–500mn sizes over 1998–2006.
- ForteBank (ALLIBK) was formed from a merger of Alliance Bank and Temirbank with ForteBank in 2015. There are two USD bonds outstanding—US$63mn of a 14% 2022 bond, originally issued by Temirbank, and US$192mn of an 11.75% 2024 bond, originally issued by Alliance Bank, which, like BTA, restructured its liabilities twice in a relatively short space of time (2010 and 2014). The 2024s were issued in December 2014, its first regular issue since its 2010 restructuring. Alliance Bank had previously issued a number of bonds of varying sizes (US$100mn–350mn) over 2005–2006, its first issue being US$150mn in 2005. It created several instruments in its 2010

restructuring, with the two main USD bonds (US$615mn 10.5% March 2017 and US$219mn 4.7% March 2020) being restructured a second time in 2014.

- ATF (ATFBP) now has just one US$100mn perpetual security outstanding. ATF Bank issued six senior USD bonds, of at least US$100mn, in 2004–2006, and the last senior bond maturity was in November 2016.
- Bank CenterCredit (CCBNKZ) has just one USD perpetual security still outstanding, although the total amount outstanding is now just under US$81mn. Bank CenterCredit previously had a series of senior USD-denominated bonds. The largest of these was a US$500mn bond, which matured in January 2014.

2009–2010 Bank Restructurings

Deep vulnerabilities in the Kazakhstan banking system were exposed by the global financial crisis, and the after-effects still reverberate in some ways today. The country experienced rapid growth over 2000–2007, as high commodity prices helped fuel a credit boom. Domestic lending to the private sector grew too quickly, and too fast, largely concentrated in the construction and real estate sectors. Between 2005 and 2007, Kazakhstan's banks borrowed the equivalent of 44% of GDP from abroad, with a substantial part lent to non-tradable sectors. However, as financing conditions tightened during the global financial crisis, banks lost access to foreign capital, forcing them to delever. The tenge was devalued by 20% in early 2009, restoring competitiveness with Russia, but exacerbating problems of creditworthiness for the private sector, as FX loans accounted for 45% of total lending. Non-performing loans (NPLs) increased rapidly from 3.5% in mid-2008 to 26% in mid-2010. The subsequent economic downturn led ultimately to bank bailouts and debt restructurings, starting in 2009.

The boom was typified by events at BTA, Kazakhstan's largest bank before the 2009 crisis, and its biggest casualty. The bank had borrowed a total of US$5.3bn in USD bonds over 2001–2008, issuing in varying sizes (ranging from US$100mn to US$1bn), and Western banks reportedly lent it over US$10bn during the oil and gas boom. BTA's foreign loans had been used to finance real estate projects in Russia and Ukraine and foreign business ventures with no clear business plan, some based in Seychelles, the British Virgin Islands and the UK, allegedly with little collateral. BTA subsequently hired investigators as corruption was suspected.

The authorities were ultimately forced to intervene in several banks, seek a restructuring of their external liabilities and introduce new banking legislation related to financial stability and bank restructurings. The government took majority stakes in three large banks (Alliance, Temirbank and BTA) and minority stakes in another two (KKB and Halyk Bank). BTA and Alliance both had to sell substantial stakes to the SK sovereign wealth fund in return for short-term liquidity. However, this was not enough to resolve their liquidity problems, and both subsequently defaulted on their debt in April 2009. Astana Finance and Temirbank subsequently defaulted too, in May 2009 and November 2009. Halyk and KKB did not default. ATF Bank and Bank CenterCredit—which had significant foreign shareholders—also did not default.

BTA, Alliance Bank, Astana Finance and Temir consequently all underwent restructuring of their external obligations. In August 2010, BTA completed a multi-billion-dollar debt restructuring, in which SK became an 81.5% shareholder. The restructuring reduced BTA's debt by 75%, from US$16.7bn to US$4.2bn. BTA issued a number of bonds in August 2010, comprising KZT-, EUR- and USD-denominated bonds (tiny scraps of un-swapped bonds remain outstanding, which have stayed in default). The government also injected US$4.5bn in cash. Alliance Bank restructured US$4.5bn, lessening its debt load by around US$3.5bn, in April 2010. Astana and Temir were both subject to smaller restructurings of around US$1bn. The table below summaries the key features of the three largest restructurings.

Government support for the banks was sizeable and came in a number of forms. The government's capital injections into the Kazakhstan banking sector are estimated to have totalled 6.4% of Kazakhstan's GDP in 2009. The total capital injection was estimated at US$6.8bn as at 1 September 2010, with BTA Bank being the main beneficiary, receiving US$1.4bn. Following the restructuring, SK had majority shares in BTA (81.5%), Temirbank (79.9%) and Alliance Bank (67%), and minority shares of KKB (21.3%) and Halyk Bank (20.9%). Sberbank, the largest bank in Russia, was reported by local press as interested in acquiring BTA, though this never happened. Government support for the banks also came from public entities placing deposits in the troubled banks by repatriating funds from abroad and reallocating from perceived stronger banks. Sectors where NPLs were extensive (mainly real estate and construction) received preferential funding. In addition, the Distressed Asset Fund was set up to remove overdue obligations from banks' balance sheets. That said, the perception at the time was that government support was insufficient—bank bonds still needed to be restructured, and the government did not 'sacrifice itself' for the banks like Russia, and others, did.

Key features of main 2010 bank restructurings

Bank	*Amount defaulted (principle & accrued)*	*Restructuring terms (haircut)*	*New issues*	*Status*
BTA	US$16,944mn	Senior Package 1—senior debt instrument (bonds, bank loans) and certain non-ECA trade finance. Offered in return a composition of cash, senior bonds, subordinated debt, equity and recovery notes. US$9036mn Senior Package 2—ECAs, other official government sector creditors and non-ECA eligible trade finance. Offered senior original issue discount bonds, sub debt, equity and recovery notes. US$954mn Senior Package 3—all non-ECA eligible trade finance debt offered Senior debt, Subordinate, equity and recovery notes. US$1037mn Junior Package 1—subordinated debt owed to Kazakh pension funds offered rollover sub debt at 8% pa interest. US$202mn Junior Package 2—all other sub debt and perpetual bonds offered equity at 4.5% of total. US$1271mn Samruk-Kazyna—includes deposits and sub debt plus accrued interest offered equity at 81.5% of total. US$4446mn	BTA Bank JSC 10.75% Step-up coupon 2018 USD, Senior Unsecured—US$2.08bn BTA Bank JSC 14.75% Step-up coupon 2018 KZT Senior Unsecured—KZT32.6bn BTA Bank JSC 0% Variable 2020 USD Bonds. Recovery Note—US$5.2bn BTA Bank JSC 3.14% Fixed 2021 OID EUR Unsecured—EUR437.1mn BTA Bank JSC 3.7% Variable 2011 OID USD Unsecured—US$384.8mn BTA Bank JSC 6.75% Fixed 2025 EUR Subordinated—EUR28.2mn BTA Bank JSC 7.2% Fixed 2025 USD Subordinate—US$496.6mn BTA Bank JSC 11.2% Fixed 2025 KZT Subordinated—KZT7.4bn BTA Bank JSC 8% Fixed 2030 KZT Subordinated—KZT28bn	No longer outstanding

Alliance Bank	US$4606mn	Option 1—senior debt fixed buy back with haircut of 77.5% (78.5% for Islamic lenders). Option 2—senior debt discounted rollover with 50% haircut Option 3—senior debt; 0% haircut replacement with a 10Y maturity Option 4—all subordinated debt, 0% haircut Option 5—allocation of 33% preferential shares with an average 77% haircut	Senior: ALLIBK '17s USD Discounts 10.5%. Amortised. 10.7% YTM—US$615mn Senior: ALLIBK '20s USD PARS. 2.7% PIK, 2.0% cash before 2017, after '17 Libor +8.5%. Amortised. 12% YTM—US$219mn Senior: ALLIBK '17s Discounts KZT 14.50%. 15.9% YTM—US$967mn Senior: ALLIBK '20s USD PARS 4.25% PIK, 4.75% cash to 2017, after 2017 12.5% to 2020. 17.3% YTM—US$1249mn ALLIBK Recovery Notes 3.4% PIK to 2017, after '17 5.8% cash to 2020. Amortised. 978,059 units.	No longer outstanding
Temir	US$1600mn	Cash—20% cash Senior bonds—7.87% of new international 12-year eurobonds with a total outstanding amount of US$60.75mn Common equity—creditors receive 20% of outstanding shares. Total number of outstanding shares is 19,472mn	Temir 17 s 14% senior USD—US$60.75mn Temir GDRs—derivative of equity in USD	Temir security is now ALLIBK 22 s

Source: Exotix, Bloomberg

2012–2014 Bank Restructurings

Despite the restructuring of some of these banks' external liabilities, they continued to face difficulties as the deceleration in growth, the collapse of real estate prices and the devaluation led to a significant build-up of NPLs. Issues with repayments resurfaced for some banks, and subsequent restructurings forced further consolidation in the sector. BTA and Alliance both underwent second restructurings, in 2012 and 2014, respectively.

In January 2012, BTA's chairman announced that it could not survive without a second round of debt restructuring and officially defaulted for the second time in three years on 17 January, after missing the 10-day grace period to make a US$160mn coupon payment. This came after BTA had made coupon payments of over US$150mn in July 2011, and repaid a US$175mn loan instalment in September 2011, as part of its 2010 debt restructuring. On 26 January 2012, shareholders voted against a debt restructuring plan, although BTA was majority-owned by the sovereign wealth fund. However, in October 2012, BTA announced that all creditors had agreed to a non-binding term sheet, except for one creditor. This would restructure existing debt for cash and new notes with a nominal amount of US$750mn, with a 5.5% coupon and maturity in 2022 (now with Halyk as obligor). Senior noteholders received US$957.8mn in cash and US$88.8mn in new notes, while recovery unit holders received US$660.2mn in cash and US$61.2mn in new notes. SK also agreed to convert its deposits into equity and issue a US$1.592bn subordinated loan. The restructuring plan was approved on 5 December 2012, with 93.8% creditor approval. The restructuring was completed in February 2013. The bank's financial indebtedness was reduced from US$11.1bn to US$3.3bn, and its average debt maturity was extended from three to 12 years.

In late 2014, Alliance Bank completed a US$1.2bn debt restructuring, its second restructuring in four years, after defaulting on 25 March 2014 on payments on its USD discounts due 2017 and pars due 2020, which had been issued in 2010. The restructuring included cancellation or restructuring of all outstanding claims and saw SK put KZT220bn (US$1.2bn) of 10-year special deposits into the bank in support. Creditors received cash, shares and/or newly issued bonds with a principal of KZT43.5bn (US$237mn). The CEO announced 90.51% shareholder approval and that the bank's debt would be reduced from US$1.2bn to US$600mn. Alliance merged with Temirbank and ForteBank, after which the combined group was called ForteBank JSC.

In February 2014, President Nazarbayev instructed SK to sell its stakes in Kazakhstan's commercial banks so as to withdraw the state's participation in the sector. SK was incentivised to increase the value of BTA to recover its investment in the bank by ensuring its return to profit. In May 2014, Samruk-Kazyna sold all of its shares in Temirbank and part of its shares (a 16% stake) in Alliance Bank to Bulat Utemuratov. Utemuratov took control of Alliance Bank in late 2014. In mid-2014, SK sold a 97.33% stake in BTA Bank to KKB (47.57%) and K. Rakishev (47.57%). The deal valued BTA at US$1bn. KKB struggled with worsening asset quality and constrained liquidity. It was reportedly granted an emergency loan in December 2016, although management denied negotiating with the government for a bailout.

Recent Developments

Halyk commenced negotiations to purchase KKB in autumn 2016, initially without state involvement. A framework agreement was signed in June 2017, and Halyk subsequently agreed to acquire 96.81% of KKB ordinary shares for KZT2 (i.e. US$0.006), and to inject KZT185bn in new capital into KKB. Halyk purchased ordinary shares held by Kenges Rakishev (who purchased shares held by certain other parties) and by SK. The agreement was conditional on the acquisition of "certain assets and loans from BTA Bank" by Kazakhstan's fund for problem loans, which would enable BTA repay the KZT2.4tn loan from KKB. It was also conditional on regulatory approvals. These conditions were met, and, although Halyk management initially stated that KKB would "remain a standalone subsidiary", both banks subsequently agreed to merge, with Halyk becoming the legal successor of KKB. Following the initial transaction, Almex Holding, which is the largest single shareholder in Halyk, boosted KKB's capital by KZT65.2bn. As a result, Almex Holding now owns just over 25% of KKB ordinary shares. The deal between Halyk Bank and KKB created the largest bank in Central Asia, holding around 40% of Kazakhstan's financial assets. The transfer of property, assets and liabilities from KKB to Halyk was completed in July 2018.

Elsewhere in the Kazakhstan banking sector, there has been significant support from the state to banks, including ATF Bank and ForteBank, in the form of subordinated capital. This support did not trigger debt restructurings at those banks—a signal that the state's stance towards the banking sector has changed.

A summary of the outstanding Kazakh bank issues is shown in the table below, and details for the two Halyk bank bonds and the Alliance bank bond are also provided.

Selected bank bond issues

BB ticker	*Name*	*Issue date*	*Maturity date*	*Issued amount (mn)*	*Outstanding amount (mn)*	*Currency*
ALLIBK	ForteBank JSC	30 June 2010	30 June 2022	60.75	63.147	USD
ALLIBK	ForteBank JSC	15 December 2014	15 December 2024	236.57	192.213	USD
ATFBP	ATF Capital BV	11 October 2006	Perpetual	100	100	USD
CCBNKZ	Bank CenterCredit JSC	3 March 2006	Perpetual	100	80.846	USD
DBKAZ	Development Bank of Kazakhstan JSC	6 March 2005	6 March 2020	100	100	USD
DBKAZ	Development Bank of Kazakhstan JSC	14 December 2017	14 December 2020	298.289	298.289	KZT
DBKAZ	Development Bank of Kazakhstan JSC	12 October 2012	12 October 2022	1425	1264	USD
DBKAZ	Development Bank of Kazakhstan JSC	5 April 2018	5 April 2023	303.099	303.099	KZT
DBKAZ	Development Bank of Kazakhstan JSC	23 March 2006	23 March 2026	150	106.666	USD
HSBKKZ	Halyk Savings Bank of Kazakhstan JSC	28 January 2011	28 January 2021	500	500	USD
HSBKKZ	Halyk Savings Bank of Kazakhstan JSC	21 December 2012	21 December 2022	750	750	USD

Source: Bloomberg

Halyk Savings Bank eurobond
Halyk Savings Bank 7.25% 01/2021
Bloomberg ticker: HSBKKZ

Borrower	Halyk Savings Bank of Kazakhstan JSC
Issue date	28 January 2011
Form	Eurobond
ISIN	XS0583796973
Issue size	US$500mn
Currency	US dollar
Denomination	Min. piece of US$200,000, increments thereafter of US$1000
Amortisation	Bullet
Final maturity date	28 January 2021
Coupon/interest	7.25% semi-annual
Method of transfer	Euroclear/Clearstream, FED FUNDS, LSE Reportable
Joint lead managers	Citi, DB, Halyk Finance

Source: Bloomberg

Halyk Savings Bank eurobond
Halyk Savings Bank 5.5% 12/2022
Bloomberg ticker: HSBKKZ

Borrower	Halyk Savings Bank of Kazakhstan JSC (formerly KKB, originally issued as part of the second BTAS restructuring in 2012)
Issue date	21 December 2012
Form	Eurobond
ISIN	XS0867478124
Issue size	US$750mn
Currency	US dollar
Denomination	Min. piece of US$1, increments thereafter of US$1
Amortisation	Callable
Final maturity date	21 December 2022
Coupon/interest	5.5% semi-annual
Method of transfer	Euroclear/Clearstream

Source: Bloomberg

Alliance Bank eurobond
Alliance Bank 11.75% 12/2024
Bloomberg ticker: ALLIBK

Borrower	ForteBank JSC
Issue date	15 December 2014
Form	Eurobond

(*continued*)

(continued)

Alliance Bank eurobond *Alliance Bank 11.75% 12/2024* *Bloomberg ticker: ALLIBK*	
ISIN	XS1153772725
Issue size	US$236.57mn
Amount outstanding	US$192.21mn
Currency	US dollar
Denomination	Min. piece of US$1, increments thereafter of US$1
Amortisation	Call/sink
Final maturity date	15 December 2024
Coupon/interest	11.75% semi-annual
Method of transfer	Euroclear/Clearstream
Agents	Bank of New York Mellon London; Luxembourg SA

Source: Bloomberg

Corporate Bond Market

Kazakhstan's private sector debt represents a high proportion of total external debt as the country's generally stable investment grade rating has opened the market to corporates. The external debt burden of the private sector accounted for 91% of total external debt in mid-2017, or 99% of GDP. The total private external debt (including intercompany lending) was US$155bn, of which US$6.2bn was owed by banks. However, data for private sector external debt (on the official BPM6 basis) may include borrowing from state-owned or government-related companies (without government guarantees), which may therefore overstate private debt. For instance, the foreign currency segment of the Kazakh corporate bond market is dominated by issuance from government entities and government-owned companies. Kazakh corporates had 254 bond issues, according to Bloomberg, in December 2017, of which most were domestic issues, but 48 were denominated in foreign currencies, 34 of which were in USD. Issuance of local currency-denominated bonds have been on the rise lately.

In contrast to the banks, Kazakhstan has seen few corporate bond defaults. One notable exception is Tristan Oil, an exploration and production oil business that lost its core assets in 2010 after the authorities brought criminal charges against the company's subsidiaries and their senior executives. The company challenged the government's decision to take over its assets in international courts. The company's US$530mn zero coupon bond due 1 January 2016 is in default, after it went unpaid at maturity. The bond itself came out of a restructuring in 2013 of its then US$531mn bonds due 2012, which fell into default in 2010. Holders are entitled to receive 70% of arbitration proceeds should the company succeed in its legal action against Kazakhstan.

The total amount outstanding of Kazakhstan corporate bonds (hard currency) is of the order US$13.5bn. A summary of the main outstanding issues (over US$200mn) is shown in the table below. KazMunayGas, the state oil and gas company, is one of the main issuers, with some US$6.4bn outstanding.

Selected corporate bond issues

BB ticker	*Name*	*Sector*	*Ownership*	*Maturity date*	*Outstanding amount (mn)*	*Currency*
KAZNMH	KazAgro Natl Mgmt Hldg	Agriculture	Government	22 May 2019	600	EUR
KAZNMH	KazAgro Natl Mgmt Hldg	Agriculture	Government	24 May 2023	961	USD
KTZKZ	Kazakhstan Temir Zholy	Transport	Government	17 November 2027	780	USD
KTZKZ	Kazakhstan Temir Zholy	Transport	Government	10 July 2042	1100	USD
KZOKZ	KazMunayGas National Co	Energy	Government	19 April 2022	500	USD
KZOKZ	KazMunayGas National Co	Energy	Government	30 April 2023	407	USD
KZOKZ	KazMunayGas National Co	Energy	Government	24 April 2025	500	USD
KZOKZ	KazMunayGas National Co	Energy	Government	19 April 2027	1000	USD
KZOKZ	KazMunayGas National Co	Energy	Government	24 April 2030	1250	USD
KZOKZ	KazMunayGas National Co	Energy	Government	19 April 2047	1250	USD
KZOKZ	KazMunayGas National Co	Energy	Government	24 October 2048	1500	USD
KZTGKZ	KazTransGas JSC	Utilities	Government	26 September 2027	750	USD
NOGLN	Nostrum Oil & Gas Fin B.V.	Energy	Corporate	25 July 2022	725	USD
NOGLN	Nostrum Oil & Gas Fin B.V.	Energy	Corporate	16 February 2025	400	USD
TENGIZ	Tengizchevroil Fin Co IN	Energy	Corporate	15 August 2026	1000	USD
TRISTN	Tristan Oil Ltd	Energy	Corporate	1 January 2016	530	USD

Source: Bloomberg

Kenya

Nominal GDP (US$mn, 2018)[a]		89,591
Population (thousand, 2018)[a]		48,033
GDP per capita (USD, 2018)[a]		1865
Credit ratings (long-term foreign currency)[b]	Fitch	B+
	Moody's	B2
	S&P	B+

[a]IMF WEO October 2018
[b]As at end-September 2018

Country Summary

- Kenya is the largest and most developed economy in East African, serving as the region's commercial and logistical hub. Agriculture remains important, but there is also an established manufacturing base. Tourism and remittances are key FX sources, and financial services and technology are also significant. By African standards, Kenya has a well-diversified economy and has invested in projects that should provide long-term growth. The global financial crisis and severe droughts exerted further strain on the economy. The countercyclical policy response led to an increased debt burden, a focal point of subsequent IMF programmes.

Exotix Capital, *Exotix Developing Markets Guide*,
https://doi.org/10.1007/978-3-030-05867-8_26

- Deeper-lying socio-ethnic tensions were exposed by political violence after the December 2007 presidential election. This led to a power-sharing government and political and constitutional reform. The successful 2013 election paved the way for a period of strong growth, low inflation and rising investor confidence. The 2017 presidential election was re-run after opposition claims of irregularities. The re-run in October was boycotted by the main opposition candidate, Raila Odinga, and incumbent President Uhuru Kenyatta won with 98% of the vote, from a 39% turnout. Over 60 people died in violence and police clashes.
- Kenya's external debt level has more than tripled since 2012. The largest increases have been seen in commercial debt, including several outstanding bank loans and four eurobonds totalling US$4.75bn. During an IMF staff visit in July/August 2018, Kenyan authorities committed to keeping public debt on a sustainable path. In 2017, election-related fiscal slippage increased borrowing.

Economic data	*Avg*[a]	*2014*	*2015*	*2016*	*2017 (e)*	*2018 (f)*	*2019 (f)*
Real GDP growth	5.3	5.4	5.7	5.9	4.9	6.0	6.1
Inflation (annual average)	8.1	6.9	6.6	6.3	8.0	5.0	5.6
Current account (% of GDP)	−6.3	−10.4	−6.7	−5.2	−6.3	−5.6	−5.3
Reserves (US$mn, end-period)[b]	5359	7895	7534	7573	7338	9291[c]	–
Reserves/imports (months)[d]	3.9	4.4	4.7	5.4	4.4	–	–
Overall fiscal balance (% of GDP)[e]	−5.0	−7.4	−8.1	−8.3	−7.9	−6.6	−5.8
Currency (ticker)	Kenya shilling (KES)						
FX regime	De jure free float and de facto peg, classified as floating by IMF. Interventions to reduce volatility.						
Key exports	Tea (23%), cut flowers (14%), textiles (9.3%), coffee (4.7%). Tourism earnings and remittances were US$2.5bn and US$1.7bn in 2016, compared with goods exports of US$6.2bn.						

Source: IMF WEO Database, Haver, ITC Trade Map, OEC

[a]10-year average to 2016 unless otherwise stated

[b]Official foreign currency reserves

[c]Latest figure, May 2018

[d]In months of the current year's imports of goods and services

[e]IMF general government net lending

Key figures		*Party*	*Since*
President	Uhuru Kenyatta	KANU/Jubilee	Apr. 2013
Prime minister	William Ruto	KANU/Jubilee	Apr. 2013
Minister of finance	Raila Odinga	ODM	Apr. 2013
Key opposition figure	Henry Rotich	–	May 2013
Central bank governor	Patrick Ngugi Njoroge	–	Jun. 2015

Notes: Kenya is a member of The Commonwealth. It gained independence from Britain in 1963

Politics

Executive power

The president is head of the government and head of state, and is elected by popular vote to serve a five-year term. In addition to receiving over half of all votes cast, the presidential candidate must also win 25% or more of the vote in over half of Kenya's provinces to avoid a run-off. A referendum on 4 August 2010 on a new constitution was approved by parliament in April 2010 and produced a resounding "yes" vote, approved by 69% of voters. The new constitution, designed to limit the powers of the president and devolve power to the regions, was signed into law on 27 August 2010.

Presidential term: Five years (two-term limit; consecutive permitted)

Parliamentary term: Five years

Legislature

Unicameral National Assembly (Bunge) usually referred to as Parliament; 349 seats, 290 members elected by popular vote to serve five years terms, 47 women elected from the counties and 12 nominated members appointed by the president, but selected by the parties in proportion to their parliamentary vote totals. The new (2010) constitution provides for a bicameral parliament, including an upper house (Senate) with 67 members plus the Speaker, who is an ex-officio member.

Parliament: 349 seats

Senate: 68 seats

Elections

Next due Presidential: December 2022; Legislative: 2022

Last legislative election (August 2017)	*Seats*	*Last presidential (Aug/Oct 2017)*	*% of vote*
Jubilee Party (JP)	171	***Original (nullified)***	
Orange Democratic Movement (ODM/NASA)	76	Uhuru Kenyatta (JP)	54.17%
Wiper Democratic Movement-Kenya (WDM-K/NASA)	23	Raila Odinga (ODM/NASA)	44.94%
Amani National Congress (ANC)	14	Others	0.89%
Forum for the Restoration of Democracy (FORD-KENYA/NASA)	12	***October re-run***	
Kenya African National union (KANU)	10	Uhuru Kenyatta	98.26%
Independents	14	Raila Odinga (boycotted)	0.96%
Other	28	Others	0.78%
Total	**348**[a]	**Total**	**100.0**

[a]The member for Kitutu Chache South constituency is still to be elected. The National Assembly has 349 seats in total.

People

The disputed general election in December 2007 that led to political and ethnic-related violence across the country revealed Kenya's underlying social tensions. The violence claimed more than 1100 lives, with 600,000 displaced according to the FCO, in a period of unrest that lasted two months. The US secretary of state at the time, Hillary Clinton, criticised Kenya in August 2009 for failing to investigate the violence after the election. Kenya's population is 46.7mn people, the main peoples being Kikuyu 22%, Luhya 14%, Luo 13%, Kalenjin 12%, and Kamba 11%. The population is 83% Christian (including 48% Protestant and 23% Roman Catholic), 11% Muslim, as well as some indigenous beliefs. The population is relatively young; almost 60% is under 25 years. Only 27% of the population live in urban areas and over 75% are employed in agriculture.

(*continued*)

(continued)

People

Kenya became a British protectorate in 1895 and a colony in 1920. The Mau Mau insurgency from 1952–59 against colonial rule and land policies took place mainly in central Kenya among the Kikuyu, a period that saw African political participation increase. Kenya gained independence in 1963, with Jomo Kenyatta (an ethnic Kikuyu) as prime minister, after the Kenya African National Union (KANU) won the 1961 general election, and later president. By 1969 Kenya was a de facto one-party state (and officially so in 1982). Kenyatta died in office in 1978 and was succeeded by vice-president Daniel arap Moi (Kalenjin).

Multi-party politics was restored in 1991 after international pressure, but KANU retained control with election victories in 1992 and 1997. Both elections were marred by violence. The opposition, under the banner of the NARC, won a landslide victory in 2002, with Mwai Kibaki elected president after defeating Uhuru Kenyatta, Moi's favoured successor. Moi himself was obliged to step down under the 1991 constitution, resulting in the ending of his 24-year rule and KANU's four decades in power. Voters rejected a draft constitution in a referendum in November 2005 as it gave the president too much power. The vote was a blow to President Kibaki, under whom it was claimed that graft cost Kenya US$1bn. International donors voiced their unease.

Kenya's score on Transparency International's corruption index has improved, though, and it ranked 145 out of 176 in 2016, compared to 154 out of 178 in 2010. The East African Common Market, of which Kenya is a member, came into being in June 2010. It allows the free movement of goods and workers across six countries (Kenya, Tanzania, Uganda, Burundi, Rwanda and South Sudan). In 2007, Kibaki again won the presidency and his PNU party came in second place in the legislative election and led a coalition (formerly NARC), brokered by UN Secretary General Kofi Annan in February 2008. It led to the creation of the office of prime minister (until 2013) and the formation of a grand coalition government, sworn in on 17 April 2008. In 2013, Uhuru Kenyatta won the presidency with 50.5% of the vote.

In August 2017, the general election indicated that Kenyatta had been re-elected with a 54% vote share. However, opponent Raila Odinga did not accept the result and challenged it at the Supreme Court, which found the result to be null and void. The presidential election was re-held on 26 October 2017, but Odinga decided to boycott, assuming that it would be interfered with as the first. Kenyatta won with 98%, although only 39% of voters participated, and the Supreme Court upheld the victory, giving Kenyatta a second and final term. Over 60 people are reported to have died in protests and clashes with police during this election period. In January 2018, three television stations covering Odinga's mock presidential swearing-in ceremony were shut down by the government. A court ordered that they be allowed to resume broadcasting, although it was nine days before all were back on air, and one of the three opposition leaders that were arrested over the mock inauguration was deported to Canada.

Debt

	2012	2017
External debt ratios (%)		
Total external debt/GDP	30.7	44.9
Public external debt/GDP	18.9	28.6
Private external debt/GDP	11.8	16.3
Total external debt/exports of goods and services	111.6	226.3
External debt service ratio	3.4	13.1
Public debt ratios (%)		
Public domestic debt/GDP	22.4	27.1
Public debt/GDP	41.3	55.7

Source: National Treasury of Kenya, IMF, Exotix

[a]Public and publicly guaranteed

Kenya's total external debt was US$43.5bn in March 2018, up from US$15.5bn in 2012 and US$35.7bn in 2017. At end-2017, this was equivalent to 44.9% of GDP and 226% of exports of goods, services and remittances. The ratio of external debt to exports has deteriorated further than with GDP. The current IMF programme (see below) includes an objective to increase resilience to external shocks and lower tourism earnings has affected export figures less than GDP figures. A small majority was public external debt, comprising 63.7% of total external debt, equivalent to 28.6% of GDP, from 18.9% in 2012. As of Q1 18, the Kenya government's largest creditor group was commercial creditors, owed almost US$8.7bn, the vast majority of which was to commercial banks. This comprises US$165mn in export credits and also the bonds and loans outlined below, including US$2bn in bonds issued in February 2018. Over the past five years, average maturities have fallen, from 26.3 years in 2012 to 20.3 in 2016, while the average interest rate has also increased, from 0.8% in 2012 to 2.6% in 2016, in part due to new non-concessional debt. Multilateral and bilateral creditors also remain large creditor groups, owed 33.3% and 31.9%, respectively, of public external debt. The proportion of bilateral debt has only changed slightly since 2012; however, multilateral debt was 60% of public external debt in 2012 and the preceding years (now 33%), as commercial creditors have emerged as a large group. The World Bank's IDA and UN's IFAD (12% of the total external debt) and China (12.1%) are the single largest creditors in each of these categories.

The World Bank has expressed concern over the cost to the taxpayer of Chinese debt, which has increased by more than a factor of 10 in the past five years.

There has been a very large increase in private sector external indebtedness, according to IMF data, although there are no details as to its composition. From US$0.6bn in 2009, private non-guaranteed external debt was US$5.1bn in 2012 and US$18.6bn in 2017. Larger Kenyan corporates have been active issuers in the domestic bond market since 2005, rather than in the international market: one issue of US$60.27mn maturing in 2019 was issued by TransCentury Ltd. in 2011, and two corporate bonds have been issued in CFA francs (XOF).

PPG external debt service was 13.1% of exports in 2017, from 3.4% in 2012, on figures provided by the IMF. The National Treasury recorded that external debt service was 31.3% of total debt service in 2016, 54% of external debt service was interest payments and the largest creditor group by debt service payments was bilaterals, receiving 45% of external debt service. Note that Kenya's Central Bank and National Treasury provide external debt and debt service ratios with exports including only goods exports in the denominator. Therefore, ratios provided by official sources can appear to be much larger than the ratios shown here. Exotix ratios are calculated with a denominator of exports of goods and services and also private remittances, which were c2.5% of GDP in 2016. It should also be noted that, in September 2014, Kenya revised the way it calculates growth, making the economy 25% bigger than previously thought and fourth biggest in Sub-Saharan Africa, although the above ratios are consistent. Total public and publicly guaranteed debt was 55.7% of GDP at end-2017. This includes domestic debt equivalent to cUS$21.5bn, which has doubled in five years. This mainly comprised government securities, with Treasury bills accounting for almost half.

Composition of external debt

External debt by creditor (Feb. 2018)	*Nominal amount outstanding (US$mn)*	*Share of total (%)*
Public and publicly guaranteed external debt	**24,913**	**57.3**
o/w Official multilateral	8297	19.1
IDA/IFAD	5237	12.0
AfDB	2045	4.7
IMF	732	1.7

(*continued*)

(continued)

External debt by creditor (Feb. 2018)	*Nominal amount outstanding (US$mn)*	*Share of total (%)*
EEC/EIB	201	0.5
Official bilateral	7942	18.3
China	5296	12.2
Japan	1022	2.4
France	643	1.5
Germany	336	0.8
Belgium	107	0.2
USA	29	0.1
Commercial creditors	8674	19.9
Commercial banks	8509	19.6
Export credit	165	0.4
Private non-guaranteed external debt	**18,574**	**42.7**
Total external debt	**43,487**	**100.0**

Source: National Treasury of Kenya, IMF, Bloomberg, Exotix

Rescheduling History

Unlike many of its Sub-Saharan African peers, Kenya did not qualify for HIPC debt relief as its debt levels were below the HIPC thresholds, despite the country's low-income status (lower-middle income since 2015). Public external debt fell over the 1990s from a peak of 103% of GDP in 1992 to 56% in 1997, although the existence of external arrears and an external debt service ratio averaging 26% over 1992–1997 pointed to the existence of some potential payments pressure. By 2002, Kenya's external debt was US$5.1bn, 49% of GDP, of which 76% was on concessional terms, while debt in NPV terms was 121% of exports (below the 150% HIPC threshold). Still, near-term balance of payments financing gaps were identified in the authorities' PRGF agreed in November 2003, which the IMF stated could be met through Paris Club rescheduling. The authorities stated an intention to seek such a rescheduling and Kenya subsequently benefitted from Houston terms flow rescheduling in the Paris Club in 2004, although as an IDA-only country it was eligible for more concessional Naples terms. Its debt levels, as stated, meant it did not qualify for HIPC terms, which was confirmed in an IMF debt sustainability analysis. In tandem, Kenya's high domestic debt was seen in 2003 as another source of concern, for which various corrective measures were identified in its PRGF arrangement of that year. Otherwise, Kenya has generally continued to service its external and domestic debt (asides from some disputed commercial arrears, now settled) and the success of the Paris Club operation has been demonstrated by the fact that further rescheduling has not been needed.

Public external debt was 28.1% of GDP in 2017, from 18.2% in 2012 and the public external debt service ratio was 5.6% in 2017, from 2.7% in 2012. These figures seem comparatively lower than the figures from the 1990s. On the latest World Bank figures, 58.7% of external debt was concessional, compared with 65.4% in 2012 and 76.4% in 2008, reflecting increased Chinese bilateral debt and the sovereign bond issues. The rising debt burden, with a smaller proportion on concessional terms and lower average maturities, presents another risk: a rising debt service requirement. Total external debt was US$33.7bn in 2017 (42.4% of GDP), of which only 66.3% was owed by the public sector. Public domestic debt has also increased to US$21bn in 2017, from US$10.3bn in 2012. The rise in both public and private debt in nominal terms is a cause of concern, and while primary and fiscal deficits are expected by the IMF to decline over the next five years, they have persisted and were a key reason for Moody's downgrading Kenya to B2 from B1 in February 2018. Real GDP growth has shown some resilience to external shocks, although risks from adverse weather, reliance on agriculture and national security may threaten the current ratios. Political stability following the peaceful 2013 elections, allowed the 2010 constitution to be implemented and growth to accelerate, especially given investment in new capital projects. Subsequent years have seen a large increase in public spending, primarily in the form of investment, rather than recurrent spending. Politics in 2016–2017 did not provide an ideal environment for private sector activity. Falling demand, an interest rate cap that restricts private sector lending, ongoing political uncertainty and the drought in 2017 have led to a continuing decline in private sector activity, as shown by the plummeting PMI figures.

More positively, London-based oil company Tullow discovered oil in Kenya in 2012. Further exploration is planned, but South Lokichar oil field may have 750mn barrels, on Tullow Oil's estimates. Tullow and the government hope that, by 2020, Kenya will have large-scale production. A pilot programme was planned for June 2017 to enter the market. Three companies used four wells initially, with a pipeline to the coast (for export) that cost Kenya US$2.1bn. The first exports were delayed until after the August 2017 general election, as the Senate needed to pass the bill regarding the distribution of revenues. Following disagreements over revenue distribution between the Turkana county government, the local community and the national government, small-scale crude exports started in June 2018 after an agreement that raised the county government's share. With many different stakeholders, satisfying every group could be an ongoing challenge. Plans to export oil to Europe for initial refining were replaced by large exports to China and India.

Relations with Multilateral Creditors

Kenya has had a sometimes difficult relationship with the multilaterals and donors alike. The country undertook numerous IMF programmes over the course of the 1980s and 1990s, but Fund (and donor) relations with Kenya were strained in 1993–2007. Over the latter period, Kenya had four successive IMF programmes, which were notable by delays in completing their reviews and their strong focus on governance. The 1996, 2000 and 2003 programmes all went off track quickly and no reviews were completed under the 1996 and 2000 arrangements. The 2000 programme was seen publicly as a resumption of aid after it was suspended following the failure of the 1996 arrangement, a fate that ultimately befell the 2000 arrangement too. The 2003 PRGF was completed, albeit with long delays. The first review was completed in December 2004, after a delay of six months, becoming Kenya's first Fund programme review to be completed in 10 years. According to the IMF's own ex-post assessment of its engagement in Kenya up to October 2008, Kenya's performance and relations with the Fund were disappointing over the period 1993–2007, until the more recent pickup of growth and implementation of structural reforms. Improved policy performance in recent years helped Kenya put this difficult past behind it, following the completed 2003–2007 PRGF and emergency support in 2009. Kenya received balance of payments support, worth 50% of its quota in May 2009 under the exogenous shock facility (ESF) and the IMF commended Kenya on maintaining macroeconomic stability throughout the post-election turmoil. Subsequent programmes have been characterised by the occasional non-observance of performance criteria, including an ongoing programme that is currently off track.

Following expansionary policies in response to the global financial crisis and other shocks over 2008–2009, the three-year ECF in 2011 was intended to deliver fiscal consolidation and build international reserves, while addressing external weaknesses. The first review was completed in June 2011 and reported continued economic recovery with strong GDP growth, despite poor weather impacting agricultural output. Performance was satisfactory, although the authorities needed to request a waiver for the non-observance of two performance criteria. Later that year, the second review was completed, with all quantitative performance criteria met. High inflation posed a threat and high international prices, with the impact of drought, led to the authorities requesting augmentation to ensure objectives could be met. Augmentation of 60% of quota was approved in December 2011, bringing the programme to 180% of Kenya's quota. The primary fiscal balance was consistent with a decline in the government debt-to-GDP ratio. Subsequent reviews highlight the successful implementation of reforms allowed by the 2010 constitution. During the fifth review, a waiver was granted by the Board for the non-observance of the performance criterion on new central government and guaranteed external payment arrears; however, economic reforms remained on course, with GDP growth showing resilience to declining exports to Europe. The sixth and final reviews were completed in December 2013, allowing full disbursements equal to 180% of quota.

In February 2015, the Board approved a 12-month SCF and SBA joint programme for total access of US$687mn (180% of quota), under precautionary measures. The funds were intended to be available for the authorities to draw for balance of payments support, should the need arise due to external shocks. The first review, completed in September 2015, reported that all quantitative performance criteria had been met; however, the continuous performance criterion on external arrears had not been met. This was due to temporary arrears, which have since been fully repaid. In January 2016, the Board approved an extension to March, to provide time for the authorities to implement fiscal and structural measures. The programme expired undrawn.

At the end of the 2015–2016 SCF and SBA joint programme, a new US$990mn (196% of quota) SCF and SBA joint programme was approved, on completion of the second and final reviews of the first. The Kenya authorities continued to treat both arrangements as precautionary, and the funds were only to be drawn for balance of payments support in the event of exogenous shocks. This came in acknowledgement of the continued threat of extreme weather and global economic conditions. The first review was completed in December 2016; however, the second review was never completed and the programme was officially considered off track as of June 2017, resulting in Kenya losing the ability to access designated funds. In March 2018, negotiations between the IMF and authorities resulted in a six-month extension of the SBA only, while the SCF arrangement expired in March. International reserves increased during H1 17, in part due to remittance inflows (2.5% of GDP in 2016). The current account also continued to improve. The funds of the SCF were not drawn and as of July 2018, the SBA funds remained undrawn.

IMF programmes

Date	*Arrangements*	*Comments*
1983–1993	Various	SBA 1983–1984, SBA 1985–1986, SFC+SBA 1988–1989, PRGF 1989–1992, PRGF 1989–1993.
1993	SMP	Six-month SMP from April 1993 after economic performance was hit in 1992 by drought, power shortages, low commodity prices, fiscal slippages, ethnic tensions ahead of elections and a suspension of donor aid. The shilling came under pressure. IMF report that external arrears reached US$600mn. Problems were exacerbated by the Goldenberg corruption scandal.
1993–1994	PRGF	One-year PRGF (formerly ESAF) from December 1993.
1996–1999	PRGF	Programme suspended after first review was not completed.
2000–2003	PRGF	A three-year programme for US$198mn approved in August 2000, due to expire in August 2003. Augmented by US$52mn in October 2000 after severe drought. Programme suspended after first review was not completed.
2003–2007	PRGF	A three-year programme for US$253mn was approved in November 2003, due to expire in November 2006, to support the authorities' economic programme, which intended to break from the past record of uneven performance and accompanied by new donor pledges of US$4.1bn. The PRGF was augmented by US$77mn in December 2004 at the time of the first review, delayed by six months. Two extensions were needed to allow time to complete the second review, with waivers for five performance criteria. At the second review, an extension to the arrangement was approved, to November 2007, along with a reduction in access by US$118.7mn, consistent with an improvement in Kenya's external position. The third and final review was approved in November 2007, with waivers for the non-observance of four performance criteria. Total disbursements under the arrangement were US$237mn.
2009 May	ESF	US$209mn disbursement approved under the rapid access component of the ESF to help Kenya respond to the negative impact of high food and fertiliser costs and the slowdown in external demand after the global financial crisis.

(*continued*)

(continued)

Date	*Arrangements*	*Comments*
2011–2013	ECF	US$509mn (120% of quota) three-year programme gained Board approval in January 2011 to implement fiscal consolidation following expansionary policies in prior years and increase reserves, while addressing weaknesses such as the external position and rising debt burden. Subsequent reviews suggested that the economy was developing resilience to external shocks, with economic growth being maintained despite declining exports. Performance was satisfactory, although the authorities needed to request a waiver for the non-observance of two performance criteria. Later that year, the second review was completed with all quantitative performance criteria met. High inflation posed a threat and high international prices, with the impact of drought, led to the authorities requesting augmentation to ensure objectives could be met; a 60% of quota augmentation was approved in December. Economic reforms continued and growth showed resilience to the external shock of declining exports and tourism earnings. The full 180% of quota was drawn.
2015–2016	SCF + SBA	Originally for 12 months, approved in February 2015 for total access of SDR488.5mn (cUS$687mn; 180% of quota), under precautionary measures, for balance of payments support in the event of exogenous shocks. Extended to March 2016, the joint programme expired undrawn.
2016–2018	SCF + SBA	Approved in March 2016 for 24 months, on successful completion of the second and final reviews of the previous SBCF and SBA, for total access of SDR709mn (about US$990mn; 196% of quota), under precautionary measures, for balance of payments support in the event of exogenous shocks, such as those from extreme weather and global economic conditions. First review was completed in January 2017; however, the second review was never completed. The SCF expired in March 2018, while the SBA was extended by six months, to allow additional time to complete outstanding reviews, expected to be completed by September 2018. The funds remain undrawn.

Source: IMF. Kenya joined the IMF in 1964

Kenya's relations with donors were perhaps even more testy than with the IMF, which even said relations with donors were often stormy. World Bank support during the 1990s was constrained by poor policy performance. Budget support was renewed with a loan in August 2000, at the same time as the IMF's PRGF, although the third tranche was cancelled and the loan closed in 2004. After the PRGF went off track, donor budgetary and project support fell. Donor support under the 2003–2007 PRGF, despite significant new pledges, remained very low. As of August 2018, the World Bank has 50 active projects in Kenya, including three new projects approved in 2018 (by the time of this writing). By commitment amount, water/sanitation, transport and other infrastructure development projects are among the highest recipients. In April 2017, the World Bank approved a new project to reduce the human and economic impact of conflict and violence, especially incurred due to refugee arrivals, causing forced displacement. The project comes with US$100mn financing. With a strong dependence on agriculture, the UN's IFAD provides significant funding to the sector in Kenya, with total IDA and IFAD lending of US$5.1bn as of February 2018, from US$3.5bn in 2012. The African Development Bank has 18 ongoing projects and has approved a further 10, with a focus on sustainable energy, agriculture and water and sanitation.

In September 2009, the World Bank suspended disbursements to two of 25 projects (education support and flood mitigation) due to suspected fraud and corruption. The government responded quickly, suspending about 50 project staff and freezing accounts. Kenya has a history of corruption problems, such as the memorable Goldenberg scandal revealed in 1992, involving a large misappropriation of Central Bank of Kenya and budgetary funds over the period 1990–1993, estimated at the equivalent of US$600mn (6% of GDP), which put additional pressure on the economy already suffering from a series of external and domestic shocks. Donor aid was subsequently limited over the following years, reflecting concerns over governance, with such concerns being magnified after the Anglo-Leasing scandal that emerged in 2004, in which government ministers were implicated. Lack of external assistance forced Kenya to rely on domestic sources of finance, helping to develop its domestic debt market, although this led to an increase in the country's domestic debt burden, creating another potential source of vulnerability.

Paris Club and Bilateral Creditors

Kenya has entered into three agreements with the Paris Club, with debt relief on each occasion taking place on non-concessional terms. According to the IMF, these mainly related to export credits from the 1980s. Even though Kenya was eligible for concessional terms (it was eligible for Naples terms in 2000 and 2004, but not HIPC), major Paris Club creditors considered that there was no reason to grant concessional rescheduling and Kenya elected for non-concessional treatment to limit potential tensions with private creditors. Kenya's 1994 agreement followed the economic decline of 1992–1993 when the economy suffered from domestic and external shocks and a large-scale corruption scandal. Donors were subsequently re-engaged and a non-concessional Paris Club rescheduling of external arrears occurred in January 1994. A Paris Club rescheduling in 2000 followed the IMF's PRGF agreed in August of that year. Another Paris Club rescheduling, and its most recent treatment, occurred in January 2004. This was a three-year flow rescheduling in response to an identified balance of payments need and took place within the context of the country's PRGF arrangement at the time.

Paris Club agreements

Date	*Terms*	*Status*	*Details*
1994	Ad hoc	Fully repaid	
2000 Nov.	Ad hoc	Active	Treated US$301mn. Treatment of arrears as of 1 July 2000, treatment of maturities falling due from 1 July 2000 up to 30 June 2001. Repayment of non-ODA credits over 18 years, with three years of grace. Repayment of ODA credits over 20 years.
2004 Jan.	Houston	Active	Treated US$353mn. Treatment of arrears as of 31 December 2003, treatment of maturities falling due from 1 January 2004 up to 31 December 2006. Repayment of non-ODA credits over 15 years, with five years of grace. Repayment of ODA credits over 20 years with 10 years of grace. Implemented in three phases: First phase: 1 Jan 2004–31 Dec 2004, on signature of agreement Second phase: 1 Jan 2005–31 Dec 2005, implemented 27 Dec 2004. Third phase: 1 Jan 2006–31 Dec 2006, implemented 15 May 2007.

Source: Paris Club

In 1998, London Club creditors rescheduled debt amounting to US$70mn and a further US$23mn in 2003–2004. None remains outstanding. Previously, Kenya has had debt cancellations from Finland, the

Netherlands and China. In 2006, Kenya entered into a debt-for-development swap agreement with the Italian government, for an amount of US$44mn.

More recently, the World Bank has expressed concerns over the amount of new borrowing from Beijing, which appears to come at a higher cost to the taxpayer; much of it is not on concessional terms. In nominal terms, the bilateral debt owed to China has increased by a factor of 10 in the past five years, to US$4.6bn in June 2017. China was a major financing contributor to the new Standard Gauge Railway (SGR) line connecting Mombasa with Nairobi, the country's biggest infrastructure project since independence. Kenyan National Assembly Speaker Justin Muturi has promoted extending the line from Nairobi to other destinations.

Sovereign Commercial Debt

Kenya's public sector external debt from commercial creditors consists of US$166mn in export credit, which has remained relatively flat, and commercial bank debt of US$8.5bn in Q1 18, which has increased very quickly over the past five years, from cUS$650mn at end-2012. Kenya had large external arrears to commercial creditors relating to fraudulent or deeply flawed contracts arising from the Anglo-Leasing scandal. The authorities obtained an external audit to assess the claims. The IMF noted that once an agreement on the amounts to be paid was reached, Kenya could refinance the payments to clear the arrears. In May 2014, a month before the sovereign bond issue, President Kenyatta ordered the payment of KES1.4bn, arguing that the ongoing dispute was affecting development projects and that international relations could deteriorate further.

The government's intention to issue a eurobond was announced in the FY2008/09 budget, presented in June 2008, for an amount of US$300mn, a transaction made easier after the country was assigned its first sovereign ratings from S&P (B+) in September 2006 and Fitch (B+) in December 2007. It repeated such intentions soon afterwards, in September 2008, saying that global market turbulence would not postpone the issue in that financial year. But events soon overtook it. This issue was subsequently postponed. Plans for a future eurobond sale were revived in early 2010, although any issue in FY2009/10 was ruled out. Prime Minister Odinga, in a Bloomberg interview in February 2010, said the country would raise between US$500mn and US$1bn to finance infrastructure, with the sale either in 2010 or early 2011. Yet a bond sale was not budgeted in the FY2010/11 budget presented in June 2010. A statement later said Kenya will wait another year before selling an international bond, although Reuters reported in November 2010 Kenyan officials saying that they could come to the market with a US$500mn bond by the end of the current financial year (i.e. before end June-2011), or early in the next financial year.

The debut sovereign eurobond joint issues in June 2014 put Kenya more firmly on the international radar, although the country was already well known in Sub-Saharan Africa (excluding South Africa) for having one of the most developed domestic debt and equity markets in the region, albeit lacking the sheer size of that of Nigeria. A five-year bullet bond was issued for US$750mn, with a coupon of 5.875% and matures in June 2019. Also issued was a 10-year US$2bn bullet bond with a coupon of 6.875% and maturity in June 2024. In February 2018, two more bullet bonds were issued, each for US$1bn. One (detailed below) has a coupon of 7.25% and matures in February 2028, and the other has a coupon of 8.25% and matures in February 2048. All four bonds are of the RegS and 144A series. Currently Kenya has four bonds outstanding, totalling US$4.75bn.

Kenya bond
Kenya 7.25% 2028
Bloomberg ticker: KENINT

Borrower	Republic of Kenya
Issue date	28 February 2018
Form	Eurobond
ISIN	XS1781710543
Issued amount	US$1000mn
Currency	US dollar
Denomination	US$200,000 and US$1000 thereafter
Amortisation	Bullet
Maturity date	28 February 2028
Coupon/interest	7.25% per annum, paid semi-annually February and August
Day count	30/360
Method of transfer	Euroclear/Clearstream
Settlement period	T + 2
Joint lead managers	Citi, JP Morgan, Standard Bank, Standard Chartered Bank Kenya Ltd

Kenya also has a number of sovereign loans. These are listed in the table and an example is detailed below. Previous loans have matured, although some recently issued loans were used for refinancing. A total of cUS$1.2bn and CNY3.4bn in loans were entered into with the Exim Bank of China during 2017, by various ministries and corporations. The loans were used to fund infrastructure and electricity projects in Kenya and mature between 2030 and 2040.

Kenya's outstanding loans

Lender	*Size*	*Issued*	*Maturity*
China Development Bank Corporation	US$600mn	Jun. 2016	2023
Afrexim Bank	US$200mn	Jun. 2016	2023
East and South Africa Trade Development Bank	US$250mn	Dec. 2016	2018
East and South Africa Trade Development Bank	US$300mn	Mar. 2017	2022
East and South Africa Trade Development Bank	US$200mn	Mar. 2017	2027
Consortium of banks	US$766mn	Mar. 2017	2019
Consortium of banks	US$234mn	Mar. 2017	2020
East and South Africa Trade Development Bank	US$750mn	Oct. 2017	2027
East and South Africa Trade Development Bank	US$750mn	Apr. 2018	2025

Source: Eurobond prospectus

Kenya loan	
Borrower	Republic of Kenya
Loan type	Term loan
Issue date	20 March 2017
Issue size	US$500mn, split across two tranches Tranche 1 = US$300mn Tranche 2 = US$200mn
Outstanding amount	US$500mn
Amortisation	Bullet
Final maturity date	Tranche 1—March 2022 Tranche 2—March 2027
Interest basis and rate	Tranche 1—Libor (6M) + margin Tranche 2—Libor (6M) + margin
Agent	East and South African Trade and Development Bank

Source: Eurobond prospectus, Exotix

Corporate Bond Markets

There has only been one USD denominated bond issued by Kenyan corporates. This is a convertible bond issue by TransCentury Ltd. (TCLKN) in March 2011, which matures in September 2019 and has a 6% coupon, listed on the Mauritius Stock Exchange. It was restructured in March 2016, along with other loan facilities and now has USD60.27mn outstanding.

Two other bonds have been issued in CFA francs (XOF): an XOF5.3mn issue by Shelter Afrique (SHELTE), which had a 6% coupon and matured in 2014, and a second bond from the same issuer for XOF20.97mn in 2014, which has a coupon of 6.6%, matures in 2021, is sinkable and has XOF14.7mn outstanding. The larger Kenyan companies have been active issuers of debt on the local market. There have been 47 KES-denominated corporate bonds from 22 issuers, listed on the Nairobi Stock Exchange, with a total of KES1.7 billion. Currently outstanding are 21 bonds, totalling KES759mn.

Mongolia

Nominal GDP (US$mn, 2018)[a]		12,724
Population (thousand, 2018)[a]		3105
GDP per capita (USD, 2018)[a]		4098
Credit ratings (long-term foreign currency)[b]	Fitch	B
	Moody's	B3
	S&P	B–

[a]IMF WEO October 2018
[b]As at end-September 2018

Country Summary

- Sandwiched between China and Russia, Mongolia, became a democratic country in 1990 after Russian influence ended following the collapse of the USSR. A new constitution, which allowed a multi-party system, led to elections for a unicameral legislature in 1992 and direct presidential elections in 1993. The Mongolian People's Party (MPP) remains the dominant party. Corruption has been a problem and a number of investigations are ongoing.
- The economy is dependent on mining and agriculture, both of which are cyclical. Falling commodity prices since mid-2011, especially copper, and a slowing of Chinese growth (major export market), led to sharply declining real GDP growth, from 17% in 2011 to 1.2% in 2016. Expansionary fiscal policies did not compensate well, and led

Exotix Capital, *Exotix Developing Markets Guide*,
https://doi.org/10.1007/978-3-030-05867-8_27

to rising public debt and declining reserves. Private sector debt has increased dramatically due to intercompany borrowing from mining sector firms with foreign partners as well as private sector banks.

- To ensure that the wealth of mineral resources can be translated into long-term economic growth, there will need to be a strong and transparent legal framework and the promotion of diversification to prevent sector overreliance. According to the ADB, the tourism sector could contribute to economic diversification and job creation.

Economic data	*Avg*[a]	*2014*	*2015*	*2016*	*2017 (e)*	*2018 (f)*	*2019 (f)*
Real GDP growth	7.5	7.9	2.4	1.2	5.1	6.2	6.3
Inflation (annual average)	9.7	12.9	5.9	0.5	4.6	7.6	8.0
Current account (% of GDP)	−11.1	−11.3	−4.0	−6.3	−10.4	−8.3	−10.8
Reserves (US$mn, end-period)[b]	1740	1650	1323	1296	3008	3256[c]	–
Reserves/imports (months)[d]	3.6	2.4	2.5	2.4	4.5	–	–
Overall fiscal balance (% of GDP)[e]	−5.3	−11.3	−8.5	−17.0	−1.9	−3.5	−5.7
Currency (ticker)	Mongolia togrog (MNT)						
FX regime	Under the current auction mechanism, the de facto and de jure exchange rates are classified as floating. The Togrog depreciated significantly during the global economic crisis of 2008–2009 due to central bank policies to maintain the then de facto conventional peg to the US dollar. In November 2008, the Bank of Mongolia (BoM) allowed flexible exchange rate movements, leading to a large depreciation. From March 2009, the BoM used a foreign exchange auction mechanism to allow the market determination of the exchange rate. There is also an official exchange rate, used in government transactions, so the authorities have created market segmentation. Since the variation of the two rates is not prevented from exceeding 2%, there may be multiplicity of rates. The BoM plans to correct this. Accelerated depreciation in 2016 and increased volatility against the US dollar led to the central bank adopting a flexible exchange rate.						
Key exports	Copper (33%), coal (20%), gold (15%), crude petroleum (6.9%)						

Source: IMF WEO Database, Haver, Bank of Mongolia, OEC

[a]10-year average to 2016 unless otherwise stated
[b]International reserves
[c]Latest figure, May 2018
[d]In months of the current year's imports of goods, services and primary income debit
[e]Overall government net lending

Key figures		*Party*	*Since*
President	Khaltmaagiin Battulga	Democratic Party	Jul. 2017
Prime minister	Ukhnaagiin Khurelsukh	MPP	Oct. 2017
Minister of finance	Khurelbaatar Chimed	MPP	Oct. 2017
Key opposition figure	Erdene Sodnomzundui	Democratic Party	Jun. 2016
Central bank governor	Bayartsaikhan Nadmid	–	Jul. 2016

Politics

Executive power

Mongolia has a presidential political system that operates alongside a parliament. The president has the ability to veto a bill in parliament that does not have a two thirds majority, as well as nominate a prime minister. He is also commander in chief of the armed forces and can make judicial appointments. Presidential candidates are nominated by parties. A popular vote elects the president to his four-year term, after having been accepted by the parliament. Each President is limited to 2 terms.

Presidential term: Four years (two-term limit) **Parliamentary term**: Four years

Legislature

Unicameral, the State Great Hural is composed of 76 seats with members elected by popular vote to serve four-year terms to a total of 26 multi-member constituencies. Election to the house is only valid if 50% of the electorate votes. Considerable power remains in the parliament: two thirds of the Hural's members are required to enact a change in legislation, the constitution or budgets.

Elections

Next due *Legislative: 2020* *Presidential: 2021*

Last legislative election (June 2016)	*Seats*	*Last presidential (June/July 2017)*	*% of vote*
Mongolian People's Party (MPP)	65	***Second round***	
Democratic Party (DP)	9	Khaltmaagiin Battulga (DP)	55.2
Other	2	Miyeegombyn Enkhbold (MPP)	44.8
Total	76	Total	100

People

Mongolia is a vast landlocked country in East Asia of sparsely populated steppe and semi-desert between Russia to the north and China to the south. It is known economically for its natural resource wealth. In the 2008 election, both major parties promised handouts for every Mongolian to distribute the nation's mining revenue. 72% of the population live in urban areas, including 1.4mn in the capital Ulaanbaatar. Ethnically, the population is 82% Khalkh and most people speak Mongolian, although Turkic languages and Russian are also spoken. The population is composed of 95% Mongol; others include Chinese and Russians. 53% of the population is Buddhist, 3% Muslim, 3% Shamanist and 2% Christian, while 39% have no registered religious affiliation. The population is young (27% of the population are under 15) with very low population density of c2 people per square kilometre. Economic activity has traditionally been based on herding and agriculture. An extremely cold winter 'zud' in 2010 killed much of Mongolia's livestock, which was particularly devastating since almost a third of the population were reliant on livestock as their main source of income. There are few opportunities in rural areas and various skills shortages. Since 2014, Mongolia has ranked high in human development and while there have been improvements in reducing inequality and poverty, many remain vulnerable of falling back into poverty.

In 1990 the country abandoned a Soviet style one-party system and opened up to political and economic reforms. Prior to this the communist Mongolian People's Revolutionary Party (MPRP) was the only official political party, and remains the dominant party today. In 1992, a new constitution prioritised human rights and freedoms, and the following year the first presidential election was won by Punsalmaagiin Ochirbat. The early 1990s saw a severe depression as the collapse of the Soviet Union created huge challenges for the Mongolian economy. GDP and per capita income in US$ terms failed to grow in line with others in the region, only returning to pre-1990 levels in 2006. A state of emergency was declared in July 2008, after riots in the capital following opposition accusations of election rigging. With this exception, all seven elections and the change to democracy since 1990 have been peaceful, with elections considered free and fair by international observers. In 2010, the MPRP changed its name back to communist-era Mongolian People's Party. Former President Nambaryn Enkhbayar set up a breakaway Mongolian People's Revolutionary Party. He was convicted of corruption in 2012. Agreements were made during 2011 on the development of the Tavan Tolgoi coal deposits and Oyu Tolgoi copper mine, although a dispute between the government and Rio Tinto led to 1700 redundancies in 2013. Water scarcity is a constraint on sustainable development. The World Economic Forum's 2016–17 Global Competitiveness Report ranked Mongolia's infrastructure at 110 out of 138 countries.

Debt

	2012	2017
External debt ratios (%)		
Total external debt/GDP	140.0	246.2
Public external debt/GDP	33.9	83.9
Private external debt/GDP	106.1	162.3
Total external debt/exports	381.2	396.3
External debt service ratio (public)	2.2	9.3
Public debt ratios (%)		
Public domestic debt/GDP	5.9	15.7
Public debt/GDP	39.8	99.6

Source: Ministry of Finance, Bank of Mongolia, IMF

On IMF figures, a dramatic increase in external debt, especially of the private sector, was seen in 2010 and continued gradually until total external debt reached US$27.4bn at end-2017. The Central Bank reports that the external debt increases in 2010 and 2011 came with the improved economic activity following the recovery from the global financial crisis, and mining company activity led to large increases in private sector external debt, which exceeded US$18bn in 2017 (66% of total external debt), from US$13bn in 2012. Intercompany external debt increased to US$11.1bn in 2015, from US$9.0bn in 2012 and US$219mn in 2009, before declining since to US$7.6bn in 2017. External debt of private sector banks (deposit-taking corporations) increased to US$2.3bn in 2017, from US$1.2bn in 2012. Sovereign and corporate bond issues during 2012 pushed total external debt up to over US$17bn by end-2012, and subsequent increases have been in private non-guaranteed debt, concessional bilateral loans, bonds and commercial bank loans.

Over 2014–2015, public sector external debt increased gradually, but increases over 2016–2017 have taken it to 84% of 2017 GDP (US$9.3bn), boosted by eurobond issues, fiscal expansion, and slow real GDP growth. According to the Ministry of Finance, the majority of this was US$-denominated. At end-2017, commercial creditors were Mongolia's largest creditor group owed 12.5% of total external debt, mostly holders of eurobonds and one-third of PED. A further 7% of total external debt was owed to bilateral creditors, especially Japan, and 6% was owed to multilateral institutions. Most multilateral and all bilateral debt was on concessional terms.

Public sector domestic debt increased to US$1.75bn in 2017, from US$725mn in 2012, bringing total public sector debt to US$11.1bn in 2017. Lower commodity prices from mid-2011 damaged export earnings, but total exports (including primary income) were higher in 2016 than in 2012, helping to limit the increase in the external debt-to-exports ratio, which rose to 396% in 2017. The PPG external debt service ratio was 9% in 2017, from 2.2% in 2012, despite the concessionality of multilateral and bilateral debt, and the bullet maturities of the sovereign eurobonds.

Composition of external debt

External debt by creditor (Dec. 2017)	*Nominal amount outstanding (US$mn)*	*Share of total (%)*
Public sector external debt	**9342**	**34.1**
o/w Multilateral creditors	1632	6.0
ADB	275	1.0
World Bank	140	0.5
IFAD	1.6	0.01
Bilateral creditors	1906	7.0
Japan	424	1.5
China	70	0.3
Korea	5.0	0.02
Austria	3.2	0.01
Germany	0.6	0.0
Commercial creditors	3419	12.5
Bonds[a]	3400	12.4
Private sector external debt[b]	**18,070**	**65.9**
Total external debt	**27,412**	**100.0**

Source: Ministry of Finance, BoM

[a]Figure from Bloomberg

[b]Includes intercompany lending

Rescheduling History

Mongolia has a very limited history of sovereign debt rescheduling, despite running high debt burdens (public and external), with its only restructuring experience in modern times related to treatment of its Soviet-era debt in 2003. Since then, it has maintained a sound track record on external debt payments, although commercial borrowing (in size) only really began in 2012. However, the sovereign was required to step in and issue new bonds in the restructuring in March 2017 of a government-guaranteed bond from Development Bank of Mongolia (DBM) after it encountered liquidity problems.

Having risen to almost 100% of GDP in 2003, and following the first Russian debt write-down (see below), Mongolia's public debt burden fell markedly in the five years to 2008 as a commodity-led boom helped the country grow out of debt vulnerabilities. But having troughed at 31% of GDP in 2008, the public and publicly guaranteed (PPG) external debt burden increased significantly in 2009 to 43% of GDP as the economy endured a slump in commodity prices, exchange rate depreciation, and a banking crisis. The rapid credit expansion of the previous period was superseded by a rapid increase in NPLs (which exceeded 20% of total loans by late 2009) which in turn precipitated sequential bank failures. PPG external debt was able to decline over the following years, as the private sector took on most of the new debt. The expansion of the mining and banking sectors has led to total external debt rising each year, to an estimated 246% of GDP in 2017.

Real GDP growth reached 17% in 2011 but an external debt crisis quickly appeared. With a massive fall in foreign investment, slowing growth in China, and falling commodity prices from mid-2011 until late 2016, both external and domestic debt rose and in 2016 the currency lost about a quarter of its value. The economy picked up in 2017, especially due to improved exports driven by the mineral sector (recovering commodity prices and investor confidence with the IMF agreement), although limited export diversification remains a vulnerability.

A shift in the balance towards the private sector had been anticipated. Privatisation, supported by successive IMF programmes and international aid, saw the private sector's share in GDP increase from 4% in 1990 to over 70% in 2000. The end of limits on non-concessional external borrowing on completion of the IMF stand-by arrangement (SBA) in 2010, the limited accession to concessional official financing due to mineral wealth, political pressure for greater development expenditure, the costs of recapitalising the banking sector and the cost of financing the government's equity share in mining projects all contributed to the private sector becoming the larger external borrower.

Each year since 2011, the government budget has been in deficit, with it reaching 17% of GDP in 2016, as expansionary fiscal policies attempted to compensate for low export revenues after commodity prices fell. In the 2008 election, both major parties promised handouts for every Mongolian to distribute the nation's mining revenue. A variation of the original universal cash handout plan was implemented as a multiyear system over 2010–2012, adding to fiscal pressures. The medium-term debt management strategy for 2016–2018 aims to create a stable tax environment and ensure fiscal stability by limiting expenses growth and making the repayment profile more favourable where possible. In January 2018, US$500mn of the 'Chinggis bond' was repaid, with the remaining US$1bn due in 2022. Tax collection efficiency may be enhanced through improved technology, and there are plans for large scale projects and privatisations.

The economy depends on gold, copper and coal mining and agriculture, which are cyclical, leaving the economy vulnerable to changes in commodity prices, which have historically led to recurring boom and bust cycles. Long periods of slow or negative growth have led to declining reserves, rising debt, and currency depreciations. While peaceful political transitions have provided stability and aided the move to a market-based economy, there remain some political risks: corruption investigations are ongoing and laws regarding foreign involvement in the mining industry have been subject to continued reviews by parliament. China is a key export market and continued slowing Chinese growth would harm Mongolian export revenue. Climate change presents a vulnerability as the more frequent extreme weather events have an adverse effect on agriculture.

In April 2015, the IMF concluded that Mongolia was at high risk of debt distress and highlighted fiscal consolidation as a key remedial step. After elections in June 2016, the central bank hiked its policy rate by 450 bps in August 2016, and parliament passed a budget in November to cut the fiscal deficit, on the IMF's definition, from 17% of GDP in 2016 to 10.6% in 2017. The 2017 extended fund facility (EFF) programme (see table below) follows the economic slowdown brought about by falling commodity prices and foreign demand. Expansionary fiscal policies only led to unsustainable public debt levels and low foreign reserves (2.9 months' import cover in 2015 and 2016). The fiscal deficit is now expected to decline over the next five years as the government is committed to fiscal consolidation, as shown by efforts made before the new programme was agreed upon and its positive progress so far. The liquidity position is fragile, dependent on the confidence of external creditors, although with high orders and a low coupon compared to the previous issue, the 2017 eurobond issue indicates creditor confidence.

After reaching staff-level agreement on the IMF EFF programme, the authorities completed an exchange offer for the publicly guaranteed DBM bonds due in March 2017. 82% of holders of the DBM bonds agreed to exchange at par for new seven-year sovereign notes. This did not impose a loss on investors relative to the original securities. Non-participating bondholders were still paid in full on the bond's maturity. The exchange relieved short-term liquidity constraints and demonstrated Mongolia's international market access.

IMF Board approval of the programme was significant because it allowed for new multilateral and bilateral disbursements, hence the improving outlooks from ratings agencies. Given the new programme, it is expected that Mongolia will be able to cover its near-term financing needs, which are large in comparison with current resources. Improving forecasts as of the first and second EFF reviews indicate lower risk of returning external liquidity pressures, partly alleviated by the debt exchange.

Relations with Multilateral Creditors

Since joining the IMF in 1991 Mongolia has undertaken six IMF programmes, the most recent of which was agreed in 2017. These included an SBA (1991–1992), ESAF (1993–1996), ESAF II (1997–2001), and PRGF (2001–2005). These programs, however, all eventually went off-track; and the 2009–2010 SBA marked the first time that Mongolia successfully completed an IMF-supported programme.

The 2009–2010 SBA, agreed in the wake of the global financial crisis, was an 18-month, US$229.2mn agreement that also received support from the World Bank, ADB and the government of Japan. The IMF commended the success of the programme; inflation was reduced, international reserves replenished, and the budget deficit lowered. The IMF also commended the Mongolian government for adhering to the structural reform conditionalities of the programme, including the fiscal stability law and central bank law. The fiscal law introduced a debt ceiling of 40% of GDP as well as a ceiling on expenditure growth and structural deficit. At the end of the programme, the IMF made a plea for prudence in anticipation of political pressures for greater expenditure on the back of the commodity boom.

After the SBA expired in 2010, the IMF continued to complete missions to Mongolia and conduct Article IV cycles, which noted that although growth was strong, government policies could lead to vulnerabilities if continued. When commodity prices started to fall, especially copper, from mid-2011, expansionary fiscal policies led to high public debt and low international reserves. In May 2017, the IMF approved a three-year EFF for Mongolia for

SDR314.5mn (cUS$434.3mn, 435% of quota) to support the economic reform programme, as part of a total financing package for Mongolia of the order of US$5.5bn. SDR28mn of IMF money (cUS$38.6mn) was disbursed immediately. The IMF programme was expected to catalyse an additional US$3bn financial package, comprising budget and project support, involving contributions from ADB, the World Bank and bilateral partners including Japan and South Korea, together with another CHY15bn three-year swap facility from the People's Bank of China. Staff-level agreement for the IMF programme was announced on 19 February 2017. The programme aims to provide assistance to the government in its attempts to stabilise the economy through fiscal and external account improvements and the restoration of debt sustainability. Institutional reforms will also be needed to ensure that the fiscal adjustment is durable. A staff-level agreement of the first review came in August 2017, and the first and second reviews were completed in December 2017. Following increased confidence of international creditors, as shown by the November 2017 bond issue and the unlocking of other official funding by the approval of the EFF, growth was reported to have been higher than expected, with improved forecasts for 2017 and 2018. The IMF also reported that reform processes had begun and all quantitative targets had been over-performed on. IMF staff agreed in February 2018 that, while performance depends on commodity prices, fiscal overperformance had allowed a reduction in public debt. A new regulatory framework and results of an asset quality review were being translated into improving balance sheets and capital adequacy of banks. All subsequent reviews, from the fifth review in June 2018 will allow for larger disbursements (SDR26.2mn) if approved. The programme is due to expire in May 2020.

IMF programmes

Date	*Arrangements*	*Comments*
1991–1992	SBA	SDR22.5mn SBA
1993–1996	PRGF/ESAF	Three-year SDR40.81mn (80% of quota) agreement was reached, lapsing in 1996.
1997–2000	PRGF	Three-year SDR33.4mn (65.4% of quota) agreement was reached although terminated just one year later in 1998.
2001–2005	PRGF	In September 2001, a three-year US$37mn agreement was reached. The second review extended the programme by 10 months and expiring in July 2005.
2009–2010	SBA	In April 2009, an 18-month US$229.9mn (300% quota) programme was agreed. All end-December performance criteria for the fourth review were met. Expired October 2010.

(*continued*)

(continued)

Date	*Arrangements*	*Comments*
2017–2020	EFF	A three-year EFF was approved in May 2017, for SDR314.5mn (cUS$434.3mn, 435% of quota) to support the economic reform programme, with SDR28mn (cUS$38.6mn) disbursed immediately. In the first and second review press releases in October 2017, the IMF reported on the authorities' continued reform commitment and upgrades to the 2017 and 2018 GDP growth projections. Once the first and second reviews were completed in December 2017, the IMF reported that strong policy implementation and a supportive external environment had helped the authorities to over-perform on all quantitative targets. The third review was released in April 2018 and the fourth review was completed in May. Efficient tax collection and spending restraints have helped the authorities to continue exceeding fiscal targets in 2018, and, although improving commodity export revenues lift growth expectations in 2018 and 2019, international prices remain an exogenous risk factor.

Source: IMF. Mongolia joined the IMF in 1991

Mongolia became a member of the World Bank Group in 1991 and, since then, the World Bank has provided over US$800mn in development financing, and currently has 15 active projects in the country. The ADB has 88 active projects in or including Mongolia, with some focused on infrastructure, education and healthcare, and other providing assistance to the government, through providing institutional support and aiming to support macroeconomic stability. Five projects were approved in H1 18. Promotion of economic diversification led by the private sector is a key priority.

Paris Club and Bilateral Creditors

Mongolian debt has never been treated by a Paris Club agreement. Following protracted negotiations in 2003, the government restructured US$11.4bn of Russian ruble debt (over 10 times Mongolia's 2003 GDP) incurred during the pre-transition period. The agreement provided for a 97.8% write-down of the debt. The financing of this transaction was controversial and violated terms of the IMF agreement, but allowed the country to normalise creditor relations. In July 2010, a bilateral agreement with Russia offered a one-time payment of US$3.8mn to resolve all outstanding debt and allow for future Russian investment inflows.

In January 2016, Russian President Putin ratified the legislation to put the agreement into effect, amid improving bilateral ties over the preceding years. Mongolia's debt stock to Russia was US$174.2mn, with 97% forgiven in the agreement. Mongolia is seen as an opportunity for Russia, as it is an importer of refined petroleum; 76% of Mongolia's imported petroleum came from Russia at the time of the agreement.

Japan agreed a US$850mn loan in March 2017 to support the economy, which almost equalled all previous Japanese loans to Mongolia since it became a democracy. South Korea is also a key bilateral donor. While rising coal prices and higher demand from China are boosting exports and growth, clearing Chinese customs is a major constraint. Queues of coal trucks waiting to enter China have stretched as far as 80 miles as Chinese customs slow imports. An upper realistic limit on coal sales to China could threaten this important economic lifeline.

Sovereign Commercial Debt

Mongolia has no history of restructuring its sovereign commercial debt. As at end-2017, it had five US$ bonds outstanding, amounting to US$3.4bn, although this fell to four issues and US$2.9bn outstanding with the payment on maturity in January 2018 of a US$0.5bn bond issued in 2012.

On several occasions in 2010, the government discussed plans to issue a sovereign bond, although the issue was delayed as the government determined that markets were not sufficiently favourable. There was pressure from Mongolian corporates for the government to issue in order to establish a benchmark, and in December 2012, Mongolia made its debut with a dual tranche five-year and 10-year bond, for a combined US$1.5bn. Further issues followed in 2016 and 2017, including a sovereign bond issued in exchange for DBM notes (see below). These issues are listed in the table below, and the most recent issue is also detailed. All sovereign eurobonds have a bullet maturity. Mongolia is currently rated B– by Fitch and S&P, and Caa1 by Moody's. In 2017, Fitch has improved its outlook on the rating to positive from stable, Moody's improved its outlook to stable from negative watch, and S&P has been stable since August 2016. Greater optimism has come from the IMF EFF programme as this also unlocked other multilateral and bilateral disbursements. IMF comments so far have been positive and forecasts have improved, easing fears of external liquidity pressures.

The government of Mongolia on 20 February 2017 launched an exchange offer for the US$580mn DBM outstanding 5.75% guaranteed notes due 21 March 2017 into new government securities. The exchange was par for par and closed on 1 March. The government set a minimum yield of 8.75% on the new notes and a seven-year bullet maturity. Holders of an aggregate principal amount of US$475.989mn of notes were validly submitted and accepted. A new US$600mn 8.75% 2024 bond was subsequently issued in March 2017. The exchange offer was a key requirement underpinning the new IMF EFF (the announcement of the exchange offer coincided with the staff-level agreement on the new IMF programme) and while not strictly a prior action, the government stated that it will only proceed with the offer if participation was sufficiently high, and if terms were consistent with debt sustainability and gross financing needs. The programme assumed that external private creditor exposure would be maintained at its prevailing level (i.e. official money would not be used to finance bondholder exits). The scheduled US$580mn DBM maturity represented half central bank's reserves (at end-January 2017, reserves were US$1.1bn).

Mongolia's outstanding eurobonds

Description	*Size*	*Series*	*Issue date*
USD 4.125% due 2018—Matured	US$500mn	RegS/144A	Dec. 2012
CNY 7.5% due 2018	CNY1000mn	GMTN	Jun. 2015
USD 10.875% due 2021	US$500mn	RegS/144A	Apr. 2016
USD 5.125% due 2022	US$1000mn	RegS/144A	Dec. 2012
USD 5.625% due 2023	US$800mn	RegS/144A	Nov. 2017
USD 8.75% due 2024	US$600mn	RegS/144A	Mar. 2017

Source: Bloomberg

Mongolia bond
Mongolia 5.625% 2023
Bloomberg ticker: MONGOL

Borrower	Government of Mongolia
Issue date	1 November 2017
Form	Eurobond
ISIN	USY6142NAB48
Issue size	US$800mn
Currency	US dollar
Denomination	Minimum of US$200,000 and then US$1000 thereafter
Amortisation	Bullet
Final maturity date	1 May 2023
Coupon/interest	5.625% per annum, paid semi-annually March and September
Day count	30/360
Method of transfer	Euroclear/Clearstream
Settlement period	T + 2
Joint lead managers	CS, DB, JPM

Source: Bloomberg

Corporate Bond Markets

Eurobond issues sourced out of Mongolia are limited, as most Mongolian names are traded on overseas exchanges (e.g. Hong Kong). Currently, following the DBM bond exchange in 2017, there are three main corporate bonds outstanding from two issuers (TDBM and MONMIN).

The Trade and Development Bank of Mongolia LLC (TDBM) has issued six US$-denominated bonds to date, although only one is still active: a five-year US$500mn bullet bond with coupon 9.375% (detailed below). The bond is senior unsecured, guaranteed by the Government of Mongolia and is listed at Singapore Stock Exchange. The TDBM is a large retail and corporate lender in Mongolia, serving around 400 firms, with SME loans of cMNT92.4bn at end-September 2017. Miat Mongolian Airlines JSC (MMAIR) has a US$20mn five-year bond, with coupon 10.7% and maturity in December 2018.

Energy Resources LLC, a wholly owned subsidiary of Mongolian Mining Corporation (MONMIN), has two outstanding eurobonds, for US$412.5mn maturing in 2022 and for US$195mn with a perpetual call, detailed below. Both of these bonds were issued in May 2017 as part of a distressed debt restructuring (bank facility, senior notes, and promissory notes), which involved a 20% haircut, the process of which started in January 2016. In December 2017, S&P upgraded its long-term rating on Mongolian Mining Corporation to B– from D with a stable outlook, citing an improved capital structure and lengthened maturity profile following the restructuring. With more flexible interest payments (amounts will be accrued as payment-in-kind when the coal price is low) and small debt amortisations only start in Q4 18. MMC does still remain sensitive to coking coal prices, and debts after the restructuring stood at US$638mn.

At the time of writing, the Development Bank of Mongolia (DBMMN) is planning a new bond issue.

Trade & Development Bank corporate bond
Trade & Development Bank Corp 2020
Bloomberg ticker: TDBM

Borrower	Trade & Development Bank of Mongolia LLC
Issue date	19 May 2015
Form	Euro MTN
ISIN	US89253YAA01
Issue size	US$500mn
Currency	US dollar
Denomination	US$200,000 minimum, increments of US$1000 thereafter
Amortisation	Bullet
Final maturity date	19 May 2020
Coupon/interest	9.375% per annum, paid semi-annually
Day count	30/360
Method of transfer	Euroclear, Clearstream, FED FUNDS
Exchange	Berlin, Frankfurt, Munich, Singapore, Stuttgart
Joint lead managers	Bank of America Merrill Lynch, DB, ING
Governing law	English

Source: Bloomberg

Energy Resources corporate bond
Energy Resources Corp 2022
Bloomberg ticker: MONMIN

Borrower	Energy Resources LLC
Issue date	4 May 2017
Form	Eurobond
ISIN	XS1598634506
Issue size	US$412.465mn
Amount outstanding	US$412.465mn
Currency	US dollar
Denomination	US$1 minimum, increments of US$1 thereafter
Amortisation	Callable
Final maturity date	30 September 2022
Coupon/interest	None
Day count	30/360
Method of transfer	Euroclear/Clearstream
Exchange	Singapore, Stuttgart
Governing law	New York

Source: Bloomberg

Energy Resources corporate bond
Energy Resources Corp Perp
Bloomberg Ticker: MONMIN

Borrower	Energy Resources LLC
Issue date	4 May 2017
Form	Eurobond
ISIN	XS1599078059
Issue size	US$194.999mn
Amount outstanding	US$194.999mn
Currency	US dollar
Denomination	US$1 minimum, increments of US$1 thereafter
Amortisation	Perpetual Call
Final maturity date	Perpetual
Coupon/interest	None
Day count	30/360
Method of transfer	Euroclear/Clearstream
Exchange	Singapore, Stuttgart
Governing law	New York

Source: Bloomberg

Mozambique

Nominal GDP (US$mn, 2018)[a]		14,601
Population (thousand, 2018)[a]		30,339
GDP per capita (USD, 2018)[a]		481
Credit ratings (long-term foreign currency)[b]	Fitch	RD
	Moody's	Caa3
	S&P	SD

[a]IMF WEO October 2018
[b]As at end-September 2018

Country Summary

- One of the poorest countries in the world, and with memories of the 14-year long civil war that ended in 1990 still fresh, Mozambique has huge proven reserves of offshore natural gas such that exports of LNG could be transformative over the next decade and more. Other key sectors include aluminium and coal. This potential has resulted in large FDI inflows since 2000, and investment in gas alone could amount to US$100bn. First gas from the project operated by ENI (Area 4) is expected in 2022, with production expected to follow from Anadarko's much bigger operations (Area 1) after that.
- Some 16 years after the granting of HIPC debt relief, Mozambique was again in debt distress and defaulted on its commercial debt over 2016–2017, including its only sovereign bond. Mozambique's bond

Exotix Capital, *Exotix Developing Markets Guide*,
https://doi.org/10.1007/978-3-030-05867-8_28

default in January 2017 was the first Sub-Saharan Africa sovereign bond default since Cote d'Ivoire's in 2010 (the Republic of Congo made some late coupon payments in 2016–2017). It was also one of the few sovereigns not even to make the first coupon payment on a bond, after the bond itself came out of a voluntary restructuring in April 2016 of the ill-fated tuna bond that was issued in 2013.

- Mozambique's default came after revelations in April 2016 that two commercial loans (amounting to 10% of GDP) had not previously been disclosed to the IMF (the so-called hidden debt). This mattered because the IMF had only just agreed to a programme for the country in December 2015. The programme was suspended and the withdrawal of IMF and donor financing, loss of confidence and resulting collapse in the currency led the government to announce in October 2016 its intention to restructure its commercial debt. Public debt was c108% of GDP in 2017. After two years, the Ministry of Finance announced on 6 November 2018 an agreement in principle on key restructuring terms for the bond (not the two loans) and hoped to complete an exchange in early 2019.

Economic data	*Avg*[a]	*2014*	*2015*	*2016*	*2017 (e)*	*2018 (f)*	*2019 (f)*
Real GDP growth	7.0	7.4	6.6	3.8	3.7	3.5	4.0
Inflation (annual average)	8.0	2.3	2.4	19.2	15.3	6.0	5.7
Current account (% of GDP)	–25.9	–38.2	–40.3	–39.3	–22.4	–18.2	–44.8
Reserves (US$mn, end-period)[b]	2254	3072	2472	1971	3299	3188[c]	–
Reserves/ imports (months)[d]	3.5	3.1	2.7	2.9	4.6	–	–
Overall fiscal balance (% of GDP)[e]	–4.8	–10.7	–7.2	–6.3	–4.4	–7.1	–7.6
Currency (ticker)	Mozambique metical (MZN)						
FX regime	The central bank maintains a flexible exchange rate regime, classified by the IMF as floating.						

(*continued*)

(continued)

Economic data	*Avg*[a]	*2014*	*2015*	*2016*	*2017 (e)*	*2018 (f)*	*2019 (f)*
Key exports	Aluminium (35%), coal products (13.6%), electricity (7.4%), gas (5.7%), raw tobacco (5.2%), refined petroleum (4.4%). LNG exports are projected to commence from 2022, which will radically change the country's export base and economic structure.						

Source: IMF WEO Database, IMF Country Reports, Haver, OEC, Exotix

[a]10-year average to 2016 unless otherwise stated
[b]Gross central bank reserve assets from Haver
[c]Latest figure, June 2018
[d]Months of the current year's imports of goods, services and primary income debits (Exotix calculation)
[e]IMF overall government net lending

Key figures		*Party*	*Since*
President	Filipe Nyusi	Frelimo	Jan. 2015
Prime minister	Carlos Agostinho do Rosario	Frelimo	Jan. 2015
Minister of economy and finance	Adriano Maleiane	Frelimo	Jan. 2015
Key opposition figure	Afonso Dhlakama	Renamo	1979
Central bank governor	Rogerio Lucas Zandamela	–	Sep. 2016

Politics

Executive power

The president is both chief of state and head of the government. Cabinet is appointed by the president from among the members of the National Assembly. The 2004 constitution established the State Council, which advises the president on issues such as dissolving parliament, declaration of war, declaration of a state of emergency and the holding of elections. The prime minister is the head of the Constitutional Council.

Presidential term: Five years (two-term limit) **Parliamentary term**: Five years

Legislature

The unicameral Assembly of the Republic (Assembleia da Republica) comprises 250 members elected by proportional representation to serve five-year terms. A party must gain 5% of the vote to get parliamentary representation.

Elections

Next due Presidential and legislative: October 2019

Last legislative election (Oct. 2014)	*Seats*	*Last presidential (Oct. 2014)*	*% of vote*
Frelimo	144	Filipe Nyusi (Frelimo)	57.0
Renamo	89	Afonso Dhlakama (Renamo)	36.6
Democratic Movement of Mozambique (MDM)	17	Daviz Simango (MDM)	6.4
Others	0		
Total	250	Total	100.0

People

One of the poorest countries in the world, Mozambique has a young population, with 66% of people under 25 in 2017. The main ethnic groups are Makhuwa, Tsonga, Lomwe and Sena. Portuguese influence is evident: Portuguese is the official language (although several others are also spoken) and Christianity is the largest religion, at 56%, with Roman Catholic being the largest denomination. Another 18% of people are Muslim. Net migration is negative, and 33% of people live in urban areas, with sparse population of the large fertile land.

In 1498, a Portuguese expedition arrived in Mozambique and colonists set up trade and mining enterprises during the sixteenth and seventeenth centuries. During the eighteenth and nineteenth centuries, Mozambique became a major part of the slave trade, until Portugal abolished it in 1842, although some did continue illegally. In 1932, Portugal broke up trading companies and imposed direct rule. This thrived during the 1950s and 1960s until the Mozambique Liberation Front (Frelimo) began a war for independence in 1964, leading to significant guerrilla control of northern areas. A new government in Portugal resulted from a coup and supported the autonomy of colonies.

Mozambique gained independence in 1975, following the Lusaka Accord the previous year. The resulting country was ruled by a single-party government led by President Samora Machel, and a Marxist-Leninist doctrine was adopted in 1977. That year also saw civil war break out between Frelimo and Rhodesia-supported Renamo. Joaquim Chissano succeeded Machel as president after he was killed in a 1986 air crash. The constitution was amended in 1990, replacing the Marxist-Leninist system with a multi-party democracy, ending the civil war. Chissana was re-elected in 1994 and 1999.

Floods in 2000 devastated agriculture and infrastructure, resulting in external debt relief and foreign aid. Chissano declined to run for a fourth term and Armando Guebuza won the election for Frelimo in 2004, taking office in 2005. Poor rainfall led to a poor harvest and hundreds of thousands in need of food aid. Guebuza was re-elected in 2009, although the opposition Renamo party alleged fraud. In March 2012, police raided a camp of 300 Renamo supporters accused of preparing to stage anti-government protests. Tensions arose again in 2013, indicating a risk of a return to civil war, especially in October when Renamo said it would pull out of the 1992 peace deal. Clashes occurred in November, and civilian fled from southern Homoine in January 2014 after government-Renamo fighting.

(*continued*)

(continued)

People
Renamo leader Afonso Dhlakama signed a peace agreement with President Guebuza in September 2014, declaring that he would run for president, while Guebuza was required to step down due to term limits. Frelimo candidate Filipe Nyusi—a former defence minister from 2008 to 2014 under Guebuza—won in 2014, leading to Renamo boycotts and protests. Peace talks continued over 2017–2018 through which Renamo has agreed to a process to lay down its weapons, thereby helping to facilitate local elections planned for October 2018 (delays were expected due to a dispute with Frelimo). The deal includes inclusion of former rebels into the police and army, and assurances that the peace process will not stop. Some complementary constitutional changes were approved by legislators in May to devolve power and a new leader has been appointed since the death of Afonso Dhlakama in May, who was given a state funeral. Violence, however, continues in the isolated and poor north of the country, escalating in May 2018, as an extremist group attempts to impose militant Islam in northern regions, including Cabo Delgado, near to one of the world's largest untapped offshore gas fields.

Debt

	2012	*2017e*
External debt ratios (%)		
Total external debt/GDP	70.9	138.7
Public external debt[a]/GDP	34.5	81.0
Private external debt/GDP	36.4	57.7
Total external debt/exports of goods and services	231.5	364.6
External debt service ratio[a]	2.1	18.2
Public debt ratios (%)		
Public domestic debt/GDP	4.8	26.7
Public debt/GDP	39.3	107.7

Source: IMF, Ministry of Finance, Bank of Mozambique

[a]Public and publicly guaranteed

Exotix estimates Mozambique's public and publicly guaranteed (PPG) external debt was US$10.3bn at end-2017, based on IMF and Ministry of Finance data. Ministry of Finance data for Q1 17 showed public external debt of US$8.7bn, although this appears to relate to central government debt only, as it excludes guaranteed debt, some other commercial debt and central bank debt (which amounted in total to another US$1.6bn). Exotix includes IMF and its own estimates for these items to produce an estimate for PPG external debt—which is roughly in line with the IMF estimate in its 2017 Article IV published in March 2018, which showed it at c80% of GDP (which equated to US$10.1bn). The creditor composition of PPG external debt, based on IMF and Ministry of Finance data, showed that 40% was owed to bilateral creditors and 39% was owed to multilateral creditors. A detailed breakdown by individual official sector creditor is not available for end-2017 although Exotix shows the position as of March 2017, based on separate Ministry of Finance figures. Around three-quarters of its bilateral debt is owed to non-Paris Club creditors. China was the biggest bilateral creditor, accounting for around half of non-Paris Club debt and 40% of bilateral debt. Portugal was the next-biggest bilateral creditor. The World Bank's IDA was the biggest multilateral creditor (65% of multilateral debt and 25% of public external debt)—indeed, IDA was the single-biggest individual creditor, ahead of China. Of the remaining 21% of PPG external debt, around two-thirds was owed to commercial creditors, either directly or through guarantees. This comprised the US$727mn MOZAM 2023 bond and the two guaranteed commercial loans (MAM and ProIndicus), all of which (the bond and two loans) are currently in default, as the government seeks a restructuring. External financing incurred late in 2017 for the Coral LNG project owed by the state-owned National Hydrocarbon Company (ENH) represented the remaining one-third of the commercial debt.

The public external debt stock figures exclude arrears, which amounted to another US$710mn at end-2017, according to IMF estimates. This comprises US$593mn in commercial debt (MOZAM, MAM and ProIndicus) on which the government entered into default over 2017, and US$117mn in bilateral debt (Brazil Paris Club debt and old non-Paris Club debt owed to Libya, Iraq, Angola, Poland and Bulgaria).

Total external debt was US$17.6bn in 2017, according to Exotix estimates, with PPG external debt comprising 58% of the total and private external debt amounting to 42%. Private external debt is estimated at US$7.3bn, based on IMF data. Private sector borrowing has been increased by investments in liquified natural gas (LNG) projects. Total external debt was therefore 139% of GDP, using 2017 estimated GDP from the IMF WEO, with public external debt of 81% of GDP and private external debt of 58% of GDP. Total external debt has risen significantly since 2012, both in nominal USD terms and as a share of GDP. Note, however, that the debt ratios would fall markedly based on 2018 GDP projections, given the expected rise in nominal GDP in local currency terms and appreciation of the metical versus the US dollar. Based on IMF WEO data, nominal GDP is expected to increase in 2018 to US$14.3bn from US$12.7bn in 2017, which would see the total external debt/GDP ratio fall to 123%, while public external debt falls to 72% of GDP, and private external debt falls to 51% of GDP (this assumes no increase in the numerator). As a share of exports, total external debt was 365% of exports of goods and services, while PPG external debt was 213% of goods and services exports. Exports of goods and services were cUS$4.8bn in 2017 on IMF figures.

Total public debt was 108% of GDP in 2017 (based on 2017 estimated GDP in the WEO), cUS$13.7bn, according to Exotix estimates. Public domestic debt amounted to US$3.4bn, according to the IMF, c27% of GDP. The estimate for the overall public debt ratio compares with the IMF figure of 112% of GDP (85% public and 27% private) in the 2017 Article IV. The public debt ratio fell last year from its peak of 128% of GDP in 2016, as per the IMF Article IV, due to FX appreciation during the year, although the ratio has increased from just 40% in 2012. The dramatic increase in the public debt/GDP ratio over this period is due to several factors, including significant new external borrowing (often on commercial terms), significantly higher domestic debt (domestic debt was only 5% of GDP in 2012), the recognition of the previously “hidden debt” (the two guaranteed commercial loans) and marked currency depreciation over this period (the metical fell from an average of MZN29 per US dollar in 2012 to US$61 in 2016). Public domestic debt has increased sharply, from US$733mn in 2012 to US$3.4bn in 2017, following large increases over 2015–2016 amid limited access to external financing due to the country’s default on its commercial borrowing and suspension of IMF programme discussions.

Composition of external debt

External debt by creditor (end-2017e)	*Nominal amount outstanding (US$mn)*	*Share of total (%)*
Public and publicly guaranteed external debt[a]	**10,271**	**58.4**
o/w Official multilateral	3989	22.7
World Bank IDAb[b]	2587	14.7
AfDF[b]	777	4.4
IMF (Bank of Mozambique)	165	0.9
IFAD[b]	132	0.8
Other[b]	328	1.9

(*continued*)

(continued)

External debt by creditor (end-2017e)	*Nominal amount outstanding (US$mn)*	*Share of total (%)*
Official bilateral	4111	23.4
Paris Club[b]	947	5.4
Korea[b]	208	1.2
France[b]	200	1.1
Brazil[b]	183	1.0
Japan[b]	113	0.6
Russia[b]	108	0.6
Non-Paris Club[b]	3164	18.0
China[b]	1693	9.6
Portugal[b]	633	3.6
Libya[b]	247	1.4
Iraq[b]	231	1.3
India[b]	180	1.0
Commercial creditors	727	4.1
MOZAM 2023 bond	727	4.1
Other	660	3.8
ENH (Coral LNG project)	660	3.8
Guaranteed debt	783	4.5
MAM and ProIndicus loans	745	4.2
Other	38	0.2
Private sector external debt	**7315**	**41.6**
Total external debt	**17,586**	**100.0**

Source: IMF, Ministry of Economy and Finance, Exotix

[a]Excluding arrears

[b]Ministry of Economy and Finance figures for Q1 17

Rescheduling History

Mozambique benefitted from debt relief under the HIPC initiative in 2001 and MDRI in 2006. The (enhanced) HIPC decision point came in April 2000 and completion point was reached in September 2001. Mozambique had earlier received US$3.7bn in debt relief (US$1.7bn NPV terms) under the original HIPC framework, under which Mozambique had reached completion point in June 1999, becoming the fourth country to do so (after Uganda, Bolivia and Guyana). It was the largest debt relief operation to have been organised under HIPC at the time. Mozambique later benefitted from an additional US$600mn in debt relief (initially US$254mn in NPV terms, later topped up to US$306mn) under the enhanced HIPC, bringing its total debt reduction under the initiative to US$4.3bn. Mozambique became the third country to reach completion point under the enhanced HIPC framework, after Bolivia and Uganda.

The total debt relief for Mozambique, under both the original and enhanced HIPC, was therefore nearly US$2bn in NPV terms, and represented a reduction of 72% in NPV terms (with a common reduction factor of 72.7%). The IMF's completion point document at the time noted that Mozambique's public external debt was US$3.4bn at end-2000 in NPV terms, after partial delivery under the original HIPC Initiative, and was expected to fall to US$1.1bn in 2001 after full delivery under traditional debt-relief mechanisms and original and enhanced HIPC Initiatives. Bilateral relief beyond HIPC was projected to reduce the NPV of the debt by a further US$140mn in 2001. The IMF and World Bank also agreed in April 2000 that additional interim debt relief, up to 100% of debt service due over the following year, would be provided in view of exceptional circumstances arising from the floods that hit the country earlier in the year. Paris Club creditors took similar action. Furthermore, in July 2006, the World Bank cancelled most of Mozambique's debt under a G8-promoted plan.

The post-debt relief period saw a resurgence in the Mozambique economy. The period from 2002 to 2012 saw real GDP growth average 7.6%, one of the highest rates in the world, buoyed by the country's commodity and natural resource wealth. Public debt, which stood at 123% of GDP in 2001 (IMF WEO), fell to just 36% in 2007, due to significant debt relief and strong growth. Public debt remained at c40% over 2007–2012. Dollar GDP tripled from 2002 to 2012 (from US$5bn to US$15bn). Major natural gas reserves were discovered in 2011—which are transformative in terms of their potential for LNG exports—and the government borrowed extensively, assuming no future financing problems. The country was lauded as a success story, hosting the IMF's Africa Rising conference in Maputo in May 2014.

Some 16 years after HIPC, though, Mozambique was again in debt distress and defaulted on its commercial debt over 2016–2017. This came after revelations of hidden debt in April 2016, first reported in the media, which led the authorities to acknowledge later that month that some US$1.4bn (10% of GDP) of external debt guaranteed by the government had not previously been disclosed to the IMF. The guaranteed debt related to two commercial loans to government-controlled companies undertaken in 2013–2014 (MAM and ProIndicus), which were in addition to the privately placed loan participation note through the EMATUM SPV in September 2013 (the MEMATU 6.305% 2020 "tuna bond"). The revelations were particularly ill-timed, coming just four months after the Fund had approved an IMF programme for the country in December 2015 in response to the commodity price shock, and just a month after the government undertook a voluntary exchange of its EMATUM bond into a new sovereign bond (MOZAM 10.5% 2023). The IMF programme was immediately suspended in April 2016, undermining donor and investor confidence, and the currency collapsed (at its peak in October, the metical had depreciated by 42% during 2016, before recovering modestly in the final months of the year). The withdrawal of IMF funding (and other donor support), on top of its existing balance of payments needs, exerted pressure on reserves and the fiscal accounts, and, with the new liabilities and currency depreciation, saw the public debt burden rise sharply to unsustainable levels. Public debt peaked at 128% of GDP in 2016 (now shown as 119% in the WEO), up from 62% in 2014. Despite some initial efforts to resume discussions with the Fund over a new programme, progress was slow and, by October 2016, starved of new external financing, the government announced its intention to restructure its commercial debt (the MOZAM bond and the two loans). The government finally presented its illustrative restructuring proposals to creditors on 20 March 2018. They implied a significant NPV loss for creditors and were immediately rejected by the bondholder committee. According to media reports on 3 August 2018, bondholders had presented a counter proposal to the government and its advisers, but few details were available. Despite this seemingly slow progress, the Ministry of Finance announced on 6 November 2018 an agreement in principle on key restructuring terms for its sovereign bond, which had the support of the majority of the restructuring committee (see below).

Relations with Multilateral Creditors

Mozambique joined the IMF in 1984 and, until 2016, had a good relationship with the Fund, and the official sector more widely, with a strong track record of engagement. It had four IMF programmes in the 1980s–1990s, mainly geared towards achieving HIPC debt reduction, and has had 10 IMF arrangements in all (including financed programmes and policy-monitoring arrangements). In fact, after completing its 2004–2007 post-HIPC ECF, Mozambique had graduated away from financed programmes and followed a number of policy support instruments (PSIs) instead, with one exception—an ESF in 2009–2010—during the global financial crisis. It would be five more years, and eight years after its last programme, before Mozambique would return to the Fund for a full programme in response to the balance of payments needs in light of the 2014 commodity price collapse.

An 18-month SCF amounting to US$283mn was approved by the Fund in December 2015. The IMF programme aimed at a sizeable, up-front correction, in order to reduce macroeconomic imbalances and rebuild reserves after the emergence of an external financing gap. The country was hit hard by the more challenging global conditions brought about by the decline in commodity prices. However, its vulnerability to the global shock was exacerbated by the country having made few savings through the good years (2011–2014) and contracting a lot of new debt. Balance of payments pressures began to build due largely to a deterioration in Mozambique's underlying current account balance and the fall in FX inflows and FDI. According to the IMF, the non-megaproject current account deficit widened by US$1.7bn over July 2014–June 2015 compared with the previous 12 months. As a result, the metical came under pressure, despite FX intervention (it fell by 25% against the US dollar in 2015, but its peak decline during the year was 40% in November). The overall balance of payments deficit amounted to US$823mn, financed in large part by a fall in reserves (US$700mn), with the remainder filled by the IMF. The IMF programme was based on three pillars: (1) monetary tightening, (2) fiscal consolidation and (3) reform of the FX market. The size of the policy adjustment sought to reduce imports by US$1bn in order to stabilise the balance of payments and rebuild reserves. The IMF programme also catalysed World Bank disbursements and other donor flows. The IMF's first review of the programme was due by end-March 2016.

The IMF suspended the SCF programme soon after. Revelations of hidden debt, first reported in the media in early April 2016, led the Fund to note in a press briefing on 15 April 2016 at the IMF/World Bank Spring Meetings that it had received confirmation that week from the authorities of the existence of a large amount of borrowing, in excess of US$1bn, that had not previously been disclosed to the IMF and that significantly changed its assessment of the country's macroeconomic outlook. The IMF also noted that it had cancelled the mission due the following week to conduct the review of the PSI and SCF, pending full disclosure and assessment of the facts. An IMF statement on 23 April 2016 noted that the authorities acknowledged that an amount in excess of US$1bn of external debt guaranteed by the government had not previously been disclosed to the Fund. Managing Director Christine Lagarde said in May 2016 that the government was "clearly concealing corruption". A staff team subsequently visited Mozambique in June, with a statement on 24 June 2016 saying that the total stock of debt had increased to 86% of GDP at end-2015 after the discovery of previously undisclosed loans, which the IMF confirmed as US$1.4bn (10.4% of GDP). The IMF noted that public debt was likely to have reached a high risk of distress and that, as a result, performance under the 2015–2017 SCF had been disappointing, with most assessment and performance criteria or indicative targets being missed at end-December 2015 and end-March 2016. The IMF statement also called for an international and independent audit of the EMATUM, ProIndicus and MAM companies and said that a resumption of programme discussions would only take place at a later stage. It noted that the authorities agreed on the need for an urgent and decisive package of policy measures to avoid a further deterioration in economic performance. In particular, staff noted the need for substantial fiscal and monetary tightening, as well as exchange rate flexibility, to restore macroeconomic sustainability, and to help alleviate pressure on the FX market and to restore supply and demand balance on the FX market A further staff visit took place in September 2016, after the president seemingly reassured the IMF about the government's willingness to work with the Fund on the terms of reference for the independent audit. The concluding statement of the staff visit on 29 September noted that a resumption of programme discussions, as requested by the government, required a solid track record of implementation of sound macroeconomic policies and an effective initiation of the audit process.

Although programme discussions did resume by the end of 2016, they had petered out within a year. The IMF confirmed on 28 November 2016 that an IMF mission would take place in December to initiate discussions on a new programme, as its two conditions had been met, not least with the selection of an independent company to conduct the audit. The concluding statement on 13 December 2016 noted that there had been several positive economic developments over the previous few months, with monetary policy tightening since October 2016 rebalancing the FX market and the current account deficit narrowing rapidly, helped by a decline in imports and higher coal prices. International reserves had started to increase, expected to stand at 3.5 months of non-megaproject imports at end-2016. However further fiscal consolidation was needed in 2017. After several months (and a short extension), a summary of the audit, undertaken by Kroll, was published on 24 June 2017, although the IMF noted at the time that information gaps remained, in particular on the use of loan proceeds, a message it repeated in its concluding statement on 19 July, following another staff mission. Programme discussions were therefore essentially put on hold, pending a response to the information gaps, but the IMF did complete its by then long overdue Article IV, with the 2017 Article IV going to the Board in March 2018 following an Article IV mission in December 2017.

At the time of writing, there had been no further progress on programme discussions. An IMF statement on 3 August 2018, following a staff visit to take stock of recent developments, noted a gradual improvement in the economy, with real GDP growth in 2017 reaching 3.75%, exceeding the Article IV projection by 0.75ppts, supported by agriculture and significantly higher mining production. Inflation had fallen to 6% in June from its peak of 26% in November 2016, reflecting tight monetary policy, exchange rate stability, and decelerating food price increases. The current account deficit had narrowed due to strong export performance and weak import growth, supporting a large accumulation of international reserves, which covered nearly 7 months of next year's projected non-megaproject imports at end-June. The central bank had begun easing monetary policy (cutting its policy rate by a 600 bps since April 2017), and the IMF noted that the government had taken important measures to contain the fiscal deficit, eliminating subsidies for fuel and wheat, adopting an automatic fuel price adjustment mechanism and increasing electricity and public transportation prices. The IMF called for realistic assumptions for the 2019 budget and noted that public debt remained in distress.

IMF programmes

Date	*Arrangements*	*Comments*
1987–1990	SAFC	Three-year structural adjustment facility commitment (SAFC) for SDR42.7mn, fully drawn.
1990–1995	ECF	Extended credit facility (ECF), previously poverty reduction and growth facility (PRGF), for SDR130.05mn, of which SDR115.35mn was drawn.
1996–1999	ECF	SDR75.6mn, fully drawn.
1999–2003	ECF	Approved in June 1999, the programme was originally for SDR58.8mn over three years, extended to SDR87.2mn in March 2000, of which SDR78.8mn was drawn.
2004–2007	ECF	SDR11.36mn (cUS$16.6mn), fully drawn. The three-year programme was agreed in June 2004 and gained Board approval in July. Disbursements began in February 2005 following the first review, which observed satisfactory performance. Only the second and final reviews needed waivers, although some performance criteria were modified at the third review in December 2005. Macroeconomic performance allowed the approval of a PSI programme.

(*continued*)

(continued)

Date	*Arrangements*	*Comments*
2007–2010	PSI	Approved in June 2007 to support the authorities' economic reforms. It overlapped with the ESF programme from 2009 and was immediately succeeded with another PSI in June 2010, as performance was at least satisfactory throughout.
2009–2010	ESF	Twelve-month exogenous shocks facility (ESF), approved in July 2009, for SDR113.6mn (cUS$176mn) to cushion the country from the effects of the global financial crisis. It was fully drawn and SDR49.7mn remains outstanding.
2010–2013	PSI	Approved following the final review of the 2007 PSI, aiming to accelerate economic development and poverty reduction. Economic performance remained strong, while inflation control became a priority and the authorities took on an ambitious development agenda.
2013–2016	PSI	Approved in June 2013 amid strong economic performance and implementation of structural reforms aiming to create sustained and more inclusive growth. Achieving this while maintaining fiscal and debt sustainability was a challenge undertaken with this programme. The outlook remained positive with investments in coal and natural gas projects. The fifth review was completed in December 2015, with waivers and modifications of three assessment criteria. No further reviews took place after the hidden debt was disclosed.
2015–2017 (suspended in 2016)	SCF	With the fifth review of the PSI, the IMF Board approved a SDR204.5mn (cUS$283mn, 90% of quota) 18-month stand-by credit facility (SCF) in December 2015 to supplement the PSI and augment reserves in response to balance of payments needs following the fall in commodity prices over 2014–2015 and its associated impact on the economy. Corrective measures included a fiscal and monetary tightening and reform of the FX market. SDR85.2mn (US$117.9mn) was disbursed immediately. The programme was, however, subsequently frozen in April 2016, before even the completion of the first review, as a result of the disclosure of "hidden debt"; with only the initial SDR85.2mn disbursement made.

Source: IMF. Mozambique joined the IMF in 1984

The World Bank currently has 42 active projects in Mozambique, the largest by commitment amounts being for the development of water supplies, electrical power, roads and other infrastructure. In 2016, the Ministry of Economy and Finance quoted debt owed to the World Bank (IDA) as US$2635mn. Recent projects by the African Development Bank (AfDB) also focus on upgrading infrastructure essential for living standards and economic growth.

Paris Club and Bilateral Creditors

Mozambique has had eight Paris club agreements, the most recent of which, its HIPC exit treatment, is still active. Mozambique reached decision point under the original framework in April 1998 (and had reached completion point in June 1999). Decision point under the enhanced framework was reached in April 2000, with completion point following in September 2001. Mozambique subsequently received its Paris Club treatment under enhanced HIPC in November 2001, becoming the third country to complete the Paris Club process under enhanced HIPC, after Uganda and Bolivia. Austria, Brazil, France, Germany, Italy, Japan, Portugal, Russia, Spain, Sweden, the UK and the US were the participating creditors.

Paris Club agreements

Date	*Terms*	*Status*	*Details*
1984	Classic	Fully repaid	Treated US$142mn under Classic terms.
1987	Ad Hoc	Fully repaid	Treated US$612mn under Ad Hoc terms.
1990	Toronto	Fully repaid	Treated US$707mn under Toronto terms, with repayment of non-ODA credits over 14 years and eight years of grace, after a cancellation to a rate of 33%. Repayment of ODA credits over 25 years with 14 years of grace.
1993	London	Fully repaid	Treated US$440mn under London terms, with repayment of non-ODA credits over 23 years and six years of grace, after a cancellation to a rate of 50%. Repayment of ODA credits over 30 years with 12 years of grace. Possibility to conduct debt swaps.
1996	Naples	Fully repaid	Treated US$663mn under Naples terms, with repayment of non-ODA credits over 23 years and six years of grace, after a cancellation to a rate of 67%. Repayment of ODA credits over 40 years with 16 years of grace. Possibility to conduct debt swaps.

(*continued*)

(continued)

Date	Terms	Status	Details
1998	Lyon	Fully repaid	Treatment under Lyon terms, with repayment of non-ODA credits over 23 years and six years of grace, after a cancellation to a rate of 80%. Repayment of ODA credits over 40 years with 16 years of grace. Possibility to conduct debt swaps.
1999	Lyon	Fully repaid	Treated US$1860mn under Lyon terms, with repayment of non-ODA credits over 23 years and six years of grace, after a cancellation to a rate of 80%. Repayment of ODA credits over 40 years with 16 years of grace. With a possibility to conduct debt swaps, a good will clause and a pullback clause.
2001	HIPC Initiative exit	Active	Of the US$2800mn owed to the Paris Club, US$2270mn in face value was cancelled (cUS$1.65bn in NPV terms) and US$530mn was rescheduled under HIPC Initiative Exit terms. There is a possibility to conduct debt swaps on a voluntary and bilateral basis. Completion point was reached on 25 September 2001.

Source: Paris Club

Mozambique has had a mixed relationship with donors. Donor support was temporarily halted in Q1 2010 due to governance concerns around the 2009 election. The government's steps to reassure donors led to the resumption of aid in April 2010. However, the revelation of hidden debt in April 2016 was a much bigger affair and led its main donors, known as the Group of 14 (G14), to suspend direct budget support on 6 May 2016, following the suspension of the IMF programme. The G14 consists of the World Bank, the AfDB, the EU, the UK, Austria, France, Portugal, Spain, Italy, Canada, Sweden, Switzerland, Ireland and Finland. The budget support for 2016 was estimated at US$265mn. Japan's International Cooperation Agency (JICA) was also reported in July 2017 to have suspended its aid and loans, amounting to US$100mn. As of January 2018, direct budget support by the donors was still suspended, although some project lending may have continued.

China is Mozambique's main bilateral creditor, based on the limited data that is available, owed about half Mozambique's non-Paris Club debt, 40% of its bilateral debt and 16% of its public external debt. Still, shortly after the commercial debt restructuring proposals in March 2018 (see below), when the authorities said that the country could not service its debts until 2023, the prime minister announced an agreement with

China and India to restructure their bilateral debt. This came "as part of efforts to bring the debt to sustainable standards" following negotiations. No details of the deal were given. In October 2017, the China government signed various agreements with Mozambique, including the partial cancellation of some bilateral obligations. Although the total outstanding debt that Mozambique owes to China was not revealed, cUS$36mn of interest was forgiven, which should have been paid by end-2017. Although a small amount relative to the total debt stock, this forgiveness allowed the government to make important budget adjustments. Other agreements included technical cooperation and a grant from the China government for the construction of a new airport, of cUS$15mn.

Relations with Russia are still strong, although former Soviet support for Mozambique was replaced by that of western donors during the 1980s. In November 2017, Russia agreed a huge debt-for-development swap, converting bilateral debt into a development fund, unlocking US$40mn for use by the UN World Food Programme to support school meal provision for 150,000 children over five years.

Mozambique also has some small bilateral arrears with six official creditors. According to the IMF Article IV in March 2018, these consist of US$94mn arrears to five creditors (Libya, Iraq, Angola, Bulgaria and Poland). These arrears are not new and date from the HIPC initiative in 2006, and to 2011 and 2015, and are subject to bilateral discussions. There are also arrears to Brazil amounting to US$23mn on US$125mn of borrowing by the state-owned airport company that had been guaranteed by the state. The loan was from BNDES. The guarantee had been called.

Sovereign Commercial Debt

Mozambique is in default on its commercial debt (a bond—MOZAM 10.5% 2023—and two loans, MAM and ProIndicus) after announcing its intention to restructure its commercial debt in October 2016. This followed the suspension of the IMF programme after the revelations of hidden debt in April 2016, and the subsequent withdrawal of donor funding, which prompted a loss of confidence, a collapse in the currency and a rise in the public debt burden to unsustainable levels (over 100% of GDP). Faced with a significant cashflow problem, the government defaulted on a coupon on its sovereign bond (MOZAM 10.5% 2023) in January 2017, its first coupon payment on the new bond following a voluntary exchange of its MEMATU bond in April 2016, and also defaulted on its MAM loan in May 2016 and ProIndicus loan in March 2017. Talks between the government and its commercial creditors on a restructuring continue.

Mozambique therefore set three records: (1) it became the first Sub-Saharan African sovereign bond default since Cote d'Ivoire's in 2010 (the Republic of Congo made some late coupon payments over 2016–2017); (2) it became one of the few sovereigns not even to make the first payment on an instrument (Cote d'Ivoire paid its first coupon in June 2010 after completing its 2010 London Club restructuring in April that year, but defaulted on its second coupon in December 2010, which remained unpaid during the grace period); and (3) it might set some kind of record for the quickest an IMF programme has gone off track (around four months).

Prior to recent events, Mozambique undertook two commercial debt rescheduling agreements over the 1980s–1990s, with the second operation (in 1991) taking the form of a debt buyback through the World Bank's debt reduction facility (DRF) at a 90% discount. At the time of its HIPC completion point in 2001, the government was said to be exploring the use of the DRF again to buy back commercial debt that was in arrears, but was not treated under the 1991 buyback. It was intended that such an operation would be on comparable terms to HIPC. However, there is no publicly available official information on whether such an operation eventually took place.

Commercial debt agreements

Date	*Details*
1987	Bank debt restructuring. Rescheduling of outstanding stock of US$253mn, including interest arrears.
1991	Bank debt restructuring. Buyback of US$124mn of commercial debt at a 90% discount funded by the DRF and donors (France, the Netherlands, Switzerland and Sweden).
2016	An exchange offer for the remaining US$697mn (face) of MEMATU 6.305% 2020 bonds was announced on 9 March, in a par for par swap into new direct government bonds, with a seven-year (2023) bullet maturity and a 10.5% coupon. After completion of the exchange, US$697mn of MEMATU notes were swapped into US$726.5mn in sovereign bonds (MOZAM 10.5% 2023). Exotix estimates that the exchange was broadly NPV neutral for bondholders.

Source: Exotix, World Bank GDF

The country's first international debt issue came in 2013 with the (now ill-fated) tuna bond. The government guaranteed loan participation notes (LPNs) of US$850mn (6% of GDP) for Empresa Moçambicana de Atum, S.A. (EMATUM), the Mozambique tuna company, which was established in

August 2013 by three public entities. EMATUM (ticker MEMATU) issued US$500mn of seven-year notes (2020 maturity) through a private placement, which was quickly tapped to US$850mn in late September because of strong demand. The proceeds were to finance the purchase of 24 tuna fishing vessels and three patrol vessels, as well as other vessels and related equipment for coastal protection and other related economic activities. The LPN had a 6.305% semi-annual coupon and began to amortise in September 2015 (at 9% of original notional semi-annually; cUS$77mn). Hence, debt service amounted to cUS$200mn annually over the first few years, with US$153mn per year in amortisation, and cUS$40mn in interest.

Talk of restructuring the EMATUM bond soon surfaced, however, perhaps not coincidentally ahead of the first amortisation payment. The idea first came to the fore in May 2015 during a parliamentary budget debate when the government referred to restructuring, but, at the time, it was taken to mean the accounting treatment of the loan—moving more of the loan onto the government's balance sheet to reflect the commercial reality of the borrowing from the loss making EMATUM's. Concerns subsequently died down and were further assuaged by the making of the September amortisation payment. However, restructuring talk resurfaced again after the government announced on 23 October that it had appointed a local bank (BNI) to advise on a debt restructuring. Evidently, the intended proceeds from tuna fishing that the borrowing was intended to support did not materialise. EMATUM was not making any money and could not afford to service the bond. The government appeared to want to reduce the debt service, with a lower coupon, reduced amortisation and a maturity extension. However, this would have imposed significant PV losses on bondholders, which investors would seek to resist, especially given the bond's 75% CAC threshold.

In the event, the government went down the voluntary exchange route, and announced on 9 March 2016 an exchange offer for the remaining US$697mn (face) of MEMATU bonds into direct government bonds. The exchange involved a three-year maturity extension, with holders of the existing 2020 bonds invited to swap par for par into a new seven-year bullet bond maturing in 2023 (MOZAM 2023). The government confirmed that the 11 March payment would be made, reducing the amount outstanding to US$697mn from its original US$850mn. The final issue price and coupon of the new bond were determined on 17 March after meetings with investors. The coupon was set at 10.5%. Accrued interest on the existing bond, from the last interest payment date (11 March) to the settlement date (6 April), was paid in cash. The new bond paid interest semi-annually on 18 January and 18 July, with a long first coupon (18 January 2017)—the bond did not make the first coupon, establishing something of a record (see below). There was also an incentive for holders to participate early. Holders who agreed to exchange before the early exchange deadline of 21 March got the early minimum exchange ratio (par for par). Holders who accepted after that, but before the final deadline of 29 March, got the base minimum exchange ratio (95%); that is, there was a 5% nominal haircut for those that did not accept early. In the event, after completion of the exchange, US$697mn of EMATUM notes were swapped into US$726.5mn of sovereign bonds and the EMATUM bond's CAC ensured that no outstanding rump remained of the exited bond. The restructuring resulted in significant (up-front) cash flow relief to the government. Exotix estimates that the exchange was broadly NPV neutral for bondholders, resulting in a modest NPV gain (7%) on the first day of trading of the new bond (the bond started trading at 89–90, according to Bloomberg), but a small NPV loss (−1%) after 30 days as a result of a near 15 point price fall in the new MOZAM bond following the hidden debt revelations that occurred shortly after the exchange was completed (the bonds fell even further in subsequent months). Bondholders were also able to move up the capital structure, swapping a guaranteed instrument to a pure sovereign bond.

Although the outcome was relatively investor friendly, the process was less so. The approach broke with best practice in terms of debtor-creditor dialogue, sharing of information and transparency, with little if any discussions with investors, and nothing transmitted to the market. And, when it did emerge, the timetable was very tight. Even more unusual was the timing itself. After stating a formal intention to look at restructuring in October, there was silence for the next six months until the announcement two days before the 11 March amortisation and coupon payment.

However, the situation quickly deteriorated and Mozambique ended up defaulting on its commercial debt over the course of 2016–2017. What was less well known at the time of the exchange was the existence of two more sizeable government guaranteed loans (MAM and ProIndicus), which later compromised debt service over the whole debt, after their eventual disclosure in April 2016 (soon after the EMATUM exchange closed) led to the suspension of the IMF programme before its first review and subsequent investigations concluded that the guarantees on the two loans and the EMATUM bond were neither legal or constitutional, according to the findings of a Mozambique parliamentary commission of enquiry in December 2016. This was because the guarantees exceeded parliamentary limits and that then Finance Minister Manuel Chang did not have the authority to sign the guarantees on his own. However, rather than use this finding to declare the loans null and void, the government, seemingly for political expediency, was committed to restructure them. Indeed, parliament subsequently declared them legal retrospectively. The hidden loans amounted to US$1.4bn, comprising mainly the US$535mn MAM loan and US$622mn ProIndicus loan, and also an additional US$221mn in a bilateral loan contracted between 2009 and 2014. The freezing of the scheduled IMF disbursements under the SCF programme, which would have amounted to US$110mn in 2016, together with the suspension of donor funding, which Fitch estimated amounted to US$300mn for the year, left a big hole in expected external financing inflows and necessitated policy tightening to close the financing gap and take the pressure off the currency. The exchange rate depreciated by 24% against the US dollar in the year to June. The IMF noted in its statement on 24 June 2016 that the discovery of the undisclosed debt increased the total stock of debt to 86% of GDP at end-2015. The debt burden was heading towards 100% and the IMF noted that public debt was now likely to have reached a high risk of distress; with implications for programme lending (i.e. it cannot lend into an unsustainable situation and would require financing assurances from creditors). The government announced on 18 May 2016 that MAM could not make the US$178mn debt payment (principal and interest) due on 23 May (it went unpaid and the guarantee was not called). Reports suggested negotiations between MAM and VTB, the lending bank, were underway. This raised concerns over the upcoming coupon due on the new MOZAM bond in January 2017 (it was a long first coupon), which was much smaller than the MAM payment and, after that, there was a much bigger payment that was due in March 2017 with the second principal repayment of US$119mn on the ProIndicus loan.

The government subsequently gave a presentation to creditors on 25 October 2016 that announced its intention to seek a restructuring of its commercial debt, i.e. the bond and two loans. The government explained that the macroeconomic and financing situation had deteriorated and, according to the government's fiscal projections, the country did not appear to have the money to pay the January coupon on the MOZAM bond. The advisors sought to complete a restructuring by January 2017 (before the January coupon), although that seemed hugely ambitious. The presentation noted that, while commercial debt was only 17% of the external debt, it was a much bigger share of overall external debt service, so that restructuring or reprofiling could provide significant cash flow relief, particularly on the MAM and ProIndicus loans. However, bondholders, who organised through the Global Group of Mozambique Bondholders (GGMB)—and reportedly represented, directly and indirectly, over 80% of the bonds—resisted. They set two pre-conditions to start talks—that the details of an IMF programme be made public and that a debt audit, as required by the IMF, was completed and results made public. Moreover, they argued that, in agreeing to a previous restructuring of the EMATUM bond, they have already provided cash flow relief, and other creditors (other commercial and bilaterals) should now shoulder the burden. The government subsequently defaulted on the MOZAM bond, announcing on 16 January 2017 that it would not make the US$59.757mn payment on the new bond, due 18 January, and failed to pay it during the 15-day grace period. As of end-July 2018, the government had missed four coupons on the MOZAM bond, amounting to US$174.2mn on Exotix calculations, with PDI equating to 24% of principal. The ProIndicus loan also went into default in March 2017.

A summary of the independent audit of the three companies (EMATUM, MAM and ProIndicus) undertaken by Kroll was published on 24 June 2017. An independent audit was a key IMF and donor requirement to renewing programme discussions, and for bondholders to start restructuring negotiations. The audit confirmed the flawed business plans of the companies concerned, weak public financial management and procurement processes, and the opaque nature of the financing arrangements. It illustrated how the three projects were intertwined, that the government overpaid for the goods relative to an external assessment, suggested the fees earned were excessive and that US$500mn of loan proceeds related to the EMATUM loan were unaudited and unexplained. Crucially, while publication of the audit was seen as paving the way to renew IMF discussions (a staff mission took place shortly afterwards in July), by the time of the annual meetings in October 2017 it was clear that there had been no progress pending more satisfactory answers to the information gaps in the Kroll debt audit, with, crucially, some US$500mn still unaccounted for.

The government and its advisers finally presented their illustrative restructuring proposals at a presentation to creditors on 20 March 2018. The government stressed that repayment capacity was limited until the gas arrives in 2023, and that it had limited ability to pay principal until 2028 and demanded low interest rates over the next five years (until 2023). The key features of the proposal were that the MOZAM bond and the two loans (MAM and ProIndicus) will be treated the same, a 50% haircut on PDI and penalties with the remaining amount capitalised, and a swap of eligible debt into new longer instruments, with very low step-up coupons, and each amortising in its last three years. Three options were presented—a 16-year maturity with no principal haircut and a step-up coupon, a 12-year maturity with 10% principal haircut and a lower step-up coupon, and an eight-year maturity with 20% principal haircut and a fixed 2.8% coupon. The proposals implied a significant NPV loss for creditors, estimated at 45–55% according to Exotix calculations, and were immediately rejected by the bondholder group (GGMB).

The bondholder committee (GGMB) was reported on 3 August 2018 to have made a formal proposal to the Mozambique government. According to the reports, the bondholders' proposal consisted of maturity extension, coupon reduction, full capitalisation of PDI and gas warrants (with payments made once a certain threshold had been reached, with the government retaining at least 97% of gas earnings). The proposal reportedly provided US$1bn in cash flow relief to the government until 2023. No further details were available.

Despite the seemingly slow progress, the Ministry of Finance surprisingly announced on 6 November 2018 an agreement in principle on key restructuring terms for the MOZAM 2023 bonds with four creditors in the bondholder committee (GGMB), owning or controlling 60% of the bonds. This was just shy of the 75% required under the bond's collective action clause, although it was felt that obtaining this threshold should be achievable. Holders of existing bonds will be invited to exchange for two new (separate) instruments, a new bond and a value recovery instrument (VRI) linked to future gas revenues (ie gas warrants). The key terms for the new bonds are: (1) no principal haircut; (2) maturity extension to 30 September 2033; (3) coupon reduction to 5.875% paid semi-annually, with 4% payable in cash and the remaining 1.875% capitalised until (and including) 30 September 2023, and the whole amount payable in cash thereafter. The coupon is payable on 30 March and 30 September each year. The first coupon payment is 30 March 2019 (accrual begins 30 September 2018); (4) principal payable in five equal annual instalments beginning 30 September 2029; and (5) nearly full capitalisation of PDI and accrued. The face value of the new bonds will be US$900mn. With principal of the existing 2023 bonds of US$726,524,000 and accrued but unpaid interest (to 30 September 2018) of US$189,441,133, this implied only a marginal (1.7%) reduction in claim. The VRI had the following basic terms, although the precise details are still to be determined: annual payment equal to 5% of the prior year's aggregate fiscal revenues from Area 1 and Area 4 gas projects, a cumulative nominal payment cap of US$500mn, and final applicable fiscal year of 2033. The agreement in principle is conditional on reaching agreement on satisfactory documentation and the ministry obtaining necessary approvals. It was hoped the restructuring will be launched in early 2019. Crucially, the proposal only concerns the bonds, not the two commercial loans.

The MOZAM 2023 bond and the two guaranteed loans of ProIndicus and MAM—all currently in default—and their key terms are summarised below.

Mozambique bond—in default
Mozambique 10.5% 2023
Bloomberg ticker: MOZAM

Borrower	Republic of Mozambique
Restructuring	Issued in exchange for EMATUM bond
Issue date	6 April 2016
Form	Eurobond
ISIN	XS1391003446
Issued amount	US$726.524mn
Currency	US dollar
Denomination	US$200,000 and US$1000 thereafter
Amortisation	Bullet
Final maturity date	18 January 2023
Coupon/interest	10.5% per annum, paid semi-annually January and July, with a long first coupon (18 January 2017)
Past due interest	US$174.184mn (up to and including July 2018, Exotix estimate)
Default date	18 January 2017
Day count	30/360
Method of transfer	Euroclear/Clearstream
Settlement period	T + 2
Governing law	English law
Joint lead managers	Credit Suisse, VTB Capital

Source: Bloomberg

ProIndicus loan—in default	
Borrower	ProIndicus SA
Guarantee	Guaranteed by the Republic of Mozambique
Issue date	15 November 2013
Issue size	US$622mn
Outstanding amount	US$597.12mn (as at October 2016)
Amortisation	US$24.88mn on 21 March 2016 and US$119.424mn on each 21 March of 2017, 2018, 2019, 2020 and 2021
Final maturity date	21 March 2021
Interest	LIBOR + 3.2% until 21 March 2014 and then 3.75% thereafter, payable annually on 21 March
Default date	21 March 2017
Arrears	Approx. US$282mn principal and interest as of 21 March 2018 (Exotix estimate)
Agent	Credit Suisse AG, London Branch
Governing law	English law

Source: Bloomberg

MAM loan—in default	
Borrower	Mozambique Asset Management SA (MAM)
Guarantee	Guaranteed by the Republic of Mozambique
Issue date	2 tranches: US$435mn on 23 May 2014 and US$100mn on 11 June 2014
Issue size	US$535mn
Outstanding amount	US$535mn (as at October 2016)
Amortisation	US$133.75mn on 23 May 2016, 2017, 2018 and 2019
Final maturity date	23 May 2019
Interest	LIBOR + 7%, payable annually on 23 May
Default date	23 May 2016
Arrears	Approx. US$503mn principal and interest as of 23 May 2018 (Exotix estimate)
Agent	VTB Capital
Governing law	English law

Source: Bloomberg

Nigeria

Nominal GDP (US$mn, 2018)[a]		397,472
Population (thousand, 2018)[a]		193,875
GDP per capita (USD, 2018)[a]		2050
Credit ratings (long-term foreign currency)[b]	Fitch	B+
	Moody's	B2
	S&P	B

[a]IMF WEO October 2018
[b]As at end-September 2018

Country Summary

- Africa's most populous nation and Sub-Saharan Africa's (SSA) largest oil producer (vying with Angola). Economic fortunes have tended to follow the oil price. Oil accounts for 10% of GDP, 80% of government revenue and over 95% of goods' exports. Collapses in global oil prices throughout 2014 and 2015 triggered a steep fall in revenue and FX reserves, as well as a worsening of current account and fiscal balances—ultimately, leading to Nigeria's first recession in 25 years in 2016. Oil production through 2017 rebounded to pre-recession levels, and a recovery in prices have led to moderate economic improvements for the country.

Exotix Capital, *Exotix Developing Markets Guide*,
https://doi.org/10.1007/978-3-030-05867-8_29

- The swearing in of President Buhari in 2015 marked the country's first-ever peaceful transition of power to an opposition candidate. Given Buhari's frequent bouts of illness, Vice President Osinbajo has served as acting president on numerous occasions, prompting questions about whether Buhari's health will prevent him from standing for re-election in February 2019.
- Despite recent increases, Nigeria's nominal debt stock and debt/GDP ratios remain relatively low; however, the debt service/revenue ratio is extremely high as a result of the low level of government revenue and inefficiencies in tax collection. This has prompted concerns about fiscal sustainability.

Economic data	*Avg*[a]	*2014*	*2015*	*2016*	*2017 (e)*	*2018 (f)*	*2019 (f)*
Real GDP growth	5.7	6.3	2.7	−1.6	0.8	1.9	2.3
Inflation (annual average)	10.5	8.0	9.0	15.7	16.5	12.4	13.5
Current account (% of GDP)	4.7	0.2	−3.2	0.7	2.8	2.0	1.0
Reserves (US$bn, end-period)[b]	39.4	34.5	29.1	25.8	38.8	47.8[c]	–
Reserves/imports (months)[d]	6.5	4.8	4.7	6.5	9.0	–	–
Overall fiscal balance (% of GDP)[e]	−0.7	−2.1	−3.5	−3.9	−5.3	−5.1	−4.5
Currency (ticker)	Nigeria naira (NGN)						
FX regime	Officially managed float, but de facto pegged to the US dollar through a multiple exchange rate regime: Official (305), Wholesale (NIFEX) (340), Investor and Exporter (NAFEX; 360), Bureau de change/parallel market rate (360). Calculations for ratios have been done using a blended rate of US$1 = NGN335.						
Key exports	Crude petroleum (81%), petroleum gas (14%), other (5%).						

Source: IMF WEO Database, IMF Country Reports, Haver, OEC

[a]10-year average to 2016, unless otherwise stated

[b]Gross foreign reserves

[c]Latest figure, June 2018

[d]In months of the current year's imports of goods, services and current transfers debit

[e]Overall government net lending

Key figures		*Party*	*Since*
President	Muhammadu Buhari	APC	May 2015
Vice president	Yemi Osinbajo	APC	May 2015
Minister of finance	Zainab Ahmed	APC	Sep. 2018
Central bank governor	Godwin Emefiele	–	Jun. 2014

Note: Nigeria is a member of the Commonwealth

Politics

Executive power

Concentrated on the president, who is both chief of state and head of government. Popularly elected, the president also heads the Federal Executive Council (cabinet) and appoints all ministers to it, although restricted to appointing at least one member from each of the 36 federal states. The president can veto any legislation passed by parliament, although parliament, in turn, can override a presidential veto with a two-thirds majority. A peculiarity in Nigeria's political structure is an unwritten agreement that the office of the presidency should rotate between the Muslim north and Christian south after two terms, while the vice president, simultaneously, represents the inverse.

Presidential term: Four years (two-term limit; consecutive allowed)

Parliamentary term: Four years

Legislature

The legislature—the National Assembly—is bicameral, comprising the Senate (upper house) and House of Representatives (lower house). Each house is elected by popular vote to serve a four-year term. The Senate comprises three members from each state and one from the capital Abuja—a total of 109 seats. The Senate acts as a review body, although it also has the power to suggest certain legislation. Each state (36 + the Federal Capital Territory—which elects a minister) has an elected governor (with a two-term constitutional limit) and an elected state assembly, below which are nearly 800 local government areas.

Senate: 109 seats

House of Representatives: 360 seats

Elections

Next due Presidential and legislative: 16 February 2019

Last legislative election[a] *(March 2015)*	*Seats*	*Last presidential (March 2015)*	*% of vote*
All Progressives Congress (APC)	225	Muhammadu Buhari (APC)	54
People's Democratic Party (PDP)	125	Goodluck Jonathan (PDP)	45
Others	10	Others	1
Total	190	Total	100.0

[a]Results shown for House of Representatives

Although there are over thirty political parties, two are dominant and the most organised; the ruling APC, the largest and with national support; the PDP, the main opposition party, whose support base is in the south. Switching between parties is common

People

Nigeria is Africa's most populous nation, housing nearly half of West Africa's population alone, and contains c250 different ethnic groups, five of which account for 80% of the population. The country is roughly divided into a predominately Muslim north and Christian south. The mostly Muslim Hausa-Fulani are found in the north and account for 30% of the population. The Yoruba (c20%) and Igbo (c18%) are also sizeable populations, and are located mostly in the southwest and southeast, respectively. The Ijaw are also found in the southeast.

Tribal and regional conflicts exposed Nigeria's fragile post-independence political structure. Most of present-day Nigeria fell under British rule in the late nineteenth century in what were then a number of protectorates. These were merged into what is now Nigeria in 1914. After independence, Nigeria became a federation of three autonomous regions (north, west and east; a fourth region, the mid-west, was added in 1964) under an overarching, but weaker, federal government. In 1967, Nigeria's four regions were replaced by 12 states in an attempt to break up regional power. However, in response to the federal centre taking back more power, further states were created due to local pressure for greater recognition. By 1996, Nigeria consisted of 36 states, with the Federal Capital Territory of Abuja having been created in 1976, giving us today's system of 36 + 1.

Divisions between the north and south, as well as along ethnic lines, fostered conflicts and power struggles as groups competed for control of the federal centre; this led to a series of coups, a bloody civil war between 1967–1970 (as the Igbo eastern region attempted to secede as the Republic of Biafra, resulting in the deaths of more than 1mn people) and long periods of military rule. According to the UK Foreign Office, in 50 years since independence, Nigeria has only had three civilian regimes (1960–1965, 1979–1983, 1999 to present).

(*continued*)

(continued)

People
Great strides have been made since civilian rule returned in 1999 under President Obasanjo (a southerner) who presided over the country's first democratic transition of power in 2007, but corruption continues to taint the country. Respect for human rights has improved since the return of civilian rule, although the UK FCO reports that abuses still occur. Meanwhile, the long-running campaign of violence, kidnapping, and extortion in the oil-rich Niger Delta is never far from the surface; it intensified in 2006, 2009, and again in 2014. More recently, the country has struggled to contain the terrorist organisation, Boko Haram (which presides primarily in the northeast), as well as the Fulani herdsman, a semi-nomadic group (located primarily throughout the middle belt/central Nigeria). Frequent clashes between military forces and both groups have led to security concerns across the country, forcing it to become a much larger piece of President Buhari's political agenda.

DEBT

	2012	*2017*
External debt ratios (%)		
Total external debt/GDP	3.3	12.6
Public external debt/GDP	1.4	5.5
Private external debt/GDP	1.9	7.1
Total external debt/exports of goods and services	5.0	87.4
External debt service ratio (public)	0.3	0.9
Public debt ratios (%)		
Public domestic debt/GDP	9.0	16.6
Public debt/GDP	10.4	22.1

Source: Nigeria Debt Management Office (DMO), Central Bank of Nigeria (CBN), IMF, Bloomberg, ITC Trademap, Exotix

Nigeria's outstanding public external debt was just under US$21bn by July 2018 (including a net US$2bn in eurobond issuances in 2018), which is 6.1% of GDP. Roughly 50% of public external debt is outstanding to multilateral creditors, of which, c80% is owed to the World Bank. There is no Paris Club debt outstanding, since it was retired in 2005. The remaining half of Nigeria's public external debt is owed to non-Paris Club creditors and commercial creditors. Prior to this treatment, public external debt stood at US$35.9bn, of which, over 80% was owed to the Paris Club. Roughly 60% of this debt received cancellation (in two stages), in addition to the retirement of most of Nigeria's London Club debt in 2006–2007. Although Nigeria's public external debt remains relatively low, it has risen significantly over the past decade following its Paris and London Club treatments, increasing by a factor of c5 times in nominal terms, however only at a factor of c2.5 as a percentage of GDP, during this time. This large increase has come mainly on the back of multiple Eurobond issues, primarily issued since the start of 2017. Since this time, Nigeria has issued US$7.3bn in commercial eurobonds including the first SSA 30-year issuance (excluding South Africa, and has since been replicated by Kenya, Ivory Coast, Angola, Ghana and Senegal, ordered first to most recent). These recent issues currently make up nearly 90% of Nigeria's US$8.3bn outstanding eurobonds. The country's Debt Management Office (DMO) has announced that it will likely issue another eurobond in late 2018 in order to gradually shift to its commercial creditor funding target of 40% external issuance and 60% domestic (currently: c18% external, 82% domestic).

Nigeria's total external debt (public and private) was just over US$47bn by March 2018; 13.2% of GDP and 91.5% of exports. Roughly 45% of this debt was attributed to the public sector, but a rapidly growing amount (US$25.8bn, c55% of total external debt, up from US$8.9bn in 2012) is owed by Nigeria's private sector, according to Bloomberg (government data on private external debt is limited). A breakdown shows that this amount is a combination of both bonds and loans, and is mainly issued by financial and energy sector firms.

Composition of external debt

External debt by creditor (end-Q1 18)	*Nominal amount outstanding (US$mn)*	*Share of total (%)*
Public sector external debt	**21,572**[a]	**45.5**[a]
o/w Official multilateral	10,929	23.0
IDA	8396	17.7
IBRD	124	0.3
AfDB/ADF	2155	4.5
Other	254	0.5
Official bilateral (non-Paris Club only)	2372	5.0
Commercial creditors	8300[a]	17.5[a]
Eurobonds	8000[a,b]	16.9[a]
Diaspora	300	0.6
Private sector external debt[c]	**25,866**	**54.5**
Total external debt	**47,438**[a]	**100.0**[a]

Source: DMO, CBN, Bloomberg

[a]Following US$500mn eurobond redemption in July 2018
[b]At the time of writing, Nigeria has announced that it plans to issue US$2.8bn in eurobonds in Q4 18
[c]Bloomberg, as of 8 August 2018

Nigeria's total public-sector (federal government plus states) debt amounted to cUS$78bn at end-17 (22.7% of GDP), according to the DMO. This amount comprised cUS$21bn (27% of total) public external debt and cUS$55bn (73% of total) domestic debt. Regarding domestic debt (federal only), most (NGN8716bn, about 70%) is in government bonds (FGNs) and treasury bills (NGN3580bn, 28%), and the balance is split between treasury bonds, FGN savings bonds, sukuk and a green bond issuance.

Rescheduling History

Although Nigeria has remained timely on servicing both its official and commercial claims in the recent past, this has not always been the case. The country has had a long history of arrears accumulation and frequent reschedulings of external obligations, which largely followed the oil price cycle and political instability. Debt restructurings were often contentious and highly politicised. There have been extended periods where key creditors have not been paid and the legislature has even set ceilings on the amount of servicing that can be paid in any year, regardless of payment schedule. Nigeria has had three commercial debt restructurings, including a Brady deal in 1992, and five Paris Club agreements. It was the last Paris Club deal in 2005, which involved significant debt forgiveness, that helped to transform the country's fortunes. Nigeria has not missed payments on its official or commercial claims since then.

Nigeria's unsustainable level of external public debt had mainly been contracted by pre-Obasanjo dictatorships. During most of the 1990s, the government paid only part of its external debt. An embargo on the contracting of new debt was imposed in 1994, yet this failed to produce the desired reduction in the debt burden. External debt stood at US$28.8bn by end-1998, with most of this (60%) in arrears, almost all to the Paris Club. To rectify this, Nigeria had for some time sought a comprehensive rescheduling, but such attempts failed due to weak policy implementation. Some payments continued to be made. US$2bn in debt service was paid in 1999, amounting to 15% of exports, including US$0.7bn to the Paris Club. However, debt service capacity remained strained and Nigeria sought debt relief from Paris Club and other creditors. Further arrears accumulation saw external debt increase to US$32.8bn by end-2003. Negotiations with Paris Club creditors led to all but four bilateral agreements under the 2000 agreement being concluded. However, it was not until the 2005 ad hoc agreement that Nigeria's Paris Club debt was normalised, in what was seen by some as a generous deal.

Relations with Multilateral Creditors

Nigeria has not had a financial arrangement with the IMF for 17 years, despite a number of external shocks since then, but historically, has shown a mixed performance under programmes it did have. These largely took the form of stand-by arrangements (SBAs) and staff-monitored programmes (SMPs), with three SBAs over 1989–2001 interspersed with an SMP in 1999 and a further SMP in 2001. However, policies exhibited a tendency to prioritise securing debt relief over reform commitments and the programmes were never drawn on. Strictly speaking, all five arrangements were completed, and the 2000 agreement was extended, but all suffered from missed targets. Interestingly, the January 1991 SBA that gave rise to Paris Club and Brady deals was particularly poor in implementation. The 1999 SMP marked the end of a seven-year break from IMF conditionality and, while 1999 saw the beginning of some reforms in Nigeria, it was not until 2004 that a structural break in performance was achieved.

Nigeria began "intensified surveillance" with the IMF in 2004, which led to a new type of fund arrangement, the policy support instrument (PSI). The intention was to provide a useful external discipline to a country's policy framework, enabling fund monitoring, but where there is no financing or balance of payments need. Nigeria obtained a PSI in 2005, a requirement of Paris Club debt relief. The two-year programme ran in tandem with the authorities' own national economic empowerment and development strategy (NEEDS) and was generally regarded as a success. The programme was completed with few waivers in October 2007 and survived a change of government. In fact, the Nigerian authorities credited the PSI framework as being pivotal in accelerating the country's reform agenda. With the conclusion of the PSI in October 2007, the authorities were said to be considering how the IMF might support its ongoing reform effort, which might include a second PSI involving external surveillance. Yet, despite the advent of the global financial crisis, no approaches to the fund were made regarding either a successor arrangement or emergency financing. In the face of the low oil price environment since 2014, Nigeria has eschewed IMF programmes, while others, instead, have requested them.

IMF programmes

Date	*Arrangements*	*Comments*
1989–1990	SBA	
1991–1992	SBA	
1999	SMP	June–December
2000–2001	SBA	Twelve-month programme for July 2000–June 2001. Treated as precautionary. The first review in December 2000 was delayed as performance went off track. In February 2001, the IMF expressed its disappointment with progress. The authorities noted their intention to complete the programme and enter a new three-year programme. The programme was extended to October 2001 when it lapsed.
2001–2002	SMP	The SBA was replaced by an SMP from October 2001 to March 2002. End-December 2001 targets were not met.
2004	Intensified surveillance	New framework designed to assist monitoring of Nigeria's NEEDS programme. Performance in 2004 was positive.
2005–2007	PSI	Two-year PSI agreed in October 2005 to cover July 2005–June 2007. Performance against the PSI was satisfactory. The fourth and final review was concluded in October 2007, based on end-June performance criteria. The reserve money target was missed and two structural reform measures were delayed, although fiscal targets were met.

Source: IMF. Nigeria joined the IMF in 1961

Paris Club and Bilateral Creditors

Nigeria underwent four Paris Club treatments prior to 2005, all of which involved flow rescheduling under Classic terms, superseded by Houston terms. Discussion with the Club committee led to anticipation that a stock treatment would follow more quickly than 2005. However, Nigeria's inability to adhere to IMF arrangements, such as the SMP over the period 2001–2002, saw the Paris Club exercise its pullback right, ceasing engagement until a clear commitment to policy reform was provided by the government. This problem had previously generated sizeable arrears and penalty interest with Paris Club creditors between the 1991 and 2000 deals. The UK, France, Germany, Japan, and Italy were the largest creditors.

Paris Club agreements

Date	*Terms*	*Status*	*Details*
1986	Classic	Fully repaid	December 1986, US$7.3bn treated.
1989	Classic	Fully repaid	March 1989, US$5.7bn treated.
1991	Houston	Fully repaid	January 1991, US$3.3bn treated. Comparability gave rise to the London Club and Trade Claims rescheduling. Following this deal, there was an eight-year period in which very little debt servicing fell due, as Nigeria made its democratic transition.
2000	Houston	Fully repaid	December 2000, US$24.5bn was outstanding to the Paris Club out of a total external debt of US$33.5bn. Paris Club treated a total of US$23.4bn; including arrears as at end-July 2000 and maturities between August 2000 and July 2001. Repayment of non-ODA credits over 18 years with three years' grace and ODA credits over 20 years with 10 years' grace. Of the US$24.5bn stock, the DMO reported 24% was penalty charges on PDI, 21% was interest on arrears and 48% was arrears on principal. This meant that only 7% of debt related to the principal balance. The agreement was considered a prelude to a stock clearance. However, as the August 2000 IMF SBA began to fail on targets, the Paris Club exercised its 'pullback clause', ending further hopes of relief. This did not affect relief from the Houston (flow) rescheduling.
2005	Ad hoc	Fully repaid	October 2005, US$30.1bn was outstanding to the Paris Club out of a total external debt of US$35.9bn (92% of exports). The deal took place in two stages, resulting in a full clearance of debt to the Paris Club: 1. Nigeria was to pay US$6.3bn (all arrears) and would receive a 33% write-off on eligible debt. 2. Conditional on successful completion of the first review of the PSI, Nigeria was to pay US$6.1bn of amounts due. Upon receipt, a further 34% of eligible debt would be cancelled. The remainder would be subject to a buyback. The March 2006 PSI review was successful, seeing the Paris Club cancel around US$18bn, or 60% of US$30bn outstanding. US$12bn was bought back by Nigeria.

Source: Paris Club

On 20 October 2005, the Paris Club announced a rescheduling arrangement (agreed upon in June of that year) to be implemented over the following six months. The agreement followed Nigeria's entrance into a two-year PSI with the IMF. Paris Club obligations stood at US$30.07bn, almost all of the country's bilateral debt. The agreement set out a schedule whereby Nigeria would clear its arrears in full, receive debt cancellation in two-stages (up to Naples terms) and buy back the remaining debt. Debt cancellation marked the culmination of a protracted process that was drawn-out by Nigeria's inability to remain committed to multilateral adjustment programmes. Yet the deal was criticised for being overly politicised; on the one hand, the authorities claimed they could not afford to make payments to the Paris Club and also suggested that much of the debt was odious in nature, having been contracted under previous military dictatorships, and its subsequent level of arrears. On the other hand, opponents argued that solvency concerns were misplaced. Medium-term debt sustainability was supported by vast oil wealth and the real concerns were over a poor payment culture and weak institutions, which debt relief would do little to improve. The final phase of the 2005 Paris Club agreement was implemented in 2006.

Sovereign Commercial Debt

Nigeria underwent three commercial bank debt restructurings, in 1987 and 1989, and a Brady deal in 1992. The authorities undertook official buybacks of London Club debt in 2002 and over 2006–2007, although informal buybacks were common throughout the 1990s. By Q1 07, virtually all London Club debt had been extinguished.

Commercial debt agreements

Date	*Details*
1987	Bank debt rescheduling of US$4.7bn of maturities due between April 1986 and December 1987, including short-term debt.
1989	Rescheduling of US$5.7bn of short-term bank debt.
1992	Brady deal. US$5.3bn of debt restructured. Deal involved cash back at 60% discount on US$3.3bn and debt exchange on US$2bn for 30-year par bond (bullet maturity with low step-up coupons). The par bond was collateralised.

(*continued*)

(continued)

Date	*Details*
2002	Voluntary exchange of par bonds, finally announced 26 November 2002. The government agreed to pay 23% for the Nigerian risk portion of the bonds, 98.5% of the principal collateral (equivalent to 44.10 percent of par) and 6.25% for the interest collateral, plus US$2.50 for each 1/250th of a warrant (see also below). The government repurchased a total of US$601mn principal of par bonds, plus warrants corresponding to US$288mn of par bonds. Because of the volume of tenders received, the government accepted only non-competitive offers. Competitive offers (effectively in excess of 23% of par for the Nigerian risk) were rejected.
2006–2007	London Club (Brady debt) buybacks and liability operations. Early repayment of par bond in November 2006, repurchase of oil warrants in March 2007 and re-assignment of obligations under the PNs in March 2007.

Source: World Bank GDF, Exotix

Following the January 1991 Paris Club deal, the authorities launched negotiations with commercial creditors. A Brady deal was concluded in January 1992. Total claims affected came to US$5.3bn (according to the World Bank). Of this, US$3.3bn was subjected to a cash buyback at 40% of face value and US$2bn was subject to an exchange. The exchange created a series of collateralised 'par bonds' and unsecured promissory notes ('PNs'), a group of trade related receivables assumed by the Nigerian government in 1988. The par bonds also carried a sweetener, the payment adjustment rights (see below), known as Nigeria oil warrants, based upon the performance of Nigeria's oil sector. Nigeria remained current on payments on the par bonds and PNs despite erratic payments to the Paris Club.

The comparability clause under the December 2000 Paris Club treatment required the authorities to revisit London Club holders. Resolution proved particularly challenging as the market viewed this rescheduling as politically motivated. This ultimately explained Nigerian Finance Minister Adamu Ciroma's November 2002 offer of a 'soft' voluntary (below par) buyback on the par bonds and warrants, rather than exercising the redemption feature in full on the par bonds. The subsequent take-up of non-competitive only tenders by the authorities meant low participation, yielding a 29% reduction in the bonds and even fewer on the warrants. Low acceptance was a blow to the government, which had been eager to settle external claims.

Following the October 2005 Paris Club treatment, the authorities renewed their efforts to eliminate the London Club debt. The par bonds were repaid, through a buyback at par, at the end of 2006 as the government exercised its call option on the November 2006 coupon date. The operation was completed at a cost of around US$1.48bn. Furthermore, in Q1 07, the authorities looked to extinguish their remaining London Club debt completely by securing holder approvals for an obligor substitution on the PNs and invited holders to tender the oil warrants in another buyback operation. The former met with successful approval and was completed in March. Ownership and obligations on the US$512mn PNs was transferred to Merrill Lynch at an outlay of US$480mn to Nigeria. Nigeria's repurchase tender for the oil warrants in March 2007 was less successful. The operation resulted in an acceptance rate of only 31.4% of those tendered at the minimum clearing price (the non-competitive price) of US$220. The warrants expire in 2020 and another operation is possible, although no further plan has been announced.

In early 2008, the Finance Ministry announced there was no intention to contract new commercial external debt. Plans for a eurobond issue, which appeared well advanced in the autumn of 2006, having received a sovereign rating from both Fitch and S&P earlier that year (both BB−). However, these plans were soon shelved, perhaps because there was little financing need. Yet the government announced in September 2008 plans for a naira-denominated 10-year bond issue to international investors to finance infrastructure spending. These plans were also shelved due to the onset of the global financial crisis. A dollar-denominated sovereign eurobond issue returned to the agenda in 2010. In October, the government announced that it had appointed Barclays Capital and FBN Capital as an adviser for a 10-year, US$500mn issue and in November selected Deutsche Bank and Citigroup as bookrunners. The issue marked Nigeria's first sovereign Eurobond issuance in January 2011, a 10-year bond (6.75%, maturing 2021) for an amount of US$500mn. This was followed by a dual tranche note in July 2013 for a five-year (5.125%, maturing 2018) and a 10-year (6.375%, maturing 2023), both US$500mn in size. There was a break of four years before Nigeria returned to the marked, issuing a US$1.5mn 15-year bond (2032) in February 2017. Nigeria has issued an additional US$5.5bn in eurobonds in four tranches since then, as well as an additional US$300mn via a diaspora bond in June of 2017. The 10-year US$1.5bn bullet bond is detailed below. In July 2018, Nigeria repaid its US$500mn 2018 maturity (issued in 2013) on time to complete its first ever principal repayment. As of end-H1 18, Nigeria has eight USD-denominated issues outstanding for a total of US$8.3bn, including its diaspora bond. At the time of writing, Nigeria has announced plans to issue US$2.8bn in eurobonds in Q4 18.

Nigeria's outstanding eurobonds

Description	*Size*	*Maturity type*	*Issue date*
USD 6.75% due 2021	US$500mn	Bullet	Jan. 2011
USD 5.625% due 2022[a]	US$300mn	Bullet	Jun. 2017
USD 6.375% due 2023	US$500mn	Bullet	Jul. 2013
USD 6.5% due 2027	US$1500mn	Bullet	Nov. 2017
USD 7.143% due 2030	US$1250mn	Bullet	Feb. 2018
USD 7.875% due 2032	US$1500mn	Bullet	Feb. 2017
USD 7.696% due 2038	US$1250mn	Bullet	Feb. 2018
USD 7.625% due 2047	US$1500mn	Bullet	Nov. 2017

Source: Bloomberg

[a]Diaspora bond

Nigeria eurobond
Nigeria 6.5% 2027
Bloomberg ticker: NGERIA

Borrower	Republic of Nigeria
Issue date	28 November 2017
Form	EuroMTN
ISIN	XS1717011982
Issue size	US$1.5bn
Currency	US dollar
Denomination	Min. US$200,000/increments on US$1000
Amortisation	Bullet
Final maturity date	28 November 2027
Coupon/interest	6.5%, paid semi-annually
Method of transfer	Euroclear/Clearstream, LSE reportable
Day count	30/360
Settlement period	T + 2
Joint lead managers	Citi, Standard Chartered Bank
Exchange	Frankfurt, London, Munich, Stuttgart
Governing law	English

Source: Bloomberg

Nigerian Payment Adjustment Warrants

These rights, dubbed 'warrants' (which is technically inaccurate), were created during the Brady bond restructuring of 1992 to enable creditors to share in any gains that Nigeria would experience from rising oil revenue. The rights are evidenced as detachable obligations of the restructured Brady par bond. Originally, each US$1mn in principal amount of par bonds was associated with 1000 payment adjustment rights, or four warrants.

Each US$1mn principal amount of par bonds is consistent with a maximum payment of US$15,000 (for warrants which have not been detached).

The rights pay if the price of Bonny Light crude exceeds an inflation-adjusted hurdle rate. The strike price was set at US$28 per barrel as of 1996 and is adjusted according to US PPI (finished goods less energy).

The warrants are direct, unconditional and general obligations of the CBN. There was a late payment on 15 November 2004 which was made finally on 14 April 2005, plus default interest of US$0.153 per right. Since this delay in payment, all subsequent payments have been paid on time.

In March 2008, the Nigerian authorities completed a buyback tender for the oil warrants. Nigeria accepted 31.4% of the warrants tendered at the minimum clearing price (and non-competitive price) of US$220. Out of the 1,759,769 warrants outstanding, 1,175,619 warrants were tendered and only 369,154 were accepted at the clearing price.

Calculation

Amounts due on the rights for payment dates 15 May and 15 November are calculated in the following manner:

Average price minus reference price multiplied by a factor of five, subject to a ceiling of US$15 per right, whereby:

- Average price is the mean price of Bonny Light crude for the six months ending sixty days before the payment date.
- Reference price is US$28 per barrel, adjusted by the percentage change in the US Labor Department's unadjusted producer price index for finished goods less energy (Exotix calculates the most recent strike price for November 2018 to be US$40.54).

The warrants have been in the money since November 2004, with almost all payments of the maximum US$15 per warrant every six months. Previously, the warrants were briefly in the money in 2000–2001. Since the publication of our last Guide in 2011, almost every payment has been subject to the maximum cap rate of US$15, except for the May 2016 payment as a result of depressed oil prices, where US$8.82 was paid.

Payments on the warrants are subject to a force majeure clause. This is defined as a condition under which Nigeria's average daily crude oil production for a six-month period (the determination period) is less than

1,618,750 barrels per day due to the occurrence of a force majeure circumstance. Force majeure events include, inter alia, acts of war, civil war, sabotage, embargoes, terrorism, natural disasters and labour disputes. Oil production is as published in the Oil Market Report (OMR) of the International Energy Agency (IEA).

Nigeria payment adjustment rights
Bloomberg ticker: NGERIA

Borrower	Central Bank of Nigeria
ISIN	XS0035901601
Issue date	21 January 1992
Amount outstanding	1,390,615 (number of warrants)
Maturity date	15 November 2020
Payment date	15 May, 15 November
Settlement period	T + 3 business days
Method of transfer	Euroclear/Clearstream
Delivery issues	There is a severe backlog of undelivered warrants that dates back to the time when warrants traded together with the Brady bonds until November 2002. Many leading EMTA members have failed to deliver. Purchasers of warrants should specify "guaranteed delivery" within T + 3 otherwise they could find themselves in a long-unresolved chain of failed deliveries. EMTA is trying to resolve this problem, although little progress has been achieved after years of negotiations.

Corporate Bond Markets

Two Nigerian banks (First Bank Nigeria and Guaranty Trust Bank) issued eurobonds in 2007 while Skye Bank was the reference entity for a convertible CLN issued by Standard Bank in the same year, unusually being a case of corporate eurobonds being issued before a sovereign Eurobond, despite Nigeria having already received its sovereign rating in the year prior. During this period, dollar-denominated loans were more common, however, the issuance of corporate eurobonds has steadily increased, with four issues in 2013, 6 in 2014, 2 in 2016, 3 in 2017, and 1 so far in 2018. These eurobonds are primarily issued by financial institutions; there have also been eurobonds issued by energy and communications firms, such as SEPLAT and IHS Towers. A summary of outstanding corporate eurobonds is detailed in the table below.

BB ticker	*Name*	*Sector*	*Rank*	*Issue date*	*Maturity date*	*Amount outstanding (US$mn)*
ACCESS	Access Bank PLC	Financial	Subordinated	24 Jun. 2014	24 Jun. 2021	400
ACCESS	Access Bank PLC	Financial	Sr. Unsecured	19 Oct. 2016	19 Oct. 2021	300
DIAMBK	Diamond Bank PLC	Financial	Sr. Unsecured	21 May 2014	21 May 2019	200
ECOTRA	EBN Finance (Ecobank)	Financial	Subordinated	7 Aug. 2014	14 Aug. 2021	250
FBNNL	First Bank Nigeria	Financial	Subordinated	31 Jul. 2013	7 Aug. 2020	300
FBNNL	First Bank Nigeria	Financial	Subordinated	17 Jul. 2014	23 Jul. 2021	450
FIDBAN	Fidelity Bank PLC	Financial	Sr. Unsecured	16 Oct. 2017	16 Oct. 2022	400
GRTBNL	Guaranty Trust Bank PLC	Financial	Sr. Unsecured	8 Nov 2013	8 Nov. 2018	277
HELTOW	IHS Towers	Communications	Sr. Unsecured	7 Aug. 2014	15 Jul. 2019	13
IHSHLD	IHS Netherlands	Communications	Sr. Unsecured	10 Dec. 2014	27 Oct. 2021	800
SEPLLN	SEPLAT Petroleum Dev.	Oil/Gas	Sr. Unsecured	21 Mar. 2018	1 Apr. 2023	350
UBANL	United Bank for Africa PLC	Financial	Sr. Unsecured	8 Jun. 2017	8 Jun. 2022	500
ZENITH	Zenith Bank PLC	Financial	Sr. Unsecured	22 Apr. 2014	22 Apr. 2019	500
ZENITH	Zenith Bank PLC	Financial	Sr. Unsecured	30 May 2017	30 May 2022	500

Source: Bloomberg

Corporate Debt Restructurings

Companies operating in Nigeria's oil and gas sector were not spared the impact of the decline in oil prices and the effect of militant activity on oil production. Afren, which was listed in London but had interests in Nigeria and several other countries, went into administration in 2015, after revenue fell and the decline in oil prices meant the issuer had to book a significant impairment charge. Afren also reported a large write-off of some oil reserves in Kurdistan, where the issuer also had exposure. Talks with various stakeholders failed to deliver the support required for a restructuring proposal that would have resulted in bondholders becoming majority owners of the company. The proposal had to be revised after production assumptions changed. Afren has three Eurobonds outstanding, still classed as in default. Seven Energy was acquired by Savannah Petroleum. The acquirer made an offer to holders of the Seven Energy USD-denominated bond, consisting of cash and shares. Bondholders were also given the option to participate in a capital raise, and to receive senior secured notes in Accugas, a midstream business within the group. At Sea Trucks Group, an oil and gas services company, bondholders approved a liquidation proposal in 2017. A restructuring plan was approved in February 2018, in which bondholders received cash equivalent to 33% of the principal of outstanding bonds, a new US$175mn senior secured bond issued by Telford Offshore Holding Ltd. (TOHL, a new company) and 100% of the shares in TOHL. TOHL acquired four multi-purpose offshore construction vessels from Sea Trucks Group following the liquidation.

Select Nigerian Corporate International Issues

Financial

Zenith Bank 7.375% 2022 *Bloomberg ticker: ZENITH*	
Borrower	Zenith Bank PLC
Issue date	22 May 2017
Form	Sr. Unsecured
ISIN	XS1619839779
Issue size	US$500mn
Currency	US dollar
Denomination	US$200,000 minimum, US$1000 thereafter
Amortisation	Bullet
Final maturity date	30 May 2022
Coupon/interest	7.375% paid semi-annually, May and November

(*continued*)

(continued)

Zenith Bank 7.375% 2022 *Bloomberg ticker: ZENITH*	
Day count	30/360
Method of transfer	Euroclear, Clearstream LUX
Settlement period	T + 2
Arranger	Citigroup, Goldman Sachs
Listing	Dublin, Frankfurt, Stuttgart
Governing law	English

Source: Bloomberg

UBA 7.75% 2022 *Bloomberg ticker: UBANL*	
Borrower	United Bank for Africa (UBA) PLC
Issue date	1 June 2017
Form	Sr. Unsecured
ISIN	XS1623828966
Issue size	US$500mn
Currency	US dollar
Denomination	US$200,000 minimum, US$1000 thereafter
Amortisation	Bullet
Final maturity date	8 June 2022
Coupon/interest	7.75% paid semi-annually, June and December
Day count	30/360
Method of transfer	Euroclear, Clearstream LUX
Settlement period	T + 2
Arranger	Barclays, Citigroup, Standard Chartered
Listing	Dublin, Frankfurt, Stuttgart
Governing law	English

Source: Bloomberg

Communications

IHS Netherlands 9.5% 2021 *Bloomberg ticker: IHSHLD*	
Borrower	IHS Netherlands Holdco
Issue date	12 October 2016
Form	Sr. Unsecured
ISIN	XS1505674751
Issue size	US$800mn
Currency	US dollar
Denomination	US$200,000 minimum, US$1000 thereafter

(*continued*)

(continued)

IHS Netherlands 9.5% 2021 *Bloomberg ticker: IHSHLD*	
Amortisation	Make Whole @50.0 until 10/27/18/ Call 10/27/18/ @ 104.75
Final maturity date	27 October 2021
Coupon/interest	9.5% paid semi-annually, April and October
Day count	30/360
Method of transfer	Euroclear, Clearstream LUX
Settlement period	T + 2
Arranger	Citigroup, Goldman Sachs, Standard Chartered
Listing	Berlin, Dublin, Dusseldorf, Frankfurt, Munich
Governing law	New York

Source: Bloomberg

Energy

Seplat 9.25% 2023 *Bloomberg ticker: SEPLLN*	
Borrower	Seplat Petroleum Development Co.
Issue date	12 March 2018
Form	Sr. Unsecured
ISIN	XS1505674751
Issue size	US$350mn
Currency	US dollar
Denomination	US$200,000 minimum, US$1000 thereafter
Amortisation	Make whole @50.0 until 04/01/20; call 04/01/18 @ 104.63
Final maturity date	1 April 2023
Coupon/interest	9.25% paid semi-annually, March and October
Day count	30/360
Method of transfer	Euroclear, Clearstream LUX
Settlement period	T + 2
Arranger	Citigroup, Natixis, Nomura, Standard Bank, Standard Chartered
Listing	Luxembourg, Stuttgart
Governing law	New York

Source: Bloomberg

Pakistan

Nominal GDP (US$mn, 2018)[a]		306,897
Population (thousand, 2018)[a]		200,960
GDP per capita (USD, 2018)[a]		1527
Credit ratings (long-term foreign currency)[b]	Fitch	B
	Moody's	B3
	S&P	B

[a]IMF WEO October 2018
[b]As at end-September 2018

Country Summary

- Pakistan has an eventful political history. The death of former Prime Minister Benazir Bhutto, the expulsion of former President Pervez Musharraf and ethnic tensions and allegations of collusion with international terrorism have meant the country has remained politically and economically unstable. Policy implementation has therefore struggled.
- Historically, the government has relied heavily on multilateral and bilateral financing to sustain economic growth and pursue infrastructure improvements. In January 2018, US President Trump threatened to cut off aid after accusing Pakistan of being deceitful in its

Exotix Capital, *Exotix Developing Markets Guide*,
https://doi.org/10.1007/978-3-030-05867-8_30

anti-terrorism stance. The country is also prone to natural disasters, including earthquakes and floods. Recently, much of Pakistan's economic growth has been fuelled by up to US$60bn of Chinese investment through the China-Pakistan Economic Corridor, as China continues to build and cement its regional economic and political dominance. However, concerns over indebtedness to China as well as a widening current account deficit based on increased Chinese imports have led to worries about fiscal and debt sustainability.

- Corruption remains high and places a burden on public projects, contributing further to public debt and the wide inequality in society. Prime Minister Imran Khan has committed to eliminating corruption, but has also been accused of having anti-Western views and appears reluctant to engage with the IMF, despite dwindling reserves. Keeping public finances and its relationship with China private are speculated factors.

Economic data	*Avg*[a]	*2014*[b]	*2015*[b]	*2016*[b]	*2017 (e)*[b]	*2018 (f)*[b]	*2019 (f)*[b]
Real GDP growth	3.9	4.1	4.1	4.6	5.4	5.8	4.0
Inflation (annual average)	9.6	8.6	4.5	2.9	4.1	3.9	7.5
Current account (% of GDP)	−2.8	−1.3	−1.0	−1.7	−4.1	−5.9	−5.3
Reserves (US$mn, end-period)[d]	14,819	14,351	19,362	21,949	18,233	13,697[c]	–
Reserves/imports (months)[e]	3.6	3.1	4.3	4.6	3.2	–	–
Overall fiscal balance (% of GDP)[f]	−5.9	−4.9	−5.3	−4.4	−5.7	−6.5	−6.9
Currency (ticker)	Pakistan rupee (PKR)						
FX regime	De jure float, de facto peg. Monetary policy is guided by multiple indicators such as economic activity, inflation rate and international reserves.						
Key exports	Textiles and clothing (60%), rice (8%). Remittances also a key source of currency inflow, c7% of GDP over 2014–2016.						

Source: IMF WEO Database, Haver, IMF Country Reports, OEC

[a]10-year average to 2016 unless otherwise stated

[b]Figure based on fiscal year between July–June following year, for instance 2015 = July 2015–June 2016 or 2015/2016

[c]Latest figure, May 2018

[d]Net reserves, end fiscal year

[e]In months of the current calendar year's imports of goods, services and income debit

[f]Overall government net lending

Key figures		*Party*	*Since*
President	Arif-ur-Rehman Alvi	PTI	Sep. 2018
Prime minister	Imran Khan	PTI	Aug. 2018
Finance adviser to prime minister	Abdul Razzaq Dawood	–	Aug. 2018
Minister of finance	Asad Umar	PTI	Aug. 2018
Key opposition figure	Shehbaz Sharif	PML-N	Aug. 2018
Central bank governor	Tariq Bajwa	–	Jul. 2017

Note: Pakistan is a member of the Commonwealth

Politics

Executive power

Pakistan is a federation of four provinces, in which the federal branch of government exercises executive control over the provincial and local governments. The President is indirectly elected to his/her post by the electoral college (composed of the Senate, National Assembly, and four Provincial assemblies). Under the Legal Framework Order (LFO) passed in compromised form in December 2003 the President is head of state, commander of the armed forces, and shares the executive branch of government with the Prime Minister. His/her scope of powers is wide ranging, even extending to dismissing government with the approval of the supreme court, triggering elections, and placing the state under martial law (as was done by Musharraf in 2007). The President can also veto legislation, although this is then sent to parliament which reviews amendments. The Prime Minister is the head of government, usually the leader of the party or coalition with the most votes in the National Assembly. The PM's primary responsibility is to appoint and oversee the cabinet and run the government's legislative agenda through parliament.

Presidential term: Five years, two-term limit (consecutive allowed)

Parliamentary term: Five years

Legislature

The Majlis-e-Shoora (Parliament) is bicameral, consisting of the Senate (upper house) and National Assembly (lower house). The President is also a vital component of the Parliament and the ceremonial figurehead. The National Assembly and its 342 members represent the formal legislative body of Pakistan's government. The leader of its largest party is the Prime Minister and often has a member preside as Speaker of the House, an equally powerful position. The Senate is a review body although now has the ability to veto bills and constitutional amendments, with the exception of finance, an extension of powers introduced by Musharraf. Power is concentrated around the President, who has the power to dissolve the National Assembly but not the Senate.

Senate: 104 seats

Chamber of Deputies: 342 seats; 272 directly elected

(*continued*)

(continued)

Legislature	
Previously 100 seats, increased by Zardari in 2011, now includes four minority members from the four provinces. Provincial assemblies elect senators to serve six-year terms. These elections take place on a biannual basis, affecting one-third of the house each time.	272 seats are elected by popular vote for a five-year term. 60 seats are reserved for women elected by proportional representation from the 272 seats. 10 seats are reserved for non-Muslims, elected in the same fashion as female seats. Seats available are weighted to the population of Pakistan's provinces. (Federal capital only has two seats; Punjab, the largest, has 183).

Elections

Next due *Presidential: Sep. 2020; Legislative: 2023*

Last legislative election[a] *(July 2018)*	*Seats*[b]		*Last presidential (Sep. 2018)*	*% of vote*
Pakistan Tehreek-e-Insaf (PTI)	116	149[c]	Arif-ur-Rehman Alvi (PTI)	53.2
Pakistan Muslim League–Nawaz (PML-N)	64	82	Fazl-ur-Rehman (MMA)	28.1
Pakistan People's Party Parliamentarians (PPPP)	43	54	Aitzaz Ahsan (PPP)	18.7
Muttahida Majlis-e-Amal	12	15		
Muttahida Quami Movement (MQM)	6	7		
Pakistan Muslim League Q (PML-Q)	4	5		
Balochistan Awami Party	4	5		
Independent politicians	13	13		
Other[d]	10	12		
Postponed	2	2		
Total	272	342	Total[e]	100.0

[a]Elections to National Assembly
[b]First column shows result of general vote. Second column shows the final allocation of all seats after the proportional distribution of 10 reserved seats for non-Muslims and 60 for women
[c]Nine of the 13 independent politicians joined the PTI, taking PTI's final total seats to 158
[d]Includes smaller parties and two seats that were postponed
[e]Of 706 votes made by the National Assembly, Senate and four provincial assemblies

People

96.4% of the 205mn population is Muslim—85% Sunni and 15% Shi'a. The remaining 3.6% are a mix of Hindu, Christian and others. Pakistan's population has historically been divided by ethnic groups. Although, as a race, almost all belong to the Indo-Iranic ancestral group, there are numerous other ethnicities by which Pakistanis identify themselves. The largest ethnic groups include the Punjabis with 98.4mn, Sindhis with 24.6mn and Pashtuns with 16.4mn, but there are millions who consider themselves to be of other groups.

Pakistan originated as a Muslim state annexing itself from the largely Hindu, British-ruled Hindu India. The Muslim state of East and West Pakistan, a separate nation for India's Muslims endorsed by the Muslim League in 1940, was formed in 1947 out of the partition of Bengal and India at the end of British rule; it became an independent commonwealth nation with a parliamentary system. Hundreds of thousands died in widespread violence and millions were made homeless during the independence process. It officially became a Republic in 1956. Bengali East Pakistan, supported by India, eventually emerged as Bangladesh in 1971 after its war for independence with West Pakistan. Civilian institutional structures were weak in the newly created country, having been crowded out by military dominance. A follow-up constitution emerged in 1962 and the most recent dates from 1973, although amendments were made by Musharraf in 2002 and later in 2010.

In 2007, political conditions deteriorated rapidly after Musharraf dismissed the Supreme Court's Chief Justice in March, sparking protests and a national strike. Over 100 people died when security forces stormed the Red Mosque in July. In October, Musharraf won early re-election as president (parliament elected the president before the 2008 legislative election) but declared a State of Emergency the following month as the Supreme Court questioned the election's eligibility. He was approved as president, despite actively serving in the military at the time of approval, but he later relinquished his military post voluntarily, amid domestic and international pressure. He was sworn in as a civilian president on 29 November for a five-year term.

In December 2007, twice former Prime Minister Benazir Bhutto was assassinated in a suicide bombing shortly after returning from exile, sparking violent riots and national strikes. The electoral commission announced that General Elections would be held on 8 January 2008; riots delayed the election until February. The two main opposition parties, the Pakistan People's Party (PPP) and Nawaz Sharif's Muslim League (PML-N), achieved a clear majority in Parliamentary elections. Musharraf's PML-Q finished third. The PPP and PML-N formed a coalition government, with PPP's Yousuf Raza Gilani elected in March by the National Assembly as prime minister. Musharraf resigned in August 2008 when the government launched impeachment proceedings against him. Nawaz Sharif pulled his PML-N out of the governing coalition, accusing the PPP of breaking its promise to reinstate all judges previously sacked by Musharraf. Asif Ali Zardari, the PPP leader, was elected president by MPs in September 2008. In November, a large IMF loan was needed due to the worsening debt crisis.

(*continued*)

(continued)

People
2010 saw many constitutional changes approved by Parliament and a large increase in political killings. The US cut aid to Pakistan after the prosecution of a doctor who helped the CIA find Osama Bin Laden. In June 2012, the Supreme Court removed Prime Minister Gilani from office over President Zardari's corruption row. Taliban attacks increased in 2012 and militant Islamists and terrorist groups continue to pose problems for the stability of Pakistan, highlighted by the 2011 assassination of Punjab governor Salman Taseer and continued suicide bombings. The 2013 elections saw PML-N as the largest party, with 166 seats, and Mamnoon Hussain as President, with 73% of the Parliamentary vote. In August 2017, Prime Minister Nawaz Sharif resigned after the Supreme Court disqualified him over corruption charges, replaced by Shahid Khaqan Abbasi. Twenty-two years after founding the PTI party, Imran Khan became prime minister after the PTI gained a large majority in the July 2018 general election. Prior to his election, Khan has frequently spoken about the need to break Pakistan's reliance on the US, prompting some to suggest that he shares anti-Western views. His public reluctance to turn to the IMF for additional financing support has also led to speculation that Chinese funding will continue to play a larger role in Pakistan's economic future.

Debt

	2012	*2017*
External debt ratios (%)		
Total external debt/GDP	26.9	28.1
Public external debt/GDP	24.1	23.7
Private external debt/GDP	2.8	4.4
Total external debt/exports of goods and services	190.1	289.9
External debt service ratio	15.0	20.2
Public debt ratios (%)		
Public domestic debt/GDP	34.9	44.3
Public debt/GDP	59.0	67.9

Source: State Bank of Pakistan, IMF, Exotix

Pakistan's total public debt stood at 67.9% of GDP as of end-2017, cUS$206bn, around double its figure seven years ago in nominal terms. There has been a shift towards domestic creditors, rather than external. This was about evenly split in 2010, but public domestic debt is now almost double public external debt. The use of domestic debt markets by the Pakistani government and central bank is significant and the authorities intend to gradually lengthen the maturity profile of domestic debt. The sustainability of this debt has fallen under question in recent years due to the ongoing budget deficits, widening current account deficit and damage caused by natural disasters. According to the IMF, public gross financing needs are high, at 29.3% of GDP in 2017, and are expected to continue to rise to 32.5% in 2022.

Of the US$85.4bn outstanding external debt, multilaterals are by far the largest creditor group, accounting for 41.4% of all external debt in 2017. This includes IMF, Asian Development Bank (ADB) and World Bank (IDA) loans, with additional funding from the Islamic Development Bank (IsDB) and the UN's IFAD. Only US$20mn is still owed to the Saudi Development Fund, a figure that has been declining since 2013. Owed 22.9% of the total, bilateral creditors are the next largest creditor group, with US$11.9bn of the US$19.6bn total bilateral debt owed to Paris Club creditors and a further US$7.7bn owed to non-Paris Club bilateral creditors, of which China is a considerable contributor. The amount owed to commercial creditors has increased dramatically in the past five years, to US$16.7bn, comprising US$7.3bn in eurobond and Sukuk issues, US$5.8bn in commercial loans and US$3.7bn in FX liabilities. Other long-term external debt in 2017 comprised only US$500mn in SAFE (a sovereign wealth fund) China deposits. The SAFE deposits were US$1bn until January 2017, obtained to support FX reserves in 2009 and 2012. The proportion of total external debt that was on concessional terms in 2016 was 48%, which has been on a downward trend since its peak at 71% in 2005, although this is due, in part, to the large increases in commercial debt.

Total public sector (PPG) external debt rose to US$71.9bn in 2017 from US$54bn in 2012. Strong real GDP growth, averaging 4.2% over this period, has led to PPG external debt falling as a proportion of GDP to 23.7% in 2017, from 24.1% in 2012. Pakistan's total external debt stock of US$85.4bn has risen as a proportion of exports of goods and services and primary income to 290% in 2017 from 190% in 2012, which is more revealing than the ratio with GDP, since the nominal value of exports declined, based on central bank figures. PPG external debt service has increased in both nominal terms and as a proportion of total exports, to 20.2% in 2017 from 15.0% in 2012; most bond maturities over this period were in domestic currency rather than foreign currency.

Total private sector external debt was US$13.5bn at end-2017 (4.4% of GDP), excluding publicly guaranteed private external debt and guarantees of state enterprises, which totalled US$1.4bn. This total comprises US$1.6bn non-guaranteed state enterprises external debt, US$4.7bn external debt of private banks and US7.2bn external debt of the wider private sector.

Composition of external debt

External debt by creditor (Dec. 2017)	*Nominal amount outstanding (US$mn)*	*Share of total (%)*
Public and publicly guaranteed external debt	**71,907**	**84.2**
o/w Multilateral creditors	35,112	41.4
IMF	6256	7.3
World Bank IDA	1460[a]	1.7
ADB	1137[a]	1.3
IsDB	903	1.1
IFAD	730[a]	0.9
Saudi Fund for Development	20	0.0
o/w Bilateral creditors	19,559	22.9
Paris Club	11,893	13.9
Non-Paris Club	7666	9.0
o/w Commercial creditors	16,736	19.7
Eurobonds/sukuks	7300	8.6
Commercial loans	5784	6.8
FX liabilities	3652	4.3
o/w Other long term	500	0.2
Private sector external debt (non-guaranteed)	**13,486**	**15.8**
Total external debt	**85,393**	**100.0**

Source: State Bank of Pakistan

[a]Latest figures, as of end-2016

Rescheduling History

Pakistan's most notable experience of debt rescheduling came at the end of the 1990s following the balance of payments crisis between 1998 and 2001. This resulted in a rescheduling of debt owed to the Paris Club, as well as bilateral and commercial creditors, and also led to higher inflows of grant aid. Pakistan's total debt had reached 115% of GDP, 624% of total government revenue, and debt servicing consumed half of government revenues. Debt covered by commercial debt rescheduling operations alone amounted to US$877.3mn in 1999 and Paris club creditors agreed on the rescheduling of some US$3.2bn in the same year, followed by an additional US$12.5bn in 2001. Following the restructuring, Pakistan's external solvency indicators were much improved. However, liquidity (and solvency) concerns re-appeared in 2007 and 2008, further IMF financing was called for over 2008–2010, although no rescheduling proved necessary.

The 1990s had seen a rapid build-up of external debt, which rose from cUS$19bn in 1990 to US$34bn at the end of the decade. Persistent current account deficits (c5% of GDP), in part reflecting poor export performance, were to blame to a degree, but economic problems also reflected ineffective public investment and an effort to raise social spending. Higher borrowing costs, meanwhile, meant that debt service became onerous at a time when FX reserves were in decline. Although balance of payments pressures had been building for some time, the crisis was triggered by UN trade sanctions following Pakistan's nuclear testing programme in May 1998, and tighter sanctions after a military coup in October 1999. Capital outflows caused a sharp loss of reserves and payment arrears were accumulated. External financing needs in 2000–2001 amounted to US$4bn, representing the large current account deficit, debt obligations due (of cUS$3.5bn), and arrears clearance. Exceptional financing across all creditors (multilaterals, bilaterals and the private sector) was necessary. The 1999 agreement saw the world's first eurobond restructuring take place as a direct result of Paris Club demands.

Pakistan also sought to restructure bilateral financing with non-Paris Club creditors. It rolled over a US$250mn deposit from the Kuwait Investment Authority at the central bank, which was due in August 2000, and sought to roll over a US$150mn deposit from the central bank of the UAE, also held at the Pakistan central bank, which was due in December 2000.

More recently, no restructurings have been necessary. Government finances could not cope with the flooding of 2010 and needed emergency financing from the IMF in September of that year. Improved energy availability developed especially during the 2013 EFF programme and structural reforms. In its most recent post-programme monitoring report (March 2018, see below), the IMF predicts 5.6% growth in 2018 and a favourable growth outlook, enhanced by Chinese investment. Private sector involvement is becoming an additional factor in reducing the losses made by public sector enterprises (PSEs) and restructuring/privatisation prospects appear encouraging.

As of end-2017, cUS$7.7bn of bilateral debt is owed to non-Paris Club creditors, based on central bank figures. Of these, China is a major contributor, especially as the China Pakistan Economic Corridor investment programme continues. Chinese investment value is currently estimated at US$60bn and may rise to US$55bn (this is an investment programme, and so does not appear as government debt). If implemented as planned, the projects hope to improve power supplies and free up oil for other uses.

Blackouts across the country are common, although they are becoming less disruptive following the most recent IMF extended fund facility (EFF) programme; the ADB has also cited energy shortages as a cause for weaker growth since 2009. Although these investments are intended to improve infrastructure and future output, medium term debt servicing requirements will increase, and if developed infrastructure does not translate into increased output, exports, and income, then future repayment ability may be uncertain. Much of the financing comes from Chinese government lending, some of which is concessional. Speculation may suggest that it comes from China's intention to access Middle Eastern oil and thus strategically surround India; India expressed concerns when China received a majority stake in Sri Lankan infrastructure projects. Furthermore, as a major trading partner, slower growth in China may lead to lower exports, remittances, and FDI for Pakistan. China is a major bilateral lender and its growth rate slowing could lead to costlier external borrowing.

Relations with Multilateral Creditors

Approximately US$6.3bn in IMF debt was held by Pakistan as of end-2017, based on central bank figures, c7.4% of total external debt. Since the Paris Club reschedulings in 2001, two new programmes have been successfully completed. The 2008 stand-by arrangement (SBA), signed in November, totalled US$7.61bn (500% of quota) with the plan to expire in 2009, requested by the Pakistan authorities as the global economic downturn led to poor economic results and, particularly, a collapse in financial reserves, which meant financial stimulus was needed. IMF financing provided emergency balance of payments support, reduced the fiscal deficit to 4.2% and boosted confidence in capital markets. The amount was raised to US$10.66bn in August 2009 and extended to 2010. In December 2010, the Pakistan government requested, and was granted, a further extension of nine months to complete policy implementations under the fifth and sixth reviews. This provided time to complete renegotiations over a general sales tax, and set new measures to repair the fiscal deficit, while taking into account the increased funding for flood damage.

The latest agreement is an EFF arrangement, approved in September 2013 by the IMF's Executive Board, which provided total disbursements equivalent to US$6.64bn to support economic reform and inclusive growth. The Fund acknowledged the natural and human resources, the progress previously made under the SBA and the ongoing challenges to political and economic stability. Improving the balance of payments, building up international reserves, and improving the fiscal position were among its objectives, with sustainability of the fiscal and external accounts cited as vulnerabilities. Improving the business environment, raising the proportion of GDP taken in taxation through institutional reform and tax efficiency were also noted as priorities. Trade liberalisation and some PSE privatisations were intended to bring about energy sector improvements, realising growth potential and protection for more vulnerable citizens from fiscal consolidation.

Reports from the 2013 EFF indicate positive performance throughout the programme, with most targets met. Where targets were missed, the authorities continued to show their commitment to the achievement of long-term goals. At the end of the 2016 fiscal year, fiscal performance was satisfactory; although the fiscal deficit was higher than programmed, the IMF reported that steps had been taken by the federal government to consolidate expenditure. Most benchmarks were met regarding structural reform. The energy sector was given certain targets in the programme: energy sector subsidies fell as a proportion of GDP from 2.0% in FY 12/13 to 0.6% in FY 15/16, power outages for industrial customers fell from nine hours per day to one hour per day over the same period, and power outages for urban consumers also saw a significant fall. Annual losses of PSEs have fallen as a proportion of GDP and, although privatisation progress has been limited, the strategy was re-assessed in 2016 and private sector participation has been sought. Monetary performance was also satisfactory, with international reserve targets being exceeded, and reaching four months of imports at end-FY 15/16, although this was forecast to decline from its temporary high in the 2017 Article IV report. Completion of quarterly reviews throughout allowed for the full disbursement amount, which remains outstanding. Real GDP growth has been on an upward trend since 2009, and is forecast in WEO figures to continue on this path to c6% over 2019–2022.

The recent agreement is the latest in a long line of Fund programmes. Successive governments have engaged in numerous adjustment facilities, although relations with the IMF can only be considered to have been on a good standing since the 1998–2001 crisis. Pakistan began implementing comprehensive economic reforms from 1988, albeit with mixed success. Only 58% of loan commitments were disbursed between 1988 and 2004 and it was only in 2001, when a short SBA was completed, that a programme had run its full course without interruption. Relations with the IMF had been further undermined by misreporting of fiscal data over the period 1997–1999, uncovered by the incoming government that took office in October 1999. Subsequent revisions to the 1997/98 budget deficit were worth 2% of GDP, pushing the deficit to 7.5% of GDP and raising the 1998/1999 deficit by 1.4% of GDP to 5.9%. The misreporting had allowed Pakistan to make purchases under the PRGF that would otherwise not have been possible. Still, the successful 2000–2001 SBA was a precursor to a three-year PRGF, which was approved in December 2001 and concluded satisfactorily in December 2004. The authorities stated their intention not to seek a successor arrangement although the country still received technical assistance on policy formulation.

IMF programmes

Date	*Arrangements*	*Comments*
1988–1990	SBA	SDR273.15mn agreement, of which SDR194.48mn was disbursed.
1988–1991	SAFC	SDR382.4mn agreement, fully disbursed under Bhutto, and then Sharif, governments.
1993–1994	SBA	Regarded a success under successive Qureshi and Bhutto administrations, although not fully drawn on. The IMF noted that the authorities intensified their efforts in 1993, with IMF support, but the situation had deteriorated by H1 1995.
1994–1995	PRGF+EFF	Terminated owing to a number of policy slippages under the Bhutto government and impending balance of payments problems. 1995 saw loose monetary policy and a worsening fiscal position. Poor weather and crop disease caused the trade deficit to widen while international reserves fell.
1995–1997	SBA	15-month US$596mn standby arrangement agreed in December 1995 to support the government's 1995/1996 economic programme. Aimed particularly at structural reforms and trade liberalisation. Extended in December 1996 owing to considerable fiscal slippages under the Bhutto government. A successful SBA was seen as providing the basis for a new PRGF programme.
1997–2000	ESAF + EFF	The US$1.55bn programme had seemed to run smoothly until the incoming administration uncovered misreporting of fiscal data in 1997–1999 by the outbound Sharif administration. The IMF stated this could have ceased or reduced disbursals under the arrangement, although its ability to take remedial action was limited. The programme opened the way for a Paris Club Houston terms flow rescheduling on US$3.25bn of debt in 1999. The Musharraf regime made repayments associated with misreporting, as specified under the agreement. Therefore, implementation was mixed, although slippages were less.

(*continued*)

(continued)

Date	*Arrangements*	*Comments*
2000–2001	SBA	Ten-month US$596mn SBA approved in November 2000. Expired successfully in September 2001. Programme paved the way for Paris Club treatment at a meeting scheduled for January 2001, following the authorities' request for rescheduling of accumulated arrears and debt service falling due. Paris Club rescheduled US$1.8bn on Houston terms. The SBA was a forerunner to the PRGF.
2001–2004	PRGF	US$1.3bn credit approved in December 2001. Regarded as highly successful, although a number of waivers were granted. The programme was crucial in securing an ad hoc Paris Club flow rescheduling on US$12.5bn across 23 to 38 years.
2008–2010 (2011)	SBA	In November 2008, the IMF approved a US$7.6bn (500% of quota) 23-month SBA after weeks of negotiations with the Pakistan authorities. The programme was requested by the authorities in response to building balance of payments pressure and exhaustion of foreign reserves. The amount was SDR5.17bn (US$7.61bn). In August 2009, an extension of the SBA programme to December 2010 and augmentation of funds by US$3.2bn was approved. The fourth review was completed in May 2010, and in December 2010, a second extension took its final expiration date to September 2011. This nine-month extension was approved by the Executive Board to allow time for continued fiscal reforms.
Sep. 2010	Emergency Financing	US$450mn provided in emergency financing under the Emergency Natural Disaster Assistance (ENDA) in the wake of flooding that covered a fifth of the country and affected 14 million people.
2013–2016	EFF	The three-year arrangement under the EFF was approved by the Board in September 2013 for SDR4.4bn (US$6.6bn, 425% of Quota) to support economic reform and inclusive growth. Summary objectives included improving growth, lowering inflation, increasing reserves and implementing structural reform. The 12th, and final review, was completed in October 2016, allowing full disbursements. The authorities did not request an extension.

Source: IMF. Pakistan became a member of the IMF in 1950

The IMF completed the first post-programme monitoring mission to Pakistan in December 2017 (concluded by the Executive Board in March 2018), welcoming the continued exchange rate flexibility and noting the strong growth; however, it commented that, to maintain the positive economic trend, strengthening economic resilience, fiscal discipline and tight monetary policy would be essential. Medium-term prospects will require sustainable private sector investment and job creation, which may be aided by continued reforms. An additional challenge is declining international reserves, forecast by the IMF to fall below two months' import cover in 2018, despite strong external financing, driven partly by the increasing current account deficit (forecast at c6% of GDP over 2017–2020). This has led to talk of another programme.

As of August 2018, the ADB had 105 active projects in Pakistan, not including an additional 10 projects that are currently approved, but not yet active. Recent projects have focussed on the energy sector, with sustainability considerations, urban development and education. In May 2017, the ADB issued a US$20mn loan to Pakistan's Khushhali Microfinance Bank Ltd. for increased lending to smaller borrowers, including agricultural firms, since these smaller firms are very significant for providing employment and reducing poverty. In September 2017, the ADB issued two new loans to Pakistan, with a combined value of US$435mn for transport development, with a focus on encouraging private sector contribution to infrastructure projects.

The IFAD had 27 active projects in Pakistan in August 2018, with a total project cost of US$2.5bn and US$730mn in financing to the government. The focus has been on poverty alleviation and livelihood support. The Saudi Fund for Development, which works to rehabilitate infrastructure in areas that have suffered destruction, either natural or man-made, has some ongoing projects with an allocation of US$11.7mn in the Swat district in Pakistan, which suffered some infrastructural damage caused by the Taliban and other militant groups. The Nordic Development Fund has one active project in Pakistan, aiming to develop renewable energy solutions and provide climate resilience in Karachi.

In August 2018, the World Bank had 62 active projects in Pakistan, including nine new projects approved in 2018. Projects receiving the largest funding include infrastructure development, especially to the wider energy sector, given the undersupply of power to citizens and firms, which hinders living standards and economic growth: at significantly higher cost, some households have to use battery-powered apparatus and many industrial and commercial firms make use of back-up diesel generators, although many firms cannot afford this and output has suffered.

In May 2018, foreign reserves stood at US$13.7bn, only c2.2 months' import cover. In September 2017, media reported that the World Bank had suspended its support programme for Pakistan and that the country was no longer eligible for IBRD loans, due to deteriorating macroeconomic indicators (three months' import cover is a requirement of IBRD loans). This was quickly denied by the Ministry of Finance, claiming that reserves exceed three months' import cover, and that recent data on FDI, tax revenue and exports are all positive. Pakistan received two short-term loans to assist with maintaining its import cover: US$153mn was borrowed from Citibank and US$77mn was borrowed from the IsDB. In December 2017, Pakistan received US$825mn in loans from the World Bank (both IDA and IBRD): US$425mn for improvements to power supplies and US$400mn for the public financial management reform programme.

The IsDB has stopped conducting development projects in Pakistan. After the completion of the 2012–2015 partnership strategy, the Bank decided to continue its research into the country and assess future partnership options. The 2012–2015 partnership review revealed that the IsDB had not approved any agriculture sector projects, citing the devolution process towards lower level government departments, which is now complete, and some agriculture sector projects may be included in a future strategy.

In general, Pakistan maintains strong links through its financial commitments with multilateral and bilateral creditors, showing strong commitment to upholding repayment schedules and performance requirements. The IMF reports positively on the authorities' commitment to long-term goals, including fiscal consolidation, further strengthening future repayment capacity. The slowing progress of fiscal consolidation since the end of the EFF is considered a macroeconomic risk, as are medium-term repayment obligations to China.

Paris Club and Bilateral Creditors

Pakistan has had various rescheduling agreements within the Paris Club going back to the 1970s, with the most recent agreements arising out of the 1998–2001 balance of payments crisis, during which Pakistan sought a restructuring of its debts with the Paris Club as payments continued to be missed. Paris Club creditors, meanwhile, demanded comparability to bail in private creditors as a pre-condition to a deal, to which Pakistan agreed.

In January 1999, the Paris Club agreed a flow rescheduling on Houston terms, covering US$3.25bn of debt (including arrears) over 18 years with three years' grace. However, the agreement was not implemented in full as

Pakistan was unable to adhere to its concurrent IMF programme. The implementation of a subsequent IMF programme in November 2000 allowed Pakistan to re-stabilise its fiscal account and rebuild reserves. This laid the foundation for a new Paris Club deal in January 2001 while the ADB and World Bank provided structural adjustment loans. A further deal followed in December 2001, post-9/11, covering US$12.5bn in debts on an ad hoc basis. This deal raised eyebrows among investors, who viewed the terms as politically motivated. The decision by Washington to provide financial assistance of US$704mn towards the end of 2001, relax export quotas and work towards further debt relief was encouraging and set the tone for other official donors.

In June 2017, Paris Club debt came to US$11.9bn, from US$14.33bn in 2011. Creditors include France, Germany, Japan and the US.

Paris Club agreements

Date	*Terms*	*Status*	*Details*
1972	Ad hoc	Fully repaid	
1974	Ad hoc	Fully repaid	
1981	Classic	Fully repaid	Conducted outside formal Paris Club.
1999 Jan.	Houston	Fully repaid	The January 1999 Houston deal treated US$3.25bn on a flow basis. It was a direct consequence of an IMF recommendation provided while Pakistan was under the 1997–2000 PRGF. The Paris Club deal rescheduled debt over 18 years with three years' grace in March after Pakistan agreed to bail in private creditors. However, the deal was not fully implemented as Pakistan did not comply with the terms of its IMF agreement.
2001 Jan.	Houston	Fully repaid	Houston treatment on US$1.75bn of arrears falling due to 30 November 2000 and maturities across December 2000 to October 2001.
2001 Dec.	Ad hoc	Active	December 2001 ad hoc flow rescheduling on US$12.5bn, with terms broadly equivalent to 'Cologne terms', representing 94% of debts owed to the Paris Club. Terms involved rescheduling US$3.7bn of commercial rate credits over 23 years with five years' grace, and US$6.8bn of non-commercial credits (ODA) over 38 years with 15 years' grace.

Source: Paris Club

Around US$7.7bn of bilateral debt is owed to non-Paris Club lenders, of which China is a major contributor, especially due to government funding for the China Pakistan Economic Corridor (CPEC). In December 2017, China decided to halt funding for CPEC-related projects following suspected corruption, which was the second problem faced by CPEC—the first was a month before, when Pakistan decided to cancel a US$14bn Diamer-Bhasha Dam project due to the strain of Chinese financing terms.

Sovereign Commercial Debt

Eurobond obligations amounting to US$610mn, maturing over 1999–2002, were restructured in 1999, the first ever eurobond exchange offer; classified by Moody's as a distressed exchange. The exchange offer, which was launched on 15 November, came just five weeks before Pakistan was due to repay one of the bonds eligible in the exchange and followed a grace period default in November 1998 on US$750mn of debt (including a eurobond). The three eligible bonds in the exchange were: US$150mn 11.5% due 22 December 1999; US$300mn libor +3.95% due May 2000; and US$160mn 6% due February 2002. Commercial creditors received a single new eurobond with a six-year maturity, three years' grace, and a flat coupon of 10%. The bond had four equal annual repayments commencing on 15 November 2002. The NPV haircut at the exit yield was 30%. The offer closed on 6 December 1999, with a reported 99% participation rate, according to the IMF. Those who did not take part in the initial exchange were invited to do so again in a second exchange on 17 December, mopping up a small rump. Virtually all investors eventually participated. The new 1999 eurobond matured without difficulty in December 2005.

A number of private loans were also rescheduled on similar terms; commercial loans amounting to US$929mn were restructured in 1998/1999 and 1999/2000. As reported by the IMF, this included US$777mn in trade-finance facilities that were rolled over on an annual basis for three years until June 2002 with a step up on the margin over libor from 100 bps in year 1 to 125bps in year 2 and 150bps in year 3. US102mn of the remaining amount was rescheduled until 2008, with a grace period until December 2002 and amortising in six equal annual instalments thereafter. The remaining US$50mn was owed to an investment bank, contracted in September 1998, and was rolled over after 2000. The authorities also sought to negotiate two further loans from commercial banks and to roll over US$500mn in deposits from the Bank of China at the central bank and some US$750mn in foreign currency deposits of institutional investors falling due in 2000/01.

Pakistan regained access to the international capital market in February 2004 with a US$500mn five-year issue. The bond matured in 2009. Four eurobond issues followed since then. Pakistan issued its first sukuk (Islamic bond) in January 2005. The US$600mn five-year note, priced at six-month USD libor + 220bps, received considerable interest from both conventional and Islamic investors across Asia, the Middle East and Europe. The issue size was increased from an original target of US$300mn–500mn due to strong demand, with total orders amounting to US$1.2bn. This issue expired in 2010, having paid the full amount and without needing a restructuring or rollover. It flowed through the Pakistan International Sukuk Company. Three subsequent sukuk bonds have been issued, each for US$1bn.

The most recent international bond issues occurred in December 2017, when the government issued US$2.5bn in the form of a 10-year US$1.5bn eurobond and a five-year US$1bn sukuk. The two issues combined received US$8bn in orders and the eurobond was priced at a record low yield. These and the other outstanding international bonds are listed in the table below. Details are also provided for the latest eurobond issue. Central bank data shows total euro/sukuk global bonds at US$7.3bn in August 2018 (8.6% of end-2017 external debt). This excludes the two PKR bonds shown below, although they are of the RegS and 144A series.

Pakistan's outstanding eurobonds

Description	*Size*	*Issue date*
USD 7.25% due 2019	US$1000mn	Apr. 2014
USD 6.75% Sukuk[a] due 2019	US$1000mn	Dec. 2014
PKR 12% due 2020	PKR96,146.7mn	Jul. 2010
PKR 12% due 2021	PKR47,802.6mn	Aug. 2011
USD 5.5% Sukuk[a] due 2021	US$1000mn	Oct. 2016
USD 5.625% Sukuk[a] due 2022	US$1000mn	Dec. 2017
USD 8.25% due 2024	US$1000mn	Apr. 2014
USD 8.25% due 2025	US$500mn	Sep. 2015
USD 6.875% due 2027	US$1500mn	Dec. 2017
USD 7.875% due 2036	US$300mn	Mar. 2006

Source: Bloomberg

[a]Sukuk (Islamic) bonds are Sharia-compliant bonds, issued by the Pakistan International Sukuk Company Limited, a public company, for and on behalf of the Islamic Republic of Pakistan

Pakistan 2027 bond
Islamic Republic of Pakistan 6.875% 2027
Bloomberg ticker: PKSTAN

Borrower	Islamic Republic of Pakistan
Issue date	5 December 2017
Form	Eurobond
ISIN	XS1729875598
Issue size	US$1500mn
Amount outstanding	US$1500mn
Currency	US dollar
Denomination	Minimum US$200,000/ increments of US$1000 thereafter
Amortisation	Bullet
Final maturity date	5 December 2027
Coupon/interest	6.875% per annum payable semi-annually, June and December
Day count	30/360
Method of transfer	Euroclear/Clearstream
Settlement period	T + 2 business days
Lead managers	Citigroup, Deutsche Bank, Standard Chartered Bank, ICBC Standard Bank PLC
Listing	EUROMTF, Frankfurt, Luxembourg, Stuttgart
Governing law	English

Source: Bloomberg

Pakistan also has a number of outstanding sovereign loans, although details are hard to come by. Creditors and agents are often Islamic banks including some Arab banks and also international banks including Credit Suisse and Standard Chartered Bank. Recent examples include a US$200mn syndicated loan arranged by Commercial Bank of Dubai, Emirates NBD and Noor Bank. The one-year loan was announced in May 2018. The Minister of Finance said that the funds would be used for fiscal purposes (amid a fiscal deficit) and to help with existing debt repayments. In addition to supporting reserves, the foreign loan will be used to repay local currency borrowing. Pakistan has loans with the Asian Development Bank, and has a partial World Bank IBRD guarantee on a 2017 issued US$700mn commercial loan.

Corporate Bond Market

The corporate bond market is described as limited; however, the Ministry of Finance, in its most recent publicly available Economic Survey, explains that a well-developed corporate bond market is essential for the growth of the economy by providing an additional avenue for raising funds in the corporate sector. The first bond issued by a Pakistani corporate was a US$45mn 5% convertible bond, issued by Dewan Salman Fibre Ltd. (DEWAN) in May 1994, with a 2001 maturity. To August 2018, 76 corporate bonds have been issued by corporates, in both USD and PKR, totalling US$3.02bn and PKR4.4bn. At present, there are six outstanding corporate bonds, totalling PKR203mn.

Rwanda

Nominal GDP (US$mn, 2018)[a]		9709
Population (thousand, 2018)[a]		12,133
GDP per capita (USD, 2018)[a]		800
Credit ratings (long-term foreign currency)[b]	Fitch	B+
	Moody's	B2
	S&P	B

[a]IMF WEO October 2018
[b]As at end-September 2018

Country Summary

- Rwanda suffered a long civil war between rival ethnic groups until a power-sharing agreement was signed in 1993. The following year, the killing of the president led to genocide due to ethnic discrimination. Criminal trials have continued since.
- Concessional borrowing remains high, at almost 70% of total external debt in 2016, from its peak of almost 95% in 1994. Foreign aid is expected to fall until 2025, which could make future borrowing more expensive, present a challenge to continued growth and place greater onus on infrastructure improvements and the private sector.
- Rwanda hopes to become a middle-income country by 2020, which will require continued growth, infrastructure improvements and poverty reduction. As a key employer and producer, the agricultural

Exotix Capital, *Exotix Developing Markets Guide*,
https://doi.org/10.1007/978-3-030-05867-8_31

sector will continue to drive growth, although urbanisation continues. Rwanda is fortunate to have large areas of arable land. Consumption and investment have driven growth as the labour force migrates to higher value-added sectors, helping the private sector lead economic development. The future of this growth will depend on the planned infrastructure improvements being realised.

Economic data	*Avg*[a]	*2014*	*2015*	*2016*	*2017 (e)*	*2018 (f)*	*2019 (f)*
Real GDP growth	7.8	7.6	8.9	6.0	6.1	7.2	7.8
Inflation (annual average)	6.6	1.8	2.5	5.7	4.8	3.3	5.5
Current account (% of GDP)	−8.5	−10.3	−14.5	−15.8	−6.8	−8.9	−9.4
Reserves (US$mn, end-period)[b]	854	951	922	1000	987	–	–
Reserves/imports (months)[c]	5.1	4.3	3.8	3.9	4.2	–	–
Overall fiscal balance (% of GDP)[d]	−1.4	−4.0	−2.8	−2.3	−2.5	−2.0	−2.1
Currency (ticker)	Rwandan franc (RWF)						
FX regime	Floating since 1995, previously pegged to the dollar						
Key exports	Gold (21%), tea (13%), refined petroleum (12%), coffee (7.1%), tourism services (24%). Private remittances are also around 2% of GDP.						

Source: IMF WEO Database, National Bank of Rwanda, OEC

[a]10-year average to 2016 unless otherwise stated

[b]Gross reserves

[c]In months of the current year's imports of goods and services

[d]IMF general government net lending

Key figures		*Party*	*Since*
President	Paul Kagame	FPR	Apr. 2000
Prime minister	Edouard Ngirente	PSD	Aug. 2017
Minister of finance	Uzziel Ndagijimana	FPR	Apr. 2018
Key opposition figure	Frank Habineza	Democratic Green	–
Central bank governor	John Rwabgombwa	FPR	Feb. 2013

Politics

Executive power

The president is both chief of state and head of government, elected by popular vote to serve a seven-year term. The limit of two consecutive terms has been respected since 1985. The prime minister and council of ministers (cabinet) are appointed by the president. Cabinet appointed by the president from among the members of the Chamber of Deputies based on the number of seats that their party holds. A 2015 constitutional change allowed for a third consecutive presidential term and, from 2024, the presidential term will shorten to five years, renewable once.

Presidential term: Seven years (five years from 2024, renewable once)

Parliamentary term: Five years

Legislature

Bicameral, comprising of the Senate (upper house) and the Chamber of Deputies (lower house). The 24 Senate members are directly appointed by the president. The Chamber of Deputies has 80 members, 53 directly elected members (proportional representation) and 27 indirectly elected from special interest groups (24 women, two representing youth and one representing the disabled).

Elections

Next due *Legislative: September 2023; Presidential: August 2024*

Last legislative election (Sep 2018)	*Seats*	*Last presidential (August 2017)*	*% of vote*
Rwanda Patriotic Front Coalition (FPR)	40	Paul Kagame (FPR)	98.8
Social Democratic Party	5	Philippe Mpayimana (Independent)	0.7
Liberal Party	4	Frank Habineza (Democratic Green Party)	0.5
Democratic Green Party	2		
Social Party Imberakuri	2		
Total	53	Total	100.0

People

For centuries, what is now Rwanda has been inhabited by both Hutus and Tutsis, who make up the majority, as well as the Twa ethnic group. Belgian colonisers stressed physical and social differences, and promoted Tutsi political domination. Almost 95% of the population of 12.1 million is Christian. The dominant language is Kinyarwanda, but English, French and Swahili are also official languages. 31% of the population live in urban areas and 75% work in agriculture, 18% in services, and 7% in industry. By 1994, the average farm size was less than one hectare, resulting in lower efficiency and private investment. Mountain streams provide potential for hydropower, but significant investment is needed.

In 1890, Rwanda became part of German East Africa until it was occupied by Belgian forces in 1916. Following the First World War, Belgium accepted the League of Nations Mandate to govern Rwanda as the Ruanda-Urundi territory, along with Congo. Ruanda-Urundi became a UN trust territory in 1946. Tutsis had been the dominant political group, and Hutu political parties formed in 1957, to give Hutus a voice reflective of their numbers. In 1959, ethnically motivated violence forced Tutsi King Kigeri V into exile in Uganda along with many other Tutsis. Rwanda gained independence in 1962, after being proclaimed a republic the previous year, with Hutu Gregoire Kayibanda as president. Many Tutsis left the country and, in 1963, c20,000 Tutsis were killed following a guerrilla invasion from Burundi. A decade later, in 1973, President Kayibanda was ousted in a military coup led by Hutu Juvenal Habyarimana, who became president under a new constitution in 1978. Ethnic violence in Burundi in 1988 resulted in c50,000 Hutu refugees arriving in Rwanda. A new multi-party constitution was introduced in 1991, after Tutsi forces invaded from Uganda in the previous year. The end of the civil war was signalled in 1993, after Habyarimana signed a power-sharing agreement with the Tutsis.

In April 1994, Habyarimana and the Burundian president were killed when their plane was shot down and Hutu militia and elements of the Rwandan military began the systematic massacre of Tutsis. The genocide saw c800,000 Tutsis and moderate Hutus killed in 100 days. The following years saw groups of refugees being pushed back into Rwanda. Unity and reconciliation were attempted after Vice-President Paul Kagame was elected president in 2000, and a new flag and national anthem were introduced in 2001. Genocide trials have continued since, although mass prisoner releases occurred over 2003–2005, and many of those released had admitted genocide involvement.

The May 2003 constitution has allowed for the multiparty parliamentary elections since. Kagame has now won his third consecutive term, after the Senate (upper house) approved a constitutional change in November 2015 to allow for a third presidential term. Kagame has succeeded in maintaining high growth, lowering poverty and tackling corruption. Since the formal end of the Second Congo War in 2003, the Rwandan government has been accused by the UN of providing military and logistical support to the M23 rebel military group, violating UN sanctions. The government has not faced any change in president or political party since the 2003 Constitution. Any political change would be unpredictable and could threaten economic stability.

DEBT

	2012	*2017*
External debt ratios (%)		
Total external debt/GDP	20.8	40.6
Public external debt/GDP	16.2	37.5
Private external debt/GDP	4.6	3.1
Total external debt/exports of goods and services	136.2	179.3
External debt service ratio	3.5	6.4
Public debt ratios (%)		
Public domestic debt/GDP	6.6	10.8
Public debt/GDP	22.8	48.3

Source: World Bank, Ministry of Finance, IMF, Exotix

Public and publicly guaranteed (PPG) external debt was US$3.4bn (37.5% of GDP) at end-2017, based on IMF figures presented in the external DSA. Private sector external debt was an additional US$283mn (3.1% of GDP). As a result, total external debt was US$3.7bn, more than double its level at end-2012. This was c40.6% of GDP and 179% of exports in 2017, with exports including goods, services and primary income. The largest foreign creditor group was multilateral creditors, owed 61.9% of total external debt, with just over US$1bn multilateral debt owed to the World Bank, as of end-2016. Bilateral creditors were owed US$343mn by Rwanda in 2017. Although this figure is fairly low, the proportion of external debt that is concessional has decreased over the past decade (peaking at 93% in 2008); subsequently, recent IMF programmes have advised that future borrowing only be on concessional terms. 70% of external debt was on concessional terms in 2016, from 83% in 2010, while IMF objectives have considered maintaining macroeconomic stability as access to foreign aid declines. On central bank figures, the role of grants, as a percentage, in the budget and meeting government financing requirements has been falling each year since 2013.

Between 2010 and 2012, public debt increased due to both external and domestic financing. External debt was mainly from large concessional loans, such as IDA project loans, but also some commercial borrowing for development projects. Domestic financing increases were mainly from treasury bills (one-year maturity), used to cover delays in donor disbursements and other cash flow needs. The rise in public debt between 2012 and 2017 was due to public investment projects, based on IMF reports.

Before 2013, Rwanda had no external commercial debt. Its first (and only to date) sovereign Eurobond issue in May 2013 was for US$400mn. This bond has a bullet maturity in 2023, and this bond amounted to 10.8% of total external debt in 2017.

Total PPG (external and domestic) debt was US$4.4bn (48.3% of GDP) on IMF figures, including US$987mn (10.8% of GDP) in domestic debt. The PPG external debt service ratio increased from 3.5% of exports in 2012 to 6.4% in 2017, based on IMF DSA figures. Debt service payments increased very quickly in 2015 and 2016. In a recent Annual Economic Report, the Ministry of Finance acknowledged that public debt rose in the fiscal year to 2016, although it cited its "efficient debt management" as the reason for its debt-to-GDP ratio remaining among the lowest in the region. It also noted that, while nominal external debt servicing increased in the fiscal year to 2016, as a proportion of exports, this remained constant, and fell slightly as a proportion of total revenue.

Composition of external debt

External debt by creditor (End 2017)	*Nominal amount outstanding (US$mn)*	*Share of total (%)*
Public and publicly guaranteed external debt	**3426**	**92.4**
o/w Publicly guaranteed external debt	377	10.2
o/w Government external debt	3049	82.2
o/w Official multilateral	2295	61.9
World Bank IDA[a]	1049	28.3
Official bilateral	343	9.2
Commercial creditors	411	11.1
Eurobond	400	10.8
Private sector external debt	**283**	**7.6**
Total external debt	**3709**	**100.0**

Source: IMF, Bloomberg

[a]Figure for end-2016 (latest)

Rescheduling History

Like many other African countries during the 1970s and 1980s, Rwanda experienced economic difficulties, resulting in a rapidly increasing government debt stock. In 2004, external debt was c90% of GDP. The enhanced HIPC initiative (completion point April 2005) and multilateral debt relief initiative (MDRI, delivery date January 2006) led to both Paris Club and multilateral debt forgiveness, resulting in a total of US$1.2bn in debt relief. Following this, the external debt stock was cUS$300mn, most of which was owed to the World Bank and AfDB. Rwanda's total public debt fell to c24% of GDP in 2006, and continued to fall to below 20% in 2008, where it stayed until 2012. It then rose to 30% in 2014, 39% in 2016 and 48% by end-2017. Total external debt has increased each year since 2006, with a large increase in 2013 when the eurobond was issued. Following the global financial crisis, investor risk aversion increased and capital was removed from Rwanda, resulting in a fall in foreign reserves.

Rwanda has had successive IMF programmes since the 1990s and currently has a standby credit facility (SCF, see below). In its ninth PSI review, the IMF predicted that real GDP growth would increase to historical averages of over 7% in 2018–2019, and 8% in 2020. After the slowdown in 2016 resulting from low international commodity prices, a drought affecting agriculture, and low lending to the private sector, real GDP growth rose again during 2017, to 6.1% and is forecast to reach 8% in 2020. 2017 inflation was fairly high at 7.1%, although this is expected to fall again to 6% in 2018. The government has run continual fiscal deficits since 2010, as the government adopted expansionary policies to counter the effects of the global financial crisis, and accommodative local policy in the face of adverse conditions, which had success in maintaining output. However, as growth increases again it is expected that the current account deficit will continue to decline as a percentage of GDP, and the primary balance to turn positive in 2021. Recurrent spending for 2016–2017 is forecast at 49% of the government budget, and fiscal outcomes have been consistent with IMF programme targets since 2016. Rwanda remains susceptible to exogenous shocks and weather patterns are becoming less predictable, threatening agriculture. Policies now focus on sustained and inclusive growth while maintaining stability, a key objective of the IMF PSI programmes over 2010–2017 (see below).

The IMF has acknowledged in its programmes' objectives that Rwanda has been dependent on foreign aid for budget support. As this becomes a less available source of funding, the use of concessional loans has become a priority, and the authorities have been encouraged to limit external debt on non-concessional terms. Delays in disbursements have required treasury bill issues for cash flow reasons. If donors delay or cancel planned disbursements, the government may struggle to meet its obligations, including debt service payments. Further, the economy is dependent on a few volatile sectors: agriculture, tourism, financial services, and IT services have become essential for output, employment, poverty reduction, and tax revenue but may be uncertain.

Vision 2020 is the government's plan to transform Rwanda into a middle-income country by 2020 (which requires GNI per capita of over US$996). Falling private sector credit growth has contributed to the weaker demand and lower real GDP growth in 2016. Although increasing nominally, as a proportion of total external debt, private sector external debt fell between 2012 and 2017. Domestic banks have also lent to small and medium-sized enterprises less than the authorities would have wanted. Government policies have included accelerating infrastructure projects and removing bottlenecks to improve private sector opportunities and improve likelihood of loan approvals. A key IMF objective over the medium term is therefore maintaining growth while changing from a public sector-led, aid-dependent economy to a more private sector-led economy. Previous IMF recommendations have been implemented to maintain the low risk rating on external debt, but to achieve middle-income status, the private sector will need to take the lead in driving growth.

The past two decades have seen ambitious development, with maintained high growth and poverty reduction: per capita GDP increased every year from 2002 to 2016. The completion of public investment projects will be important for tourism, developing infrastructure and paving the way for the private sector to lead growth. Various reforms are being completed by the government, including those of the public financial management system and on the improvement of national data accuracy. A weakness in government monitoring will be addressed when an integrated system is introduced to consolidate accounting information, currently scattered in different software systems and in different government departments. Rwanda has a more robust institutional framework than that of most other Sub-Saharan African countries, and the control of corruption is a strong government focus. However political risks remain, due to the uncertainty of the period after Kagame leaves office, and poor accountability remains a problem.

Rwanda is a land-locked country, so its main export countries are its neighbours, such as the Democratic Republic of the Congo and the East African Community countries. Rwanda has been trying to widen its export base for the diversification benefits. The macroeconomic framework comes with government plans for the new Bugesera Airport (construction started in August 2017), which could open up new export markets. Debt sustainability should not suffer from the airport's construction, as the government has a minority share in a public-private partnership with a diversified set of investors. The government is expected to take on cUS$37mn in debt over 2017–2019 for this project.

Relations with Multilateral Creditors

Since joining the IMF in 1963, Rwanda has had many programmes. Successive stand-by arrangements (SBAs) were completed during the 1960s and 1970s, as listed in the table below. Most of these were fully disbursed. In August 2002, the Executive Board approved a three-year poverty reduction and growth facility (PRGF, now extended credit facility or ECF) for an amount of SDR4mn (cUS$5mn) after the poverty reduction strategy was deemed acceptable for IMF concessional financing. Additional interim assistance was also approved under the enhanced HIPC initiative for SDR0.838mn (cUS$1mn) for debt service assistance. The PRGF (ECF) is intended to provide concessional funding for low income countries. Rwanda's specific targets included resolving the security situation, working towards macroeconomic sustainability, and strengthening institutions. Some waivers were granted for non-observance of performance criteria, although continued access to concessional funds was approved. All funds were drawn by the end of the programme and have since been repaid. On successful completion of the fourth review in April 2005, the Board approved a six-month extension.

On successful completion of the sixth review of the 2002 PRGF, the IMF Executive Board also approved a new three-year PRGF (ECF) programme, despite further waivers for non-observance of performance criteria. The new programme starting June 2006 was for SDR8.01mn (about US$12mn). The Board noted that growth was strong and policy implementation was on track, although structural changes still needed further progress. Every review during this programme required waivers to be granted for the non-observation of various performance criteria. The authorities' response to the global financial crisis led to a worsening of the fiscal stance during the programme and a loan from the ExIm Bank of China on less concessional terms than allowed under the programme was taken on.

Within a year of completing the PRGF (ECF) programme, inflation stood at just 2.3% in 2010 (from a high of 15.4% in 2008) and the maintenance of macroeconomic stability and broad-based growth had been achieved. The Board approved the authorities' request for a policy support instrument (PSI) in June 2010 with an aim to consolidate stability, sustain growth and reduce the dependency on foreign aid. This transition to a PSI is indicative of the Board's acknowledgement of Rwanda's previous success under IMF programmes and the likelihood of continued progress. Successive reviews came with positive reports by IMF staff, although it was noted in the third review in 2012 that high growth was bringing high inflation, in particular, through high food and fuel prices increases. The Board decided to extend the programme by seven months to January 2014 on successful completion of the sixth review. The seventh and final review was completed in December 2013, with one waiver for non-observance of a non-concessional borrowing ceiling criterion. A new three-year PSI was also approved on 2 December 2013. The second review was completed alongside the 2014 Article IV consultation, with IMF commendations for the authorities and reports that the fiscal stance was within reach of its objectives. Despite the strong policy implementation, the fall in international commodity prices had made the growth outlook more uncertain, as highlighted in the fourth review, completed in January 2016.

The fifth review of the PSI was completed in June 2016, and the Board also approved an 18-month stand-by credit facility (SCF) for SDR144.18mn (cUS$204mn, 90% of quota). The PSI was extended until the end of 2017, and then again to December 2018. The sixth review of the PSI and first review of the SCF were completed in January 2017, reporting that programme implementation had been strong and the agreed upon policy strategy remained appropriate. Growth had declined in 2016, as expected, while food prices pushed the inflation rate up. Similar comments were made following the seventh PSI review and second SCF review in July 2017, although growth expectations were high for 2017–2018 due to strong harvests and domestic production. Most targets had been met, but it was noted that private sector activity would be essential for Rwanda to reach middle-income status. The latest review was the ninth PSI review in June 2018 and reports strong programme implementation, improving external position and also a stronger-than-expected 2017 growth rebound, at 6.1%.

IMF programmes

Date	*Arrangements*	*Comments*
1966–1980	Various	SBAs: 1966–1967, 1967–1968, 1968–1969, 1969–1970, 1979–1980.
1991–1994	SAFC	Agreed for SDR30.66mn in April 1991. SDR8.76mn was disbursed.
1998–2002	ECF	Agreed for SDR71.4mn in June 1998. SDR61.88mn was disbursed.
2002–2005 (2006)	ECF	Approved by the Board in August 2002 as a three-year programme for SDR4mn (cUS$5mn) with additional enhanced HIPC debt service assistance for debt owed to the IMF. Some waivers were granted by the Board for non-observance of performance criteria, although the programme was completed successfully, fully drawn, after a six-month extension was granted following the fourth review in April 2005. Loans now fully repaid.
2006–2009	ECF	Immediately following the completion of the 2002 ECF, the Board approved a new programme with SDR8.01mn (cUS$12mn), starting in June 2006. Every review required waivers for non-observance of various performance criteria. This programme's funds were also fully drawn and, as of October 2017, SDR1.152mn remains outstanding.
2010–2013 (2014)	PSI	After the 2006–2009 ECF, the authorities demonstrated their commitment to continued development, stability and poverty reduction, and the IMF approved a PSI, a programme that is designed for countries that do not need balance of payment financial support and are developing economic programmes for IMF approval. This programme focused on future stability and continued growth despite the expected reduction in foreign aid. Extended after the sixth review, to January 2014.
2014–2017 (2018)	PSI	After the extension of the previous PSI, this programme was to continue the progress made towards maintaining stability, following satisfactory performance under the first PSI. Extended until end-2017, overlapping with the successor SCF, and again until December 2018.
2016–2018	SCF	On successful completion of the fifth review of the 2014 PSI, an SCF was approved in June 2016, with SDR144.18mn (cUS$204mn), 90% of Rwanda's quota. Growth slowed in 2016, as expected, although growth for 2017–2018 is forecast to approach 7% per annum. Reviews so far indicate that most targets have been met. A continued objective must be to increase private sector activity. Low credit to the private sector may have contributed to the 2016 slowdown in economic growth. The IMF highlighted encouraging private sector-led growth as essential for reaching middle-income status.

Source: IMF. Rwanda joined the IMF in 1963

Rwanda began cooperating with the World Bank in 1998 and so far has had 133 projects, some of which have enabled the involvement of other development partners, both multilateral and bilateral. As of August 2018, the World Bank has 27 active projects in Rwanda, with a focus on poverty reduction and infrastructural development, and has four more in the pipeline. The AfDB has 12 ongoing projects that aim to promote sustainable development, social progress and poverty reduction.

Paris Club and Bilateral Creditors

Rwanda has had three Paris Club agreements, as detailed in the table below, the most recent two being as part of HIPC debt relief. In 2000, the IMF and the World Bank found Rwanda eligible for the enhanced HIPC initiative and completion point was reached in April 2005. Participating creditors in the 2005 agreement were Austria, Belgium, Canada, Denmark, France, Germany, Italy, Japan, the Netherlands, the UK and the US.

Paris Club agreements

Date	*Terms*	*Status*	*Details*
1998 July	Naples	Fully repaid	Treated US$54mn, falling due from July 1998 to November 2000. The Naples terms provided a cancellation of 67% over three phases. There was the possibility to conduct debt swaps.
2002 Mar.	Cologne	Fully repaid	Treated US$1mn, falling due from December 2000 to June 2005, as part of the HIPC debt relief initiative. The cologne terms provided cancellation of 90%, with Austria, Canada, France, Japan, the Netherlands and the US participating. Possibility to conduct debt swaps.
2005 May	HIPC Initiative Exit	Fully repaid	Treated US$90.4mn (US$82.7mn cancelled, US$7.7mn rescheduled) following HIPC completion point in April 2005.

Source: Paris Club

Bilateral debt is currently a low proportion of total external debt, at just 9.2% at end-2017. The nominal amount of this debt has increased since 2012 but, as a proportion of total external debt, it has fallen from 16.1% in 2012.

Sovereign Commercial Debt

Rwanda has no experience of restructuring its commercial debt, as far as Exotix is aware. Historically, it has had a conservative borrowing strategy, which has eschewed commercial sources of finance in favour of concessional loans, although debt owed to commercial creditors is now c14% of total public external debt. Most of its commercial debt is accounted for by the country's sole sovereign eurobond.

Rwanda issued its first (and still only, to date) sovereign eurobond in 2013, the details of which are in the table below. The US$400mn fixed rate bullet bond was issued in May 2013 and has a 10-year maturity. The bond has a coupon of 6.625% and was priced to yield 6.875% (the issue price was 98.213). Final pricing was well below the initial guidance of 7–7.5%, as orders exceeded US$3bn, even though the size of the issue meant that it was not index-eligible. At the time, the coupon of 6.625% per annum was a premium over other Sub-Saharan African eurobonds, but the priority was on issuing the optimal amount of debt, according to sources. Proceeds were to be used for the repayment of the government's existing external loans in relation to the Kigali Convention Centre and the RwandAir strategic development plan (US$120mn to repay two outstanding loans on the Kigali Convention Centre, and US$80mn to repay an outstanding loan to RwandAir), as well as financing the completion of the Kigali Convention Centre (US$150mn) and to finance the Nyabarongo hydro power project (US$50mn). Rwanda already had a rating from Fitch and S&P (since 2006 and 2011, respectively) and was rated single B by both agencies at the time the bond was issued. The bond issue was seen as an indication of the country's recovery from the 1994 genocide and its new position in the international community following its HIPC debt relief. Reports in the summer of 2014 suggested the government would seek a return to the market in 2015 with a second bond, of as much as US$1bn, but this failed to materialise because of the deterioration in market conditions.

Rwanda bond
Rwanda 6.625% 2023
Bloomberg ticker: RWANDA

Borrower	Republic of Rwanda
Issue date	2 May 2013
Form	Eurobond
ISIN	XS0925613217
Issued amount	US$400mn
Currency	US dollar
Denomination	US$200,000 and US$1000 thereafter
Amortisation	Bullet
Final maturity date	2 May 2023
Coupon/interest	6.625% per annum, paid semi-annually May and November
Day count	30/360
Method of transfer	Euroclear/Clearstream
Settlement period	T + 2
Governing law	English
Joint lead managers	BNP Paribas, Citi

Source: Bloomberg

Corporate Bond Markets

There has only ever been one corporate bond issued on the Rwanda Stock Exchange. This was a 10-year sinkable issue for RWF1.84mn by I&M Bank Rwanda Ltd. (IMBRW), which matured in January 2018. This bond was a private placement.

The Rwanda Stock Exchange was incorporated in 2005 and is still very limited. Some of its activity has been from cross-listings from the Nairobi Securities Exchange in Kenya.

Senegal

Nominal GDP (US$mn, 2018)[a]		24,240
Population (thousand, 2018)[a]		16,319
GDP per capita (USD, 2018)[a]		1485
Credit ratings (long-term foreign currency)[b]	Fitch	NR
	Moody's	Ba3
	S&P	B+

[a]IMF WEO October 2018
[b]As at end-September 2018

Country Summary

- Senegal is regarded as a stable and relatively democratic country in an otherwise unstable region, and saw a transition from government to opposition in 2012. President Macky Sall reduced the presidential term from seven years to five, following concerns over the president's influence under his predecessor. This was seen as a strong example for other countries in the region, where leaders sometimes hold on to power beyond the end of their term.
- Senegal is now one of the best-performing economies in Sub-Saharan Africa (SSA). Growth has averaged 5.5% over the past five years (albeit weaker than Cote d'Ivoire's 8.5% average), helped by new structural reforms and a more diversified export base, and the government plans to raise the rate to 7–8% over the 20-year period of its

Exotix Capital, *Exotix Developing Markets Guide*,
https://doi.org/10.1007/978-3-030-05867-8_32

Plan Sénégal Emergent (PSE). This will require steadfast action to reduce patronage and rent-seeking so as to open up economic space for small and medium-sized enterprises (SMEs) and FDI. Senegal has historically been reliant on agriculture, especially groundnut production, and foreign aid. Other main areas of activity are fishing and mining (including phosphates, gold, iron ore, Zircon). The discovery of offshore oil in July 2017 suggests further potential, but it is still a relatively poor country.

- Senegal has seen a sharp rise in its debt burden over the past five years, with public debt now at over 60% of GDP, more than a decade on from HIPC debt reduction. Since its eurobond debut in 2009, it has been one of the more active SSA borrowers on the market, but debt service appears to have remained manageable and, unlike many other frontier and SSA sovereigns, Senegal did not need to go the IMF for a financial arrangement following the 2014 oil price crash, although policy discipline is maintained under close IMF monitoring.

Economic data	*Avg*[a]	*2014*	*2015*	*2016*	*2017 (e)*	*2018 (f)*	*2019 (f)*
Real GDP growth	4.2	6.6	6.4	6.2	7.2	7.0	6.7
Inflation (annual average)	1.7	−1.1	0.1	0.8	1.3	0.4	0.9
Current account (% of GDP)	−6.8	−7.0	−5.4	−4.0	−7.3	−7.7	−7.1
Reserves (US$bn, end-period)[b]	–	13.0	12.4	10.4	13.0	17.6[c]	–
Reserves/ imports (months)[d]	–	4.8	5.0	3.9	4.2	–	–
Overall fiscal balance (% of GDP)[e]	−3.8	−3.9	−3.7	−3.3	−3.0	−3.5	−3.0
Currency (ticker)	Member of the CFA franc zone (XOF)						
FX regime	The CFA franc is pegged against the euro at a rate of CFAF655.957 per euro. The CFA franc floats freely against other currencies.						

(*continued*)

(continued)

Economic data	*Avg*[a]	*2014*	*2015*	*2016*	*2017 (e)*	*2018 (f)*	*2019 (f)*
Key exports	Fish (16.2%), gold (12.5%), mineral fuels (10.7%), petroleum products (9.7%), cement (7.4%) and phosphoric acid (7.0%). Remittances are also a key source of foreign exchange earnings, reaching 13.6% of GDP in 2016.						

Source: IMF WEO Database, IMF Country Reports, Haver, Bloomberg, OEC, Exotix

[a]10-year avg. to 2016 unless otherwise stated
[b]WAEMU gross official reserves from IMF reports
[c]Latest April 2018
[d]Months of WAEMU imports of GNFS from IMF reports
[e]General government net lending (IMF WEO)

Key figures		*Party*	*Since*
President	Macky Sall	APR	Apr. 2012
Prime minister	Mahammed Dionne	Independent	Jul. 2014
Minister of finance	Amadou Ba	Independent	Sep. 2013
Key opposition figure	Abdoulaye Wade	PDS	Apr. 2012[a]
Central bank governor	Tiémoko Meyliet Koné (Governor of BCEAO)	n/a	Sep. 2011

[a]Abdoulaye Wade was president from 2000 to 2012, when he lost the election to Macky Sall, and has been leader of the PDS party since it was founded in 1974

Politics

Executive power

The president is elected by popular vote, with a run-off if no candidate achieves an absolute majority. In a referendum in March 2016 to amend the constitution, President Sall won approval to reduce the presidential term from seven to five years, but the change will only take effect when the current seven-year term expires (i.e. from 2019), with a maximum of two consecutive terms.

Presidential term: Five years (from 2019) **Parliamentary term**: Five years

Legislature

Unicameral National Assembly consisting of 165 seats. 90 are elected by first past the post in 35 constituencies, 60 are elected by national proportional representation and 15 are elected by overseas voters.

Elections

Next due *Presidential: February 2019; Legislative: December 2022*

Last legislative election (July 2017)	*Seats*	*Last presidential (2012)*	*% of vote*
Benno Bokk Yakaar Coalition	125	*First round (February)*	
Winning Coalition Wattu Senegal	19	Abdoulaye Wade (PDS)	34.8
Manko Taxawu Senegal	7	Macky Sall (APR)	26.6
Party for Unity and Rally	3	Moustapha Niasse (AFP)	13.2
Patriotic Convergence Coalition	2	Tanor Dieng (PSS)	11.3
Others	9	Others	9.7
		Second round (March)	
		Macky Sall	65.8
		Abdoulaye Wade	34.2
Total	165	Total	100.0

People

Of the population, 95% is Muslim and 5% Christian/with indigenous beliefs. The largest ethnic groups are the Wolof, Pular and Serer, constituting 39%, 27% and 15% of the population, respectively, which speak various languages, although French is the official tongue. Population growth is fast (2.4% per year), with a young population, a low rate of literacy and high youth unemployment. Life expectancy is 60 years (men) and 64 years (women). 44% of the population live in urban areas. Agriculture employs 77.5% of the working population, with groundnut being the chief crop. Traditional exports of groundnuts and cotton have become less significant.

Senegal became independent from France in April 1960, forming in June the Federation of Mali with French Sudan (now Mali). In August, Senegal declared national independence and withdrew from the federation. Leopold-Sedar Senghor was elected president in September. By 1963, Senegal had become a de facto one-party state. Multiparty politics was restored in 1974. Senghor, after being re-elected three times, resigned in 1980. He was succeeded by Abdou Diouf, also of the Parti Socialiste Senegalais (PS) from 1981 to 2000. Abdoulaye Wade, leader of the Senegalese Democratic Party (PDS) opposition, was elected president in 2000 ending 40 years of Socialist rule. Wade's legacy as an anti-corruption reformer was, however, marred by the country's fall in Transparency International's corruption perceptions' index and concern over the intimidation of journalists and insufficient dialogue between the government and opposition parties. There had also been concerns about the increasing power of the president under Wade, who appointed his son Karim as a "super minister" in 2009, a move that was widely seen as an attempt by his aging father to groom his son to be his successor.

President Wade did, however, oversee a democratic transition in government after his 2012 defeat to Macky Sall. Karim was subsequently charged with corruption in 2013 and jailed for six years in 2015, but was pardoned by Sall in 2016 and left the country. A generally peaceful and stable country, protests were held in the capital against the detention of opponents to the president in April 2017. Meanwhile, a separatist movement in the impoverished Casamance region of southern Senegal continues, despite numerous attempted peace processes.

Senegal is the second biggest of the eight countries that make up the West Africa Economic and Monetary Union (WAEMU), which also includes Benin, Burkina Faso, Cote d'Ivoire (the biggest), Guinea-Bissau, Mali, Niger and Togo, comprising 15% of its GDP and 14% of its population.

DEBT

	2012	2017
External debt ratios (%)		
Total external debt/GDP	62.7	73.2
Public external debt/GDP	31.4	52.0
Private external debt/GDP	31.3	21.3
Total external debt/exports of goods, services and remittances	157.1	171.7
External debt service ratio (public)	4.8	7.2
Public debt ratios (%)		
Public domestic debt/GDP	11.0	14.5
Public debt/GDP	42.4	66.5

Source: Eurobond prospectus, IMF, Exotix

The latest official data provided for Senegal's external debt is for end-2017, as contained in the prospectus for the 2028 and 2048 eurobonds issued in March 2018. Exotix has used this data, together with private external debt derived from IMF data, to calculate the external debt ratios. Currency conversions from the CFA franc to the US dollar were made using the end-period exchange rates also provided in the prospectus. For the creditor composition shown in the below, however, in order to provide the most representative position, Exotix has added the net issuance from its March 2018 bond sales to the end-2017 stock to provide a proxy for the overall Q1 18 external debt position. Note also that for the debt/GDP ratios, GDP is taken from the April 2018 IMF WEO. The authorities have since updated their national accounts data, using a new GDP series with a base year of 2014, previously 1999, under which GDP is c30% higher in nominal terms compared with the previously reported GDP data, which would therefore result in lower debt/GDP ratios than those reported here.

Senegal's total external debt at end-2017 was US$12.1bn (73.2% of GDP), comprising public external debt of US$8.6bn (52% of GDP) and private external debt of US$3.5bn (21.3% of GDP). Public external debt was mostly owed to multilateral and bilateral creditors (accounting for 40% and 32% of public external debt, respectively). The World Bank was by far the biggest multilateral creditor (accounting for 57% of multilateral debt), followed by the African Development Bank (AfDB) (19% of multilateral debt). Jointly, OPEC, the Islamic Development Bank (IsDB) and the Arab Bank for Economic Development in Africa (BADEA) were owed US$364mn by Senegal. Major bilateral creditors include France, other

EU countries, the US and China, although exact figures are not provided. Commercial creditors were owed cUS$2.4bn at end-2017 (28% of public external debt). Most of this was owed to bondholders. At end-2017, the stock of outstanding eurobonds amounted to US$2.1bn in three issues. In addition, commercial loans owed to banks (Credit Suisse and the African Export-Import Bank) have been accumulating since 2014 and totalled US$296mn.

However, public external debt (and total external debt) increased in Q1 18 due to net issuance from Senegal's 2018 eurobond operations in March 2018. These operations consisted of the issuance of a US$1bn 2048 bond and EUR1bn 2028 bond (cUS$1.2bn equivalent), as well as the purchase of US$200mn of the 2021 bond, so that outstanding eurobond issuance by end-March 2018 increased to US$4.1bn. Public external debt increased by the same amount to US$10.6bn (all other items unchanged)—c54% of 2018 projected GDP in the IMF WEO—and total external debt increased accordingly to US$14.1bn (71% of 2018 projected GDP). The net issuance also results in a marked change in the composition of public external debt such that now it is mostly owed to commercial creditors. Commercial creditors account for 41.8% of public external debt (and 31.4% of total external debt), with the bulk of this in the form of Eurobonds (39% of public external debt and 29% of total external debt), while the share of public external debt owed to multilaterals and bilaterals falls to 32.6% and 25.5%, respectively. The increase in commercial debt (including bank loans and bridge loans) has also contributed to the lower proportion of external debt that is on concessional terms. The government continues to favour concessional financing and has stated its preference of concessional debt with traditional creditors over new financing sources, although the IMF identified recent (non-concessional) bond issues as a challenge for public debt sustainability. Bilaterals accounted for 32% of public external debt.

As a proportion of GDP, public sector external debt has increased over 2012–2017, from 31.4% to 52.0%, leading to an increase in total external debt as a proportion of GDP, from 62.7% in 2012 to 73.2% in 2017. Nominal GDP in USD terms rose by 16% over this period, suggesting much of the increase in the debt ratios was due to higher levels of public debt (i.e. government borrowing). Private sector external indebtedness has fallen, standing at 21.3% of GDP in 2017, down from 31.3% in 2012, based on IMF figures. Total external debt as a percentage of exports of goods, services and remittances, increased from 157% to 172%. Private remittances are included in the denominator because of their significance (they reached

13.6% of GDP in 2016). The public sector external debt service ratio rose from 4.8% to 7.2% between 2012 and 2017, according to the IMF.

Total public debt rose to 66.5% of GDP in 2017 (the IMF WEO says 61%), up from 42.4% in 2012; and up considerably from its post-HIPC low of just 22% in 2006 (based on IMF WEO data). Public domestic debt was 14.5% of GDP in 2017. Domestic public debt is denominated in local currency (CFA franc), and is mostly held by regional banks, and includes significant treasury bill issuance. Domestic issuance in WAEMU is now centralised through a separate debt management agency called Agence UMOA-Titres.

Composition of external debt

External debt by creditor (est Mar. 2018)[a]	*Nominal amount outstanding (US$mn)*	*Share of total (%)*
Public sector external debt	**10,587.7**	**75.1**
o/w Official multilateral	3456.7	24.5
World Bank	1958.7	13.9
AfDB	666.9	4.7
IMF	104.1	0.7
OPEC/IsDB/BADEA	364.0	2.6
Official bilateral	2703.8	19.2
OECD	237.9	1.7
Arab countries	86.5	0.6
Commercial creditors	4427.2	31.4
Eurobonds[b]	4131.4	29.3
Commercial bank loans	295.8	2.1
Private sector external debt[c]	**3502.5**	**24.9**
Total external debt	**14,090.2**	**100.0**

Source: 2028/2048 Eurobond prospectus, IMF, Bloomberg, Exotix

[a]External debt as of end-2017 plus net Eurobond issuance in March 2018

[b]We include the 2028 and 2048 Eurobond issue and partial repurchase of the 2021 Eurobond in March 2018

[c]Derived from IMF data

Rescheduling History

Senegal was deemed eligible for HIPC debt relief, achieving decision point in June 2000, after a series of debt reschedulings on both its Paris Club and commercial bank debt during the 1980s and early 1990s. It benefitted from multilateral and bilateral debt reduction after reaching HIPC completion point in April 2004, and has had an unblemished payment experience since.

HIPC debt relief reduced Senegal's debt significantly, with total multilateral debt falling by XOF1,069.7bn (US$1.7bn at the average exchange rate in 2004), of which XOF841.1bn was from the IDA and XOF163.9bn from the AfDB. With a common reduction factor (CRF) of 19%, based on the fiscal criterion, it obtained debt reduction of 73% in NPV terms after taking account of traditional debt relief mechanisms. External public debt fell from 33% of GDP at end-2005 to below 20% at end-2008. HIPC debt relief was projected to reduce NPV external debt/exports from 179% in 2002 to 139% in 2004 and further to 100% by 2010, while NPV external debt/revenues was projected to fall from 242% in 2002 to 183% in 2004 and 122% in 2010. External debt in 2006 was US$2.2bn in nominal terms, some 144% of exports, and rose further to 172% in 2009. Since HIPC completion and the MDRI (multilateral debt relief initiative), total public sector debt has been rising. In 2016, at 60.5% of GDP, public debt exceeded its 2003 level (pre-HIPC completion point). Bilateral debt and commercial debt have both been rising, in both absolute terms and as a proportion of total external debt, and domestic debt almost doubled in 2011–2016. However, the use of funds from some non-concessional loans has been for infrastructure projects, which should drive future growth and debt servicing capacity.

Relations with Multilateral Creditors

Senegal has a long history of IMF involvement and generally maintains a good relationship with the Fund. Indeed, it has pretty much been under some form of IMF engagement nearly every year for the past four decades, although this has taken the form of policy monitoring rather than a financed programme in the past eight years. A number of these arrangements have been in place since achieving HIPC completion point in 2004 in order to foster post-HIPC policy discipline. It has had 15 financing arrangements in all, its last one being an exogenous shock facility (ESF) over 2008–2010 in part a response to balance of payments problems that emerged in 2008 due to high global food and energy prices and the subsequent global financial crisis. It has had three policy-monitoring arrangements (policy support instruments—PSI). Its most recent PSI was approved in June 2015, initially for a three-year period, but was extended by one year (to June 2019) at the time of the fourth review in June 2017. The sixth review of the PSI was approved in July 2018. The IMF noted performance was mixed.

IMF programmes

Date	*Arrangements*	*Comments*
1980s	Various	1979–1980 (SBA), 1980–1981 (EFF), 1981–1982, 1982–1983, 1983–1984, 1985–1986, 1986–1987, 1987–1988 (all SBAs), 1986–1988 (structural adjustment facility commitment).
1988–1992	ECF	Formerly PRGF. Fully drawn.
1994	SBA	From March to August. Not fully drawn.
1994–1998	ECF	Formerly PRGF. Fully drawn.
1998–2002	ECF	Formerly PRGF. Four-year SDR107mn programme approved in April 1998. Not Fully drawn.
2003–2006	ECF	Formerly PRGF. Three-year SDR24.3mn (US$35.1mn) programme agreed in April 2003. In completing the reviews, a waiver for the non-observance of performance criteria was granted. Expired April 2006. Fully drawn.
2007–2010	PSI	Three-year PSI agreed in November 2007. The first review was completed satisfactorily in June 2008 despite fiscal slippage and a waiver for non-observance of the criterion for domestic payment arrears. The second review was completed in December 2008, with three waivers. The third review was completed in June 2009, with waivers. The fourth review was completed in December 2009 and the fifth review in May 2010. The sixth and final review was completed in December 2010.
2008–2010	ESF	The IMF approved in December 2008 a one-year SDR48.5mn (US$75.6mn) ESF arrangement, running in parallel with the 2007–10 PSI, at the same time as the second review of the PSI. The ESF was intended to help finance the balance of payments impact of higher food and energy prices. US$37.8mn was available immediately. Financial support under the ESF was increased by SDR72.8mn to SDR121.4mn (by US$112mn to US$186mn) at the completion of the first review of the ESF in June 2009 (coinciding with the third review of the PSI). The ESF was also extended from 12 to 18 months. The second review of the ESF was competed in December 2009. The third and final review of the ESF was completed in May 2010 with waivers on the basic fiscal balance and non-concessional external debt. The ESF was fully drawn with total disbursements of US$178mn.
2010–2014	PSI	A new three-year PSI arrangement was approved in December 2010 at the time the sixth and final review of the previous PSI was completed. Performance was satisfactory, except for a breach in non-concessional external debt, which was considered "not material for debt sustainability." All structural benchmarks were met. The programme was extended by one year to end-2014, as requested by the authorities at the time of the fifth review in June 2013. The eighth and final review was concluded in December 2014.

(*continued*)

(continued)

Date	*Arrangements*	*Comments*
2015–2019	PSI	A third three-year PSI was approved by the Board in June 2015, to support the implementation of macroeconomic reforms, to reduce poverty and work towards debt sustainability. The fourth review was completed in June 2017, and noted that growth had steadily increased, inflation had remained low and the fiscal deficit had fallen to 4.2% of GDP in 2016. On completion of this review, a one-year extension to June 2019 was also approved. The fifth review was completed in December 2017, which noted the economic outlook was positive, although continued implementation of structural reforms was needed to maintain the high growth rates of recent years. Program performance through September 2017 was seen as satisfactory. All end-June 2017 assessment criteria and indicative targets were met, except for the indicative target on tax revenue, which was missed due to lower-than-projected oil-related revenue. Two of the three structural benchmarks were met. The sixth review of the PSI was completed in July 2018, although performance was mixed. A waiver was granted for end-December 2017 non-observance of the central government overall net financing assessment criteria, and two end-December 2017 indicative targets were missed, including the floor on tax revenue, which led to the modification of assessment criteria. Five of the seven end-March 2018 indicative targets were met. Three of the five structural benchmarks set for the sixth review were met, while substantial progress was made on the other two.

Source: IMF. Senegal joined the IMF in 1962

The World Bank and AfDB are Senegal's biggest official multilateral creditors. The World Bank currently has 35 active projects in Senegal, including a Dakar transport project with a commitment of US$300mn, aiming to enhance urban mobility through a Bus Rapid Transit corridor. The World Bank has also agreed to provide US$29mn IDA credit for the development of institutions needed to negotiate agreements in the extractive industries, including negotiating oil and gas development projects that are in line with the public interest. Several oil and gas discoveries off the coast were announced during 2017. The AfDB began working with Senegal in 1972, and 66 projects had been financed to 2017, with accumulated investment totalling US$1.1bn. Infrastructure projects account for c40% of the Bank's investments. The social sector, rural development and private sector are also key recipients.

The four private sector projects to date received around US$250mn in financing. AfDB agreed to provide US$212mn in July 2017 for a project to link Dakar with the main airport, by a 29-mile urban railway. It came after US$348mn was already agreed with the IsDB and US$235mn from France. The government has also pledged US$219mn. Most daily journeys in Dakar are still made on foot. In addition to easing road traffic congestion, transport infrastructure development is intended to facilitate further economic growth and improve the living standards of local people. The IsDB also has a number of ongoing projects in Senegal, with a focus on developing infrastructure to drive future growth. Several major projects aim to improve drinking water supplies and the transport infrastructure and stimulate urban modernisation, while educational improvements aim to reduce youth unemployment and provide the supply-side expansion necessary to enable growth without increasing inflation.

Paris Club and Bilateral Creditors

Senegal has undergone 14 Paris Club treatments, which Exotix counts as the most of any sovereign debtor, the most recent of which (the HIPC exit treatment in 2004) is still outstanding. In June 2004, US$463mn of the total US$968mn Paris Club debt was treated under HIPC. Participating creditors were Belgium, Brazil, Canada, France, Italy, the Netherlands, Norway, Spain, the UK and the US.

Paris Club agreements

Date	*Terms*	*Status*	*Details*
1981–1986	Classic	Fully Repaid	Various: 1981, 1982, 1983, 1985, 1986
1987	Ad Hoc	Fully Repaid	Treated US$74mn.
1989	Toronto	Fully Repaid	Treated US$136mn. Repayment of non-ODA credits over 14 years, with eight years of grace, after cancellation to a rate of 33%. Repayment of ODA credits over 25 years with 14 years of grace.
1990	Toronto	Fully Repaid	Treated US$107mn. Repayment of non-ODA credits over 14 years, with eight years of grace, after cancellation to a rate of 33%. Repayment of ODA credits over 25 years with 14 years of grace.
1991	Toronto	Fully Repaid	Treated US$233mn. Repayment of non-ODA credits over 14 years, with eight years of grace, after cancellation to a rate of 33%. Repayment of ODA credits over 25 years with 14 years of grace. Possibility to conduct debt swaps.

(*continued*)

(continued)

Date	*Terms*	*Status*	*Details*
1994	London	Fully Repaid	Treated US$233mn. Repayment of non-ODA credits over 23 years, with six years of grace, after cancellation to a rate of 50%. Repayment of ODA credits over 30 years with 12 years of grace. Possibility to conduct debt swaps.
1995	Naples	Fully Repaid	Treated US$168mn. Repayment of non-ODA credits over 23 years, with six years of grace, after cancellation to a rate of 67%. Repayment of ODA credits over 40 years with 16 years of grace. Possibility to conduct debt swaps.
1998	Naples	Fully Repaid	Treated US$427mn. Treatment of arrears as of 17 June 1998, treatment of maturities falling due from 1 June 1998 up to 31 December 2000, treatment of the stock as of 17 June 1998. Pullback clause.
2000 Oct	Cologne	Fully Repaid	Following HIPC decision point in June 2000. Treated US$22mn, of which US$22mn being cancelled. Treatment of maturities falling due from 22 June 2000 up to 31 December 2003. Good will clause.
2004 Jun	HIPC Initiative Exit	Active	Following HIPC completion point in April 2004. Treated US$463mn, of which US$127mn being cancelled, US$336mn rescheduled. Treatment of arrears as of 31 March 2004, treatment of the stock as of 1 April 2004. Possibility to conduct debt swaps.

Source: Paris Club

Other bilateral creditors (grants and concessional loans) include Exim Bank China, Exim Bank Korea, Exim Bank China (Taiwan) and Exim Bank Turkey. An increasing share of foreign aid is coming from China and the Gulf Arab states.

Sovereign Commercial Debt

Senegal undertook a few commercial debt restructuring operations in the 1980s and a World Bank-sponsored debt buyback of its commercial debt in 1996. From then, until its first eurobond issue in 2009, it was largely off the international capital markets' radar although it was assigned a B+ rating from S&P in December 2000. Since then, Senegal has returned to the market to issue more bonds and entered into various loan agreements with international banks.

Commercial debt agreements

Date	*Details*
1984	Rescheduling of US$96mn of bank debt maturities in May 1981–June 1984.
1985	Rescheduling of US$20mn of bank debt maturities in July 1984–June 1986.
1989	Rescheduling of US$37mn.
1996 Dec.	Debt buyback at 8 cents per US dollar of US$80mn owed to commercial banks funded by the World Bank's DRF.

Source: World Bank GDF

Senegal has issued six eurobonds, since its debut in 2009, five of which are still outstanding. Its first sovereign eurobond was issued in December 2009, as Senegal became only the fourth country in SSA (excluding South Africa) to issue a plain vanilla bond outside a restructuring, after benchmark issues in Ghana and Gabon in 2007, and the Seychelles' small issue in 2006. The US$200mn issue had a five-year maturity (2014) and a coupon of 8.75%, but was priced to yield 9.25%. Proceeds of the bond issue were used exclusively to finance the Dakar-Diamniadio toll road. It was the intention on issue to establish an escrow account abroad to provide for the repayment of principle at maturity. The 2014 maturity was called on 13 May 2011 and, at the same time, Senegal issued a new US$500mn 10-year bond (8.75% 2021), some of the proceeds of which were used to effect the early repayment of the 2009 issue. The 2011 issue had a coupon of 8.75% and was priced to yield 9.125% (the issue price was 97.574). Four further bonds have been issued. A US$500mn 10-year bond was issued in July 2014. The bond had a coupon of 6.25% and was issued at par. Part of the proceeds of the 2014 issue was used to repay to Credit Suisse a EUR150mn loan due in January 2015. It returned to the market after a three-year break in May 2017 with a US$1.1bn 15-year amortising bond. The bond had a coupon of 6.25% and was issued at par. The government intended to use a portion of the proceeds of the bond to repay in full a bridge loan, a US$150mn term facility loan at a rate of three-month LIBOR plus 3.25% from Standard Chartered Bank and Citibank in order to finance certain infrastructure project, which Senegal entered into in March 2017. Senegal also entered into a new EUR150mn loan in March 2015 with a maturity of five years at a rate of six-month EURIBOR plus 5.15% from Credit Suisse. Senegal's most recent issuance came in a dual tranche USD and EUR offering in March 2018, with a EUR1bn 10-year bond and a US$1bn 30-year bond. Both denominations were issued at par. Part of the proceeds of this issuance was used for liability management purposes. The government launched a cash repurchase offer for the 2021 bond, paying down 40% of the principal, thereby reducing the outstanding principal to US$300mn. The repurchase was at 113.5% and closed on 14 March 2018.

A summary of its five outstanding bonds is shown in the table below.

Senegal's outstanding eurobonds

Description	*Amount outstanding*	*Maturity type*	*Issue date*
USD 8.75% due 2021	US$300mn[a]	Bullet	May 2011
USD 6.25% due 2024	US$500mn	Bullet	Jul. 2014
EUR 4.75% due 2028	EUR1000mn	Sinkable	Mar. 2018
USD 6.25% due 2033	US$1100mn	Sinkable	May 2017
USD 6.75% due 2048	US$1000mn	Sinkable	Mar. 2018

Source: Bloomberg

[a]Following US$200mn repurchase in March 2018

Senegal bond
Republic of Senegal 6.75% 2048
Bloomberg ticker: SENEGL

Borrower	Republic of Senegal
Issue date	13 March 2018
Form	Eurobond
ISIN	XS1790134362
Issue size	US$1000mn
Currency	US dollar
Denomination	Minimum of US$200,000 and US$1000 thereafter
Amortisation	Repayment in three equal instalments on 13 March 2046, 13 March 2047 and 13 March 2048.
Final maturity date	13 March 2048
Coupon/interest	6.75% paid semi-annually, March and September
Day count	30/360
Method of transfer	Euroclear/Clearstream
Settlement period	T + 2 business days
Governing law	English
Listing	Dublin
Joint lead managers	Citi, Deutsche Bank, BNP Paribas, Standard Chartered Bank, Société Générale, Natixis

Source: Bloomberg

Seychelles

Nominal GDP (US$mn, 2018)[a]		1564
Population (thousand, 2018)[a]		95
GDP per capita (USD, 2018)[a]		16,377
Credit ratings (long-term foreign currency)[b]	Fitch	BB−
	Moody's	NR
	S&P	NR

[a]IMF WEO October 2018
[b]As at end-September 2018

Country Summary

- Politically stable, Seychelles has the highest GDP per capita in Africa according to the World Bank and its development indicators are among the most favourable in the world.
- Small, open economy based on high-end tourism and fishing and more recently has developed an offshore financial services centre. In 2016, tuna fishing made up 60% of goods exports while tourism earnings, which make up 47% of services exports, are cUS$500mn a year (about one-third of GDP). In recent years, to improve resilience to external shocks, the government has tried to diversify the economy. In June 2018, Seychelles signed an economic partnership agreement with the EU, removing trade barriers. 58% of Seychellois exports go to European markets.

Exotix Capital, *Exotix Developing Markets Guide*,
https://doi.org/10.1007/978-3-030-05867-8_33

- A decade after its 2008 default, the country has experienced a robust recovery, supported by debt reduction and a strong policy response under successive IMF programmes. The fiscal effort has been impressive, with primary surpluses averaging 5.5% of GDP over the past seven years, and the authorities now aim to reduce public debt to below 50% of GDP by 2021. The default came after the global financial crisis exposed Seychelles' vulnerabilities—one of the highest public debt burdens in the world (reaching 200% of GDP in 2001), an unsustainable exchange rate peg and a very low level of reserves. However, the primary surplus target is now planned to soften to 2.5% of GDP over the medium term (compared to a 3% target over 2017–2018) as the government embarks on large infrastructure spending projects as set out in the President's State of the Nation Address in March 2018.

Economic data	*Avg*[a]	*2014*	*2015*	*2016*	*2017 (e)*	*2018 (f)*	*2019 (f)*
Real GDP growth	4.7	4.5	4.9	4.5	5.3	3.6	3.3
Inflation (annual average)	8.0	1.4	4.0	−1.0	2.9	4.4	3.7
Current account (% of GDP)	−17.7	−23.1	−18.6	−20.1	−20.5	−18.4	−18.0
Reserves (US$mn, end-period)[b]	310	464	536	523	545	569[c]	–
Reserves/imports[d]	2.6	3.7	4.8	4.3	3.8	–	–
Overall fiscal balance (% of GDP)[e]	1.2	3.7	1.9	0.2	0.4	1.0	1.1
Currency (ticker)	Seychelles rupee (SCR)						
FX regime	Officially floating after the currency's devaluation in November 2008 although the rupee has been fairly stable against the US dollar since mid-2010.						
Key exports	Processed fish (53%), oil re-exports (26%). Services' exports (half of which are tourism revenues) are now more important, amounting to nearly twice that of goods' exports.						

Source: IMF WEO Database, Central Bank of Seychelles, OEC

[a]10-year average to 2016 unless otherwise stated

[b]Official reserve assets

[c]Latest figure, May 2018

[d]In months of the current year's imports of goods, services and primary income debit

[e]Overall government net lending

Key figures		*Party*	*Since*
President	Danny Faure	PL	Oct. 2016[a]
Vice president	Vincent Meriton	PL	Oct. 2016
Minister of finance, trade and planning	Dr Peter Larose	PL	Oct. 2016
Key opposition figure	Wavel Ramkalawan	SNP	1998
Central bank governor	Caroline Abel	–	Mar. 2012

[a]Faure became president after James Michel resigned

Politics

Executive power

Centred on the president who is both chief of state and head of government. Under the 1993 constitution, the president has the capacity to rule by decree. The president is directly elected and responsible for cabinet appointments (Council of Ministers). A run-off vote is required if the leading candidate fails to get over 50% in the first round. The cabinet has 10 members including the president.

Presidential term: Five years, three-term limit (consecutive allowed)

Parliamentary term: Five years

Legislature

Unicameral, the National Assembly, elected by popular vote to serve five-year terms. Of 33 seats, 25 are elected by popular vote and eight are allocated based upon proportional representation.

Elections

Next due *Presidential: 2020* *Legislative: 2021*

Last legislative election (September 2016)	*Seats*	*Last presidential (December 2015)*	*% of vote*
Linyon Demokratik Seselwa (LDS)	19	*First round*	
Parti Lepep (formerly Seychelles People's Progressive Front) (PL)	14	James Michel (PL)	47.8
		Wavel Ramkalawan (SNP)	33.9
		Others	3.5
		Second round	
		James Michel (PL)	50.15
		Wavel Ramkalawan (SNP)	49.85
Total	33	Total	100.0

People

The Republic of Seychelles is an archipelago located 1500 km off the east coast of Africa, just south of the equator in the Indian Ocean. Mahe, the main island, houses 90% of Seychellois people. Creole is the predominant grouping at over 90% of the population, although most people can claim African/French descent. There are small numbers of Arab, Indian and Chinese too.

Around 90% of people are Christian. Originally settled by French plantation owners, the islands fell under British control in 1812. After independence was granted from the UK in 1976, a period of instability followed. President James Mancham was overthrown in a coup in 1977 by supporters of PM France Albert Rene, which saw the country enter a period of one-party rule until multiparty democracy was reinstituted in 1991 and a new constitution in 1993. Stability has endured since, with the PL (formerly SPPF)—in power continuously until 2016—dominating politics for over three decades, first under President Rene, who then handed the reins to James Michel in April 2004. The Seychelles became a de facto two-party state with the SNP being the main opposition since 1994; it had previously been three different parties. Michel was re-elected in 2006 and legislative elections in 2007 secured a large majority for his party, which was increased further in 2011 when other parties boycotted the election. Michel won a third (and final) term in the 2015 presidential election run-off by just 193 valid votes, but the following year, the opposition coalition Linyon Demokratik Seselwa (LDS) won a majority in the National Assembly with 19 seats. Michel resigned as a result and Danny Faure became president.

Debt

	2012	*2017*
External debt ratios (%)		
Total external debt/GDP	148.8	100.4
Public external debt/GDP	48.5	31.2
Private external debt[a]/GDP	100.3	69.1
Total external debt/exports of goods and services	144.3	95.3
External debt service ratio (public)	1.8	3.6
Public debt ratios (%)		
Public domestic debt/GDP	36.6	33.7
Public debt/GDP	80.1	64.9

Source: Central Bank of Seychelles, Ministry of Finance, IMF, Exotix

[a]Excludes intercompany lending

Seychelles's total external debt was c100% of GDP in 2017, compared to nearly 150% in 2012, according to central bank data based on BPM6 methodology (excluding intercompany lending). The decline in the external debt/GDP ratio is due to the strong increase in nominal GDP over the period (up about 40% in US$ terms, from US$1.06bn to US$1.48bn on IMF WEO data). In nominal USD terms, total external debt has been relatively stable over the period, declining over 2012–2015 (mainly due to a fall in private external debt) but rising over 2015–2017.

Total external debt stood at US$1.5bn at the end of 2017. Of this, public external debt (including the monetary authority, ie central bank) amounted to US$463mn, c31% of the total and 31% of GDP, comprising general government external debt of US$404mn and external debt of the monetary authority of US$59mn. Private external debt (excluding intercompany lending) was US$1bn, about 69% of the total and 69% of GDP. Intercompany lending is significant however, amounting to another US$1.7bn at end 2017 (albeit declining from US$2.1bn at end-2012), so amounting to an additional 114% of GDP. The ratio of total external debt to exports of goods and services has also fallen from nearly 145% to 95%, due to higher export earnings (especially tourism). The public debt service ratio remains low, even as, being a high-income country since 2015 (World Bank update), access to concessional debt is limited. Coupon payments on the 2026 eurobond however stepped up again in 2015 and bond amortisations started in July 2016. As a result, external debt service in 2016 was double that of 2013, in nominal USD terms.

A basic creditor composition of public external debt is provided in separate data in the central bank's monthly statistical bulletin (although it appears to exclude the monetary authority, so we assume it relates only to general government debt), although the most recent detailed breakdown by creditor dates from August 2017, as provided by the Ministry of Finance's 2018–2020 Debt Management Strategy. Hence, Exotix shows the main totals, and subtotals, from both sources, although it means figures don't always add up. Commercial creditors are the biggest creditor group, which comprised mainly the 2026 eurobond, plus a small amount of bank debt. They accounted for 42% of general government external debt at end-2017. The eurobond, which was issued in February 2010 following an exchange offer for commercial debt, had an outstanding US$143.6mn at end-2017. This amounted to 35% of general government external debt and 10% of total external debt. Multilaterals were 35% of general government external debt, and 10% of total external debt. There is no breakdown available by multilateral creditor. Bilateral creditors were 23% of general government external debt, and 6% of total external debt. The MOF report showed that, at least as of August 2017, bilateral creditors were roughly evenly split between Paris Club and non-Paris Club creditors.

Total public debt (including guarantees) was 65% of GDP at end-2017, based on Exotix estimates. This comprised public external debt of 31.2% of GDP and public domestic debt of 33.7% of GDP. The central bank's monthly statistical bulletin showed that public debt was 62% of GDP at end 2017, comprising public external debt of 28.1% of GDP, but this excludes external debt of the central bank, and public domestic debt of 34%. The IMF's latest report (the first review of the PCI, from June 2018) put public debt at end-2017 at 67.2% of GDP (with external of 30.4% of GDP and domestic of 36.8% of GDP). Another difference in the calculation of these ratios may be the level of GDP. Domestic debt includes debt issued for monetary purposes, which is c40% of domestic debt (c14% of GDP) according to IMF figures. Unwinding monetary debt will be a key macroeconomic challenge given its fiscal and monetary impacts. Still, the public debt ratio has fallen sharply from 80% of GDP in 2012 and 192% in 2008 (when it rose from 144% after the currency was devalued). The ratio peaked at 200% in 2001, and averaged 160% over the period 1994–2008, since when debt reduction, fiscal consolidation (running large and persistent primary surpluses over the past decade) and strong growth have helped to put the debt ratio on a firmly downward trend. The authorities' fiscal target is to reduce debt/GDP to 50% by 2021.

Composition of external debt

External debt by creditor (Feb. 2018 estimate)[a]	*Nominal amount outstanding (US$mn)*	*Share of total (%)*
Public sector external debt	**462.5**	**31.1**
General government	406.0	27.3
o/w Official multilateral	143.6	9.7
Official bilateral	92.1	6.2
Paris Club[b]	48.6	3.3
Non-Paris Club[b]	41.5	2.8
Commercial creditors	170.3	11.4
Eurobond (8% 2026)	143.6	9.7
Banks[b]	31.1	2.1
Monetary authorities (incl. IMF)	58.7	3.9
Private sector external debt[c]	**1024.8**	**68.9**

(continued)

(continued)

External debt by creditor (Feb. 2018 estimate)[a]	*Nominal amount outstanding (US$mn)*	*Share of total (%)*
Total external debt	**1487.3**	**100.0**

Source: Central Bank of Seychelles, Ministry of Finance, Bloomberg, Exotix

[a]Note components may not add up to totals as figures based on different methodologies. Public sector and private sector totals taken from gross external debt figures from BOP statistics (BPM6), while general government debt figures taken from public debt statistics
[b]As of August 2017 from Ministry of Finance
[c]Excluding intercompany lending

Rescheduling History

Seychelles defaulted on its commercial debt in 2008, after a period of running arrears on official sector loans, and subsequently undertook a comprehensive debt restructuring. Since then, it has had an unblemished payment experience on its external debt. Performance was helped by two successful IMF programmes since the default, and the use of innovative financial operations, including a currency conversion effected through the African Development Bank in 2014 and a debt-for-nature swap through its below par buyback of Paris Club debt in 2015.

One of the most heavily indebted countries in the world at the time, and already in default on most of its bilateral and multilateral debt by 2000, Seychelles defaulted on its foreign commercial debt in 2008 after failing to repay a private placement and missing a coupon payment on its eurobond. Public debt was 146% of GDP (half of which was external) in the year before the commercial default, after peaking at 200% of GDP in 2004 (subsequent data revisions have reduced these figures). Yet, until 2008, and despite ongoing arrears with official creditors, Seychelles had no prior history of rescheduling its debt. Still, the high debt burden and a dangerously low level of reserves (which often led to foreign exchange shortages) left the country in a constantly fragile state and exposed to external shocks, such as the global financial crisis when it came. Moreover, these weaknesses meant the country had limited access to external finance. Commercial loans were generally beyond its reach (those it had obtained tended to be expensive) and access to even bilateral loans was restricted on occasion. This sometimes meant that foreign exchange earnings were pledged to creditors and held in escrow accounts of the creditor banks.

While the increase in Seychelles' external indebtedness was a relatively recent phenomenon, the arrears problem dates from much further back and began accumulating under past governments. Public debt was contracted by successive governments of the Seychelles Progressive People's Front (SPPF), under the leadership of France-Albert René, but the external debt/GDP ratio over the second half of the 1990s was only 30–40% of GDP, with generally two thirds of the debt owed to bilateral and multilateral creditors. Government borrowing increased over 1996–1999, reflected in rising imports and a worsening current account deficit. In order to continue with the managed exchange rate regime, foreign exchange was rationed. Foreign exchange and trade restrictions were imposed, which often led to foreign exchange shortages. Official reserves were very low. On a net basis, they were only US$10mn in 1997, rising to US$15mn in 1999, equivalent to just 1.7 weeks of imports. Arrears mounted particularly in the wake of 9/11 when the associated drop in tourism arrivals devastated foreign reserves. Reserves stood at just US$67mn at end-2003 and fell dangerously low to US$34mn in 2004. Nonetheless, after the handover of power in early 2004, President James Michel and his SPPF government (re-elected in 2006) attempted to rein back public spending and adopted an official debt management strategy. This targeted a long-term public debt to GDP ratio of 60%. A Macro Economic Reform Programme (MERP) 2003–2006 aimed to achieve overall fiscal surpluses that, along with refinancing operations, made inroads into reducing the debt stock. Seychelles used commercial borrowing to pay off some of the country's arrears, deploying part of the proceeds from the eurobond issue in 2006 for this purpose. Arrears to the World Bank were cleared in October 2006, while those to the AFDB and almost all amounts to the EIB were discharged by the end of 2006. Addressing commercial creditors, the eurobond enabled the clearance of a US$64mn syndicated loan that had been led by Bank of Tokyo Mitsubishi. In total, arrears—owed mainly to bilateral and multilateral creditors—were reduced by just over two-fifths by end 2006 to stand at US$102mn. With the eurobond proceeds, reserves rose to US$113mn by the end of 2006, although this was equivalent to just 1.3 months of import cover, but they quickly resumed their downward trend. By the end of 2007, reserves were virtually exhausted—reported by the IMF at US$9.8mn, less than a week of import cover—and considerably less than the punishing coupon payment on the 2011 eurobond (with a coupon of 9.125%, annual interest amounted to US$21mn).

After the commercial debt default, the government sought advice from the IMF securing a two year Standby Agreement and subsequently announced its intention to pursue good faith negotiations with bilateral and commercial creditors in order to secure debt restructuring, necessary as fiscal consolidation alone, despite the authorities' commitment, could not restore solvency. In their IMF Letter of Intent (October 2008), the government stated that "no plausible fiscal adjustment" can deliver debt sustainability. A restructuring was therefore a key part of the government's economic reform programme. In the absence of a restructuring, the authorities stated that public debt would increase to 169% of GDP in 2009 from an average of c148% over 2007–2008 and 140% in 2006. Given the debt burden, it seemed likely that all creditors would be asked to participate in good faith negotiations. 40% of public external debt (amounting to US$323mn) was by then in arrears to Paris Club and commercial creditors (mainly the private placement). The government announced in September 2008 that it would seek to restructure US$800mn in external debt owed to its official and commercial creditors, aiming to deliver sustainability to debt service payments and debt levels, supported by a front-loaded fiscal adjustment over several years.

Relations with Multilateral Creditors

Seychelles joined the IMF in 1977 and prior to 2008 had never had a fund programme. In the build up to the crisis, the IMF noted in the press release for its 2008 Article IV in November 2008 that Seychelles had experienced an acute balance of payments and public debt crisis. Expansionary monetary and fiscal policy was not compatible with the pegged exchange rate regime and competitiveness had been undermined. Foreign exchange shortages arose and external debt became unsustainable. While reform efforts since 2003 brought some improvement, they were insufficient, while higher oil and food prices over 2007 and 2008 produced additional pressures.

In November 2008, the IMF approved a US$26mn two-year Standby Arrangement (SBA). Following July's default event the government sought IMF advice and in September, a mission visited the country. Discussions culminated in approval of the SBA with US$9mn made available immediately and the balance disbursed over two years in seven quarterly instalments, subject to performance. The programme sought to support the authorities' "bold" economic reform programme, which involved a significant fiscal adjustment, targeting a primary balance surplus over 2008–2010 averaging c6.5% of GDP per year after a primary deficit in 2006 and 2007 (–2.3% of GDP). The government would also pursue good faith negotiations with bilateral and commercial creditors in order to secure debt restructuring. In addition, the EU provided US$1.6mn in financial assistance in 2008. For 2009, programme financing was intended to be covered by the IMF (US$3.85mn), multilateral creditors (US$15mn) and external debt relief (US$85mn).

The IMF approved a successor programme, a three-year EFF, in December 2009 and cancelled the previous SBA arrangement upon the conclusion of its third review. Performance under the EFF was satisfactory and a one-year extension was granted to the original three-year EFF programme in December 2012. Reviews to this point found that policy implementation and structural reform was positive. Debt as a proportion of GDP did not improve as much as expected during the 2009 EFF, despite consistent primary surpluses and strong real GDP growth over this period. By the programme's end, public sector debt was intended to be 57% of GDP. The realised figure was 65%, although down from 80% in 2012. Policies were described as "appropriate and consistent with falling public debt over the medium term". The 2013 extension was approved to support the reform programme, including the increased oversight necessary to ensure fiscal discipline and aid future debt sustainability. Previous implementation had been strong, such as the introduction of VAT in January 2013, which was a milestone in modernising (and simplifying) the tax system. The eighth and final review was concluded in December 2013, allowing full augmented disbursements and the programme was completed successfully, with the key objectives of external and fiscal sustainability achieved.

A second three-year EFF was approved in June 2014. This continued to improve fiscal sustainability, while reducing external vulnerabilities and improving sustained and inclusive growth. A key sustainability target was for public sector debt to fall to 50% of GDP in 2018, down from its 2013 level of 65%. The sixth and final review was completed in June 2017. In its Debt Management Strategy (DMS) for 2017–2019, the government confirmed its commitment to bring government debt down to 50% of GDP by 2020 (previously an IMF target for 2018), a target which was reiterated in its 2018–2020 DMS published in October 2017—although the target date has since been pushed back to 2021.

The IMF Board approved a new three year Policy Coordination Instrument (PCI) in December 2017. Seychelles was the first IMF member to request the new facility, which it did in September 2017. Under the PCI, which doesn't involve the use of Fund resources, programme reviews take place on a fixed semi-annual basis. The PCI may help unlock financing from multiple sources while successful completion is seen as helping to demonstrate Seychelles' commitment to continued strong economic policies and structural reforms. The programme aims to support the authorities' efforts to consolidate macroeconomic stabilisation and foster sustained and inclusive growth. The first review of the PCI was approved by the IMF Board in June 2018. It noted macroeconomic performance in 2017 and programme implementation continued to be strong, with the authorities committed to reducing public debt to below 50% of GDP by 2021, as the government adopts a slightly lower primary surplus target of 2.5% of GDP over the medium term (2019–2023) in order to support its large infrastructure projects. This compares to the 3% target held over 2017–2018, which itself was a loosening compared to the 2014–2016 outturns of 4.9%, 4.3% and 3.4%.

IMF programmes

Date	*Arrangements*	*Comments*
2008–2009	SBA	Initial two-year programme approved in November 2008 was cancelled in December 2009 at the time of the third review, and was therefore not fully drawn. The programme was for SDR17.6mn (US$26.1mn, 200% of quota), front-loaded with an initial disbursement of 70% of quota to cover remaining financing needs for 2008. The first and second reviews were completed in March 2009 and June 2009. Although some waivers were granted in the first review and performance criteria were modified in the second, performance was generally satisfactory.
2009–2013	EFF	Originally a three-year programme approved in December 2009 for an amount of SDR19.8mn (US$31.1mn, 182% of quota). Due to expire in December 2012. The first review was completed in June 2010 and the second review in December 2010. The completion of the sixth review in December 2012 allowed for the disbursement of the originally agreed amount and a one-year extension, to support the reform programme. Augmentation of access by SDR6.6mn (61% of quota) brought the total amount drawn to SDR26.4mn.

(*continued*)

(continued)

Date	*Arrangements*	*Comments*
2014–2017	EFF	In June 2014, the IMF approved a second three-year programme for SDR11.5mn (105% of quota in 2014 and 50% of quota at programme end; the quota more than doubled in February 2016), which was fully drawn. The first review was completed in December 2012, the second in June 2015, the third in December 2015, the fourth and fifth in January 2017 and the sixth and final in June 2017 with performance criteria being met throughout, despite some modifications.
2017–2020	PCI	The IMF Board approved a new three-year Policy Coordination Instrument (PCI) for Seychelles on 13 December 2017. Seychelles is the first IMF member country to request a PCI, an arrangement that does not involve the use of IMF resources although requires the same level of policy oversight as a financed programme. The PCI will build on the lessons from the previous programs supported by the IMF, aiming to support the authorities' efforts to consolidate macroeconomic stabilisation and foster sustained and inclusive growth. Program reviews take place on a semi-annual fixed schedule. The first review was completed in June 2018.

Source: IMF. Seychelles joined the IMF in 1977

Seychelles is a member of the World Bank and the African Development Bank, although as an upper middle income country its access to concessional lending was restricted (now a high income country). Due to its arrears to multilaterals, Seychelles went into non-accrual status with the World Bank in 2001 and, indeed, most multilateral agencies, which meant that Seychelles was precluded from all lending activities. Technical assistance however continued. Seychelles cleared its arrears in full to the World Bank in October 2006, with payments enabled by the 2011 eurobond issue, lifting the country out of non-accrual status and by February 2007 all outstanding principal to the IBRD had been repaid.

The World Bank has had 18 projects in Seychelles but only one is currently active. This is for disaster risk management and comes with a commitment amount of US$7mn. The Board of the African Development Bank approved a new strategy for Seychelles in early 2016, lasting until 2020, with the aims of diversifying the economy to provide resilience to external shocks and provide employment, improving energy infrastructure and enhancing environmentally sustainable growth.

Paris Club and Bilateral Creditors

Seychelles had not previously had a Paris Club rescheduling until its 2008 default, after which it engaged in constructive talks with all creditors. It secured a Paris Club rescheduling agreement in April 2009. The agreement also required comparability of treatment (in net present value terms) with all external commercial and bilateral creditors. The Paris Club agreement itself saw rescheduling in three phases. The third and final stage was delivered in July 2010. Overall debt cancellation under the Paris Club agreement was 45% in nominal terms. This delivered NPV reduction at the 6-month CIRR discount rate of 50%. Participating creditors were Belgium, France, Germany, Italy, Japan, Russia, Spain and the UK. A debt restructuring agreement was also reached on US$12.1mn owed to EXIM Bank of Malaysia on similar terms to that of the Paris Club.

The Seychellois President announced in February 2015 that the Paris Club and South Africa had agreed with Seychelles a debt buyback of over 90% of debt to Paris Club members maturing over 2015–2021, at a discount. The government of Seychelles will then issue to the Seychelles Conservation and Climate Adaptation Trust (SeyCCAT), a marine conservation and climate adaptation initiative, debt obligations to pursue sustainable economic development. About US$30mn was transferred to the SeyCCAT and a further 5% debt reduction was given by creditors, thereby reducing external debt service, keeping more money in the national economy and working towards sustainable growth and further resilience to external shocks (Seychelles is highly dependent on tuna and tourism exports, and the economy was damaged by the effects of both 9/11 and the global financial crisis). Creditor participation was at the highest rate ever achieved in a market-based debt buyback transaction involving Paris Club debt, according to the Seychellois Government. National media in March 2016 reported that the financial stage of the process had been completed successfully, and the agreed area of 400,000 square kilometres would be managed for conservation within an originally agreed five years.

Paris Club agreements

Date	*Terms*	*Status*	*Details*
April 2009	Ad hoc	Active	Treatment covered all external debt owed to the Paris Club, amounting to US$163mn at the end of 2008, out of total external debt of US$760mn. Treatment was in three phases according to the following schedule: 1. Immediate rescheduling and deferral of arrears due as of 31 October 2008 and maturities due from 1 November 2008 to 30 June 2009. 2. First reduction. Cancellation of 22.5% of the outstanding amounts as of 1 July 2009. This entered into force on 17 July. 3. Second reduction. Cancellation of 29.03% of the remaining outstanding amounts as of 1 July 2010. This entered into force on 23 July. Remaining amounts were to be rescheduled over 18 years with five years' grace.

Source: Paris Club

Gulf countries, particularly the UAE (and especially Abu Dhabi), have become an increasingly important source of financial and economic support to Seychelles. The UAE has financed development projects, including infrastructure. Abu Dhabi Airports agreed to redevelop Seychelles Airport, hoping to bring more UAE visitors. Much of this investment has been driven by the President of the UAE, Sheikh Khalifa bin Zayed al-Nahyan, who also built a new palace on the islands.

During 2016, Seychelles maintained cordial relations with various bilateral creditors. A new Agreement on Economic and Technical Cooperation was signed with China, providing a US$15mn grant for infrastructural projects. In February 2016, Air Seychelles launched its first nonstop flight to Beijing. The Chinese government also financed a new primary school in March. An Indian government grant covered the cost of 34 buses from India's Tata Company. The defence and surveillance of Seychelles maritime zone was also enhanced by a third vessel from India. The EU signed an agreement with Seychelles to finance climate adaptation projects. This came in February 2016, as the EU also provided EUR2.2mn for sustainable development.

Sovereign Commercial Debt

Until its 2008 default, Seychelles had not previously had a commercial debt rescheduling, although it had suffered from persistent payments problems. After defaulting on most bilateral and multilateral creditors by 2000, Seychelles turned to increasingly expensive commercial financing and refinancings after 2001. Perhaps in a sign of things to come, Seychelles cleared cUS$70mn in arrears to commercial banks in August 2002 through new borrowing. But it was the onset of the global financial crisis that finally tipped Seychelles over the edge, with its low level of reserves exposing the country's vulnerability to external shocks. After two of its commercial refinancing operations over 2006 and 2007 fell into default by 2008, Seychelles was pretty much in default on everything.

Seychelles issued its first ever sovereign eurobond in October 2006. The US$200mn (nominal) five-year bullet bond had a coupon of 9.125% and was due to mature in 2011 (the bullet repayment was roughly two thirds of projected 2011 revenues). The bond was rated B from S&P at issue. The intention of the bond was for proceeds to help build reserves and clear arrears. But by the time proceeds were used to settle some long-standing arrears to multilateral and bilateral creditors, repatriate foreign dividends and refinance certain private (securitised) loans, little of the money went to the government. The bond enabled the government to amortise US$166.5mn with net proceeds of US$71.9mn. The domestic debt burden was also reduced by US$94.6mn. The issue was tapped in August 2007 for a further US$30mn. The bond's rating was however placed on negative outlook by S&P in December 2007 on concerns over the size of the current account deficit and weak fiscal outturns.

Yet, by the end of October 2008, Seychelles was in default on its two internationally traded commercial debts, including the 2006 eurobond, following the near exhaustion of foreign reserves by the middle of that year. The first default occurred on a portion of a privately-placed euro denominated EUR54.75mn amortising loan note due 2011 after a payment due on 1 July 2008 was missed. Creditors of the loan note, which was reportedly placed in 2007, subsequently issued a notice of default published in the Financial Times at the end of July. While creditors exercised their rights under the prospectus to accelerate payments on the note, the non-payment reportedly reflected the Seychellois authorities questioning the legality of the debt. Lack of reserves would be another explanation. At the time, it was not certain whether the default on the note would represent an isolated incident or reflect wider credit difficulties. On 7 August 2008, Standard and Poor's downgraded Seychelles's country rating to Selective Default (SD) and the US$230mn eurobond issued in 2006 to CCC–. This action followed a downgrade from B– to CCC only three days before. The downgrade also reflected perceived weakness in the economy, public finances and debt management, as well as foreign exchange difficulties. Cross default to the eurobond was not triggered by creditors however and it was left to see whether the eurobond's scheduled coupon payment on 3 October would be made. In the event, the coupon payment (totalling US$10.5mn) was missed on its due date and it was not paid in the grace period. Subsequently, Seychelles appointed financial and legal advisors to provide advice on a comprehensive debt restructuring.

After lengthy discussions, Seychelles presented its long-awaited debt restructuring proposal on 7 December 2009 (this was a revised, and enhanced, proposal compared to the initial proposal presented in March 2009). Holders of cUS$320mn (nominal) in eligible debt were invited to tender in an exchange offer for new notes. Eligible debt comprised: (1) US$230mn 9.125% 2011 Notes (the eurobond); (2) EUR54.75mn (cUS$83mn equivalent) 2011 Amortising Notes (the privately placed loan); (3) Term Loan Agreement dated 22 March 1999 as amended and restated on 23 March 2004 between Seychelles Marketing Board, Seychelles and ABN Amro; and (4) Facility Agreement dated 2 June 2003 between Public Utilities Corporation of Seychelles, Central Bank of Seychelles, Seychelles, ABN Amro, Commerzbank and Cooperatieve Centrale Raiffeisen Boerenleenbank. Together (3) and (4) were known as the Existing Loans and were for a combined amount of US$9mn.

Holders were offered the following new notes:

- Discount bond maturing in 2026 with a step up coupon, amortising from 2016 and a 50% principal reduction. It also has a partial interest guarantee from the African Development Bank; or
- Par bond maturing in 2041. This bond would have a fixed 2% coupon, amortising in seven equal semi-annual instalments from 2038 but with no principal reduction. It would not have any guarantee. The par bond was subject to a minimum size. In the event, the US$50mn threshold for the par bonds was not reached and only the discount bond was issued.

The exchange offer had some interesting features: (1) A goodwill payment. Tendering holders would receive a goodwill payment in lieu of past due interest (PDI), which was written off in the exchange. PDI comprised three missed coupons (October 2008, April 2009 and October 2009), plus accrued interest between October and December 2009, amounting to cUS$37mn. This resulted in an estimated claim of 116% of principal. By way of some compensation, holders in the exchange, receiving either the discounts or pars, would receive a goodwill payment, amounting to US$10.44 per US$100 face on the discount bonds or US$5.22 per US$100 face on the par bonds (ie equivalent between the two bonds after taking into account the 50% reduction on the discounts). This amounted to a cash payment of US$12mn for the eurobond, out of US$18mn altogether which was ring-fenced by the Seychelles from its own resources. The amount was judged to be the most the country could afford to pay, after negotiations with creditors and the IMF, and was equivalent to a 3% interest rate; a rate which was below the contractual rate, over the default period (3 April 2008 to 31 December 2009). (2) Principal reinstatement. Holders tendering into the discount bond would benefit from a principal reinstatement clause such that they would receive additional bonds (25% more) if Seychelles did not pass the first review of its successor IMF programme by end-2010. This condition was requested by bondholders to bring the terms of the bond into line with the Paris Club agreement. Despite some moral hazard concern, Seychelles was willing to concede the condition as the authorities were confident in their ability to perform against the IMF programme and implement their reform agenda. (3) Partial interest guarantee from the African Development Bank (AFDB). This applied to the discount bonds only and is subject to a maximum amount of US$10mn. It was a new feature in the exchange offer compared to the original proposal presented in March 2009.

The offer, which closed on 14 January 2010, was a success and participation was high. Debt totalling US$283mn was tendered in the exchange (giving a participation rate of 89%). The authorities had reserved the right to terminate the offer if the total principal tendered was less than US$304mn (i.e. participation less than 95% of the eligible debt). But what really mattered, in terms of ensuring a successful exchange—and thereby restoring debt sustainability—was reaching the 75% threshold to activate the Collective Action Clause (CAC) on the 2006 eurobond, which was issued under English law. The threshold was achieved, with participation on the eurobond at 84% (participation on the other eligible debts was

100% for each instrument). As a result, the authorities were able to sweep in non-participating holders and, through the approval of an extraordinary resolution on 8 February 2010, holders of the 16% of the eurobond that was not tendered received the new discount bonds, which were finally issued on 11 February (a description of the bond is given below). As a result, holdouts were completely eradicated and there was no illiquid rump of outstanding eligible bonds left. Seychelles became only the fourth modern sovereign exchange to use CACs in a sovereign restructuring after Ukraine (2000), Moldova (2002) and Belize (2007). The NPV haircut was 56.2%, according to the Cruces and Trebesch database.

Seychelles bond
Republic of Seychelles 8% 2026
Bloomberg ticker: SEYCHE

Borrower	Republic of Seychelles	
Issue date	11 February 2010 (interest accrued from 1 January 2010)	
Form	Global	
ISIN	XS0471464023	
Issue size	US$168.894mn	
Amount outstanding	US$126.671mn (as of 1 July 2018)	
Currency	USD	
Denomination	US$100 minimum; US$100 thereafter	
Amortisation	20 equal semi-annual instalments commencing 1 July 2016	
Final maturity date	1 January 2026	
Coupon/interest	Step up, payable semi-annually in January and July, according to the following schedule:	
	From 1 January 2010 to and excluding 1 January 2012	3%
	From 1 January 2012 to and excluding 1 January 2015	5%
	From 1 January 2015 to and excluding 1 January 2018	7%
	From 1 January 2018 to and excluding 1 January 2026	8%
Goodwill payment	US$ 10.44 per US$100 face amount on 12 April 2010	
Collateral/guarantor	Partial interest guarantee from the African Development Bank (AFDB) subject to an aggregate maximum amount of US$10mn.	
Day count	30/360	
Method of transfer	Euroclear/Clearstream	
Settlement period	T + 2 business days	
Governing law	English	
Listing	UK	

Source: Bloomberg

Seychelles has not returned to the market since its restructured eurobond was issued in 2010. However, the government is exploring the possibility of a liability management operation to swap the current US dollar obligations of the 2026 global bond into euros, in order to take advantage of favourable conditions in the market for euro denominated debt. The swap is expected to reduce the interest cost on the bond, while also reducing exchange rate risk, as the country's earnings are mostly in euros. The swap may take place in the second half of 2018. In the absence of commercial finance, borrowing requirements continue to be filled with long-term financing from multilateral and bilateral development institutions. Specifically, the 2018 financing requirement will be met by project loans from the Arab Bank for Economic Development in Africa (BADEA), Opec Fund for International Development (OFID), Kuwait Fund, India, Agence Française de Développement (AFD) and the European Investment Bank (EIB).

The government has, however, sought to issue a Blue Bond to support its blue economy strategy and the transition to sustainable fisheries. It is another Seychelles' innovation aimed at making use of impact investors to finance ocean-related environmental projects and programmes. The issue, which had been discussed for some two years now, had been expected to amount to US$15mn over 10 years and include a World Bank guarantee with the support of the Global Environment Facility resources to secure attractive terms. 80% of the proceeds from the Blue Bond will be used to provide loans, administered by the Development Bank of Seychelles (DBS) through a Blue Investment Fund, for projects consistent with the provisions of the fisheries management plans. The remaining 20% will be transferred to Seychelles Conservation and Climate Adaptation Trust (SeyCCAT) to establish a Blue Grants Fund for grants to be made available to the public and private entities on a project proposal basis. On 11 October 2018, the government issued a US$15mn 6.5% 2028 amortising bond with a World Bank partial guarantee (33%), according to Bloomberg (while it looks like the Blue Bond, other details were not available at the time of writing).

In February 2018, the Seychelles government announced that it had implemented an innovative debt-for-nature swap, agreed in 2016, which provided debt reduction in exchange for the protection of a large area of ocean. It is the first debt swap for ocean conservation in the world, and covers two marine parks spread over 80,000 square miles. Under the swap, a charity and investors will repay a portion of public debt, amounting to US$22mn, in exchange for future payments (lower than debt service payments would have been) to SeyCCAT to fund new projects for the protection of marine life. The investors purchased the debt from the governments of the UK, France, Belgium and Italy.

Sri Lanka

Nominal GDP (US$mn, 2018)[a]		92,504
Population (thousand, 2018)[a]		21,688
GDP per capita (USD, 2018)[a]		4265
Credit ratings (long-term foreign currency)[b]	Fitch	B+
	Moody's	B1
	S&P	B+

[a]IMF WEO October 2018
[b]As at end-September 2018

Country Summary

- The end of the Civil War promoted a surge in capital flows, helping the economy recover from the negative impact of the global financial crisis. But macroeconomic imbalances remain: high inflation, wide budget and trade deficits, and a high public debt burden.
- Fast growing economy despite long conflict. Traditionally based on agriculture (Ceylon tea and rubber) and textiles and garments, tourism and ICT/services have now emerged as important economic activities. Market-oriented economic policies were adopted in 1977 and reform has been continued by successive governments, developing growth prospects and economic resilience.

Exotix Capital, *Exotix Developing Markets Guide*,
https://doi.org/10.1007/978-3-030-05867-8_34

- Record public debt servicing will fall due in 2019, amid lower-than-anticipated output creation from post-civil war infrastructural project borrowings. The prime minister previously warned that 2018–2020 would be "tough years". There may have been a possibility of rescheduling, although a new US$1bn loan from the China Development Bank was accepted in May 2018 to cover other loans coming due.

Economic data	*Avg*[a]	*2014*	*2015*	*2016*	*2017 (e)*	*2018 (f)*	*2019 (f)*
Real GDP growth	6.1	5.0	5.0	4.5	3.3	3.7	4.3
Inflation (annual average)	6.9	2.8	2.2	4.0	6.5	4.8	4.8
Current account (% of GDP)	−3.9	−2.5	−2.3	−2.1	−2.6	−2.9	−2.7
Reserves (US$mn, end-period)[b]	5661	8208	7304	6019	7959	9248[c]	–
Reserves/ imports (months)[d]	3.4	3.9	3.5	2.8	3.4	–	–
Overall fiscal balance (% of GDP)[e]	−6.3	−6.2	−7.0	−5.4	−5.5	−4.6	−3.6
Currency (ticker)	Sri Lankan rupee (LKR)						
FX regime	De facto managed float but de jure free float. The IMF now classifies it as a crawl-like arrangement.						
Key exports	Textiles and garments (49%), tea (12%), rubber and plastics (8.4%). Services exports of US$7.9bn forecast for 2017 (72% of goods exports), including tourism (US$3.5bn a year) and telecoms/ICT. Remittances worth US$7.25bn in 2016 (70% of goods exports).						

Source: IMF WEO Database, Haver, Central Bank of Sri Lanka, IMF Country Reports, OEC

[a]10-year average to 2016 unless otherwise stated

[b]Gross official reserves

[c]Latest figure, June 2018

[d]In months of the current year's imports of goods, services and primary income debit

[e]Overall government net lending

Key figures		*Party*	*Since*
President	Maithripala Sirisena	UPFA	Jan. 2015
Prime minister	Ranil Wickremesinghe	UNP	Jan. 2015
Minister of finance	Mangala Samaraweera	UNP	May. 2017
Key opposition figure	Rajavarothiam Sampanthan	ITAK	Sep. 2015
Central bank governor	Indrajit Coomaraswamy	–	Jul. 2016

Note: Sri Lanka is a member of the Commonwealth

Politics

Executive power

Concentrated in the president who is chief of state, head of government and commander-in-chief of the armed forces. Directly elected for five-year terms, the president is responsible for cabinet appointments with the advice of the prime minister, who is also appointed by the president from the leading party in the legislative. Given the preponderance of political parties, and no party able to command a majority, ruling parties rely on a series of alliances and coalitions. The cabinet is made up of the president, the prime minister and 45 ministers.

Presidential term: Five years with a two-term limit (since the 2015 constitutional amendment)

Parliamentary term: Five years

Legislature

Unicameral. The Parliament consists of 225 popularly elected seats. 196 seats are on a first-past-the-post system, and the remainder are decided on the proportional representation of 22 provinces. Parliamentary and presidential elections are held by popular vote every six years, although not on the same cycle.

Elections

Next due *Legislative/presidential: 2021*

Last legislative election (August 2015)	*Seats*	*Last presidential (January 2015)*	*% of vote*
United National Party (UNP & CWC)	106	Maithripala Sirisena (UPFA)	51.3
United People's Freedom Alliance (UPFA)	95	Mahinda Rajapaksa (UPFA)	47.6
Tamil National Alliance	16	Other	1.1
People's Liberation Front	6		
Others	2		
Total	**225**	**Total**	**100.0**

People

Almost three-quarters of the population are Sinhalese, with a further 15% of Tamil descent. Around 70% of the population are Buddhist; Muslim and Hindu account for a combined 20%. Sri Lanka, then known as Ceylon, has been a member of the Commonwealth since it achieved independence from Britain in 1948.

The Tamils are most numerous in the north and east of the country, where fighting for Tamil independence was fiercest. Troubles originated from a change in political structure that occurred in 1931, while the country was still under governorship, that saw communal representation dropped in favour of universal franchise. Suddenly, the Tamil minority, who hail from southern-India, were faced with losing what had been an equitable say in the country's rule, while the majority north-Indian Sinhalese gained dominance.

Sinhalese nationalisation began to take hold over the mid-twentieth century, alienating the Tamil regions of the north and east, so that the 1970s saw the emergence of the radical JVP party, leading to a six-year state of emergency. In 1976, amid increasing ethnic tension, the Liberation Tigers of Tamil Eelam (LTTE), "Tamil Tigers", were formed, fighting for an independent homeland. In 1983, a full-scale civil war erupted between Tamil rebels and Sri Lankan armed forces, marking the beginning of intensive and sporadic violence under successive governments that continued until 2009. Peace talks frequently failed. In 1987–1991, the Tamil region achieved marginally greater autonomy. Indian peacekeepers were deployed, initially more on the behalf of Tamils. Indian troops departed in 1990, having become embroiled in violence. Indian support of Tamils was completely withdrawn after Tamil elements assassinated India's prime minister Rajiv Gandhi, in 1991.

A ceasefire was declared by the LTTE in December 2001, formalised in a memorandum of understanding in February 2002, brokered by Norway. Temporarily, the Tamil's call for independence was dropped. After the LTTE ended talks in 2003, the country returned to full-blown conflict in 2004 and the ceasefire was declared officially over by the government in January 2008 (despite its de facto end in 2004) as the conflict intensified after the government stepped up its military campaign. International concern mounted over the humanitarian situations of thousands of civilians trapped in the battle zone, prompting calls for a ceasefire, which were rejected by the government.

Rebel leader Velupillai Prabhakaran was reported as having been killed in fighting in May 2009, and the government declared the Tamil Tigers defeated after fighters surrendered. President Rajapaksa capitalised on his success in ending the 26-year-long civil war, winning re-election as president in January 2010, while his UPFA party won in legislative elections in April of that year. After his defeat in that election, retired army general Fonseka, who led the war against Tamil rebels, was arrested and charged with committing military offences, including involvement in politics while in active service. He was found guilty by a military court in August 2010 and stripped of all military ranks. A second court martial in September found him guilty of corruption in arms procurement and sentenced him to three years in jail. He was released after serving 30 months, on condition that he would not run for political office for seven years. Parliament approved a constitutional change that would allow him to seek an unlimited number of terms; however, in January 2015, he lost by a small margin to Maithripala Sirisena. The United National Party is now the largest parliamentary party, albeit without an overall majority.

Debt

	2012	*2017*
External debt ratios (%)		
Total external debt/GDP	54.2	59.2
Public external debt/GDP	37.5	38.1
Private external debt/GDP	16.7	21.1
Total external debt/exports of goods and services	270.5	268.8
External debt service ratio (public)[a]	11.9	10.9
Public debt ratios (%)		
Public domestic debt/GDP	37.2	41.6
Public debt/GDP	74.7	79.7

Source: Central Bank of Sri Lanka, Ministry of Finance, Haver, Exotix

[a]Excludes SOEs

Sri Lanka's total external debt was US$51.8bn (59.2% of GDP) at end-17, on central bank figures. It is worth noting that some figures for the past few years have been revised; in September 2016, the prime minister admitted to parliament that "we still don't know the exact total debt number".

The latest official figures are for end-17, although, in April 2018, the government issued US$2.5bn in eurobonds (see below) and this amount has been added to the end-17 composition figures, to give a proxy for the total external debt after the bond issuance, assuming no large changes in other external debt categories. This gives our composition table below, with total external debt of US$54.3bn, US$35.9bn of which was owed by the public sector. With large bond issues every year since 2014, commercial creditors (mostly bondholders) have become the largest creditor group. Multilateral creditors accounted for most public external debt until 2010, with the ADB and World Bank being the main creditors. Although they are still significant creditor group, bilateral creditors are now a larger group, owed 18% of the total. Japan was the largest bilateral creditor, while India and China make up most of the remainder; issues surrounding the investment by the Chinese government and firms are explained below. Concessional debt no longer accounts for the greater proportion of the government's foreign debt: c45%, according to separate central bank figures, with non-concessional debt amounting to 55% of the total. Multilateral concessional debt was 80% of all multilateral debt, and bilateral concessional debt was 78% of all bilateral debt. The large stock of debt now owed to commercial creditors reduces the overall proportion of external debt that is on concessional terms. Private sector borrowing has increased from 5.8% of GDP in 2009, to 16.7% in 2012 to 21.1% in 2017, including inter-company lending. Factors in this include political moves towards a social market economy, the end of the civil war and some corporate firms accessing the international bond markets.

Public domestic debt, as a percentage of GDP, increased from 37.2% in 2012 to 41.6% in 2017, although this is lower than the 49.8% in 2009. Strong real GDP growth (averaging 6.2% over 2010–2016, reaching 9.1% in 2012) has kept the ratio presented here fairly low: total public sector debt was 44.3% in Q1 17, which is higher than in 2012 (37.2%), but lower than the 49.8% seen in 2009. Exports have increased each year since 2010, allowing a decline in external debt as a proportion of exports and external debt service as a proportion of exports since 2012. Now higher USD interest rates and a weaker rupee will contribute to higher repayments and an outflow of foreign reserves, allowed by weaker exchange control regulations. Debt increases since 2009 have been largely for infrastructure projects that have not (yet) increased output or exports, so there is future potential for the above ratios to improve.

Composition of external debt

External debt by creditor (Apr. 2018)	*Nominal amount outstanding (US$mn)*	*Share of total (%)*
Public sector external debt	**35,868**	**66.0**
o/w Official multilateral	7749	14.2
ADB	4018	7.4
World Bank	3157	5.8
Official bilateral	9758	18.0
Japan	3444	6.3
China	2870	5.3
Commercial creditors	13,693	25.2
International sovereign bonds	12,150	22.4
Other	4668	8.6
Private non-guaranteed external debt	**18,455**	**34.0**
Total external debt	**54,323**	**100.0**

Source: Central Bank of Sri Lanka, Ministry of Finance, Exotix

Rescheduling History

Despite a persistently high public debt burden, Sri Lanka has a near perfect debt service history. Until 2005, it had never rescheduled its debts and only entered into a Paris Club rescheduling following the 2004 tsunami. It was one of three countries (along with Bhutan and Laos) to reject enhanced HIPC debt relief when it was considered eligible under the IMF's "ring-fenced" policy in 2006, as the Sri Lanka authorities pointed out that the debt indicators for 2005 were below the 2004 qualifying levels used by the IMF. Yet, the tsunami in December 2004 affected the debt ratios and the Paris Club extended a one-year unconditional moratorium on servicing falling due throughout 2005. The global financial crisis also forced Sri Lanka to turn to the IMF in 2009 as central bank reserves were quickly eroded but debt rescheduling was avoided.

The government has run a primary deficit every year since 1993. Although fiscal consolidation is expected to bring this to surplus by 2018, real GDP slowed sharply after 2012, due in part to a slowdown in domestic demand, but maintained by disappointing returns from government infrastructure investment. In January 2017, then Finance Minister Ravi Karunanayake said the government was engaged in a mission to bring investment to the country thereby generating employment and income and potentially saving the country from the existing foreign debt burden, reported local media. With IMF support, the government aims to widen the tax base, simplify tax laws and increase tax revenue. "Under the current complicated income tax framework, we have faced several risks. Sri Lanka has become one of the countries which gets the lowest tax revenue in the world," new Finance Minister Mangala Samaraweera said in Parliament. Current laws do not allow the government to exceed the annual borrowing as set out in the Budget. With record debt servicing due in 2019, there have been plans to reschedule some loans to ease the 2018 and 2019 repayments. "The new liability management bill will help to reschedule some loans to smoothen the debt repayment," deputy treasury secretary S.R. Attygala, told Reuters. This is planned to provide the government with various options, the secretary said, including buybacks and reissuance of existing debt.

According to the Ministry of Finance, US$2.9bn was owed by the government to China at end-2017, with high interest rates on Chinese loans. Reuters reported Junior Economy and Planning Minister Harsha de Silva in 2015 as saying that the first Hambantota port loan came with a fixed 6.3% interest rate. Economic conditions, reflected in the debt ratios, are not ideal to make these repayments. In addition, some Chinese debt is being converted to equity stakes in state-owned enterprises (SOEs) and the Hambantota Port by this government, despite violent protests at the plans. The government criticised the previous regime for paying too much to borrow. After unsuccessfully attempting to renegotiate the terms with China, in

January 2017, after a framework agreement had been drafted for an 80% equity deal for Hambantota port, controversy led to the government renegotiating: India was concerned over China's presence there and the opposition in Sri Lanka saw it as a sell-out of the country's assets to China. A US$1.12bn deal was later signed for a 70% equity stake in July 2017. Indian concerns over the possible presence of Chinese military vessels at the port led Sri Lanka to revise the deal to rule out military vessel docking, and a 99-year lease was agreed. Separately, the government has also been considering selling stakes in two state-owned banks (Bank of Ceylon and People's Bank) and an insurance company (Sri Lanka Insurance). Government officials cited debt obligations as a key reason for this consideration.

Foreign debt doubled from US$9bn in 2000 to US$18.6bn in 2009. In early 2007, the government launched a ten-year horizon development plan, which targeted "mega infrastructure projects"; focusing on investment in infrastructure (including power, roads and ports) to maintain growth momentum and regenerate the country following decades of internal conflict. However, these projects did not lead to the output anticipated by President Rajapaksa's government. Based on estimates (in September 2016, the prime minister admitted the figures were uncertain) between 2009 and 2014, total government debt tripled and external debt doubled to US$43bn (c54% of GDP). In January 2015, the new government sought to address the rising debt burden, but by July 2016 it had reached US$47.4bn (falling slightly by January 2017). Rajapaksa has criticised public spending on subsidies and cash transfers to the poor, given that it did not lead directly to improving infrastructure.

There are some other notable hindrances that the current government is hoping to address. In 2016, Forbes reported that "it's now becoming evident that the previous government also utilized [SOEs] to take out additional loans on its behalf. While the full extent of this extracurricular lending seems unknown, current estimates peg it at a minimum of US$9.5bn—which is all off the books of the Finance Ministry." Although some official debt figures have been revised up, it is unclear if all borrowings are now included in our figures above. The legal framework is outdated, and a poor fit for the modern business environment. Over 60% of legislation is over 50 years old, including laws regarding education, excise and customs ordinance, based on a September 2017 report. These are important for economic development, but they remain mostly unchanged since their historic introductions. The introduction of new tax laws comes with the fiscal structure reforms, enacted in October 2017 and implemented in April 2018, one year later than planned, which should expand the tax base, including by removing certain VAT exemptions. The finance minister is optimistic about the 2018 Budget, which came with plans to reduce public sector debt to 70% of GDP in 2020.

Relations with Multilateral Creditors

Sri Lanka has pursued a number of programmes with the IMF over the years although performance has often been mixed. Until the 2009 programme, relations were defined by the 2004 tsunami. Sri Lanka sought to obtain a new ESAF/PRGF in 1997 but none materialised, in part due to fiscal slippage in 1998. Serious macroeconomic imbalances emerged, as the current account widened sharply and the rupee came under pressure. The currency was floated in January 2001 after large current account deficits and declining reserves. Ethnic tensions with the Tamil Tigers also reignited after the re-election of President Kumaratunga in December 1999. The authorities requested a quicker disbursing programme and the IMF approved a 14-month stand-by arrangement (SBA) in April 2001. This was seen as a prelude to a PRGF as and when the political and economic situation improved. A PRGF was finally agreed in April 2003, following satisfactory performance and policy implementation, albeit with some delays, under the SBA. The first review was delayed for over a year and the programme eventually expired in 2006 without a review taking place. This followed from the difficult political environment and a period of elections that prevented progress on structural reforms. However, this lack of compliance has not been detrimental to Sri Lanka's multilateral relations.

Sri Lanka obtained emergency assistance from the IMF in March 2005, to help the government to respond to the devastation of the tsunami. The IMF approved a sizeable programme (cUS$2.5bn) in July 2009 to support international reserves, which fell to low levels by December 2008 (just 1.5 months of imports) following the global financial crisis. The IMF programme also supported the country's reconstruction effort after the end of the civil war in April 2010. The key IMF requirement was reducing the fiscal deficit to a sustainable level. There was tension between the government and the IMF throughout, over the speed of deficit reduction; some reviews were delayed due to fiscal underperformance. The eighth and final review acknowledged strong economic activity and made recommendations, which were later considered in the extended fund facility (EFF) that was approved in June 2016.

The EFF aims to address the macroeconomic challenges facing Sri Lanka over 2016–2019, as large debt repayments need to be made and there is still significant underachievement of policy goals. Targets to create output from the expensive infrastructure projects undertaken since 2009 and fiscal consolidation, including through tax reform, are among the priorities; a primary surplus is needed to cover interest payments expected from 2018. Reducing the fiscal deficit to 3.5% of GDP by 2020 is a key goal for the programme and the reviews echoed performance in previous programmes: while some targets were missed, progress towards achieving the overall outcome is strong. There were some delays in increasing VAT, but the fiscal target was met. Transparency of five SOEs has improved and international reserves are back above the minimum threshold, from US$6.02bn in 2016 (2.9 months of imports) to a projected US$7.25bn in 2017 (3.3 months of imports). The IMF has projected foreign reserves reaching 3.9 months of imports by 2021, and monetary policy is ready to be tightened further should inflationary pressure require it. Programme summaries are shown in the table below.

IMF programmes

Date	*Arrangements*	*Comments*
1983–1995	Various	SBA (1983–1984), ESAF (1988–1991), ESAF (1991–1995)
2001–2002	SBA	Programme extended to August 2002. The programme was completed satisfactorily despite some policy delays and in the face of external shocks.
2003–2006	PRGF+EFF	Approved in April 2003. The EFF ran concurrently with the PRGF. The programme expired without completion of the first review.
2009–2012	SBA	A 20-month arrangement was approved in July 2009, and extended in June 2010, for an amount of SDR1.65bn (about US$2.5bn), some 400% of quota. The first review was completed in November 2009. The second and third reviews were completed together in June 2010, after a period of several months during which the programme was on hold following the non-observance of the end-December 2009 domestic budget borrowing ceiling. The overrun was due to faster-than-expected infrastructure project disbursements, higher interest payments, weak revenue, and post-conflict rehabilitation spending. As a result of the breach in the deficit target, election-related delays in preparing the 2010 budget, and implementing tax reform; the IMF approved the government's request to extend the SBA by one year through end-2011. In April 2012, the Board approved an extension to 23 July to allow for the completion of the eighth and final review. This was completed in July and concluded that GDP had grown and economic activity was strong, although global demand had dropped.

(*continued*)

(continued)

Date	*Arrangements*	*Comments*
2016–2019	EFF	A 36-month EFF was approved in June 2016 for an amount of SDR1.1bn (cUS$1.5bn), equivalent to 185% of quota, with the aim of supporting economic reform with the recommendations from the previous SBA. The first review was completed in December 2016, which reported progress towards stability and structural reforms, with appropriate policies implemented, allowing further fund disbursement. The second review was published in August 2017. Growth in 2016 withstood the adverse fiscal and weather shocks, allowing tax revenue to meet the target improvements. The IMF reported progress towards structural reform and the passing of the Inland Revenue Act, which modernises the income tax system, allowing for a US$167.2mn disbursement, taking the current disbursements (and total amount owed to the IMF) to SDR360mn (about US$502mn). December 2017 saw the third review completed, noting the meeting of fiscal targets, income tax reform, and international reserves accumulation under greater exchange rate flexibility. June 2018's Fourth review recommended greater implementation of structural reforms, but also recognised important progress already made.

Source: IMF. Sri Lanka joined the IMF in 1950

The World Bank is currently operating 19 active projects as of August 2018, with an additional eight projects currently in pipeline, for a wide variety of sectors. Among all active projects, Colombo urban development, the health sector and water supply and sanitation improvement projects receive the largest World Bank commitment amounts.

The ADB currently has 78 active projects in or including Sri Lanka as of August 2018, although 11 others have been approved and 13 more proposed. Active projects include six new projects approved so far in 2018, for small and medium-size enterprise (SME) and corporate financing.

Paris Club and Bilateral Creditors

Sri Lanka's only Paris Club treatment came in May 2005, following the December 2004 tsunami. Reflecting the special circumstances, the treatment was on an ad hoc basis, granting a one-year moratorium on debt servicing. There was no comparability clause, although some multilaterals are thought to have extended a similar arrangement.

Paris Club agreements

Date	*Terms*	*Status*	*Details*
May 2005	Ad hoc	Fully repaid	Treated US$227mn of total Paris Club debt of US$6.235bn as of January 2005. Deferred 100% of principal and interest due during 2005.

Source: Paris Club

The 2004 tsunami saw the mobilisation of the international community in providing relief and financial support. Reconstruction was estimated to cost US$2.2bn over a three-to-five-year period. The international community pledged US$2.8bn for reconstruction with a further US$260mn granted from Paris Club creditors in a debt moratorium and US$157.5mn in emergency assistance from the IMF.

The official termination of the ceasefire by the Sri Lankan authorities on 2 January 2008 strained bilateral relations. In mid-2007, the UK (minor donor) and Germany (more significant—yet both not considerable) had already cut back aid to Sri Lanka over escalating violence and what were seen as human rights abuses by the government, particularly in security operations. On 31 January 2008, Japan (both the largest and least politically divisive creditor) stated it might reconsider its aid policy as fighting intensified after the government pulled out of the 2002 ceasefire.

In September 2016, the US, the UK, Germany and France announced that they would cooperate with Sri Lanka to minimise its debt burden. Ambassadors met with the finance minister in September 2016 to discuss possible solutions. Plans to reschedule some government debt to ease near-term debt service payments are recent (September 2017) and the inclusion of bilateral creditors is not yet known.

China provided over US$5bn to Sri Lanka in various forms between 1971 and 2012, and US$2.9bn was outstanding at the end of 2017. Some debt has been converted to equity and infrastructure leases to Chinese firms, leading to protests in Sri Lanka. Most recently, in May 2018, the government accepted a US$1bn loan from the China Development Bank, ahead of debt service payments on existing loans due in 2018 and 2019. This was chosen over three other potential creditors, as it offered an eight-year tenure.

Sovereign Commercial Debt

Sri Lanka strengthened its international profile and signalled to commercial creditors the government's confidence in its ability to service its external debt by its decision to reject HIPC treatment, despite meeting the two criteria. Commercial borrowing by the government, both externally and domestically, is becoming more significant, at over one-quarter of all external debt in 2017.

In October 2007, Sri Lanka issued its first sovereign eurobond. The US$500mn five-year issue, rated B+, was 1.5 times oversubscribed. The issue was aimed in part at retiring more expensive domestic debt. By November 2007, according to the central bank, around two-fifths of the issue had been used to retire debt. The eurobond's strong reception prompted the authorities to consider a further medium-term issue of the order US$300mn. In February 2008, the government (via the central bank) invited numerous international and local banks to raise this finance in a syndicated loan. Standard Chartered Bank was selected as the preferred arranger for an initial amount of US$150mn for a three-year maturity, incorporating annual put options, at LIBOR + 259bps. The issue could be upsized to US$250mn depending on demand. Deustche Bank won a mandate to raise a further US$50mn for a five-year maturity at LIBOR + 370bps. The government intended to use the proceeds from the syndicated loans, which were subject to obtaining the necessary approvals, to finance infrastructure projects. However, the syndicated loan was not raised due to market conditions. Also in February 2008, S&P changed its ratings outlook from stable to negative, stating that the fiscal position would likely be jeopardised by the formal end of the ceasefire.

The government has issued 13 further eurobonds since the debut 2007 issue, of which 12 are currently outstanding as of August 2018, as listed below. A US$500mn bond was issued in October 2009 at 7.4%, which matured in 2015. All have a bullet maturity type. Plans were announced in January 2018 to issue US$500mn in Sri Lanka development bonds (SLDBs) in a process of divesting two state-owned hotels, amid large debt servicing requirements during 2018. SLDBs are guaranteed by the government and US$2.5bn will mature in 2018. This is part of the US$3bn in SLDB that the cabinet approved for 2018.

All of the eurobonds listed below have a bullet maturity. US$2.5bn is expected to mature over 2019–2020, and Sri Lanka started seeking proposals from banks in March 2018 to issue more securities, with longer maturities. The central bank governor has said that a maturity to get the country past its upcoming maturing debt hump was the intension, while the prime minister warned that the country would face "tough years" over 2018–2020. A solution has been found in the April 2018 issued bonds, of a total US$2.5bn, split equally between a five- and a 10-year maturity. These bonds are detailed below. The five-year tranche was 2.4 times oversubscribed and the 10-year tranche was 2.8 times oversubscribed.

Sri Lanka's outstanding eurobonds

Description	*Size*	*Issue date*
USD 6% Due 2019	US$1000mn	Jan. 2014
USD 5.125% Due 2019	US$500mn	Apr. 2014
USD 6.25% Due 2020	US$1000mn	Oct. 2010
USD 6.25% Due 2021	US$1000mn	Jul. 2011
USD 5.75% Due 2022	US$500mn	Jul. 2016
USD 5.875% Due 2022	US$1000mn	Jul. 2012
USD 5.75% Due 2023	US$1250mn	Apr. 2018
USD 6.125% Due 2025	US$650mn	Jun. 2015
USD 6.85% Due 2025	US$1500mn	Nov. 2015
USD 6.825% Due 2026	US$1000mn	Jul. 2016
USD 6.2% Due 2027	US$1500mn	May 2017
USD 6.75% Due 2028	US$1250mn	Apr. 2018

Source: Bloomberg

Sri Lanka bond
Republic of Sri Lanka 5.75% 2023
Bloomberg ticker: SRILAN

Borrower	Republic of Sri Lanka
Issue date	18 April 2018
Form	Eurobond
ISIN	USY8137FAK40
Issued amount	US$1.25bn
Amount outstanding	US$1.25bn
Currency	US dollar
Denomination	US$20,000 and US$1000 thereafter
Amortisation	Bullet
Maturity date	18 April 2023
Coupon/interest	5.75% per annum, paid semi-annually
Day count	30/360
Method of transfer	Euroclear/Clearstream

(*continued*)

(continued)

Sri Lanka bond *Republic of Sri Lanka 5.75% 2023* *Bloomberg ticker: SRILAN*	
Settlement period	T + 2
Exchange	Berlin, Frankfurt, Munich, Singapore, Stuttgart
Joint lead managers	Citi, Deutsche Bank, HSBC, JP Morgan, Standard Chartered
Governing law	New York

Source: Bloomberg

Sri Lanka bond *Republic of Sri Lanka 6.75% 2028* *Bloomberg ticker: SRILAN*	
Borrower	Republic of Sri Lanka
Issue date	18 April 2018
Form	Eurobond
ISIN	USY8137FAL23
Issued amount	US$1.25bn
Amount outstanding	US$1.25bn
Currency	US dollar
Denomination	US$20,000 and US$1000 thereafter
Amortisation	Bullet
Maturity date	18 April 2023
Coupon/interest	6.75% per annum, paid semi-annually
Day count	30/360
Method of transfer	Euroclear/Clearstream
Settlement period	T + 2
Exchange	Berlin, Frankfurt, Munich, Singapore, Stuttgart
Joint lead managers	Citi, Deutsche Bank, HSBC, JP Morgan, Standard Chartered
Governing law	New York

Source: Bloomberg

Sri Lanka also has a number of outstanding sovereign loans, including various bilateral deals, although details are hard to come by. Creditors and guarantors are often export credit agencies or development banks, such as a recent US$1bn syndicated loan announced in April 2018 and accepted in May to repay existing loans maturing in 2018. The eight-year loan was accepted from the China Development Bank, from four bidding for the loan. The CDB was able to offer the longest tenure with US$100mn repayments biannually over five years and a three-year grace period, with an effective rate of return of 5.3%, according to two Ministry of Finance officials in media reports.

Corporate Bond Markets

A total of 10 eurobonds have been issued by Sri Lankan corporates as of August 2018. Current outstanding corporate eurobonds are as follows. Bank of Ceylon and DFCC Bank PLC have previously issued eurobonds, and Sri Lanka Telecom PLC (SLTL) also issued a US$100mn bond at 6.875% in 2004, which matured in 2009.

Sri Lanka corporates' outstanding eurobonds

Issuer	*Description*	*Size*	*Series*	*Issue date*
National Savings Bank (NSBLK)	USD 8.875% Due Sep. 2018	US$750mn	RegS/144A	Sep. 2013
DFCC Bank PLC (DFCCSL)	USD 9.625% Due Oct. 2018	US$100mn	–	Oct. 2013
Sri Lankan Airlines Ltd (SRAILT)	USD 5.3% Due Jun. 2019	US$175mn	–	Jun. 2014
National Savings Bank (NSBLK)	USD 5.15% Due Sep. 2019	US$250mn	RegS/144A	Sep. 2014

Source: Bloomberg

27 companies have issued 131 LKR-denominated corporate bonds as of August 2018. There are currently 27 Sri Lankan rupee corporate debt securities outstanding, totalling LKR982.2mn, seven of which were issued by Hatton National Bank PLC (HNBSL) and another 5 issued by National Development Bank (NATDB). Bank of Ceylon (BAKCEY) and Singer Finance Lanka PLC (SIFILK) have also been issuers.

Sudan

Nominal GDP (US$mn, 2018)[a]		33,249
Population (thousand, 2018)[a]		41,985
GDP per capita (USD, 2018)[a]		792
Credit ratings (long-term foreign currency)[b]	Fitch	NR
	Moody's	NR
	S&P	NR

[a]IMF WEO October 2018
[b]As at end-September 2018

Country Summary

- Sudan (Khartoum) separated from South Sudan (Juba) following the South's independence referendum in 2011, a vote which came out of the 2005 Comprehensive Peace Agreement (CPA) that ended a 22-year civil war. Economically, Sudan has struggled since, with the loss of three-quarters of its oil reserves (located in South Sudan) and the subsequent loss of foreign exchange earnings in addition to lower oil prices. Oil exports began in 1999 and, before 2011, oil accounted for almost all export earnings and half government revenue. Gold has become an important export but severe FX shortages have since emerged, while inflation jumped to 64% yoy in June 2018. Bashir replaced the entire cabinet in September 2018 amid a growing economic crisis, and also reduced the number of ministries to 21 from 31, to lower costs.

Exotix Capital, *Exotix Developing Markets Guide*,
https://doi.org/10.1007/978-3-030-05867-8_35

- Omar Al-Bashir, Sudan's President, gained power in 1989. International arrest warrants were issued by the ICC against Bashir in 2009 and 2010 for crimes against humanity, war crimes, and genocide in the western region of Darfur, although the case remains at pre-trial stage. Conflict continues between government forces and rebel groups in Darfur, and the southern states of South Kordofan and Blue Nile. Rural poverty is still prevalent as rainfall dictates agricultural output. Infrastructure is often poorly developed and recent figures show that less than half of the population have electricity access (below 30% in rural areas).
- Sudan's debt is unsustainable. External debt (PPG) is high, and mostly in arrears. While eligible for HIPC debt relief, under which Khartoum agreed to retain all external liabilities of the former unified Sudan under the 'zero option', reaching decision point requires Sudan to meet a number of conditions. Moreover, the state sponsor of terrorism listing by the US (despite the lifting of certain trade and financial sanctions in 2017) is also a barrier to debt relief.

Economic data	*Avg*[a]	*2014*	*2015*	*2016*	*2017 (e)*	*2018 (f)*	*2019 (f)*
Real GDP growth	0.8	4.8	1.3	3.0	1.4	−2.3	−1.9
Inflation (annual average)	20.2	36.9	16.9	17.8	32.4	61.8	49.2
Current account (% of GDP)	−7.9	−5.8	−8.3	−7.6	−10.5	−14.2	−13.1
Reserves (US$mn, end-period)[b]	1409	1461	1003	875	970	830	872
Reserves/imports (months)[c]	1.7	1.7	1.4	1.4	1.4	1.1	1.1
Overall fiscal balance (% of GDP)[d]	−2.5	−3.6	−3.9	−3.6	−3.8	−4.1	−4.8
Currency (ticker)	Guinea (or new pound) (SDG). The guinea replaced the Sudanese dinar after a redenomination at the rate of SDG1 = SDD100 on 1 July 2007.						
FX regime	Classified by the IMF as multiple exchange rates. The *de jure* regime is a managed float and the *de facto* is now 'other managed' (previously a managed peg to the US$). There are two set exchange rates: an 'indicative' rate and an 'official' rate which applies to public transactions and customs valuations. The SDG was devalued against the US$ in January 2016. It was devalued again by 63% in January 2018 and 40% in February 2018.						

(*continued*)

(continued)

Economic data	*Avg*[a]	*2014*	*2015*	*2016*	*2017 (e)*	*2018 (f)*	*2019 (f)*
Key exports	Oil (10%), gold (12%), livestock and animal products (12%) in 2016. Oil was 37% of exports in 2013 and c90% of Sudan's exports pre-secession.						

Source: IMF WEO Database, IMF Country Reports, OEC, Exotix

[a]10-year average to 2016 unless otherwise stated
[b]Gross international reserves (IMF 2017 Article IV, December 2017)
[c]Months of the next year's imports of goods and services (IMF 2017 Article IV, December 2017)
[d]Overall government net lending

Key figures		*Party*	*Since*
President	Omar Hassan Ahmad-al-Bashir	NCP	Oct. 1993[a]
First vice president	Bakri Hassan Saleh[b]	NCP	Dec. 2013
Second vice president	Osman Yusuf Kubur	NCP	Sep. 2018
Prime minister	Moutaz Mousa Abdallah	NCP	Sep. 2018
Minister of finance and economic planning	Abdallah Hamdok	NCP	Sep. 2018
Key opposition figure	Mohamed Osman Al-Mirghani	DUP	–
Central bank governor	Vacant[c]	–	–

[a]al Bashir came to power after a military coup in 1989 toppled the democratically elected government that followed elections in 1986. In October 1993, he dissolved the military junta and declared himself civilian president. He has since been re-elected four times (1996, 2000, 2010 and 2015), albeit amid claims that elections have been unfair, flawed and often boycotted by the opposition
[b]Saleh also served concurrently as prime minister from March 2017 to September 2018
[c]Governor Hazim Abdegadir Ahmed Babiker died in June 2018, no replacement has yet been announced

Politics

Executive power

Concentrated around the president who is chief of state and head of government. This is reflected in appointments to the Council of Ministers (cabinet) that are mostly made up of National Congress Party (NCP) members. The president is elected by popular vote, although irregularities have been common in Sudanese ballots. The role of prime minister was reinstated by President Bashir in March 2017 (the role had been abolished when he came to power after a 1989 coup).

Presidential term: Five years, no term limits **Parliamentary term**: Six years

Legislature

Bicameral National Legislature consisting of the Council of States (upper house), elected indirectly by each state, and an appointed National Assembly (lower house). Members in both houses serve six-year terms. Law-making has typically been dictated by Sharia practice (not exclusively).

Council of States (54 seats)
Three members from each state are elected by the Assembly (two additional observers may be elected by Abyei Area Council but do not have voting rights).

National Assembly (426 seats)
426 members appointed according to: 213 elected by constituency simple majority voting, 128 seats reserved for women (proportional representation) and 85 directly elected by proportional representation.

Elections

Next due *Presidential: 2020; Legislative: 2021*

Last legislative election (April 2015)[a]	*Seats*	*Last presidential (April 2015)*[a]	*% of vote*
National Congress Party (NCP)	323	Omar Ahmad-al-Bashir (NCP)	94.05
Democratic Unionist Party (DUP)	25	Fadl el-Sayed Shuiab (Federal Truth)	1.43
Democratic Unionist Party (Jalal al-Digair)	15	Fatima Abdel Mahmoud (Socialists)	0.85
Other parties	44	Others	3.67
Independents	19		
Total	**426**	**Total**	**100.0**

[a]The majority of opposition parties boycotted the 2015 elections, although 44 parties put forward candidates

People

Sudan was formerly the largest country in Africa, bigger than Western Europe, and sharing a border with nine other countries, until South Sudan's independence from Sudan in July 2011. The former country was split between the Arab/Muslim north (which accounted for some 30 million of Sudan's total population of 39 million before the secession of South Sudan) and the African South, mainly Christian and animist. In the country now, a 2017 estimate of the population was 40.8 billion, mostly Sunni Muslim and 70% of the Sudanese Arab ethnic group. The official languages are Arabic and English, although others are also spoken. The population is young, with 39% below age 15 and a median age of 20.

(*continued*)

(continued)

People
Decades of civil war in former Sudan, between north and south, formally ended with the signing of a Comprehensive Peace Agreement (CPA) in 2005, although unrest still persists in some regions, and ultimately led to the South's independence (and the creation of South Sudan, the world's youngest country). After independence in 1955, a first civil war (1955–1972) was followed by a second civil war (1983–2005), in a period dominated by military governments, military coups and intraregional conflicts between the ruling elite in northern Sudan and marginalised peoples elsewhere in this vast country. With the status of an Anglo-Egyptian Condominium from 1899, nationalist sentiment gained ground after the First World War, culminating in independence in 1956; by which time it was already effectively in a north/south civil war, with the northern dominated legislative in Khartoum failing to adhere to the promise of a federal republic. A 1972 peace agreement between the government and southern rebels granted autonomy to the south, thereby ending 17 years of civil war. But it failed (especially after oil was discovered in the south in 1979) and civil war between the government of the mainly Muslim north and southern rebels of the Sudan People's Liberation Army/Movement (SPLA/M) erupted again in 1983. A transition to peace was set out in the Machakos Protocol in 2002, but it was the 2005 CPA that finally ended over 20 years of civil war between north and south. It promised nationwide elections at presidential, parliamentary and state level in 2008 or 2009. They were finally held in 2010, the first democratically contested elections since 1986. It also agreed that a referendum could take place in Southern Sudan on secession from the North, which was held on 9 July 2011, and led to the independent country of South Sudan. However, only some two years later, conflict erupted in South Sudan in December 2013 between government and opposition forces after President Kiir accused his former deputy, Riek Machar, of attempting a coup. The situation quickly escalated into civil war. An international grouping of the US, UK and Norway (the Troika), along with the UN and AU, has helped to support South Sudan's peace process. A power sharing agreement was signed in August 2018, which sees rebel leader Machar return to government as one of five vice-presidents. A previous peace deal in 2015 failed a year later. According to the UN, the civil war has seen tens of thousands killed while more than 4 million have been displaced, c2 million of whom have fled to neighbouring states.

(*continued*)

(continued)

People
Sudan has seen conflict in a number of its other regions, including in the westerly region of Darfur since 2003, and the southern states of South Kordofan and Blue Nile since 2011. The UN, which maintains operations in Darfur through the African Union-United Nations Hybrid Operation in Darfur (UNAMID), reported in April 2018 that the overall security situation in the region had calmed, although low-level skirmishes continued and a stalemate in the Darfur peace process persisted. Indeed, reports in June 2018 said clashes had returned between the Sudan Liberation Army and Government of Sudan forces as well as inter-tribal violence in the Jebel Marra region. The situation in Darfur escalated over 2002/03 with the overt involvement of government forces, supporting the militia groups known as Arab Janjaweed, and the emergence of two African Darfuri rebel elements (Sudan Liberation Movement/Army (SLM/A) and Justice and Equality Movement (JEM)) opposing Khartoum. In January 2004, the army attempted to stop a rebel uprising in Darfur and fighting led to widespread suffering, famine and displacement. Pro-government forces carried out civilian killings in the region. The UN estimates that 300,000 have been killed and up to 3mn displaced. In 2005, the UN Security Council authorised sanctions against those violating a ceasefire in Darfur and referred the war crimes accused to the International Criminal Court (ICC). International arrest warrants have since been issued by the ICC against Bashir. In 2009, Sudan's President al-Bashir became the first sitting president to be wanted by the ICC for crimes against humanity and war crimes, and later in 2010, the crime of genocide. Neither of the two warrants of arrest against him have been enforced, and he is not in the Court's custody. In a surprise move, the outgoing administration of President Obama in the US announced on 10 January 2017 an amendment to OFAC's Sudanese Sanctions Regulations to authorise all prohibited transactions, effective 12 July 2017 (ie after a 180-day period to ensure compliance with agreed upon acts, including inter alia, the situation in Darfur). The US imposed sanctions on Sudan in 1997. But the Obama move followed ongoing US-Sudan bilateral engagement and positive developments in the country. In the event, it fell to the new Trump administration to complete the six-month review to make the cancellation permanent. The US government announced on 6 October 2017, delayed from July, that certain sanctions were revoked effective 12 October 2017. The lifting of some US sanctions in October 2017 came following humanitarian efforts, in addition to progress in anti-terrorism and a commitment not to purchase arms from North Korea. Notably however, Sudan remains on the US State Sponsor of Terrorism List (SSTL). However, the lifting of sanctions has not been accompanied by an economic rebound: international firms/ banks have still not returned, being cautious because of the SSTL designation and debt situation, while continuing conflicts (meaning high security spending) and President Bashir's international arrest warrants may be further deterrents to new investment. Protests across the country in mid-January 2018 followed IMF austerity policies such as ending subsidies on bread, sugar and electricity, and led to violence and a government crackdown.

Debt

	2012	*2016*
External debt ratios[a] (%)		
Total external debt/GDP	63.8	90.9
Public external debt/GDP	61.2	88.0
Private external debt/GDP	2.6	3.0
Total external debt/exports	688.0	1035.0
Total external debt/revenue	860.0	1282.0
External debt service ratio (PPG)	33.1	33.0
Public debt ratios[a] (%)		
Public domestic debt/GDP	12.9	8.4
Public debt/GDP	74.1	96.4
Memo		
PV PPG external debt/exports	–	1859.5
PV PPG external debt/revenues	–	1932.0

Source: IMF, Exotix

[a]IMF figures for GDP based on weighted average exchange rate

Sudan's public external debt is unsustainable. The debt is high and mostly in arrears, and its distressed status means that it is eligible for HIPC debt relief. Some 85% of its public external was in arrears in 2016, the most recent data available, according to the IMF. Total external debt was estimated at US$52.4bn in 2016 according to the IMF, with most of it (97%) public and publicly guaranteed (PPG) debt. The structure of its public external debt has also been stable over the past decade, given limited new financing options. PPG external debt was US$50.7bn in 2016, of which three-quarters was owed to bilateral creditors and roughly equally divided between Paris Club and non-Paris Club creditors. Multilaterals were owed 11% of PPG external debt, while commercial debt (including defaulted London Club debt) was 14%. Only a small amount of total external debt was private debt owed to suppliers (US$1.7bn, 3% of the total).

Exotix calculates total external debt was 91% of GDP in 2016, based on IMF WEO GDP (estimated at US$57.6bn), with public external debt (PPG) of 88% of GDP (the IMF DSA in its 2017 Article IV stated 110.8% and 107.8% respectively). Total external debt was therefore 1035% of exports of goods and services and 1282% of fiscal revenue. However, based on HIPC criteria (NPV of debt to exports and revenue), the debt burden is even higher, projected at c1900% each in 2016; suggestive of significant debt reduction to reach the relevant thresholds of 150% and 250% respectively. The decline in oil exports following the secession of South Sudan, which holds three-quarters of the former country's oil reserves, as well as the impact of lower oil prices over 2014–2016, also contributed to a significant increase in debt to exports and debt to revenue ratios. Oil exports fell from US$1.8bn in 2013 to US$0.3bn in 2016, while total exports fell from US$4.9bn to US$3.1bn. Public domestic debt was 8% of GDP in 2016, giving total public debt of 96% of GDP (the IMF DSA in its 2017 Article IV stated total public debt was 116.2% of GDP in 2016).

Public external debt continues to grow, mainly due to accumulation of arrears. New borrowing has been limited over recent years, averaging less than 1% of GDP annually over 2012–2016, with Sudan cut off from external financing because of the historical presence of sanctions and arrears. New borrowing has generally been restricted to non-Paris Club bilateral creditors, including Gulf countries, and has mainly been on non-concessional terms. According to the IMF, US$319mn of new debt was contracted in 2016, all from bilateral creditors, while only one bilateral loan of US$170mn was contracted in 2017 by November. In addition, official creditors from Gulf countries deposited an estimated US$1.6bn in the Central Bank of Sudan in 2015 and US$0.8bn in 2016. In January 2017, it was reported that the United Arab Emirates (UAE) Abu Dhabi Fund for Development (ADFD) deposited the equivalent of US$400.5mn into the central bank. Sudan is however reported to be making selective payments on its debt; partial payments to most multilateral creditors and paying bilateral creditors that have provided new financing.

Meanwhile, the debt/GDP burden increases with the devaluation of the currency. The Sudanese pound was devalued by 63% against the US dollar in January 2018 (from 6.7 to 18), although the black market rate at the time was 40. The pound was devalued again by 43% in February 2018 (from 18 to 30). The large difference between the official and parallel market exchange rates complicates the measurement of nominal GDP in USD terms. In its 2017 Article IV (published in December 2017), the IMF calculated Sudanese nominal US dollar GDP on a weighted exchange rate basis (taking a weighted average of the parallel and official rate) to adjust for the significant overvaluation in the official rate. On that basis, US dollar GDP fell to US$57.6bn in 2016 and US$60.8bn in 2017 compared with projections in the 2016 Article IV a year earlier of US$94.1bn and US$112.2bn for the same years, respectively. Moreover, the IMF

WEO for April 2018 projected nominal GDP falling to US$41.7bn in 2018, following an implied 50% average devaluation in the currency in 2018. Assuming the same level of PPG external debt in 2018 as in 2016, given the only gradual increase in the public debt stock over time, this would equate to an increase in PPG external debt to 121.5% in 2018.

Composition of external debt

External debt by creditor (2016)	*Nominal amount outstanding (US$mn)*	*Share of total (%)*
Public and publicly guaranteed external debt[a]	**50,668**	**96.7**
o/w Official multilateral	5697	10.9
World Bank IDA	1192	2.3
Official bilateral	38,090	72.7
Paris Club	18,360	35.0
Non Paris Club	19,730	37.7
Commercial creditors[b]	6881	13.1
Private non-guaranteed external debt	**1715**	**3.3**
Total external debt	**52,383**	100.0

Source: IMF, World Bank

[a]Including principal and interest arrears and late interest to end-2016
[b]Includes London Club claim calculated by IMF

Rescheduling History

Sudan is eligible for HIPC debt relief, although it has yet to meet all the qualification requirements, and remains "pre-Decision Point". Traditional debt relief mechanisms alone will not be able to address Sudan's unsustainable debt burden. It has undertaken debt reschedulings in the past with both official and commercial creditors, but this has not proved sufficient or comprehensive enough and Sudan remains in arrears to most of its external creditors (multilaterals, including the IMF, World Bank and AfDB, and the Paris Club and London Club); 85% of external debt (PPG) was in arrears in 2016.

Sudan's debt problems stem from the early 1970s. Khartoum had borrowed heavily and was hurt by subsequent increases in global interest rates. By 1984, drought and inflation led to capital flight and a foreign exchange crisis. This led to goods shortages while donor disbursements, on which Sudan had relied, were reduced. The World Bank and other official donors, as well as the IMF, worked in Sudan in the 1970s and 1980s promoting economic reform and market liberalisation. Arrears began accumulating (and have been accumulating since). But it was the outbreak of civil war in the early 1980s that caused the debt problems to intensify while international relations deteriorated, exacerbated by the toppling of the democratically elected government by the military in 1989. This caused many Western donor governments to suspend non-humanitarian aid, despite attempts to implement economic reforms at the time. However a four-year economic reform programme in 1988 was not implemented and a further programme was announced in 1989. It took roughly another ten years before Sudan was able to re-engage with the IFIs.

Securing debt reduction under the HIPC initiative remains a key policy goal for Khartoum. There are three requirements to meet the first stage, HIPC Decision Point. First, to obtain sufficient financing assurances from a large majority of creditors holding at least 70% of HIPC eligible debt. Second, to establish a track record of strong policy performance with the IMF. Good performance under successive Staff Monitored Programmes (SMPs) may count towards this track record. Third, to clear its arrears with the IMF, and have a plan and timetable to clear arrears with the World Bank and AfDB. Historically, the presence of US sanctions (now removed) and Sudan's SSTL designation have been a barrier to obtaining support for debt relief. Removal from the SSTL is necessary for the elimination of statutory prohibitions on US aid to Sudan, which blocks progress toward debt relief and the clearance of IMF arrears.

As part of its debt relief strategy, following the South's independence in 2011, Sudan and South Sudan agreed to work towards a 'zero-option' for dealing with the external debt in September 2012, whereby Sudan would retain all external liabilities on two conditions; first that South Sudan joined Sudan in outreach efforts for debt relief for Sudan, and second that the international community gave firm commitments to the delivery of debt relief within two years of the secession. This followed a joint World Bank-IMF Technical Workshop held in Khartoum in December 2010 to discuss Sudan's debt issues. Following the announcement that both Sudans would pursue the zero option, a Technical Working Group (TWG) on Sudan's external debt, co-chaired by the IMF and World Bank, as well as the African Union's High Implementation Panel (AUHIP), chaired by President Mbeki, gave added impetus to the debt relief process and encouraged Sudan to enter into another SMP with the Fund in 2014. However, the sanctions remained a barrier to progress and ultimately led Khartoum to question its efforts. The 2014 SMP was not renewed and the two year deadline was not (and still has not been) met, although it has been rolled over a few times since then. It was extended by two years in 2014 and again in 2016. It is next due to expire in October 2018. Failure to adopt the zero option for dealing with both Sudans' debt would lead to it being apportioned between Khartoum and Juba, which would be a more complicated exercise and debt relief parameters would themselves become more uncertain.

Relations with Multilateral Creditors

Sudan has had 10 formal IMF programmes since becoming a member in 1957, although most of these occurred in the 1960s and 1970s, with only three in the 1980s (all but one of the ten arrangements were SBAs, with the other being an EFF). Its most recent programme ended in 1985. Since then, Sudan has maintained a generally good track record of cooperation with the IMF through successive staff monitoring programmes (SMPs), surveillance programmes which do not involve any Fund financing, with the hope that these could count towards a policy track record towards achieving HIPC debt relief; a key barrier to the approval of a new formal programme being its longstanding arrears to the Fund. Sudan has had 14 SMPs in all, according to the IMF, with the last one being in 2014. In its latest 2017 Article IV report, published in December 2017 following the Board in November, the IMF noted the authorities' interest in a new SMP, to pursue optimal macroeconomic policies, as a pre-condition to reaching the HIPC decision point. Sudan is officially classified by the IMF as a pre-decision point country, just one of three countries remaining in the HIPC process (the other two being Eritrea and Somalia).

That said, relations with the IMF and other official creditors have at times been strained because of sizeable ongoing arrears; Sudan was threatened with expulsion from the IMF in the 1990s. Following the difficulties of the 1980s and early 1990s, Sudan became the IMF and World Bank's largest debtor in 1993, upon which normal relations with both institutions were suspended. The withdrawal of Sudan's voting rights in the IMF in 1993 followed a warning in September 1990 when the IMF announced its "Declaration of Non Co-operation". At the same time, the World Bank suspended lending to Sudan, as did other donors, including the EU. These actions added to Sudan's arrears problem. In February 1997, the IMF threatened to expel Sudan from being a member of the Fund, due to persistent payment failures, although action was deferred and scheduled payments were made in 1997 and 1998. Noting the commitment since February 1997 to making scheduled payments to the IMF, and progress on implementing economic reforms, the IMF lifted its declaration of non cooperation on 27 August 1999. At the same time, the IMF noted it could consider lifting the suspension on voting rights subject to satisfactory performance over a twelve-month evaluation period. The suspension on voting rights was lifted on 1 August 2000.

Sudan remains in sizeable arrears to the Fund. It is now just one of two "protracted arrears" cases (defined as having amounts due that are six or more months overdue), the other being Somalia, after Zimbabwe cleared its arrears to the Fund in October 2016. Sudan has been in arrears to the IMF since 1984. Its arrears to the Fund are large, at SDR965.3mn (cUS$1.4bn) as at January 2018. Dealing with its overdue financial obligations to the IMF remains a government priority: partial payments to the Fund resumed in 1995, and Sudan has been making repayments to the IMF averaging cUS$10mn annually since 2014, according to the IMF, with US$5mn paid in 2017 by the time of the 2017 Article IV. Sudan also has arrears of US$582mn to the World Bank and US$251mn to the African Development Bank (as at June 2010), bringing its total arrears to these institutions and the IMF to US$2.3bn.

IMF programmes

Date	*Arrangements*	*Comments*
1980s	Various SBAs	1982–1983, 1983–1984, 1984–1985
1997	SMP	March–December. Performance was satisfactory.
1998	SMP	
1999–2001	SMP	A medium-term SMP was agreed in May 1999 based on the government's four-year economic recovery strategy, which could lead to a Rights Accumulation Programme. Performance weakened in 2001, because of external factors and policy slippages, and a payment to the IMF in the final quarter was missed as debt service capacity was sharply reduced.
2002	SMP	The IMF noted performance was encouraging. Agreed payments of US$24mn to the Fund were made.
2003	SMP	Performance was in line with the programme. Agreed payments to the Fund of US$27mn were made.
2004	SMP	Performance was in line with the programme. Payments to the Fund of US$32.4mn were made, slightly above the programme target. From 1997 to 2004, Sudan made payments to the IMF totalling US$366mn.

(continued)

(continued)

Date	Arrangements	Comments
2005	SMP	
2006	SMP	Performance was mixed as macroeconomic imbalances built up in the second half of 2006. Increased payments to the IMF were planned, at US$45mn, from US$30mn in 2005.
2007–2008	SMP	July 2007–December 2008.
2009–2010	SMP	July 2009–December 2010. The SMP focused on maintaining macroeconomic stability and building foreign exchange reserves. Structural reforms aimed at raising non-oil revenues and improving the quality of government spending. Lower oil revenues and overall tax revenues were offset by reduced current and capital expenditures. Uncertainty over the January 2011 South Sudan referendum weighed on the economy.
2014	SMP	A new SMP covering January–December 2014 was approved in March 2014. The programme supported the authorities' economic adjustment programme, in response to the economic challenges caused by the secession of South Sudan. Most targets in the first review (May 2014) were met and Q1 figures indicated economic improvement. The second review was concluded in November 2014, reporting that performance had been broadly satisfactory and most targets were met, although inflation remained high. Performance continued to be satisfactory up to the third review in December 2014, again with most targets met, and a good harvest set a strong outlook for 2015, with strong growth and lower inflationary pressures.

Source: IMF. Sudan joined the IMF in 1957

Partly due to large multilateral arrears and to US sanctions (revoked in October 2017), Sudan has had fewer multilateral arrangements than some other African countries. There have, however, been various development projects helping to address the poor standard of infrastructure. The Islamic Development Bank (IDB) has provided significant project funding, including US$100mn for three projects in 2014; its projects have included the development of electricity infrastructure, dam construction and agriculture. The African Development Bank (AfDB) has also had various projects, and the World Bank's IDA has long been a multilateral creditor. The World Bank played a major role in Sudan's reconstruction during the 1970s and 1980s, following the 1972 peace agreement. But the Bank withdrew between 1992 and 2002 while it suspended IDA disbursements in April 1993 following Sudan's default on its IDA loans. Payments began in 1999 although arrears have accumulated. The World Bank re-engaged with Sudan in 2003 upon peace with the South. Sudan is also a member of the Arab Bank for Economic Development in Africa. A donor conference, the Sudan Consortium, was held on 9–10 March 2006. In September 2010, a High Level Meeting on Sudan was convened by the UN Secretary General with fourteen heads of states and governments. It urged all development partners to support peace in Sudan.

Paris Club and Bilateral Creditors

Official bilateral creditors (Paris Club and non-Paris Club) have been significant sources of assistance to Sudan. This includes western creditors such as the Netherlands, Italy and Germany (and historically the US) and Middle Eastern creditors such as OPEC, and also Kuwait and Saudi Arabia, traditionally providing Sudan with many individual loans, some for infrastructure projects, and others without a particular use identified. Many date back to the 1970s and 1980s, and are in arrears. Sudan has seen only a few Paris Club agreements, with four treatments all on Classic terms. However, the lack of recent Paris Club deals testifies more to a difficult relationship with multilaterals than to an improved debt payment record. There are continuing arrears to the Paris Club and all its debt agreements are still active.

Paris Club agreements

Date	*Terms*	*Status*	*Details*
1979	Classic	Active	US$487mn treated.
1982	Classic	Active	US$270mn treated.
1983	Classic	Active	US$516mn treated.
1984	Classic	Active	US$263mn treated. ODA and non-ODA credits rescheduled on a case-by-case basis.

Source: Paris Club

In the presence of US sanctions, China, Middle Eastern countries—notably Saudi Arabia and the United Arab Emirates (UAE)—and Turkey have been the most prominent foreign investors in Sudan. With over 50 years of bilateral ties, China has been a major investor in Sudan's oil, construction, agriculture and other sectors. Chinese loans pay for the maintenance of infrastructure in Sudan and Chinese companies operating in the country now total c160. Sudan's debt to China was estimated at US$10bn, before debt relief of US$160mn was announced in August 2017, with an additional US$75mn in financial assistance. Turkish company Summa agreed in March 2018 to build the new Khartoum international airport for US$1.15bn.

Sovereign Commercial Debt

While Exotix understands trading in Sudanese London Club debt by US investors is now permitted, investors should make their own legal enquiries. Effective 12 October 2017, OFAC (the US Office of Foreign Assets Control) sanctions under sections 1 and 2 of Executive Order (EO) 13067, along with all of EO13412, were revoked. The sanctions under EO13067, which had been in place since November 1997, imposed a ban on US persons granting or extending credits or loans to the Government of Sudan. The sanctions had the effect of preventing US investors from holding and trading Sudanese commercial debt, which significantly reduced the secondary market liquidity in Sudanese debt. Certain sanctions still remain on Sudan, and Sudan remains on the US State Sponsor of Terrorism List.

Sudan has been in default on its commercial (London Club) debt since 1985, and Exotix estimates the total claim (principal plus past due interest) is now equivalent to EUR1.9bn (US$2.3bn) on a simple interest basis, excluding penalty interest (as of April 2018). Sudan's commercial bank debt was partially restructured in 1981 as part of London Club negotiations. In fact, Sudan received five bank debt restructuring agreements in the 1980s (1981, 1982, 1983, 1984 and 1985). The currency of the 1981 refinancing agreement was in US$, after the conversion of the original multi-currency loans. A resulting US$ loan was converted into CHF in October 1985, about the same time as the loan default, after being divided into two tranches with a combined principal amount of CHF1.641bn, which is equivalent to EUR1.36bn (US$1.66bn) today (at the end April 2018 exchange rate). Sudan has been unable to repay any instalments on its restructured bank debt and therefore the principal has been in default for over 30 years. The last interest payment occurred in 1985 and considerable unpaid and penalty interest has accrued since then. As of April 2018, Exotix estimates PDI on a simple interest basis, excluding penalty interest, stood at 141% of principal for Tranche A and 125% of principal for Tranche B. This rises to 175% and 158%, respectively, on a simple interest basis including penalty interest.

Regarding new bank financing, Sudan has accessed trade financing, particularly from Middle Eastern banks, although Exotix believes ME banks became more reluctant to lend to Sudan after the global financial crisis and have demanded additional guarantees and security when doing so. There have also been reports of bilateral agreements to repay or reschedule commercial debt, although terms have not been published. Middle Eastern banks are believed to have benefited most from this. In December 2007, the Sudan Government was able to place privately a sukuk issue through a SPV ("Sudan Salam Sukuk Company" (SSSC)) registered at the Central Bank of Bahrain. The issue was denominated in euros and guaranteed by the Central Bank of Sudan and the Sudanese Ministry of Finance and National Economy. The SSSC, jointly owned by Liquidity Management Centre (LMC) and The Arabic Investment Company (TAIC), issued EUR75–100mn worth of notes due in 2010. The issue was backed by oil revenues. In 2010, Sudan was also reported to have sold EUR100mn (US$140mn) of notes to Gulf investors, although there are no details. In 2012, another sukuk, which was fully subscribed, raised an equivalent of cUS$160mn, to make up for the loss in oil revenue after the secession of South Sudan. But in the absence of external finance, Sudan became more active in borrowing from local banks. In 2015, media reported that South Sudan had agreed to borrow US$500mn from Qatar National Bank (QNB).

Sudan Refinancing Agreement 1981

Borrower	The Democratic Republic of Sudan/Bank of Sudan
Issue date	The Refinancing Agreement dated 30 December 1981 made between the Democratic Republic of the Sudan as Borrower (obligor), the Bank of Sudan as Guarantor, certain financial institutions and Citicorp International Bank Limited as Servicing Institution as amended from time to time (amended in March 1982, March 1983, March 1984, September 1985)
Restructuring	Under the second amendment in March 1983, all amounts outstanding under the refinancing agreement (both principal and interest) were consolidated and treated as a single loan referred to as the "Consolidated Loan". Furthermore, under the amendment in September 1985, the Consolidated Loan was divided into two portions, and subsequently converted into CHF, as follows: Tranche A: amount equal to the principal amount plus interest outstanding as of 31 December 1981 Tranche B: amount equal to 100% of accrued interest since 1 January 1982
Form	Registered loans
Amount outstanding	Tranche A: CHF1156.09mn Tranche B: CHF484.93mn
Currency	CHF
Coupon/interest	Tranche A: LIBOR + 1 3/4% Tranche B: LIBOR + 1 1/4% All past due and accrued interest trades for free and at no extra cost for the account of the Buyer.
Method of transfer	Contractually, by full assignment with consent from the Borrower. However, in practice, consent has not been forthcoming from the Borrower for some years. Transactions have therefore settled on a sub participation basis.
Agency fees	N/A based on above
Settlement period	T + 20 business days
Agent	Citibank International Plc is acting as the servicing institution.
Governing law	English

Source: Exotix

Suriname

Nominal GDP (US$mn, 2018)[a]		3840
Population (thousand, 2018)[a]		590
GDP per capita (USD, 2018)[a]		6506
Credit ratings (long-term foreign currency)[b]	Fitch	B–
	Moody's	B2
	S&P	B

[a]IMF WEO October 2018
[b]As at end-September 2018

Country Summary

- Suriname has a somewhat volatile past, with a history of coups and political violence since independence from the Netherlands in 1975. Desiré Bouterse has been President since 2010 and was previously military ruler between 1980 and 1987, but was convicted in absentia in 1999 for drug smuggling and was one of 25 people granted amnesty in 2012 for 1982 political executions.
- Suriname is a small open economy dependent on gold and a few other commodities. After gold prices started to decline from 2012, oil prices from 2014 and Alcoa's alumina refinery closed in 2015, the country fell into a three-year long recession. But the economy is expected to recover in 2018 and medium-term prospects could be

Exotix Capital, *Exotix Developing Markets Guide*,
https://doi.org/10.1007/978-3-030-05867-8_36

supported by new gold investment and oil, where there are high hopes after recent large offshore oil finds in neighbouring Guyana.

- Suriname turned to the IMF in May 2016 after the resulting balance of payments crisis, which saw pressure on reserves give way to a sharp currency devaluation, and a growing debt burden following large fiscal deficits. But the IMF programme never made the first review and was suspended by the authorities a year later. Suriname issued a debut eurobond in October 2016. Public debt has risen to 60% of GDP and the liquidity position remains tight.

Economic data	*Avg*[a]	*2014*	*2015*	*2016*	*2017 (e)*	*2018 (f)*	*2019 (f)*
Real GDP growth	2.5	0.3	−2.6	−5.1	1.9	2.0	2.2
Inflation (annual average)	11.8	3.4	6.9	55.5	22.0	7.8	6.0
Current account (% of GDP)	2.4	−7.9	−16.3	−5.2	−0.1	−3.3	−2.4
Reserves (US$mn, end-period)[b]	629	625	330	381	424	762[c]	–
Reserves/imports (months)[d]	3.5	2.6	1.4	2.6	2.7	–	–
Overall fiscal balance (% of GDP)[e]	−3.2	−8.6	−9.4	−7.8	−7.4	−7.3	−7.5
Currency (ticker)	Surinamese dollar (SRD)						
FX regime	De jure floating but de facto pegged, with a dual rate, which the IMF describes as a stabilised arrangement. The peg to the US dollar was devalued in November 2015 and March 2016, for a cumulative amount of c55%, and was devalued previously in 2011. In November 2015, a dual rate was established for official transactions and commercial market transactions.						
Key exports	Gold (49.4%), alumina (12.6%), oil (8.4%).						

Source: IMF WEO Database, Central Bank of Suriname, OEC

[a]10-year average to 2016 unless otherwise stated

[b]Official reserve assets

[c]Latest figure, May 2018

[d]In months of imports of goods, services and transfer debits

[e]Overall government net lending

Key figures		*Party*	*Since*
President	Desiré (Dési) Bouterse	NDP	Aug. 2010[a]
Vice president	Ashwin Adhin	NDP	Aug. 2015
Minister of finance	Gillmore Hoefdraad	NDP	Aug. 2015
Key opposition figure	Chan Santokhi	VHP	Jan. 2015
Central bank governor	Glenn Gersie	–	Feb. 2016

[a]Dési Bouterse was Suriname's de facto leader from 1980–1987 after a military coup

Politics

Executive power

Concentrated on the president, who is both chief of state and head of government, in accordance with the Constitution of 1987. Indirectly elected by the National Assembly following a legislative election. If the National Assembly fails to elect a president with a two-thirds majority after two votes, then the election will go to the wider People's Assembly of Suriname, which consists of 893 representatives from the national, local and regional councils, where a simple majority only is needed.

Presidential term: Five years **Parliamentary term**: Five years

Legislature

Unicameral, the Nationale Assemblée (National Assembly), consisting of 51 directly elected seats using proportional representation in 10 multi-member constituencies, based on the 10 administrative districts of Suriname.

Elections

Next due *Legislative: 2020*

Last legislative election (May 2015)	*Seats*	*% of vote*
National Democratic Party (NDP)[a]	26	45.5
Progressive Reform Party (VHP/V7 Alliance)	18	37.3
A-Combination (AC)	5	10.5
Party for Democracy and Development through Unity (DOE)	1	4.3
Progressive Workers' and Farmers' Union (PALU)	1	0.7
Others	0	1.7
Total (directly elected)	**51**	**100.0**

[a]The NDP is part of the Megacombinatie ("Mega combination") alliance, which also includes PALU, New Suriname (NS) and the Party for National Unity and Solidarity (KTPI)

People

Hindustanis make up 27.4% of the population, Maroons 21.7%, Creoles 15.7%, Javanese 13.7%; the remainder are mixed or other groups. The largest religions are Christianity at 49.6%, Hinduism at 22.3% and Islam at 13.8%. The official language is Dutch, although English and native languages are widely spoken. Spanish explorers visited and named Suriname in the late sixteenth century. After various settlement attempts by the Spanish, Dutch, British and French, a British settlement was established at Paramaribo, now the capital city, in 1651, which was ceded to the Netherlands in 1667 in exchange for New Amsterdam (later called New York City). Using African slave labour, Dutch rulers established coffee and sugar plantations. Slavery was abolished in 1863. American firm Alcoa began mining bauxite in 1916, which became Suriname's main export, until Alcoa's subsidiary (Suralco) decided to close its alumina refinery in 2015; it no longer operates in Suriname, contributing to the recession. In 1954, Suriname gained self-governance from the Netherlands, with the exception of defence and foreign affairs, and in 1975 gained full independence, with Johan Ferrier as President and Henck Arron of the Suriname National Party (NPS) as prime minister. More than one-third of the population emigrated to the Netherlands. A 1980 military coup ousted Arron's government, but Ferrier did not recognise the military regime and appointed Henk Chin A Sen of the Nationalist Republican Party (PNR) as civilian leader, who was then made President by the army. Chin A Sen acted as president and prime minister until 1982, when a second coup, led by Lieutenant-Colonel Desiré Bouterse set up the Revolutionary People's Front. The Netherlands and US cut off economic aid when 15 opposition leaders were executed. In 1985, the ban on political parties was lifted. A guerrilla war was started by the Surinamese Liberation Army (SLA) of mostly escaped African slaves in 1986. The following year, 97% of the electorate approved a new civilian constitution and, in 1988, former agriculture minister Ramsewak Shankar was elected President. He reached a peace accord with the SLA, which was rejected by Bouterse in 1989, who assisted a coup against Shankar in 1990. Civilian rule was restored in 1991, when Johan Kraag (NPS) became interim President and reached a 1992 peace accord with the SLA. Bouterse ally, Jules Wijdenbosch, was elected President in 1996. A Dutch international arrest warrant for Bouterse was refused by Suriname in 1997, but a Dutch court convicted Bouterse for drug smuggling in absentia in 1999. Wijdenbosch was succeeded as President in 2000 by Ronald Venetiaan, who was re-elected in 2005. The 2010 elections saw Bouterse return as President, following a coalition in the National Assembly presidential elections, and an amnesty law was passed by Parliament in 2012 for Bouterse and 24 others accused of 1982 political executions. Bouterse was re-elected as President following the 2015 general election. Bouterse's son was sentenced to over 16 years in prison in 2015 after pleading guilty to charges of offering Suriname as a home base to Lebanese paramilitary group Hezbollah. The country's medium-term economic prospects could be supported by offshore oil, where recent large oil finds in neighbouring Guyana have raised hopes for Suriname's own potential. However, Kosmos Energy announced in June 2018 that it had abandoned one offshore well after failing to find oil or natural gas, although its exploration programme continues in other wells.

DEBT

	2012	*2017 Q2*
External debt ratios (%)		
Total external debt/GDP	21.9	78.2
Public external debt/GDP	11.4	46.7
Private external debt/GDP	10.5	31.6
Total external debt/exports of goods and services	38.0	128.5
External debt service ratio (public)	2.0	6.3
Public debt ratios (%)		
Public domestic debt/GDP	10.1	17.2
Public debt/GDP	21.5	63.9

Source: Ministry of Finance, Central Bank of Suriname, IMF, Exotix

The Surinamese authorities provide debt data using both the international definition and also the Suriname national debt act (NDA) definition. We use the conventional international definition. Note that debt statistics may appear to be higher if the NDA definition is used because it includes amounts that have not yet been disbursed.

Suriname's total external debt in June 2017 was US$2.6bn, according to Ministry of Finance figures. Of this, US$1.56bn (60% of the total) was owed or guaranteed by the public sector. Since 2016, and the issue of Suriname's debut eurobond, public external debt has been owed mainly to commercial (43% of the total) and multilateral (40%) creditors. The eurobond accounted for 82% of commercial debt and 35% of public external debt. The remaining commercial debt is banks loans, the biggest being from the Industrial and Commercial Bank of China (ICBC). Most of the multilateral debt is owed to the Inter-American Development Bank (IADB), c83% of multilateral debt and 33% of public external debt. The next biggest multilateral creditor is the Caribbean Development Bank (CDB), at just 8% of multilateral debt. This means that the bulk of Suriname's public external debt (68%) is concentrated in just two creditor groups, the eurobond and IADB. Most multilateral debt is, however, concessional. Bilateral creditors account for 17% of public external debt, the single biggest bilateral creditor being China, followed by France and India. Private non-guaranteed external debt amounted to US$1.06bn (40% of the total). No further details are provided on the composition of private external debt although no companies in Suriname appear to have access to the international bond market.

The level and composition of Suriname's public external debt has changed dramatically over the past several years. Public external debt has tripled in nominal USD terms since 2012, when it was just US$567mn. Half the increase is due to the eurobond, while most of the remaining increase is due to increased IADB lending. At the same time, bilateral lending has become a less significant share in overall public external debt, although in nominal USD terms it has fallen by just 16% since then. In 2012, bilateral creditors accounted for just over half the debt.

Total external debt was therefore 78% of GDP in 2017, up from 30% in 2012. The increase reflects both the higher numerator (more external debt), and also currency depreciation. Nominal GDP was projected at 33% lower in USD terms in 2017 than in 2012, according to the IMF WEO. Total external debt was 129% of exports of goods and services, which has increased from 38% in 2012, due in part to lower exports. The external debt service ratio has more than tripled since 2012 to 6.3% of exports. This ratio is still relatively low since, before 2013, external debt was fairly low and exports were high.

Overall public debt was 64% of GDP in 2017, an increase from 22% in 2012. The increase is due to the primary deficit, and higher (mainly external) debt, and the more depreciated exchange rate. Public domestic debt increased from US$503mn in 2012 (10% of GDP) to cUS$576mn in 2017 (17% of GDP). It comprises domestic currency bonds and commercial bank debt.

Composition of external debt

External debt by creditor (June 2017)	*Nominal amount outstanding (US$mn)*	*Share of total (%)*
Public sector external debt[a]	**1562**	**59.7**
o/w Official multilateral	625	23.9
IADB	519	19.8
CDB	50	1.9
IsDB	39	1.5
OFID	13	0.5
EIB	3	0.1
Official bilateral	266	10.2
China	197	7.5
France	43	1.6
India	26	1.0

(*continued*)

(continued)

External debt by creditor (June 2017)	*Nominal amount outstanding (US$mn)*	*Share of total (%)*
Private creditors	671	25.6
Bonds	550	21.0
Commercial banks	121	4.6
o/w ICBC	49	1.9
Private sector external debt[b]	**1057**	**40.3**
Total external debt	**2619**	**100.0**

Source: Ministry of Finance

[a]Excludes monetary authorities' external debt
[b]Includes intercompany lending

Rescheduling History

Modern debt rescheduling has been minimal. Suriname has a modest history of incurring arrears in the past, but these have tended to be mostly with official bilateral creditors and dealt with on a bilateral basis, rather than through more comprehensive debt restructuring agreements. Some external arrears with bilateral creditors built up and were cleared between 2008 and 2012, with some written-off, most notably with Brazil and the US.

Suriname avoided the serial debt reschedulings endured by other countries in the region during the 1980s although this gave way to a high inflation episode in the early 1990s. Its initial starting point, as a result of its independence from the Netherlands in 1975, may have insulated it from debt problems seen elsewhere, although political turmoil through the 1980s saw a deteriorating fiscal balance, which was financed through seigniorage (printing money) rather than foreign debt. A high inflation experience followed in the early 1990s, with inflation averaging over 140% in 1994, although why it took so long to develop remains something of a puzzle. External creditors pressured the government to undertake a structural adjustment programme (SAP) in 1994, although the adjustment took its toll on the population. The government had to rein in spending, including subsidies for the private sector. Critics point to examples such as an end to subsidised milk and unemployment brought about by austerity.

Suriname subsequently experienced relative economic prosperity due to production and exports from its extractive sector. Macroeconomic performance improved significantly during the 2000s and until 2012. Annual economic growth was strong, averaging 4.9% between 2005 and 2011, with the highest growth rate in 2011 at 5.8%. Growth was driven by the extractive sector, especially gold and oil, and due to public infrastructure investment. Per capita GDP increased by c35% between 2008 and 2012. Rating agency upgrades and GDP growth were among the highest in the region due to strong commodity prices and political stability.

However, balance of payments pressures began to re-emerge. Over-reliance on the extractive sector and commodity exports was exposed when commodity prices started to fall, especially with the decline in gold prices in 2012, while counter-cyclical policies, led by central bank financing of the fiscal deficit, stoked inflation and put pressure on reserves. Gross international reserves dropped to 1.9 months of imports in 2015, from 4.4 months in 2012, and the currency had to be devalued. The run up to the 2015 general election also drove fiscal expansion, as some consolidation targets were abandoned. The government's commitment to fiscal consolidation in late 2015 opened the door to multilateral support and an IMF programme, although policy discipline was ultimately short-lived.

Relations with Multilateral Creditors

Relations with the IMF are somewhat patchy. Suriname has only ever had one IMF programme which was approved in May 2016, but this was terminated before the conclusion of the first review. On a positive note, the IMF announced on 23 January 2018 that Suriname had implemented data standards under its enhanced general data dissemination system (e-GDDS) designed to help data transparency and surveillance.

The need for an IMF programme followed a difficult period of lower commodity export prices and the closure of Alcoa's alumina refinery in late 2015, which saw the country fall into recession and put pressure on the external accounts. The current account deficit shifted from a surplus of 3.3% of GDP in 2012 to a deficit of 16% in 2015. Central bank reserves fell by nearly 70% from their peak of US$1bn in 2012 to US$330mn by end-2015, forcing the currency to be devalued. Inflation peaked at 79% in October 2016. Real GDP stagnated in 2014, and then fell by 2.6% in 2015 and by 5.1% in 2016 (reported at −10.5% in previous WEOs, but GDP has since been revised up). In its 2016 Article IV, which was concluded by the IMF Board in December 2016, the IMF stated that "the drop in international gold and oil prices and the cessation of alumina production resulted in large fiscal and current account deficits and the onset of a deep recession in 2015. During the boom, there was no institutional arrangement to save resources for future price corrections, and implementation of IMF advice on strengthening the policy framework was limited. Suriname has thus had a much sharper recession, steeper exchange rate depreciation, and larger rise in inflation and government debt than most commodity exporters."

The authorities launched an adjustment plan in late 2015 and eventually sought IMF financial assistance to support the balance of payments, with a programme approved in May 2016. However, this showed mixed performance by the time of the staff visit in August 2016 to conduct the first review. The fiscal deficit had been kept close to the programme's path and some reforms had been implemented, including preparations for a value-added tax (a broad-based tax in 2018 was an IMF priority). Electricity subsidies were reduced gradually and tariffs were increased. However, higher prices were met by over 5000 protestors in the capital and, when the budget deficit fell as a proportion of GDP in 2016, the government partially reversed the tariff rise, against IMF advice, abandoning the target of eliminating electricity subsidies by December 2016. Interest rates had also been kept low, despite rising inflation. Although higher expected gold production from the Merian mine, operated by the US company Newmont, which commenced operations in October 2016, may have eased the immediate balance of payments needs and the need for IMF support, arguably it was the government's reluctance to follow austerity policies under the IMF programme that prompted it to suspend the programme. In May 2017, the government announced that it had cancelled the SBA programme, without concluding the first review, with no further disbursements, on the grounds that its citizens could not bear the conditions.

IMF programmes

Date	*Arrangements*	*Comments*
2016–2018 (terminated early)	SBA	A two-year SBA was approved in May 2016 for SDR342mn (US$478mn, 265% of quota). It enabled an immediate disbursement of SDR58mn (US$81mn) and supported the authorities' home-grown programme aiming to facilitate the country's adjustment to the fall in commodity export prices. This included fiscal consolidation to restore fiscal and external stability. The programme was expected to catalyse support from other IFIs, including the Caribbean Development Bank (CDB), the IADB, the Islamic Development Bank and the World Bank, as well as bilaterals. The programme was subsequently terminated by the authorities in April 2017 before completion of the first review.

Source: IMF. Suriname joined the IMF in 1978

Since 2011, total multilateral debt has more than tripled to US$625mn (as of June 2017), although this has been driven largely by IADB lending. The IADB is Suriname's largest multilateral creditor, accounting for 85% of multilateral credit. The IADB's strategy in Suriname until 2020 aims to support economic stabilisation, modernisation and policy reform. Dominating projects in terms of funding are in energy and the reform and modernisation of the state. The World Bank is less active and has undertaken two projects in Suriname. The first was a project to support fiscal reforms, the private investment climate and disaster risk management that was planned in 2016; however, a corporate review decided not to proceed. The second is still awaiting approval: It will aim to improve transparency in extractive revenues and seek multi-stakeholder dialogue on the governance of oil and mining. In July 2015, the Ministry of Trade and Industry agreed with the CDB on projects to improve Suriname's implementation of both the CariCom single market and economy (CSME) and the European Union economic partnership agreement (EPA). The two projects aimed to boost competitiveness, increase export earnings and attract foreign investment. Notably, to overcome macroeconomic challenges, the Islamic Development Bank (IsDB) is increasing its concessional funding to Suriname, the only country in the region to receive its funding. As of June 2017, IsDB had US$39mn outstanding with Suriname. A board of governors meeting in May 2017 outlined a concessional support plan, up to 2021, worth US$1.8bn in financial and technical support. European DFIs are less important. Lending from the European Development Fund (EDF) has centred on transport infrastructure and, under the current six-year plan, sustainable agriculture. Suriname also benefits from the EU's special assistance framework for traditional banana suppliers and has received over EUR20mn in the past 10 years, to increase efficient production. A major banana producer, SBBS, was privatised in early 2014 (with Belgian fruit company Univeg owning 90%), and is expected to improve efficiency further. Other European Commission projects in Suriname have included a renewable energy project (2013–2017) and a drinking water supplies project (2012–2016).

Paris Club and Bilateral Creditors

Suriname has not received any restructuring within the Paris Club, although it has incurred bilateral arrears in the past and has attempted to obtain debt restructuring from its creditors on an individual basis. The Netherlands has traditionally been the main bilateral creditor to Suriname; however, since 2007, China and India have become more significant donors. China is still the largest bilateral creditor (US$226mn in June 2016), followed by France (US$42.4mn) and India (US$30.1mn). Although not a major creditor, Germany has projects in Suriname and the wider region. In 2008, 71% of external arrears were to Brazil. In 2009, Suriname cleared these Brazilian arrears, totalling US$118mn, including a write-off of US$44mn. In 2012, Suriname cleared US$26.6mn with the US, including significant penalties.

In June 2018, media reported that India, through the Export-Import Bank of India, had provided US$51mn in development aid to Suriname, through a combination of a US$31mn credit line and US$20mn concessional financing. The bulk of the line of credit was to support a power-transmission project, while the concessional financing was for a solar project to provide clean energy across a number of villages. The new line of credit took the total number extended by Exim Bank to seven, amounting to US$78mn.

Suriname has had outstanding debt with Venezuela, through the PetroCaribe concessional oil financing: Venezuela supplies oil with a loan term of 25 years with a two-year grace period and 2% interest rate. Part of the 2016 bond issue was intended to repay US$54mn under the scheme.

Sovereign Commercial Debt

Suriname historically, until 2016, had very little or even no public external debt owed to commercial creditors, and therefore has only a modest history of commercial debt restructuring. There was one instance of bank debt restructuring back in 2001. Commercial debt was zero over 2007–2013, according to central bank figures, but it increased modestly in 2014 and 2015. Commercial debt jumped significantly higher in 2016 with the issue of a eurobond. There were, however, reports of commercial arrears. In preparing for its SBA in 2016, the IMF was made aware that Suriname had built up arrears in early 2016 with a private sector creditor in the Netherlands, who was in discussions with the authorities regarding rescheduling the payment (through good faith efforts). The only other arrears identified by the IMF in 2016 were to the Government of the People's Republic of China.

Commercial debt agreements

Date	*Details*
2001 Dec.	Clearing of US$36mn principal arrears owed to commercial banks.

Source: World Bank GDF

Suriname issued its first (and, to date, only) international bond in October 2016, the details of which are in the table below. The US$550mn 10-year bullet bond was issued at a relatively high 9.25% coupon, which reflected the challenging market conditions at the time. Reuters reported the issue was well received by investors, despite possible political and economic risks. Suriname already had a rating from S&P (since 1999) and Fitch (since 2005), and was rated B+ by both agencies at the time of issue. Moody's assigned its first rating of B1 for the bond issue. Proceeds of the bond issue would be used to cover existing loan payments, including senior notes due in September 2017, the US$27mn payment of an equity investment in Suriname Gold Project CV, repayments to Venezuela under the PetroCaribe oil scheme, financing for a state oil company Staatsolie and for general budgetary purposes.

Bloomberg reported in December 2017 that Suriname had mandated Oppenheimer to arrange an 18-month private placement financing of up to US$75mn. Proceeds were intended to be used to pre-fund a portion of the government's upcoming asset sales. There are no publicly available deals on the terms or the amount raised.

Suriname bond
Suriname 9.25% 2026
Bloomberg ticker: SURINM

Borrower	Republic of Suriname
Issue date	26 October 2016
Form	Eurobond
ISIN	USP68788AA97
Issued amount	US$550mn
Currency	Dollar
Denomination	US$200,000 and US$1000 thereafter
Amortisation	Bullet
Maturity date	26 October 2026
Coupon/interest	9.25% per annum, paid semi-annually April and October
Day count	30/360
Method of transfer	Euroclear/Clearstream
Settlement period	T + 2
Governing law	State of New York
Joint lead managers	Oppenheimer, Scotia

Source: Bloomberg

Tajikistan

Nominal GDP (US$mn, 2018)[a]		7350
Population (thousand, 2018)[a]		9107
GDP per capita (USD, 2018)[a]		807
Credit ratings (long-term foreign currency)[b]	Fitch	NR
	Moody's	B3
	S&P	B–

[a]IMF WEO October 2018
[b]As of end-September 2018

Country Summary

- Tajikistan has really only known one leader since its independence in 1991 after the fall of the USSR, namely current President Emomali Rahmon. It remains a transitional democracy with still maturing political institutions. The next presidential election is in 2020 but a change in the constitution in 2016 exempts President Rahmon from a two-term limit and allows for his indefinite re-election.
- The poorest of the five central Asian countries that emerged from the break-up of the USSR. Its economy is traditionally based on agriculture, although the share that is industry is growing. Manufacturing is dominated by the state-owned Tajik Aluminium Company ("TALCO") aluminium plant, the largest aluminium manufacturing plant in Central Asia and Tajikistan's largest state-owned enterprise.

Exotix Capital, *Exotix Developing Markets Guide*,
https://doi.org/10.1007/978-3-030-05867-8_37

The country also has substantial hydroelectric power potential. Gold, other minerals, cotton, and remittances are major foreign exchange earners. Its main trading partners are Kazakhstan, Afghanistan, and until recently Russia.

- Tajikistan became one of the poorest countries to issue a eurobond after its debut issuance in September 2017, a ten-year US$500mn bond. The proceeds were used to help finance the ongoing construction of the massive Rogun Hydropower Plant project. It has resulted in public debt increasing to 50% of GDP, of which public external debt is about 75%, although higher borrowing, a sharp depreciation in the local currency and the collapse in current account earnings has all seen external debt ratios pick up.

Economic data	*Avg*[a]	*2014*	*2015*	*2016*	*2017 (f)*	*2018 (f)*	*2019 (f)*
Real GDP growth	6.8	6.7	6.0	6.9	7.1	5.0	5.0
Inflation (annual average)	8.9	6.1	5.8	5.9	7.3	5.8	5.5
Current account (% of GDP)	−5.9	−2.8	−6.0	−5.2	−0.5	−4.7	−4.3
Reserves (US$mn)[b]	427	511	494	653	701	758	911
Reserves/imports[c]	1.4	1.8	2.0	2.3	2.3	2.2	2.5
Overall fiscal balance (% of GDP)[d]	−2.8	0.0	−1.9	−9.8	−6.8	−7.7	−6.8
Currency (ticker)	Tajikistani somoni (TJS)						
FX regime	Managed float against the US dollar, reclassified by the IMF as de facto "other managed" regime in 2015 from crawl-like. The exchange rate was devalued by 25% against the US$ in 2015 and a further 12% in 2016 and 11% in 2017.						
Key exports	Metals (31%), minerals (20%), precious metals (17%). Net remittance inflows amounted to US$2.2bn in 2016, or c31.4% of GDP, from Tajikistan citizens working abroad, mostly in Russia.						

Source: IMF WEO Database, National Bank of Tajikistan, IMF country reports, eurobond prospectus, OEC

[a]10-year average to 2016 unless otherwise stated

[b]Gross official reserves (IMF 2017 Article IV, historical and projections)

[c]In months of the next year's imports

[d]General government net lending/borrowing

Key figures		*Party*	*Since*
President	Emomali Rahmon	People's Democratic Party	Nov 1994[a]
Prime minister	Kokhir Rasulzoda	People's Democratic Party	Nov 2013
Minister of finance	Fayiddin Qahhorzoda	People's Democratic Party	Jan 2018
Leading opposition figure	Muhiddin Kabiri	Islamic Renaissance Party	Aug 2006
Central bank governor	Jamshed Nurmahmadzoda	–	May 2015

[a]Effectively leader since 1992. Rahmon was elected a People's Deputy to the Supreme Soviet in 1990 but resigned in August 1992, soon after the civil war started. Until November 1992, Akbarsho Iskandarov was acting President, and that month Rahmon was also elected by the Supreme Soviet members to be Chairman of the Supreme Assembly of the Republic, and became acting President, until the post of President of the Republic was officially restored in November 1994. Rahmon has held this position since

Politics

Executive power

Tajikistan is a presidential republic in which the president, who is elected directly, is both head of state and head of government. The president appoints the members of the cabinet, including the prime minister who is responsible for the day-to-day activities of the government. President Rahmon has formally been the President since 1994 after serving as interim head of state. After the presidential election in 1999, the constitution (as amended in 2003) set a limit of two seven-year terms for the president, thereby making President Rahmon eligible to serve until 2020. He subsequently won elections in 2006 and 2013. However, following a referendum in May 2016 to amend the constitution, Rahmon, became exempt from any presidential limits under his sole status as 'Leader of the Nation'. The referendum was approved by 94.5% of the vote cast. Turnout was 90%. A second amendment lowered the minimum age for presidential candidates from 35 to 30, seen as a way to allow Rahmon's son, Rustam Emomali, 27, to potentially stand for president in 2020.

Presidential term: Seven years, two term limit (Emomali Rahmon exempt)

Parliamentary term: Five years

Legislature

Bicameral, known as the Majlisi Oli (Supreme Assembly), introduced in 1999; previously unicameral. The lower chamber is the Assembly of Representatives (Majlisi namoyandagon) and the upper chamber is the National Assembly (Majlisi milli). The People's Democratic Party of Tajikistan, a centre-left party, has controlled both chambers of parliament since the 2005 election.

(*continued*)

(continued)

Legislature	
Assembly of Representatives (63 seats) 41 MPs are directly elected in single-seat constituencies and 22 MPs are elected in a single nationwide constituency by proportional representation. It meets all year-round and members serve five-year terms.	**National Assembly (33 seats)** Strictly 34 seats but only 33 seats are filled. 25 members are indirectly elected by local representative assemblies, eight are appointed directly by the president, and one seat is reserved for the former president (but Tajikistan does not have one). It meets at least twice a year and members serve five-year terms.

Elections

Next due *Legislative: Spring 2020; Presidential: Autumn 2020*

Last legislative election (Mar. 2015)	*Seats*	*Last presidential (Nov. 2013)*	*% of vote*
Assembly of representatives		Emomali Rahmon	83.1
People's Democratic Party	51	Ismoil Talbakov	5.0
Agrarian Party of Tajikistan	5	Tolibbak Bukhoriev	4.6
Party of Economic Reforms	3	Olimjon Boboyev	3.9
The Communist Party of Tajikistan	2	Abdulhalim Ghafforov	1.5
The Socialist Party	1	Saidja'tar Ismonov	1.0
The Democratic Party	1	Other	0.9
Total	**63**	**Total**	**100.0**

People

A landlocked area in Central Asia, Tajikistan is bordered to the north by Uzbekistan, Kyrgyzstan and China to the east, and Afghanistan and Pakistan to the south. The territory that now constitutes Tajikistan was previously home to several ancient cultures and ruled by numerous empires and dynasties, and became part of the Soviet Union (later USSR) in 1924. Tajikistan declared independence in September 1991 shortly before the dissolution of the USSR in 1991 and almost immediately plunged into a five-year long civil war from 1992–1997 between Moscow-backed pro-government forces and a coalition of democratic, regional and Islamist factions which ended with the signing of a United Nations-brokered peace agreement in June 1997. Up to 50,000 people were killed and over one-tenth of the population fled the country.

After the office of president of Tajikistan was abolished in November 1992, having been established in 1990, Emomali Rahmon was the nominal head of state during an interim period and was elected president in 1994. He has remained in power ever since, winning elections in 1999, 2006, and 2013. Tajikistan has an estimated population of 8.8mn. Most of them belong to the Tajik ethnic group. An estimated 1.4mn Tajikistan citizens live in Russia, with another 600,000 living in other countries. Mountains cover 93% of the country. The country is rich in natural resources (approximately 55% of the water resources in Central Asia are in Tajikistan), but the mountainous nature of the country makes extracting them difficult.

Debt

	2012	*Q3 17 (estimate)*
External debt ratios (%)		
Total external debt/GDP	46.5	74.4
Public external debt/GDP	28.6	38.5[a]
Private external debt/GDP[b]	18.0	35.9[c]
Total external debt/exports of goods, services & remittances	168.7	313.2
External debt service ratio[d] (public debt only)	5.1	9.8
Public debt ratios (%)		
Public domestic debt/GDP	7.6	11.6[c]
Public debt/GDP[a]	36.2	50.1

Source: 2017 eurobond prospectus, MoF BoP Report 2016, MoF BoP Report 2013, IMF WEO, Exotix

[a]Q2 17 figure plus US$500mn eurobond issued in September. Includes external debt of the central bank

[b]Includes intercompany lending

[c]2016 figure

[d]Debt service to exports of goods, services and remittances

Exotix estimates that public external debt was cUS$2.8bn by September 2017, c39% of GDP. Public external debt stood at US$2.27bn at the end of 2016, according to official figures, and rose slightly to US$2.30bn in June 2017. Virtually all the debt at the time was owed to official and bilateral creditors, on concessional terms. Bilateral creditors accounted for 60% of the total and multilaterals c38%. China Eximbank was the single largest creditor, accounting for nearly half the total, followed by the World Bank and Asian Development Bank. In September 2017, Tajikistan issued its debut US$500mn eurobond (c22% of the existing debt stock and 7% of GDP) thereby drastically changing the composition of the debt (see 'sovereign commercial debt' section). Exotix therefore estimates total public external debt based on adding the eurobond issue to the end-2016 debt stock (when more detailed data on creditor composition is available); and we illustrate the resulting creditor composition in the table below. On that basis, the eurobond accounted for 18% of the total, becoming the second single biggest creditor after China Eximbank (43% of public external debt). Indeed, before the eurobond, public external debt had remained relatively flat in nominal US$ terms since 2012.

Total external debt amounted to an estimated US$5.4bn, c74% of GDP, in 2017. This was split roughly 50:50 on Exotix estimates between public external debt and private external debt. Although private external debt rose faster than public external debt, most of that increase came from higher intercompany lending, which now represents about half of the total private external debt portfolio. External debt rose to an estimated 313% of exports of goods, services and remittances in 2017, up from 169% in 2012, as a result of not only the rise in the debt in nominal terms (in both public and private debt) but also because of the sharp depreciation of the currency (the somoni) relative to the US dollar, which lost more than 45% of its value over this period, and a sharp fall in the denominator. This follows a decline in exports to Russia, traditionally Tajikistan's primary export market, following the slowdown in the Russian economy and a tightening in Russian immigration rules. Goods exports, which fell by 36% between 2012 and 2014, have since recovered although remittances and services income remain subdued. Remittances have traditionally been a significant source of FX inflows (mainly family remittances from the significant Tajikistan population living in Russia). Remittances may have fallen by 40% from 2012 levels in 2017. Services income may have fallen by 60%. As a result of currency depreciation, the public sector external debt service ratio increased to 16% (as a percent of goods only) although when expressed as a percent of goods, services and remittances, it has increased to 10%.

Total public debt rose to an estimated 50% of GDP in 2017 from 36% in 2012. Roughly 75% of public debt is owed to external creditors. Domestic public debt is now nearly 12% of GDP, up from 7.6% in 2012. Domestic public debt had fallen to 5.2% of GDP in 2014, but it increased significantly in 2016 due to the issuance of government bonds to the central bank (NBT) in connection with the recapitalisation of distressed banks in December 2016.

Composition of external debt

External debt by creditor (Sep. 2017, estimate)	*Nominal amount outstanding (US$mn)*	*Share of total (%)*
Public external debt	**2775**	**51.5**
Central government debt	2720	50.5
o/w Official multilateral	862	16.0
World Bank	293	5.4
ADB	225	4.2
Islamic Development Bank	115	2.1
IMF	107	2.0
Eurasian Development Bank	65	1.2
OPEC Fund	40	0.7
EBRD	11	0.2
EIB	5	0.1

(*continued*)

(continued)

External debt by creditor (Sep. 2017, estimate)	*Nominal amount outstanding (US$mn)*	*Share of total (%)*
Official bilateral	1358	25.2
China Eximbank	1197	22.2
Saudi Fund for Development	45	0.8
Kuwait Fund for Development	39	0.7
France	25	0.5
KfW (Germany)	22	0.4
Abu Dhabi Fund for Development	13	0.2
China	10	0.2
United States	7	0.1
Private creditors (Eurobond)	500	9.3
Other (guaranteed and non-guaranteed)	55	1.0
Private sector external debt[a]	**2611**	**48.5**
Total external debt	**5385**	**100.0**

Source: Ministry of Finance, 2017 eurobond prospectus. Numbers are estimates. All figures are from end-of-year 2016, apart from eurobonds, which are added (issued in September 2017)

[a]Includes intercompany lending

Rescheduling History

Tajikistan has only a very limited history of debt rescheduling, in part because it had very limited debt to start with. Upon its independence in 1991, Tajikistan had practically no foreign debt, with Russia assuming all the former Soviet Union's assets and liabilities under a 1994 Zero Option agreement with the ex-Soviet Republics. Throughout the 1990s, foreign debt rose rapidly, in part due to the 1998 financial crisis in Russia, which led to a deteriorating external environment for Tajikistan with government debt rising from 60% to c110% of GDP in 1997–2000 (on IMF WEO figures). The 2000s were characterised by a significant improvement in foreign debt levels with a shift to concessional financing through debt restructuring deals with the country's key creditors, notably Russia. In 2002, it reached a restructuring agreement with some of its key bilateral creditors, including a US$250mn write-off of the country's US$300mn debt to Russia. And in 2005, the IMF extended debt relief under MDRI on all of Tajikistan's outstanding debt to the IMF incurred before 2005. Tajikistan has never entered into any restructuring deals with commercial creditors.

Relations with Multilateral Creditors

Tajikistan has undertaken four programmes since becoming a member of the IMF in 1993, all of which have been extended in the form of concessional loans for implementation of economic reform programmes. It also had two emergency post-conflict assistance (EPCA) facilities in the late 1990s and, following policy deficiencies, a SMP in 2008. Tajikistan has seen two episodes of mis-reporting go to the Executive Board (2002 and 2008). In December 2005, as part of its multilateral debt relief initiative (MDRI), the IMF extended 100% debt relief for Tajikistan on all its debt incurred before 1 January 2005 that remained outstanding (this amounted to cUS$99mn).

Tajikistan is not currently under an IMF programme. Its most recent programme (a three-year ECF which was augmented to SDR104mn, 120% of quota) was approved in 2009 and responded to a deterioration in global economic conditions, which reduced remittance inflow and adversely affected export demand. The programme was concluded in 2012.

A statement on 29 May 2018, following an IMF staff visit, noted the authorities indicated they wish to resume discussions on a possible IMF programme. The authorities had noted a previous intention to pursue discussions on a possible IMF programme following a Staff Article IV mission in May 2017, although—until now—there had been no further progress. The 2017 Article IV went to the IMF Board in November 2017, over two years after the previous Article IV Board discussion which took place in June 2015. In common with previous Article IV reviews, the latest staff paper has not been published. Directors commended the authorities' response to external shocks since 2014, including allowing greater exchange rate flexibility, containing the government wage bill, and accumulating reserves, but noted that the country continued to face vulnerabilities, which required maintaining prudent macroeconomic policies and stepping up reforms, especially in the banking sector. The IMF's recent statement in May noted that negotiations on a programme could start in coming months after demonstrating further reform progress, especially in the financial sector.

IMF programmes

Date	*Arrangements*	*Comments*
1996	SBA	A six-month SDR15mn (US$22mn, 25% of quota) SBA programme approved in May with the aim of reducing inflation, improving balance of payments, and slowing the decline in real incomes. All money was drawn. The programme ended in December.
1997	EPCA	The IMF approved SDR7.5mn (US$10mn) Emergency Post Conflict Assistance (EPCA) for Tajikistan in December 1997 after renewed violence interrupted the authorities' stabilisation program.
1998	EPCA	The IMF approved a second EPCA for SDR7.5mn (US$10mn) in April 1998. It was seen as a transitional phase, possibly leading to a program supported by loans under the enhanced structural adjustment facility (ESAF).
1998–2001	ECF[a]	A three-year SDR96mn (US$128mn, 110% of quota) ESAF (subsequently known as a PRGF and now ECF) programme approved in June 1998 (augmented by SDR4.3mn to SDR100.3mn in December 1998) to support an economic reform program, including privatisation of state-owned assets, consolidation in the cotton sectors, and bank restructuring to accommodate further domestic savings. SDR78mn was drawn. In February 2002, the Board reviewed three non-complying disbursements under the programme relating to the second and third reviews (totalling SDR25.3mn) as, subsequent to the PRGF disbursements in January 2000, April 2001, and July 2001, it became apparent that the information on Tajikistan's external arrears at the time of approval of the disbursements was incorrect. This related to arrears accumulated in connection with two government guarantees. The Board agreed that Tajikistan could repay the IMF in four quarterly tranches beginning June 2002 and completing repayment no later than March 2003.
2002–2006	ECF[a]	A three-year SDR65mn (US$87mn, 75% of quota) PRGF (now ECF) programme approved in December 2002 to accelerate structural reform and maintain exchange rate stability. The programme ended in February 2006 after the conclusion of the sixth and final review. All money was drawn. In November 2006, the president confirmed the intention to work towards a policy support instrument (PSI) instead of a successor PRGF although, in the event, it was not forthcoming. In March 2008, the Board met to discuss another misreporting episode involving the provision of inaccurate data to the Fund (involving the level of international reserves, net domestic assets of the NBT, and the issuance of directed credit by the NBT) over the past six years. This had seriously undermined the credibility of the authorities with IFIs and other donors. The Board agreed that Tajikistan repay early the three noncomplying disbursements (amounting to SDR29.4mn) that were not discharged under MDRI relief. It also noted that the authorities needed to take decisive actions to restore policy credibility in the form of a staff-monitored program (SMP) to run in parallel with a proposed special audit of the NBT.

(*continued*)

(continued)

Date	*Arrangements*	*Comments*
2008	SMP	An SMP was approved in June 2008 lasting through to the end of the year. It came after a significant slowdown in growth early in the year, due to severe weather conditions and related energy shortages, and targeted a reduction in inflation (which had reached 20% in March) and a balanced budget. However, central to the SMP were measures to address governance and management problems at the central bank (NBT), for which a special audit was being conducted.
2009–2012	ECF[a]	A three-year SDR78mn (US$116mn, 90% of quota) PRGF (now ECF) programme was approved in April 2009 with the aim to facilitate external adjustment, achieve structural reforms in the areas of central bank governance and the agriculture sector, and to ensure no build-up of external debt. The programme was augmented in June 2010, at the time of the combined first and second review, to SDR104.4mn, cUS$153mn (an increase of 30% of quota to 120%). The programme was concluded satisfactorily with the sixth review in May 2012. All money was drawn.

Source: IMF

[a]Previously, poverty reduction and growth facility (PRGF)

Tajikistan became a member of the World Bank and the Asian Development Bank (ADB) in 1993 and 1998, respectively. Tajikistan's relationships with these development banks have focused on achieving sustained economic growth, fostering development of the private sector, improving social services, and enhancing regional connectivity. As of June 2017, the World Bank Group's active portfolio in the country included 21 projects totalling cUS$583mn (including US$225.7mn committed for the Nurek HPP rehabilitation project). Tajikistan's borrowing from the World Bank has been mainly on concessional terms through the IDA, which has provided US$1.1bn in grants and concessional credits to Tajikistan since 1996. As of June 2017, the ADB has approved cUS$1.5 bn in credits to the country, mainly in the form of concessional loans and grants to public sector projects.

Paris Club and Bilateral Creditors

Tajikistan has not entered into any rescheduling agreement with the Paris Club.

China is the country's main bilateral creditor, accounting for 89% of all bilateral debt, and is the single biggest creditor overall, accounting for 43% of public external debt. Most of its Chinese debt is owed to China Exim Bank.

Sovereign Commercial Debt

Tajikistan has no prior history of restructuring commercial credits, probably because until recently it had very little commercial debt.

In September 2017, Tajikistan issued its debut eurobond, a ten-year US$500mn bond maturing in 2027 with a coupon of 7.125%. This made it one of the poorest countries to issue a eurobond, just ahead of Ethiopia (2014), Ghana (2007), Rwanda (2014) and Mozambique (if one includes EMATUM in 2013). According to the published data the bond issue was heavily oversubscribed, with Tajikistan receiving more than US$4bn in bids, which resulted in pricing below the 8% yield that was initially indicated. However, the bond rarely traded above par post issue. More than 60% of the new issue went to US and UK investors, with fund managers accounting for 85%. Tajikistan used the proceeds to finance parts of the ongoing construction of the Rogun Hydropower plant, lending the proceeds to 96.6% state-owned company Open Joint Stock Company Rogun HPP (OJSC Rogun HPP). The Rogun Hydropower plant will cost an estimated US$3.9bn and will be the country's largest hydropower plant and the world's tallest dam upon its estimated completion in 2032.

Tajikistan bond
Tajikistan 7.125% 2027
Bloomberg ticker: TAJIKI

Borrower	Tajikistan
Issue date	14 September 2017
Form	International
ISIN	XS1676401414
Issue size	US$500mn
Currency	USD
Denomination	Minimum US$200,000; increments of US$1000 thereafter
Amortisation	Six equal semi-annual installments paid on 14 March and 14 September of each year commencing on 14 March 2025
Final maturity date	14 September 2027
Coupon/interest	7.125%, payable semi-annually, March and September
Day count	30/360
Method of transfer	Euroclear/Clearstream
Settlement period	T + 2 business days
Governing law	State of New York
Listing	Luxembourg
Arranger	Citibank, Raiffeisen Bank

Source: Bloomberg

Tanzania

Nominal GDP (US$mn, 2018)[a]		55,645
Population (thousand, 2018)[a]		51,046
GDP per capita (USD, 2018)[a]		1090
Credit ratings (long-term foreign currency)[b]	Fitch	NR
	Moody's	B1
	S&P	NR

[a]IMF WEO October 2018
[b]As at end-September 2018

Country Summary

- One of Africa's more politically stable countries, Tanzania has known only five presidents since independence in 1961, and the dominant political party (CCM) has been in power for over 50 years. 2015 saw the fifth election since multi-party politics was restored in 1992, with President John Pombe Mangufuli elected, after previously serving in several ministerial positions.
- Traditionally based on agriculture, mining has emerged in the past decade as important for Tanzania—the country has large deposits of natural resources, including chrome, tin, platinum, gold and diamonds. A new graphite exploration project is planned by Volt Resources. A history of state domination in the economy has resulted in a poor business environment, but foreign investment opportunities

Exotix Capital, *Exotix Developing Markets Guide*,
https://doi.org/10.1007/978-3-030-05867-8_38

offer huge potential. Diversification has seen other sectors develop, including tourism and business services. Economic transformation goals include improving industrialisation from its currently low level.

- External debt levels remain low, but have been increasing, and the IMF forecasts a similar trend over the medium term. External debt service has increased quickly in recent years, as the government uses non-concessional borrowing for public investment projects.

Economic data	*Avg*[a]	*2014*	*2015*	*2016*	*2017 (e)*	*2018 (f)*	*2019 (f)*
Real GDP growth	6.5	7.0	7.0	7.0	6.0	5.8	6.6
Inflation (annual average)	8.9	6.1	5.6	5.2	5.3	3.8	4.7
Current account (% of GDP)	−8.6	−10.1	−8.4	−4.5	−2.8	−4.3	−5.5
Reserves (US$mn, end-period)[b]	3535	4377	4094	4326	5906	–	–
Reserves/imports (months)[c]	4.1	3.9	3.9	4.9	7.4	–	–
Overall fiscal balance (% of GDP)[d]	−3.3	−3.0	−3.3	−2.2	−1.4	−2.9	−4.1
Currency (ticker)	Tanzanian shilling (TZS)						
FX regime	De jure free floating, but de facto managed.						
Key exports	Precious metals (36%), tobacco and substitutes (8.4%), fruit and nuts (7.8%), ores, slag and ash (7.5%). Tourism is also significant, total (wider) contribution to GDP was 13.3% in 2016.						

Source: IMF WEO Database, Haver, IMF Country Reports, OEC

[a]10-year average to 2016 unless otherwise stated
[b]Gross official reserves for end of the fiscal year (June)
[c]In months of the current year's imports of goods and services
[d]Overall government net lending

Key figures		*Party*	*Since*
President	John Pombe Magufuli	CCM	Nov. 2015
Vice president	Samia Suluhu	CCM	Nov. 2015
Prime minister	Kassim Majaliwa	CCM	Nov. 2015
President of Zanzibar	Ali Mohamed Shein[a]	CCM	Nov. 2010
First vice president of Zanzibar	Seif Sharif Hamad[a]	CUF	Nov. 2010
Minister of finance	Philip Mpango	CCM	Dec. 2015
Key opposition figure	Tundu Lissu	Chadema	–
Central bank governor	Florens Luoga	–	Jan. 2018

(*continued*)

(continued)

Notes: Tanzania is a member of the Commonwealth, gaining independence from Britain in 1961
[a]Shein, the respected former vice-president of Tanzania, was elected president of Zanzibar after winning 50.1% of the vote compared with Seif Sharif Hamad's 49.1%. Hamad subsequently accepted a position in the coalition government when he was appointed Zanzibar's vice president. In 2015, Hamad won the election against Shein, but the election commission cancelled the election. Shein remains president

Politics

Executive power

The president is chief of state and head of the government, elected by popular vote to serve a five-year term. The limit of two consecutive terms has been respected since 1985. The vice president is the second-highest political position. The prime minister is responsible for supervision and control of the activities of certain ministries and the leader of government business in the National Assembly. The cabinet is appointed by the president from among the members of the National Assembly. The semi-autonomous island of Zanzibar elects a president who is head of government for its internal matters.

Presidential term: Five years (two consecutive) **Parliamentary term**: Five years

Legislature

Unicameral National Assembly (Bunge), with 367 seats in the 2015 elections; 264 members elected by popular vote (although seven members were not returned, leaving 257), 113 seats were reserved for women, five members are chosen by the Zanzibar House of Representatives, 10 additional members are appointed by the president (25 women were directly elected, so are not counted twice) and one further seat reserved for the Attorney General.

Elections

Next due *Legislative/presidential: October 2020*

Last legislative election (October 2015)	*Seats*	*Last presidential (October 2015)*	*% of vote*
Chama Cha Mapinduzi (CCM)	189	John Pombe Magufuli (CCM)	58.5
Chadema	34	Edward Lowassa (CHADEMA)	40.0
Civic United Front (CUF)	32	Other	1.5
Other	2		
Total (directly elected)[a]	**257**	**Total**	**100.0**

[a]Of the 264 directly elected seats, seven members were not returned, leaving 257 directly elected to the National Assembly

People

Tanzania (with the largest population in East Africa) now forms part of the East African Common Market, which came into force in June 2010. There are 120 ethnic groups in Tanzania, none of which exceed 10% of the population, and also some Asian and expatriate minorities. Christianity and Islam are the main religions, comprising c61% and 35% of the population, respectively, and some traditional beliefs. The country was under many influences, including Portuguese, Omani Arabs, British, and German, through the nineteenth century, until after WWI, when Tanganyika (as it was then known) passed to the UK under a League of Nations mandate. After WWII, Tanganyika became a UN trust territory under British control but with increasing moves towards self government, until independence was granted in 1961. A union with the semi-autonomous island of Zanzibar was formed in 1964, and Tanzania was born, the name a portmanteau moniker. Under the country's first president, Julius Nyerere (1961–1985), Tanzania saw single-party socialist rule. Although Nyerere presided over unbroken political stability and fostered a strong national identity, his rule coincided with economic decline. By the late 1970s, Tanzania was a highly state-controlled economy. A war with Uganda and external shocks resulted in major macroeconomic imbalances, with per capita income seeing a marked decline over a 15-year period.

Economic transformation began in the mid-1980s, but Tanzania remains a poor country and ranks low on levels of human development, placing 151st out of 188 countries in the UN Human Development Index in 2016, comparable to Kenya (146) and Uganda (163). Around 70% of the population live in rural communities and two-thirds are employed in agriculture, which accounts for just 25% of GDP. Almost 90% of the land is not arable, meaning the areas available for farming are concentrated by the coastal plains. It is Africa's fourth-largest producer of coffee (after Ethiopia, Uganda and Ivory Coast) and fourth-largest gold exporter (after South Africa, Ghana and Mali). Gas reserves were discovered off the coast in 2012 and East Africa's first major oil pipeline is being built in an agreement with Uganda (completion expected by 2020). Anti-corruption policies have been stepped up in recent years, illustrated by the dismissal of six ministers by President Kikwete in 2012 for "rampant misuse of funds". In September 2017, opposition politician Tundu Lissu was shot and wounded by unknown gunmen in Dar es Salaam. President Magufuli has promised the delivery of a referendum for constitutional change, initiated by his predecessor.

Zanzibar, which consists of two main islands and several smaller ones off the Tanzanian coast, has a population of 1mn (2% of Tanzania's). It is the scene of much of Tanzania's political instability. The mainland government carried out a brutal crackdown on political opponents on Zanzibar and the neighbouring island of Pemba in 2000 after protests organised by the island's opposition party (CUF) against the elections. Zanzibar's elections in 2005 were again marred by violence, intimidation and claims of fraud and vote-rigging by the CUF, which announced an indefinite boycott of Zanzibar's parliament that only ended in 2009. Zanzibar is 98% Islamic.

Debt

	2012	2017
External debt ratios (%)		
Total external debt/GDP	27.3	37.1
Public[a] external debt/GDP	22.5	29.5
Private external debt/GDP	4.8	7.6
Total external debt/exports of goods and services	121.1	190.2
External debt service ratio	1.5	8.9
Public debt ratios (%)		
Public domestic debt/GDP	8.4	11.6
Public[a] debt/GDP	30.9	41.1

Source: Bank of Tanzania, IMF, Exotix

[a]Public and publicly guaranteed

Public and publicly guaranteed (PPG) external debt was US$15.8bn (27.9% of GDP) in March 2018 on central bank figures, slightly lower than at end-2017 as shown above, partly due to an amortisation of the floating rate note (FRN) in March. Private sector external debt, was an additional US$4.3bn (7.7% of GDP). As a result, total external debt was US$20.2bn, c35.5% of GDP. This total nominal amount has roughly doubled since end-2009, although high GDP growth has prevented such large changes in the ratios. PPG external debt comprised US$14.9bn of disbursed debt and US$877mn in interest arrears. The difference between PPG debt and central government debt comprises the debt owed by public corporations. The largest foreign creditor group was multilateral creditors, owed 47.4% of total external debt, with US$5.6bn multilateral debt owed to the World Bank, as of end-2016. This was through the World Bank's IDA facility, after IBRD lending to Tanzania ended in 2003. Other multilateral creditors include the African Development Bank (AfDB) and the IMF. Around US$150mn was still owed to the IMF from previous programmes. Bilateral creditors' share has decreased, to 10.2% in March 2018, from 16.5% in 2012 and 18.9% in 2009. Bilateral creditors include China, Germany, Japan, the UK, and the US, following the September 2017 Brazilian debt cancellation (see below). The share of commercial creditors has increased from 13.9% in 2009 to 21.1% in 2012, now to 30.8% in March 2018. This was cUS$6.2bn, and a further US$2.3bn in export credits, but these figures include both the public and private sectors and, since no further breakdown is provided by official sources, this leaves a total commercial debt and export credits owed by the public sector of US$4.2bn, and a separate US$4.3bn owed by the private sector. The increasing external commercial debt is owed to commercial banks, and the FRN issued for US$600mn in March 2013, which had US$267mn outstanding in March 2018.

Total PPG (external and domestic) debt was US$22.1bn (39% of GDP) according to the central bank, including US$6.3bn (11.1% of GDP) in domestic debt; 39.2% of domestic public debt securities were held by commercial banks and another 26.9% were held by pension funds. The domestic debt comprises 20.6% of treasury bills and 67.0% of government bonds. On separate figures, Tanzania's domestic debt roughly doubled between 2010 and 2014, and also rose sharply over 2017-Q1 2018, explained by the inclusion of government obligations in pension funds' portfolios.

Over our comparison period of 2012–2017, total external debt increased from 27.3% of GDP to 37.1%, and from 121% of exports of goods and services to 190% (in NPV terms, the debt ratios are lower). External debt service (public and private sectors) also increased from 1.5% of exports in 2012 to 8.9% in 2017. The government's domestic debt increased to 11.6% of GDP, bringing total government debt to 41.1% of GDP at end-2017.

Composition of external debt

External debt by creditor (Mar. 2018)	*Nominal amount outstanding (US$mn)*	*Share of total (%)*
Public and publicly guaranteed external debt	**15,812**	**78.4**
o/w interest arrears	*877*	*4.4*
o/w central government external debt	**15,572**	**77.3**
o/w interest arrears	*846*	*4.2*
o/w official multilateral	9552	47.4
World Bank IDA[a]	5621	29.9
Official bilateral	2057	10.2
Commercial creditors and export credits	4203	20.8
Bond (FRN)	267	1.3
Private sector external debt	**4345**	**21.6**
o/w interest arrears	*812*	*4.0*
Total external debt	**20,157**	**100.0**
o/w interest arrears	*1689*	*8.4*

Source: Bank of Tanzania

[a]Provided separately by the World Bank, latest figure for end-2016

Rescheduling History

Tanzania was an early beneficiary of HIPC debt relief under the enhanced framework. It reached decision point in April 2000 and completion point soon after in November 2001. Tanzania received debt relief of US$2bn in NPV terms. Its common reduction factor was 54%, implying overall debt reduction in NPV terms, after including traditional debt relief mechanisms, of 84.8%. The advent of the multilateral debt relief initiative (MDRI) in 2006 provided 100% cancellation of eligible debt owed to the International Development Association (IDA), the IMF and the AfDB.

Tanzania's debt problems originated from the economic decline seen over the period 1970–1985, over which time it was a highly state-controlled economy. Over this period, policy was based on a familyhood model of society (Ujamaa Socialism) envisaged by the country's first president Julius Nyerere. This helped unify the country socially but, by the mid-1980s, Tanzania suffered from widespread shortages, high inflation, declining agricultural production (the mainstay of the economy since the 1970s), declining exports of cash crops and FX shortages. Since the mid-1980s however, Tanzania has seen three phases of economic transformation. The first, over 1986–1995, saw the gradual liberalisation of the economy. Prices were adjusted to market rates, the exchange rate was liberalised, government intervention in the economy was reduced and trade was liberalised. These reforms began to pay off in the mid-1990s, while the homegrown growth and poverty-reduction strategy (MKUKUTA on the mainland and MKUZA on Zanzibar) gave greater domestic ownership to the reform process. The second phase, over 1996–2006, saw stabilisation and structural reforms gain momentum following the first multi-party elections, held in October 1995. IMF guidance and HIPC debt relief set the stage for improving economic performance over the last decade. At decision point in 2000, the NPV of external debt to exports was projected at c180% in 2001/2002. A better-than-expected export performance, however, meant that debt indicators were significantly better at completion point than had been expected; debt/exports was just over 100% in 2001/2002, followed by a modest rise but still well below decision point projections. Moreover, the actual debt/exports ratio saw a decline from 2004/2005, outperforming even the completion point projections, falling to 92% in 2006/2007. By 2008/2009, the NPV of external debt/exports (PPG basis) had declined to 55%, while debt on the same basis was 21% of GDP. The third phase has been the period since 2006, which has seen the consolidation of reforms such as a post-HIPC mature stabiliser, as reflected by the IMF policy support instrument (PSI) programmes from 2007, detailed below. Since these PSIs started, successive waivers for fiscal slippages have been granted, often due to inadequate tax revenues, in part caused by the large informal sector.

The government's reform programme, which is now in a second five-year development plan, aims to enable economic development and improved public service delivery using management of the macroeconomy, resources, and the budget. The IMF has described the economic reform plan as ambitious and is aiding the fiscal stance with anti-corruption and tax evasion policies, yet the implementation of structural reforms has been slow. Private sector activity could lead future growth, but this will need a predictable business environment, helped by the reform programme. Greater external financing has been used for public investment, while increasing credit to the private sector has also been a target, although future monetary policy must be tied to fiscal developments, which remain slower than planned under the current PSI.

Many debt obligations have medium- and long-term maturities. As of July 2017, the average time to maturity was 11.9 years, so the effect of debt repayment on the government budget is relatively low. In March 2017, an economist from the Bank of Tanzania said that the total government debt/GDP ratio was "below the acceptable ratio of 56%". This suggests that the economy has the capacity to repay its debts without difficulty, especially if infrastructure projects yield the results envisaged. Many longer-maturity loans have been used to finance transportation projects, a gas pipeline and power projects, which can provide the facilities needed for sustained future growth. Given the Bank of Tanzania's positive view on the debt burden, and the long list of new infrastructure projects that the government already has to ensure continued growth (including liquified natural gas, sugar factories and national power projects), it is likely that the government will consider its options for further borrowing.

In 2017, macroeconomic performance was strong, although growth has recently decelerated, from almost 7% in 2016 to 6% in 2017, and inflation has moderated, expected to fall to the authorities' target of 5% in

2018. The slow budget implementation remains a key risk according to the IMF, due to financing shortfalls, including from tax revenue. In September 2017, Tanzania benefitted from the cancellation of US$203mn of debt owed to Brazil, with the hope that new bilateral trade can now be established.

Relations with Multilateral Creditors

The IMF has been supportive of Tanzania since 1976, and particularly since 1996 with back-to-back programmes supporting the authorities' economic programmes. Although the early years were borne out of some necessity (the need for financial assistance and the road to debt relief), more recent performance demonstrates a greater seriousness and maturity about policy making. The IMF's long history of engagement in Tanzania dates back to the mid-1970s. Tanzania had two IMF programmes between 1975–1985 (SBAs over 1975–1976 and 1980–1982), but reform moved slowly and the programmes went off track. While this early period was marked by the country's general economic decline, recent experience—especially in the 2000s—has been much better. Economic performance began to improve after the economic liberalisation that began in 1986, culminating in the delivery of HIPC debt relief in 2001. This process was supported by IMF PRGFs over 1996–2000 and 2000–2003, programmes that were completed successfully.

Since 1996, Tanzania has had consecutive IMF programmes, including an exogenous shocks facility (ESF) and a standby credit facility (SCF) that also ran concurrently with the PSIs. The 2003–2007 programme perhaps marked a watershed moment for Tanzania as it graduated out of debt relief. In April 2006, the authorities expressed interest in a successor programme in the context of a PSI in light of Tanzania's position as a mature stabiliser. A PSI is intended for countries that do not need balance of payments support, but need assistance in designing effective economic programmes that signal to the international community the IMF's endorsement of the government's policies. In February 2007, the IMF approved a three-year PSI, acknowledging its endorsement of the policies outlined in the programme. Despite some waivers, and, crucially, the advent of the global financial crisis, performance under the 2007–2010 PSI, which expired in June 2010, was seen as strong.

The PSI's performance was recognised by the IMF and enabled rapid agreement on the ESF, approved in May 2009, an emergency facility that Tanzania was able to tap when it needed it most—when the global financial crisis hit. Foreign reserves maintenance and balance of payments support were objectives after traditional export receipts declined (a 26% decline in the price of cotton) and tourism and FDI inflows also fell. The IMF concluded that the ESF played a valuable role in maintaining confidence and limiting contagion.

A new three-year PSI was approved in June 2010 upon the completion of the 2007–2010 PSI. An SCF was approved in July 2012, on completion of the fourth review of the 2010–2013 PSI, with access to SDR149mn (cUS$225mn) of which SDR74.6mn (cUS$116mn) was drawn. It was treated as precautionary, initially for 18 months, and intended to provide a financial cushion against declining external demand and limited international financing options, as the planned bond debut was never issued. See the table below for performance details. In December 2013, the Board approved an extension to April 2014 to allow time for the third and final review, which named fiscal consolidation, through more efficient tax collection and contained expenditure, as an objective. The programme expired in April 2014.

In July 2014, a new three-year PSI was approved following the completion of the SCF's final review, with objectives of supporting macroeconomic stability, preservation of debt sustainability, job creation and equitable growth over the medium term. The Board noted the need for fiscal consolidation and efficiency in public spending. The first review was completed in January 2015 with a waiver for the non-observance of one criterion (the non-accumulation of external arrears). The third, fifth and sixth reviews were also completed with waivers granted for the non-observance of criteria, especially due to the difficulty the government has encountered in meeting fiscal targets, as widening the tax base has proved a challenge, in part due to the very large informal sector. A six-month extension was granted to January 2018, to allow time for negotiations of a successor PSI. As of July 2018, SDR101.448mn (cUS$142βmn) remains outstanding, comprising SDR51.714mn from the ESF and SDR49.733 from the SCF.

IMF programmes

Date	*Arrangements*	*Comments*
1986–1988	SBA	
1987–1990	SAFC	
1991–1994	ECF	
1996	SMP	Staff programme adopted by the newly elected government for the first half of the year. Performance was broadly satisfactory.
1996–2000	PRGF (ECF)	Now known as an extended credit facility (ECF). The IMF commended the authorities for the strong record in stabilising the economy under this programme.
2000–2003	PRGF (ECF)	A three-year agreement for SDR135mn (cUS$181.5mn) was approved in April 2000. At completion of the fifth review in November 2002, the programme was extended until June 2003 to allow time for the final review. Waivers were approved for the non-compliance on procedures for foreign borrowing and non-accumulation of external arrears. The sixth and final review was completed in July 2003. A waiver was granted for the non-observance of end February 2003 performance criteria.
2003–2007	PRGF (ECF)	On the completion of the sixth review of the 2000–2003 review in July 2003, the IMF approved a new three-year agreement of SDR19.6mn (cUS$27mn), effective August 2003. The first review was completed in February 2004, with a waiver. The third was in February 2005, with a waiver for net international reserves and modification to criteria on banking law amendments. At the fifth in April 2006, the authorities expressed interest in a successor programme in the context of a PSI. The sixth and final review was completed in February 2007.
2007–2010	PSI	The IMF approved a three-year PSI in February 2007, at the same time as the completion of the sixth and final review of the previous ECF. The first review was completed in June 2007, with a waiver for a missed ceiling on reserve money. In the third review completed in May 2008, the IMF noted recent allegations of fraud and corruption and that the authorities had taken remedial action after a breach of Article VIII (provision of accurate information to the Fund). The fourth review was completed in December 2008, with waivers for a breach of the reserve money ceiling and the delay in signing a memorandum of understanding delineating responsibilities between the Ministry of Finance and the central bank on liquidity management and financial operations. By the time of the fifth review mission in March 2009, the authorities had also sought additional financial support from the IMF (via an ESF) due to the impact of the global financial crisis. A waiver was granted for non-observance of the ceiling on net domestic financing, which was narrowly missed. The sixth and seventh reviews were rescheduled after the authorities requested an extension of the PSI to end-May 2010 (later extended to early June) to ensure full consistency between the PSI and ESF programmes. The sixth review was completed in November 2009. The IMF Board completed the seventh review on 4 June 2010 and also approved a new three-year PSI.

(*continued*)

(continued)

Date	*Arrangements*	*Comments*
2009–2010	ESF	A 12-month ESF for an amount of SDR219mn (cUS$336mn, 110% of quota) was approved in May 2009, at the same time as the fifth review of the PSI, after the authorities requested high access financial support. The first disbursement of US$244mn was available immediately. The first and second reviews of the ESF were scheduled to take place at the same time as the sixth and seventh reviews of the PSI. In May, the IMF Board approved an extension to 18 June to permit completion of the second review. Two challenges were highlighted as the programme ended: inflation was persistently high amid a low interest environment and, while private sector activity was improving, it displayed greater future potential
2010–2013	PSI	A new three-year PSI was approved in June 2010 upon the completion of the 2007–2010 PSI arrangement. The first of the second PSI took place in December 2010. Despite adverse shocks, the economy exceeded performance expectations. The IMF reported the authorities had limited non-concessional borrowing and remained committed to the debt management strategy, infrastructural projects and structural reform. On completion of the fourth review in July 2012, the IMF Board approved an SCF, which continued beyond this PSI.
2012–2013 (14)	SCF	In July 2012, following completion of the PSI's fourth review, the IMF approved an SCF for SDR149mn (US$225mn) of which SDR74.6mn (US$116mn) was drawn. This was initially for 18 months, under precautionary measures. The first review in January 2013 reported declining inflation and favourable growth with appropriate fiscal and structural reforms aiding fiscal sustainability and private sector activity. Macroeconomic stability was facilitated by the floating exchange rate regime. The second review in May 2013 identified the success of monetary policy in continuing disinflation and then in the following December, the Board approved an extension to April 2014 to allow time for the third and final review, which named fiscal consolidation, through more efficient tax collection and contained expenditure, as an ongoing objective.
2014–2017 (18)	PSI	In July 2014, a new three-year PSI was approved following the completion of the SCF's final review. The first review was completed in January 2015 with a waiver for the non-observance of one criterion (the non-accumulation of external arrears). The second review was completed in July 2015, and the third in January 2016 with a modification of an assessment criterion and a waiver for a missed assessment criterion in June 2015. The October 2015 elections were cited as a cause for slowing policy implementation, while macroeconomic performance remained strong. Along with the Article IV consultation, the fourth review was completed in July 2016, as the IMF noted the continuing growth of almost 7% and moderate inflation. Before completing the fifth review, waivers were granted for the non-observance of end-June 2016 assessment criteria on fiscal consolidation and domestic expenditure arrears, which were excused since slippages were only minor. The sixth review, completed in June 2017, again came with waivers for missed criteria due to missed tax revenue targets. A six-month extension was granted to January 2018 to allow time for negotiations for a successor PSI, although the seventh review in January 2018 was concluded without a successor programme in place. Waivers were granted for minor fiscal slippages during 2017.

Source: IMF. Tanzania joined the IMF in 1962

The World Bank has had many ongoing projects in Tanzania and has provided US$183mn since 2000 to improve transportation. As of August 2018, 37 projects are active in the country, including two new projects in 2018. The AfDB also has several active projects in the country and offers support to small private sector businesses. The AfDB has "High 5" priorities for Tanzania: electrical power provision, food availability and optimal use of arable land, industrialisation, regional integration, and quality of life improvements, including education.

Paris Club History

Tanzania has had seven Paris Club agreements since 1986, six of which are still active, as of August 2018. Its most recent treatments, in 2000 and 2002, followed from debt relief under the HIPC initiative after it reached completion point in November 2001. At that time, this represented the cancellation of 56% of total Paris Club debt and the overall treatment (cancellation or rescheduling) of 71% of outstanding Paris Club debt.

Paris Club agreements

Date	*Terms*	*Status*	*Details*
1986	Classic	Fully repaid	
1988	Toronto	Active	Amount treated US$341mn. Repayment of non-ODA credits over 14 years, with eight years of grace, after cancellation to a rate of 33%. Repayment of ODA credits over 25 years with 14 years of grace.
1990	Toronto	Active	Amount treated US$199mn.
1992	London	Active	Amount treated US$691mn. Repayment of non-ODA credits over 23 years, with six years of grace, after cancellation to a rate of 50%. Repayment of ODA credits over 30 years with 12 years of grace.
1997	Naples	Active	Amount treated US$1608mn. Treatment of arrears as of 30 November 1996, treatment of maturities falling due from 1 December 1996 up to 30 November 1999. Repayment of non-ODA credits over 23 years, with six years of grace, after cancellation to a rate of 67%. Repayment of ODA credits over 40 years with 16 years of grace.
2000 Apr.	Cologne	Active	Amount treated US$711mn. Treatment of arrears as of 31 March 2000, treatment of maturities falling due from 1 April 2000 up to 31 March 2003. Repayment of non-ODA credits over 23 years, with six years of grace, after cancellation to a rate of 90%. Repayment ODA credits over 40 years with 16 years of grace.
2002 Jan.	HIPC initiative exit	Active	Treated US$1245mn, of which US$973mn being cancelled and US$272mn being rescheduled in an agreement with 14 participating creditors. Treatment of stock as of 1 January 2002.

Source: Paris Club

In September 2017, Brazil cancelled US$203mn of debt owed by Tanzania from a loan in 1979 for the construction of the Morogoro-Dodoma road. This loan had previously hindered their trade relationship. It is hoped that this will open new bilateral trade and finance opportunities. Among all African countries, BRICs (Brazil, China, India, and Russia) are the largest trading partners and are large creditors and investors.

Sovereign Commercial Debt

Public external debt from commercial creditors and export credits is small but increasing, to 20.8% of total external debt in Q1 18 from 10.4% in 2012, reflecting mainly increased debt owed to foreign commercial banks. Historically, Tanzania has had a conservative borrowing strategy, which has eschewed commercial sources of finance in favour of concessional loans, and which saw one commercial debt agreement (a small debt buy-back operation) in 2001.

Commercial debt agreements

Date	*Details*
April 2001	Buyback of US$156mn of debt comprising US$76.6mn of eligible principal debt and US$79.2mn of interest. Buyback price set at 12 cents per US dollar of principal. Funded by the World Bank's DRF and governments of Germany and Switzerland.

Source: World Bank GDF

The government said in May 2008 that it intended to get a sovereign rating and potentially issue a eurobond, but plans were put on hold with the advent of the global financial crisis. A bond issue was, however, back on the authorities' agenda in May 2010 as new external financing was deemed both sustainable and needed for projects. Indeed, the authorities' then new three-year PSI, approved in June 2010, allowed for non-concessional borrowing of US$1.5bn over the three-year period, at a roughly even pace over the period.

Tanzania issued its first (and still only, to date) sovereign eurobond in 2013, the details of which are in the table below. The US$600mn floating rate note (FRN) was issued in March 2013 with a final maturity in 2020 and an average life at issue of five years. The bond began amortising in March 2016, leaving just US$266.7mn outstanding after the March 2018 amortisation. Proceeds were to be used for selected infrastructure projects. Despite previous suggestions that the country would obtain a rating first, this did not happen and Tanzania became an unusual example of where a bond was issued without the existence of a sovereign rating. During 2017, it was reported that the government was again pursuing a rating and, in March 2018, Moody's assigned a first-time rating of B1 to the Government of Tanzania, with a negative outlook due to the effect on businesses of unpredictable policy. The government hopes to issue a eurobond to fund infrastructure projects; the process to issue a US$700mn bond was restarted in 2017. It is likely to clear domestic arrears and establish a repayment reputation, before attempting to issue while global interest rates remain low.

Tanzania FRN bond
United Republic of Tanzania FRN 2020
Bloomberg ticker: TNZNIA

Borrower	United Republic of Tanzania
Issue date	8 March 2013
Form	Eurobond
ISIN	XS0896119897
Issue size	US$600mn
Issue outstanding	US$266.7mn
Currency	US dollar
Denomination	US$20,000 and US$1000 thereafter
Amortisation	11.1% amortising every March and September, commencing 8 March 2016
Final maturity date	18 April 2023
Coupon/interest	Floating, US 6m LIBOR plus 600bps (currently, 8.24%), paid semi-annually March and September
Day count	30/360
Method of transfer	Euroclear/Clearstream
Settlement period	T + 2
Governing law	English
Managers	Standard Bank PLC

Source: Bloomberg

Corporate Bond Markets

There is currently one outstanding 144A USD bond issued by a Tanzanian corporate. This is the five-year Swala Oil & Gas (Tanzania) PLC bond issued in January 2018. There have been six other USD-denominated bonds issued by two corporates in Tanzania (DEDE Reality Ltd and Wentworth Resources Ltd), although all of these have matured. The domestic corporate bond market is very limited. There are only two corporate bonds outstanding on the DSE, out of 12 that have been issued, according to Bloomberg in October 2017.

In October 2017, graphite exploration company Volt Resources appointed Exotix to raise funds from African institutions, with plans to raise up to US$40mn using a seven-year USD-linked TZS-denominated Tanzanian bond issue, on the DSE, before its planned first production in Tanzania before the end-18. This bond is currently awaiting approval from the Tanzanian regulator (CMSA). A Chinese offtake partner, China National Building Materials General Machinery, gave positive feedback on samples from Volt's Bunyu project in Tanzania. Its fire-retardant properties make graphite a useful building material and its use in batteries for electric vehicles could see a rise in demand in the coming years.

In January 2018, Swala Oil & Gas (Tanzania) plc ("Swala"), the first oil and gas company listed on the Dar es Salaam stock exchange with a significant local ownership, announced that it had arranged acquisition financing through Exotix after reaching an agreement with Orca Exploration Group Inc. ("Orca") under the terms of which the company's subsidiary Swala (PAEM) Limited ("SPL") shall acquire up to 40% of Orca's wholly owned Mauritius subsidiary, PAE PanAfrican Energy Corporation ("PAEM") for a total consideration of up to US$130mn. Exotix placed a gross US$25mn from US institutions under an early bird 144A USD bond offering, a first for a Tanzanian company. Tanzanian, East African and international investors will be accessed in September for a follow-on tranche of US$50mn fundraising via a Mauritian bond and additional tapping of the 144A USD bond. The Mauritian US$50mn bond was launched on 31 August 2018 as a five-year (non-call 2) USD bond.

Trinidad and Tobago

Nominal GDP (US$mn, 2018)[a]		23,284
Population (thousand, 2018)[a]		1375
GDP per capita (USD, 2018)[a]		16,931
Credit ratings (long-term foreign currency)[b]	Fitch	NR
	Moody's	Ba1
	S&P	BBB+

[a]IMF WEO October 2018
[b]As at end-September 2018

Country Summary

- Trinidad and Tobago, culturally diverse, has established itself as the Caribbean's main industrial and financial centre, driven by significant oil and gas revenues. About half of the country's natural gas production is converted into liquefied natural gas (LNG) at the Atlantic LNG facility in Trinidad and exported under long-term contracts and on the spot market. Trinidad and Tobago is the single largest supplier of LNG to the United States and the fifth largest exporter of LNG in the world. Real GDP growth averaged 6% over the noughties, and the country built significant fiscal and external buffers, with low public debt and high reserves cover.
- Lower energy prices and output since 2014 however, have contributed to a period of weak growth, widening fiscal deficits and a rising public

Exotix Capital, *Exotix Developing Markets Guide*,
https://doi.org/10.1007/978-3-030-05867-8_39

debt burden. Real GDP growth is projected to turn positive (just) in 2018 after a two-year recession, although growth has actually struggled to recover on a consistent basis since 2008 (real GDP growth has averaged −1.0% over the nine years 2009–2017—a near decade long recession). The government is aware of the high dependence on earnings from the energy sector and is encouraging diversification away from it.

- Headline external debt ratios look low, but gross public debt at a wider consolidated level, including contingent liabilities, is high and rising (c80% of GDP in 2017), mainly driven by rising domestic public debt. Despite foreign public debt more than doubling in USD terms since 2012, it remains low (16% of GDP, 33% of exports). Commercial creditors (mainly bonds) now account for most of its public external debt. However, fiscal consolidation is required to put public debt on a sustainable path and the weak financial situation at Petrotrin, the state-owned oil company, poses another vulnerability, especially with a bond maturity in August 2019. Reserves cover, though, remains strong and savings (in the oil stabilisation fund, HSF) amount to a further 25% of GDP, so net debt may be much lower.

Economic data	*Avg*[a]	*2014*	*2015*	*2016*	*2017 (e)*	*2018 (f)*	*2019 (f)*
Real GDP growth	1.4	−1.2	1.7	−6.1	−2.6	1.0	0.9
Inflation (annual average)	7.2	5.7	4.7	3.1	1.9	2.3	3.1
Current account (% of GDP)	17.1	14.7	7.6	−2.9	10.2	10.7	7.3
Reserves (US$mn, end-period)[b]	9447	11,497	9933	9466	8370	7965[c]	–
Reserves/imports (months)[d]	10.9	12.7	11.2	11.6	11.0	–	–
Overall fiscal balance (% of GDP)[e]	−2.1	−4.7	−8.1	−12.0	−11.0	−6.0	−4.6
Currency (ticker)	Trinidad and Tobago dollar (TTD)						
FX regime	De jure floating but in practice classified as a de facto stabilised arrangement by the IMF which is heavily managed against the US dollar.						
Key exports	Petroleum gas (36.4%), ammonia and chemicals (33.5%), refined petroleum (12.6%), iron and metals (6.8%). Goods exports were US$9.5bn in the four quarters to Q3 17, while services exports were just US$1.1bn.						

Source: IMF WEO Database, IMF Country reports, Central Bank of Trinidad and Tobago, OEC

[a]10-year average to 2016 unless otherwise stated

[b]Net official reserves

[c]Latest figure, May 2018

[d]Average over 2011–2016 only, months of the current year's imports of goods, services and private transfers

[e]Overall government net lending

Key figures		*Party*	*Since*
President	Paula Mae Weekes	–	Mar. 2018
Prime minister	Dr Keith Rowley	PNM	Sep. 2015
Minister of finance	Colm Imbert	PNM	Sep. 2015
Key opposition figure	Kamla Persad-Bissessar[a]	UNC	Sep. 2015
Central bank governor	Dr Alvin Hilaire	–	Dec. 2015

[a]Previously Prime Minister from May 2010 until September 2015. The then President appointed her opposition leader following the 2015 elections.

Politics

Executive power

Concentrated on the President, who is both chief of state and head of government, replacing the British monarch in 1976. The President, who is indirectly elected by an electoral college comprised of members of the country's House of Representatives and the Senate, also heads the cabinet and has the power of veto, although constitutional amendments in 1995 mean this can be overturned by the legislature on a simple majority. A runoff vote is avoided if a candidate obtains either 40% of the vote or 35% and a 5pp lead over the nearest rival. The President appoints a Prime Minister following legislative elections, usually the leader of the winning party, to serve a five-year term.

Presidential term: Five years, renewable indefinitely **Parliamentary term**: Five years

Legislature

Bicameral parliament consists of the Senate, which has 31 seats, 16 members appointed by the ruling party, 9 by the president and 6 by the opposition party, to serve a maximum of five years. The House of Representatives has 41 seats; members are elected by popular vote to serve five-year terms. Parliament approved an increase in the number of seats in the House of Representatives from 36 to 41 in 2005.

Senate (31 seats)
16 members are appointed by the ruling party, 9 by the president and 6 by the opposition party.

House of Representatives (41 seats)
Directly elected.

Tobago has a unicameral House of Assembly with 12 members serving four-year terms, established in 1980 to rectify some disparities between the two islands. It is separate from, and has limited power in comparison with, the national government.

Elections

Next due	*Legislative: March 2020; Presidential: March 2023*	
Last legislative election[a] *(September 2015)*	*Seats*	*% of vote*
People's National Movement (PNM)	23	51.7
United National Congress (UNC)	17	39.6
Congress of the People (COP)	1	6.0
National Joint Action Committee (NJAC)	0	0.8
Other	0	1.9
Total	**41**	**100.0**

[a]House of Representatives

People

The main ethnic groups are East Indian (35.4%), African (34.2%), mixed African/East Indian (7.7%) and other mixed (15.3%). English is the official language, but Spanish and others are widely spoken. Christianity is the dominant religion, with all denominations combined accounting for 55% of the population, followed by Hinduism at 18% and Islam at 5%. In 1498, Christopher Columbus landed in Trinidad, claimed it for Spain and named it after the Catholic Holy Trinity. In 1596, Tobago was claimed by the British and Tobago's first Assembly was established in 1769. Various European forces disputed rights over Tobago until the French captured it in 1781, converting it into a sugar colony. The Spanish ceded Trinidad to Britain in 1802 under the Treaty of Amiens and the French ceded Tobago to Britain in 1814 under the Treaty of Paris. 1801 saw a slave uprising in Tobago and the first Chinese workers were brought to Trinidad in 1806, one of several labour-importations that led to the very diverse society in the country today. Slavery was abolished in 1834 and indentured workers were brought in from India to work on the sugar plantations. Labour from other islands, Portugal, Syria and Lebanon were subsequently brought to the country. The first oil well was drilled in Trinidad in 1857 and commercial oil production later began in 1908. The first national elections were held in 1925, although universal suffrage was only introduced in 1945. Politics has traditionally been ethnically divided, with Afro-Trinidadians supporting the PNM, the current ruling party which was founded in 1956, and Indo-Trinidadians supporting various India-majority parties, such as the United National Congress (UNC), currently the main opposition party. Trinidad and Tobago gained its independence from Britain in 1962. A period of unrest followed with violent protests over economic conditions in 1970, multiple sector strikes in 1975, politically motivated shootings and attacks in 1980, and an attempted coup by over 100 Islamist radicals in 1990. The 2010 election for the House of Representatives was called two years earlier than required by law by the then Prime Minister Patrick Manning (PNM), to thwart an opposition motion of no confidence against him. The move back-fired. The People's Partnership coalition (led by the UNC), led by Kamla Persad-Bissessar, won a majority of 29 of the 41 seats and Ms Persad-Bissessar became the country's first female PM. The PNM under Keith Rowley won the following election in 2015 with 23 seats, versus 18 for the People's Partnership coalition. In March 2018, Paula Mae Weekes succeeded Anthony Carmona as president. She was the only nominee and so was deemed elected without a vote actually taking place. As the second largest country in the English-speaking Caribbean, Trinidad and Tobago takes a prominent role in the Caribbean Community and Common Market (CARICOM) and supports CARICOM economic integration. It is also active in the Summit of the Americas process and supports the establishment of the Free Trade Area of the Americas (FTAA).

Debt

	2012	2017
External debt ratios (%)		
Total external debt/GDP	5.8	16.2
Public external debt[a]/GDP	5.8	16.2
Private external debt/GDP	n/a	n/a
Total external debt/exports of goods and services	8.3	32.9
External debt service ratio (public)[a]	1.0	2.0
Public debt ratios (%)		
Public domestic debt[a]/GDP	31.6	46.1
Public debt[a]/GDP	37.3	62.3
Public debt (including contingent liabilities)/GDP	53.9	82.7

Source: Central Bank of Trinidad and Tobago, IMF, Exotix

[a]Central government

External debt owed by Trinidad's central government stood at US$3.5bn at the end of 2017, according to the central bank. Commercial creditors were its largest single creditor group, amounting to 59% of the total (10% of GDP). This was mainly in the form of bonds (totalling cUS$2bn), along with some other, smaller commercial bank debt. Multilateral creditors are the next largest creditor group and accounted for 30% of the total, while bilateral creditors represented 8% of the total. No further breakdown of multilateral or bilateral creditors is given, although the central bank noted that the government contracted a number of new loans in the second half of 2017 totalling about US$130 mn from the IADB, and US$23 mn from the Export-Import Bank of China. Official figures do not include private sector external debt, and such statistics are not available from other sources.

Both the level and composition of Trinidad's central government external debt have changed significantly over recent years. Central government external debt was just US$1.5bn in 2012, so debt has more than doubled in US$ terms since then, and at the time, multilateral creditors accounted for nearly half the debt, while bonds (amounting to just US$500mn) accounted for a third. Not only has the US$ amount increased, but the debt has nearly tripled as a share of GDP; although at just 16% of GDP, it remains low by most standards. This rise in the debt/GDP ratio is also due to a fall in nominal GDP, due to lower oil prices since 2014, although we note that the level of nominal GDP reported by the authorities has historically been higher than the IMF. For instance, the central bank reported nominal GDP in 2017 at TT$156bn (cUS$23.2 bn), a 7% increase on the IMF's latest

WEO figure (from April 2018) of TT$146bn (US$21.6bn)—although the IMF looks to have closed the gap now, with upward revisions to its 2016 and 2017 nominal GDP figures according to the end-of-mission statement for the 2018 Article IV published on 6 July (this showed nominal GDP in 2017 at TT$154.4bn, up nearly 6% from the WEO estimate). Exotix uses the IMF WEO figures in calculating debt/GDP ratios here (using the central bank's GDP figure, CG external debt would be 15.1% of GDP). Debt to exports was just 33%, although the ratio has also increased due to the rise in the nominator and the fall in the denominator. Exports of goods and services have fallen by 40% since 2012, from US$17.7bn to US$10.7bn (the figure for 2017 is based on the first three quarters of the year on an annualised basis), with most of this fall being driven by the fall in goods exports (goods exports account for 90% of goods and services exports). The central government external debt service ratio was just 2% in 2017.

Trinidad's central bank reports public debt figures at a number of levels. Central government domestic debt was 46% of GDP in 2017 (using IMF WEO GDP—it was 43% of GDP using the central bank's GDP figure), up from 32% in 2012, although in local currency terms the rise was only 30%, much lower than the rise in CG external debt. This means overall central government debt (domestic and external) was 62% of GDP (58.3% using central bank GDP), up from 37% in 2012. However, Trinidad also reports other public sector debt owed to state enterprises and statutory authorities, collectively referred to as contingent liabilities, which amounted to another 20% of GDP (19% using central bank GDP) in 2017 (up from 16.5% in 2012), and adds this to central government debt to give total gross public debt. On that basis, total gross public debt in 2017 was 83% of GDP (77.3% using central bank GDP), which amounted to cUS$18bn, up from 54% of GDP in 2012. The central bank also reports net central government and net public debt, both net of open market operations (OMOs)—central bank sterilisation activities—at c27% of GDP and 62% of GDP respectively. The IMF's latest figures in its 2018 Article IV mission in July 2018 put central government debt at 42% of GDP in 2017, up from 24% in 2014, and remaining at c43% over 2019–2023, while gross public sector debt (NFPS basis) was 61% of GDP in 2017, up from 40% in 2014, and remaining at c64% over 2019–2023.

However, to some extent, the gross debt position is partially offset by savings in the country's oil stabilisation fund, the Heritage and Stabilisation Fund (HSF). HSF assets amounted to 25% of GDP in 2017 according to IMF figures. This could mean net public sector debt is much lower, at only 35% of GDP.

Composition of external debt

External debt by creditor (end-2017)	*Nominal amount outstanding (US$mn)*	*Share of total (%)*
Public sector external debt[a]	**3501.1**	**100.0**
o/w Official multilateral	1076.2	30.7
Official bilateral	287.8	8.2
Private creditors	2137.2	61.0
Bonds	2047.7	58.5
Banks	89.5	2.6
Private sector external debt	**n/a**	**n/a**
Total external debt	**3501.1**	**100.0**

Source: Central Bank of Trinidad and Tobago

[a]Central government

Rescheduling History

Trinidad and Tobago has limited experience of debt restructuring, but has not needed to reschedule any debt since 1990. Successive governments have always honoured commitments of previous administrations, since the country's international bond debut in 1992. Panama is the only other Caribbean or Central American country to achieve significant debt reduction in the past 25 years without defaulting.

Previous restructuring experiences (both official and commercial debt) came after the fall in oil prices in the 1980s. The national reliance on oil exports dates back to the 1970s, when oil prices rose and the country became dependent on the extraction and exportation of one product, allowing the rest of the economy to fall behind, becoming inefficient and uncompetitive. Until oil prices started to fall in the 1980s, Trinidad and Tobago built up large international reserves, government spending had increased and the economy had specialised, adapted to high government expenditure. When oil prices fell, a severe knock-on effect impacted other sectors, and it became difficult to obtain credit on the international credit markets. During the second half of the 1980s, the government began putting greater emphasis on the use of domestic financial markets as a source of financing. Despite some fiscal consolidation and divestment attempts, Trinidad and Tobago was forced to restructure some bilateral and commercial debt between 1989 and 1990, which included the deferral of external debt repayments falling due between 1988 and 1992 for four years, to be restarted in 1993. This effectively closed off the external credit market to Trinidad and Tobago for this period. The only exceptions were the funds derived from drawdowns on loan contracts that had been signed before September 1988 and from an IMF stand-by facility. Despite the external environment improving significantly since then, the government has shown reluctance to enter into international financing arrangements. In any case, its financial position improved markedly over the 1990s, when the primary surplus averaged 4% per year, rising to 4.4% per year over the noughties, according to IMF WEO data, and real GDP growth averaged over 5% over the twenty years to 2010. Per capita income rose five-fold between 1993 and 2008.

However, macro concerns have resurfaced in recent years with the fall in the oil price since 2014. Indeed, the fiscal position began to weaken even before then, with the primary surplus falling to just 1% in 2011 and close to balance in 2012 (according to WEO data), as counter-cyclical policies meant the surpluses seen before the global financial crisis were not repeated. A primary deficit of 1.3% was recorded in 2013, and this widened over the following years to 10% of GDP in 2016, only easing slightly to 8% in 2017, due to lower oil prices and weaker growth. The country saw a double dip recession, with a small contraction in 2014, followed by a short rebound in 2015, and recession again over 2016–2017 (with real GDP falling a cumulative 8.5%), although growth is expected to return in 2018 (just, with growth projected at 1% according to the IMF's 2018 Article IV mission in July, up from its WEO forecast of 0.2%). But even before the 2014 recession, growth averaged only 0.7% over 2011–2013, and in reality, barring a couple of positive years, growth has struggled to recover on a consistent basis since 2008. Real GDP growth has averaged −0.7% over the nine years 2009–2017—marking a near decade long recession. As a result, the debt burden (gross government debt, IMF WEO definition) has risen to over 40% of GDP in 2017 (41.3%) from a low of 14% in 2008, and is expected to remain at this level over the medium term. In particular, the financial situation at Petrotrin, the state-owned oil company, has weakened. However, international liquidity, judged by net international reserves, remains strong, which Exotix calculates at around 11 months of imports of goods and services at end-2017. Savings in the Heritage and Stabilisation Fund (HSF) also provide a liquidity cushion.

Relations with Multilateral Creditors

Trinidad and Tobago has only ever had two IMF programmes, both of which were a long time ago (the most recent ended in 1991). These programmes coincided with the two Paris Club agreements and a commercial debt restructuring in 1989, which became necessary after oil prices fell in the 1980s. The IMF continues to provide Article IV assessments, which are on the standard annual cycle, although these have not always been regular. The most recent, the 2017 Article IV, was approved by the IMF Board in November 2017. The IMF published a detailed end-of-mission statement for the 2018 Article IV visit on 6 July 2018.

In its 2017 Article IV review, the IMF noted that low energy prices and production and weakness in the non-energy sector had taken their toll on the fiscal and external positions, with risks tilted to the downside. The authorities were urged to use its buffers to smooth out the pace of adjustment. The IMF noted that the draft FY2017/18 budget constituted a significant step along the needed fiscal adjustment path, although restoring macroeconomic stability, managing external imbalances, and supporting broad based and inclusive growth would require additional fiscal consolidation, measures to restore balance in the foreign exchange market and structural reforms. In particular, while commending the steps taken in the FY2016/17 and FY2017/18 budgets towards fiscal adjustment, including the introduction of property, excise and gaming taxes, royalties on natural gas production and elimination of fuel subsidies, the IMF stated that more adjustment is needed. The budget introduced processes to improve revenue collection, streamline expenditure and achieve full cost recovery pricing, yet the Fund notes in addition the need to further broaden the VAT base, raising the overall VAT rate to the regional average, finalise reforms of the fiscal regime for oil and gas, and reduce the cost of transfers and subsidies through better targeting.

IMF programmes

Date	*Arrangements*	*Comments*
1989–1990	SBA	Amount agreed was SDR99mn (58% of Quota, US$130mn equivalent), of which all was drawn and since repaid.
1990–1991	SBA	Amount agreed was SDR85mn (50% of Quota, US$111mn equivalent), of which all was drawn and since repaid.

Source: IMF. Trinidad and Tobago joined the Fund in 1963

Trinidad and Tobago has had no lending programme with the World Bank since graduation in 2003. However, technical and advisory services have been provided, with a focus on promoting a better investment climate, economic diversification and increased competitiveness, AML/CFT, strengthening institutional capacity; and, building a modern and efficient public sector. The IADB's country strategy for the period 2016–2020 aims to remove constraints to economic diversification and encourage policy changes to adapt to new lower commodity prices, by strengthening government institutions and encouraging private sector development. The active portfolio consists of 10 loans for a total of US$504mn, 64% of which is undisbursed. Projects for the development of water and sanitation are the largest recipients of funding. The Caribbean Development Bank (CDB) has no major projects, although its country goals include knowledge-driven development, enhancing competitiveness through innovation and improving environmental sustainability.

Paris Club and Bilateral Creditors

Trinidad and Tobago had two agreements with the Paris Club, in the late 1980s/early 1990s, both of which have been repaid in full. Both agreements included creditor countries Austria, Canada, France, Germany, Italy, Japan, the UK and the USA. The 1989 agreement also included Switzerland.

Paris Club agreements

Date	*Terms*	*Status*	*Details*
Jan 1989	Classic	Fully repaid	US$209mn treated
Apr 1990	Classic	Fully repaid	US$110mn treated

Source: Paris Club

Bilateral creditors are small relative to overall government external debt, accounting for 8% of the total, and under 2% of total government debt. The bilateral debt stock has been increasing gradually since 2000, standing at cUS$290mn over 2016–2017 compared to US$100mn in 2012. The US, the UK and Canada, and previously Germany, are among its bilateral creditors. China is also a bilateral creditor. Japan and India are among its main bilateral direct investors. Across the Caribbean region, there is a strong presence of Canadian banks, acting as subsidiaries.

Sovereign Commercial Debt

Trinidad has seen one episode of commercial bank debt rescheduling, back in 1989, although has not restructured since. The amount treated was US$473mn (c10% of GDP) with an extension of maturities.

Commercial debt agreements

Date	*Details*
Dec. 1989	Restructuring of US$473mn of maturities over September 1988—August 1992 into a new US$450mn floating rate bond (LIBOR + 93.75bp) maturing in 2000.

Source: Exotix, World Bank GDF

Trinidad and Tobago has four outstanding US$ eurobonds, totalling US$1.95bn. Trinidad began issuing bonds in the international market during the 1990s, and even issued a very small GBP bond (GBP50mn) in 1984, but with the exception of a US$450mn FRN US$ bond issued in its 1989 restructuring agreement, subsequent bonds were very small (generally cUS$200mn or less). After the FRN, its first issue was a 5-year 11.5% US$100mn issue (144A eligible) in 1992, one of seven bonds issued during the decade, through to 2000, mostly in US$, although a yen-denominated bond (2036 maturity) was also issued in 2000 along with a twenty-year US$ bond of US$250mn (which is still outstanding). A break then came until 2007, which saw the issue of a twenty-year bond (2027), but again it was only US$150mn in size. Trinidad's first proper, REGS/144A, bond of benchmark size came in 2013 (only five years ago), with a US$550mn ten-year issue (4.375% 2024). This was followed in 2016 with a US$1bn 4.5% ten-year bond (2026). It therefore has four US$ bonds outstanding, although only its most recent two are of any size.

The current outstanding US$-denominated eurobonds are shown in the table below, and details for the most recently issued US$1bn 4.5% 2026 bond, issued in August 2016, are also given.

Trinidad and Tobago's outstanding sovereign US$ bonds

Description	*Size*	*Maturity type*	*Issue date*
US$ 9.75% Due 2020	US$250mn	Bullet	Jun. 2000
US$ 4.375% Due 2024	US$550mn	Bullet	Dec. 2013
US$ 4.5% Due 2026	US$1000mn	Bullet	Aug. 2016
US$ 5.875% Due 2027	US$150mn	Bullet	May 2007

Source: Bloomberg

Trinidad and Tobago bond
Trinidad and Tobago 4.5% 2026
Bloomberg ticker: TRITOB

Borrower	Trinidad and Tobago
Issue date	4 August 2016
Form	Eurobond
ISIN	USP93960AG08
Issue size	US$1000mn
Currency	US dollar
Denomination	Minimum of US$200,000 and US$1000 thereafter
Amortisation	Bullet
Final maturity date	4 August 2026
Coupon/interest	4.5%, semi-annually February and August.
Day count	30/360
Method of transfer	Euroclear/Clearstream
Settlement period	T + 2 business days
Governing law	New York
Lead manager	DB

Source: Bloomberg

Corporate Bond Markets

Trinidadian corporates have US$2.1bn in international bonds outstanding, as of October 2017, made up of four REGS/144A bonds from three issuers. The Petroleum Company of Trinidad and Tobago (Petrotrin), the state-owned oil and gas company, has two outstanding issues, a US$850mn 9.75% 2019 bond issued in 2009 and a US$250mn 6% 2022 bond issued in 2007. The 2022 bond was US$750mn in size at issue, and has been amortising semi-annually since November 2010 (c4.2% each payment). These are the only two bonds the company has issued. There is no explicit government guarantee on either of Petrotrin's bonds. The National Gas Company of Trinidad and Tobago (NGCTT), a state-owned natural gas company, has one bond outstanding, a US$400mn 6.05% 2036 bond issued in 2006. The bond is the company's only issue. Trinidad Generation UnLtd (TRNGEN), a JV between the government and AES of the US, has one bond outstanding, a US$600mn 5.25% 2027 bond issued in 2016. The bond is the company's only issue.

Petrotrin will face a US$850mn bullet bond maturity in August 2019 and Prime Minister Keith Rowley has expressed concern over the state of infrastructure and debt sustainability of Petrotrin and other state enterprises (see below). After undertaking a large upgrade to its refinery, completed in 2015, the company has been left highly indebted, due to its issuance of the two bonds currently outstanding used to finance the refinery. First, a US$750mn bond was issued in July 2007, which had initially been scheduled for just US$350mn, to finance a gasoline optimisation project (GOP). A second bond of US$850mn was issued in August 2009 for the financing of the latter stages of the GOP, despite it being over a year behind schedule and US$3.6bn over budget. This was the Caribbean's largest ever investment-grade bond, issued for refinery upgrade projects. The GOP was planned at a cost of US$600mn, but national media reported the company president's announcement in December 2013, after its completion, that it had over-run by US$560mn. Petrotrin's president said that a number of projects had suffered cost overruns due to procurement methods. The energy minister expressed concern over the capacity of the company to service the debt, amid scepticism over whether the GOP will have the potential to produce sufficient revenue to meet the debt servicing requirements. The fall in crude oil prices and declining refinery margins had contributed to a 50% fall in the company's revenue between 2012 and 2016, and cashflow problems had led to significant unpaid taxes. In September 2017, the prime minister announced that Petrotrin would be restructured and a new board would be installed to do this. As of end-2017, requirements have been met. However the new company president Fitzroy Harewood described debt repayments, including the US$850mn 2019 bullet maturity, as "a huge challenge". Responding to its difficulties, the loss-making company announced at end-August 2018 that it will close the Pointe-a-Pierre refinery, as part of its corporate restructuring plan. The company reported at the time that it had TT$12bn in debt (US$1.8bn), was projected to lose TT$2bn (US$0.3bn) annually, owed TT$3bn (US$0.4bn) in taxes and royalties to the government, and needed a TT$25bn (US$3.7bn) cash injection to remain in operation. Subsequently, in September, media reported that the company was expected shortly to launch a request for proposal (RFP) to consider refinancing options for the 2019 maturity.

Descriptions for Petrotrin's 2019 bonds and the National Gas Company and Trinidad Generation bonds are given below.

Petrotrin bond
Petrotrin 9.75% 2019
Bloomberg ticker: PETRTT

Borrower	Petroleum Company of Trinidad and Tobago Ltd
Issue date	14 August 2009
Form	Eurobond
ISIN	USP78954AC19
Issue size	US$850mn
Amount outstanding	US$850mn
Currency	US dollar
Denomination	US$100,000 minimum, increments of US$1000 thereafter
Amortisation	Bullet
Final maturity date	14 August 2019
Coupon/interest	9.75% per annum, paid semi-annually, February and August
Day count	30/360
Method of transfer	Euroclear, Clearstream, DTC, FED FUNDS
Exchange	Berlin, Luxembourg, EUROMFT
Settlement period	T + 2 business days
Joint lead managers	Credit Suisse, JP Morgan, BNP Paribas, Deutsche Bank, Morgan Stanley

Source: Bloomberg

National Gas Company bond
National Gas Company 6.05% 2036
Bloomberg ticker: NGCTT

Borrower	National Gas Company of Trinidad and Tobago
Issue date	20 January 2006
Form	Eurobond
ISIN	USP70809AB71
Issue size	US$400mn
Amount outstanding	US$400mn
Currency	US dollar
Denomination	US$100,000 minimum, increments of US$1000 thereafter
Amortisation	Bullet
Final maturity date	15 January 2036
Coupon/interest	6.05% per annum, paid semi-annually in July and January
Day count	30/360
Method of transfer	FED FUNDS, DTC
Exchange	Berlin
Settlement period	T + 2 business days
Joint lead managers	Citibank, Lehman Brothers

Source: Bloomberg

Trinidad Generation bond
Trinidad Generation 5.25% 2027
Bloomberg ticker: TRNGEN

Borrower	Trinidad Generation Company UnLtd
Issue date	4 November 2016
Form	Eurobond
ISIN	USP9400VAA90
Issue size	US$600mn
Amount outstanding	US$600mn
Currency	US dollar
Denomination	US$200,000 minimum, increments of US$1000 thereafter
Amortisation	Sinkable
Final maturity date	4 November 2027
Coupon/interest	5.25% per annum, paid semi annually
Day count	30/360
Method of transfer	Euroclear, Clearstream
Exchange	Singapore
Settlement period	T + 2 business days
Joint lead managers	Bank of Nova Scotia, Credit Suisse

Source: Bloomberg

Ukraine

Nominal GDP (US$mn, 2018)[a]		126,390
Population (thousand, 2018)[a]		42,639
GDP per capita (USD, 2018)[a]		2964
Credit ratings (long-term foreign currency)[b]	Fitch	B–
	Moody's	Caa2
	S&P	B–

[a]IMF WEO October 2018
[b]As at end-September 2018

Country Summary

- Since independence from the Soviet Union in 1991, Ukraine has wavered politically between Russia and the West, which has produced periods of social unrest and turmoil, as well as economic crisis. Most recently, the political crisis that followed the public's rejection of President Yanukovych's shift away from the EU and towards Russia in November 2013, just a decade after the 'Orange revolution' of 2004, brought with it another period of turmoil, including conflict with Russia over its illegal occupation of Crimea, which still continues.
- The resulting 2014–2015 crisis still shapes Ukraine's economy. Nominal GDP in USD terms fell by 50% from peak to trough over 2013–2015, inflation rocketed and the currency collapsed. But the international support umbrella and IMF-led financing helped to

Exotix Capital, *Exotix Developing Markets Guide*,
https://doi.org/10.1007/978-3-030-05867-8_40

stabilise the economy—at the time of writing, the IMF announced staff agreement on a new stand-by agreement (SBA) to replace the stalled extended fund facility (EFF). Growth has recovered, but private sector confidence remains weak and the impact of fiscal austerity and structural reform have weakened the government of President Poroshenko ahead of the next presidential election in March 2019, partly also because he is perceived as not doing enough to tackle corruption.

- Ukraine has seen a number of commercial debt restructurings and IMF programmes, with varying degrees of success, over the past 20 years. The 2014–2015 crisis was no different. Ukraine was forced to restructure much of its bonded debt as part of its IMF bailout. However, bondholders were able to secure relatively favourable terms. Many banks and corporates also had to restructure their commercial debt. Public debt eased to 72% of GDP in 2017, although it remains high, while growth and investor confidence remain highly dependent on IMF engagement. Ukraine even managed to return to the market with a new 15-year bond issue in autumn 2017, just two years after its sovereign debt restructuring.

Economic data	*Avg*[a]	*2014*	*2015*	*2016*	*2017 (e)*	*2018 (f)*	*2019 (f)*
Real GDP growth	−0.5	−6.6	−9.8	2.4	2.5	3.5	2.7
Inflation (annual average)	14.1	12.1	48.7	13.9	14.4	10.9	7.3
Current account (% of GDP)	−3.9	−3.9	1.7	−1.5	−1.9	−3.1	−3.9
Reserves (US$bn, end-period)[b]	24.7	7.5	13.3	15.5	18.8	18.0[c]	–
Reserves/imports (months)[d]	3.7	1.2	2.9	3.2	3.3	–	–
Overall fiscal balance (% of GDP)[e]	−3.4	−4.5	−1.2	−2.2	−2.2	−2.5	−2.6
Currency (ticker)	Hryvnia (UAH)						
FX regime	De jure floating, according to the IMF. The central bank intervenes to smooth fluctuations in the currency. The IMF classifies Ukraine as maintaining exchange restrictions and having multiple currency practices.						
Key exports	Metals (26%), agriculture (21%), machinery (10%)						

Source: IMF WEO Database, IMF Country Reports, Haver, OEC, Exotix

[a]10-year average to 2016 unless otherwise stated

[b]Foreign reserves from Haver

[c]Latest figure, June 2018

[d]In months of the current year's imports of goods, services and primary income debit, Exotix calculation

[e]General government net lending/borrowing from WEO (excludes Naftogaz balance)

Key figures		*Party*	*Since*
President	Petro Poroshenko	Poroshenko Bloc	Jun. 2014
Prime minister	Volodymyr Groysman	Poroshenko Bloc	Apr. 2016
Minister of finance	Oksana Markarova	Independent	Jun. 2018[a]
Key opposition figure	Yulia Tymoshenko	Fatherland	Mar. 2010
Central bank governor	Yakiv Smoliy	–	Mar. 2018

[a]Acting since June, officially confirmed in November

Politics

Executive power

Ukraine became a parliamentary democracy after constitutional reforms were accepted in 2006. The president is head of the state, and the prime minister and his cabinet of ministers represent the senior executive body. It is the role of the president to nominate the prime minister, who must be elected by parliament. The prime minister subsequently appoints a cabinet, although the appointed cabinet requires parliamentary approval. The exceptions are the foreign and defence ministers, nominated by the president, with approval of deputies.

Presidential term: Five years **Parliamentary term**: Five years

Legislature

Unicameral, the Supreme Council of Ukraine or Verkhovna Rada (450 seats); members voted on a mixed voting system (50% under party lists and 50% under simple-majority constituencies) with a proportional basis to those parties that gain 5% or more of the national electoral vote. Members serve five-year terms. In the 2014 elections, only 438 seats will be filled, with the remaining 12 seats reserved for the contested region of Crimea.

Elections

Next due *Presidential: March 2019; Legislative: November 2019*

Last legislative election (2014)	*Seats*	*Last presidential (2014)*	*% of vote*
Petro Poroshenko Bloc	132	Petro Poroshenko (Independent)	54.70
People's Front	82	Yuliya Tymoshenko (Fatherland)	12.81
Self-Reliance Party	33	Oleh Lyashko (Radical Party)	8.32
Opposition Bloc	29	Anatoliy Hrystenko	5.48
Radical Party of Oleh Lyashko	22	Serhiy Tihipko	5.23
All-Ukrainian Union "Fatherland"	19	Mykhailo Dobkin	3.03
Freedom Party "Svoboda"	6	Vadim Rabinovich	2.25

(*continued*)

(continued)

Elections			
Next due Presidential: March 2019; Legislative: November 2019			
Last legislative election (2014)	*Seats*	*Last presidential (2014)*	*% of vote*
Other	100	Other	8.18
Total	**423**[a]	**Total**	**100.0**

Source: IFES Election Guide

[a]27 seats remained unfilled as voting was not provided in the annexed Autonomous Republic of Crimea and Sevastopol, or some parts of Donetsk and Luhansk

People

Ukraine's population of c40mn live in Europe's second-largest country by land mass, with vast swathes of agricultural plains. The population, which has declined due to net emigration, is comprised of 77.8% Ukrainians, Russians 17.3% with the remaining ethnic groups from surrounding countries. The official language is Ukrainian, although a minority uses Russian as its first language.

Part of the first eastern Slavic state, Kievan Rus, Ukraine was absorbed into the Russian Empire in the late eighteenth century. It was independent for a short period after the fall of czarist Russia, before being reconquered and incorporated in the Soviet Union. In 1921, two-thirds of Ukraine became the Ukrainian Soviet Socialist Republic and the western third became part of independent Poland until the Soviet invasion of Poland in 1939. Millions of deaths were caused by two forced famines in 1921–1922 and 1932–1933, and again during World War II. Since independence from the Soviet Union in 1991, Ukraine has wavered politically between Russia and the West. Pro-Russian Viktor Yanukovych was prime minister in 2002–2004. The "Orange revolution" in late 2004, launched by opposition leader Viktor Yushchenko over rigged elections, appeared to mark a sea-change, resulting in Yushchenko defeating Viktor Yanukovych in a re-run election marred by electoral fraud. However, Yanukovych's comeback was completed by his victory in the February 2010 presidential election, and his coalition government set aside plans to join the EU and NATO as they looked to re-establish stronger ties with Russia. Yanukovych abandoned a trade and cooperation agreement with the EU in November 2013 leading to protests, including the three-month occupation of Kiev's central square (known as Euro-Maidan). The government broke this up in February 2014, resulting in scores of deaths and international condemnation. Yanukovych fled Ukraine for Russia, bringing new elections in June, which saw pro-West Poroshenko become president.

Soon after Yanukovych's departure, Russia invaded Ukraine's Crimean Peninsula, claiming to be attempting to protect ethnic Russians living there. A referendum was held two weeks later to integrate Crimea into the Russian Federation, which was condemned as being illegitimate by the Ukraine government, the EU, the US and the UN General Assembly. Russia has continued to support proxies in Ukraine's eastern Donbas region, fighting against the government. The Minsk Protocol and Memorandum in September 2014 ended the conflict, but fighting continued.

A new agreement in February 2015 has led to steps to implement the peace deal. However, the events took its toll on the economy, causing a deep recession and, ultimately, led to an IMF-led bailout and sovereign default. After real GDP growth was flat in 2013 (and had only grown by 0.2% in 2012), there was a contraction of –6.6% in 2014 and –9.8% in 2015. Real GDP fell by 16% in 2012–2015. Although the new government has brought greater stability to Ukraine, institutions and governance remain weak; Ukraine is ranked low in Transparency International's Corruption Index, 130 out of 180 in the 2017 survey.

Debt

	2012	*2017*
External debt ratios (%)		
Total external debt/GDP	76.8	104.6
Public external debt/GDP	18.4	41.5
Private external debt/GDP	58.5	63.0
Total external debt/exports of goods and services	155.6	216.8
External debt service ratio (PPG[a])	8.2	4.8
Public debt ratios (%)		
Public domestic debt/GDP	14.8	25.9
Public debt/GDP[b]	36.9	72.2

Source: Haver, Ministry of Finance, IMF, World Bank IDS, 2032 Eurobond prospectus, Exotix

[a]MLT plus IMF, Exotix calculation

[b]Based on public finance methodology, so does not equal sum of public domestic and public external debt

Ukraine's overall public debt burden has increased sharply over the past five years, in large part due to the impact of currency devaluation following the 2014–2015 economic and financial crisis. Nominal GDP halved in US dollar terms in 2013–2015. Public debt rose by c4.5 times between 2012 and 2017 in local currency terms, and by just 18% in US dollar terms, despite the fiscal consolidation over the latter half of this period, due to high budget deficits and FX-linked debt. Total public debt (defined as state debt including guarantees) was US$76.3bn at end-17, according to the Ministry of Finance, equating to c72% of WEO GDP, double its share of GDP in 2012. Around 64% of public debt was external (direct debt and guarantees) and 36% was domestic (denominated in local currency or USD). 87% of public debt (external and domestic) was direct, while 13% was guaranteed debt (external and domestic guarantees). In 2017, public external debt (including guarantees) was 46.4% of GDP and public domestic debt (including guarantees) was 25.9% of GDP. Public debt peaked at 81.5% of GDP in 2016, and the ratio fell in 2017 due to a sizeable rebound in nominal GDP in USD terms that year, because of higher inflation.

Ukraine's total external debt was 105% of GDP in 2017. Total external debt was US$116.6bn, based on BPM6 methodology, according to Haver. This was down from US$134.6bn in 2012 (and US$142.1bn in 2014), although the collapse in US dollar GDP during the crisis caused the external debt/GDP ratio to rise sharply from 77% of GDP in 2012 to a peak of 132% in 2015, before falling in 2017. External debt rose from 156% of exports of goods and services in 2012 to 217% in 2017 (having peaked at 248% in 2015) as exports (goods and services) fell by nearly 40%. According to BPM6 methodology, public external debt (general government and central bank) was US$46.3bn (41.5% of GDP) in 2017, while private external debt (banks, corporates and inter-company lending) was US$70.3bn (63.0% of GDP). However, note that public external debt differs modestly between BPM6 and public finance methodologies (c5ppts in 2017). Meanwhile, the external debt service ratio (PPG MLT plus IMF repayments) fell over the period, despite the fall in exports of goods and services, in part due to the fall in debt service following the sovereign restructuring. Exotix calculates public external debt service fell from US$7.2bn in 2012 to US$2.6bn in 2017. However, repayments to the Fund have been a significant portion of overall public sector external debt service over recent years, with heavy principal repayments to the Fund over 2012–2014, averaging cUS$4bn a year, according to the IDS, arising from drawings under previous programmes. After easing over 2016–2018, repayments to the Fund are expected to pick up again over 2019–2022, to cUS$1.6bn a year.

The creditor composition of public external debt, as of May 2018, according to Ministry of Finance figures, is shown in the table below. The composition changed markedly due to the 2014–2015 crisis, with an increased share of official sector debt due to lending from the IMF, the World Bank and European institutions. Total public external debt was US$47.1bn (c39.5% of 2018 projected GDP in the IMF WEO). Direct government external debt (ie excluding guarantees) was c80% of this (US$37.6bn), of which the official sector was owed c45%. This mainly comprised three institutions, the IMF (owed 16%), the World Bank (13%) and the European institutions (EIB, EBRD, and EU) (12%). Other bilateral creditors included Russia, Japan, Canada, and Germany, although these comprised less than 5% of the total. Bondholders accounted for 54% of direct government external debt, cUS$20.5bn in total. This consisted of the US$11.5bn outstanding in bonds issued in the 2015 restructuring (which comprised the original issuance, additional issuance and after allowing for those retired in the 2017 LMO), the US$3bn 2032 bond issued in September 2017, the three UST-guaranteed issues (US$1bn each issued in 2014, 2015 and 2016), and the US$3bn Russia bond (which is subject to litigation). Hence, the US$14.5bn in marketable eurobonds (those that came out of the 2015 restructuring and the new 32s) amounted to 71% of all bonds, 39% of central government direct external debt and 31% of PPG external debt. Government-guaranteed external debt was an additional US$9.5bn. Private external debt was US$70bn (as at March 2018).

Composition of external debt

External debt by creditor (May 2018)	*Nominal amount outstanding (US$bn)*	*Share of total (%)*
Public and publicly guaranteed external debt	**47.1**	**40.3**
o/w Central government direct debt[a]	37.6	32.2
Multilateral	12.1	10.4
IMF	6.0	5.1
World Bank	4.8	4.1
EIB	0.7	0.6
EBRD	0.6	0.5
Bilateral	5.1	4.4
EU	3.3	2.8
Other	1.8	1.5
Eurobonds	20.5	17.6
Guarantees	9.5	8.1
Private external debt[b]	**69.7**	**59.7**
Total external debt	**116.8**	**100.0**

Source: Ukraine Ministry of Finance, Haver, Exotix

[a]Excluding GDP warrants
[b]As of end-March 2018

Rescheduling History

In December 1994, Ukraine accepted the 'Zero Option', under which Russia assumed liability for all Soviet debt allocated to Ukraine (equivalent to just over US$10bn), in exchange for its share of former Soviet assets. This effectively allowed Ukraine to begin with a clean slate regarding external debt.

Ukraine began to accumulate liabilities rapidly from the mid-1990s and, by 1999, public debt had increased to 59% of GDP (IMF WEO). Russia's crisis of 1998 was the catalyst for the Ukraine crisis that followed, and the seeds were similar. Ukraine had a pegged exchange rate, had financed its budget deficits in part by offering high-yielding local currency debt to foreign investors. When demand dried up, so did foreign currency reserves, and with domestic economic policy disjointed, Ukraine attempted piecemeal restructurings before undertaking a more comprehensive restructuring in 2000. In 1999, Ukraine reopened the 16% 2001 bond, in the amount of DEM538mn. But this did not resolve solvency problems and, early the following year, the government proposed an exchange of its five outstanding bonds (which had complicated features) for two new conventional eurobonds, one denominated in dollars and the other in euros.

Prime Minister Yushchenko had little choice but to make a fairly generous offer to secure agreement from a diverse group of international investors. Several other external debts were also rescheduled, including Ukraine's liabilities to the Paris Club and natural gas debt owed to Russia's Gazprom. In October 2001, Ukraine agreed to issue US$1.4bn in 10-year bonds in exchange for NaftoGaz Ukrainy's debt to Russia's Gazprom at terms similar to the July Paris Club restructuring.

The 2008–2009 global financial crisis saw Ukraine turn to the IMF again, but the sovereign avoided payment problems. There were, however, a number of corporate debt restructurings (see Corporate Bond Market section below). In particular, NaftoGaz's problems returned in 2009 and its reform was central to the prevailing IMF programme. A combination of below-market price sales and weak payment discipline led to large cash deficits. The government transferred c2.5% of GDP in 'recapitalisation' bonds to NaftoGaz while, in October 2009, NaftoGaz restructured US$1.6bn of eurobond and bank debt.

Ukraine's most recent and biggest financial crisis came in the aftermath of the country's political crisis in 2013–2014 and Russia's annexation of Crimea and subsequent conflict in the Donbass region of eastern Ukraine, prompting a sovereign default and restructuring and a wave of corporate debt restructurings. Ukraine quickly sought IMF financial assistance in early 2014 through a two-year SBA approved in April (after reserves had already fallen by a quarter), but the crisis triggered a substantial depreciation in the hryvnia, which fell by 48% against the US dollar during 2014, while real GDP fell that year by 6.6% (with a decline of 14% yoy in Q4). Reserves fell by around half, from US$20.4bn at end-2013 to US$7.5bn at end-2014 (and reached a low of US$5.6bn in February 2015). As the SBA went off track, a new four-year IMF EFF was approved in March 2015, which called for a bolder policy response (in part, because of the weak policy response in the previous SBA, but also because the starting point was now lower, as the conflict worsened and the economic situation deteriorated more than expected, leading to bigger financing gaps). The UAH was allowed to float, falling by 53% against the US dollar from UAH/US$16 at end-January 2015 to its peak of UAH34 a month later (the overshooting was soon corrected and the hryvnia settled in a range of 20–25 for the rest of the year). All told, the Ukraine currency fell by c67% against the US dollar from end-2013 to end-2015. Real GDP fell by 9.8% in 2015, and a cumulative 16% over 2013–2015, while nominal GDP fell by 50% in US dollar terms between 2013 and 2015. CPI inflation peaked at 61% yoy in April 2015, although had declined to 9.8% a year later. Recession and increased fiscal expenditure associated with the conflict in eastern Ukraine put added strain on the public finances, and liquidity conditions. Public debt rose to 79% of GDP in 2015, up from just 37.5% in 2012 (IMF WEO) Crucially, the IMF set as a pre-condition for moving forward with the SBA that the government approach its debtholders for a "debt operation" intended to strengthen debt sustainability. Out of the US$40bn (30% of GDP) financing package fronted by the IMF EFF, the IMF's gross contribution was US$17.5bn and other multilaterals and bilaterals provided US$7.2bn. The remaining US$15.3bn was to come from debt operations with holders of public sector debt.

Relations with Multilateral Creditors

Since gaining membership in 1992, Ukraine has had nine financial arrangements with the IMF and the country has been in an IMF programme for all but seven of those years. Its current arrangement, a four-year EFF, was approved in March 2015 and is due to expire in March 2019.

Fund relations have not always been smooth, however. An independent report found the central bank's (NBU) reserves were overstated by between US$391mn in September 1997 to US$713mn in December 1997, following which the IMF agreed to conduct quarterly audits of the reserve position of the NBU. And, in 2009, the programme—an SDR11bn SBA agreed in response to the financial crisis—went off track, as Yushchenko signed a bill to raise the minimum wage by 20%, meaning the IMF could not complete the programme review. More recently, the 2014 SBA went off track within a year as the conflict worsened and the economic situation deteriorated more than expected, leading to bigger financing gaps, while the current 2015 EFF programme has seen numerous delays in completing reviews.

The IMF Board approved a two-year SBA for US$17.01bn (800% of quota) in April 2014 in the aftermath of the country's political crisis and Russia's annexation of Crimea. The programme aimed to provide Ukraine with financial support to implement a reform agenda aimed at addressing large fiscal and current account deficits. The agenda was focused on five key policy areas: exchange rate and monetary policy, financial sector stabilisation, fiscal adjustment, energy sector reform and other structural reforms (especially to fight corruption). The first review was completed in August 2014, but the programme was terminated soon after, due to the worsening conflict and deteriorating economy. The decline in GDP was greater than expected, with a later recovery, due to disruption in industrial production and exports, while inflation was expected to peak at more than double what had been projected in the first review. The real exchange rate was much weaker, the current account deficit wider, reserves lower, and public debt higher (expected to peak at 100% of GDP compared with 70% in the first review). In consequence, the IMF concluded that Ukraine's balance of payments and adjustment needs had increased to levels beyond what could be achieved under the SBA. The programme was subsequently cancelled in favour of a new facility.

The IMF approved a new four-year EFF programme worth US$17.5bn (900% of quota) in March 2015. This followed staff-level agreement reached in February 2015. In approving the programme, the IMF noted that Ukraine faced an exceptionally large financing gap of cUS$40bn over the programme period (2015–2018), equivalent to 31.25% of estimated 2014 GDP. Some three-quarters of the gap resulted from the need to gradually strengthen official reserves to adequate levels, judged to be cUS$18.3bn at end-2015 and cUS$35.2bn at end-2018. The financing gap was expected to be filled by a combination of official and private funds, as well as a comprehensive economic adjustment programme. In particular, official financing was expected to fill 60% (US$24.7bn) of the financing gap, with other multilateral and bilateral lenders providing another US$7.2bn, on top of the IMF money. Private creditors were expected to provide the remaining 40% (US$15.3bn) through a debt operation (see Commercial Debt section below).

Performance under the EFF, which was scheduled to end in March 2019, has been somewhat mixed. Its successes include macro-financial stabilisation, with a pick-up in growth, lower inflation, fiscal discipline and improved stability in the financial system. A significant fiscal adjustment, amounting to 8% of GDP in the overall balance (including Naftogas) in one year (from 10.0% in 2014 to 2.2% in 2015) was a notable achievement, with the overall balance being maintained within 2.5% of GDP since then. However, other structural reforms have lagged and reviews are behind schedule. The first review was approved in July 2015. The second review was approved late, in September 2016, after the political crisis that erupted in February 2016, sparked by the resignation of the Economy Minister Aivaras Abromavicius, who cited political pressure over the reform agenda, and a rift between President Poroshenko and Prime Minister Arseniy Yatsenyuk. This led to real concerns over the possible collapse of the government (Yatsenyuk was later replaced by Groysman). The intervening uncertainty and distraction caused the programme to go off track. The third review was therefore also subject to a lengthy delay, finally being approved in April 2017; in turn, setting the dubious record of being the first time any Ukraine programme had got that far. Crucial to the third review was the passage of an IMF-compliant 2017 budget, structural benchmarks on anti-corruption, notably including the asset declaration register for high-ranking officials, and progress on financial sector reform. Pension reform and land reform were pushed back to the fourth review (land reform was subsequently pushed back to the fifth review). The fourth review was still ongoing at the end of September 2018, again subject to a long delay. Of the five key structural benchmarks for the fourth review, three had been met; namely pension reform (passed in October 2017), passage of a privatisation law (the law became effective in March 2018) and passage of legislation to establish the anti-corruption court (adopted on 7 June 2018). However, two structural benchmarks were ongoing, concerning the budget and an increase in retail gas tariffs. Moreover, the slippage meant that, by then, new structural benchmarks were necessary as the 2019 budget was coming into view, which brought with it Fund concerns over the President's plans for an exit capital tax.

As of July 2018, SDR6.18bn (US$8.38bn) had been drawn under the EFF. Completion of the fourth review was expected to lead to an IMF disbursement of another US$2bn. After the fourth review, there were then another six reviews scheduled, after the rephasing in September 2016 (at the conclusion of the second review) to bring the total to 10 reviews in all (11 disbursements). The EFF originally scheduled 15 reviews (16 disbursements).

The IMF announced on 19 October 2018 that it had reached staff-level agreement on a new SBA to replace the existing EFF. Mindful of the delays to the fourth review of the EFF, the looming expiry of the arrangement (March 2019) and limited prospects for structural reform in 2019 (given the heavy election calendar that year), the IMF took the unusual step ahead of an election of seeking to replace the existing arrangement with a new 14-month SBA. The new SBA was anticipated at SDR2.8bn (US$3.9bn, c140% of quota). A new programme was expected to allow the IMF to remain engaged with the government (and potentially the next one) at a crucial time. The programme was conditional on parliamentary approval of an IMF-compliant 2019 budget and an increase in household gas and heating tariffs. It was hoped that Board approval for the programme would follow later in the year.

IMF exposure to Ukraine was SDR7.8bn (cUS$11.1bn) as at end-July 2018. Ukraine's repayments to the Fund are expected to pick up over coming years, rising from SDR860mn in 2018 to SDR1.3bn in 2019, and then amounting to cSDR1bn a year over 2020–2022.

IMF programmes

Date	Arrangements	Comments
1995–1996	SBA	One-year stand-by credit totalling SDR1247mn (US$1.96bn) with the aim of reducing critical levels of inflation to around a monthly figure of 1%. Structural reforms also comprised a key part of the IMF programme.
1996–1997	SBA	Nine-month stand-by credit of SDR599mn (US$867mn) to implement economic policies, most notably a major reduction in the budget deficit.
1997–1998	SBA	One-year SBA approved in August 1997 for SDR399mn (US$542mn) to strengthen the external reserve position of the National Bank of Ukraine.
1998–2002	EFF	Three-year EFF approved in September 1998 for SDR1646mn (US$2.2bn) in response to regional shocks—the aim was to stabilise macro performance through tighter fiscal policy and debt restructuring. SDR1193mn drawn.
2004–2005	SBA	12-month SBA approved in March 2004 for SDR412mn (US$605mn). Expired March 2005 undrawn.
2008–2010	SBA	Two-year SBA approved in November 2008 for SDR11bn (US$16.4bn, 802% of quota). The programme entailed exceptional access and was approved under the Fund's fast-track emergency financing mechanism. Approval allowed an immediate disbursement of SDR3bn (US$4.5bn). The arrangement was cancelled in July 2010 with SDR7bn drawn.
2010–2012	SBA	29-month SBA approved in July 2010 for SDR10bn (US$15.15bn, 730% quota) Expired December 2012. SDR2.25bn was drawn.
2014–2015	SBA	In April 2014, the IMF approved a two-year SBA amounting to SDR10.976bn (US$17.01bn, 800% of quota) to support a reform agenda aimed at addressing large fiscal and current account deficits, with an immediate disbursement of SDR2.058bn (US$3.19bn), of which SDR1.29bn (US$2bn) was allocated to budget support. The first review was completed in August 2014, with a disbursement of SDR915mn (US$1.39bn). The programme was, however, terminated soon after (and a year ahead of schedule) in favour of a new EFF, with only SDR2.97bn drawn (US$4.51bn).
2015–2019	EFF	In March 2015, the IMF approved a four-year EFF for SDR12.348bn (US$17.5bn, 900% of quota) under the Fund's exceptional access policy. The EFF is due to expire in March 2019. At the same time, Ukraine cancelled its 2014 SBA. Approval of the EFF enabled the immediate disbursement of SDR3.546bn (US$5bn), with SDR1.915bn (US$2.7bn) being allocated to budget support. The first review of the EFF was approved in July 2015 with a disbursement of US$1.7bn. The second review was approved in September 2016, subject to waivers, with US$1bn disbursed. The third review was approved in April 2017 with US$1bn disbursed. At July 2018, SDR6.18bn (US$8.38bn) had been drawn.

Source: IMF. Ukraine joined the IMF in 1992

Paris Club and Bilateral Creditors

Ukraine's only Paris Club treatment came in July 2001. US$578mn of the total US$1.1bn Paris Club debt was treated under classic terms, whilst total external debt was US$12.4bn. Ukraine was under its IMF EFF at the time, which was approved in December 2000. The agreement allowed for the rescheduling of debt on a case-by-case basis to the appropriate market rate. The participating Paris Club members consisted of France, Germany, Italy, Japan and the US. Ukraine agreed to seek comparable treatment from non-Paris Club creditors.

Paris Club agreements

Date	*Terms*	*Status*	*Details*
2001	Classic	Active	Treated US$578mn out of US$1.1bn in Paris Club debt. Treatment of arrears as of 19 December 2000, treatment of maturities falling due from 19 December 2000 up to 3 September 2002. Repayment of non-ODA credits over 12 years, with three years of grace.

Source: Paris Club

Ukraine is in a legal dispute with Russia over a US$3bn loan provided in December 2013 by the Russian government to the then Ukraine government of President Yanukovych. The loan took the form of a bond issue, which is solely held by Russia (the "Russia bond"). The bond had a coupon of 5%, below prevailing bond yields at the time, and was due to mature in December 2015. It was included as eligible debt in Ukraine's 2015 bond restructuring. However, Russia declined to participate on the grounds that the bond was sovereign bilateral debt rather than commercial debt; the IMF subsequently determined that the December 2013 bond was official debt too. Kiev refused to make the repayment upon its schedule maturity date, arguing that Russia should have participated in the restructuring. The bond is now subject to legal proceedings in the High Court of England and Wales, after the trustee (acting on behalf of the holder) filed a lawsuit on 17 February 2016 against Ukraine seeking full payment (principal and accrued interest). The High Court's first instance summary judgement issued on 29 March 2017 in favour of the claimant (Russia) was appealed by Ukraine. After a hearing in January 2018, London's Court of Appeal is due to rule in September 2018. A final resolution, however, could remain distant, as domestic politics in Ukraine may oppose making such a large payment to Russia. Moreover, a most-favoured creditor clause in the new bonds issued in the 2015 restructuring stated that Ukraine shall not pay the old bonds or enter a settlement with any of the old notes on better terms without offering the same terms to holders of the new notes (an Argentina-style RUFO clause). In November 2015, ahead of the scheduled maturity date, Russia reportedly proposed that Ukraine repay the bond in three equal annual instalments starting in 2016.

Sovereign Commercial Debt

Ukraine has experienced two major sovereign bond default episodes over the past 20 years (over 1998–2001 and 2015), with its most recent—and biggest—arising out of Russia's annexation of Crimea in 2014 and the subsequent conflict and associated economic disruption. Before then, it saw commercial debt restructurings of mainly short-term debt and bonds (and domestic debt) in four stages over the course of 1998–2001. The largest occurred in 2000, which tried to deal more comprehensively with short-maturity bonds, after the failure of a series of exchanges prior to it. In 1998, a moratorium on debt service for certain bearer bonds was announced. Only those entities willing to identify themselves and convert to local currency accounts were eligible for debt repayments, which Moody's classified as a distressed exchange. In January 2000, Ukraine announced that it would miss the repayment of the 16.75% USD bond and, in February 2000, it missed the coupon payment on its 16% DEM bond due in 2001. In an exchange proposal, holders were offered seven-year amortising bonds in two different currencies (USD and DEM). According to Moody's, over 90% of holder agreed to restructure. The exchange used CACs in three eurobonds governed by Luxembourg law.

Commercial debt agreements

Date	*Details*
1998	Debt exchanges with holders of domestic T-bills (OVDPs) in August followed in October by a loan placed by Chase Manhattan in October 1997. T-bills were exchanged for longer-term bonds with small haircuts for resident holders (<10%) and larger haircuts (40–60%) for non-residents.
Jul. 1999	Agreement to restructure a 10-month US$163mn eurobond repayment (principal and interest) that had been due in June 1999. The restructuring included a 20% cash repayment and the remaining 80% was exchanged into a DEM-denominated three-year eurobond with a 16% coupon.

(*continued*)

(continued)

Date	*Details*
Feb. 2000	Agreement to restructure US$2.7bn of short-term obligations. Creditors were offered a new seven-year eurobond denominated in either US dollars or euros, with 11% and 10% coupons, respectively. There was no reduction in principal, and all accrued interest was paid in full in cash.
Mar. 2001	Exchange of US$21.5mn of external debt into a new six-year eurobond, denominated in either EUR at a 10% interest rate, or USD at an 11% interest rate. Eligible bonds were: DEM 16% February 2001, EUR 10% amortising notes due March 2007 and USD 11% amortising notes due March 2007.
Nov. 2015	Agreement to restructure US$18.4bn in 14 outstanding sovereign and government-guaranteed eurobonds (cUS$18bn in principal and US$0.3bn in accrued interest). Holders of two 2015 bonds exchanged into a single 2019 maturity. The 12 remaining bonds exchanged into an equal share of 2020–2027 bonds, plus a residual amount of the 2019s. The new bonds had a 7.75% coupon. Principal was subject to a 20% haircut and accrued interest was capitalised. Holders also received GDP warrants. Exotix estimates the NPV haircut was c15–20% (excl. the value of the GDP warrants).

Source: Exotix, World Bank GDF, Moody's

Ukraine has been regularly issuing bonds in the international capital markets since 1997, denominated in various foreign currencies. Ukraine had US$7.7bn of eurobonds outstanding at end-2010. It issued four sovereign bonds with total nominal amount of US$3.1bn in the final four months of 2010, on the back of its IMF programme. The September 2010 issues (US$1.5bn 10-year and US$0.5bn five-year) were important insofar as they marked Ukraine's return to international markets nearly two years after the previous issues in November 2007 (US$0.7bn 10-year and US$0.5bn five-year). Ukraine also issued a US$568mn "financing of infrastructure" bond in October 2010, maturing in 2017, and a US$500mn one-year bond in December 2010.

Ukraine's biggest default came in the aftermath of Russia's annexation of Crimea in 2014 when private sector involvement (PSI), through a debt operation, was a key condition of the resulting IMF EFF programme that was approved in March 2015. The IMF demanded that the government quickly negotiate a comprehensive restructuring of its US$18bn in sovereign and sovereign-guaranteed eurobonds, of which US$8.5bn was scheduled to mature during the term of the EFF programme. Although the specific terms of the debt operation would be determined following consultations with creditors, the IMF ensured that the debt operation would be guided by three targets: (1) generate cUS$15bn in financing during the program period; (2) bring public and publicly guaranteed debt/GDP ratio below 71% of GDP by 2020; and (3) keep the budget's gross financing needs at an average of 10% of GDP (maximum of 12% of GDP annually) in the post-programme period (2019–2025). The debt operation was expected to be concluded by the time of the first programme review. Ukraine's Cabinet of Ministers subsequently passed a resolution on 4 April 2015 permitting the restructuring of certain state and state-guaranteed debt obligations in order to be able to meet its financing obligations under the EFF. Ukraine's financial advisor was Lazard Freres and its legal advisor was White and Case. An ad-hoc creditor committee (AHC) was formed, comprising five creditors, holding in aggregate cUS$10bn of instruments within the perimeter of Ukraine's debt operation.

The government's investor presentation on 17 April 2015 outlined the perimeter of the debt operation. External debt to be included in the debt operations included government eurobonds and eurobonds of the Ukraine Infrastructure Fund (Fininpro), foreign currency loans of state-owned entities (SOEs) benefiting from a sovereign guarantee (Ukravtodor, Ukrmedpostach, and Yuzhnoe State Design Office), and City of Kiev eurobonds. Non-guaranteed external debt of certain state-owned entities (Oschadbank, Ukreximbank, and Ukrzaliznytsia—Ukrainian Railways) were also included, in order to contribute to Target 1, but each was subject to its own restructuring process. According to the IMF, the total debt of all these instruments to be restructured amounted to US$22.7bn, with the sovereign eurobonds and the City of Kiev amounting to US$16.8bn, Finipro bonds amounting to US$1.8bn, the SOE-guaranteed loans of US$0.7bn and the non-guaranteed SOE liabilities of US$3.4bn. According to Moody's, restructuring negotiations with sovereign bondholders were well enough advanced that creditors had already agreed that Ukraine's eurobonds maturing in September and October 2015 and the eurobond coupons due on bonds from September through December would be included in the restructuring. The first default occurred on 23 September 2015, with missed payment of principal and interest on the 6.875% 09/2015 bond due that day, and it remained unpaid after the expiry of the grace period 10 days later. It was the first principal payment since June 2014 with the US$1bn due on the maturity of the 7.95% 06/2014. A second default occurred on 13 October 2015, again with missed payment of principal and interest, this time on the 4.95% 10/2015 bond due that day, and it also remained unpaid after the expiry of the grace period 10 days later.

The Ukraine government announced indicative heads of terms (IHT) on 27 August 2015 after coming to an agreement with the AHC on restructuring its sovereign eurobonds and Fininpro bonds. The deal envisaged a 20% principal haircut, a 7.75% coupon on all new bonds and a maturity extension of four years. The old bonds were to be rescheduled into nine new bonds due between 2019 and 2027. Accumulated interest at the time of the exchange date was rolled into the new bonds (capitalised and without haircut). The interest accrual date on the new bonds was from 1 September 2015. In addition, bondholders would be entitled to 20-year GDP-linked warrants with potential payments over 2021–2040, conditional on achieving certain conditions (see below).

The designated (eligible) securities comprised 14 bonds amounting to a total nominal amount outstanding of US$18bn (see table below). This included US$16.15bn in 11 sovereign bonds (including the September and October 2015 maturities and the US$3bn 5% December 2015 "Russia bond"), and US$1.81bn in three government guaranteed bonds (UKRINF bonds). The AHC held c60% of the eligible bonds (excluding the Russia bond), ie not far from the 75% CAC threshold. The only holdout was the Russia bond, as Moscow was unwilling to accept the same terms offered to the other bondholders (see Paris Club and bilateral history section above). Hence, only 10 of the 11 sovereign bonds, and 13 of the 14 eligible bonds were swapped.

Eligible bonds in 2015 sovereign debt restructuring

Ticker	*Coupon (%)*	*Maturity*	*Currency*	*Amt outs (US$mn)*	*CAC (Y/N)*
1. Sovereign bonds					
UKRAIN	6.875	23 September 2015	USD	500	Y (2/3)
UKRAIN	4.95	13 October 2015	EUR	600	Y (2/3)
UKRAIN	5	20 December 2015	USD	3000	Y (2/3)
UKRAIN	6.25	17 June 2016	USD	1250	n/a
UKRAIN	6.58	21 November 2016	USD	1000	Y (2/3)
UKRAIN	9.25	24 July 2017	USD	2600	Y (2/3)
UKRAIN	6.75	14 November 2017	USD	700	Y (2/3)
UKRAIN	7.75	23 September 2020	USD	1500	Y (2/3)
UKRAIN	7.95	23 February 2021	USD	1500	Y (2/3)
UKRAIN	7.8	28 November 2022	USD	2250	Y (2/3)
UKRAIN	7.5	17 April 2023	USD	1250	Y (2/3)
				16,150	
2. Government-guaranteed bonds					
UKRINF	8.375	3 November 2017	USD	568	n/a
UKRINF	9	7 December 2017	USD	550	n/a
UKRINF	7.4	20 April 2018	USD	690	n/a
				1808	
Total				**17,958**	

Source: Exotix, Bloomberg, Exchange prospectus

The government announced final restructuring terms on 23 September 2015, just five months restructuring talks began, and the exchange closed on 12 November. The final terms were amended slightly from the previously announced IHT. The key change concerned the two 2015 maturities—23 September (USD) and 13 October (EUR). Originally in the IHT, holders of all 14 eligible bonds were to receive an equal share of a series of nine new bullet bonds maturing from 2019–2027 (ie a strip, similar to the Greek PSI deal), but the revised terms gave holders of both the aforementioned 2015 bonds special treatment (as implied in the name given to them in the exchange, that of Priority Notes). The two 2015s exchanged into a single 2019 maturity. Holders of the remaining 12 bonds exchanged into an equal share of 2020–2027 bonds, plus a residual amount of the 2019s. By drawing this distinction with the shortest bonds, the government succumbed to the threat of potential holdouts in the September 2015 bond (who may have been able to reach a blocking minority). These holders faced the longest extension in the swap, under the initial terms, and hence would have suffered the largest PV loss. By making this sweetener, the government was able to increase the participation rate and reduce the chance of any future legal battles. Other terms were unchanged, including the 20% principal haircut. Indeed, the sense was that a concentrated, robust and well-coordinated set of creditors managed to secure a good deal for bondholders. The 20% haircut seemed to be a compromise between the government seeking something higher (40%) and bondholders insisting on no haircut at all, arguing instead that it was not a solvency crisis. Rather, it was a liquidity crisis that required maturity extension. The addition of GDP warrants was also seen as favourable to bondholders.

Ukraine issued US$11.951bn in new bonds originally in the exchange, although the total issue size of the new bonds rose to US$13.043bn after additional issuance to settle other obligations. A number of other debt operations also followed on other bonds included in the perimeter of the restructuring in order to meet the EFF targets. Most of the additional issuance of US$1.092bn was created on 2 March 2016, mainly in the 2019s and some in the 2020s, and again on 12 May 2016, again mainly in the 2019s and some in the 2020s, and some spread relatively evenly over the other maturities. According to the 2032 prospectus, further tranches of Ukraine's new eurobonds and GDP warrants were issued in 2016 in exchange for the termination of state-guaranteed loans of Ukravtodor with Sberbank, VTB and a syndicate of banks, respectively, as well as a state-guaranteed loan to Yuzhnoye State Design Office. In addition, other entities in the perimeter completed their own restructurings, although these did not lead to additional exchange bonds. Ukreximbank and Oschadbank (the two largest state-owned banks) successfully reprofiled their bonds on 7 July 2015 and 3 August 2015, respectively (see section on Banks below). The City of Kiev authorities announced on 22 December 2015 the successful restructuring of the majority of its US$250mn 8% LPN due 2015 and all of its US$300mn 9.375% LPN due 2016. Ukrainian Railway on 14 March 2016 successfully completed the exchange of its US$500mn 9.5% LPN due 2018 for a new US$500mn 9.875% LPN due 2021 (see Corporate section below). Hence, the sovereign restructuring was formally completed in June 2016 (excluding the Russia bond which remains subject to litigation).

It is fair to say that Ukraine's new sovereign bonds traded very well after the debt exchange. The new bonds generally traded up to the mid- to high-90s by mid-November, with some bonds (the shorter 2019 and 2020 maturities) rising close to par. The bonds may even have been seen as a bit rich, as yields declined to 8%. However, estimates for recovery values or bondholder losses vary. The old bonds traded at around 79–80 just before the exchange (the two 2015 maturities were a little higher), implying market estimates of bondholder losses of c20%, a figure also reported by Moody's. However, comparing the PV of the new bonds with the PV of the old bonds, at the same discount rate—regarded as a more accurate way of assessing bondholder losses—Exotix estimates an NPV loss of c15–20%, albeit in a highly stylised way to keep the calculation tractable. This calculation excludes the two 2015 maturities, which had preferential treatment into the 2019s, and is based on a simple average of short, medium and long eligible bonds exchanging into one new medium-term bond rather than the strip (a simplifying assumption, especially as the yield curve was inverted at the time). It implies an initial NPV loss of 17% (the first day of trading the new bonds was 13 November) at an average discount rate of 8.9%, but falling to a 15% loss after the fourth day (when bond prices peaked, on 18 November), with the average discount rate falling to 8.2%. However, after 30 days, the NPV loss had risen to 18%, when the average discount rate had risen to 9.9%. However, the presence of the GDP warrants in the exchange package also helped recoveries. The GDP warrants were indicated as high as the high 40s (mid) after the exchange. Taken together, investors may have broken even in the exchange, if not making money, even after the 20% reduction in principal. However, despite the restructuring (and 20% haircut), public debt sustainability was far from assured. Although it provided cash flow relief, the restructuring covered just 20% of public debt, and likely reduced public debt by 3ppts of GDP, other things unchanged, on Exotix's calculations. Public debt after the exchange was still 70% of GDP, which meant sticking to fiscal consolidation and structural fiscal reform remained important under the IMF programme in order to support debt dynamics.

Ukraine returned to the market in September 2017 for the first time since its 2015 restructuring, with a new sovereign bond issue and a liability management operation. The government issued US$3bn in a new 15-year bond (2032 maturity) at par with a coupon of 7.375%. The notes redeem in four equal semi-annual instalments over the last two years of its life, commencing in March 2031. The bonds' documentation specifically excludes default and acceleration of the Russia bond as an event of default on the new notes. Part of the proceeds of the bond issue was used to finance the purchase of outstanding eurobonds through a tender offer, which the government had been talking about earlier in the year. The government focused on the front end of its curve (the 2019 and 2020 bonds) in order to reduce potential refinancing risks, at a time when the IMF EFF programme was due to expire and the country holds its next elections. The operation retired US$1.6bn in the two maturities, comprising US$1.2bn of the 2019s and US$0.4bn of the 2020s. Net issuance was therefore just US$1.4bn.

Additionally, Ukraine issued a short-dated (six-month) zero-coupon bond on 28 August 2018 through a private placement. The issue was for US$725mn, in REGS/144A form, with a scheduled maturity on 28 February 2019. The issue was priced at 95.551, implying a yield at issue of c9.3%, and contained a call at 98.551 until 28 November 2018 that would make the prospective IRR >10%. The notes were intended to be used for general budgetary purposes and listed on the Vienna Stock Exchange, and ostensibly provided bridging finance ahead of the expected (but subsequently delayed) IMF disbursement.

Ukraine returned to the market again on 1 November 2018 with a US$2bn dual tranche USD sale. Ukraine issued US$750mn in a new long five-year maturing in February 2024. The bond was issued at par with a coupon of 8.994%. It also issued US$1.25bn in a new 10-year maturing in November 2028. That bond was also issued at par with a coupon of 9.75%. Part of the proceeds of the sale was used to repay the entirety of the US$725mn zero coupon bond that had been issued in August 2018. The bond sale followed the announcement of an IMF agreement on a new SBA on 19 October 2018.

Ukraine's outstanding stock of marketable eurobonds, as at November 2018, was therefore US$16.5bn (ie excluding the Russia bond and UST-guaranteed bonds). Its main outstanding bonds, including the latest issues, are summarised in the table below. A description of the 2032 bond is also given.

Ukraine's outstanding eurobonds

Description	*Amount issued*[a] *(US$mn)*	*Amount outstanding (US$mn)*	*Maturity type*	*Issue date*
USD 5% due 2015[b]	3000.0	3000.0	Bullet	Dec. 2013
USD 7.75% due 2019	1822.2	661.3	Bullet	Nov. 2015
USD 7.75% due 2020	1779.8	1364.7	Bullet	Nov. 2015
USD 7.75% due 2021	1409.3	1409.3	Bullet	Nov. 2015
USD 7.75% due 2022	1383.7	1383.7	Bullet	Nov. 2015
USD 7.75% due 2023	1355.2	1355.2	Bullet	Nov. 2015
USD 8.994% due 2024	750.0	750.0	Bullet	Nov. 2018
USD 7.75% due 2024	1339.1	1339.1	Bullet	Nov. 2015
USD 7.75% due 2025	1328.9	1328.9	Bullet	Nov. 2015
USD 7.75% due 2026	1317.9	1317.9	Bullet	Nov. 2015
USD 7.75% due 2027	1307.2	1307.2	Bullet	Nov. 2015
USD 9.75% due 2028	1250.0	1250.0	Bullet	Nov. 2018
USD 7.375% due 2032	3000.0	3000.0	Sinkable	Sep. 2017

Source: Bloomberg

[a]After additional issuance in the new restructured bonds in exchange for certain other loans
[b]Held by Russia, subject to legal proceedings in English courts

Ukraine bond
Ukraine government 7.375% 2032
Bloomberg ticker: UKRAIN

Borrower	Ukraine government
Issue date	25 September 2017
Form	Eurobond
ISIN	XS1577952952
Issue size	US$3000mn
Issue outstanding	US$3000mn
Currency	US dollar
Denomination	US$200,000 and US$1000 thereafter
Amortisation	Four equal amortisations on 25 March 2031, September 2031, March 2032 and September 2032
Final maturity date	25 September 2032
Coupon/interest	7.735% per annum, paid semi-annually March and September
Day count	30/360
Method of transfer	Euroclear/Clearstream
Settlement period	T + 2
Joint lead managers	BNP Paribas, Goldman Sachs, JP Morgan
Exchange	Berlin, Dublin, Frankfurt, Stuttgart, PFTS
Governing law	English

Source: Bloomberg

Ukraine GDP Warrants

All existing bondholders in the 2015 debt exchange received, as well as new bonds, 20-year value recovery rights ("GDP-linked securities"). Payouts on these securities are dependent on real GDP growth over 2019–2038 and subject to certain conditions being met. In short, provided nominal GDP exceeds US$125.4bn, there will be payments on the GDP-linked securities if real GDP growth in any year exceeds 3%. Payments, which are made in US dollars, are essentially a share of GDP. If growth is 3% or below, no payments will be made. The payment related to performance in any particular year is made two years later. Payments are subject to a payment cap of 1% of GDP over the period 2021–2025. Thereafter, payments are theoretically unlimited. The cap seems more generous than with Greek and Argentine GDP warrants.

The warrants have a 20-year life (and, hence, 20 possible annual payments) over the reference years 2019–2038. The first payment date is May 2021, in respect of the 2019 reference year, and the last payment date is May 2040, in respect of the 2038 reference year. Hence, the payment life is 2021–2040.

Other important features are explicit cross default to the new bonds (removing one area of uncertainty that has historically plagued other value recovery instruments), independent verification of GDP (GDP is taken from the IMF WEO, learning the lesson from Argentina) and a holder-put option that gives some protection to reclaim par under certain events. The warrants are governed under English law.

Ukraine GDP Warrants
Ukraine 0% 2040
Bloomberg ticker: UKRAIN

Borrower	Ukraine government
Issue date	12 November 2015
Form	GDP-linked security
ISIN	XS1303929894
Issue size	US$3.214bn
Amount outstanding	US$3.214bn
Payment currency	US dollar
Denomination	Minimum of US$1000 and US$1000 thereafter
Payments	Variable rate subject to a payment formula
Final maturity date	31 May 2040, in respect of the 2038 reference year
First payment date	31 May 2021, in respect of the 2019 reference year
Payment trigger	No payment if nominal GDP in US$ terms <US$125.4bn, or real GDP growth is <=3%. For growth between 3–4%, 15% of excess GDP. For growth greater than 4%, 40% of excess GDP.
Payment cap	Cap on the annual payments such that the reference amount shall not exceed 1% of nominal GDP (measured in UAH) over the reference years 2019–2023 inclusive. Thereafter, there is no payment cap.
Calculation date	30 April two years after the relevant reference year
Calculation currency	Ukrainian hryvnia
Other features	Holder put option
Day count	30/360
Method of transfer	Euroclear/Clearstream
Governing law	English
Listing	Berlin, Dublin, Frankfurt, Munich, Stuttgart

Source: Bloomberg, Exotix, Exchange prospectus

Ukraine Bank Debt Restructuring

Over 2014–2016, Ukraine's banking sector suffered a severe crisis. Almost half of the banks went bankrupt and losses incurred by the state and banking sector clients exceeded US$20bn. Ukraine's major banks with outstanding eurobonds (including Ukreximbank, Oschadbank, First Ukrainian International Bank, and Privatbank) all had to restructure their eurobonds and certain loans over the course of 2014–2015 amid the country's financial crisis. The total amount covered was US$3.4bn. At Privatbank, the largest lender in Ukraine, senior and subordinated Eurobonds were bailed in as part of its nationalisation.

The NBU passed a resolution on 14 April 2015 to oblige the two largest state-owned banks, Ukreximbank and Oschadbank, to restructure their external obligations as per the 4 April Cabinet of Ministers Resolution. This followed as a direct result of the government's own restructuring need. These bank restructurings generally took the form of seven-year maturity extensions with higher coupons and did not impose nominal haircuts. First Ukrainian International Bank also restructured, even before the two state-owned banks, with a maturity extension through consent solicitation in 2014 (after restructuring its liabilities in 2009). Privatbank, also restructured its bonds, but soon after, in December 2016, NBU declared Privatbank insolvent and the government backed its nationalisation and recapitalisation to protect its 20mn customers and to preserve financial stability.

The authorities in Ukraine have made significant progress in their efforts to clean up the banking sector, and more than 80 banks have been closed. With both support and pressure from the West, significant policy implementation and regulation have helped to clean up the sector. The surviving banks are, on average, bigger than before. Regulators have more powers to supervise related-party lending, and the NBU also strengthened other prudential requirements, including credit risk provisioning. More stringent regulation has led to significant improvement in banking sector health, although this is ongoing. After Privatbank's nationalisation, state banks dominate, with over 50% market share.

A summary of the restructuring experiences of four banks mentioned above over this period is shown below. Other lenders with Eurobonds outstanding, such as VAB Bank, also restructured these bonds, but have since gone into bankruptcy or liquidation.

Summary of key bank restructurings in 2015

Bank		*Eligible debt*	*New securities*
Oschadbank	State owned	Restructuring on 3 August 2015 of US$1.3bn in debt comprising: • US$700mn 8.25% 2016 eurobond. • US$500mn 8.875% 2018 eurobond. • US$100mn subordinated loan due 2017.	Three new securities created. Bonds were swapped for new amortising notes with seven-year maturity extensions and coupon increases. • 16s swapped into 9.375% 2023 with US$700mn outstanding amortising by 60% in March 2019 and the remainder redeemed in eight equal semi-annual instalments starting in September 2019. • 18s swapped into 9.625% 2025 with US$500mn outstanding amortising by 50% in March 2020 and the remainder redeemed in 10 equal semi-annual instalments starting in September 2020. Holders of the 2016 and 2018 notes were able to elect to receive either new 2023 notes or new 2025 notes, although there were issuance limits on the size of each one. The 2017 subordinated loan was swapped for loan participation notes with a seven-year maturity extension to 2024, a coupon increase to USD six-month Libor plus 6.875% and a 50% amortisation in January 2020, with the remaining principal redeemed in eight semi-annual instalments starting in July 2020.

(*continued*)

(continued)

<table>
<tr><th>Bank</th><th></th><th>Eligible debt</th><th>New securities</th></tr>
<tr><td>Ukreximbank</td><td>State owned</td><td>Restructuring on 7 July 2015 of US$1.5bn in debt comprising:
• US$750mn 8.375% eurobond due April 2015.
• US$125mn subordinated bond due February 2016.
• US$600mn 8.75% eurobond due January 2018.
The US$750mn bond had already been extended by three months to allow for negotiations; its original maturity was 27 April 2015.</td><td>In a similar agreement to that with Oschadbank, noteholders agreed to extend maturities by seven years with higher coupons.
• 15s into 9.625% 2022 with US$750mn outstanding.
• 16s into FRN 2023 with US$125mn outstanding.
• 18s into 9.75% 2025 with US$600mn outstanding.
On 27 March 2015, Ukreximbank solicited the approval of the holders of the Ukreximbank's note maturing in April 2015 for the extension of the final maturity and repayment date from 27 April 2015 to 27 July 2015. Approval was eventually given.</td></tr>
<tr><td>First Ukrainian International Bank</td><td>Private sector</td><td colspan="2">FUIB has just one senior USD-denominated eurobond, which has had two maturity extensions. The original issue came out of the consolidation of two loans in 2007 into US$275mn 9.75% 2007:
1. 2010: Maturity extension from the original 16 February 2010 to 31 December. 2014. Coupon increased from 9.75% to 11% and payments made quarterly, rather than semi-annually. A partial principal repayment on 16 February 2010, of US$17.576mn, favouring holders who had supported the new terms and conditions.
2. 2014: Maturity extension by four years to 2018, considered by Moody's to be distressed exchange. Partial redemption on the previous maturity date of US$44.928mn, and FUIB agreed to make quarterly principal amortisation repayments from 30 September 2016 to 31 December 2018. A US$10mn principal amortisation was also made at end-2015.</td></tr>
</table>

(*continued*)

(continued)

Bank		*Eligible debt*	*New securities*
Privatbank	Private sector	Two bonds subject to restructuring: • US$200mn 9.375% 2015 bond. • US$150mn 5.799% 2016 subordinated bond. A proposal in June 2015 to amend terms of its two bonds was rejected. The proposal to amend the 2015 notes was passed but the proposal to amend the 2016 notes was not, and the proposal was conditional on both being passed. In July, Privatbank attempted to extend the imminent maturity of the 2015 notes from September to December, but this also was not passed in meetings with noteholders. In September 2015, creditor meetings led to agreement to extend the 2015 maturity to 15 January 2016, if no restructuring deal for the US$150mn notes maturing 9 February 2016 could be reached before then, or 23 January 2018 if the 2016 notes were extended. Agreement for an exchange for the 2016 eurobond was reached in October, with the new bond issued on 17 November 2015, before the deadline associated with the extended January maturity for the 10.25% bond, which was then further extended to January 2018. Its other outstanding issue (US$175mn 10.875% February 2018 LPN) was untouched.	2015s extended to 23 January 2018, with higher coupon 10.25%. In line with the agreement, a 20% amortisation payment was made (US$40mn) on 23 August 2016. This was the only principal repayment before default, leaving US$160mn outstanding. 2016s swapped into new US$220mn 10.25% subordinated note due in February 2021 in November 2015. In January 2017, the NBU stated that "no payments will be made" on Privatbank bonds. Holders of the senior bonds have since launched arbitration proceedings. At the time of writing, Privatbank had requested information regarding the bondholders from the Trustee. Privatbank is seeking to show that the bonds were held by parties related to the former shareholders. Several lawsuits are in progress, involving the former shareholders as well as the previous auditors of Privatbank.

Source: Bloomberg, Exotix

State Savings Bank of Ukraine via SSB 9.375% 2023
Bloomberg ticker: OSCHAD

Borrower	State Savings Bank of Ukraine via SSB
Issue date	1 September 2015
Form	Eurobond
ISIN	XS1273033719
Issue size	US$700mn
Currency	US dollar
Denomination	US$200,000 and US$1000 thereafter
Amortisation	Sinkable
Final maturity date	10 March 2023
Coupon/interest	9.375% paid semi-annually
Collateralisation	Senior unsecured
Day count	30/360
Method of transfer	Euroclear/Clearstream
Exchange	Dublin, Stuttgart
Governing law	English

Source: Bloomberg

Ukreximbank via Biz Finance PLC 9.625% 2022
Bloomberg ticker: EXIMUK

Borrower	Ukreximbank via Biz Finance PLC
Issue date	27 April 2015
Form	Eurobond
ISIN	XS1261825977
Issue size	US$750mn
Currency	US dollar
Denomination	US$150,000 and US$1000 thereafter
Amortisation	Sinkable
Final maturity date	27 April 2022
Coupon/interest	9.625% paid semi-annually
Collateralisation	Senior unsecured
Day count	30/360
Method of transfer	Euroclear/Clearstream
Exchange	Berlin, Dublin, Stuttgart
Governing law	English

Source: Bloomberg

Corporate Bond Market

Ukraine corporates have generally been active issuers over the last decade, although issuance has been punctured by episodes of sovereign debt distress (eg in 2000, 2009–2010, and 2013–2015), especially for those companies with FX mismatches (FX-denominated debt and local currency revenues). MHP, for instance, issued its first eurobond in November 2006 (due 2011), while a number of first-time issuers came to the market after the 2009–2010 crisis, eg DTEK, Metinvest and Avangard. Ukraine corporate (non-financial) external debt stood at US$54bn at end-17, according to official data on BPM6 methodology (excluding intercompany loans). This was down from US$77bn in 2013, as the subsequent crisis forced a number of companies to deleverage and restructure.

A number of corporate defaults occurred during 2009–2010 due to the global financial crisis. Naftogaz, the cash-strapped state-owned Ukrainian gas company, announced in September 2009 plans for a debt restructuring of a US$500mn bond coming due at the end of the month (the 8.125% 2009 bond, issued in 2004, was its first and at the time only bond). Naftogaz subsequently refused to make the principal repayment, thus triggering a failure-to-pay credit event. The exchange offer involved a maturity extension of five years and a higher 9.5% coupon. Although a group of investors had threatened to block the restructuring, the vast majority of bondholders accepted the offer by 8 October, which was the early participation deadline. Ultimately, over 93% of bondholders accepted the offer, with the remaining holders being bound in via collective action clauses contained in the old bonds. In addition, Naftogaz succeeded in renegotiating its debt owed to Western banks and other bilateral creditors, with all old claims being exchanged into a new five-year eurobond amounting to US$1.595bn, which was guaranteed by the government. The exchange completed in November 2009. The new bond had a final maturity date of 30 September 2014. It was fully repaid on 1 October 2014. Overall, the bond restructuring techniques used in the exchange resembled more closely those in corporate debt exchanges rather than in sovereign practice (Lareya, 2010). MHP launched an exchange offer on 12 April 2010 for its US$250mn 10.25% bond issued on 30 November 2006, which was due to mature on 30 November 2011. The company offered to pay an exchange fee to the bondholders accepting the exchange offer, while any non-consenting holders were bound despite not giving consent. Concurrently with the exchange offer, an offering of new US$330mn notes was issued, fungible with the exchanged notes, bringing the total post-exchange issue to US$585mn. 97% of the 2011 notes were refinanced by the exchange and the new issue, maturing in 2015, had the same annual coupon of 10.25%.

A wave of corporate distress followed over 2015–2017 after the 2013–2015 country crisis. This came after economic activity was disrupted by conflict in the east of the country, which impacted industrial production and exports, due to the loss of mining, electricity generation and distribution assets in the conflict zone of the east of the country, and a trade blockade with Donbass, and due to the sharp fall in the currency (impairing those companies with significant dollar debt). A risk premium has been assigned to assets located near the conflict zone.

A summary of the restructuring experiences of four companies over 2015–2017 (Metinvest, Ferrexpo, DTEK, and state-owned Ukrainian Railway) is shown below, which generally involved maturity extensions and no principal haircuts.

Summary of some recent corporate restructurings

Corporate	*Eligible debt*	*New securities*
Metinvest	Restructuring completed in March 2017 of US$2.3bn in debt comprising: • Guaranteed notes due 2016. • Guaranteed notes due 2017. • Guaranteed notes due 2018. • Four PXF syndicated loan agreements.	Guaranteed notes replaced with new senior secured notes totalling almost US$1.2bn, due December 2021, with 7.5% coupon. The PXF agreements were combined into one facility of cUS$1.1bn, due June 2021. The new term for the securities extended maturities by five years, including, in respect of the new PXF facility, two years of grace period on the scheduled amortisation of principal. This repayment schedule was better aligned with the company's production and investment objectives over the five years, improving profitability, according to management. Subsequently, in March 2018, the company announced a buy back of the complex secured bonds issued in its (total) US$2.3bn debt restructuring in March 2017, financed by two new (RegS/144A) US dollar offerings. A US$945mn 7.75% bond due 2023 and US$648million bond due 2026 were issued on 4 April 2018. US$117million of the original restructuring bond remain outstanding. All three outstanding bond issues rank pari passu with senior unsecured debt.

(*continued*)

(continued)

Corporate	*Eligible debt*	*New securities*
Ferrexpo	Ferrexpo's two outstanding bonds both came out of a restructuring of its US$500mn 2016 notes into new notes due April 2019 and cash. Falling commodity prices led the company to seek debt restructuring.	Initially, in February 2015, only some bondholders (of US$214.3mn) participated in the exchange. Three months later, the remaining holders of the 2016 notes accepted, giving two 10.35% 2019 bonds that have the same economic terms and are pari passu, but are not fungible and have different ISINs. Both have half principal amortising in April 2018 and half in April 2019, and the coupon was increased to 10.375% from 7.875%. • February 2015: Holders of US$214.3mn of 2016 bonds due 7 April approved an exchange into new bonds, receiving US$160.7mn in 2019 notes and US$54mn in cash. The new bond was issued on 24 February 2015. • May 2015: The company announced a new exchange offer and consent solicitation for the outstanding amount of its eurobonds due in April 2016 for holders who refused to exchange the securities in February 2015. 99.42% voted in favour, above the 75% majority required. Viewed as a distressed exchange by Moody's and a limited default. US$185.664mn was issued 6 July 2015.
DTEK	2015–2016 restructuring, two affected bonds: • US$500mn 9.5% senior bond due April 2015. • US$750mn 7.875% senior bond due 4 April 2018.	In spring 2015, DTEK turned to English courts to extend the maturity of its 2015 notes, which were due imminently; this was the first time that a bond's governing law was changed to effect an independent path to English jurisdiction. An exchange offer swapped the 2015 maturity into new notes issued by the English company DTEK Finance PLC, with an extended maturity in March 2018 and higher 10.375% coupon, after successfully changing jurisdiction to England. DTEK subsequently implemented a standstill on 26 April 2016 of the US$750mn 7.875% senior bond due 4 April 2018 and the 2015 notes, again through an English scheme. The standstill was in effect until 28 October 2016. On 18 November 2016, DTEK agreed restructuring terms with creditors (bondholders and bank lenders), to cancel the notes (the remaining US$160mn of the extended 18s, and the US$750mn 18s) and replace them with new 10.75% senior PIK notes due 31 December 2024, issued 29 December 2016, with a total aggregate principal of US$1.275bn. Creditors voted 90% in favour. An important feature, given the diversity of the creditor group, was the option for bank lenders to choose to swap their debt into new restructured notes up to an aggregate US$300mn, which gave bank lenders the option to be treated as noteholders, thereby demonstrating equitable treatment of all creditors (with different risk preferences). Beyond US$300mn, amounts could be exchanged on a pro rata basis. This also reduced the number of bank lenders in negotiations, as they became noteholders. The bond deal preceded the bank deal, but all creditors were included, to all groups' satisfaction.

(*continued*)

(continued)

Corporate	*Eligible debt*	*New securities*
Ukrainian Railway	The state-owned company had one outstanding USD bond—US$500mn 9.5% May 2018 issued in 2013. The company's bond was in the perimeter of the government's debt restructuring operation, with its maturity falling due during the life of the IMF programme.	Restructuring, with a new bond issued in March 2016 involving maturity extension and higher coupon, and no principal haircut. Holders swapped into a new US$500mn 9.875% 2021 maturity, issued via a LPN structure through Shortline Plc.

Source: Bloomberg, Exotix

The US$7.4bn-strong Ukraine corporate bond market is concentrated around several major issuers and the leading industrial companies in the country. MHP, a vertically integrated poultry producer and one of the first corporates to ever issue Eurobonds in Ukraine, has three bond issues outstanding, with a total amount of US$1.13bn, and Kernel, a sunflower oil and grain producer, has a US$500mn bond issue. These have traded at lower yields than the sovereign, which reflects their sound management, remoteness from the conflict-hit east of the country, robust balance sheets and increasing reliance on export markets for cash flow. At the time of writing, Naftogaz was planning to issue a eurobond—a five-year US$ benchmark bond. It currently has no eurobonds outstanding.

Metinvest and DTEK were both affected by the conflict in the east of the country and some of their assets were seized in the temporary uncontrolled territories. Both companies completed bond restructurings (see table above) and their restructured and newly issued bonds are part of the corporate universe. The proximity of Metinvest's and DTEK's assets to the conflict zone and certain idiosyncratic risks place their eurobonds firmly above the sovereign yield curve.

There is a stack of still-unrestructured bonds, including those issued by agricultural companies Avangard and Mriya (at the time of writing, Mriya announced a restructuring) and Ukrlandfarming, and industrials Interpipe and Industrial Union of Donbass.

Descriptions of the Metinvest 2023, Metinvest 2026, MHP 2024, MHP 2026, DTEK 2024, and Kernel 2022 below.

Metinvest BV 7.75% 2023 *Bloomberg ticker: METINV*	
Borrower	Metinvest BV
Issue date	23 April 2018
Form	Eurobond
ISIN	XS1806400534
Issue size	US$944.515mn
Currency	US dollar
Denomination	US$200,000 and US$1000 thereafter
Amortisation	Callable
Final maturity date	23 April 2023
Coupon/interest	7.75% paid semi-annually
Collateralisation	Senior unsecured
Day count	30/360
Method of transfer	Euroclear/Clearstream
Joint lead managers	Deutsche Bank, ING, Nataxis, UniCredit
Exchange	Dublin, Munich, Stuttgart
Governing law	English
Guarantee type	Multiple
Guarantors	Subsidiaries
Guarantee level	Pari passu with senior unsecured

Source: Bloomberg

Metinvest BV 8.5% 2026 *Bloomberg ticker: METINV*	
Borrower	Metinvest BV
Issue date	23 April 2018
Form	Eurobond
ISIN	XS1806400708
Issue size	US$647.661mn
Currency	US dollar
Denomination	US$200,000 and US$1000 thereafter
Amortisation	Callable
Final maturity date	23 April 2026
Coupon/interest	8.5% paid semi-annually
Collateralisation	Senior unsecured
Day count	30/360
Method of transfer	Euroclear/Clearstream

(*continued*)

(continued)

Metinvest BV 8.5% 2026 *Bloomberg ticker: METINV*	
Joint lead managers	Deutsche Bank, ING, Nataxis, UniCredit
Exchange	Dublin, Munich, Stuttgart
Governing law	English
Guarantee type	Multiple
Guarantors	Subsidiaries
Guarantee level	Pari passu with senior unsecured

Source: Bloomberg

MHP 7.75% 2024 *Bloomberg ticker: MHPSA*	
Borrower	MHP SE
Issue date	10 May 2017
Form	Eurobond
ISIN	XS1577965004
Issue size	US$500mn
Currency	US dollar
Denomination	US$200,000 and US$1000 thereafter
Amortisation	Bullet
Final maturity date	10 May 2024
Coupon/interest	7.75% paid semi-annually
Collateralisation	Senior unsecured
Day count	30/360
Method of transfer	Euroclear/Clearstream
Joint lead managers	ING, JP Morgan
Exchange	Berlin, Dublin, Frankfurt, Stuttgart
Governing law	New York
Guarantee type	Multiple
Guarantors	Subsidiaries
Guarantee level	Pari passu with senior unsecured

Source: Bloomberg

MHP Lux SA 6.95% 2026
***Bloomberg ticker:** MHPSA*

Borrower	MHP Lux SA
Issue date	3 April 2018
Form	Eurobond
ISIN	XS1713469911
Issue size	US$550mn
Currency	US dollar
Denomination	US$200,000 and US$1000 thereafter
Amortisation	Bullet
Final maturity date	3 April 2026
Coupon/interest	6.95% paid semi-annually October and April
Collateralisation	Senior unsecured
Day count	30/360
Method of transfer	Euroclear/Clearstream
Joint lead managers	ING, JP Morgan, UBS
Exchange	Dublin, Berlin, Stuttgart
Governing law	New York
Guarantee type	Multiple
Guarantors	Parent & subsidiaries
Guarantee level	Pari passu with senior unsecured

Source: Bloomberg

DTEK Finance PLC 10.75% 2024
***Bloomberg ticker:** DTEKUA*

Borrower	DTEK Finance PLC
Issue date	29 December 2016
ISIN	XS1543030222
Issue size	US$1275.114mn
Amount outstanding	US$1343.774mn
Currency	US dollar
Denomination	US$2000 and US$1000 thereafter
Amortisation	Call/sink
Final maturity date	31 December 2024
Coupon/interest	10.75% paid quarterly (PIK)
Collateralisation	First lien
Day count	30/360
Method of transfer	Euroclear/Clearstream
Exchange	Frankfurt, Stuttgart
Guarantee type	Multiple
Guarantors	Parent & subsidiaries
Guarantee level	Pari passu with first-priority lien
Guarantor restrictions	Merger

Source: Bloomberg

Kernel 8.75% 2022
Bloomberg ticker: KERPW

Borrower	Kernel Holding SA
Issue date	31 January 2017
Form	Eurobond
ISIN	XS1533923238
Issue size	US$500mn
Currency	US dollar
Denomination	US$200,000 and US$1000 thereafter
Amortisation	Bullet
Final maturity date	31 January 2022
Coupon/interest	8.75% paid semi-annually January and July
Collateralisation	Senior unsecured
Day count	30/360
Method of transfer	Clearstream/DTC
Joint lead managers	ING, JP Morgan
Exchange	Dublin, Frankfurt, Stuttgart
Governing law	English
Guarantee type	Multiple
Guarantors	Subsidiaries
Guarantee level	Pari passu with senior unsecured

Source: Bloomberg

Selected corporate and financial bond issues

BB ticker	*Name*	*Sector*	*Issue date*	*Maturity date*	*Coupon*	*Issued amount (US$mn)*	*Outstanding amount (US$mn)*	*Currency*
AVINPU	Avangardco Investments	Food & Beverage	8 Oct. 2010	29 Oct. 2018	10%	200	213.725	USD
DTEKUA	DTEK Finance PLC	Mining & Power	28 Apr. 2015	28 Mar. 2018	10.375%	160	0	USD
DTEKUA	DTEK Finance PLC	Mining & Power	29 Dec. 2016	31 Dec. 2024	10.75%	1275.114	1343.717	USD
EXIMUK	Ukreximbank via Biz Finance PLC	Financial	2 Mar. 2018	2 Mar. 2021	16.5%	4051	4051	UAH
EXIMUK	Ukreximbank via Biz Finance PLC	Financial	27 Apr. 2015	27 Apr. 2022	9.625%	750	750	USD
EXIMUK	Ukreximbank via Biz Finance PLC	Financial	20 Jul. 2015	9 Feb. 2023	US LIBOR + 700	125	125	USD
EXIMUK	Ukreximbank via Biz Finance PLC	Financial	17 Jul. 2015	22 Jan. 2025	9.75%	600	600	USD
FXPOLN	Ferrexpo Finance PLC	Mining	24 Feb. 2015	7 Apr. 2019	10.375%	160.724	80.362	USD
FXPOLN	Ferrexpo Finance PLC	Mining	6 Jul. 2015	7 Apr. 2019	10.375%	185.664	92.832	USD
KERPW	Kernel Holding SA	Agriculture	31 Jan. 2017	31 Jan. 2022	8.75%	500	500	USD
METINV	Metinvest BV	Industrial	23 Apr. 2018	23 Apr. 2023	7.75%	944.52	944.52	USD
METINV	Metinvest BV	Industrial	23 Apr. 2018	23 Apr. 2026	8.5%	647.661	647.661	USD
MHPSA	MHP SE	Agriculture	10 May 2017	10 May 2024	7.75%	500	500	USD
MHPSA	MHP Lux SA	Agriculture	3 Apr. 2018	03 Apr. 2026	6.95%	550	550	USD
OSCHAD	State Savings Bank of Ukraine via SSB	Financial	1 Sep. 2015	10 Mar. 2023	9.375%	700	700	USD
OSCHAD	State Savings Bank of Ukraine via SSB	Financial	1 Sep. 2015	20 Mar. 2025	9.625%	500	500	USD
PUMBUZ	First Ukrainian International Bank CJSC via Green Finance PLC	Financial	14 Feb. 2007	31 Dec. 2018	11%	275	102.554	USD
RAILUA	Ukraine Railways via Shortline PLC	Transport	14 Mar. 2016	15 Sep. 2021	9.875%	500	500	USD

Source: Bloomberg

Venezuela

Nominal GDP (US$mn, 2018)[a]		96,328
Population (thousand, 2018)[a]		29,187
GDP per capita (USD, 2018)[a]		3300
Credit ratings (long-term foreign currency)[b]	Fitch	RD
	Moody's	C
	S&P	SD

[a]IMF WEO October 2018
[b]As at end-September 2018

See p. 771 for an important update on OFAC sanctions on Venezuela.

Country Summary

- After some 15 years in power, under which the economic model became increasingly dependent on oil revenues, the death of President Hugo Chavez in 2013 saw his nominated successor Nicolas Maduro take over the presidency. Maduro's rule has seen the build-up of an intense political rivalry with the opposition at a time of economic collapse and a growing humanitarian crisis following the period of low oil prices over 2014–2016.
- The country is now in a period of hyperinflation, amid fiscal dominance and FX shortages. Inflation is expected to reach 2.5mn percent by end-2018 according to the IMF. Real GDP is projected to have

Exotix Capital, *Exotix Developing Markets Guide*,
https://doi.org/10.1007/978-3-030-05867-8_41

fallen by 35% over 2013–2017 according to IMF WEO figures, while nominal GDP in USD terms could have halved in 2018 compared with 2017 (depending on what FX rate is used). Public debt could have risen to 150% of GDP.

- The government declared an intention to restructure its foreign debt (sovereign and PDVSA) on 2 November 2017, amid a severe tightening of liquidity conditions, and is now in default on most of its sovereign and PDVSA bonds. However, even if Venezuela wanted to, US sanctions preclude any restructuring under this government. Moreover, sizeable external debt, a complex capital structure, different legal rankings, with the presence of significant non-traditional bilateral creditors (China and Russia) and arbitrations claims, added to the collapse of the economy, all suggest the restructuring process could be one of the most complicated sovereign debt restructurings yet.

Economic data	*Avg*[a]	*2014*	*2015*	*2016*	*2017 (e)*	*2018 (f)*	*2019 (f)*
Real GDP growth	−0.3	−3.9	−6.2	−16.5	−14.0	−18.0	−5.0
Inflation (annual average)	57.5	57.3	111.8	254.4	1087.5	1.4mn	10mn
Current account (% of GDP)	3.2	2.3	−6.6	−1.6	2.0	6.1	4.0
Oil production (avg m bpd)[b]	2.30	2.34	2.36	2.22	1.94	1.49[c]	–
Reserves (US$bn, end-period)[d]	26.2	22.1	16.4	11.0	9.5	8.7[e]	–
Reserves/ imports (months)[f]	5.6	4.1	4.2	5.1	–	–	–
Overall fiscal balance (% of GDP)[g]	−10.6	−16.5	−17.6	−17.8	−31.8	−30.5	−30.0
Currency (ticker)	Bolivar (VEF, also abbreviated Bs).						

(*continued*)

(continued)

Economic data	*Avg*[a]	*2014*	*2015*	*2016*	*2017 (e)*	*2018 (f)*	*2019 (f)*
FX regime	Historically pegged against the US dollar and periodically devalued, high and hyperinflation since 2015 has destroyed the currency. The government stated on 26 July 2018 plans to roll out a new currency (Sovereign Bolivar), with five zeros removed, linked to the country's Petro cryptocurrency. The official DICOM FX auction rate was VEF/EUR201,364 on 27 July 2018 (implying VEF/US$178,200).						
Key exports	Mineral fuels including oil (83%), gems and precious metals (10%). Before the oil price fall in 2014–2016, oil accounted for 96% of goods exports.						

Source: IMF WEO Database, Haver, Bloomberg, WTEx. World Bank, Exotix

[a]10-year average to 2016 unless otherwise stated
[b]Bloomberg
[c]Average for January–July
[d]International reserves incl. gold from Haver
[e]Latest figure, July 2018
[f]Months of imports of goods and services, using imports data from World Bank WDI, Exotix calculation
[g]General government net lending

Key figures		*Party*[a]	*Since*
President	Nicolas Maduro	PSUV/GPP	Apr. 2013
Prime minister	Delcy Rodriguez	PSUV/GPP	Jun. 2018
Minister of finance	Simon Zerpa[b]	PSUV/GPP	Oct. 2017
Key opposition figure	Henri Falcon	Progressive Advance	2018
Central bank governor	Ramon Lobo[b]	PSUV/GPP	Oct. 2017

[a]After his re-election in 2006, President Chavez proposed the creation of a unified socialist party, the United Socialist Party of Venezuela (PSUV), to consolidate the parties aligned with his administration. These parties are not obligated to join the PSUV and can remain independent. The PSUV was officially registered at the National Electoral Council (CNE) in April 2008, comprising six political parties. The Great Patriotic Pole (GPP) was an alliance of the PSUV with other parties in support of Hugo Chavez's re-election in 2012

[b]Ramon Lobo was the Finance Minister until being appointed the central bank governor in October 2017. PDVSA CFO Simon Zerpa was then appointed acting Finance Minister

Politics

Executive power

Centred on the president who is chief of state and head of government. The cabinet is made up of a council of ministers appointed by the president.

Under President Chavez (1998–2013), there were various attempts (some successful, some not) to increase the power of the presidency. After taking office in February 1999, Chavez oversaw the approval of a new constitution in December extending the presidential term to six years (from five) and allowed presidential re-election. An election was subsequently held on 30 July 2000 under the terms of the new constitution, which Chavez won. In December 2007, proposals from both President Chavez and members of the National Assembly to amend the 1999 constitution, which included the further extension of the president's powers and term length, as well as increasing the powers of the State, were rejected in a referendum. In December 2008, President Chavez submitted a proposal to the National Assembly to amend the 1999 constitution to eliminate all term limits on elected officials, including the presidency. The changes were approved in a national referendum held in February 2009. In December 2010, the outgoing parliament passed legislation that gave President Chavez considerably more power to rule by decree. This was achieved before the new parliament session began in January 2011, and before the increased representation from the opposition following September 2010's legislative election. There have been no further constitutional changes; President Maduro's PSUV/GPP no longer has a parliamentary majority following the last legislative elections in 2015.

President Maduro called for a new National Constituent Assembly (NCA), tasked with the writing of a new constitution, for which elections were held on 30 July 2017. The opposition boycotted the election while the government reported more than eight million people voted. The NCA, which has 545 members, has wide-ranging powers and its authority exceeds that of the National Assembly and the President. In August 2017, the NCA extended the time it will meet from six months to two years. A number of countries have refused to recognise the authority of the NCA, including the US, the EU, Argentina, Brazil, Colombia, Mexico, Panama and Peru.

Presidential term: Six years, no term limits **Parliamentary term**: Five years

Legislature

Unicameral National Assembly (167 seats). 164 members elected by popular vote to serve five-year terms; three seats reserved for the indigenous peoples of Venezuela.

Elections

Next due *2020 (Legislative)/2024 (Presidential)*

Last legislative (December 2015)	*Seats*	*Last presidential (May 2018)*	*% of vote*
Democratic Unity Roundtable (catch-all opposition)	109	Nicolas Maduro (PSUV/GPP)	67.8
Great Patriotic Pole (Pro-PSUV)	55	Henri Falcon (Progressive Advance)	21.0
Other	0	Javier Bertucci (Independent)	10.8
		Reinaldo Quijada (UPP89)	0.4
Total	**164**	**Total**	**100.0**

People

Official name the "Bolivarian Republic of Venezuela", coined by President Chavez and named after Simon Bolivar who secured the independence of Gran Colombia, an area that covers modern day Venezuela, Colombia, Ecuador and Panama (and some other areas), from Spain in 1821. Venezuela seceded in 1830. Almost 90% of the population live in urban areas, especially in the north of the country. In addition to mestizo/ indigenous people, Europeans are predominant, particularly Spanish and Italian. There are also a considerable number of ethnic Arabs and Africans. Following a series of coups and military intervention beginning in 1947, and into the 1950s, democracy returned and the first civilian handover of power occurred in 1964. Venezuela went on to enjoy three decades of stable democracy into the 1990s. After the prosperity of the 1970s, as the country enjoyed the decade's oil price spikes and nationalised the oil and steel industries, boom turned to bust with the oil price collapse in the 1980s that led to a four-year recession. Hugo Chavez, a former paratrooper and coup leader in 1992, emerged out of the 1980s economic hardship, a champion of the poor and opposing the traditional wealthy and political elite, and was elected President in 1998. After surviving a political crisis over 2002–2004 (which included a two-day coup in April 2002 and a major strike at PDVSA), he sought to deepen his Socialist Revolution, including nationalisations beyond the oil sector. The country polarised further under his rule, with economic mismanagement and rising crime, and various attempts to increase the power and term length of the president. Chavez won a fourth term in the presidential election in October 2012 against Henrique Capriles (with 55.1% of the vote against 44.3%), but died in March 2013, leading to a snap election the following month, narrowly won by PSUV candidate and Chavez's chosen successor, Nicolas Maduro, with 50.6% of the vote to Capriles' 49.1%; a difference of just 225k votes. Inflation was already on the rise when Maduro took over, reaching 57% by end-2013, and his adoption of one-year emergency powers prompted opposition protests. Violence erupted in February–March 2014 in the student protests and opposition marches, while the later fall in the oil price put the economy under even greater pressure—leading to a deep (and continuing recession), hyperinflation, a sharp fall in reserves, FX shortages, and default. The opposition Democratic Unity coalition won a majority in the 2015 legislative elections, although in January 2016, three Democratic Unity deputies resigned from the National Assembly under Supreme Court pressure, removing the two-thirds majority needed to block Maduro's legislation proposals. Still, an emboldened opposition following its parliamentary election triumph now focussed its efforts on how to oust President Maduro, but a divided strategy played into the government's hand and finally the National Electoral Council (CNE) suspended the process of a recall referendum on 20 October 2016. The opposition demanded an early election, holding an unofficial referendum in July 2017, ahead of elections for the new Constituent Assembly that Maduro had called for. Maduro eventually called an early election, brought forward from December 2018, which was held in May 2018. Maduro won a second term, but his two closest rivals, Falcon and Bertucci, rejected the result due to irregularities (other leading opposition figures such as Henrique Capriles and Leopoldo Lopez were unable to run, by this time in prison or under house arrest). Turnout was less than half of all voters. Amid Venezuela's economic collapse, concern has grown over a humanitarian disaster, while over a million Venezuelans have reportedly left the country through Colombia over the 15 months to August 2018, many continuing to Ecuador and Peru.

Debt

	2012	*2017e*
External debt ratios (%)		
Total external debt/GDP	39.5	78.9
Public external debt/GDP	34.1	70.0
Private external debt/GDP	5.3	8.9
Total external debt/exports of goods and services	133.6	604.6
External debt service ratio (central government)	1.5	4.7
Public debt ratios (%)		
Public domestic debt/GDP	15.6	0.3
Public debt/GDP	49.7	70.3

Source: Central Bank, Ministry of Finance Office of Public Credit, World Bank IDS, IMF WEO, Exotix

There are no up-to-date or comprehensive statistics for Venezuelan debt from government sources. The Ministry of Finance's office of public credit publishes central government debt (external and domestic) with the most recent figures for June 2017. However, not only is that dated, the external debt figures appear to omit other lending, such as from China, and because it is central government, it excludes public corporations (such as PDVSA). The Office of Public Credit also publishes central government domestic debt to June 2017. The central bank publishes public sector and private sector external debt, although its most recent figures are for 2015. Its definition of public sector is not clear, however; it should relate to a wider level of government, although the figure it gives for bonds does not accord with the outstanding stock of sovereign and PDVSA bonds. Nor is it clear how the ministry's central government debt figures marry up to the central bank's public sector debt figures. Exotix therefore combines the different sources and its own estimates to derive external debt ratios for 2012 and 2017. There is also significant uncertainty over the level of US dollar GDP, given the hugely depreciated parallel exchange rate. Exotix uses IMF WEO figures for nominal GDP. Up-to-date figures for exports are also absent. Central bank figures for exports (and balance of payments in general) only go to Q3 15. Exotix uses World Bank WDI figures for subsequent years, although the WDI currently only goes to 2016.

Total external debt in 2012, according to the central bank, was US$130.8bn, comprising US$113.1bn in public sector external debt and US$17.7bn in private external debt. Central government external debt was US$45.4bn, according to the Office of Public Credit. As a share of WEO GDP, total external debt was 40% of GDP in 2012, with public external debt of 34% of GDP (and central government external debt of 13.7%) and private external debt of 5% of GDP (nominal GDP in US dollar terms in the WEO was US$31.5bn in 2012, with an implied average FX rate of VEF/US$4.9). Total external debt amounted to 134% of exports of goods (based on the central bank exports' figure of US$98bn). Public (central government) domestic debt was 15.6% of GDP in 2012, based on Office of Public Credit figures and WEO GDP. Hence, Exotix estimates that total public debt was 49.7% of GDP in 2012.

Total external debt in 2017, according to Exotix estimates, was cUS$66bn, comprising Exotix's own estimate of US$147bn in public sector external debt and holding constant the central bank figure of US$18.7bn in private external debt in 2015. Central government external debt was US$46.4bn in June 2017, according to the Office of Public Credit. As a share of WEO GDP, total external debt was 79% of GDP in 2017, with public external debt of 70% of GDP (and central government external debt of 22.1%) and private external debt of 9% of GDP (nominal GDP in US dollar terms in the WEO was projected at US$210.1bn in 2017, with an implied average FX rate of VEF/US$1397). Total external debt amounted to 605% of exports of goods (based on holding constant the latest WDI figure for 2016 of US$27bn in 2017—this is a strong assumption as oil production fell in H2 17 following PDVSA's own technical and cashflow problems, and after the imposition of US sanctions). Public (central government) domestic debt was 0.3% of GDP in 2017, based on office of public credit figures and WEO GDP. Hence, Exotix estimates that total public debt was 70.3% of GDP in 2017.

Exotix's best estimate for total external debt in 2017 is shown in the creditor composition table below. Exotix's own estimate of US$147bn in public external debt consists of central government external debt of US$46.4bn as of June 2017, according to Office of Public Credit figures, and an estimated US$100.3bn in other public sector external debt. Regarding central government external debt, over three-quarters of it is in the form of sovereign eurobonds, with an outstanding stock of US$36.1bn (nominal). Eurobonds have consistently been the single biggest creditor group in central government external debt since the official figures began in 1996, accounting for 70–85% of the debt. In June 2017, multilateral debt was US$5.3bn, c11% of central government external debt, which comprised mainly just two creditors, CAF and IADB. Bilateral debt was US$4bn in June 2017, c2.4% of central government external debt, three-quarters of which was owed to Russia. In terms of other public sector external debt, estimates are subject to significant uncertainty because of the lack of up-to-date data and transparency in lending (except, for other bond issues). Exotix groups other public sector external debt into four main categories: (1) other bilateral debt, estimated at cUS$25bn, including China (which Exotix estimates at US$20bn, based on media reports) and Rosneft (US$4.6bn outstanding at end-2017); (2) debt of public corporations. This comprises mainly PDVSA. Exotix estimates PDVSA debt as US$60bn, comprising cUS$40bn in financial debt (based on its accounts, which show it as fairly constant around this level, and which includes US$28.8bn in PDVSA bonds), and assuming some US$20bn in other debt, a figure which is subject to huge uncertainty (for example, debt owed to its joint ventures (JVs), as PDVSA has increasingly turned to its JV partners, asking them to handover oil planned for export for no payment, and arrears). The ELECAR bond is also included in public corporations; (3) other arrears, assumed to be US$10bn, which again is subject to huge uncertainty; and (4) arbitration awards of US$5bn. According to Exotix estimates, bonds (sovereign, PDVSA and ELECAR) amount to US$65.5bn, which is c45% of the public external debt.

Public external debt has likely increased over recent years, due to a rise in "other" public sector debt. This is mainly Chinese debt, arrears and other claims. Public external debt in 2015 (the latest year available) was US$120.2bn, according to central bank data, compared with US$113.1bn in 2012 (and just US$88.7bn in 2010). According to Exotix's best estimate for public sector external debt, it has risen by some US$27bn since 2015. The government has occurred some new (bilateral) debt since then, although the decline in Chinese debt probably outweighs any new debt, while the amount of bonds outstanding is broadly unchanged—new bonds came out of the off-market transactions (VENZ 36 and PDVSA 22) while there were some maturities over 2016–2017 and the PDVSA debt swap, but there have not been any significant new issues. Hence, the main driver of the increase in public external debt, on Exotix estimates, comes from arrears that have really built since the fall in the oil price in 2014, and arbitration claims.

Notably, assuming the same level of public external debt in 2018, the public external debt/GDP ratio increases from the estimated 70% in 2017 to 146% in 2018 because of the projected fall in US dollar GDP. The IMF WEO assumed nominal GDP of US$100.8bn (half as much of its estimated 2017 level). This is due to the assumed further devaluation in the exchange rate (the implied average FX rate in the WEO is VEF/ US$348,656). The IMF WEO projects gross general government debt at 162% of GDP in 2018.

Public external debt service (central government only) declined during our comparison period, to US$1.3bn in 2017 (almost two-thirds of which was interest) from US$1.5bn in 2012, based on Ministry of Planning and Finance figures. As a result, the external debt service ratio rose from 1.5% to 4.7%. However, separate World Bank figures show this increasing dramatically when publicly guaranteed debt is included, to US$6.6bn for 2016 (latest); only a small proportion of total external debt is concessional. Moreover, Venezuela began to default in certain sovereign and PDVSA bonds during the last quarter of 2017.

Composition of external debt

External debt by creditor (est 2017)	*Nominal amount outstanding (US$mn)*	*Share of total (%)*
Public sector external debt	**146,690**	**88.7**
o/w Central government[a]	46,440	28.1
Multilateral	5273	3.2
CAF	3252	2.0
IADB	2016	1.2
Bilateral	3953	2.4
Russia	3020	1.8
Brazil	756	0.5
Japan	107	0.1
Spain	66	0.0
Sovereign bonds	36,080	21.8
Banks and other financial institutions	1142	0.7
Suppliers	(8)	0.0
Other public sector debt (estimated)[b]	100,250	60.6
China	20,000	12.1
Rosneft	4600	2.8
PDVSA	60,000	36.3
o/w bonds	28,880	17.5
ELECAR bond	650	0.4
Arrears	10,000	6.0
Arbitration awards	5000	3.0
Private sector external debt[c]	**18,655**	**11.3**
Total external debt	**165,665**	**100.0**

Source: Ministry of Finance Public Credit Office, IMF, Exotix

[a]Central government debt as at end June 2017 from the Office of Public Credit

[b]Exotix estimates

[c]Latest figure (for 2015) from central bank

Rescheduling History

Venezuela is currently in default on most of its sovereign and PDVSA bonds after President Maduro announced on 2 November 2017 the government's intention to restructure all of its foreign debt (sovereign and PDVSA). This came after the period of low oil prices over 2014–2016 took its toll, amid an already deteriorating economy, with growing imbalances and a limited policy response. However, as at the time of writing, there had been no substantive talks with bondholders although bilateral rescheduling agreements with Russia and China have been reported. The latest debt crisis is the first since the 1990 Brady deal which occurred after a succession of commercial bank reschedulings in the 1980s. The country also suffered from short-lived technical defaults on commercial debt obligations in 1999 and 2005.

Relations with Multilateral Creditors

The IMF has no relationship with the Venezuela government and has not conducted an Article IV consultation since 2004. Venezuela's relations with the Bretton Woods institutions deteriorated under President Chavez, who essentially saw them as US imperialists, to the extent that Venezuela became largely isolated from them after being one of the IMF's founding members. Relations have seen no major improvements under President Maduro. Venezuela does not owe any money to the IMF. The outstanding balance was repaid in 2001 while its last programme finished in 1997. In fact, it was probably out of the experience of IMF austerity measures in the early 1990s imposed by Carlos Perez of the Democratic Action Party (AD), who was elected president in 1989, that in part laid the foundation for Chavez's subsequent ascent and his criticism of the Washington orthodoxy. Perez introduced austerity measures, including hikes in gas prices and public transport fares, with the help of an IMF loan, but these met with violent riots, particularly in Caracas (known as the "Caracazo"), and martial law. A general strike followed, in a period which saw hundreds die. President Chavez's anti-IMF stance reached its peak in April 2007 when he announced that Venezuela would withdraw from the IMF and World Bank, saying that the institutions did not help the poor. However, having paid back all its obligations to these institutions (five years ahead of schedule, saving US$8mn), immediate withdrawal was put on hold pending a proper evaluation of the matter. The backtracking came after the realisation that no longer being a member of the IMF would trigger a technical default on its global bonds, owing to membership clauses under the terms of the bonds. No formal steps were taken by Venezuela to withdraw its membership from the IMF and World Bank. However, Chavez announced the creation of a regional bank, the Bank of the South, established in September 2009, saying that the IMF and the World Bank were in crisis.

In November 2017, the IMF's Executive Board approved a decision that found Venezuela in breach of its obligation under Article VIII, Section 5 for the failure to provide certain data and key economic indicators. The Board expressed its hopes that Venezuela would consider strengthening its relations with the Fund and would consider Venezuela's progress again with six months. The Board met again in May 2018 to consider progress in implementing remedial measures approved in November 2017. The Board found that Venezuela had not implemented the remedial measures and had failed to provide information as required. The Fund subsequently issued a declaration of censure against Venezuela and the Board agreed to meet again in six months to consider progress in implementation.

IMF programmes

Date	*Arrangements*	*Comments*
1960–1961	SBA	
1989–1993	EFF	SDR3.9bn of which SDR2.0bn was drawn. Venezuela secured IMF assistance following its economic decline during the early 1980s as the Perez government implemented tough—and unpopular—austerity measures.
1996–1997	SBA	One-year SBA for SDR976mn, of which SDR350mn was drawn.

Source: IMF. Venezuela joined the IMF in 1946

The Inter-American Development Bank (IADB) is a relatively small creditor, but has active projects in Venezuela, especially in the energy sector. Developing infrastructure has been a focus, including electrical power, water and sanitation and resilience to natural disasters. The other major multilateral creditor, the Andean Development Corporation (CAF), has a similar focus on infrastructural development, with projects also in transport and urban development. The World Bank has had 52 projects in Venezuela, although six were dropped. Of the other 46, the latest new project approval was in June 2005, and no projects remain active.

Paris Club and Bilateral Creditors

Venezuela has never had a Paris Club agreement but has, recently, sought to restructure its bilateral debt.

Before its current economic problems started with the lower oil price from mid-2014, Venezuela had extended its own influence (and its role as a creditor) with countries in the region and beyond through a number of bilateral trade and development agreements. It used abundant oil revenues to provide an alternative credit market for Latin America and agreed a series of bilateral deals for the provision of cheap oil, through its Petrosur and PetroCaribe initiatives. The latter included agreements with Bolivia and Cuba made in April 2006, and the addition of Honduras, Nicaragua and Dominica, in initiatives that covered trade, health and energy. It also reached agreements to construct gas pipelines from Venezuela to Colombia, Brazil, Argentina, Uruguay, Paraguay and Bolivia. Several agreements had to be suspended after the oil price fell; Cuba in particular suffered from the loss of bilateral agreements. Strapped for cash, Venezuela accepted agreements from some countries, the Dominican Republic (2015) and Jamaica (2015), to buy back their PetroCaribe debt at significant discounts. The Dominican Republic bought back its US$4bn PetroCaribe debt at a 52% discount (only US$1.93bn was paid to satisfy the debt) while Jamaica repurchased its US$3.2bn PetroCaribe debt at 46 cents on the dollar.

President Chavez was also instrumental in the creation of the Banco del Sur (Bank of the South). The bank was established in 2009 via a treaty signed by seven countries (Argentina, Brazil, Bolivia, Ecuador, Paraguay, Uruguay and Venezuela) with initial capital of US$7bn (agreed in March 2009). It aims to foster regional integration through the financing of integration projects across the southern cone and is seen by members as a viable alternative to traditional multilaterals for the funding of economic and infrastructure projects in the region. There were three 'Bonds of the South' issues (in 2006 and 2007). However, its activities have been limited. Banco del Sur has experienced delays in receiving funds (it did not get its first deposits as scheduled by 2016) and in May 2017, Ecuador President Correa said he did not expect a solution in the short term, after the programme had been put on hold. A final regional initiative is the Bank of the ALBA which was created in January 2008. This built on Chavez's Bolivarian Alliance for the Americas (ALBA) established in December 2004, his alternative to the FTAA.

China and Russia have emerged as Venezuela's most important bilateral creditors over the past decade, a situation that only strengthened after 2014 following the decline in oil prices and the absence of other sources of external finance. According to figures from the Dialogue, China lent Venezuela US$62.2bn over 2007–2017. However, the terms of China's lending are not publicly available and it is not clear how much of the total has been repaid, although media reports in September 2016 citing local sources said that China was still owed US$20bn of the US$60bn it had lent to Venezuela. Venezuela's official figures appear to omit China's lending. Media reports suggest that Russia had lent Venezuela up to US$20bn over the past decade. The terms of its lending are not publicly available, but Venezuelan figures put bilateral debt with Russia at US$3bn.

Much of China's lending has occurred since the creation of the China-Venezuela Joint Fund in 2008 to channel billions of dollars into state projects in Venezuela, under which Venezuela shipped 524,000 barrels of crude oil and derivatives to China per day, nearly half of which went towards paying the loans. A US$20bn long-term facility with the China Development Bank was agreed in August 2010. After the oil price fall in 2014, Venezuela appeared to turn to China first. Media reports in November 2014 said that a US$4bn loan from China was added to reserves. President Maduro then led a trip to China in January 2015 (before heading to Qatar) to secure new financing, with media reports of loan pledges of up to US$20bn. The first US$5bn tranche of a US$10bn loan from the China Fund would be signed in March, with the remaining US$5bn in June. However, the Dialogue's figures show China's appetite to continue to provide new lending has appeared to wane, with only US$2.2bn agreed in 2016 and no lending in 2017, perhaps as Venezuela struggled with repayments. According to media reports in May 2016, a China foreign ministry spokesman confirmed that they had agreed to increase flexibility in bilateral financing cooperation to take account of changes in international oil prices although no details were given. In June 2016, Venezuela was reportedly in talks with China to obtain a grace period in its oil-for-loans deal, seeking a one-year grace period in which it would only pay interest on the loans. Meanwhile, in December 2017, a US subsidiary of China's state-owned Sinopec sued PDVSA in a US court for US$23.7mn relating to a 2012 steel rebar contract. Sinopec had agreed to invest US$14bn in a Venezuelan oilfield in September 2013, but the lower oil price from mid-2014 and lower production contributed to debt repayment difficulties. The lawsuit may indicate weakening relations and patience from China.

Venezuela has instead increasingly turned to Russia in the last few years. According to media reports, Rosneft agreed in February 2016 to pay US$500mn to PDVSA to increase its stake in their Petromonagas crude-processing joint venture, increasing its stake from 16.7% to 40%, and provided a US$1.5bn loan to PDVSA in December 2016 collateralised by a 49.9% pledge in Citgo Holding, PDVSA's US refining subsidiary. However, reports of a default to Russia surfaced in June 2017, after Russia announced that Venezuela had failed to make payments on a debt it renegotiated in September 2016, and by September 2017 there were media reports that Russia was in talks with Venezuela over a possible restructuring of its bilateral debt. In November 2017, Venezuela agreed with Russia to restructure US$3.15bn of sovereign debt. The deal allowed the repayment of the debt over 10 years, with minimal payments required in the first six years. It applied to sovereign bilateral debt only and not PDVSA's debt owed to Russia's Rosneft, which totalled around US$6bn in oil-guaranteed loans. At the time, Rosneft said it had no current plans to provide further financial support, and that debt servicing was continuing on schedule. According to Rosneft, PDVSA's debt to Rosneft declined by US$1bn to US$3.6bn in H1 2018.

The US has imposed various sanctions on Venezuela. This followed the Venezuela government's holding of elections to a National Constituent Assembly on 30 July 2017. The US State Department had threatened on 17 July to take "strong and swift economic actions" if the government proceeded with the NCA, which it did. Additional sanctions announced by the US Treasury on 26 July 2017 brought the number of Venezuela ministers/officials/military on OFAC's list of specially designated nationals (SDN) to 28, some of whom were already listed under President Obama, while the then vice president Tareck El Aissami was listed on the "kingpin" list in February 2017. The sanctions faced by those on the SDN list include an asset freeze in the US and prohibit US persons from dealing with them. US sanctions have intensified since then. In August 2017, OFAC extended sanctions under General Licence 3 to certain financial instruments and new borrowing, although permitting secondary market trading in most sovereign and PDVSA bonds (except VENZ 2036s). The impact of these sanctions was to prohibit trading in any new debt that comes out of an exchange that is not endorsed by the National Assembly (ie the opposition), in order not to provide financial support to the government. Sanctions were extended again in May 2018 following Maduro's election victory, although stopping short of a bank on US imports of

Venezuela's oil, including a ban on the purchase of debt or accounts receivables issued by the government and PDVSA and trading or purchase of any equity interest in which the Venezuela state owns more than 50%. 14 Latin American countries also agreed to increase financial scrutiny of sanctioned Venezuela officials.

Sovereign Commercial Debt

Important notice: Readers should be aware that, after the cut-off date for information in this book, the US Treasury's Office of Foreign Assets Control (OFAC) imposed a raft of new sanctions on Venezuela on 28 January 2019 which, inter alia, designated PDVSA as an SDN and restricted the trading of PDVSA bonds (under General Licence 9b). Trading restrictions were also extended to Venezuela sovereign bonds (General License 3c). The new US sanctions followed the emerging and now broad international recognition of opposition leader Juan Guaido as the country's legitimate president, after he was declared interim leader by the National Assembly on 23 January 2019, following the swearing in for a second six-year term of Nicolas Maduro as president on 10 January 2019. The situation in Venezuela remains fluid and investors are advised to seek legal advice on the sanctions regime.

Venezuela is currently (as at the time of writing) in default on most of its sovereign and PDVSA bonds, since announcing an intention to restructure its foreign debt in November 2017. Before this, Venezuela had generally remained current on its commercial debt for the preceding 18 years after seeing a number of commercial debt restructuring agreements, the most recent relating to its Brady deal in 1990, which followed earlier bank debt reschedulings during the 1980s.

In June 1990, Venezuela announced the terms of an exchange of medium term bank debt. The exchange, known as the 1990 Financing Plan, was along the lines of a Brady deal restructuring and followed from the 1980s Latin American debt crisis which Venezuela did not escape. The debt crisis of 1983–1988 was heightened by an unexpected drop in oil prices in 1986. This led to the restructuring of US$21.1bn of public debt in 1986 on terms that reflected expectations of future foreign exchange earnings. The interest margin was 0.875% over selected funding rates, becoming effective in November 1987. The Brady deal followed after a series of revisions to the 1986 agreement. The Brady deal repackaged between US$18bn–20bn of restructured bank debt. The menu of options consisted of debt and debt service reduction or new money and collateralised bonds. Funds for the purchase of collateral were provided by the IMF, World Bank, own resources and other sources. The exchange was completed in December 1990. The new instruments included par bonds, discount bonds, debt conversion bonds, new money bonds, FLIRBS and short-term notes, with different currencies being available. Holders of the par and discount bonds due 2020 were issued oil-indexed payment obligations (oil warrants). In March 2006, Venezuela completed the repurchase of US$699.55mn (principal amount) of dollar denominated discount bonds due 2020. The operation was done in a private transaction. Later, in May 2006, it redeemed all its outstanding par and discount bonds. All other bonds under the 1990 Financing Plan (except for the oil obligations) had matured by the end of 2008.

Commercial debt agreements

Date	*Details*
1986	Bank debt restructurings. Multi-year rescheduling agreement of US$21bn in maturities due over 1983–1989.
1987	Bank debt restructurings. Revision to the 1986 agreement, reducing the spread and extending maturities. US$100mn in new long-term money.
1988 Sep.	Bank debt restructurings. Revision to the 1986 agreement, reducing the spread. Covered US$20.3bn in debt.
1988 Dec.	Bank debt restructurings. Exchange of debt for bonds outside the main agreement.
1990 Dec.	Brady deal. Total of US$19.7bn of debt covered. The menu comprised: exchange for bonds at 30% discount (US$1.81bn), exchange at par for reduced fixed rate interest bonds (US$7.46bn), exchange for bonds at par with interest reduction (US$3.03bn), new money combined with debt conversion bonds (US$6.02bn) and buyback of 91-day collateralised short-term notes (US$1.41bn). The NPV haircut was 36.7%, according to the Cruces and Trebesch database.

Source: Exotix, World Bank GDF

Until 2017, Venezuela generally remained current on its public external debt since the 1990 Financing Plan, including its commercial debt. There were however two episodes of non-payment on public debt obligations which were quickly cured. In July 1998, the coupon on local currency bonds that were held by local residents was not paid. It was made a week later although the event counted as a technical default. The non-payment was due to a bureaucratic problem (the person who signed the cheques was not in the office). Such an event had been known to occur before, but the delays were not seen as intentional. Afterwards, Venezuela introduced automatic payment procedures to ensure such an event would not happen again. At the time, Moody's downgraded its rating from B2 to Caa1. In January 2005 a delay in the completion of the calculation to determine the payment under Venezuela's oil warrants prompted S&P to lower its rating to selective default (SD). The Venezuelan authorities blamed the delay, which affected the October 2004 payment, on problems stemming from the 2002–2003 works' stoppage at PDVSA. The payment was eventually made in March 2005, plus accrued interest from the scheduled payment date, and totalled US$350,000. S&P subsequently returned its rating to B.

Venezuela issued a number of global bonds after the 1990 Financing Plan, although its last regular sovereign bond issue was in 2011, while PDVSA's last regular issue was in 2014 (PDVSA also issued a new collateralised 2020 bond in a liability management operation in October 2016—see below). The sovereign returned to the market with a couple of issues each in 1997 and 1998 followed by a string of issues in 2001, 2003, 2004 and 2005, all of which are still outstanding. Operations tended to refinance maturities. Three-dollar issues amounting to US$4.6bn and a EUR1bn 10-year issue in 2005 for example enabled the prepayment of US$3.9bn in Brady Bonds, as well as US$843mn of obligations to multilaterals and private banks, including US$243bn to the World Bank, a year later in March 2006. In November 2007, the government issued a US$825mn bond with a coupon of 7% maturing in 2038 (subsequently tapped to US$1.25bn). The terms of the bond excluded the provision of default in the event that Venezuela ceases to be a member of the IMF. In November 2008, the government was reported to have repurchased US$800mn of bonds, including part of the 2027 maturity, although details were not provided. There were further issues annually over 2008–2011. Many of its existing bonds were also subsequently tapped. At the end of December 2016, the government issued a US$5bn sovereign bond (6.5% 2036) in what was considered an opaque transaction. According to media reports, the bonds was sold to a state-owned bank and subsequently offered to foreign investors at 20 cents on the dollar. Trading in the bond by US persons is sanctioned by OFAC. Meanwhile, Venezuela faces the maturity of its VENZ 13.625% 08/2018s Olds and News on 15 August 2018, for a combined amount of US$1.05bn, and a US$1bn maturity of its VENZ 7% 12/2018 on 1 December 2018, although repayment looks unlikely given the default situation. Prior to these, it had annual maturities over 2013–2016, with its most recent sovereign maturity the 5.75% 02/16 for US$1.5bn.

In November 2006 Venezuela issued US$1bn of the Bono Sur I, "Bond of the South". This was a mix of Argentina dollar-denominated Boden bonds and Venezuelan local debt securities (TICCs—denominated in US dollars but can be traded in bolivars). Further issues were made in 2007. Venezuela sold US$1.5bn of the Bono Sur II in February, which included US$750mn of 7% Bodens due 2015 and US$750mn of 5.25% TICC bonds due 2019. In September, Venezuela issued US$1.2bn of Bono Sur III, comprising US$600mn of 7.0% Bodens due 2015 and US$600mn 7.125% TICCs due 2015. Both times, Venezuela purchased the Bodens from Argentina. There have been no further issues.

Petroleos de Venezuela (PDVSA), the state-owned oil company, has also been an active issuer. The company has nine bonds outstanding as of July 2018 for a total nominal amount of US$27.9bn. Most of its outstanding bonds were issued between 2011–2014. PDVSA did a mega bond issue in April 2007, when it issued US$7.5bn in total in three maturities (2017, 2027 and 2037). In another opaque transaction, the US$3bn PDVSA 6% 10/22 were issued in 2014 but sold to the central bank, before being offered to investors in June 2017, at a reported 31 cents on the dollar. The bonds became known as the Hunger Bonds.

PDVSA completed a liability management operation in October 2016. As financing concerns grew during 2016, the government stated in May 2016 that it was studying proposals for a voluntary debt reprofiling. It was not clear whether the government meant the sovereign or PDVSA or both but by September, PDVSA had published details of a proposed bond swap after lengthy discussions with market participants, amid some concern that given depressed market prices at the time, investors may demand too much to make such an operation work. At the time, PDVSA was confronted with a debt repayment hump in late 2016/early 2017, including a US$1bn bullet maturity of its 5.125% 10/2016 due on 28 October, the second amortisation payment of US$2.05 of its 8.5% 11/2017 (17n) due on 2 November, and US$3bn bullet maturity of the 5.25% 04/2017 (17o) due 12 April. Eligible bonds were the April 2017 bullet and November 2017 amortising bonds (US$3bn 5.25% 2017 and US$4.1bn 8.5% 2017), with an eligible amount therefore of US$7.1bn. The 5.125% 10/2016 bullet was not included and was repaid. In the swap PDVSA offered a new 8.5% 2020 bond with a 1:1 exchange ratio to be repaid in four equal annual payments starting at the first anniversary. Crucially, in order to sweeten the deal, the bonds were to be secured by a first-priority security interest on 50.1% of the capital stock of CITGO Holding. The oil minister said the swap was voluntary and that the government was prepared to meet debt obligations if the swap was declined by bondholders; probably a requirement to avoid it being classed as a distressed exchange. The PDVSA swap was concluded on 24 October after a few delays and while the government presented it as a success, participation was lower than it would have wanted, at 39.4%. Only US$2.8bn was tendered. PDVSA confirmed it will waive the condition of getting at least 50% of the principal eligible amount for the swap to be consummated. The split of amounts tendered was: US$942mn of 17o bonds and US$1857mn of 17n bonds; participation was 31.4% and 45.3%, respectively. More than two-thirds of the amount of 17o elected to hold out on the expectation of getting par upon maturity in the following April. US$3367mn of new 2020 amortising bonds would be issued in exchange for bonds tendered. Expected settlement date was 27 October. Cash flow savings were estimated at US$1.9bn through to November 2017.

President Maduro announced on 2 November 2017 that Venezuela would seek a renegotiation of its foreign debt after making a US$1.1bn payment that was due the same day. The payment was the final amortisation of the unswapped PDVSA 17n. Maduro had steadfastly chosen not to default in the immediate aftermath of the oil price decline from mid-2014, despite rising pressure on liquidity and declining reserves, instead squeezing imports to adjust to declining export revenues (goods' imports fell by 75% between 2012 and 2016, according to World Bank WDI data, to just US$16.3bn) and reaching out, initially, to China and then to Russia to secure new funding, as well as trying to buy time through the PDVSA debt swap. For some observers, the surprise was not that Venezuela defaulted, but why it took so long. Various arguments were put forward by market participants as to why the government rejected default, including the fear that it would lead to creditors seizing oil and foreign assets, it would hurt senior politicians, officials and military leaders who allegedly held the bonds, and/or that it would lead to the collapse of the government. But it seemed that the government bowed to the inevitable by the autumn of 2017, confronted with heavy debt repayments. Amid market confusion over the government's intentions, the government organised a meeting in

Caracas for bondholders on 13 November although attendance was reportedly low. The meeting was hosted by the then vice president Tareck El Aissami, who had been selected to lead the debt negotiations, but investors were concerned that attending the meeting would be breach of the sanctions given he was on the US sanctions list. Moreover, the US sanctions would appear to prevent a restructuring from taking place anyway as they prohibit the issuance of the new securities that would be needed to execute an exchange (unless authorised by the National Assembly, which is difficult to envisage), suggesting that any attempt to restructure will have to wait for political change.

After the restructuring announcement, Venezuela began to use grace periods to delay payments and seemed to pay some bonds selectively over others, after delays, although over time most coupons on both sovereign and PDVSA bonds were being missed except for the PDVSA 2020 collateralised bond (which remains current), while the situation on the VENZ 36s, which is subject to OFAC sanctions, is unclear. Arrears have been accumulating since on all other bonds. The government also failed to repay the maturing VENZ 18s (old and new) on 15 August 2018.

Exotix calculates that total past due interest and accrued as at end July 2018 was US$5.4bn, comprising US$3.3bn on sovereign bonds (excluding VENZ 36s) and US$2.1bn on PDVSA bonds (excluding PDVSA 20s). As of the end of July, none of the bonds had been accelerated by bondholders.

Bondholders in the US and Europe began to organise informally even before the government announced its intention to restructure. The IIF also helped to facilitate creditor coordination. At least one creditor committee has since been formed, according to media reports. The Venezuela Creditors' Committee, consisting of creditors holding US$8bn of bonds issued by the Republic, PDVSA and ELECAR, issued a statement on 25 June 2018 stating that it will not support a restructuring that did not respect the principle of fair treatment of all creditors of equal rank.

A summary of Venezuela's outstanding eurobonds (sovereign and PDVSA) is shown below. As of July 2018, there were 16 sovereign bonds outstanding, including the 36s, for a total nominal amount of US$36.1bn, and there were nine PDVSA bonds outstanding, including the 22s, for a total nominal amount of US$28.8bn. A description of the VENZ 27s (in default) and the PDVSA collateralised 20s (current) is also given.

Venezuela's outstanding eurobonds—sovereign and PDVSA

Description	*Size (US$mn)*	*Issue date*	*CAC (Y/N and threshold)*	*First missed coupon payment*[a]
Sovereign (Bloomberg: VENZ)				
US$ 13.625% Due 8/2018	753	6 August 1998	No	15 March 2018
US$ 13.625% Due 8/2018	300	27 September 2001	No	15 March 2018
US$ 7% Due 12/2018	1000	1 December 2003	Yes (85%)	1 January 2018
US$ 7.75% Due 10/2019	2496	13 October 2009	Yes (75%)	13 November 2017
US$ 6% Due 12/2020	1500	9 December 2005	Yes (75%)	9 January 2018
US$ 12.75% Due 8/2022	3000	23 August 2010	Yes (75%)	23 March 2018
US$ 9% Due 5/2023	2000	7 May 2008	Yes (75%)	7 December 2017
US$ 8.25% Due 10/2024	2496	13 October 2009	Yes (75%)	13 November 2017
US$ 7.65% Due 4/2025	1600	21 April 2005	Yes (75%)	21 November 2017
US$ 11.75% Due 10/2026	3000	21 October 2011	Yes (75%)	21 November 2017
US$ 9.25% Due 9/2027	4000	18 September 1997	No	15 April 2018
US$ 9.25% Due 5/2028	2000	7 May 2008	Yes (75%)	7 December 2017
US$ 11.95% Due 8/2031	4200	5 August 2011	Yes (75%)	5 March 2018
US$ 9.375% Due 1/2034	1500	14 January 2004	Yes (85%)	13 February 2018
US$ 6.5% Due 12/2036[b]	5000	29 December 2016	n/a	n/a
US$ 7% Due 3/2038	1250	15 November 2007	Yes (75%)	30 April 2018
PDVSA (Bloomberg: PDVSA)				
US$ 8.5% Due 10/2020	3368	28 October 2016	n/a	Current
US$ 9% Due 11/2021	2394	17 November 2011	n/a	17 December 2017
US$ 12.75% Due 2/2022	3000	17 February 2011	n/a	17 March 2018

(continued)

(continued)

Description	*Size (US$mn)*	*Issue date*	*CAC (Y/N and threshold)*	*First missed coupon payment*[a]
US$ 6% Due 10/2022	3000	28 October 2014	n/a	28 May 2018
US$ 6% Due 5/2024	5000	16 May 2014	n/a	16 December 2017
US$ 6% Due 11/2026	4500	15 November 2013	n/a	15 December 2017
US$ 5.375% Due 4/2027	3000	12 April 2007	n/a	12 November 2017
US$ 9.75% Due 5/2035	3000	17 May 2012	n/a	17 December 2017
US$ 5.5% Due 4/2037	1500	12 April 2007	n/a	12 November 2017

Source: Bloomberg, Exotix. As of end-July 2018

[a]Date shown is the expiry of grace period
[b]Trading of this bond is prohibited under US OFAC sanctions

Venezuela eurobond—in default Venezuela 9.25% 2027 Bloomberg ticker: VENZ	
Borrower	Republic of Venezuela
Issue date	18 September 1997
Form	Global
Other features	The bonds do not include collective action clauses (CACs)
ISIN	US922646AS37
Issue size	US$4bn
Currency	US dollar
Denomination	Min. piece of US$1000/increments thereafter of US$1000
Amortisation	Bullet
Final maturity date	15 September 2027
Coupon/interest	9.25% per annum, paid September and March
Default date	15 March 2018
Day count	30/360
Method of transfer	Euroclear/Clearstream, FED FUNDS, DTC
Settlement period	T + 2 business days
Exchange	Berlin, Dusseldorf, EuroTLX, Frankfurt, HI-MTF, LIMA, Luxembourg, Munich, SIX, Stuttgart
Joint lead managers	Chase Manhattan International, Goldman Sachs
Governing law	New York

Source: Bloomberg

PDVSA Eurobond
PDVSA 8.5% 2020
Bloomberg ticker: PDVSA

Borrower	Petroleos de Venezuela SA (PDVSA)
Issue date	27 October 2016
Form	Eurobond
Collateral	Secured by first-priority lien on 50.1% of the capital stock of CITGO Holding
ISIN	USP7807HAV70
Issue size	US$3.368bn
Amount outstanding	US$2.526bn (after October 2017 amortisation payment)
Currency	US dollar
Denomination	Min. piece of US$150,000/increments thereafter of US$1000
Amortisation	Four equal annual payments commencing 28 October 2017
Final maturity date	27 October 2020
Missed payment	27 October 2017 (subsequently paid after expiry of 30-day grace period)
Coupon/interest	8.5% per annum
Day count	30/360
Method of transfer	Euroclear/Clearstream
Settlement period	T + 2 business days
Exchange	Berlin, Dusseldorf, Frankfurt, Munich, Stuttgart
Governing law	New York

Source: Bloomberg

Venezuela is the subject of a number of arbitration claims. According to media reports, there are 41 public claims lodged against the country in the World Bank's International Centre for Settlement of Investment Disputes (ICSID) alone. Claims against Venezuela include those by gold and oil companies whose assets were expropriated by the government. Exotix is aware of three gold company claims. Gold Reserve signed a settlement agreement with Venezuela in June 2017 after an ICSID award in its favour. Under the terms of the Agreement, Venezuela agreed to pay the Company US$792mn to satisfy the award and US$240mn for the mining data for a total of cUS$1.032bn. Rusoro Mining was awarded US$1bn (plus interest) in August 2016 following an arbitration claim filed in ICSID. Rusoro submitted a claim for US$3.03bn in 2013. In May 2018, Rusoro announced that it had filed lawsuits in Houston and

Calgary as it sought to enforce its judgments. Crystallex was awarded US$1.2bn (plus interest) against Venezuela in April 2016 in a claim brought before ICSID. Crystallex subsequently registered the judgement in the US (Delaware) and sought to collect on its judgement through attaching shares PDVSA owns in PDV Holding, its US subsidiary. PDV Holding, 100% owned by PDVSA, owns 100% of Citgo (PDVSA's US refinery). Crystallex alleged PDVSA was the alter ego of the State and thus it was allowed to seize PDVSA's property to satisfy its judgement. The US District Court for the District of Delaware ruled on 9 August 2018 granting Crystallex's motion, which is subject to appeal.

In the oil sector, PDVSA was ordered to pay ConoccoPhillips US$2.04bn by the International Chamber of Commerce (ICC) in April 2018 in compensation for expropriation of the company's assets in 2007. Conoco had sought up to US$22bn from PDVSA. The company has also filed a separate arbitration case against Venezuela in ICSID. ExxonMobil has also brought two separate arbitration claims before ICSID and the ICC after the nationalisation of its assets in 2007. In 2017, an ICSID ruling annulled an award made in 2014 for Venezuela to pay damages of US$1.6bn to the company. The company had been seeking compensation of up to US$10bn.

Venezuela's Oil Warrants

Venezuela's Oil-Indexed Payment Obligations ("oil warrants") were created during the Brady bond restructuring of 1990 to enable creditors to share in any gains that Venezuela would experience from rising oil revenues. Payments are due, subject to certain conditions, twice a year (April and October) if they are in the money. According to the Fiscal Agent there were 24,779,805 obligations outstanding in December 2017. The warrants are due to expire in April 2020.

The warrants are currently in default, as of 16 April 2018, after the Fiscal Agent notified that the Republic failed to deposit funds to pay monies due on the obligations on 16 April 2018.

The warrants pay if Venezuela's oil export price (reference price) exceeds an inflation-adjusted hurdle rate (strike price), although payments are capped at US$3 per obligation per semi-annual payment. The reference price is calculated as the average of Venezuela's oil export price in the twelve months through to February for the April payment and the twelve months through to August for the October payment. The strike price was set at US$26 per barrel as of April 1996 and is adjusted at each payment date according to the US producer price index (PPI Finished Goods less Energy, not seasonally adjusted). The most recent officially published strike price for the October 2017 payment, as given by the fiscal agent, was US$37.52pb. The published reference price was US$41.42. Venezuela's oil export price trades at a (variable) discount to WTI reflecting the high sulphur content (heaviness) of Venezuelan crude.

Payments on the warrants are subject to a force majeure (ie payments can be suspended if certain conditions are met). This requires meeting two conditions. First, a decline period must be satisfied. This means any six-month period ending on the last day of a determination period (February and August) for which there is a decline of at least 7.5% in the volume of crude oil exports (in barrels) compared to the volume of crude oil exports for the six consecutive six-month periods immediately preceding the decline period. Second, the decline must be the direct result of the occurrence of a suspension event. These are specified in the prospectus and include acts of God, acts of war, civil war, sabotage, embargoes, revolution, riot, civil disturbance, natural disasters and labour related disruptions, such as strikes, etc. Upon a force majeure being triggered, as determined by the Calculation Agent at the request of the Republic, payments are suspended. A make-up clause ensures that suspended payments are paid upon a resumption report being issued by the Calculation Agent.

Although the warrants were eligible to pay in April 1996, payments did not begin until 2004 as until then the oil price did not exceed the trigger. The first payment (being US$ 0.01) was made on 15 October 2004. Since then, payments from 15 April 2005 until October 2015 inclusive were made at the US$3 cap. With the subsequent decline in oil prices over 2014–2016, the payment fell to US$0.65 in April 2016. There were no payments due in October 2016 or April 2017. The payment due in October 2017 was at the US$3 cap. However, it was not paid on the payment date itself. The Fiscal Agent notified on 26 October 2017 a change to the record date to 13 November 2017 and a change to the payment date to 20 November 2017. The total amount due was US$74.3mn. Default interest on the late October 2017 payment amounting to US$0.008 per obligation (a total of US$190,509.61) was subsequently paid on 12 January 2018. Exotix calculations suggest a payment was also due at the most recent payment date in April 2018, but this was not made.

Venezuelan oil warrants
Bloomberg ticker: VENZ

Borrower	Republic of Venezuela
ISIN	XS0029484945
Issue date	18 December 1990
First payment date	15 April 1996
Last payment date	15 April 2020
Payment dates	15 April, 15 October
Calculation formula	Excess of Reference Price over Strike Price on Determination Date.
Strike price	US$26.00 as of 5 April 1996, inflated by the US producer price index (PPI index—finished goods less energy, not seasonally adjusted).
Reference price	Price per barrel of crude equal to the ratio of Venezuelan oil export revenues to volumes (barrels) during the Determination Period.
Payment cap/each payment	US$3.00
Determination date	5 April for 15 April payment and 5 October for 15 October payment of each year.
Determination period	12-month period ending on 28 February and 31 August of each year.
Warrant detachment	Effective 2 January 2002, trades separately from par and discount bonds.
Notional amount of warrants per bond	0.5% of face of pars. 0.714% of face of discounts.
Settlement period	T + 3 business days
Method of transfer	Euroclear/Clearstream
Fiscal agent	Bank of New York Mellon

Source: Bloomberg

Corporate Bond Markets

Aside from sovereign and PDVSA bonds there is one other bond of note, that issued by the state-owned company Electricidad de Caracas (ELECAR). The company is now in default on its US$650mn principal that was due on 10 April 2018. The company had previously defaulted on a coupon in October 2017. ELECAR is a subsidiary of PDVSA but not a significant subsidiary in bond document terminology. The corporate bond does not have a state guarantee and does not cross default to either the government or PDVSA.

ELECAR eurobond—in default
ELECAR 8.5% 2018
Bloomberg ticker: ELECAR

Borrower	CA La Electricidad de Caracas (ELECAR)
Issue date	10 April 2008
Form	Eurobond
ISIN	XS0356521160
Issue size	US$650mn
Currency	US dollar
Denomination	Min. piece of US$1000/increments thereafter of US$1000
Amortisation	Bullet
Final maturity date	10 April 2018
Coupon/interest	8.5% per annum, paid semi-annually April and October
Default date	Coupon: 10 October 2017; Principal: 10 April 2018
Day count	30/360
Method of transfer	Euroclear/Clearstream
Manager	ABN Amro
Exchange	Berlin, Frankfurt, Luxembourg, Munich, SIX, Stuttgart
Governing law	New York

Source: Bloomberg

Vietnam

Nominal GDP (US$mn, 2018)[a]		241,434
Population (thousand, 2018)[a]		94,575
GDP per capita (USD, 2018)[a]		2553
Credit ratings (long-term foreign currency)[b]	Fitch	BB
	Moody's	Ba3
	S&P	BB–

[a]IMF WEO October 2018
[b]As at end-September 2018

Country Summary

- Although a one-party communist state, under the firm control of the Communist Party of Vietnam (CPV), a process of economic transformation (market-based reforms) began under a policy of Doi Moi in 1986. Industrialisation has since contributed to a decline in agriculture's share of economic activity, although it still employs almost half of the labour force. However, a significant wealth gap exists between rural and urban areas. There is political and religious suppression and opposition activists have been convicted without actual criminal acts.
- One of the fastest-growing Asian economies over the past decade (averaging over 6% annually), despite a series of exogenous shocks, economic development has been spurred by WTO accession in 2007. Low labour

Exotix Capital, *Exotix Developing Markets Guide*,
https://doi.org/10.1007/978-3-030-05867-8_42

costs provide international competitiveness. Near-term policy challenges include tackling economic overheating, rising inflation, the large budget deficit and the recent reliance on short-term debt. Vietnam has the third-largest proven oil reserves in Asia, after those of China and India.

- Since its Brady deal in 1998, Vietnam has had a generally sound track record on debt payments, barring a default in 2010 at Vinashin, the state-shipping company, an event that spurred long overdue reform of inefficient state-owned enterprises (SOEs). Public and external debt have both risen over the past several years, with government debt at over 60% of GDP in 2016 (up-to-date official statistics are not available), although Vietnam only has two outstanding eurobonds.

Economic data	*Avg*[a]	*2014*	*2015*	*2016*	*2017 (e)*	*2018 (f)*	*2019 (f)*
Real GDP growth	6.1	6.0	6.7	6.2	6.8	6.6	6.5
Inflation (annual average)	8.8	4.1	0.6	2.7	3.5	3.8	4.0
Current account (% of GDP)	−1.1	4.9	−0.1	2.9	2.5	2.2	2.0
Reserves (US$bn, end-period)[b]	23.5	34.3	28.4	36.7	42.2	–	–
Reserves/imports (months)[c]	2.3	2.5	1.9	2.3	2.3	–	–
Overall fiscal balance (% of GDP)[d]	−3.9	−6.3	−5.5	−4.8	−4.5	−4.6	−4.7
Currency (ticker)	Vietnam dong (VND)						
FX regime	De jure floating, but de facto peg to the dollar, with a trading band around a central rate quoted by the State Bank of Vietnam. The IMF classifies the regime as a stabilised arrangement. In November 2009, the State Bank of Vietnam (SBV) devalued the dong, lowering the dollar-dong central rate by 5.5%, within a revised band of +/−3%. It lowered the central rate again in February 2010 (by 3.3%), in August 2010 (by 2%), in February 2011 (by 8.5%) and in August 2015 (by 1%).						
Key exports	Machinery (40.8%), clothing and footwear (25.2%), vegetable products (5.8%), metals (3.1%), crude petroleum (2.0%).						

Source: IMF WEO Database, Haver, IMF Country Reports, OEC

[a]10-year average to 2016 unless otherwise stated

[b]Gross international reserves

[c]In months of the current year's imports of goods, services and primary income debit

[d]Overall government net lending

Key figures		*Party*	*Since*
President	Dang Thi Ngoc Thinh[a]	CPV	Sep. 2018
Prime minister	Nguyen Xuan Phuc	CPV	Apr. 2016
CPV general secretary	Nguyen Phu Trong	CPV	Jan. 2011
Minister of finance	Dinh Tien Dung	CPV	Apr. 2016
Central bank governor	Le Minh Hung	–	Jan. 2016

[a]Serving as acting president following the death of President Tran Dai Quang on 21 September 2018

Politics

Executive power

Vietnam is a one-party communist state controlled by the CPV, with executive power shared among a tripartite consisting of the president (who is chief of state), the prime minister (who is head of government) and the CPV general secretary. All three are members of a 15-person Politburo (effectively, a joint executive) that determines government policy, although the supreme party organ is the National Congress held every five years (next due in January 2021). The president is elected by the legislature and is responsible for appointing the prime minister, affirmed by the legislature. The CPV elects the secretary general.

Presidential term: Five years (consecutive terms allowed)

Parliamentary term: Five years

Legislature

Unicameral, the 500-seat Quoc Hoi (National Assembly), the main legislative body, is elected by popular vote to serve five-year terms. It meets twice a year. Candidates stand for the CPV or CPV-approved independents. There is no legal opposition to the CPV. The National Assembly has become more assertive and enjoys some legislative freedom (it was previously a rubber stamp organisation), although the Politburo still heavily guides policy-making and the CPV remains in firm control.

Elections

Next due *Presidential and legislative: 2021*

Last legislative election (May 2016)	*Seats*	*Last presidential (April 2016)*	*% of vote*
Communist Party of Vietnam (CPV)	475	Tran Dai Quang (CPV)	91[a]
Non-party members (pro-CPV)	21	(running unopposed)	
Total	**496**[b]	**Total**	**100**

[a]The presidential candidate is indirectly elected by the legislature from within the politburo. Members are asked if they approve the candidate or not and, in 2016, 91% did

[b]Four seats were left vacant as some provinces had no candidates earning the requisite 50% of votes. Two CPV candidates-elect were disqualified before the first session of the newly elected National Assembly, and the party's number of seats declined to 473

People

Vietnamese account for c85% of the population, although there are another 50 ethnic groups. According to a 2010 Pew study, c45% of the population follow indigenous religions, followed by Buddhism, Christianity and other faiths; however, the 2009 census found that around four-fifths of the population are not religious. Approximately 40% of the population is under 25, and the median age is 30. Net migration is very slightly negative, and 35% of population live in urban areas (2017). Although Hanoi is the capital city, with a population of 7.4mn, Ho Chi Minh City (formerly Saigon), population 8.4mn, is the largest, and the main economic centre.

Vietnam's French colonial rulers were ousted by Japanese forces during World War II. After Japan's surrender, a communist nationalist group, called Viet Minh, under the leadership of Ho Chi Minh, took advantage of the power vacuum and declared independence in 1945. The French did not withdraw for another nine years under the Geneva Agreement and Vietnam was divided into communist North (the Democratic Republic of Vietnam) and non-communist, western-backed South (the Republic of Vietnam). The Vietnam war followed over 1961–1973 when, after several years of northern incursion, South Vietnam's president requested US military aid in December 1961. The Paris Accords were signed in January 1973, officially ending the war and dividing South Vietnam between non-communists and the southern-Viet Cong (communist militia group). However, fighting continued as North Vietnam invaded the South, taking Saigon on 30 April 1975, which was followed by formal unification of the country in July 1976 creating today's Socialist Republic of Vietnam. In 1986 CPV leader Nguyen Van Linh led the 'Doi Moi' liberal and economic reform agenda and a new constitution was approved in 1992.

Vietnam continues peacefully under a socialist one-party state, not dissimilar to the Chinese model. Although formal clandestine democratic political groups began to emerge in 2006, the State still takes a hard line on dissent and criticism of the regime and has been accused of clamping down on the freedom of expression. Six democracy activists were sentenced for up to six years in prison in 2009 for "spreading propaganda" against the government by hanging pro-democracy banners on a road bridge.

Vietnam has normalised its international standing. Relations with the US were fully restored in 1995, and Vietnam joined the WTO in January 2007 after 12 years of negotiations, and took up a two-year non-permanent seat on the UN Security Council in January 2008, but has not taken a seat since. The years since the 1980s reforms have also seen continued economic progress and industrialisation. In January 2018, several senior communist figures were convicted following losses at state oil firm PetroVietnam. Although this was explained as cracking down on corruption and holding executives accountable for mismanagement, observers suggested it may have also been intended to remove officials who opposed political leaders.

The country has traditionally been agriculture-based, although agriculture's share of GDP declined from 32% of GDP in 1990 to c16% in 2015, while still employing 48% of the labour force. Challenges remain, however, as Vietnam remains a poor country. There is still massive under-development and high poverty in the remote ethnic-minority regions, which is much greater than the national average. Large foreign aid and multilateral support have helped to improve infrastructure, and numerous organisations have development programmes in the country.

DEBT

	2012	*2016*
External debt ratios (%)		
Total external debt/GDP	39.6	43.2
Public external debt[a]/GDP	26.0[b]	24.1[b]
Private external debt/GDP	5.7[b]	12.2[b]
Total external debt/exports of goods and services	49.4	45.9
External debt service ratio	1.8	1.8
Public debt ratios (%)		
Public domestic debt[a]/GDP	21.0	33.0
Public debt[a]/GDP	47.0[b]	57.1[b]

Source: World Bank IDS, IMF, Exotix

[a]Public and publicly guaranteed
[b]Including only MLT external debt

Vietnam's total external debt at end-16 was US$87bn, based on World Bank figures, with the majority (55.7%) being MLT debt owed by the public sector. Much of the public sector's foreign debt was on concessional terms and was still owed to official creditors. Public and publicly guaranteed (PPG) MLT external debt amounted to US$48.5bn in 2016, up from US$40.4bn in 2012. Another US$14bn was short-term external debt, although it is not specified how much of this is owed by the public sector and private sector. The main public sector multilateral creditors remain the World Bank (both IDA and IBRD) and the Asian Development Bank (ADB). Bilateral creditors accounted for 40% of MLT PPG and over 22% of all external debt at end-16. PPG MLT commercial creditors accounted for US$7.7bn, most of which is owed to banks, although there was US$1.5bn in bonds, based on World Bank figures. The maturity profile of government bonds has shortened: 10% of government bonds had a maturity of one-to-three years in 2004; this rose to 60% in 2014. Vietnam has taken on concessional debt since the 1990s to develop infrastructure, contributing to foreign debt rising by more than a factor of six between 2001 and 2015, compounded by inefficient management of public investment. Some debtors with government-guaranteed loans also lost their repayment ability, passing on the burden on to the government. At end-16, on official figures, Vietnam's total public debt (excluding short-term external debt) stood at 57% of GDP, up from 47% in 2012.

Total external debt in 2016, therefore, stood at a modest 43% of GDP and 46% of exports of goods and services (and primary income), from 40% and 49%, respectively, in 2012. Debt-to-exports improved due to a significant increase in the export earnings over this period. PPG MLT external debt fell from 25% of GDP to 24%. Given the extent of concessional debt in the total, the present value of the debt is lower still. Vietnam has historically made use of official (concessional) creditors, who provide financing with favourable conditions and maturities, keeping debt service payments manageable. In its latest annual report, the Ministry of Finance has expressed the government's intension to increase the proportion of debt owed to domestic creditors, which has accounted for most new debt stock accrued since 2008. The report also noted plans to address shortening maturities by issuing longer-dated bonds, in line with the government's self-imposed limits. After becoming a middle-income country and graduating from IDA eligible status in 2015, access to concessional external financing has declined due to the slow withdrawal of official creditors. As a percentage of total external debt, concessional debt has declined from over 70% in 2008 to 40% in 2016, on World Bank figures. Public debt increases have followed the primary deficit (4.5% of GDP in 2016), which has declined slightly as the global economy has experienced recovery. Public domestic debt as a proportion of GDP has increased to 33% in 2016, from 21% in 2012 and 18% in 2009, and the government has expressed its aim to maintain growth of domestic issuance by at least 10% per year, while limiting total public debt.

Composition of external debt

External debt by creditor (end-2016)	*Nominal amount outstanding (US$mn)*	*Share of total (%)*
Public sector external debt (MLT PPG)	**48,461**	**55.7**
o/w Official multilateral	21,158	24.3
World Bank	13,090	15.1
IMF[a]	423	0.5
Official bilateral	19,199	22.1
Commercial creditors	7673	8.8
Bonds	1521	1.7
Commercial banks and other creditors	6152	7.1
Other	431	0.5

(continued)

(continued)

External debt by creditor (end-2016)	*Nominal amount outstanding (US$mn)*	*Share of total (%)*
Private non-guaranteed external debt	**24,484**	**28.2**
Short term external debt	**14,008**	**16.1**
Total external debt	**86,953**	**100.0**

Source: World Bank IDS

[a]Use of IMF credit

A complication in the analysis of the public debt is the treatment of debt owed by SOEs and other guaranteed corporations. Vietnam's public debt statistics shown here include the debt owed and guaranteed by autonomous public bodies. Details are, however, limited and the composition of this debt (between domestic and foreign debt for example) is unclear. SOEs accounted for c30% of GDP in 2017. In its 2017 Article IV, the IMF noted that good progress had been made on the legal framework for SOE reforms, but that SOEs retained key advantages over private sector firms, including access to credit. The IMF recommends forbidding SOE involvement in non-core areas of the economy, where the private sector could take over and predicts that improvements to the business environment could help to boost GDP growth to 7% per annum in the long run.

Rescheduling History

Vietnam carried over an unsustainable debt burden as it began the transition to a market economy in the late 1980s. Severe financial difficulties were caused by the collapse of the Soviet Union, which represented a significant share of Vietnam's established export market; its end in 1989 removed both Russia and the Eastern European bloc as a source of revenue. Due to the US trade embargo that was in place at the time, Vietnam was barred from accessing funds from the IMF, the World Bank and the ADB, and was therefore unable to secure the funds it needed to diversify its export market. Consequently, it went into default. A Paris Club restructuring in 1993 was followed by a London Club Brady deal in 1997, born out of the Paris Club's comparability requirement. Vietnam was considered for HIPC debt relief in 2000, but its debts were subsequently judged to be sustainable. An agreement was reached with Russia, also in 2000, over its ruble-denominated debt. Since then, the sovereign has been current on all its debts, even being able to access the international bond markets for a debut issue in 2005 and a subsequent bond issue in 2010.

In 1996, Vietnam's external debt (MLT) consisted of US$8bn of debt in convertible currency (35% of GDP) while a further US$10bn of debt (42% of GDP) related to non-convertible currency debt (denominated in Russian rubles). Of the convertible currency debt, US$5bn was public sector debt and US$3bn was owed by the private sector (mostly FDI related). Most public sector debt was made up of official loans (US$3bn), with US$1bn of London Club debt. The combined amount of external debt was, therefore, 78% of GDP, over 200% of exports, while the debt service ratio (due) was 13% (6% on a paid basis). This structure was broadly maintained until 2000, even following the Brady deal; in fact, debt in non-convertible currency declined by c5ppts by 1999, when a rescheduling agreement with Russia was reached, thereby eliminating nonconvertible debt. Debt rose to 40% of GDP in 2000, up from below 35% in 1999 (as the residual Russian debt was consolidated) and rose gradually thereafter to peak at 45% of GDP in 2003. Meanwhile, the debt/exports ratio fell sharply in 2000, to below 80%, a level at which it remained until 2005, while the debt service ratio fell below 10% by 2002, illustrating the improved solvency conditions of the country. External debt was 40% of GDP in 2009, around which it has oscillated since.

One current government target is keeping total public debt below 65% of GDP in 2016–18. The objective was set at a medium-term debt management programme for 2016–2018 recently approved by the prime minister. The programme is meant to limit debt service and ensure debt sustainability. Based on official statements in June 2017, Vietnam's total public debt will reach a record high over 2017–2018, before gradually falling in subsequent years. "Assuming the country's GDP growth rate is around 7% this year [2017], public debt will reach 64.8% of GDP. The amount will remain as high as 64.7% in 2018 before falling to 63.7% by 2020. The Finance Ministry and the government will adopt solutions to restructure the State budget, ensuring public debt never surpasses the 65% ceiling set by the National Assembly." Vietnam has also not been able to borrow official development assistance (ODA) at preferential interest rates and terms since July 2017. The country will pay higher interest rates on loans with shorter repayment terms. "Since Vietnam officially became a middle-income country in 2010, many donors have significantly reduced their preferential treatment for loans to the country." Debt financing costs have increased, since interest rates on domestic debt and international bonds are much higher than those on concessional external debt. This applied to loans from the World Bank, the ADB and Japan, its three biggest donors, from July 2017. The Debt Management Agency revealed last year that new interest rates could rise by up to 3.5% per annum and the maturities could be halved. The World Bank has agreed with government projections. The mounting debt will impose a steadily increasing burden on Vietnam's economy and make it ever harder to cut the budget deficit, the bank said in a report released last year.

Economic growth has been fast over the past decade, with average real GDP growth over 6% annually on WEO figures. Opportunities for private sector firms and infrastructural improvements have been enabled by public-private partnerships, particularly useful due to government fiscal constraints. Support from abroad has come from both loans to the public and private sectors, and in the form of FDI, forecast at almost 7% of GDP in 2017.

According to the latest Ministry of Finance report, the government aims in the 2016 budget (latest) to restructure state expenditures, lower recurrent expenditure from 66.9% of GDP in 2015 to 64.7% in 2016, reduce tax collection inefficiencies and tax evasion, strictly control public debt through careful inspection of new loans (including publicly guaranteed), and aim to lengthen maturities with appropriate interest rates. The debt structure has moved towards domestic borrowing. Growth in the stock of public debt has been high, averaging growth of 18.4% per year over 2011–2015. Vietnam became a middle-income country in 2010, so now gets less favourable conditions on official loans. Public debt management has remained fragmented and inefficient: debt management is separate from borrowing agencies.

Aims for 2016–2020 include keeping public debt below 65% of GDP and the country's external debt below 50% of GDP. Government bond targets include the maintenance of growth of domestic issuance by at least 10% per year and extension of average maturity by 6–8% per year and keeping annual foreign debt repayments under 25% of exports of goods and services. The strategy to achieve this is to continue to improve the institutional framework, enhance control of the debt safety and security of national finances, strengthen risk management, develop the domestic market, and combine this with favourable foreign debt conditions. Over 2016–2020, the number of SOEs will continue to fall, and those that remain will be restructured to improve efficiency and competitiveness. Vietnam intends to be a developed nation by 2020; hence, the deadline.

Relations with Multilateral Creditors

Although Vietnam's transition to a market economy began as early as 1986, the continuation of the Cold War eroded its relationship with multilateral institutions. Although the transition was piecemeal at first, a comprehensive reform drive began in March 1989. Relations with the IFIs soon normalised during the 1990s and several years of positive economic performance ensued until the Asian crisis in the late 1990s, at the same time as domestic structural weaknesses came to a head. These weaknesses were primarily centred around capital-intensive investment by public enterprises in uncompetitive sectors that could not be sustained and a business environment that stifled the private sector. The fiscal cost of supporting public enterprises mounted and pressures built in the banking sector. Vietnam emerged in 1999 from this difficult period and reforms began to accelerate. Having now been through three adjustment facilities, two specifically designed for low-income countries, Vietnam is not presently under an official IMF programme, although it continues to receive technical assistance on policy formation, including upgrading the tax administration organisation and modernising the monetary policy framework.

IMF programmes

Date	*Arrangements*	*Comments*
1993–1994	SBA	The October 1993 stand-by arrangement (SBA), although not crucial, was a considerable factor in procuring the Paris Club treatment on London terms. The SBA was extended by a systemic transformation facility in 1994.
1994–1997	ESAF	The enhanced structural adjustment facility (ESAF, forerunner of the poverty reduction and growth facility, PRGF) was initially heralded a success by all parties. The programme, approved in November 1994, made available some US$535mn in loans. Some delays in implementing structural policies were seen, but macroeconomic performance in the first two programme years was good, with economic growth of 9%, rising exports and increases in FDI inflows. However, economic performance began to weaken in the late 1990s and the ESAF was allowed to lapse in 1997 as agreement on the final-year programme could not be reached. Poor performance was exacerbated by the impact of the Asian economic crisis of 1997–1998.

(*continued*)

(continued)

Date	*Arrangements*	*Comments*
2001–2004	PRGF	Three-year PRGF approved in April 2001 worth US$368mn. Concluded with reasonable success in April 2004, but the third review's completion was delayed. 'Equitization' and withdrawing support from SOEs proved the most problematic measures to implement, although audit practice at the central bank also delayed PRGF dispersals in the later stages. The World Bank simultaneously approved a US$400mn poverty reduction support credit (PRSC) over three years.

Source: IMF. Vietnam joined the IMF in 1956

In its 2017 Article IV, the IMF said it expects strong imports to reduce the current account surplus, although WEO figures predict this remaining positive until at least 2022. Resilience to external shocks has developed as a result of government reform successes and bilateral trade agreements. The EU trade agreement was also implemented relatively quickly.

Vietnam is also a founding member of the ADB; however, relations ceased for over 13 years (1979–1992). The ADB resumed lending in 1993 and now has many projects in Vietnam, with two new projects approved in H1 18, for tourism and financial safety. Other active projects focus on infrastructural development and sustainable economic growth.

The World Bank also resumed lending to Vietnam in 1993. As of March 2017, it had provided US$22.5bn in grants, credits and concessional loans to Vietnam, with US$13bn outstanding (IDA and IBRD) on latest World Bank figures (2016). After becoming a middle-income country in 2010, Vietnam received its first IBRD loan in that year, now totalling US$3.3bn. The Bank's country strategy includes a socio-economic plan, private sector support, public service sustainability, poverty reduction among ethnic minorities and environmental sustainability.

The World Bank has many active projects in Vietnam, with the largest funding amounts going to infrastructural projects. In July 2016, the World Bank agreed three projects with the State Bank of Vietnam, worth a total of US$371mn to support economic competitiveness and environmental sustainability. World Bank projects aim to improve financial sector stability, reform SOEs and improve the business climate. Almost US$120mn, over various projects, aims to develop water and sanitation in 10 cities across the country, with consideration for river pollution.

Paris Club and Bilateral Creditors

Vietnam's only Paris Club treatment occurred in December 1993. The agreement treated US$544mn of debt and saw debt reduction of 50% (London terms) on eligible debt. Total forgiveness was estimated at US$3.8bn of principal and arrears valued at the time of agreement, with complete delivery conditional on reaching comparability with other creditors. This was hard won, as detailed below. However, following resolution with private creditors at the beginning of 1998, full relief was granted and Vietnam's external public debt stock stood at just US$10.6bn by year-end, just over half of the stock recorded two years before. The deal involved most of the Paris Club's permanent members although Japan, Vietnam's largest bilateral creditor, did not participate.

Paris Club agreements

Date	*Terms*	*Status*	*Details*
1993	London	Active	Treated US$544mn. Commercial credits saw a reduction of 50% with the remainder rescheduled over 23 years, with six years' grace. ODA credits rescheduled over 30 years with 12 years' grace.

Source: Paris Club

In the early 1990s, a donor group (the Consultative Group for Vietnam) was formed. The group was a response to the challenges faced by Vietnam in moving to a market economy and poverty reduction, and comprises 51 donors: 28 bilaterals and 23 multilaterals. The first meeting was in Paris in November 1993, resuming the relationship between Vietnam and the development finance institutions, and meetings have continued annually since, the latest being in 2017. According to the Ministry of Planning and Investment, the World Bank acts as the coordinator of the donor community and has now held 20 group meetings. Funding dropped significantly from 2011, as the future strategy changed. Vietnam agreed in 2015 with the World Bank to change this group into the Vietnam Development Partnership Forum (VDPF), with a 2016–2020 strategy to develop modern market economy features, infrastructure and human resources.

Vietnam reached a rescheduling agreement with Russia in September 2000. The agreement wrote-off 85% of Vietnam's debt (original loan amount) to Russia. The remaining amount, cUS$1.7bn, was to be repaid over 23 years at a 5% interest rate. This represented annual repayments of US$100mn. Vietnam's Soviet-era debt arose from years of Soviet sponsorship and amounted to US$10bn. When confirmation was announced six months later, a number of trade and military agreements were struck, bringing the two countries closer together. Since this time, bilateral relations have been on good terms.

The July 2016 World Bank project agreement (described above) included co-financing of US$12mn from the Swiss and Canadian governments. Australia is a major bilateral partner of Vietnam. In 2015–2016, Vietnam received AUD90.2mn (cUS$67.5), with education and infrastructure as the largest recipient areas. Ministers from the two countries agreed upon recent successes at the Tenth Australia-Vietnam Joint Trade and Economic Cooperation Committee, held in 2011. In September 2016, India announced US$500mn in credit for Vietnam for defence spending.

Sovereign Commercial Debt

Vietnam has only seen one significant sovereign debt restructuring, its Brady deal in 1998, although the state shipping company Vinashin defaulted on some of its commercial debt in 2010, which led to a restructuring but no sovereign distress.

The Socialist Republic of Vietnam issued a series of Brady bonds to resolve its defaulted commercial bank claims after the Paris Club restructuring. London Club claims made up US$1.6bn in 1996, out of total external obligations of US$26.7bn (including Soviet-era convertible ruble debt), which equated to 110% of GDP. Full delivery of Paris Club relief had been made conditional on comparability. But the process was drawn out and agreement on restructuring London Club claims in a Brady deal was eventually reached only in December 1997 although the Commercial Bank Advisory Committee announced in May 1996 a package of Brady-style proposals for the restructuring of Vietnam's London Club debt, with commercial creditors agreeing to consolidate an amount broadly equivalent to Paris Club terms. Vietnam's Brady bonds were issued in March 1998. Two of these Brady's are still outstanding and are detailed below, although trading is very limited. Their outstanding amount is now only US$207mn combined.

Commercial debt agreements

Date	*Details*
1998 Mar.	Brady deal. Agreement to restructure nearly US$800mn of debt, comprising US$310mn of principal and US$486mn of past-due interest (PDI). Principal of US$20.4mn was repurchased at 44 cents per dollar, US$51.6mn was exchanged for a 30-year bullet discount bond at a 50% discount, and US$238.9mn was exchanged for a 30-year par bond which amortised from year 15. The discount bond paid LIBOR+13/16 while the par bond had step up coupons. The discount bond was 100% collateralised by zero-coupon US Treasuries, with a six-month rolling interest guarantee, while 50% of the par bond was collateralised. Regarding PDI, US$15mn was paid at closing, US$294.8mn was exchanged for a PDI bond maturing in 2016, with seven years' grace and step-up coupons, non-collateralised, while US$21.8mn was repurchased at 44 cents on the dollar and US$154.6mn was written off. The NPV haircut was estimated at 52% according to the Cruces and Trebesch database.

Source: Exotix, World Bank GDF

The three main rating agencies (Fitch, Moody's, and S&P) all downgraded Vietnam's sovereign rating during 2010, citing weaker external finances, the risk of a balance of payments crisis and rising inflation, and risks from the banking system, which could require direct government support. Gradual improvements look set to continue: Fitch upgraded Vietnam from B+ to BB– with a stable outlook in November 2014, while Moody's and S&P changed their outlook on the rating from stable to positive during 2017.

Vietnam has two eurobonds outstanding as well as its Brady bonds. Its first foray into the international capital markets since the Brady deal was a privately placed eurobond in November 2005, which was followed by a second eurobond issue in January 2010, and its third, and most recent, in November 2014. The US$750mn 10-year issue in 2005, repaid successfully in January 2016, was six times oversubscribed, with total bids of US$4.5bn. Establishing a new benchmark for Vietnamese external commercial rate debt, proceeds were for Vinashin, the state-owned shipbuilding company (see next section). The Vinashin bond was seen as a prelude to a series of essentially investment-driven eurobonds in other state sectors and further issues were mooted. However, with strong capital inflows that accompanied surging portfolio investments, FDI and increased exports, the authorities delayed further issues. The government's plans for a US$1bn sovereign eurobond in 2008, postponed from 2007, were again postponed even after

Barclays, Citibank and Deutsche Bank were appointed joint lead managers in July 2007 and the Ministry of Finance reconfirmed its intentions that December. Proceeds from the issue were to be on-lent to SOEs, particularly to PetroVietnam for the purpose of constructing an oil refinery, as well as in shipping and construction. However, the 2007 issuance was postponed due to concerns over excess liquidity already in the banking system, and further delays were experienced as the government waited for more favourable market conditions. Finally, Vietnam successfully issued a 10-year US$1bn international bond in January 2010. This was oversubscribed, but priced at 98.576 to yield 6.95%, above a similarly rated Philippines bond. Proceeds were on-lent to state-owned oil refineries (US$700mn), Vinashin and other projects (US$300mn). A cash buyback in November 2014 repurchased US$254.5mn (at 114%), reducing the outstanding principal to US$745.451mn. A second 10-year US$1bn bond followed, issued in November 2014, priced at par with a lower coupon of 4.8%, shortly after a rating upgrade: in July 2014, Moody's upgraded Vietnam to B1 from B2, citing its recent macroeconomic stability, the strengthening of its balance of payments and the easing of banking sector risks.

In its most recent annual report, the Ministry of Finance said that, from 2011–2015, c55% of domestic capital for the state budget was mobilised by the bond market, with an average growth rate of 36% per year. Falling interest rates allowed the state budget to raise capital at low cost and high efficiency. Over this period, the Ministry reported completing the legal framework, to conform with international market practice. The Ministry has also been gradually diversifying the investor base to focus on longer-term and foreign investors in government bonds. Commercial bank holdings of government bonds fell to 77% of total government bonds; as of 2015, holdings of insurance companies and investment companies rose to 13%. The government also has pension funds in mind when setting policy to attract longer-term investors. The Ministry's aims for 2016–2020 are to enhance transparency, to coordinate with the SBV to ensure smooth issuance of government bonds, to research the secondary market for government bonds and to perfect the clearing payment system. The government hopes to change its bond term profile: bonds with maturity one-to-three years were c10% of the total in 2004 (a recent low), but rose to just over 60% in 2014. The Ministry wants longer-term issues, with acceptable interest, to relieve near-term debt service.

Of the US$-denominated bonds, there are four outstanding, the two remaining Brady bonds and the two outstanding eurobonds, all four totalling US$1.96bn outstanding, with the eurobonds amounting to US$1.7bn combined.

Vietnam bond
Socialist Republic of Vietnam 6¾% 2020
Bloomberg ticker: VIETNM

Borrower	Socialist Republic of Vietnam
Issue date	29 January 2010
Form	Eurobond
ISIN	USY9374MAF06
Issue size	US$1bn
Amount outstanding	US$745,451,000
Currency	US dollar
Denomination	US$100,000 minimum, increments of US$1000 thereafter
Amortisation	Bullet
Final maturity date	29 January 2020
Coupon/interest	6 3/4% payable semi-annually in January and July
Day count	30/360
Method of transfer	Euroclear/Clearstream
Settlement period	T + 2 business days
Joint lead managers	Barclays, Citi, Deutsche Bank
Governing law	US

Source: Bloomberg

Vietnam bond
Socialist Republic of Vietnam 4.8% 2024
Bloomberg ticker: VIETNM

Borrower	Socialist Republic of Vietnam
Issue date	19 November 2014
Form	Eurobond
ISIN	USY9384RAA87
Issue size	US$1bn
Amount outstanding	US$1bn
Currency	US dollar
Denomination	US$200,000 minimum, increments of US$1000 thereafter
Amortisation	Bullet
Final maturity date	19 November 2024
Coupon/interest	4.8% payable semi-annually
Day count	30/360
Method of transfer	Euroclear/Clearstream
Settlement period	T + 2 business days
Joint lead managers	Deutsche Bank, HSBC, Standard Chartered
Governing law	US

Source: Bloomberg

Vietnam par bond
Socialist Republic of Vietnam 4% 2028
Bloomberg ticker: VIETNM

Borrower	Socialist Republic of Vietnam
Issue date	12 March 1998
Form	Registered
ISIN	XS0085134145
Issue size	US$228.2mn
Amount outstanding	US$190.2mn
Currency	US dollar
Denomination:	US issue: US$250,000 Non-US issue: US$1000
Amortisation	31 semi-annual instalments after 15 years' grace: Instalments 1–30: 1.67% Instalment 31: 50%
Final maturity date	12 March 2028
Coupon/interest	Step up coupon, paid semi-annually: Years 1–2: 3.00% Years 3–4: 3.25% Years 5–6: 3.50% Years 7–9: 3.75% Years 10–20: 4.00% Years 21–30: 5.50%
Day count	30/360
Collateral	50% of principal collateralised by 30-year US Treasury zero-coupon bonds
Method of transfer	Euroclear/Clearstream
Settlement period	T + 3 business days
Main agent	Tokyo-Mitsubishi Securities Limited
Governing law	US

Source: Bloomberg

Vietnam discount bond
Socialist Republic of Vietnam FRN 2028
Bloomberg ticker: VIETNM

Borrower	Socialist Republic of Vietnam
Issue date	12 March 1998
Form	Registered
ISIN	XS0085134574
Issue size	US$24.55mn
Amount outstanding	US$24.55mn

(*continued*)

(continued)

Vietnam discount bond
Socialist Republic of Vietnam FRN 2028
Bloomberg ticker: VIETNM

Currency	US dollar
Denomination	US issue: US$250,000 Non-US issue: US$1000
Amortisation	Bullet
Final maturity date	13 March 2028
Coupon/interest	6M US LIBOR +13/16%, paid semi-annually March and September
Day count	30/360
Collateral	Principle secured by 30-year US Treasury zero-coupon bonds, with six-month rolling interest guarantee
Method of transfer	Euroclear/Clearstream
Settlement period	T + 2 business days
Main agent	The Bank of Tokyo-Mitsubishi
Governing law	US

Source: Bloomberg

Corporate Bond Markets

The Vietnamese corporate bond market is limited and includes SOEs and private companies. State-owned company Vietnam National Coal and Mineral Industries Group (Vinacomin) cancelled a planned US$500mn 10-year issue on 23 November 2010. It had been expected to be priced at 7.25%. PetroVietnam is another SOE that issues corporate debt.

Vietnam Shipping Industry Group (Vinashin) defaulted on its foreign debt in December 2010 after it missed a portion of a principal payment due on 20 December (which was extended to 23 December). Media reports had suggested in November 2010 that the state-owned shipbuilder would seek to delay the repayment of a US$60mn instalment on a commercial bank loan facility, the first principal repayment due under a US$600mn unsecured loan arranged by Credit Suisse in 2007. But it defaulted instead after creditors appeared unwilling to accept the government's restructuring proposal (the loan had 10 scheduled loan repayments every six months). The company had sought a one-year extension to allow time for asset sales. Accrued PDI came to US$26.79mn. The company had experienced growing financial difficulties over 2010, after a period of rapid business expansion. As of June 2010, Vinashin had debts totalling VND86tn (US$4.5bn), c5% of GDP, and total assets of VND104tn (US$5.4bn). Its problems ultimately forced the government to intervene and support the struggling company. In November 2010, Prime Minister Nguyen Tan Dung announced approval of a corporate restructuring plan for Vinashin over 2011–2013. In late December 2010, after the default, the government was reported to have extended an interest free-loan to the company, apparently to pay employees. Restructuring began in March 2011, and shipbuilding capacity dropped by almost half in 2012 as this developed. Shipbuilding Industry Corporation (SBIC) replaced the original company in 2013. A restructuring plan for the syndicated loan facility plan was later sanctioned by the High Court of England in September 2003 under a Scheme of Arrangement, nearly three years after the loan default, reportedly the first time the English Scheme had been used successfully by an Asian company. Since restructuring began, SBIC has restructured US$135mn of foreign debts and VND80 trillion of domestic debts.

In its restructuring of commercial debt, Vinashin issued a government-guaranteed 2025 PIK Note (DEBTAS), which is in RegS/144A form. Details for this bond are given below. The government has since bought back selective exposures, leaving US$388mn outstanding.

Vinashin corporate bond
Vinashin Corp 2025
Bloomberg ticker: DEBTAS

Borrower	Debt and Asset Trading Corp
Issue date	10 October 2013
Form	Eurobond
Guarantor	Ministry of Finance
ISIN	USY2031QAA23
Issue size	US$626.799mn
Amount outstanding	US$387.991mn
Currency	US dollar
Denomination	US$200,000 minimum, increments of US$1000 thereafter
Amortisation	Callable (at any time at par with 14 days' notice)
Final maturity date	13 March 2025
Coupon/interest	1% per annum simple interest PIK
Day count	30/360
Method of transfer	Euroclear/Clearstream
Settlement period	T + 2 business days
Main agent	Citibank
Governing law	English

Source: Bloomberg

No Va Land Investment Group bond
No Va Land Investment 5.5% 2023
Bloomberg ticker: NVLVN

Borrower	No Va Land Investment Group
Issue date	27 April 2018
Form	Eurobond
ISIN	XS1808317892
Issue size	US$160mn
Amount outstanding	US$160mn
Currency	US dollar
Denomination	US$200,000 minimum, increments of US$1000 thereafter
Amortisation	Convertible
Final maturity date	27 April 2023
Coupon/interest	5.5% per annum, paid semi-annually
Day count	30/360
Method of transfer	Euroclear, Clearstream
Exchange	Singapore
Settlement period	T + 2 business days
Lead manager	Credit Suisse
Governing law	New York

Source: Bloomberg

In Vietnam, much of the agriculture and other sectors are made up of smaller firms, which have decided typically not to invest in new technology. So, for future productivity, investment is needed for modernisation of these industries. A domestic corporate bond market began in the early 1990s, but it was very limited until 2005. Rapid growth occurred in 2006 and 2007. As of April 2018, 188 domestic currency bonds had been issued and 54 domestic bonds were active. Corporate bonds are listed on the Hanoi Stock Exchange and some are listed on the Ho Chi Minh Stock Exchange. 11 international bonds have been issued by Vietnamese corporates, with a total amount issued of US$1.59bn, of which only two remain active (detailed below).

Vinpearl JSC bond
Vinpearl JSC 3.5% 2023
Bloomberg ticker: VINPRL

Borrower	Vinpearl JSC
Issue date	14 June 2018
Form	Eurobond
ISIN	XS1836357357
Issue size	US$325mn
Amount outstanding	US$325mn
Currency	US dollar
Denomination	US$200,000 minimum, increments of US$200,000 thereafter
Amortisation	Convertible/putable
Final maturity date	6 June 2023
Coupon/interest	3.5% per annum, paid semi annually
Method of transfer	Euroclear, Clearstream
Exchange	Berlin, Singapore
Settlement period	T + 2 business days
Joint lead manager	Credit Suisse, Deutsche Bank
Governing law	English

Source: Bloomberg

Zambia

Nominal GDP (US$mn, 2018)[a]		25,778
Population (thousand, 2018)[a]		17,773
GDP per capita (USD, 2018)[a]		1450
Credit ratings (long-term foreign currency)[b]	Fitch	B–
	Moody's	Caa1
	S&P	B–

[a]IMF WEO October 2018
[b]As at end-September 2018

Country Summary

- Zambia has been transformed by the emergence of multiparty politics in 1991 and, following multilateral debt relief over 2005–2006, the onset of macroeconomic stabilisation, although the trickle down in terms of wider social benefits has been slow. The country has seen a number of democratic transitions in elections, although the more authoritarian rule under President Lungu could have tarnished its image.
- Dependent on a single commodity, Zambia is a major copper producer, recently ranked the world's eighth-largest producer. After finally beginning to enjoy the macroeconomic benefits of its natural resource wealth over 2005–2015, after years of waste, the commodity price crash in 2014 had a significant adverse impact on the economy, which

Exotix Capital, *Exotix Developing Markets Guide*,
https://doi.org/10.1007/978-3-030-05867-8_43

is still being felt, most notably in terms of weaker public finances, higher public debt and a low level of international reserves.

- Debt sustainability concerns have resurfaced just over a decade after Zambia benefited from significant debt relief under HIPC/ MDRI. Public debt/GDP virtually doubled over 2014–2016, and could now be c60%, due to a significant rise in new borrowing, much of it on commercial terms, and a weaker currency following the fall in copper prices. The authorities eventually sought IMF help, but the Fund suspended programme discussions in October 2017, after some two years of negotiations, pending greater clarity on the government's fiscal and borrowing plans. The government subsequently issued statements in June and July 2018 trying to clarify the debt position, having also said in February 2018 that it will seek a restructuring of its Chinese debt (its biggest single creditor, after bondholders). At the time of going to press, the situation remained somewhat fluid.

Economic data	*Avg*[a]	*2014*	*2015*	*2016*	*2017 (e)*	*2018 (f)*	*2019 (f)*
Real GDP growth	6.6	4.7	2.9	3.8	3.4	3.8	4.5
Inflation (annual average)	10.2	7.8	10.1	17.9	6.6	8.5	8.3
Current account (% of GDP)	1.5	2.1	−3.9	−4.5	−3.9	−4.0	−3.4
Reserves (US$mn, end-period)[b]	2505	3103	2967	2366	2081	1785[c]	–
Reserves/imports (months)[d]	3.4	3.4	3.8	3.3	2.4	–	–
Overall fiscal balance (% of GDP)[e]	−1.9	−5.7	−9.3	−5.8	−7.8	−9.8	−10.9
Currency (ticker)	Zambian kwacha (ZMW)						
FX regime	Free float with interventions to reduce volatility. Previous high inflation led to a currency rebasing in 2013.						
Key exports	Metals are c80% of goods exports, mainly copper (74%), plus cobalt and gold. Exports also include foodstuffs. Goods' exports were US$8.2bn in 2017, services exports were just US$0.9bn.						

Source: IMF WEO Database, IMF Country Reports, OEC, Haver

[a]10-year average to 2016 unless otherwise stated
[b]Gross international reserves
[c]Latest figure, April 2018
[d]Months of imports of goods, services and primary income
[e]IMF overall government net lending

Key figures		*Party*	*Since*
President	Edgar Lungu	PF	Jan. 2015[a]
Vice president	Inonge Wina	PF	Jan. 2015
Minister of finance	Margaret Mwanakatwe	MMD	Feb. 2018
Key opposition figure	Hakainde Hichilema	UPND	2006[b]
Central bank governor	Denny Kalyalya	–	Feb. 2015

Note: Zambia is a member of the Commonwealth. It gained independence from Britain in 1964

[a]Following the death of President Sata (of the PF party) in October 2014, then vice-president Guy Scott assumed the role and responsibilities of the president until January 2015's presidential by-election, when Edgar Lungu was elected to serve out the remainder of Sata's term. Lungu was re-elected for a second term in August 2016

[b]Hakainde Hichilema was the candidate for the UDA party in 2006, coming third, against incumbent president Levy Mwanawasa of MMD and PF candidate Michael Sata. Hichilema ran as the UPND candidate in the 2008 election, following the death of President Mwanawasa, again coming third. He came third in 2011 and second in 2015 and 2016

Politics

Executive power

The president is both chief of state and head of the government. Cabinet is appointed by the president from among the members of the National Assembly. The vice president appointed by president. Multi-party politics was established by President Kaunda in 1991 with a new constitution that ended the UNIP monopoly of power, providing for more than one presidential candidate (who need not be from the UNIP) and increasing the size of the National Assembly. In 1996, President Chiluba forced through changes to the constitution, imposing a retroactive two-term limit on the presidency, which still applies. The constitution requires an election within 90 days from the day the office of president becomes vacant. The president is directly elected by an absolute majority popular vote and a run-off is held if no candidate wins outright.

Presidential term: Five years (two-term limit) **Parliamentary term**: Five years

Legislature

Unicameral national assembly: following the Constitutional amendment of 2016, 156 members are directly elected on the basis of a simple majority, up to eight are appointed by the President, plus the Vice President, the Speaker and First and Second Deputy Speakers. There is also a 27-member advisory body, the House of Chiefs.

Elections

Next due *Presidential and legislative: 2021*

Last legislative election (Aug. 2016)	*Seats*	*Last presidential (Aug. 2016)*	*% of vote*
Patriotic Front (PF)	80	Edgar Lungu (PF)	50.4
United Party for National Development (UPND)	58	Hakainde Hichilema (UPND)	47.6
Movement for Multiparty Democracy (MMD)	3	Others	2.0
Forum for Democracy and Development (FDD)	1		
Independents	14		
Total (directly elected)	**156**	**Total**	**100.0**

People

Zambia's population is highly urbanised, with 42% living in a few urban zones. There are over 70 ethnic groups, the major ones being the Bemba, Tonga, Chewa and Lozi. Christianity is the main religion, with c95% of the population practicing Protestantism or Catholicism, and some Muslims and Hindus. Indigenous beliefs also exist. English is the main official language, but there are over 70 local languages and dialects. Bemba is spoken by 30% of the population.

British influence dates back to 1890 when Cecil Rhodes's British South Africa Company signed a series of treaties with local leaders obtaining mineral rights concessions and leading to the establishment in 1911 of Northern Rhodesia (now Zambia) and Southern Rhodesia (now Zimbabwe). In 1953, the two Rhodesias were joined with Nyasaland (now Malawi) to form the Federation of Rhodesia and Nyasaland, but it was short-lived as African demands for greater political participation ultimately led to its collapse in 1963 and independence a year later.

In 1973, a new constitution enshrined Zambia as a one-party state, with the UNIP as the only legal party. Kenneth Kaunda, Zambia's leader at independence, was elected president as the sole candidate in 1973, and was subsequently re-elected in 1978, 1983 and 1988. Under its first president, Zambia also played a leading role in the liberation of neighbouring states in the 1970s and 1980s, supporting UNITA in Angola, the ANC in South Africa, SWAPO in Namibia and Zimbabwe's ZAPU.

(*continued*)

(continued)

People

By 1990, however, years of economic mismanagement had taken their toll (inflation reached close to 200% by the mid-1990s) and an attempted coup started the process of political change. In 1991, the opposition MMD, under its leader Frederick Chiluba (president from 1991–2001), was swept to power in the country's first multiparty presidential and parliamentary elections, thus ending 27 years of UNIP rule.

The arrival of a reform minded government marked the beginning of a reversal in economic fortunes. Chiluba began to liberalise the economy and privatise industry, although corruption allegations marred his administration, particularly in its later years. He stood down in 2001 after his unsuccessful attempt to change the constitution to allow a third term resulted in MMD candidate Levy Mwanawasa being elected president by a narrow margin. Mwanawasa won again in 2006, defeating the PF candidate Michael Sata, but died in Paris in August 2008, leaving vice president Rupiah Banda (MMD) as acting president until elections were held in October 2008 to see who would see out the remaining term, which Banda won, defeating PF candidate Michael Sata.

Sata subsequently won the 2011 elections, defeating Banda, and following protests, Banda was charged with abuse of power. Sata died in office in October 2014 and vice president Guy Scott became acting president until elections were held in January 2015 to see who would see out the remaining term, which PF candidate Edgar Lungu won, defeating UPND candidate Hakainde Hichilema ("HH") by just 28,000 votes. Lungu was re-elected in 2016, defeating HH, by a margin of 200,000 votes. The opposition UPND alleged the election was rigged and HH was subsequently charged with treason in April 2017 for allegedly obstructing the president's motorcade. The charges were dropped in August, but have led to concerns that the government is becoming more authoritarian. A constitutional referendum was also held in August 2016 and, although a majority (55%) voted 'Yes' in favour of the proposed amendments, the voter turnout (44%) did not meet the required 50% to validate the results.

Social challenges remain. 60% of the population lives in poverty with unemployment and underemployment as serious problems. Only 27% of the population have electricity access. Zambia's rank remains low on the UN Human Development Index. The World Economic Forum still cites corruption as an impediment to investment. Added to this, Zambia has a very high rate of HIV infection, with 12% of the population infected by HIV/Aids and life expectancy at birth of 53 years, up from 39 in 2011.

Resource nationalism and China's presence have continued as political issues; the privatisation of mines occurred in 2000, with the government further reducing its stake since, and Chinese relations pre-exist independence. A change to mining royalties announced in 2015, under President Lungu, also threatened to undermine investment in the mining sector at a time of declining copper prices. From January 2015, royalties increased to 20% from 6% on open pit mines and to 9% from 6% on underground mines, but by April, the negative impact on output led to a policy reversal and the President setting both at 9% before lowering underground mines to 6% from July. In March 2018, Canadian mining company First Quantum Minerals Ltd. received a US$7.9bn tax bill from the Zambian Revenue Authority for historical unpaid import duties, penalties and interest.

Debt

	2012	2017
External debt ratios (%)		
Total external debt/GDP	15.7	70.0
Public external debt/GDP	12.0	34.3
Private external debt/GDP	3.7	35.7
Total external debt/exports of goods and services	38.2	169.8
External debt service ratio (public)[a]	2.7	6.8
Public debt ratios (%)		
Public domestic debt/GDP	12.0	19.1
Public debt/GDP	24.0	53.4

Source: Ministry of Finance, Bank of Zambia, IMF, Haver, Exotix

[a]Public and publicly guaranteed from IMF

Zambia's public debt has shown a sharp increase in the past few years, due to new borrowing, often on commercial terms, to fund wider deficits as a result of the fall in copper revenues, and due to currency depreciation. According to the IMF WEO, public debt peaked at 62% of GDP in 2015 (and remained at this level since then), up from a low in 2010 of 19%. Public debt had fallen to 25% of GDP in 2006, after the delivery of HIPC debt relief, from 76% in 2005, and 130% in 2004 (it had reached 261% of GDP in 2000). The increase in overall public debt reflects a significant rise in both its external and domestic debt. According to Ministry of Finance data, external public debt has tripled since 2012 from US$3bn to US$9bn in 2017 (and it was only US$1.3bn in 2010). According to Exotix calculations, since 2012, public external debt has nearly tripled as a share of GDP, while public domestic debt has risen by one-third. Indeed, through significant new borrowing, Zambia's debt ratios have returned to levels seen prior to HIPC debt relief, while the composition of its external debt has altered dramatically (shifting from mainly concessional to commercial debt).

Exotix estimates Zambia's total public debt was US$13.6bn at end-2017. This was c53% of WEO 2017 estimated GDP, up considerably from just 24% of GDP in 2012. Public external debt was reported as US$8.7bn at end-2017 in the Ministry of Finance's 2017 Annual Report (c34% of WEO GDP), compared with US$7.5bn in June 2017 in its 2017 Mid-Year Review. This followed US$6.9bn in 2016 and US$6.7bn in 2015.

The inclusion of US$590mn in fuel debt that was reconsolidated as external debt (included as other commercial debt) accounted for around half the difference in the final 2017 figure. Most of the remaining difference was accounted for by higher debt from Export Import Bank of China (EXIM Bank of China) and multilaterals (World Bank and AFDB). The Annual Report put public domestic debt (excluding arrears) at ZMK48.4bn at end-2017 (cUS$4.9bn and c19% of GDP). Domestic debt, which is mostly in the form of government securities, rose by 47% in 2017 compared with 2016, and has nearly doubled since 2015, due to increased issuance of government bonds (as external financing sources dried up). However, Exotix calculations may underestimate public debt. The government figures for public external debt might be for central government debt only, added to which there might be another cUS$1bn in external debt, according to the IMF, owed by public enterprises/guarantees, so total public external debt would have been cUS$9.7bn. The IMF's DSA in its 2017 Article IV in October 2017 noted PPG external debt was US$8bn in 2016, of which US$7bn was central government external debt and US$0.8bn was publicly guaranteed external debt. In addition, domestic arrears were cZMK12.7bn in 2017 on official figures (US$1.3bn). This means that total public debt (including arrears and guarantees) might have been as high as US$15.7bn in 2017 (61% of WEO 2017 estimated GDP). Note that these figures are similar to IMF figures. The IMF's aforementioned DSA showed public debt (public and publicly guaranteed) at 55.6% of GDP in 2017 (cUS$14.2bn). Of this, 32.9% of GDP was public external debt, which implied cUS$8.4bn, and 22.7% of GDP was public domestic debt (which implied US$5.8bn).

The creditor composition of public external debt, as at end-2017 (taken from the Annual Report) is shown below. Most of this (around half) was commercial debt, of which nearly 70% comprised Zambia's three outstanding eurobonds, 5.375% 2022 (US$750mn), 8.5% 2024 (US$1000mn) and 8.97% 2027 (US$1250mn)—US$3bn in total. The bonds alone amounted to 34% of public external debt. Most of the remaining commercial debt was specified as "other", which included the reclassified fuel debt. Multilateral creditors accounted for 20% of the public external debt, with half of this owed to the World Bank/IDA, and one-quarter owed to the AFDB. Bilaterals accounted for just 4% of public external debt, mostly owed to non-Paris Club creditors. Bilateral debt was less than half of its 2012 level, partly due to an agreement with Brazil in 2016 to cancel 80%

of the outstanding amount (see below). The remaining 25% of public external debt was in the form of export and suppliers' credit, with most of this (nearly 90%) owed to EXIM Bank of China (the terms of which are not clear—whether it is on soft terms or commercial terms). Together with a small amount of commercial debt owed to China Development Bank (CDB), this means that total Chinese debt was about US$2.2bn (c25% of public external debt). That is, some 60% of Zambia's public external debt is owed to just two creditor groups—bondholders and China. On 13 February 2018, the government (via the President's office) announced plans to restructure bilateral debt with China and the Ministry of Finance confirmed in July that talks would began in August 2018. At the time of writing, no further details were available.

Total external debt was 70% of GDP in 2017. This was an over four-fold increase from 2012, as public external debt tripled as a share of GDP, while private external debt saw an even bigger increase (rising from less than 4% of GDP to c36% of GDP). Private external debt rose from US$0.9bn in 2006 to US$2.3bn in 2009, according to central bank figures. It stood at US$9.1bn in June 2017, although it should be noted that new data collection methods that include more firms are used to estimate private external debt and make comparisons difficult, especially since 2014. The increase in the debt/GDP ratio was mainly due to much higher debt, as nominal GDP in US dollar terms was broadly unchanged over the period (although the point-to-point comparison masks a rise in nominal GDP over 2012–2014, and a sharp fall over 2015–2016 due to kwacha devaluation). Total external debt in 2017 was split roughly evenly between public external debt and private external debt. Private external debt was estimated at US$9.1bn (35.7% of GDP) based on IMF data. Total external debt was 170% of exports of goods and services, a marked increase from just 38% in 2012. The increase is due to the higher debt (numerator) and lower export earnings (denominator). Exports of goods and services fell by 14% over this period, mainly due to the fall in copper prices. Meanwhile, external debt service (public sector only) was US$504mn in 2017, up from US$300mn in 2015, and comprised US$342mn in interest and US$162mn in principal, according to Ministry of Finance figures. The external debt service ratio (public sector only) was 5.6%. The IMF show a slightly higher DSR based on PPG debt. The DSR has increased, in part due to lower export earnings, but also to an increase in non-concessional debt (and hence a higher interest service ratio). New borrowing increased a lot in 2016 and 2017. The Annual Report noted that the government contracted 18 new loans in 2017, amounting to US$1.75bn, compared with 26 loans in 2016 amounting to US$3.1bn, although it is not clear how much was disbursed.

The Ministry of Finance in a statement on 14 June 2018 gave further details on its debt position, albeit some three months after it had promised, in response to market concerns over the true level of Zambia's debt that emerged through the course of 2018, amid reports that it was substantially higher than reported, following the suspension of IMF programme talks in October 2017. The government had previously said in March 2018 that it would present an updated DSA at the April 2018 IMF/World Bank Spring meetings. This did not happen. In its June statement, the Ministry noted that, after full reconciliation of the debt stock and an updated DSA, total public external debt at end-March 2018 amounted to US$9.3bn. It noted public external debt was US$8.7bn in 2017 (unchanged from its Annual Report). There were no details as to the cause of the increase during Q1. The domestic debt stock (government securities) amounted to ZMK53.5bn (US$5.6bn), up from ZMK48.4bn at end-2017. Exotix calculates that the government's figures implied total public debt of US$14.9bn (presumably still excluding guarantees and arrears), c57% of WEO 2018 estimated GDP (comprising public external debt of 35.5% of GDP and public domestic debt of 21.5% of GDP). The government also announced in its statement on 14 June that it will address the pace of debt contraction, in order to bring debt down to moderate risk. The government noted that it will indefinitely postpone the contraction of all pipeline debt, cancel some current contracted but not yet disbursed loans, undertake refinancing of bilateral loans, cease issuance of guarantees to commercially viable projects, cease issuance of letters of credit and guarantees to insolvent state-owned enterprises and carry out liability management operations to improve cash flow. In a further development, the President was reported on Turkish TV at end-July as saying that the country was seeking help from an unspecified Turkish company to refinance its 2022 eurobond maturity, which prompted the Ministry of Finance to issue a statement to clarify that it remained committed to honouring the debt (see Commercial Debt section below).

Composition of external debt

External debt by creditor (end-2017)	*Nominal amount outstanding (US$mn)*	*Share of total (%)*
Public sector external debt	**8739**	**49.0**
o/w Official multilateral	1740	9.8
World Bank IDA	892	5.0
AfDB/AfDF	433	2.4
IMF	125	0.7
Official bilateral	374	2.1
Paris Club	128	0.7
Non-Paris Club	246	1.4
Commercial creditors	4435	24.9
Eurobonds	3000	16.8
CDB	255	1.4
Other	1179	6.6
Export and suppliers' credit	2190	12.3
EXIM Bank of China	1947	10.9
Other	244	1.4
Private sector external debt	**9105**	**51.0**
Total external debt	**17,844**	**100.0**

Source: Ministry of Finance, IMF

Rescheduling History

Zambia benefitted from significant debt relief over 2005–2006 under HIPC and MDRI, which transformed its debt stock. The country reached HIPC decision point in 2000 with completion point coming in April 2005. MDRI relief followed in January 2006. Completion point had been expected in 2003–2004, but was delayed after fiscal performance went off track in 2003. Debt relief amounted to cUS$6bn. Before debt relief, Zambia's debt stood at US$7bn (nominal) in 2003. Even after traditional debt relief mechanisms, the NPV of debt was US$4.9bn, equivalent to 432% of exports (on a three-year average basis as defined under HIPC). HIPC reduced public external debt to just US$1bn in 2006. At completion point, HIPC and additional bilateral relief were projected to reduce the debt on an NPV basis to 174% of exports. Although this was higher than the 150% threshold, the IMF/World Bank agreed a common reduction factor of 62.6%, implying total debt reduction in NPV terms after traditional debt relief mechanisms of 87.7%. The NPV of external debt would be reduced in 2003 from 113% of GDP to 45%. Public debt (in nominal terms) subsequently continued to fall as a proportion of GDP, to below 19% in 2010. And, whereas multilaterals used to be the main creditors, with one-third owed to the World Bank Group and 23% to the IMF, followed by bilateral creditors (over two-thirds of which was owed to Paris Club creditors), commercial creditors, through the issue of eurobonds, became the largest creditor group. Publicly guaranteed debt also increased—by more than five times since 2012—most of which was for ZESCO (state-owned electricity company) and ZAMTEL (state-owned telecommunications company). Moreover, private external indebtedness has also increased since debt relief was granted, as Zambia's credit ratings improved.

Zambia's historical debt problems stemmed from a long period of deteriorating economic performance and reliance on a single commodity export (copper), which left the economy vulnerable to commodity price shocks. Poor economic management and failure to diversify the economy, notably into agriculture, were also factors. Economic performance declined after independence in 1964 as a socialist economic model under a one-party state saw the country turn from one of Africa's seemingly more prosperous, resource-rich countries to one with one of the highest foreign debts per capita in the world by the mid-1990s, according to the US State Department, as the collapse in global copper prices in the 1970s and 1980s and rise in oil prices that began in the early 1970s led the government to borrow its way out of trouble. Increased borrowing, mainly from multilateral agencies, later gave rise to debt service problems. Meanwhile, copper production also experienced a secular decline over the 30 years to 2000. Production fell from a high of 700,000mt in 1973 to 221,000mt in 2000, reflecting the inefficiencies of state ownership and a lack of investment. Privatisation of the mines occurred in 2000, since when production took a rising trend, but it has since fallen, in part due to lower global prices, but also due to inadequate exploration since 2011. Initial efforts at economic stabilisation through the 1980s under various IMF programmes failed because of their strict conditionality. But the arrival of a reform-minded government in 1991 ushered in a period of change and marked the beginning of a reversal in economic fortunes. Market-based reforms and gradual economic liberalisation, combined with macroeconomic stabilisation, supported—this time successfully—by the IMF in successive programmes and other donors, saw inflation fall to below 30% in 1997 from over 180% in 1993 and set the stage for the granting of debt relief.

Public debt is now back to levels not seen since 2005, since HIPC debt relief was granted. After HIPC, Zambia's economy subsequently performed well, until recently, helped by significant debt relief and the global commodity boom over the rest of the noughties and through the early part of this decade. Zambia saw strong growth (averaging 7.3% in the 10 years to 2014) and moderate inflation (averaging 10.2% in the 10 years to 2014). But the commodity price crash that came in H2 2014 hit the country particularly badly, as both lower copper prices and lower copper production (with the shutting of production in a number of mines, notably Glencore) took their toll. Moreover, a more persistent fiscal weakness has been observed. The primary deficit reached a peak of 6.5% of GDP in 2015 as counter-cyclical policies, partly in the lead up to the 2016 elections, contributed to a fiscal deficit of almost 10% of GDP; higher domestic spending such as wages and subsidies also played their part. The exchange rate also weakened sharply, by c50% against the US dollar, over 2013–2016. This has contributed to a rise in the public debt burden to 60% of GDP in 2016, up from 27% in 2013, and a low of 19% in 2008 (on IMF WEO figures), leading to renewed concerns over debt sustainability.

Relations with Multilateral Creditors

Zambia has a long history of IMF engagement, dating back to the early 1980s. Although initial programmes were unsuccessful, and finished prematurely, performance improved with the 1999–2003 ECF, which took the country to HIPC decision point. However, progress towards completion point was interrupted after severe fiscal underperformance in 2003, forcing the country onto a temporary staff monitored programme (SMP) in order to get policy back on track. This was duly achieved and a three-year ECF was approved in June 2004. It was completed successfully, albeit with a few waivers on the way, in September 2007. A successor three-year ECF programme was approved in June 2008. This programme was considerably augmented in size in May 2009 with the onset of the global financial crisis. Performance under the ECF was generally satisfactory. Various waivers were granted for non-observance of debt limits and concessionality requirements on new debt. The sixth and final review was completed in June 2011, and the programme expired fully drawn. The authorities expressed interest in a successor programme at the time, but this failed to materialise.

Zambia's relationship with the Fund has arguably become more challenging over the past year as discussions on a new programme were suspended by Staff in autumn 2017, the third false dawn in as many years. Programme discussions had been ongoing (and on and off) for some three years beforehand, prompted by the challenging external environment and fiscal imbalances that emerged with the onset of the 2014 commodity price fall, and the resulting sharp fall in international reserves (with gross reserves falling from a peak of US$4bn in July 2015 to US$2.2bn in October 2016). Indeed, Zambia had publicly stated as early as June 2014 its intention to start talking to the Fund, although it was not clear what kind of engagement Zambia was aiming for at the time (for instance a proper standby agreement (SBA) or a policy support instrument (PSI), with no money attached), or when discussions would be completed. An IMF press release on 6 June 2014 following a Staff visit noted that the government had requested the Staff team to return in early September for discussions on a Fund-supported programme. However, talks seemed to proceed more slowly than anticipated, partly because of the looming 2015 Budget in October and domestic political considerations given the then President's ill-health, which may have distracted policymakers, while the sovereign eurobond in April probably reduced the urgency.

In the event, a programme never materialised, probably because of the then President's death in October 2014 and the subsequent presidential by-election in January 2015, which saw Edgar Lungu take over. The authorities then seemed close to securing a programme in November 2015, after a period of negotiations, when President Lungu announced a set of measures—which if they were adhered to could have led to a Fund programme—but the measures (which included an increase in electricity tariffs) were reversed within a few weeks in response to protests. By early 2016, the economy was under intense pressure and government finances were under immense stress, according to an IMF statement in March, but by this time the window for approval of an IMF programme had become too short ahead of the approaching presidential election in August 2016. This meant Zambia was on its own until then, and suggested any programme (if one was still needed) was unlikely to be approved before mid-December 2016 at the earliest.

With President Lungu's re-election, optimism over an imminent deal seemed to increase ahead of the IMF's Spring meetings in April 2017. The finance minister and the Fund later suggested that a programme would go to the Board by August 2017, according to media reports. However, this did not happen and the subsequent scheduling of an Executive Board meeting for the long overdue Article IV consultation on 6 October 2017 gave the impression that programme discussions had again ground to a halt. This was confirmed during the IMF's Annual Meetings in October 2017, and made clear in the 2017 Article IV report that was published subsequently. The IMF's updated DSA (contained in the 2017 Article IV review) now assessed Zambia to be at high risk of debt distress (although this merely confirmed what investors already knew). It noted that, under current policies, the PV of the external debt/GDP ratio breached the 40% threshold during 2019–2023, while the debt-service-to-revenue ratio temporarily breached its threshold in 2022 and 2024 when eurobonds mature. As a result, the IMF suspended programme discussions pending clarification on the government's fiscal and borrowing plans, which were seen as being inconsistent with the Fund's DSA. The Ministry of Finance's subsequent statement on 14 June 2018, although long overdue and lacking in detail, in which it announced a set of measures aimed at addressing debt sustainability concerns, was therefore a useful step towards re-engaging with the Fund. But, as noted in the IMF press briefing on 12 July, the Fund was still awaiting specifics on the authority's new debt plans and revised budget numbers.

A statement from the Ministry of Finance on 24 August 2018 did suggest that the authorities were still keen on a programme, although, at the time of writing, there had been no further progress or indication as to when programme discussions would resume.

IMF programmes

Date	*Arrangements*	*Comments*
1980s–1990s	Various	SBA 1984–1986, SBA 1986–1987, SAFC 1995–1996, ECF 1995–1998.
1999–2003	ECF	US$349mn ECF (formerly ESAF, then PRGF) agreed in March 1999. The programme came after Zambia's economy suffered in 1998 from a 39% fall in the currency as metal prices fell 35%. Reserves dropped to below two weeks' import cover. The first review was completed in July 2000. The fifth review was completed in November 2002. The programme was due to expire in February 2003.

(*continued*)

(continued)

Date	*Arrangements*	*Comments*
2003–2004	SMP	A six-month SMP was approved for July–December 2003. A revised 2003 economic programme was agreed after large projected budget overruns in the wage bill and related allowances were identified. Initial negotiations on a new ECF took place in November 2003. Performance under the SMP, however, was not satisfactory and it was extended to June 2004. Performance through March 2004 was strong, paving the way for a new ECF arrangement.
2004–2007	ECF	Three-year agreement of US$320.4mn approved in June 2004, scheduled to run to June 2007. The first review was completed in December 2004, with some waivers. The second review was completed in April 2005, with waivers. The third review was completed in January 2006, with a waiver. The fourth review was completed in July 2006. The fifth and sixth reviews (the sixth being the final review) were completed in June 2007, with waivers. In May 2007, the programme was extended to September 2007.
2008–2011	ECF	Three-year arrangement of SDR48.9mn (US$79.2mn) approved in June 2008. The first and second reviews were completed in May 2009 when financial support under the arrangement was increased by SDR172mn (US$256.4mn) to SDR220.1mn (US$329.7mn) to help Zambia cope with the impact of the global financial crisis. Waivers relating to both domestic and external borrowing were granted with subsequent reviews. The programme expired in June 2011 after the sixth and final review, with which a waiver was granted for domestic financing. The programme was fully drawn.

Source: IMF. Zambia joined the IMF in 1965

The World Bank currently has 23 active projects in Zambia, with the largest by commitment amount being focused on rural road improvements, irrigation and electricity transmission. Of the 19 African Development Bank projects currently active in Zambia, a wide variety of objectives are pursued, including agriculture and electricity infrastructure.

Paris Club and Bilateral Creditors

Zambia has had nine Paris Club agreements. Its three most recent agreements are still active, the last two being related to HIPC debt relief in 2002 and 2005. Debt due to the Paris Club was US$1.9bn in 2005, of which US$1.8bn was treated in the 2005 agreement, out of total external debt of US$7.0bn. All Paris Club creditors had provided beyond-HIPC relief by January 2008, except one full member, Russia, and Brazil—which was invited to participate in the Paris Club meeting—although both by then had started bilateral discussions. In 2006, US$99.2mn of outstanding Russian debt was consolidated in an agreement, using the remaining amount to fund development projects. In 2016, Brazil agreed to cancel 80% of the US$113.4mn that remained outstanding, and a final bilateral agreement was announced on 20 December 2017. The remaining 20% (US$22.7mn) was to be repaid in two equal instalments, by March 2018. The savings were planned to support the country's poverty reduction initiatives. The Brazil settlement came 12 years after the 2005 Paris Club Agreement and six years after the bilateral minute's agreement. Zambia's nine non-Paris Club creditors included China, India, Bulgaria, Iraq, Kuwait, Romania and Yugoslavia. The latter three had sold their claims on Zambia to private creditors and were fully repaid.

Paris Club agreements

Date	*Terms*	*Status*	*Details*
1980s	Classic	Fully repaid	Three separate agreements: 1983, 1984, 1986.
1990	Toronto	Fully repaid	Treated US$963mn. Repayment of non-ODA credits over 14 years, with eight years of grace, after cancellation to a rate of 33%. Repayment of ODA credits over 25 years with 14 years of grace.
1992	London	Fully repaid	Treated US$918mn. Repayment of non-ODA credits over 23 years, with six years of grace, after cancellation to a rate of 50%. Repayment of ODA credits over 30 years with 12 years of grace.
1996	Naples	Fully repaid	Treated US$566mn. Repayment of non-ODA credits over 23 years, with six years of grace, after cancellation to a rate of 67%. Repayment of ODA credits over 40 years with 16 years of grace.
1999	Naples	Active	Treated US$1062mn. Treatment of arrears as of 30 June 1999, treatment of maturities falling due from 1 April 1999 up to 31 December 2000. Repayment of non-ODA credits over 23 years, with six years of grace, after cancellation to a rate of 67%. Repayment of ODA credits over 40 years with 16 years of grace.

(*continued*)

(continued)

Date	*Terms*	*Status*	*Details*
2002	Cologne	Active	Decision point treatment in December 2000. Treatment of maturities falling due from 1 January 2001 up to 30 June 2005. Repayment of non-ODA credits over 23 years, with six years of grace, after cancellation to a rate of 90% Repayment of ODA credits over 40 years with 16 years of grace.
2005	HIPC initiative exit	Active	Completion point treatment in May 2005. Treated US$1763mn of which US$1403mn being cancelled and US$360mn rescheduled. Treatment of arrears as of 31 March 2005, treatment of the stock as of 1 April 2005.

Source: Paris Club

China has been an active partner for Zambia since even before its independence and is now its single biggest bilateral and official creditor. China was the largest non-Paris Club creditor in 2006, with much of its US$217mn debt written off after Chinese President Hu Jintao visited Zambia in early 2007. A landmark project was the Chinese-financed and built Tanzania-Zambia railway (Tan-Zam or Tazara) constructed between 1970 and 1976, which linked Zambia's Copperbelt to the port of Dar es Salaam in Tanzania. The railway reduced Zambia's dependence on the Rhodesian and South African trade routes. At the time, the cost of US$500mn made it China's biggest overseas aid project in the world.

The creation of Special Economic Zones in 2007 cemented the Zambia-China relationship. Current Chinese investments include airport, road and rail projects in particular, with total project finance of cUS$10bn in June 2017, based on media reports. Also in June 2017, Zambia sought additional loans and grants from China, potentially reaching US$8bn. On 13 February 2018, the Zambia government announced plans to restructure its bilateral debt with China, presumably to secure cash flow relief.

Sovereign Commercial Debt

Before its first eurobond issue in 2012, the Zambia government had a relatively small amount of debt owed to external commercial creditors and had seen two commercial debt agreements over the 1980s–1990s. Commercial debt amounted to US$140mn in 2009, c9% of the public sector's external debt, and related to commercial banks and suppliers, although there is not much additional information available.

Unlike some other African/HIPC countries, Zambia had little by way of commercial (ie London Club) claims although those commercial creditors with outstanding arrears were offered settlement terms similar to those offered by the Paris Club. Arrears to private creditors generally accumulated because of limits on the availability of foreign exchange before 1985. In 2005, commercial claims (on IMF data) were only 1% of GDP as a relatively conservative borrowing strategy generally eschewed commercial sources of finance in favour of concessional or multilateral loans.

Commercial debt agreements

Date	*Details*
1984	Bank debt rescheduling of US$74mn of maturities, including arrears as of February 1983.
1994	Donor funded commercial debt buyback, treating US$570mn

Source: World Bank GDF, IMF

Zambia has three eurobonds outstanding for a total amount of US$3bn (nominal). Its debut eurobond issue came in September 2012, for US$750mn. The bond had a 5.375% coupon (with an issue price of 98.108) and a bullet maturity in 2022. The spread at issue was 383bps. This came after the government had stated in 2008 that it would seek to obtain a sovereign rating. Although this was widely seen as a prelude to a debut sovereign bond, the authorities publicly stated they had no such plans. With the death of the president in 2008 and onset of the global financial crisis, the authorities' plans for a rating were put on hold. These were, however, revived in 2010 and the government confirmed in May that a rating was back on the agenda, as was a bond issue, coming after a 2009 IMF comment that Zambia had some space for non-concessional borrowing. The second issue was in April 2014 for US$1bn, with a coupon of 8.5% (priced to yield 8.625% at issue) and a bullet maturity in 2024. The third and most recent eurobond issue was a 12-year bond (2027 maturity) in July 2015 for US$1.25bn. It had an 8.97% coupon and was priced to yield 9.375% (the issue price was 97.257), with a spread of 710bps, after initial guidance of 9.5%. The bond amortises in three equal annual payments over its last three years.

In a surprise, and perhaps off the cuff, statement, the President was reported on Turkish TV on 28 July 2018 as saying that the country was seeking help from a Turkish company to refinance its 2022 eurobond maturity. The US$750mn maturity amounted to some 42% of current gross international reserves. The President's comments prompted the Ministry of Finance to seek to clarify the situation with a quickly issued statement on Monday 30 July saying, inter alia, that the country was committed to meeting bond payments on time and in full, that, while it was open to discussions on refinancing the bond, it would not take action without consulting holders, and that the government was in the process of engaging financial advisors. It also noted that discussions on its Chinese debt would take place in August. The comment came just a day after Moody's downgraded Zambia to Caa1 from B3 and just a few weeks after the Ministry's own statement on 14 June about the debt situation and future borrowing policy.

Zambia's outstanding sovereign bonds are listed in the table below and details for the 2027 bond are also shown.

Zambia's outstanding eurobonds

Description	*Size*	*Maturity type*	*Issue date*
USD 5.375% Due 2022	US$750mn	Bullet	Sep. 2012
USD 8.5% Due 2024	US$1000mn	Bullet	Apr. 2014
USD 8.97% Due 2027	US$1250mn	Sinkable	Jul. 2015

Source: Bloomberg

Zambia bond *Zambia 8.97% 2027* *Bloomberg ticker: ZAMBIN*	
Borrower	Republic of Zambia
Issue date	30 July 2015
Form	Eurobond
ISIN	XS1267081575
Issued amount	US$1250mn
Currency	US dollar
Denomination	US$200,000 and US$1000 thereafter
Amortisation	Amortises in three equal instalments on 30 July 2025, 2026 and 2027
Final maturity date	30 July 2027
Coupon/interest	8.97% per annum, paid semi-annually January and July
Day count	30/360
Method of transfer	Euroclear/Clearstream
Settlement period	T + 2
Governing law	English
Joint lead managers	Barclays Bank, Deutsche Bank

Source: Bloomberg

Although not active in the bond market over 2016–2017, the government received a number of bank loans. In 2017, the government contracted several commercial bank loans, which Exotix calculates as amounting to some US$622mn, based on Ministry of Finance figures. This included a two-year placement by Standard Chartered Bank for US$134mn in March 2017, which trades in the secondary market. The loan matures in March 2019.

Corporate Bond Markets

Zambia has a very limited domestic corporate bond market and no domestically issued USD corporate bonds. However, the Canadian mining company First Quantum Minerals Limited (ticker: FMCN), which has operations in Zambia, has six active eurobonds: two issued in 2018, two issued in 2017 and two issued in 2014. The total outstanding amount is some US$6.02bn (nominal). All of these are of the RegS/144A series and all have a callable maturity type. These are summarised in the table below, and an example of one of its 2018 issues also given. Three bonds had previously been issued in 2012 and one other in 2014, but these were called before maturity. First Quantum operates six mines globally, two of which (Kansanshi and Sentinel) are located in Zambia. First Quantum's bonds are included in the JPM CEMBI corporate bond index under Zambia.

First Quantum's outstanding eurobonds

Description	*Size (US$mn)*	*Issue date*
USD 7% Due Feb. 2021	1120.5	Feb. 2014
USD 7.25% Due May 2022	850	May 2014
USD 7.25% Due Apr. 2023	1100	Mar. 2017
USD 6.5% Due Mar. 2024	850	Feb. 2018
USD 7.5% Due Apr. 2025	1100	Mar. 2017
USD 6.875% Due Mar. 2026	1000	Feb. 2018

Source: Bloomberg

First Quantum bond
First Quantum 6.875% 2026
Bloomberg ticker: FMCN

Borrower	First Quantum Minerals Ltd			
Issue date	27 February 2018			
Form	Eurobond			
Ranking	Senior Unsecured			
ISIN	USC3535CAJ74			
Issue size	US$1000mn			
Currency	US dollar			
Denomination	Minimum of US$200,000 and US$1000 thereafter			
Amortisation	Callable from:	1 March 2021	At price:	105.156
		1 March 2022		103.438
		1 March 2023		101.719
		1 March 2024		100.000
Final maturity date	1 March 2026			
Coupon/interest	6.875% paid semi-annually			
Day count	30/360			
Method of transfer	Euroclear/Clearstream			
Settlement period	T + 2 business days			
Joint lead managers	ABSA Capital, BNP Paribas, Credit Agricole Securities, Credit Suisse, ING Financial Markets, JP Morgan, Societe Generale, Standard Chartered Bank			

Source: Bloomberg

Zimbabwe

Nominal GDP (US$mn, 2018)[a]		19,367
Population (thousand, 2018)[a]		15,263
GDP per capita (USD, 2018)[a]		1269
Credit ratings (long-term foreign currency)[b]	Fitch	NR
	Moody's	NR
	S&P	NR

[a]IMF WEO October 2018
[b]As at end-September 2018

Country Summary

- Zimbabwe was one of Sub-Saharan Africa's (SSA) most developed economies in the 1990s. Agriculture and industry have since declined, partly due to land reform and government intervention that crowded out the private sector. There is spare capacity in the primary and secondary sectors, enabling output growth without increasing inflation. Large numbers of skilled workers have emigrated since the economic decline.
- Zimbabwe's debt situation is unsustainable. A large debt burden amid fiscal deficits has caused arrears to accumulate with external creditors, while total public domestic debt has increased almost tenfold since 2013. A strategy to clear external arrears was developed with IMF support, but its implementation, among other reforms,

Exotix Capital, *Exotix Developing Markets Guide*,
https://doi.org/10.1007/978-3-030-05867-8_44

was delayed. Continued economic challenges and political transition could cause further delays, but could also bring policy change.

- External arrears, political concerns, and human rights issues have left Zimbabwe isolated, with various sanctions still in place. Despite the removal of former President Mugabe, the Trump Administration announced the extension of sanctions on Zimbabwe for another year while the post-Mugabe transformation continues. President Mnangagwa has stated his intention to carry out political and economic reform, and large USD inflows since Mugabe's departure have begun to help ease currency shortages and service external debts. Mnangagwa remains president after the first election since 1980 without Mugabe as a candidate.

Economic data	*Avg*[a]	*2014*	*2015*	*2016*	*2017 (e)*	*2018 (f)*	*2019 (f)*
Real GDP growth	3.6	2.8	1.4	0.7	3.7	3.6	4.2
Inflation (annual average)	11.9	−0.2	−2.4	−1.6	0.9	3.9	9.6
Current account (% of GDP)	−8.9	−14.2	−9.5	−3.4	−4.1	−5.8	−5.6
Reserves (US$mn, end-period)[b]	295	303	339	310	221	201	181
Reserves/imports (months)[c]	0.5	0.5	0.6	0.6	0.4	0.4	0.4
Overall fiscal balance (% of GDP)[d]	−2.0	−1.4	−1.0	−8.4	−12.7	−10.8	−9.1
Currency (ticker)	US dollar (USD)						
FX regime	Official dollarisation occurred in 2015, but other foreign currencies are still used. In November 2016, the government began issuing bond notes with a one-to-one exchange ratio with USD as a parallel currency in response to currency shortages following years of trade deficits. In February 2018, the RBZ governor announced measures to attract foreign trade, increase exports and liberalise the FX market. The deputy finance minister also said Zimbabwe may bring back its own currency when it has six months' import cover; he predicted this would take 2–3 years.						
Key exports	Tobacco (32%), gold (30%), nickel ore (10%), diamonds (4.2%), ferroalloys (4.2%). Remittances came to 11.5% of GDP in 2016.						

Source: IMF WEO Database, IMF Country Reports, OEC

[a]10-year average to 2016 unless otherwise stated
[b]Gross international reserves
[c]In months of imports of goods and services
[d]IMF Overall government net lending

Key figures		*Party*	*Since*
President	Emmerson Mnangagwa	ZANU-PF	Nov. 2017
First vice president	Constantino Chiwenga	ZANU-PF	Dec. 2017
Second vice president	Kembo Mohadi	ZANU-PF	Dec. 2017
Minister of finance	Mthuli Ncube	Independent	Sep. 2018
Key opposition figure	Nelson Chamisa	MDC Alliance	Feb. 2018
Central bank governor	John Panonetsa Mangudya	–	May 2014

Note: Zimbabwe was a member of the Commonwealth until its membership was suspended in March 2002 following that year's presidential election, which was marred by violence. It gained independence from Britain in 1980

Politics

Executive power

The president is both chief of state and, since the office of prime minister was abolished in 2013, head of government. Cabinet is appointed by the president from among the members of the House of Assembly. Vice presidents are appointed by the president. The president is directly elected by absolute majority vote (with two rounds if necessary) to serve a five-year term[a]. Two co-vice presidents are appointed by the president.

Presidential term: Five years (two-term limit) **Parliamentary term**: Five years

[a]As of constitutional change in 2013. This rule did not apply to incumbent President Mugabe

Legislature

The bicameral parliament comprises the Senate (upper house) and the House of Assembly (lower house). Members of the Senate and House of Assembly serve five-year terms.

Senate: 80 seats
60 members are directly elected, with six seats in each of the 10 provinces, 16 are indirectly elected by the regional governing councils, two are reserved for the National Council Chiefs and two are reserved for disabled members.

House of Assembly: 270 seats
210 members are directly elected in single-seat constituencies by simple majority vote and 60 seats are reserved for women directly elected by proportional representation.

Elections

Next due *Presidential and legislative: 2023*

Last legislative election (July 2018)	*Seats*	*Last presidential (July 2018)*	*% of vote*
Zimbabwe African National Union – Patriotic Front	180	Emmerson Mnangagwa (ZANU-PF)	50.8
MDC Alliance	87	Nelson Chamisa (MDC Alliance)	44.3
MDC-Tsvangirai	1	Thokozani Khupe (MDC-T)	0.9
National Patriotic Front	1	Others	4.0
Independents	1		
Total	**270**	**Total**	**100.0**

People

The population of Zimbabwe is almost entirely of African origin, while a small white minority are of European ancestry, although after independence their number declined. Christianity is the dominant religion, with all denominations accounting for a combined 87% of the population. There are 16 official languages, with the most widely spoken being Shona, Ndebele and English.

From 1830 to 1890, Europeans explored the region from the south and, in 1889, Cecil John Rhodes' British South Africa Company (BSA) gained a British mandate to colonise what later became Southern Rhodesia. An uprising against BSA was crushed in 1893 and the BSA administration continued until the white minority gained self-governance in 1922. A 1930 Land Apportionment Act restricted land ownership of the black population and forced many to work for wages, rather than subsistence. Black opposition to colonial rule grew over the following decades. In 1953, Britain created the Central African Federation, comprised of Southern Rhodesia (Zimbabwe), Northern Rhodesia (Zambia), and Nyasaland (Malawi). The Federation broke up in 1963 when Zambia and Malawi gained independence. Southern Rhodesia remained a British colony and nationalist groups including the Zimbabwe African National Union (ZANU) emerged in the 1960s. A guerrilla war followed attempts to gain independence with rival groups, including ZANU, operating out of neighbouring countries. Talks were held at Lancaster House in London in 1979 with all parties to reach a peace agreement and a new constitution, which would guarantee minority rights. Independence was granted in 1980 and pro-independence leader Robert Mugabe and his ZANU party won elections that year, making Mugabe prime minister, and Southern Rhodesia was renamed Zimbabwe. Joshua Nkomo, leader of ZAPU, a rival group during the independence talks was included in the cabinet, until Mugabe removed him in 1982, accusing him of preparing to overthrow the government. Land reform began in 1980 as overpopulation and poor distribution of land between subsistence farmers and European Zimbabweans was cited as a cause of growing poverty. Land reform planned to redistribute land to the subsistence sector without reducing the economic contribution of the commercial farming sector. Independence allowed the reforms to begin, with some financing from the British government under Thatcher. The government is accused of killing thousands of civilians during the following years, as it fought rebel groups.

(*continued*)

(continued)

People
In 1987, Mugabe and Nkomo merged their parties to form ZANU-PF, which ended violence in southern areas. Mugabe also changed the constitution in 1987 to make him president. Subsequent attempts to change the constitution were unsuccessful. In 1997, Tony Blair brought to a halt land reform financing. UK development aid ended and sanctions were imposed on Mugabe and his inner circle. An economic crisis began in 1998, and severe food shortages led to a state of disaster being declared in April 2002. In June of that year, almost 3000 white farmers were given 45 days to leave their land. During 2003, there were various protests and strikes, leading to arrests, including that of opposition leader Morgan Tsvangirai, who received multiple charges of treason. The UN estimated that 700,000 people had been left homeless after urban slums were cleared in 2005. Annual inflation had become very high by 2006 and demonstrations against the government resulted in violence. Mugabe won the 2008 presidential election, although the opposition accused the government of intimidation. In July, the US and EU extended sanctions. The office of prime minister was brought back and opposition leader Tsvangirai was appointed to the role in 2009 in an attempt at power-sharing, although by 2011, he had accused the government of disregard for the arrangement. The run up to the 2013 elections saw numerous opposition rallies shut down. Mugabe won a seventh term and the opposition dismissed the election as fraudulent. In 2015, the RBZ formally phased out the Zimbabwean dollar and formalised the multi-currency system, but a currency shortage in 2016 resulted in the issuance of domestic bond notes valued at par with the US dollar. In November 2017, the military took control and within days, Mugabe resigned as president, succeeded by Emmerson Mnangagwa until elections in July 2018. The EU deployed observers to Zimbabwe to monitor the poll, following invitation from the government. Tsvangirai died due to cancer in February 2018, and Nelson Chamisa now leads the main opposition party. Mnangagwa narrowly won the presidential election without the need for a second round, but ZANU-PF won 180 of 270 seats in the House of Assembly. Although the campaign was considered free by international observers, many incidents of food and agricultural assistance and media bias to secure ZANU-PF votes were reported. Chamisa rejected the result and attempted a legal challenge (rejected by the Constitutional Court in August), and protests ended in violence. However, regional observers believed the poll was orderly and lawful.

Debt

	2012	*2017*
External debt ratios (%)		
Total external debt/GDP	54.2	74.3
Public external debt/GDP	49.1	52.4
Private external debt/GDP	5.2	21.9
Total external debt/exports of goods and services	156.9	243.6
External debt service ratio[a]	0.4	5.0
Public debt ratios (%)		
Public domestic debt/GDP	2.0	28.2
Public debt/GDP	51.1	80.6

Source: RBZ, IMF

[a]Public and publicly guaranteed

Zimbabwe's public and publicly guaranteed (PPG) external debt stood at just under US$9bn at the end of 2017, up from US$6.9bn in 2012. This comprised US$7bn central government external debt, US$490mn RBZ external debt and US$1.4bn publicly guaranteed external debt of public enterprises. Although the nominal PPG external debt stock rose, 2017 nominal GDP was almost 22% higher than in 2012, causing the ratio of PPG external debt with GDP to increase only slightly over this period, to 52% in 2017. This debt was owed to multilateral and bilateral creditors only. Including all arrears, multilaterals were owed US$3.1bn, the largest creditor being the World Bank (US$1.4bn on 2016 figures). Bilaterals were owed the remaining US$5.3bn. US$3bn was owed to Paris Club creditors on the latest 2016 figures. The creditors of the US$490mn RBZ debt are not reported, although it is categorised as short term.

Zimbabwe still has no debt owed to commercial creditors, as there are no eurobonds and various sanctions imposed under Mugabe's rule limit the potential commercial credit options to the government. Despite some crowding out effects of the continuous fiscal deficits and interventions of the government, private sector borrowing has led to an increase in private sector external debt from US$726mn in 2012 (5.2% of GDP) to US$3.8bn in 2017 (22% of GDP). This contributed to the total external debt of Zimbabwe reaching US$12.7bn at end-2017, 74% of GDP and 244% of exports of goods, services and workers' remittances. PPG external debt service increased from 0.4% of exports in 2012 to 5% in 2017, due partly to a decline in concessional debt, but also caused by the accumulation of arrears.

A large external debt burden caused Zimbabwe to fall into arrears, and recent accumulations of domestic debt have led to debt distress. Driven by the government's rising spending and poor international relations that limit access to IFIs, the domestic debt stock has rapidly increased as the government has become reliant on domestic financing. The IMF identifies T-bill issuance and the use of an RBZ overdraft as key drivers (the legal limit of the government's RBZ overdraft was exceeded in 2016). Between 2013 and 2016, domestic borrowings of the central government and RBZ increased by a factor of nine. Over our comparison period, public domestic debt increased from US$287mn in 2012 to US$4.8bn in 2017. As a percentage of GDP, public domestic debt increased from 2% in 2012 to 28% in 2017. Total PPG debt (external and domestic), therefore, totalled US$13.8bn at end-2017, equivalent to 81% of GDP.

Composition of external debt

External debt by creditor (end-2017)	*Nominal amount outstanding (US$mn)*	*Share of total (%)*
Public and publicly guaranteed external debt	**8966**	**70.5**
o/w Official multilateral	3148	24.8
World Bank	1402[a]	11.0[a]
AfDB	642[a]	5.0[a]
EIB	250[a]	2.0[a]
Official Bilateral	5328	41.9
Paris Club	3041[a]	23.9[a]
Non-Paris Club	1142[a]	9.0[a]
Commercial creditors	0	0.0
Other (RBZ)	490	3.8
Private sector external debt	**3751**	**29.5**
Total external debt	**12,717**	**100.0**
Memo: PPG external debt composition		
Central government external debt	7057	55.5
RBZ external debt	490	3.8
Publicly guaranteed external debt	1419	11.2

Source: RBZ, IMF

[a]Latest figures are for end-2016, hence do not add to the totals

Rescheduling History

Since being a well-developed economy in the 1990s, increasing debt, political concerns, and human rights issues have left Zimbabwe internationally isolated. In 2000, the US and EU imposed sanctions on Zimbabwe following their accusations that former president Mugabe had violated human rights, rigged elections and reduced press freedom. Human rights and democracy violations resulted in US travel and economic embargoes on certain politicians, military figures and state-owned enterprises (SOEs). EU sanctions were lifted in 2014, with the exception of those applying to Mugabe and his wife.

Despite the removal of Mugabe in November 2017, the Trump administration announced in March 2018 the extension of sanctions on Zimbabwe for another year while the post-Mugabe transformation continues, and the degree to which the 2018 elections were free and fair would be closely observed. President Mnangagwa has stated his intention to carry out political and economic reform. Two British diplomats visited Zimbabwe in

February 2018 to meet Mnangagwa, although UK sanctions remain in place. The UK provided US$100mn in loans for the Zimbabwe private sector in May 2018 amid a currency shortage, which was criticised by the opposition in Zimbabwe as it was timed before the first election without Mugabe as a candidate. The UK later expressed concern over election violence.

Large arrears to multilateral and bilateral creditors have contributed to Zimbabwe's international isolation, although some have been cleared. Poor access to external financing has slowed progress towards reform implementation and SOE transformation. Increasing government expenditure has caused continuous fiscal deficits since 2013 and the domestic debt stock has rapidly risen, as external financing options were limited. The IMF identifies T-bill issuance and the use of an RBZ overdraft as key components of domestic debt: between 2013 and 2016, domestic borrowings of the central government and RBZ increased by a factor of 9. This is unlikely to improve under current policies, although Mnangagwa is pursuing reforms. The IMF sees fiscal consolidation, structural reform (including mining sector transparency) and external assistance (debt relief) as key components in the solution.

Falling exports due to lower export prices, lower FDI inflows and a fall in rand remittance value following a depreciation versus the US dollar created worsening currency shortages in 2016 and the need for the RBZ to issue its own bond notes, for domestic use only, with a par value to the US dollar. Some current and capital account controls were put in place in May 2016 to reduce imports and currency outflows; there are exchange restrictions in place and some importers face delays. In February 2018, RBZ governor John Mangudya announced measures to attract foreign trade, increase exports and liberalise the FX market.

Zimbabwe is in debt distress, as evaluated by the IMF. However, it is not currently eligible for debt relief under the highly indebted poor country (HIPC) initiative, which has resulted in significant debt forgiveness for several SSA countries, as its debt is too low (in terms of its export and fiscal revenue ratios as per HIPC criteria), although improving international relations under Mnangagwa could lead to a willingness of creditors to provide debt relief. An ad hoc treatment may make it easier (and quicker) to provide debt relief because Zimbabwe would not need a track record, as is required for HIPC.

GDP growth exceeded mid-year forecasts for 2017, following increased agricultural output brought on by ideal weather conditions, as well as stronger exports of gold, chrome and tobacco, as export commodity prices increased. Medium-term forecasts have also been revised up by the IMF and prospects will depend on reform implementation and international relations, which could provide debt relief and restore debt sustainability. The level of infrastructure and human capital are favourable, and there is capacity for greater production in the primary and secondary sectors without creating inflationary pressures. Fiscal discipline can also help to limit inflation and create greater opportunities for the private sector.

Relations with Multilateral Creditors

Zimbabwe had seven programmes with the IMF during the 1980s and 1990s, including a simultaneous extended fund facility (EFF) and extended credit facility (ECF) over 1992–1995. In 2013, Zimbabwe agreed its first arrangement with the IMF in over a decade, in the form of a staff-monitored programme (SMP). An SMP is an informal agreement between the authorities and the IMF, to monitor the implementation of the authorities' economic programme. It does not come with any financial assistance. A successor SMP was approved in October 2014, although the IMF reports that political circumstances constrained the reform agenda. The IMF provided support and advice over the two SMPs regarding fiscal policy, bank risk management and structural reforms. The commitment of the authorities, the meeting of quantitative targets, and continued economic difficulties were consistently reported, and an arrear-clearance strategy, among others, was developed. However, reform implementation following the second SMP was delayed. Weakening fiscal discipline, slow reform of SOEs and increasing private sector debt meant that imbalances were not addressed, while disappointing structural reform implementation did not reduce stakeholder perception of corruption.

IMF programmes

Date	*Arrangements*	*Comments*
1981–1982	SBA	SBA for SDR37.5mn, fully drawn and repaid.
1983–1984	SBA	SBA for SDR300mn, of which SDR175mn was drawn and fully repaid.
1992	EFF	EFF for SDR373.8mn, of which SDR71.2mn was drawn and fully repaid.
1992–1995	EFF+ECF	EFF for SDR114.6mn, of which SDR86.9mn was drawn and simultaneous ECF for SDR200.6mn, of which SDR151.9mn was drawn and fully repaid.

(*continued*)

(continued)

Date	*Arrangements*	*Comments*
1998–1999	SBA	SBA for SDR130.65mn, of which SDR39.2mn was drawn and fully repaid.
1999–1900	SBA	SBA for SDR141.36mn, of which SDR24.74mn was drawn and fully repaid.
2013 (14)	SMP	An SMP, initially covering April–December 2013, was approved in June, and, at the authorities' request, a six-month extension was approved in January 2014. Putting public finances on a sustainable course and increasing diamond revenue transparency were among priorities, in recognition of large current account deficits, low international reserves and accumulating arrears. The first and second reviews were completed in June 2014, noting broadly satisfactory performance in a difficult election year. The third review was completed in October 2014. Although the economic situation remained difficult, all quantitative targets and structural benchmarks were met amid renewed commitment from the authorities.
2014–2015	SMP	Acknowledging the difficult political and economic circumstances in Zimbabwe, the IMF agreed a successor SMP along with the third review in October 2014. This programme would cover the period October 2014 to December 2015, with the objective of helping the authorities to normalise relations with the international community in the future, by strengthening the external position to clear arrears, restore financial stability and get external debt on a sustainable path. The first review in April 2015 noted the continuing economic difficulties, but also the progress made in implementing macroeconomic and structural reforms. In September 2015, the second review was completed, noting the continued commitment of the authorities to the reform programme and the development of an external arrears-clearing strategy. The third review was completed with the Article IV in March 2016, and came after the economic shock caused by the El Nino-induced drought, worsened by lower export commodity prices and an appreciating US dollar. All quantitative targets and structural benchmarks were met, although maintaining fiscal discipline remained a priority.

Source: IMF. Zimbabwe joined the IMF in 1980

From February 2001, Zimbabwe remained in continuous arrears to the IMF, and the Board considered the compulsory expulsion of the country from the Fund on several occasions between 2003 and 2006, although formal action was never taken. There has been limited success in arrears clearance since the end of the SMPs, although all PRGT (ECF) obligations to the IMF were cleared in October 2016, as announced in a clearance plan a year previously. Discussions on arrears clearance between the authorities and the World Bank and African Development Bank (AfDB) continue. Following a favourable World Bank technical assistance mission to Zimbabwe in early 2017, the authorities have good incentives to clear arrears and continue development programmes. RBZ deputy governor Khupikile Mlambo said in March 2018 that Zimbabwe hoped to clear all multilateral arrears by September. Arrears to bilateral creditors also need resolution. The IMF mission chief said in November 2017 that, for any future financing request to be considered, Zimbabwe would need to clear its arrears to the World Bank, AfDB and EIB, among other reforms.

In media reports in March 2018, Deputy Finance Minister Terence Mukupe quoted IMF Managing Director Christine Lagarde as saying that, if the 2018 elections were declared free and fair, then she would be one of the first people on their doorstep, and would likely announce "something for us within 48 hours". He said that all multilaterals were "talking about pressing the reset button". He also suggested that Zimbabwe's problem was not the debt level, but its ability to repay, due to political reasons; however, significant inflows to the country already since Mugabe's departure were helping it to accumulate reserves and service its debt. He reported progress in the reform and potential privatisation of SOEs and significant interest among potential buyers.

On Ministry of Finance and Economic Development figures for 2016 (latest), other significant multilateral development partners were the Global Fund and the AfDB, providing development partner support disbursements of US$164mn and US$15mn, respectively, in 2016. The Global Fund is a partnership between international organisations to accelerate the end of epidemic diseases, and is also a financing institution. As of August 2018, the AfDB has 16 active projects focused on infrastructure development and improving financial management. Meanwhile, debt owed to the World Bank was mostly arrears in 2016. Recently approved projects (the largest were for financial management, water infrastructure and the health sector) had relatively small commitment amounts relative to projects approved in the 1990s (now closed).

Paris Club and Bilateral Creditors

Zimbabwe has never had a Paris Club agreement, despite large outstanding Paris Club debt and significant arrears. Finance Minister Patrick Chinamasa visited France in June 2016 for talks with Paris Club officials to resolve arrears. The latest figures for end-2016 showed that, of the US$3.041bn that Zimbabwe owed to Paris Club creditors, only US$223mn was outstanding principal and US$2.818bn was arrears (large PDI).

The most significant bilateral development partners, as of 2016, were the UK, China and the EU, providing total development support (including outstanding bilateral loans) of US$109mn, US$63mn and US$31mn respectively. It was reported in April 2018 that China had written off debt owed to its institutions, among other bilateral deals, although few details have been provided.

Sovereign Commercial Debt

Zimbabwe has never issued any eurobonds and has no marketable commercial debt. Access to international financing (commercial and official sectors) is limited due to large arrears and sanctions imposed by various countries. Restoring access would depend in part on improving international relations, an arrears-clearance strategy and securing debt relief.

Corporate Bond Markets

According to Bloomberg, in September 2018, only four bonds have been issued by Zimbabwean corporates to date, and three remain outstanding. The first issue was for US$50mn, issued by CBZ Holdings Ltd. (CBZBNK) in April 2011 with an 8.5% coupon. It had a bullet maturity in April 2014. The three outstanding bonds are shown in the table.

Zimbabwe's outstanding corporate bonds

Issuer	*Amount issued*	*Amount outstanding*	*Maturity*	*Coupon*	*Issue date*
GetBucks Financial Services Ltd (GTBKCS)	US$5.44mn	US$5.44mn	Oct. 2019 (Bullet)	11%	Apr. 2017
Infrastructure Development Bank of Zimbabwe (INFZIM)	US$15mn	US$4.5mn	Dec. 2019 (Sinkable)	8%	Dec. 2014
Infrastructure Development Bank of Zimbabwe (INFZIM)	US$50mn	US$15mn	Dec. 2019 (Sinkable)	8%	Dec. 2014

Source: Bloomberg

In May 2018, the UK government's development finance institution, the Commonwealth Development Corporation (CDC), announced that US$100mn in loans would be issued to the Zimbabwe private sector, the first such commercial arrangement between London and Harare in over 20 years, and was finalising a list of recipients with partner Standard Chartered Bank, with whom the CDC had lent to Sierra Leone in 2015, during the Ebola epidemic. Zimbabwe opposition politicians criticised the timing of the decision, including former Finance Minister Tendai Biti, who said that foreign government lending should wait until credible elections have taken place. However, the CDC points out that the lending is to the private sector, which is struggling to operate with US dollar shortages, and does not represent an endorsement of the government.

Annex A: Supranational Bonds Issues

There are a number of hard currency bond issues from various supranational and regional financial institutions that trade actively in the secondary market. Descriptions are given below for the more actively traded, longer maturity bonds from six such issuers.

African Export-Import Bank

The African Export Import Bank was established in Abuja, Nigeria in October 1993 by African governments, African private and institutional investors as well as non–African financial institutions and private investors. It launched in 1994 with headquarters in Cairo. Its purpose is financing, promoting and expanding intra-African and extra-African trade. Shareholders come in four categories: (A) African governments, central banks and regional institutions; (B) African private investors and financial institutions; (C) Non-African financial institutions, export credit agencies and private investors; (D) other institutions and individuals. Its first major bond issue, a US$300mn five-year bond with a coupon of 8.75%, came in November 2009. The bond matured in 2014. More bonds followed, with US$500mn five-year issues in 2011 and 2013, both of which have since matured. It now has four outstanding eurobonds, amounting to a total of US$2.85bn notional, following its most recent issue, a US$500mn five-year bond, in October 2018. Details are given below.

Exotix Capital, *Exotix Developing Markets Guide*,
https://doi.org/10.1007/978-3-030-05867-8

African Export-Import Bank bond
Afreximbank 4.75% 2019
Bloomberg ticker: AFREXI

Borrower	The African Export-Import Bank
Issue date	29 July 2014
Form	EuroMTN
ISIN	XS1091688660
Issue size	US$700mn
Currency	US dollar
Denomination	Min US$200,000/increments on US$1000
Amortisation	Bullet
Final maturity date	29 July 2019
Coupon/interest	6.5%, paid semi-annually
Method of transfer	Euroclear/Clearstream
Day count	30/360
Settlement period	T + 2
Lead manager	HSBC
Exchange	Dublin, Frankfurt, Munich, Stuttgart
Governing law	English

Source: Bloomberg

African Export-Import Bank bond
Afreximbank 4% 2021
Bloomberg ticker: AFREXI

Borrower	The African Export-Import Bank
Issue date	24 May 2016
Form	EuroMTN
ISIN	XS1418627821
Issue size	US$900mn
Currency	US dollar
Denomination	Min US$200,000/increments on US$1000
Amortisation	Bullet
Final maturity date	24 May 2021
Coupon/interest	4%, paid semi-annually
Method of transfer	Euroclear/Clearstream
Day count	30/360
Settlement period	T + 2
Joint lead managers	Barclays, RMB International
Exchange	Berlin, Dublin, Dusseldorf, Frankfurt, Stuttgart
Governing law	English

Source: Bloomberg

African Export-Import Bank bond
Afreximbank 5.25% 2023
Bloomberg ticker: AFREXI

Borrower	The African Export-Import Bank
Issue date	11 October 2018
Form	EuroMTN
ISIN	XS1892247963
Issue size	US$500mn
Currency	US dollar
Denomination	Min US$200,000/increments on US$1000
Amortisation	Bullet
Final maturity date	11 October 2023
Coupon/interest	5.25%, paid semi-annually
Method of transfer	Clearstream
Day count	30/360
Settlement period	T + 2
Joint lead managers	Barclays, HSBC, MUFG, RMB, Standard Chartered
Exchange	Berlin, Stuttgart
Governing law	English

Source: Bloomberg

African Export-Import Bank bond
Afreximbank 4.125% 2024
Bloomberg ticker: AFREXI

Borrower	The African Export-Import Bank
Issue date	20 June 2017
Form	EuroMTN
ISIN	XS1633896813
Issue size	US$750mn
Currency	US dollar
Denomination	Min US$200,000/increments on US$1000
Amortisation	Bullet
Final maturity date	20 June 2024
Coupon/interest	4.125%, paid semi-annually
Method of transfer	Euroclear/Clearstream
Day count	30/360
Settlement period	T + 2
Joint lead managers	Barclays, Commerzbank, HSBC, MUFG Securities, Standard Chartered
Exchange	Dublin, Frankfurt, Stuttgart
Governing law	English

Source: Bloomberg

Eastern & Southern African Trade and Development Bank

The Eastern and Southern African Trade and Development Bank, headquartered in Burundi, commonly known as the TDB (formerly, the PTA Bank), was established on 6 November 1985. This was the beginning of the Preferential Trade Area for the Eastern and Southern African States (PTA), which was later transformed into the Common Market for Eastern and Southern Africa (COMESA). There are 18 African country members plus the People's Republic of China (joined in 2000) and the African Development Bank. The bank's mission is to provide development capital and promote increased trade and project financing. The bank has supranational status and has two outstanding hard currency bonds, although one matures in December 2018 (issued in 2013). The remaining bond is shown below. A previous bond issued in 2010 matured in 2016.

Eastern and Southern Africa Trade and Development Bank (PTA) bond
PTA Bank 5.375% 2022
Bloomberg ticker: PTABNK

Borrower	The Eastern and Southern Africa Trade and Development Bank
Issue date	14 March 2017
Form	EuroMTN
ISIN	XS1520309839
Issue size	US$700mn
Currency	US dollar
Denomination	Min US$200,000/increments on US$1000
Amortisation	Bullet
Final maturity date	14 March 2022
Coupon/interest	5.375%, paid semi-annually
Method of transfer	Euroclear/Clearstream
Day count	30/360
Settlement period	T + 2
Joint lead manager	Commerzbank, MUFG Securities, Standard Chartered
Exchange	Dublin
Governing law	English

Source: Bloomberg

Black Sea Trade & Development Bank

Black Sea Trade & Development Bank, headquartered in Greece, offers various financial services. The Bank provides term loans, credit lines, equity and guarantees for projects and trade financing in both the public and private sectors. Black Sea finances the economic development, regional cooperation and enterprise development of various countries geographically located near to the Black Sea. Its members are Albania, Armenia, Azerbaijan, Bulgaria, Georgia, Greece, Moldova, Romania, Russia, Turkey and Ukraine. It was established in 1997 and commenced operations in 1999. It has one outstanding USD bond shown below. A previous bond issued in 2009 matured in 2012.

Black Sea Trade and Development Bank bond
Black Sea Trade and Development Bank 4.875% 2021
Bloomberg ticker: BSTDBK

Borrower	The Black Sea Trade and Development Bank
Issue date	6 May 2016
Form	EuroMTN
ISIN	XS1405888576
Issue size	US$500mn
Currency	US dollar
Denomination	Min US$200,000/increments on US$1000
Amortisation	Bullet
Final maturity date	6 May 2021
Coupon/interest	4.875%, paid semi-annually
Method of transfer	Euroclear/Clearstream
Day count	30/360
Settlement period	T + 2
Joint lead manager	HSBC, JP Morgan
Exchange	Berlin, Dublin, Frankfurt
Governing law	English

Source: Bloomberg

Africa Finance Corporation

AFC provides banking solutions: project development, technical advisory, principal investing, corporate finance and financial advisory services. Founded in 2007 and headquartered in Nigeria, AFC serves power, infrastructure, oil & gas, telecoms, chemical, manufacturing, cement, agro-processing, maritime and logistics sectors in Africa. Its members include 19 African countries. The Central Bank of Nigeria is also a large shareholder, along with some private investors. AFC has two main USD bonds outstanding.

Africa Finance Corporation bond
Africa Finance Corp 4.375% 2020
Bloomberg ticker: AFRFIN

Borrower	Africa Finance Corporation
Issue date	29 April 2015
Form	EuroMTN
ISIN	XS1225008538
Issue size	US$750mn
Currency	US dollar
Denomination	Min US$200,000/increments on US$1000
Amortisation	Bullet
Final maturity date	29 April 2020
Coupon/interest	4.875%, paid semi-annually
Method of transfer	Clearstream
Day count	30/360
Settlement period	T + 2
Joint lead manager	Citi, Mitsubishi UFJ, Standard Chartered, Standard Bank
Exchange	Berlin, Dublin, Frankfurt, Munich
Governing law	English

Source: Bloomberg

Africa Finance Corporation bond
Africa Finance Corp 3.875% 2024
Bloomberg ticker: AFRFIN

Borrower	Africa Finance Corporation
Issue date	13 April 2017
Form	Eurobond

(*continued*)

(continued)

Africa Finance Corporation bond *Africa Finance Corp 3.875% 2024* *Bloomberg ticker: AFRFIN*	
ISIN	XS1598047550
Issue size	US$500mn
Currency	US dollar
Denomination	Min US$200,000/increments on US$1000
Amortisation	Bullet
Final maturity date	13 April 2024
Coupon/interest	3.875%, paid semi-annually
Method of transfer	Euroclear/Clearstream
Day count	30/360
Settlement period	T + 2
Joint lead manager	Citi, JP Morgan, MUFG Securities, Standard Chartered
Exchange	Dublin
Governing law	English

Source: Bloomberg

Eurasian Development Bank

The Eurasia Development Bank, headquartered in Almaty, Kazakhstan, was established in 2006 by founding members the Russian Federation and Republic of Kazakhstan to finance economic development and integration of the member states. Armenia and Tajikistan joined as members in 2009, followed by Belarus in 2010 and Kyrgyzstan in 2011. It has two outstanding USD-denominated bonds, shown below, and also ruble- and tenge-denominated bonds. A repurchase tender for both USD bonds took place in November 2015. A previous USD bond issued in 2009 matured in 2014.

Eurasian Development Bank bond *Eurasian Development Bank 5% 2020* *Bloomberg ticker: EURDEV*	
Borrower	Eurasian Development Bank
Issue date	26 September 2013
Form	Eurobond
ISIN	XS0972645112
Issue size	US$500mn

(*continued*)

(continued)

Eurasian Development Bank bond *Eurasian Development Bank 5% 2020* *Bloomberg ticker: EURDEV*	
Amount outstanding	US$296.331mn
Currency	US dollar
Denomination	Min US$200,000/increments on US$1000
Amortisation	Bullet
Final maturity date	26 September 2020
Coupon/interest	5%, paid semi-annually
Method of transfer	Euroclear/Clearstream/LSE Reportable
Day count	30/360
Settlement period	T + 2
Joint lead manager	BNP Paribas, Deutsche Bank, HSBC, JP Morgan
Exchange	London
Governing law	English

Source: Bloomberg

Eurasian Development Bank bond *Eurasian Development Bank 4.767% 2022* *Bloomberg ticker: EURDEV*	
Borrower	Eurasian Development Bank
Issue date	20 September 2012
Form	EuroMNT
ISIN	XS0831571434
Issue size	US$500mn
Amount outstanding	US$335.812mn
Currency	US dollar
Denomination	Min US$200,000/increments on US$1000
Amortisation	Bullet
Final maturity date	20 September 2022
Coupon/interest	4.767%, paid semi-annually
Method of transfer	Euroclear/Clearstream/LSE Reportable
Day count	30/360
Settlement period	T + 2
Joint lead manager	BNP Paribas, Citi, HSBC, VTB Bank
Exchange	Berlin, Frankfurt, London
Governing law	English

Source: Bloomberg

BOAD

The West African Development Bank (BOAD), headquartered in Togo, disburses long- and medium-term loans, maintains cooperation relations, and supports the private sector, economic integration and resource-mobilisation services. It was founded in 1973 to serve French- and Portuguese-speaking countries in West Africa; it has eight member states. In 1994, it became the development agency for the West African Economic and Monetary Union (WAEMU). It has two USD bonds outstanding and a few issues denominated in local CFA francs (XOF).

Banque Ouest Africaine de Developpement bond
BOAD 5.5% 2021
Bloomberg ticker: BOAD

Borrower	Banque Ouest Africaine de Developpement
Issue date	6 May 2016
Form	Eurobond
ISIN	XS1350670839
Issue size	US$750mn
Amount outstanding	US$750mn
Currency	US dollar
Denomination	Min US$200,000/increments on US$1000
Amortisation	Bullet
Final maturity date	6 May 2021
Coupon/interest	5.5%, paid semi-annually
Method of transfer	Euroclear/Clearstream
Day count	30/360
Settlement period	T + 2
Joint lead manager	BNP Paribas, Deutsche Bank, JP Morgan, Standard Bank
Exchange	Luxembourg
Governing law	English

Source: Bloomberg

Banque Ouest Africaine de Developpement bond
BOAD 5% 2027
Bloomberg ticker: BOAD

Borrower	Banque Ouest Africaine de Developpement
Issue date	27 July 2017
Form	Eurobond
ISIN	XS1650033571
Issue size	US$850mn
Amount outstanding	US$850mn
Currency	US dollar
Denomination	Min US$200,000/increments on USD1000
Amortisation	Bullet
Final maturity date	27 July 2027
Coupon/interest	5%, paid semi-annually
Method of transfer	Euroclear/Clearstream
Day count	30/360
Settlement period	T + 2
Joint lead manager	Citi, JP Morgan, Natixis, Standard Bank
Exchange	Luxembourg
Governing law	English

Source: Bloomberg

Annex B: Paris Club Terms

The Paris Club in an informal group of bilateral creditors who cooperate to resolve unsustainable debt situations in their debtor countries. There are 22 permanent members: Australia, Austria, Belgium, Brazil, Canada, Denmark, Finland, France, Germany, Ireland, Israel, Italy, Japan, the Netherlands, Norway, Russia, South Korea, Spain, Sweden, Switzerland, the UK and the US. Other official creditors can also participate in Paris Club negotiations on an ad hoc basis, subject to the agreement of permanent members and the debtor country. The following creditors have participated on an ad hoc basis: Abu Dhabi, Argentina, China, Kuwait, Mexico, Morocco, New Zealand, Portugal, South Africa, Trinidad and Tobago and Turkey. Often under an IMF programme, debtor countries implement reforms aiming to ensure long-term debt sustainability through institutions, policies and economic management, while Paris Club creditors provide a debt treatment, such as principal/arrears reduction, reduced debt service payments or extended repayment profiles. To date, there have been 433 agreements provided to 90 debtor countries, starting in 1956, when Argentina agreed to meet its public creditors in Paris. A total of US$583bn has been treated under the Paris Club framework. This involves treatments under one of the following terms:

Exotix Capital, *Exotix Developing Markets Guide*,
https://doi.org/10.1007/978-3-030-05867-8

Paris Club standard terms of treatment

Terms	*Debtor eligibility*	*Description*
Classic	Any country with an appropriate IMF programme showing the need for Paris Club debt relief.	Credits (ODA or non-ODA) are rescheduled at the appropriate market rate with a case-by-case negotiated repayment profile.
Houston	Assessed case-by-case by creditors, considering previous PC or IMF engagement, and meeting at least two of the following: (1) low per capita income (below US$2995), (2) high indebtedness (at least two of the following: debt to GDP higher than 50%, debt to exports higher than 275%, scheduled debt service over exports higher than 30%), (3) bilateral debt stock of at least 150% of private debt.	Non-ODA credits are rescheduled at the appropriate market rate over c15 years with two-to-three years' grace and progressive payments raising year by year. ODA credits are rescheduled at an interest rate at least as favourable as the original concessional interest rate applying to the loans, over 20 years with a maximum 10-year grace period. Creditor countries can conduct debt swaps.
Naples	Assessed on a case-by-case by creditors, considering previous PC or IMF engagement. Criteria include high indebtedness, only being eligible for IDA financing from the World Bank and a low per capita income (US$755 or less).	Now replaces the previous Toronto and London terms. Non-ODA credits are cancelled to a 67% level. Creditors may choose to implement this reduction by various options. ODA credits are rescheduled at an interest rate at least as favourable as the original concessional interest rate applying to the loans. Creditor countries can conduct debt swaps.
Cologne	Implemented case-by-case, but a debtor country must be eligible for Naples terms, have a sound track record with the PC and have been declared eligible for enhanced HIPC by the IMF and World Bank boards.	Now replaces the previous Lyon terms. Non-ODA credits are cancelled up to a 90% level or more if necessary in the context of the HIPC initiative. ODA credits are rescheduled at an interest rate at least as favourable as the original concessional interest rate applying to the loans. Creditor countries can conduct debt swaps.
Evian	A new approach for non-HIPC eligible countries introduced in 2003. It is only granted to countries facing imminent default. This may be due to unsustainable debt or a liquidity problem.	Case-by-case decision to provide debt treatment reflecting the debtor's financial needs, to ensure long-term debt sustainability. If debt is unsustainable, PC creditors will agree a treatment if the debtor will seek comparable debt treatment from other external creditors. If debt is sustainable, but a liquidity problem exists, a treatment may be designed to avoid default.

Source: Paris Club